BALLOONS TO BUCCANEERS

Yorkshire's role in aviation since 1785

A new sound in Yorkshire's skies. The Shorts Tucano training aircraft frequently transits North Yorkshire and the East Riding.

Shorts of Belfast

BALLOONS TO BUCCANEERS

Yorkshire's role in aviation since 1785

BY

BRIAN CATCHPOLE

 MAXIPRINT

Printed and Published by
Maxiprint
Designers and Colour Printers
Kettlestring Lane
York
YO3 4XF
First published 1994

ISBN 1 871125 12 X

Maps researched and drawn by
Brian Catchpole

Dedicated to all, friend or foe alike,
who have flown in Yorkshire's air space,
but especially to the aircrews
of No 4 Group Royal Air Force and
No 6 Group Royal Canadian Air Force

Acknowledgements

Crown Copyright material in the Public Record Office is reproduced by permission of the Controller of Her Majesty's Stationery Office, as are the excerpts from the listed publications of HMSO. © Crown copyright/MOD photographs are reproduced with the permission of the Controller of HMSO. Where possible, I have acknowledged their current source. Similarly, short extracts from Public Record Office and Air Historical Branch Files, together with Cabinet Office papers that have become progressively available, are wherever possible listed in the Chapter Notes under previously published works more accessible to the reader. I am grateful to the Science Museum for permission to reproduce the photograph of the Cayley silver disc.

Many publishers and individuals have kindly allowed me to use their copyright materials. These are indicated in full in the Chapter Notes or are credited adjacent to illustrations. A work of this nature must lean heavily on the wealth of aviation history already written by experts and if I had to choose one work to acknowledge in particular it would be *The Bomber Command War Diaries* by Martin Middlebrook and Chris Everitt for this has become an indispensable source for those who research the Second World War.

I am grateful for the quotation from A. H. Jones, *War in the Air,* by permission of Oxford University Press; for the October 1928 commentary on the Blackburn Iris by permission of The Times Newspapers Ltd; for the description of the helicopter rescue courtesy of the Editor of the *Yorkshire Post;* for the extract relating to the German fighter pilot Wilhelm Johnen from *The War in the Air* (ed. Gavin Lyall) by permission of Random House UK Limited; for the extract from *Action Stations 4, Military Airfields of Yorkshire,* by Bruce Barrymore Halpenny, by permission of Patrick Stephens Limited, an imprint of Haynes Publishing; for permission to use the excerpts from *Reap The Whirlwind: The Untold Story of 6 Group, Canada's Bomber Force of World War II* by Spencer Dunmore and William Carter, Ph.D., published by Crecy Books, Canada; for the excerpt from *Gulf War Debrief,* courtesy Aerospace Publishing.

I have made every effort to locate copyright holders of texts long out of print and of old postcards and photographs in my collection. In cases where even the resources of the Publishers' Association and the Society of Authors have been defeated and I have not been able to place an acknowledgement, copyright holders may wish to write in the first instance to the publishers and corrections will be made in any future editions of the work.

Museums and their archivists have been invaluable and I am indebted to the Trustees and Members of the Yorkshire Air Museum, especially Rachel Semlyen, Ian Robinson, Derek Reed, Dave Tappin, Ron Pontefract, Ian Wormald, Dick Chandler, David Lamb, the Rev Leonard Rivett, Gerald Myers and Guy Jefferson. Mike Wood, official photographer and photographic archivist at the Yorkshire Air Museum, was unstinting in his help to secure photographs with a Yorkshire context, many of them contributed anonymously by former Bomber Command/Coastal Command aircrew.

Other museums and archive collections proved invaluable and my thanks go to Captain W. J. Flindell, Director FAA Museum, and his research officer, David Richardson; to Michael Dorrington, Archivist at York Minster Museum; to Catherine Walker and Mary Kennedy at Hornsea Museum; to Rob Stanley, Jill Crowther and the staff of Hull Local Studies Museum; to John Flexton of Pickering Beck Isle Museum; and to Philip Johnson, Archivist at The Records Office, York.

I owe much to Molly Sedgwick in Eastbourne who allowed me to use photographs from her mother's autobiography; to Aphra Burley in Coulsdon, an aviation enthusiast now so sadly missed, daughter of test pilot Rowland Ding; and to Stuart Leslie who let me plunder his archives at Scalby. British Aerospace unhesitatingly provided photographs and I must thank in particular D. R. Russell of BAe Regional Aircraft Ltd, Prestwick Airport, Simon Raynes of BAe Farnborough, Andrew Bunce of BAe Warton and the staff of BAe Military Division, Brough, especially Nicola Dean, Liz Naylor, Eric Barker and Doug Black, for access to so many photographic records. My thanks also go to Peter Batten of Westland Helicopters, Yeovil, to Don Scott at Heliyorks, to Margaret Gomersall at Yorkshire Gliding Club and to the Photographic Department of Shorts of Belfast.

Sub-Lieutenant Gordon Hyams DFC generously recalled his flights from Hornsea Mere in World War I. Three Halifax pilots allowed me to record their World War II experiences: Flight Lieutenant Desmonde Moss DFC (Halifax); Squadron Leader Frank Lord DFC (Bideford); and Squadron Leader Harry Woodhatch DFC (Hessle). Three former WAAFs added their memories: Joan Haigh (4 Group crew driver), Margaret Henriksen and Barbara Wake (both Special Duties). Two of Europe's aviation historians, Frank Weber in Denmark and Jukka Raunio in Finland, kindly let me have the use of their research materials on the Second World War.

Many friends and correspondents produced logbooks, diaries, letters, photographs and memorabilia: Ted Rowland, Darrell Bell, Derrick Banyard, Bob Tyers (Melbourne, Australia), Pat Trowell, Bill Storr, Harry Flinton, Patricia Sage, Mike Swanborough, Bob Fewlass, Charles Batte, Gordon Chapman, Lieutenant Colonel Wythe, Bob Rosner, David Wall, David Banks, Norrie Grove, Frank Southern, Emile Krieps (Chamber of Deputies, Luxembourg), Desmond Penrose, G. Swales, Stan Smith, Ted Rowland, Dennis Ireland, Ian Hawkins, Doug Taylor and Bernard Reuben. Joe Rotherham and his daughter, Mary, who do so much to preserve 4 Group memories at Holme-upon-Spalding Moor, were especially helpful. Ed Solman, former Flight Engineer on Halifaxes with the Canadians, air test observer on the unusual Mosquito TT39, the GAL 56/03 'V' Wing Glider, the Mk 1 WF 320 Freighter and ultimately Head of Flight Tests on the Buccaneer, was raconteur extraordinary and worth a book in his own right.

Six friends whose contributions I treasure passed away while the book was still in manuscript: Colonel Dick Sage and Alan Paton, both of Wool, Dorset, Group Captain Joe Saunders (Elloughton), Doug Bridger (Lockington); Dr Peter Farrar (Hessle) and Wing Commander Bobby Sage, OBE, AFC.

Service personnel were ever helpful: Wing Commander Andy Kirk at Strike Command, Flight Lieutenant Maggie Pleasant WRAF, Community Relations Officer at Leeming, Captain Bob Petrie, 672 Squadron Army Air Corps, Dishforth, and MALM Dave Allen of D Flight No 22 Squadron at Leconfield.

Special thanks must go to Geoffrey Geddes, Managing Director of Maxiprint, to Carrie Geddes, Marketing Executive, and to Ian Ross, Commercial Director, for their interest, support and tolerance; to Malcolm Hill at Maxiprint who designed the book and accommodated all my updates; and to Derek Reed who read the manuscript, corrected my blunders and dispensed aviation gems from his 'Cockpit' in The Shambles, York. David Henderson piloted the Grumman for the aerial photography. Babs, my wife, was book researcher, driver and photocopier. To those whose names I may have missed and who succumbed to my requests for interviews and illustrations or let me copy photographs from family albums, I thank you for your patience and hospitality.

Brian Catchpole
Goodmanham 1994

Contents

List of Maps

Preface

Balloons to Buccaneers sets out to place in its historical and international context the extraordinary contribution that Yorkshire has made to the history of aviation over the last two hundred and fifty years. My brief is not just the story of invention and manufacture of balloons, airships and aeroplanes within the County but also the achievements of aircrew of all nationalities who have flown from or to Yorkshire in times of war and peace. Consequently, the scene may often change to the icy cold of the cruel North Sea in wartime or the flaming skies en route to Berlin and Nuremberg. Similar excursions in more peaceful times will take the story to the Schneider Trophy Races or to an airship mooring mast in Canada, though there is plenty to highlight within the County from the earliest days of aviation.

The first tentative balloon flight in the County took place in 1785, a mere two years after a sheep, a cockerel and a duck had flown in a Montgolfier "aerostatic machine" at Versailles. Just over sixty years later the County could lay claim to man's first flight in a heavier than air machine, the product of the genius of Sir George Cayley. In his footsteps came other local pioneers of aviation – Blackburn, Bell and Slingsby – while Doncaster had earned its place in the history of international air races even before the First World War.

Aviation and those wonderful aviators in their flying machines were by then firmly established in northern provincial culture though the construction of balloons and aeroplanes – apart from one local entrepreneur – was firmly anchored in the south. When one glances through the pages of *Flight* for April 1913 the sole manufacturer of flying machines in Yorkshire, advertising before the First World War, was the Blackburn Aeroplane Company of Leeds.

During that conflict, Yorkshire was one of the first Counties to experience German naval and air attack and stood compelled to develop primitive methods of air defence. Its strategic importance was marked by a growing aeroplane industry – Sopwith Camels were erected by Marsh, Jones & Cribb Ltd in Leeds and the Phoenix Dynamo Co. built flying boats in Bradford – and by the anti-submarine operations carried out by airships and seaplanes of the Royal Naval Air Service based in Yorkshire. By 1918 Howden had become the biggest patrol base in Britain. When peace came, Howden and Barton remained centres of airship construction while Blackburn supplied the Royal Navy with a remarkable variety of aeroplanes first from Leeds and then from Brough. During the Thirties the County was earmarked, somewhat belatedly, for the development of bomber bases.

These led to Yorkshire's major claim to fame during the Second World War. Not only was it a vital centre of bomber manufacture and repair but it also housed the headquarters of *three* Bomber Command Groups: at Bawtry (No 1 Group); at Heslington (No 4 Group) and at Allerton Park Castle (No 6 Canadian Group). During 1939-1941 Bomber Command's Whitleys, Hampdens and Wellingtons flew their missions from the County until they were gradually replaced by the mighty Halifaxes and Lancasters that equipped the squadrons of No 4 Group and No 6 RCAF Group. The importance of what was in progress between 1942 and 1945 may be gauged from the fact that over 25% of the entire strength of Bomber Command's offensive against Germany was ultimately based in Yorkshire. The County's infrastructure – aircraft manufacturing centres, a host of front-line and training airfields, repair centres, bomb dumps, communication and supply systems – was unique and far more complex than in any other shire of the realm. Yorkshire was vital to the war effort and consequently presented a tempting, accessible and enduring target for the Luftwaffe crews who, for a variety of reasons, chose to pulverise Hull more than any other city in Yorkshire.

The County can also lay claim to another 'record' during the Second World War: the first German aeroplane to be shot down in England crashed in Yorkshire in 1940; and five years later the last Luftwaffe aircraft to crash in England met its doom near Elvington. As I relate particular aspects of the two World Wars, I am conscious that Squadron and Group locations sometimes transgress the ever-changing boundaries of Yorkshire, and I hope that residents of Durham and Cleveland will not object to their inclusion in the tales of Redcar, Seaton Carew and the exploits of 6 Group.

When the Second World War ended the great bomber fleets were scrapped, their airfields usually placed on Care and Maintenance before being abandoned. Within two years, the onset of the Cold War revived an interest in the strategic value of the County and its new role reflected the changing fashions in manned and unmanned interceptors, V-bombers and the electronic surveillance of the stratosphere. As technology grew more expensive and the prospects of peace improved, the surviving airfields were gradually eroded until Leeming became the solitary front-line RAF base in the County. Training, Search and Rescue were swiftly centralised and long-serving, well-equipped airfields such as Church Fenton and Holme-upon-Spalding Moor became redundant.

By the end of 1993 it was clear that Leeming's three Tornado squadrons were not immune from Options for Change and No 23 Squadron was disbanded in 1994. Elsewhere, several BAe factories shut down their production lines though the highly skilled engineers at Brough's British Aerospace Military Division were in part reprieved by international demand for their brilliant Hawk trainer/ground-attack fighter. The decline of the RAF presence in Yorkshire was a high price to pay in the cause of financial "efficiency".

Inventiveness, skill, courage and determination have been the characteristics of all who have reached for the skies and Yorkshire's role in the history of aviation demonstrates that the County possesses these qualities in abundance. It is vital that they be preserved for, irrespective of where the next enemy may appear, the military defences of the north-east are neglected at our peril. The primary duty of government is the defence of the realm and it would never be appropriate for our leaders to ignore the long coastline and rich manufacturing centres of the biggest County in the United Kingdom, a County that produced the Father of Aviation and the Buccaneers that were so crucial in the Gulf.

Foreword

This book makes a good story, especially for anyone with Yorkshire connections. For many people, perhaps, the interest will come from memories revived, of people, places, danger, courage – and often of tragedy. Since Yorkshire is as near to Germany as anywhere in Britain, and large parts of it are flat – ideal for aircraft – much of the story is inevitably about military flying. Much of it was new to me. To my shame, I was surprised to learn of the enormous debt we owe to the many volunteers from the Commonwealth and Europe who were serving beside the RAF in Yorkshire by the end of the 2nd World War. By 1945 there were some 39 active air stations in the county.

For many people, the interest will be more personal. I was reminded of Howden Airship Station, where we lived when I was a very small boy – of fetching milk from Mrs Jones' dairy (it was always cool on hot days), then picking mushrooms for dinner and going on to "The Shed" to wonder at my father, a tiny spider crawling far up in the skeleton of R100.

More generally, there are some fascinating vignettes: of Cayley's coachman complaining after a 'flight' that he was hired to drive, not fly. Or of the two lady balloonists (at least one in daring trousers and boots!) sharing a parachute to earth after the release gear on the other parachute failed. Or again of how, at the beginning of the war, an optimistic RAF predicted that they could drop a delayed fuse bomb down the funnel of the *Emden*. Though they did have the sense to add, "or at least penetrate its deck".

Then, seriously, I was made to think again about the war time strategy of 'area' bombing, which reached its peak during Arthur Harris's time as AOC C-in-C Bomber Command. Why does every generation have to denigrate the actions of its fathers? The 'area' bombing strategy had been laid down before Harris went to High Wycombe. A commander cannot be blamed for actively doing his job – and must not be suspected of criticising the policy, if only for the sake of his men's morale. At one of the worst moments, Churchill minuted that the only way he could see of defeating the Germans was to attack from the air. But did it work? As I read this book, the evidence is not conclusive: it seems that the first one or two raids on a locality actually stiffen morale, but that persistent repetition does seriously affect it – as Goebbels noted in his diary towards the end of the war.

Would the strategy work with modern technology? And what of the people who would have to operate it? I do devoutly hope that no-one will need to try. The past has gone, and we must learn from it.

My hope lies in education. And I welcome the collaborative educational work now being planned between the Yorkshire Air Museum and the Barnes Wallis Trust (see page 58)

We can only be grateful, both to Ian Robinson of the Museum for sponsoring this project, and to Brian Catchpole for making it his own, and for the research he must have done.

BARNES WALLIS, MA(CANTAB) M.PHIL. C.ENG. M.R.AE.S.

Abbrevations

ABC	Airborne Cigar
AD	Air Department (Admiralty)
ADF	Automatic Direction Finding
ADGB	Air Defence of Great Britain
ATA	Air Transport Auxiliary
AVM	Air Vice Marshal
BAFF	British Air Forces in France
BAT	Blind Approach Training
BE	British Experimental
Cpl	Corporal
DME	Distance Measuring Equipment
ECM	Electronic Counter Measures
ELG	Emergency Landing Ground
FAA	Fleet Air Arm
FIDO	Fog Investigation Dispersal Operation
F/Lt	Flight Lieutenant
F/O	Flying Officer
F/Sgt	Flight Sergeant
FTR	Failed to return
G/Capt	Group Captain
GP	General Purpose
HCU	Heavy Conversion Unit
ILS	Instrument Landing System
KptLt	Kapitän Leutnant
MALM	Master Air Loadmaster
NCO	Non-commissioned officer
OTU	Operational Training Unit
QGH	Controlled descent through cloud
QFE	Airfield barometric pressure
P/O	Pilot Officer
RAF	Royal Air Force
RAAF	Royal Australian Air Force
RCAF	Royal Canadian Air Force
RFC	Royal Flying Corps
RNAS	Royal Naval Air Service (Royal Naval Air Station)
ROC	Royal Observer Corps
SAM	Surface to Air Missile
SBA	Standard Beam Approach
Sgt	Sergeant
S/Ldr	Squadron Leader
SOC	Sector Operations Centre
TIs	Target Indicators
TRE	Telecommunication Research Establishment
VOR	Very High Frequency Omni-directional Radio
W/Cdr	Wing Commander
WO	Warrant Officer
WOP/AG	Wireless Operator/Air Gunner
WAAF	Women's Royal Air Force
W/T	Wireless Telegraphy

Chapter One

Sir George Cayley, Gliders and Balloons

Above the grassy slopes of Brompton Dale in North Yorkshire, possibly in the spring of 1849, an apparatus called the 'old flyer' lifted a boy a few yards off the ground. This was the first flight of a full-size aeroplane in the modern sense of the word. It flew in stable flight; it had an adjustable tail-unit that could be trimmed; and it had its own pilot-operated rudder and elevator. Although we do not know the precise date of the event or the name of the young aviator, we are told by Sir George Cayley, designer of the old flyer, that when willing hands hauled the apparatus downhill against a gentle breeze

"a boy of about ten years of age was floated off the ground for several yards."

There was no national recognition of the importance of what had just happened. No journalists came to Brompton that day although not long before they had attended Hull's Zoological Gardens to record Lt G.B. Gale's ascent in a 'Monster Balloon' called the *Cremorne*, "being the First Balloon Ascent from Hull for upwards of twenty years."

Of course, Sir George Cayley's old flyer lacked the sensationalism attaching to the story of Thomas Pelling, described as 'The Flying Man' in contemporary newspapers. Fascinated by the prospect of flight, he was one of those individuals who approached the problem rather differently from Sir George. As Cayley later wrote in his Triple Paper on Aerial Navigation: "The whole problem is confined within these limits - to make a surface support a given weight by the application of power to the resistance of air." Pelling had no knowledge of these fundamental principles and All Saints Church, Pocklington, records on a recently restored memorial stone the fate of this ill-prepared 'flying man' who met his death forty years before Cayley was born:

In memory of Thomas Pelling, Burton Stather, Lincolnshire, commonly called 'The Flying Man' who was killed against the battlement of Ye Choir when coming down the rope from the Steeple of this Church. This Fatal Accident happened on the 10th of April. He was buried on the 10th April 1733 exactly under the place where he died.

Apparently Pelling had fitted a pulley to the heel of a shoe in order to slide down a rope running from the church to a windlass located in the Star Inn that once stood opposite. Attached to his arms and legs were bird-like wings and a large crowd gathered to witness the flight of a man who looked "like a bat" as he stood silhouetted against the sky. Unfortunately, it seems that the windlass operator allowed the rope to slacken just as Pelling began his downward glide.

Of course, Sir George may not have publicised the old flyer because he was alive to the risks that inventors ran in those days: ridicule and theft. Those who tried to fly in

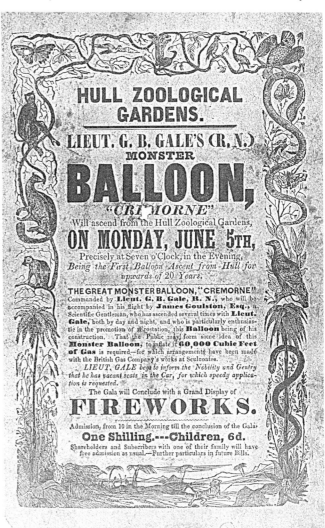

Contemporary advertisement of the 'Cremorne' ascent at Hull Zoological Gardens.

Hull Local Studies Library

ornithopters equipped with paddles and flapping wings were usually regarded as amiable lunatics; while some who produced a good idea but were slow to patent it were robbed of their own ingenuity by unscrupulous imitators. Moreover, Cayley's work in designing the 'old flyer' would have been known to very few during 1848-9 simply because the media of the day was disenchanted with the subject of 'flying machines'. Nor was it especially impressed by Sir George Cayley's views on the design of power units for the propulsion of aerial carriages.

A book entitled Aerial Navigation, written by Daedalus Britannicus, had just been published and it drew a careful distinction between *floating* and *flying* in the air. *Chambers's Edinburgh Journal*, published on 6 May 1848, devoted several pages to Daedalus, flying machines and the problem of aerial navigation, concluding that while ballooning had already 'attained perfection' it remained a toy, simply because it could not be steered. Everyone agreed that the challenge facing ambitious aeronauts was one of propulsion or navigation through the skies but the idea that this could be best achieved by hoisting a steam engine aloft was impracticable. The Journal went on to refer to Sir George Cayley though its editor had plainly never heard of the Yorkshireman's *current* experiments with gliders:

> "Sir George Cayley, an accurate mathematician and a sound philosopher, clung with invincible tenacity to the steam-propulsion idea, and proposed the use of a balloon made of Mackintosh's India-rubber cloth, filling it with *steam*, and at the same time propelling the car by a steam-engine beneath."

The editor then selected some of Cayley's favourite lines from Dr. Darwin:

> "Soon shall thy arm, unconquered steam ! afar
> drag the slow barge, or drive the rapid car;
> Or on wide-waving wings expanded, bear
> The flying chariot through the fields of air."

but gave this idea scant credibility, dismissing steam-engined propulsion units as "a hopeless drag". So in the 1840s Cayley's name was associated with the un-attainable: the use of a steam-engine to secure propulsion through the air. There was no acknowledgement of his immense contribution to the theory of flight and its application to the design of the 'old flyer'.

Yet there was ever-increasing *public* interest in what the magazines and journals of the day described as *aerostation*, supporting an apparatus in the air statically. This interest was as developed in Yorkshire as in any other part of the

United Kingdom. Among Cayley's contemporaries were starry-eyed experimenters who dreamed of the day when people would fly over hill and dale in aerial carriages. The Hull artist, Thomas Walker (c.1785-1835), was such a dreamer. He had read Cayley's aeronautical papers and published his own *Thoughts upon the Art of Flying by Mechanical Means* in 1810. However, his claim to have flown a successful ornithopter was the product of his own vivid imagination while George Cayley's claim to have designed the first successful aeroplane in the modern sense of the word remains secure.

★ ★ ★

Born in Scarborough in 1773, George Cayley was nine and a half years old when the Montgolfier brothers' first unmanned hot-air balloon reached a height of over six thousand feet above Paris on 4 June 1783. When he was about twenty-two, Cayley was working on an idea for 'mechanical flight' and produced a helicopter toy fitted with two contra-rotating rotors. So as early as 1796 Cayley understood the significance of the airscrew or propeller though he would always fight shy of fitting an airscrew to the glider designs for which he later became famous. Evidence of this appears in 1799 when he carefully engraved on a silver disc the outline of a fixed-wing monoplane. All agree it was the "first modern configur-ation aeroplane design of history with the system of lift divorced from the system of thrust", crewed by a pilot whose task was to work the paddles as well as to fly the aircraft.[1] On the obverse of this disc Cayley drew the very first lift-drag-thrust diagram, the foundation of modern international aeronautical science.

Cayley's problem was that, although he was the first to grasp the principles of mechanical flight, he was forever frustrated by the lack of a device to produce thrust. What

The silver disc initialled and dated by Sir George Cayley and preserved in the Science Museum.
(C.H Gibbs-Smith, Sir George Cayley's Aeronautics, HMSO 1962 p.3)

he needed, he said, was "a prime mover". He well understood the relationship between the weight of an aeroplane, the lift provided by its wings and the drag created by the air through which it flew. But how could he impel the aeroplane forward to overcome these forces, maintain the thrust and keep the aeroplane aloft ? His genius led to the design of successful model gliders of modern aeronautical configuration in 1804 and 1808/9 but, of course, it was muscle power that provided the thrust for these experiments. From then on, Cayley's main aim was to enable men to fly in fixed wing aeroplanes which would be propelled through the air, as he put it, "when we can get a hundred horsepower into a pint pot". So, aside from a brief period in 1843 when he designed an 'Aerial Carriage', part aeroplane, part helicopter, Cayley devoted such time as he could spare from his many other interests to building man-carrying gliders.

For Cayley was a man of many parts. In his twenties, he displayed an intelligence adored by his mother but resented by some with whom he was in daily contact. He had a quick, logical, enquiring mind and could be devastating in an argument. This he balanced with plenty of charm and wit and girls liked this tall, auburn-haired young man. Little 'Miss Phil' was the first to succumb. She was his cousin, Philadelphia Cayley, who dreamed of a romantic attachment to George, especially when he succeeded to the baronetcy after his father died in 1792. He confided in her one day:

> "I have ideas, lots of ideas that must be made to work. This must be the best-run property in Yorkshire, with the happiest tenants in all England, if I can so make it . . ."[2]

To Miss Phil's dismay, George was attracted to Sarah Walker, a very bright and gorgeous redhead. He had first met her at the home of his private tutor, the Reverend George Walker of Nottingham, and married her in 1795, the year before he made his helicopter toy.

His contributions to aeronautical science, though profound, proceeded with many interruptions to permit the invention of devices as varied as a mechanical hand for an injured estate worker and a self-righting lifeboat. In a spurt of original thought and practice between 1804 and 1818 (a period dominated by the Napoleonic Wars and the peacemaking after the defeat of Napoleon at Waterloo in 1815), Cayley wrote his *Triple Paper On Aerial Navigation*. Published during 1809-1810, it was the first ever to deal with theoretical and practical aeronautics. Equally exciting, he designed and launched "the first full-size glider of history", either in 1808 or 1809. Cayley was delighted with the tests he carried out at Brompton.

"It was very beautiful," he wrote, "to see this noble white bird sail majestically from the top of a hill to any given point of the plain below, according to the set of its rudder . . . descending in an angle of about eight degrees with the horizon."[3]

In 1816 he published his second paper, this time on the design and propulsion of an airship, and though his designs did not result in a practical flying machine they proved a fruitful source of data for later airship builders. Cayley actually inscribed some of his airship plans on his workshop doorpost and these are still on view today, as the illustration overleaf shows.

Meanwhile, his contemporaries either followed the path he was treading or concentrated on building man-

A view of Sir George Cayley's Workshop in 1992.

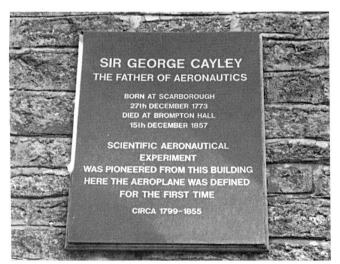

Plaque on wall of Sir George Cayley's Workshop.

The famous 'airship scratching' now urgently in need of preservation.

Rev. Leonard Rivett

This is a rather faint engraving of the The Royal Balloon taken from the frontispiece of "An Account of Mr James Deeker's Two Aerial Expeditions from the City of Norwich", describing Deeker's balloon ascents two months before he and Weller came to York. It was printed by John Crouse in Norwich during 1785.   *York City Archives, The Horner Collection*

carrying balloons, some of which were displayed in Yorkshire. Although Rolt properly credits Lunardi with a "triumphantly successful ascent"[4] from Kettlewell's Orchard, York Minster, on 23 August 1786, perhaps the earliest recorded balloon ascent in the County was made by a Mr Weller in somewhat imperfect weather conditions from the same site close to York Minster in 1785. Weller had borrowed an "aerostatic globe" belonging to the English pioneer balloonist, James Deeker. According to the following extract from a scrapbook compiled by the Rev. Robert William Bilton Hornby, Deeker's 'Royal Balloon' had an exciting though short-lived ascent.

"Yesterday... Messrs Weller's and Deeker's Balloon ascended from Kettlewell's Orchard at the back of the Minster, the process of filling the Balloon (by oil and vitriol) began at 11 am and occupied two hours. After Mr Walker had got into the car the balloon was liberated and seemed to ascend with majestic grandeur but a sudden gust of wind caused the Balloon and Car to strike against a high wall and a tree by which they were both much injured.

Mr Weller threw out sand and the Balloon was disengaged. It however was thrown by the violence of the wind against the Riding House. On quitting this it struck the top of Alderman Bacon's house and chimney by which the netting was rent from top to bottom and the Balloon was turned upside down. The silk near the top gave way and the valve which fastened the netting was left with it on the chimney by which means the Car was supported against the roof of the house and Mr Weller was miraculously preserved.

The Balloon escaped but being instantly deprived of inflammable air was taken up in Blake Street about 150 yards from the roof of the house where it had left Weller, the shattered car and the netting."[5]

Hornby mistakenly places these events as taking place on 1 September 1785 but the *York Courant* (from which Hornby had copied his data and which may be found in the J.G Horner Collection in the York City Archives) describes the first flight as taking place on 25 August 1785. In fact the balloon and its car had already been exhibited at the Judges Lodgings in Coney Street at the relatively high entrance fee of one shilling for 'Ladies and Gentlemen' and sixpence each for 'Servants etc.' Apparently, no broadsheet depicting the *Royal Balloon* was ever issued in York but the car was described as "an elegant Chinese Temple, decorated and ornamented in a style of unparalleled elegance which had been allowed by the many thousands (who have already seen it) as the most superb and complete Vehicle ever seen in this Kingdom".

After Weller's first flight in York, during which he had travelled about 400 yards, he and Deeker managed to persuade the local citizens to fund the cost of hydrogen manufacture for a second attempt on 31 August 1785. This time, Weller chose to fly from the Knavesmire where a grandstand could accommodate the spectators. Again, weather conditions were against him. Spectators were beoming cold and impatient, someone spilt a bottle of acid, there was a commotion and the balloon escaped from its handlers. The crowd turned into an angry mob and Deeker and Weller, in fear of their lives, disappeared from the Knavesmire and from the history of aviation.

This event illustrates why early aeronauts were sometimes seen as charlatans, charging high spectator fees for flights that so often ended in failure. Fortunately for Vincenzo Lunardi, his ascent in York was a triumph in August 1786, followed by an even more successful flight on 14 December 1786 when his hydrogen balloon astonished the citizens of Leeds by ascending from the White Cloth Hall and landing at Thorp Arch after a forty minute flight. In 1814 William Windham Sadler (1796-1824), a professional aeronaut at the age of seventeen, arrived in York to demonstrate an ascent on 24 August. Three weeks later he was in Pontefract and took up a Miss Thompson. Sadler was back in Yorkshire in 1823 and on 4 September he took off in his crimson and white balloon from the Coloured Cloth Hall in Leeds and flew across country to South Cliffe near Market Weighton. He hired a chaise in Market Weighton and returned to Leeds with his balloon strapped on top. On Friday 5 September an equally famous aeronaut named Charles Green (1785-1870) ascended at the White Cloth Hall in Leeds in his *Royal Coronation* balloon. His balloons were the first to be

inflated with coal gas, readily available in many of Britain's new industrial cities. Some reports claimed the *Royal Coronation* was the biggest balloon yet seen in Yorkshire, with a circumference of 107 feet and a gas capacity of 136,210 gallons. The flight was not without incident. As he was landing at Haxey, nine miles north of Gainsborough in Lincolnshire his anchor cable snagged a tree and snapped. Green fell to the ground. He was unhurt but the balloon immediately shot into the air, crossed the North Sea and came down in Holland! The Leeds Mercury carried advertisements for its recapture and Green offered £10 reward. However, the Dutchman who found it demanded £18 before he would restore it, torn and missing its valuable barometer, to its owner.

Despite these hazards, balloon ascents were profitable for both the aeronauts and the organisers of the spectacle. They rapidly became the high spot of local fairs and galas and were much in demand. Sadler returned to York a fortnight after Green's accident at Haxey and thrilled the crowds with a flight to Selby on 22 September. The following year Charles Green was in Halifax and on 19 April 1824 he took off from the Piece Hall (the spire of the Congregational Church had not been built then) and flew his balloon to Hornby Castle, seat of the Duke of Leeds, sixty-three miles away at Bedale. It was said that 50,000 people assembled on the hills outside Halifax for a free view of Green's departure. Not to be outdone, Sadler launched his balloon from Hull Citadel on 11 August 1824. More than 60,000 people came to watch Sadler and his passenger Rees Davies fly from Hull to Preston.

Balloonists such as Green and Sadler were heroes of their day and their activities brought a very real excitement into the lives of Yorkshire people. Thus it was with a sense of shock that they heard news of Sadler's death in the autumn of 1824. Sadler's balloon had collided with the chimney of a house at Foxhill Bank near Blackburn on 29 September and the aeronaut was killed when the impact hurled him from his basket to the ground. He had earned his place in aviation history by making the first aerial crossing of the Irish Sea and his fatal flight that September day was his thirty-first ascent. Though not the first air fatality in northern England - one of Lunardi's assistants, Ralph Heron, had died during a faulty ascent at Newcastle in August 1786 - his death was keenly felt. For Sadler had been one of the first of the great band of balloonist showmen who provided millions with their vicarious thrills of flying in the early nineteenth century.

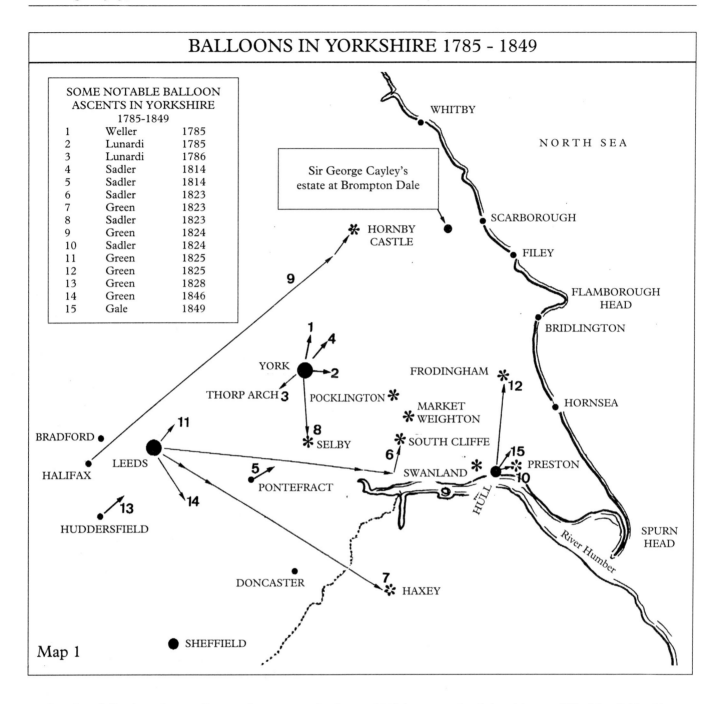

BALLOONS IN YORKSHIRE 1785 - 1849

SOME NOTABLE BALLOON
ASCENTS IN YORKSHIRE
1785-1849

1	Weller	1785
2	Lunardi	1785
3	Lunardi	1786
4	Sadler	1814
5	Sadler	1814
6	Sadler	1823
7	Green	1823
8	Sadler	1823
9	Green	1824
10	Sadler	1824
11	Green	1825
12	Green	1825
13	Green	1828
14	Green	1846
15	Gale	1849

Sir George Cayley's
estate at Brompton Dale

Map 1

In the following June, Green demonstrated the reliability of his giant balloons before a breathless crowd at the Coloured Cloth Hall, Leeds, by taking aloft a lady passenger, Miss Stocks, on his thirty-second ascent (9 June 1825). It was a busy summer for Green and his much admired ascents included one from the Hull Gas Company Station near Sculcoates Church, landing at Frodingham after a 'highly successful aerial voyage'. In 1828 he entertained the citizens of Huddersfield with two impressive ascents and was the most popular of all performers on the north of England gala circuit. By 1841 Green had the reputation of being one of Europe's most experienced aeronauts and in the September he was due to make his 289th ascent from the Hull Citadel. During the night a storm ripped across the city and Green's balloon was "torn from the grasp of thirty men." Five

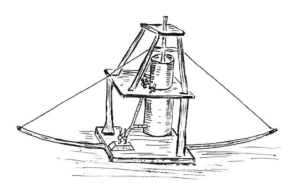

Cayley's sketch for a 'gunpowder explosion engine.'

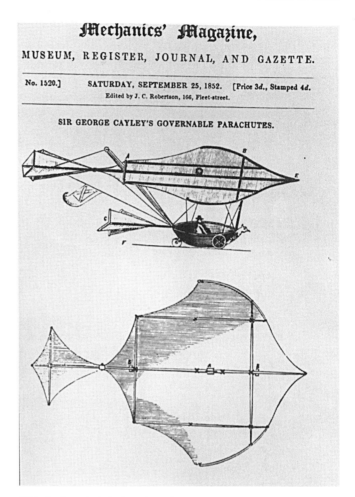

This is the 1852 design though there is no evidence that it was adopted for the 1853 'New Flyer'. However, Lt Cmdr J Sproule copied the design in 1971 and flew a 16lb model off Brompton Dale. In 1974 he made a replica of the 1852 design and, towed by a motor car, the glider made a successful flight at Brompton with Derek Piggott at the controls.

Leonard Rivett & Jim Matthew, Sir George Cayley,
The Father of Aeronautics, YAM, 1991, P.19

years later, in 1846, the City Fathers of Leeds were anxious to celebrate the Repeal of the Corn Laws. They declared that Friday afternoon, 7 August 1846, would be a public holiday and to make it memorable they hired Charles Green to thrill the people with a balloon ascent from the White Cloth Hall.

This was also the year in which the aviation pioneer William Samuel Henson (1805-1888) first described George Cayley as the "Father of Aerial Navigation". An avid student of Cayley's publications, Henson had optimistically registered a patent for his "Machine for conveying goods, letters and passengers from place to place through the air" and he tried to persuade Parliament to let him set up an Aerial Steam Transit Company. He was particularly receptive to Cayley's ideas on the need for a light-weight engine to power a fixed wing aeroplane. In fact, Cayley had been working on the basic principle of an internal combustion engine in which the piston would be fired by a gas explosion - or even a gunpowder explosion !

In partnership with John Stringfellow (1799-1883), Henson managed to build a little steam engine and he used this to power *Ariel*, a model monoplane fitted with two pusher airscrews. Though it conformed to most of the aeronautical principles laid down by Cayley, *Ariel* failed to fly. Disenchanted and short of cash, Henson emigrated to America, leaving Stringfellow to improve on the design of both the monoplane and the steam engine during 1848. This was the year in which Cayley was trying to perfect his man-carrying glider and, as we have already seen, he met with remarkable success at Brompton Dale in 1849. Then, on 30 August 1849, at the age of seventy-six, this extraordinary man recorded the first flights of the most sophisticated fixed wing glider to date, with the upright rudder riding on top of the elevator.

Cayley was now confident that he could construct a full-scale man-carrying glider and published his

arguments and specifications in the *Mechanics' Magazine* for 25 September 1852. His article had a most unlikely title: *Sir George Cayley's Governable Parachutes.*

But it becomes more acceptable when we understand that Cayley designed the glider to be *dropped* from a balloon and controlled by a pilot in its glide to the ground.

His governable parachute had all the characteristics of an aeroplane as we understand it today: fixed wings set at an angle of incidence with dihedral to give lateral stability in flight; fin and tailplane to provide directional stability; a rudder and elevator control for the pilot who sat in a fuselage equipped with a three-wheel undercarriage. It is reasonable to suppose that Cayley's 1852 design, perhaps modified as a biplane or triplane by his versatile mechanic, Mr.Vick, was the man-carrying glider of 1853. Sadly, no photograph or drawing of this "new flyer" has ever been found but we are lucky to have a a verbal record from Mrs Dora Thompson (1843-1933), grand-daughter of Sir George Cayley.

Dora was only ten when the Brompton villagers gathered on the dale to watch one of Sir George Cayley's staff clamber into the fuselage of the "new flyer". Again, we do not know who he was. Dora remembered him as her grandfather's coachman.[6] Everyone expected the machine to soar into the Yorkshire skies and the villagers thronged the high east side of the dale, pressing forward to get a good view of the start. No doubt the launching system was similar to the one used for the "old flyer" and the aeroplane lifted up and flew rapidly across the dale. Dora thought "it came down in rather a shorter distance than we expected. The coachman got himself clear and, when the watchers had got across, he shouted,

'Please, Sir George, I wish to give notice. I was hired to drive, and not to fly !' "[7]

We have little reason to doubt Dora's veracity though she could remember little else except that the "new flyer" was stored in a barn roof and that she often used to sit in it to hide from her governess!

Such was the first flight of a man-carrying aeroplane in Yorkshire and in the world, almost exactly fifty years before the Wright brothers took off in Flyer No. 1 on 17 December 1903 at Kill Devil Hill in the United States of America. In a speech to the Aero Club in London (1909), Wilbur Wright properly acknowledged his debt to a Yorkshire baronet:

"About a hundred years ago an Englishman, Sir George Cayley, carried the science of flying to a point it had never reached before."

So it seems odd that, in Europe, Cayley's work remained largely ignored for the rest of the nineteenth century. Though his scientific achievements were in part acknowledged by the Aeronautical Society of Great Britain in 1876, they appeared to have little or no

Sir George Cayley
1773-1857.

Yorkshire Air Museum Publication: 'Sir George Cayley - The Father of Aeronautics', Leonard Rivett & Jim Matthew, 1991.

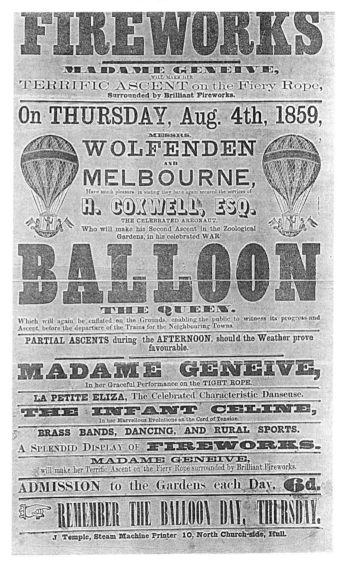

Coxwell's War Balloon - 4 August 1859.

Hull Local Studies Library

influence on the world of aviation for the forty years or so after Cayley died (15 December 1857).

Ballooning and gliding remained the passion of the pioneer aeronauts. In Yorkshire, memories of Gale's *Cremorne* were eclipsed by Henry Coxwell's War Balloon, *The Queen*, that flew from the Hull Zoological Gardens on a hazy July day with the wind from the east. It made a safe landing in Swanland. After another flight on 4 August 1859 with his sponsor, R.R.Melbourne, he descended in the grounds of Burton Constable where the noble owner ordered the balloon to be packed up and shipped to Hull, wined and dined the pilot and his passenger, and then sent them home in his private carriage. Henry Coxwell was a worthy successor to Green, with an altitude record (1862) and a permanent niche at the York gala every year from 1859 to 1885.

Less well known was the pioneer work of Otto Lilienthal (1848-96) in Germany. He was Europe's leading glider expert and had certainly read George Cayley's *Triple Paper*. He too studied the flight of birds but seemed to ignore most of Cayley's findings, choosing to study the flight of hand-reared storks as the basis of his own aerodynamics. Lilienthal lacked a Brompton Dale and had to build an artificial hill near his home at Lichterfelde. His man-carrying gliders were averaging flights of fifty yards and were much admired by Percy Sinclair Pilcher (1866-1899) who visted Lilienthal to learn the German's flying techniques. Lilienthal, who also enjoys the title 'Father of Modern Aviation', crashed and died in 1896.

Undeterred, Pilcher built a glider called the *Hawk* that managed a flight of 250 yards in 1897. In 1899 he was designing a Cayley-like triplane glider to which he planned to fit a lightweight engine and propeller. He might have been the first man to make a sustained powered flight but fate decreed otherwise. Pilcher crashed the *Hawk* and died from his injuries on 2 October 1899.

Four years later the Wright brothers, themselves disciples of Cayley and Lilienthal, flew at Devil Hill, Kittyhawk, USA.

Chapter Two

Magnificent Men, Magnificent Women and their Flying Machines 1901 - 1914.

Samuel Franklin Cody, a US citizen, was the first aviator to fly a powered aeroplane in Britain. He was a professional showman at Alexandra Palace, headquarters of his Wild West cowboy show and the site of the workshop where he experimented with kites and hot air balloons. Having aroused the interest of the War Office in the kite's military potential, he laid on a demonstration at Holbeck Moor near Leeds in December 1901. He was performing his current show, the *Klondyke Nugget*, when Major F. Trollope of the Grenadier Guards arrived in Leeds to announce that the War Office was indeed interested in the man-carrying kite. But the middle of a Yorkshire winter was not the best time to demonstrate his latest aeronautical design. However, the major encouraged him to go ahead and Cody's pilot kite, followed by the 'lifters' quickly disappeared into ominously low clouds. So did Cody's son, Leon, who was on board the man-carrying kite and acting as a reluctant observer. Fortunately, Leon was linked to earth by telephone and soon told his father how cold Yorkshire stratus could be. Cody rapidly pulled his frost-encrusted son back to earth to be greeted by a highly impressed Major Trollope. Despite a glowing report on the military implications of a man-carrying kite, the War Office did not share the major's enthusiasm.

Cody's response to rejection was two-fold: to pester the War Office through his friendship with like-minded army officers and to keep his kite-flying ideas before the British public at every opportunity. Eventually, he won a contract for man-carrying kites and was appointed the Army's first Kiting Instructor. Ever persuasive, he managed to convince the military of the need for a heavier-than-air flying machine and the soldiers solemnly set aside £50.00 for research purposes. Thus was born the idea of Army Aeroplane No. 1 and it was this machine that made the first powered flight in Britain on 16 October 1908 when the aeroplane covered 1390 feet in twenty-seven seconds. In the same year, Richard 'Bobby' Allen, the 'flying policeman' from Bradford, hoped for similar success. He had built an elaborate winged bicycle and at the 1908 Peel Park Gala Reuben Bramhall's balloon was scheduled to release Allen and his flying bicycle at 200 feet. The balloon began to rise and Allen pedalled with all his might. Almost immediately, a wing fell off, followed by the flying policeman.

Aviation truly came of age the following year. European enthusiasts perceived that flying machines and the people who flew them were of special fascination to the public who would willingly pay to watch or read about any form of aviation that was presented as 'daring' and 'spectacular'. From its beginnings, therefore, aviation was marketed as a commercial commodity and it was with this in mind that Louis Blériot flew across the English Channel on 25 July 1909 in his specially modified Model XI monoplane. His motive was to advertise and sell Blériot aeroplanes though, at the time, the media recognised his flight as a great technological and human achievement that carried with it an unpalatable fact: Britain was no longer an island. This was a statement calculated to create a sense of unease in the minds of the insular British and to motivate them into taking an interest in aeronautics. Accordingly, when Europe's first Air Show was held at the Reims Aviation Meeting in August 1909, it was reported in terms of 'speed records', 'distance records' and 'height records', phrases designed to inject a sense of competitive sport and excitement into the public's perception of aeronautics. Newspapers, especially the indefatigable *Daily Mail*, rapidly transformed Britain into an air-minded nation. Within weeks, local councils were competing with one another to attract pilots of powered aircraft to their Gala Days.

Blackpool was the first municipality to sign up the 'big names' and, not to be outdone, Doncaster did the same. Aviation's own 'War of the Roses' had begun. In Leeds the Yorkshire Light Aeroplane Club held its inaugural meeting in the Metropole Hotel and by the time the eight-day Doncaster Air Races began on 15 October 1909 the club boasted two hundred members. Many were young businessmen who by 1909 had already bought the new powerful motor-cars that were coming on the market. If they were willing to pay over £1000 just for the rolling chassis of a 1909 60 hp Napier then a Blériot XI that could fly across country and land at low speed in a meadow must have seemed an exciting investment at £480. As scores of French and British aeroplanes took part in festivities, gala days and exhibition flying across the County over the next four years, Yorkshire began to reach for the skies.

However, to attract Cody and his *Cathedral* biplane in 1909, Doncaster had to pay out £2000 - £500 in advance - and the sponsors must have wondered if they would get their money's worth. The Press had been told that the curious 'gull wing' effect of the lower wing on Cody's aeroplane was technically a 'katahedral' and from then on everyone called it *The Flying Cathedral*, especially as it towered above all the other competitors. Cody's flying was spectacular. Scorning the French pilots who made short flights to inspect the course, Cody throttled the *Cathedral* at full power, skimmed a Farman [1] and wheeled round for a fly-past in front of the shilling enclosure and then climbed away. As *The Times* later commented:

"It was a spectacle never to be forgotten."

Then came the accident. As Cody landed, the *Cathedral's* wheels sank into a ditch and this mishap kept him out of the impressive list of prize-winners.

Cody took out naturalisation papers during the Doncaster Air Races so the Cathedral was technically one of the three British entries. Of the other British aeroplanes at Doncaster, one was A.E.Mine's tiny pusher aircraft called the *Dot*. Its eight horse-power engine lacked the necessary thrust and the aeroplane refused to leave the

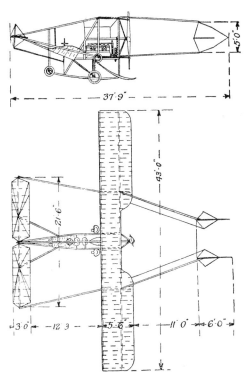

This is a contemporary drawing of the CODY TYPE V BIPLANE that won the British Military Trials (1912). It was almost identical with the 'Round Britain Race' biplane, apart from modified rudder shape. Much interest focused on the divided front elevator in which the two halves were operated to maintain lateral balance and were used in conjunction with wing warping to effect turns. Pegamoid fabric covered the wings and elevators. There was no covering on the horizontal tailplane.

ground. Even less successful was Captain Windham's 'Special'. Its air-frame collapsed as he wheeled it out of the hangar. It was left to the French aviators to provide the air races. Roger Sommer won the Doncaster Cup with his outstanding Farman biplane; Delagrange put up a new speed record of 53 mph in his Gnôme-engined Blériot; Schrenk demonstrated his up-dated Wright Flyer. No British aeroplane entered the Doncaster Air Races in September 1910 and so the

Mlle Hélène Dutrieux

Farmans and Blériots, plus the attractive little stagger-winged biplane 'Goupy III' (designed by Ambroise Goupy but built by Blériot), collected all the prizes. An unusual feature of the meeting was the competitiveness of the three women pilots, all of whom flew Farmans: Hélène Dutrieux (the first woman in Belgium to gain a pilot's licence), Mlle Beau and Bruneau de Laborie. These three, together with Ladougne, pilot of the Goupy, and de Lesseps and Mamet who flew the Blériots, displayed the speed and manoeuvrability of French designs. The Yorkshire crowds had hoped that Britain's first licensed pilot, Claude Graham-White, would land at Town Moor racecourse to repeat his earlier success at the Halifax Air Display (June 1910) but the aviator and his Farman biplane were left out of the programme.

Still, the British were doing their best. A Hull marine engineer, Thomas Leonard Bell, designed and built a monoplane at his garage in Newington during 1909. This aeroplane was displayed at the Central Hall, Pryme Street, Hull, in May 1910 and was publicised as 'the

Thomas Leonard Bell (1886-1923) Hull's first aeronautical designer.   *Darrell Bell*

Yorkshire - Lancashire Rivalry 1909

(As recorded in *How to Fly* by Richard Ferris, published by Thomas Nelson & Sons in 1910)

16 October 1909	Sommer, with biplane, at Doncaster, England, flies 9.7 miles in 21 minutes and 45 seconds, making the record for Great Britain. Delagrange, with monoplane, at Doncaster, flies 5.75 miles in 11 minutes and 25 seconds. Cody, with biplane, at Doncaster, flies 3000 feet, when his machine is wrecked and he is injured.
18 October 1909	Paulhan, with biplane, at Blackpool, flies 14 miles in 25 minutes and 58 seconds. Rougier, with biplane, at Blackpool, flies 17.7 miles in 24 minutes and 43 seconds, winning the second prize. Farman, with biplane, at Blackpool, flies 14 miles in 23 minutes.
19 October 1909	Le Blon, with monoplane, at Doncaster, flies 15 miles in a gale. Paulhan, with biplane, at Blackpool, flies 15.7 miles in 32 minutes and 18 seconds, winning the third prize.
20 October 1909	Farman, with biplane, at Blackpool, flies 47 miles in 1 hour, 32 minutes and 16 seconds, winning the first prize - £2000. Le Blon, with monoplane, at Doncaster, makes a spectacular flight in a fierce gale.
22 October 1909	Latham, with monoplane, at Blackpool, flies in a squally gale blowing from 30 to 50 mph. When headed into the wind the machine moved backward in relation to points on the ground. Going before the wind, it passed points on the ground at a speed of nearly 100 mph. This flight twice round the course is the most difficult feat accomplished by any aviator up to this date.
26 October 1909	Sommer, with biplane, at Doncaster, flies 29.7 miles, in 44 minutes and 53 seconds, winning the Whitworth Cup. Delagrange with monoplane at Doncaster, flies 6 miles in 7 minutes and 36 seconds - a speed of over 50 mph.

Newington monoplane'. Invitations to the 'Aeroplane Exhibition' promised that this aircraft, "every part of which has been built at Hull by local workmen", would be test-flown in Hull at "an early date". Few details of its brief career still exist but a 'Newington Monoplane' was certainly tested at Hedon in 1910 on the old racecourse that closed the previous year. There it suffered crankshaft failure due to its oversize propeller. Matters were not helped along by the attentions of an irate bull. Thomas Bell may by then have rebuilt the Mark I; or perhaps he built an entirely new aeroplane - a Newington 'Mk II'? Was it the 'Mark II' - seen opposite with Thomas Leonard's youngest brother, William, posed beside it - that flew at Hedon? Certainly several new

propellers made by a joiner, Walter Jackson, (one of which still survives in Walkington) were fitted in an effort to improve the flying qualities of this early design. However, the experiments were unsuccessful and the Newington monoplane never entered the competition for which it had been originally designed, the London *Daily Mail* £1000 prize for the first British aeroplane to fly a continuous mile. J.T.C. Moore-Brabazon, holder of the Royal Aero Club's first pilot licence, won this prize flying a Short-Wright biplane in October 1909.

During 1910 a new Northern Aero Syndicate formed in Bradford and bought a 25 hp Blériot. They hangared the aeroplane at Airedale Aerodrome on Rawdon Meadow and during August transported the Blériot to

Photograph of French aviators at the 1909 Doncaster Aviation Meeting.
J.M.Bruce/G.S.Leslie collection

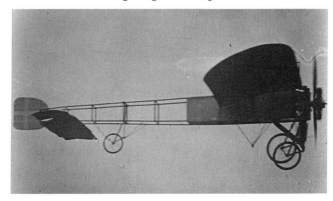

Delagrange's Blériot at Doncaster 1909. Note the propeller behind the engine.
J.M.Bruce/G.S.Leslie collection

J.W. House swings the propeller of the Blériot purchased by the Northern Aero Syndicate, August 1910, at the foot of the Filey slipway.   *J. M. Bruce/ G..S Leaslie collection*

The 'Newington Monoplane' displayed in Hull during 1910.   *Darrell Bell*

The 'Newington Mk II', with William Bell standing by its side. The machine clearly owed a lot to the influence of Blériot though its precise origins and fate remain unknown.   *Darrell Bell*

Filey to test it on the long stretch of unobstructed sands. Filey, an ideal flying ground, had already been selected as a test centre by Yorkshire's second aviation genius, Robert Blackburn.

Robert Blackburn was born on 26 March 1885 in Leeds where his father managed the manufacturing firm

Robert Blackburn in the wicker chair of the 'First Monoplane'   *British Aerospace, Brough*

The First Monoplane engaging local interest on the sands at Filey.   *British Aerospace, Brough*

of Thomas Green & Sons. Robert graduated from Leeds University with an honours degree in engineering and the prospect of a career designing steam-engines and lawn-mowers for his father. Eventually, father and son agreed to differ on this subject and by 1908 Robert was working for a French company in Rouen. Passionately interested in aeroplanes, he regularly took time off to watch Wilbur Wright, Louis Blériot and Henry Farman fly their aeroplanes at Le Mans and Issy. He was especially taken by the lines of the elegant Antoinette machines. [2] His long-suffering French employers, less interested in aeroplanes than he, encouraged Robert to return to the UK at the end of the year and, thanks to parental generosity, Robert was able to build a small workshop in Benson Street, Leeds. He was fortunate to have as his mechanic one of Green's apprentices, Harry Goodyear, who had been approached by George Blackburn to "help our Bob build this contraption of his..." It was at the Benson Street workshop that Robert Blackburn and Harry Goodyear built the 'First Monoplane' and maintained an unsteady cash flow selling wooden propellers at £1.75 a foot. Robert also advertised an unproven ability to manufacture ready-to-fly aeroplanes at £700 a time.

Blackburn soon finished his 'First Monoplane' and tested it in April 1909 on the sands between Marske and Saltburn where the machine hopped along for a few yards 'sand-scratching' but refused to engage in sustained flight.

Back at the drawing board, Blackburn designed a Second Monoplane inspired by the graceful Antoinettes he had seen at Issy. His new aeroplane came on the market at £500 but there were no takers. Blackburn transported it to Filey in 1910 and rented a small bungalow and a hangar on top of the cliffs. Before carrying out taxying trials and test flights he had to winch or manhandle his monoplane down a concrete slipway to Filey Sands. Harry Goodyear accompanied the Second Monoplane to the international flying meeting held at Squire's Gate, Blackpool, and it was there that he and Blackburn first met Bentfield Hucks who was acting as flying manager to Graham-White. Blackburn persuaded Bentfield to join his organisation (now known as Blackburn Aeroplanes) which was reconditioning Blériot machines in Leeds and selling them to private owners. Bentfield was attracted by the other aspect of Blackburn's work - the Filey venture which was now publicised as the 'Blackburn Flying School'. Here Robert was offering student pilots the chance to fly either in a reconditioned Blériot or in the

Second Monoplane, more robust now it was fitted with a stronger undercarriage. Harry Goodyear was then appointed as Bentfield Hucks' mechanic and given responsibility for maintaining the training aircraft in good flying condition.

This unexpected success at the Filey Flying School meant that Blackburn could now expand his Yorkshire enterprise. He opened new workshops in Balm Street, Leeds, and these became the headquarters of 'The Blackburn Aeroplane Co.' Helped by Harry Goodyear, Mark Swann and George Watson, Blackburn constructed Mercury I, a two-seat version of the Second Monoplane powered by a 50 hp Isaacson radial engine. Realising that student pilots were bound to make some heavy landings during their training, he fitted the Mercury with a four-wheel undercarriage protected by a complicated ash-framed skid system. *Mercury I* was now a sturdy machine and after being displayed at the 1911 Olympia Air Show in London it joined the Second Monoplane as a trainer at Filey. Bentfield Hucks was both instructor and test pilot and in his skilled hands *Mercury I* set up a height record for Northern England: 1200 feet on 17 May 1911.

1911 was the year of the *Daily Mail* £10,000 Circuit of Britain Air Race. Backed by Stuart Hirst, a keen air-minded businessman who had already offered a prize of £50 to the first airman to fly into Leeds in a Yorkshire-built aeroplane, Blackburn constructed two special single-seat *Mercury IIs*. One flown by Hucks had a Gnôme engine; the other piloted by Conway Jenkins was fitted with an Isaacson. A week before the race, Hucks tried to win the £50 prize in his *Mercury II* but had to force-land at East Heslerton Grange, wrecking Mercury's undercarriage in the process. Robert Blackburn repaired the aircraft and both *Mercury IIs* reached Hendon where the race started on 22 July 1911.

The first official stop was to be in Yorkshire on the Stray at Harrogate where interest in Air Races had never been higher. Proclaimed the *Harrogate Advertiser*, "The great aviation meeting on the Stray formed one of the most succesful attractions we have had in Harrogate." Local newspapers estimated that some 70,000 people paid between sixpence and five shillings to secure a place on the Stray while another 100,000 found their spots free of charge. Roads into Harrogate were blocked with traffic; over one thousand motor cars were parked on the Stray; a train arrived from Hull packed with aviation enthusiasts who were to witness "some of the finest descents and ascents ever made in connection with aviation." The huge grandstand had acetylene lighting in case any of the aircraft arrived after dusk though the organisers at

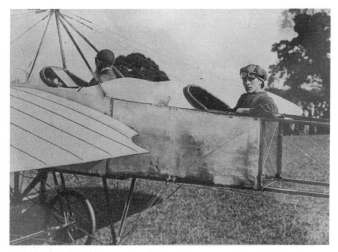

Harry Goodyear became well known among the small but ever-growing band of pioneer aviators and often flew with them. He is sitting in the rear cockpit of a Blériot prior to a flight from Norwich in 1914.   *Mr H Goodyear via J.G.A Swales*

Blackburn's Second Monoplane at Filey. Note the hangar detail and the skids fitted on the wingtips of the monoplane.

Bruce Leslie collection.

Bentfield Hucks in the cockpit of Mercury I on the cliff-top at Filey.   *Bruce Leslie collection.*

Hendon hoped to avoid this by starting the race at four in the morning.

Blackburn was to have no luck with his *Mercury IIs*. Conway Jenkins crashed his aeroplane as he was taxying prior to take-off; Hucks had to make a forced-landing near Luton and retired from the race. More than anything else, Robert Blackburn wanted a racing win to establish himself in the forefront of British aircraft designers. But the first British pilot to arrive at the Stray was in a French aeroplane - James Valentine flying a Deperdussin. He promised the delighted crowds that "All my life, I'll be your Valentine!" and the organisers presented him with a solid silver tea service and tray for his achievement. Cody's great biplane, the Cody No III, just missed the top of the Royal Hotel as he came in low over the trees. Everyone thought he looked the usual immaculate aviator but he had actually had a difficult and demanding flight with two unscheduled stops to repair a radiator at Rotherham and then a cracked petrol pipe just before he reached Harrogate. When interviewed about his misfortunes and the fact that he had no support team of

mechanics as did the French entrants, Cody is reputed to have replied with a defiant toss of his grey beard:

"But then I know how to nurse little things of this sort. I know this machine, sir, and it's British through and through."

Many other competitors also had their problems. Gustav Hamel arrived and "swooned" as his machine touched down. Doctors rushed to his aeroplane to find him slumped in his seat, his hands clenched round the 'steering wheel'. They administered brandy and after five hours' rest Hamel was on his way again. Lt Reynolds had to force-land his Howard-Wright biplane in a cornfield near Doncaster and then employ a team of men to carve a runway with their scythes so he could take off again. Howard Pixton was flying a Bristol biplane when he crashed at Rudding Park to the south of Harrogate. Lt Cammell had to abandon his wrecked machine at

Cody's great machine.

Bruce Leslie collection

'Giant of a man in a giant of a machine': Cody at the controls.

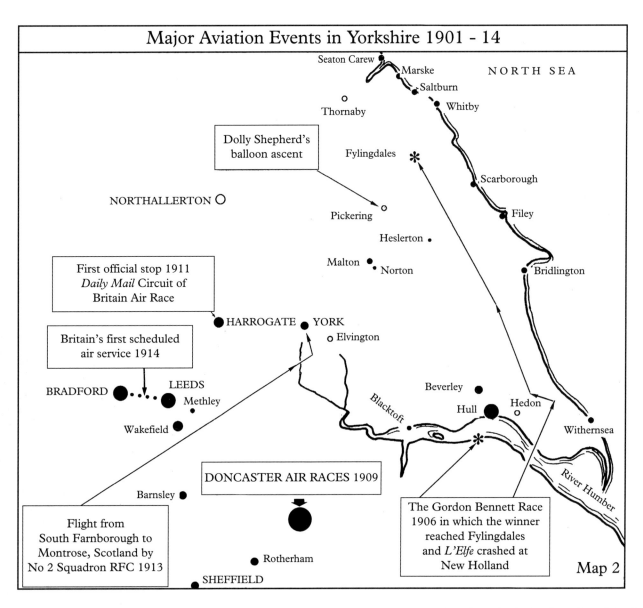

Major Aviation Events in Yorkshire 1901 - 14

NORTH SEA

Seaton Carew
Marske
Saltburn
Thornaby
Whitby

Dolly Shepherd's
balloon ascent

Fylingdales
Scarborough

NORTHALLERTON O

Pickering
Filey
Heslerton
Malton
Norton
Bridlington

First official stop 1911
Daily Mail Circuit of
Britain Air Race

HARROGATE   YORK
Elvington

Britain's first scheduled
air service 1914

BRADFORD   LEEDS
Methley
Wakefield

Beverley
Blacktoft
Hull   Hedon
Withernsea

DONCASTER AIR RACES 1909

River Humber

Barnsley

Flight from
South Farnborough to
Montrose, Scotland by
No 2 Squadron RFC 1913

Rotherham

SHEFFIELD

The Gordon Bennett Race
1906 in which the winner
reached Fylingdales
and *L'Elfe* crashed at
New Holland

Map 2

Methley. Nevertheless, times were impressive for the flights from Hendon. The official timekeepers were Fattorini & Co., of Bradford, and they recorded the times at the Harrogate, Newcastle and Carlisle controls. It is interesting to note that Cody's Aeroplane No III was the only British aeroplane and the sole biplane to complete the course.

HENDON TO HARROGATE TIMES July 1911

	hrs	min	secs
Vedrines	3	3	4
Beaumont	3	7	30
Valentine	3	39	8
Cody	4	45	49
Hamel	7	40	43

Though disappointed by the lack of result at Hendon, Blackburn sent Hucks off on a tour of the West Country and went on to build six Mercury IIIs. The first of these was a three-seater, crashed by pilot Hubert Oxley at Filey on 27 November 1911. Oxley and his passenger, Robert Weiss, both died after the machine lost most of its fabric covering in a dive estimated to have reached 150 mph. The fourth *Mercury III* featured cutaway wing roots and Jack Brereton flew this aeroplane from Filey on 29 May 1912 in an attempt to win Hirst's elusive £50. He also failed to reach Leeds, coming down at Norton Parks near Malton. By then Robert Blackburn had unveiled a completely new design - the Type E Monoplane.

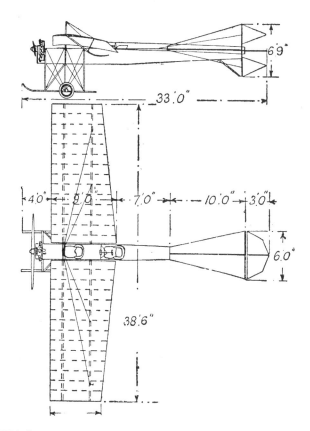

Brereton on Bridlington beach with a Mercury III 15 July 1912.
Bruce/Leslie collection

Salmet's Blériot over the fishing fleet at Scarborough 28 August 1913.   *Bruce/Leslie collection*

This is a contemporary drawing of one of the early Blackburn monoplanes with a tapering wing chord, presumably the Mercury Passenger Type that lost its wing fabric over Filey and crashed on the sands on 6 December 1911. It poses one or two interesting questions. A.J.Jackson states that this machine was the only one with a tapered wing chord and that it had a 60 hp Renault V-8 engine. It is now known that Blackburn was experimenting with various V-8 engines at this time, including the very rare American Rinek recently discovered by Dave Tappin in Leeds and now in Yorkshire Air Museum. However, the copywriter in 1911 stated that the aeroplane in the drawing had a 50 hp Isaccson, quite different from the V-8 powered, tapered wing Passenger Type illustrated below.

His *Type E* was a response to the first military specification issued by the War Office. The military needed a two-seat reconnaissance aeroplane that could loiter at 4500 feet for an hour. Designers at government-financed Farnborough, as well as Avro, Short, Vickers and Handley Page, were all seeking contracts for the manufacture of warplanes. With admirable foresight, Blackburn decided that the Type E would be a stronger version of the *Mercury IIIs* , with many metal components and a fuselage covered in sheet aluminium. He chose an 80 hp Renault engine as its powerplant but the so-called 'military two-seater' proved far too heavy to fly. To his disappointment, Blackburn aeroplanes were denied a place in the 1912 Trials on Salisbury Plain. Anyway, events beyond his control were about to dictate future aeroplane design. During the autumn of 1912 monoplanes had been involved in several accidents and the War Office decided on safety grounds to equip the new Royal Flying Corps solely with biplanes. That is why the first contracts were issued for the 'British Experimental No. 2' biplane (the B.E.2) designed by Geoffrey de Havilland at Farnborough.

Yorkshire Air Museum

Understandably, Blackburn felt he needed a base at the heart of British aviation. Leeds and Filey were too far away from Hendon and Brooklands. He chose to settle at Hendon and in September 1912 the School moved there under the direction of a new Chief Instructor, Harold Blackburn - no relation to Robert. Aircraft production continued in Balm Street and there Robert built the *Single-Seat Monoplane* for a recently qualified pilot named Cyril Foggin. Harold Blackburn test flew it in 1912 and then displayed it at Lofthouse Park, Leeds, and over Wakefield during Easter 1913. On 29 April he landed on the Stray, Harrogate, and in July he was making regular deliveries of *The Yorkshire Post* between Leeds and York. Cyril Foggin sold the machine to Montague Glew who crashed it at Wittering in 1914. Glew began a rebuild with the intention of installing a bigger engine but once the Great War began, he stored the airframe and all his spares in a barn. Twenty years later R.O.Shuttleworth salvaged everything he could find at Wittering and brought the components back to Old Warden. After a lengthy restoration, the *Single Seat Monoplane* still flies as part of the Shuttleworth Collection though there is now some doubt that the aeroplane is actually the original built for Foggin back in 1912. [3]

Others beside Blackburn were now making an impact on Yorkshire aviation. Gustav Hamel (1889-1914) was the first fixed wing pilot to fly into Hull and he arrived at the old racecourse at Hedon in July 1912. He flew a 50 hp Blériot and was the first aviator to cross the Humber, from Hedon to Grimsby Municipal College, on 17 July 1912. He put on several displays and flew over Hull docks, Withernsea, Preston and Sutton. Blackburn was, of course, familiar with Blériots; but he was astonished by the speed and power of a new biplane that appeared in 1913, the Avro 504 that had been built in "considerable secrecy". [4] Blackburn had not yet converted to biplane design and he was currently working on a new private-venture, the Blackburn *Type 1*. This was a bigger aeroplane with a span of 38 feet and a powerful 80 hp Gnôme engine. Its new owner, Dr M.C. Christie, hired Harold Blackburn as his professional pilot and Blackburn confidently challenged Lancashire to another aerial War of the Roses. The Avro 504 flew up to Leeds to compete against the *Christie Type 1* and the *Yorkshire Evening News* put up the prize-money. On 2 October 1913 the two aircraft set out to fly a hundred mile circular course: Leeds, York, Doncaster, Sheffield, Barnsley and back to Leeds. In appalling visibility, the Avro had to land near Barnsley while the *Christie Type 1* went on to win - Robert Blackburn's first racing success.

Aviation swiftly enters the world of popular culture. This is a Christmas card of c.1910.

Another manufacturer, Handley Page, had also made his mark in the Yorkshire skies. Handley Page built the famous *Yellow Peril* and hired a test pilot, Ronald Whitehouse, for a series of exhibition flights in the Midlands, in Hull and Beverley. Whitehouse and the *Yellow Peril* arrived in Hull and flew from a large field next to Endike Lane. On Thursday and Friday, 10-11 July 1913, Whitehouse enthralled the crowds; on the Saturday they were horrified when the *Yellow Peril* suffered engine failure on take-off. Apparently, Whitehouse did not try to land straight ahead but banked sharply in an effort to return to the field. The aeroplane stalled and nose-dived into Barmston Drain. Whitehouse was unhurt and he and his mechanic replaced the distinctive crescent-shaped wings, shorn off in the crash, to be ready for the Sunday air display. To his dismay, Hull's Mayor was unwilling to let Whitehouse fly within the city limits on the Sabbath and invoked the 1625 Lord's Day Observance Act to show how serious he was. Hull Education Committee and the local Wesleyan Mission were loud in their support of the Mayor though they did not deter Whitehouse who announced he intended to fly. Accordingly, on Sunday 13 July 1913 the police arrived to take the names of 7000 air-minded atheists who had congregated to cheer the defiant aviator. In the event, the Hull magistrates were

Lining up for the 'Great Air Race' - the War of the Roses
2 October 1913.
Bruce/Leslie collection

Ronald Whitehouse taking off in Yellow Peril.
Bruce/Leslie collection

Blackburn's entry taking off, War of the Roses 1913.
Bruce/Leslie collection

Captain Beck's B.E.2a No 217 of No 2 Squadron down near
Doncaster en route to Montrose.   *P Jarret via G.S.Leslie*

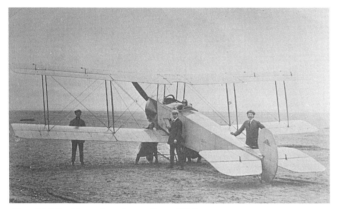

Harold Blackburn's private Avro 504.
Bruce/Leslie collection

Lt R.W.L Hubert flew this Farman Longhorn pusher No 266
into York during the RFC visit (21 February 1913).
Bruce/Leslie collection

disinclined to issue a summons against Whitehouse.
Apparently. some legal mind had pointed out that the
Yellow Peril could be defined as an arrow and, under a
much earlier Act of Parliament, archery practice was
permissible on a Sunday. Hull's citizens showed how they
felt about the matter. At the end of his display, they
presented Whitehouse with "a purse of gold sovereigns".

Even more spectacular was the arrival of the first Royal
Flying Corps machines to visit Yorkshire. Five RFC
aircraft of 2 Squadron took off on an epic flight from
South Farnborough in February 1913. Their destination
was Montrose, Scotland's first military airfield. It took
them thirteen days and one of their scheduled stops was
York's Knavesmire racecourse. Three aircraft actually

No 2 Squadron at York: The B. E. 2a was flown by Captain Longcroft; the Maurice Farman by Lieutenant Hubert.
Bruce/Leslie collection

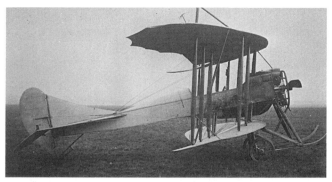

The Handley Page G/100.   *Bruce/Leslie collection*

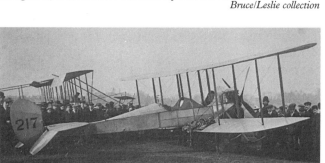

No 2 Squadron at York: The public displays great interest in B. E. 2a No 217.   *Bruce/Leslie collection*

The Avro 504 Daily Mail waterplane at Scarborough, runner-up in the 1913 War of the Roses.   *T. Foreman via G.S.Leslie*

The first Blackburn Type 1 Monoplane about to take off with original cowling.   *Bruce/Leslie collection*

Low-flying Tornado, 1914 style. This is B.C.Hucks taking off over spectators in College Lane, Scarborough. In the background is the old Orleston School, now Scarborough's Teacher Training College.   *Bruce/Leslie collection*

reached York and the first of these was Capt. Longcroft's new B.E.2 No. 218. His two wingmen, Lt. Hubert and Lt. Waldon, piloted Farmans fitted with pusher airscrews. The two missing pilots, Capt. Beck and Capt. Dawes, had force-landed elsewhere. All five aeroplanes eventually reached Montrose.

A later flight led to tragedy. In May 1914 Major Charles James Burke commanded 2 Squadron on the return flight from Montrose. It was the first attempt to show off the aeroplanes of the Royal Flying Corps to the public and the Squadron made slow progress down to Seaton Carew near Thornaby. Burke checked all the aeroplanes carefully and warned pilots not to continue their flights if they encountered fog: "in the event of machines going into a fog, the machines must land in the best place in the clear." Three of the aeroplanes landed safely on York's Knavesmire and it was soon obvious that other members of the flight must have force-landed. One pilot, Captain Todd, was deputed to locate the missing fliers. A telephone message then came through with the news that a milkman on his round near Northallerton had discovered the body of Lt Jack Empson in the wreck of a B.E.2a. Jack Empson and his crewman, Air Mechanic George Cudmore, had encountered the dreaded

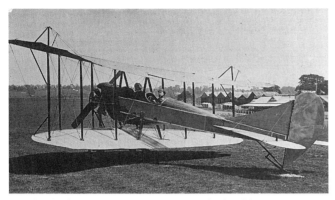

Rowland Ding (1885-1917), seen here in the G/100 went on to instruct on Blackburn Mercury seaplanes at Lake Windermere; to test-fly the Blackburn Type L Seaplane; to take delivery of the famous "White Falcon"; and to test scores of B.E.2c aeroplanes produced by Blackburn at his Olympia factory in Leeds. It was while testing a B.E.2c that he inexplicably dived to his death on 12 May 1917.   *Author's collection via Aphra Burley (née Ding)*

Yorkshire clag and had touched down in nil visibility at Hutton Bonville near Northallerton. Careering across a field, the B.E.2 had embedded itself in an unseen hedge. Both men had died instantly. Lt Empson's home was at Yokefleet Hall, Blacktoft, in the East Riding and his grief-stricken family had been awaiting his triumphant arrival on Knavesmire racecourse.

Two months later Handley Page's display pilot, Rowland Ding, also came a cropper at Northallerton. One of Britain's most brilliant pilots, he had learnt to fly at Hendon in April 1914 and during the summer he began a very successful season of barnstorming displays in Yorkshire and, flying from the Stray in Harrogate, had taken up a total of seventy-eight joy-riders in the new G/100 biplane.

On a short-field approach with a passenger at the Northallerton Carnival, the G/100 hit a small obstruction and tipped over on its nose. It returned to Hendon aerodrome by train.

Aeroplanes were not the only aviation attraction at local fairs and carnivals. Balloonists and aeronauts had become even more adventurous and none more so than the remarkable Dolly Shepherd (1886-1983). She had met the handsome Samuel Cody at Alexandra Palace, then one of the most popular entertainment centres in the country. As she was shown round Cody's aeronautical workshop she became totally enthralled with the world of balloons, kites and parachutes. Cody introduced her to Capt. Auguste Gaudron, a famed balloonist and parachutist, who invited her to make a parachute descent from a balloon - and this was before the Wright brothers

had made their flight at Kittyhawk. Dolly Shepherd soon won a national reputation for her parachute descents. A very attractive woman, she dressed in a distinctive aeronaut's uniform. Her jacket carried a parachute emblem on its lapel; she wore, daringly for the day, trousers tucked into high boots. A peaked cap perched on top of her bushy hair. She gauged her height by means of a small aneroid barometer on her wrist and always petrified the crowds by holding on to her trapeze with one hand and waving a silken Union Jack with the other.

Dolly Shepherd.

Dolly Shepherd was the unchallenged star of the show at Pickering's Grand Gala held on 26 July 1911. Captain Gaudron supervised the excavation of the fire trench over which the balloon's 'big mouth' was carefully positioned. There was never any shortage of local volunteers to hold the balloon in position and when all was ready Dolly Shepherd began her ascent. The balloon dragged her through tree tops at the beginning of the flight and a broken branch became tangled with her parachute cords. Despite this, she waved her little flag at the crowds and soon reached the mandatory 1500 feet, the height Gaudron had advised her to 'pull away'. Dolly Shepherd yanked hard on the ripping cord and began her parachute descent. Above her the balloon was transformed into a dramatic

Her famous aerial rescue 1908.

Filling her balloon at the Scarborough Show.

sight. It had turned turtle, spilling hot air from its open mouth in a great belch of black smoke. Dolly Shepherd landed safely to be met by wildly enthusiastic crowds*.

At the Yorkshire Show the same year, three balloons provided tethered flights and seven or eight passengers at a time would pay their half-crowns for the experience of a lifetime. For the six men and two women who went up on 15 June 1911 it certainly was a memorable flight. A steam traction engine was winching down their balloon - owned by Capt. Gaudron - when the cable broke and the passengers began a totally unscheduled free flight into the Yorkshire skies. The hero of the hour was one Limery, assistant to Captain Gaudron, who first pulled the gas release cord (which also broke) and then climbed the balloon's netting, from which dangerous position he managed to reduce the gas pressure. By then the passengers had a clear but unwelcome sight of York Minster and were grateful when the balloon finally came down at Elvington.

Among the dedicated band of balloonists were those who were primarily interested in racing and the most celebrated balloon race was the annual Gordon Bennett contest. It began in 1902 and Gordon Bennett[3] offered a second prize to the winner of an international balloon race to be governed by the regulations of the FAI *(International Aeronautic Federation)*. This became a long-distance balloon race starting from Paris under the rules of the Aéro Club de France. Sixteen balloons from seven countries set off from Paris on 30 September 1906. Three of these balloons managed to cross the Channel and the winner, the American balloonist Frank P. Lahm, reached Yorkshire to land at Fylingdales. Second place went to *L'Elfe*, the Italian entry crewed by Lt Cianetti and Alfred Vanwiller. On 2 October 1906 *L'Elfe* began its descent over the Humber and finally crashed on a house at New Holland, near Hull, on Monday afternoon, 2 October 1906. Local residents in Summercroft Avenue brought a ladder and rescued the crew from the balloon's car firmly embedded in the roof.

* Three years earlier, she saved the life of her fellow parachutist, Louie May, whose parachute had become entangled with the balloon. Both women desended on one parachute - from 13,000 feet! - at Longton in 1908.

Balloons and aeroplanes were soon to be called upon to perform even more dangerous tasks as conflict in the Balkans highlighted the rivalry between the Great Powers and the ever-present danger of a great war. In Yorkshire, Blackburn was busily modifying the *Christie Type 1* after its success in the War of the Roses Race. The engine cowling had two large holes to facilitate cooling and a better carburettor intake. This aeroplane, together with a new freight-carrying Type 1, made a great impression at air displays in the North of England. Harold Blackburn delivered the *Sheffield Independent* to Chesterfield during Sheffield's Aviation Week (29 March-4 April 1914); and in July he used the *Christie Type 1* to begin Britain's first scheduled air service between Leeds and Bradford. By then Robert Blackburn had raised £20,000 capital in £1 shares to establish the Blackburn Aeroplane & Motor Co Ltd (June 1914) with Stuart Hirst, his old friend and patron, as one of its directors. He had also moved to new premises at the former Olympia Skating Rink in Roundhay Road, Leeds.

The first aeroplane to emerge from the Olympia Works was the *Type L* seaplane entered for the 1914 *Daily Mail* Circuit of Britain Seaplane Race. *The Daily Mail*, which had done more than any other newspaper to transform Britain into an air-minded nation, had bought the 'War of the Roses' Avro 504 as a private publicity aircraft to which floats could be fitted. With the newspaper's name emblazoned along its fuselage, the 504 was often seen at coastal resorts during 1914. One of its pilots was Henri Salmet, well-known for his low level runs in a Blériot over Scarborough's beaches in 1913. Blackburn's Type L was a biplane, a dramatic departure from earlier designs but necessitated, of course, by the government's ban on monoplanes in the armed services. Before the race could begin, Britain had declared war on Germany (4 August 1914) and the Admiralty commandeered the Type L seaplane as well as the *Daily Mail's* Avro 504. In this way, and much to Robert Blackburn's surprise, his company began its long aeronautical association with the Royal Navy.

Chapter Three

The First World War 1914 - 1918

Zeppelins over Yorkshire

In June 1914 the Prime Minister of Serbia advised the Austrian government that it would be unwise to allow their Archduke Franz Ferdnand and his wife to visit the Bosnian town of Sarajevo, then part of the Austrian Empire. He had information that a terrorist group called the Black Hand Gang planned to murder the Archduke. In their wisdom the Austrians decided not to tell the Archduke of the risk he ran and the unfortunate heir to the Austrian throne died when Gavril Princip shot him at close range.

Was Serbia party to this appalling affair? Austria thought so and, backed by her German ally, she delivered an ultimatum to the Serbs who agreed to all but two of the Austrian demands. Despite this, an inflexible Austria hauled her howitzers into position and shelled Belgrade. When Russia mobilised her army to protect the Serbs the Germans decided it was time to implement their infamous Schlieffen Plan. This was a scheme designed to win total mastery of Europe in a matter of weeks. German troops would advance through Belgium, catch the French army unawares, occupy Paris and force France to surrender. Using the efficient German railway system the victorious troops would pile into trains, chug across the Continent and then rout the weary Russian soldiery trudging across the Polish plains. "What about Britain?" This was the question that Kaiser Wilhelm II asked his army commander, Field Marshal von Moltke. "The British?" answered the Field Marshal "They have the biggest navy in the world but their army is tiny. They can do nothing."

As history shows, they did quite a lot. A totally professional army, the British Expeditionary Force crossed to France in 1914 to honour the nation's promise to defend Belgian neutrality under the 1839 Treaty of London. With it went sixty-three of its 179 aeroplanes. This was the war footing of the Royal Flying Corps, formed on 13 May 1912. It had its roots in the balloon detachments that had already served in the 1884 Bechuanaland Expedition, then in the Sudan campaign of 1895-96 and at Magersfontein and Ladysmith during the Boer War of 1899-1902. Their success persuaded the government to move the detachments to the new Balloon Factory at South Farnborough in 1905. It was here, on 28 February 1911, that the Royal Engineers formed Britain's first Air Battalion, a

> "body of expert airmen . . . ready to take to the field with troops and capable of expansion by reserve formations."

No 1 Company had airships; No 2 Company, at Larkhill, had aeroplanes. Expansion was rapid and when the RFC came into being in 1912 it had an aircraft factory, or park, at South Farnborough, and three squadrons: No 1 (Airships); No 2 (Aeroplanes) and No 3 (Aeroplanes). It was some of No 2 Squadron's aircraft that had landed at York en route to Montrose in 1913. The Royal Navy had been quick to imitate the army's example. It formed an Air Instruction School at Eastchurch (March 1911) and by the time Britain declared war on Germany (4 August 1914) it had thirty-two aeroplanes, six airships and fifty-two balloons. It had even managed to fly aeroplanes off ships. In July 1914, on the eve of the First World War, the Naval Wing became the Royal Naval Air Service (RNAS) and took charge of all airship flying and development. From September 1914 to February 1916 the RNAS had responsibility for the air defence of Great Britain.

Ranged against the RFC, the RNAS and 138 French military aeroplanes were the aircraft and airships of the German Military Aviation Service. Founded in October 1912, its total strength on the outbreak of war was 246 aeroplanes, half of which were the famous Gotha-Taube machines, and seven operational Zeppelins, four of which were on the Western Front. The German Naval Airship Division saw its own small fleet of Zeppelins as 'aerial cruisers' capable of bombing key military targets in France and Britain. Both Germany and Britain had practised warlike manoeuvres with their aircraft and airships and a few crews had some experience of machine-guns, wireless telegraphy, artillery spotting and air photography. RNAS crews had even tried dropping bombs on moving and stationary targets - as had the Germans, one of whom, Lt Franz von Hiddeson, bombed the outskirts of Paris on 13 August 1914.

Despite this rapid progress, very few of the aircraft on either side were equipped for any kind of aerial warfare. Lord Kitchener, Britain's Secretary of War, was nevertheless wise to take precautions against possible attack and it was he who required the Admiralty to take over the air defence of Great Britain. The First Lord of the Admiralty was Winston Spencer Churchill who expected Zeppelin raids from Germany in the very near future. Had he not already promised the House of Commons in 1913 that "the fighting aeroplane, rising lightly laden from its base, armed with incendiary bullets, would harry, rout and burn these gaseous monsters." ?

But Yorkshire had seen very little of the "fighting aeroplane". There was no military airfield in the County; Blackburn was still Yorkshire's sole aircraft manufacturer. In September 1914 the RNAS showed the flag and sent a modified Short S.41 coded No 20 to Bridlington for a few days and such an aeroplane might have proved useful on the morning of 16 December 1914 when five German battle-cruisers commanded by Admiral Hipper loomed out of the mist to bombard the Yorkshire coastline. Suddenly and without any warning Yorkshire was very much involved in war. Protracted shelling of Hartlepool killed over a hundred people and, unhindered, the German fleet steamed south to attack Whitby and Scarborough where more than forty people died from enemy shelling. Though public protest was unprecedented it had no effect on the Army and Navy who were slow to recognize the vulnerability of Yorkshire's long coastline and its strategic importance in a new kind of war against Germany.

On the other side of the North Sea were the German airship bases at Evere, Berchem and Gontrode in occupied Belgium and at Nordholz and Hage in north-west Germany. The word 'Zeppelin' was applied generally by the British public to the dreaded airships that raided England and Scotland from 1915 to 1918 though two manufacturers built the airships used in the air war: the SL or Schütte-Lanz and the LZ or Luftshiff-Zeppelin. Both types employed rigid frame construction enclosing numerous hydrogen-filled balloons or 'cells'. They equipped the German Army and Navy and were continuously developed and improved until, in 1918, the Germans brought the 693 feet long Zeppelin L-71 (LZ-113) into service. Fitted with six 260 hp Maybach engines, it had a speed of 73 mph and an operational ceiling of 23,000 feet, beyond the best of the British fighters.

Zeppelin L-3, commissioned in 1914 and of rather primitive design, was the first German airship to attack Britain. These early Zeppelins had been designed not as long-range bombers but, at best, as reconnaissance and escort airships. Yet as early as 1914 there was a desire among the German people to strike directly at England

and even the children could be heard singing this song:

> *Zeppelin, flieg*
> *Hilf uns im Krieg*
> *Fliege nach England*
> *England, wird abgebrannt*
> *Zeppelin flieg !*

Already the German people saw the Army and Navy crews as popular heroes:

> *Fly, Zeppelin*
> *Help us to win this war*
> *Fly to England*
> *England shall be destroyed by fire*
> *Fly, Zeppelin !*

The challenge of making a strategic attack upon an enemy target was a great temptation to the German airship crews and this was the main reason why the L-3 crossed the North Sea on 19/20 January 1915. It had open gondolas, poor endurance and the Yorkshire coastal area was about the limit of its range.

On the night of 19/20 January 1915 L-3 was under orders to attack the Humber ports but navigational problems caused Kapitänleutnant Hans Fritz to miss his objective by more than eighty miles. He therefore steered L-3 southwards and dropped his load of eight 110 bombs and ten 62 lb incendiaries on the unlucky port of Great Yarmouth. Here the defences were barely prepared for an aerial assault by a 520 foot monster and L-3 escaped without interference either from the RNAS seaplanes that took off rather late in a fruitless attempt to find the invader or from the RFC crews in Vickers Gunbus aircraft who pursued the Zeppelin with Lewis gun, a carbine and petrol bombs carried in the cockpit. East Anglians were not impressed by these efforts. They had seen the L-3 over Yarmouth and its sister-ship, the L-4 (Kptlt Magnus von Platen-Hallermund) over King's Lynn. There were seaplanes and guns on the East Coast so why had the Zeppelins been allowed to get away ? The Admiralty had no answer and, ironically, it was left to the elements to wreak their revenge on L-3. On 17 February 1915 bad weather forced the airship down on Fäno Island in neutral Denmark where the crew set fire to the Zeppelin before they were marched away to internment.

War returned to Yorkshire on 4/5 June 1915 when SL-3 came in over Flamborough Head and dropped three bombs near Driffield. Kptlt Fritz Bömack later said that he had cruised around the East Riding in SL-3 for over two hours and encountered no opposition from the RNAS and RFC. Far more serious was the attack on Hull during

GERMAN AIRSHIP BASES – AND THEIR PROXIMITY TO YORKSHIRE

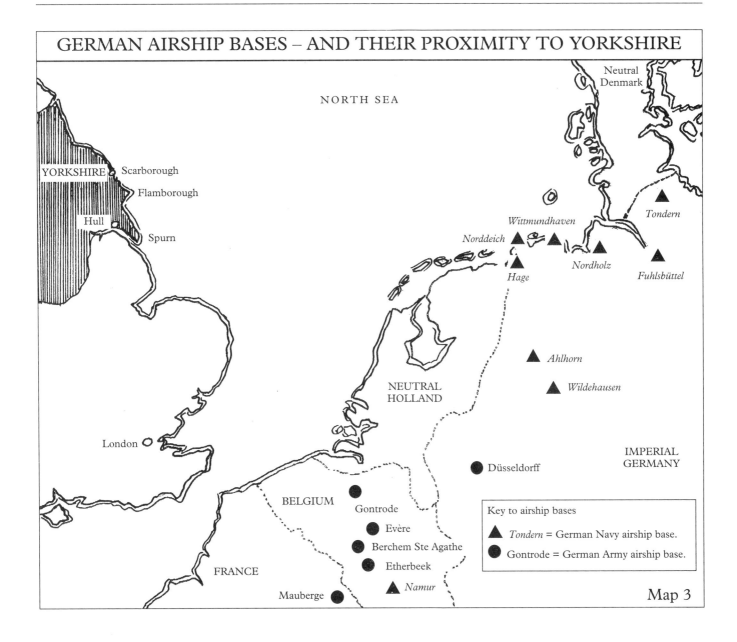

Key to airship bases

▲ *Tondern* = German Navy airship base.

● Gontrode = German Army airship base.

Map 3

the night of 6/7 June 1915. Kptlt Heinrich Mathy, commander of the L-9, overflew Spurn Head, identified Bridlington and then headed south to Hull. For twenty minutes L-9 lingered over the city, destroying houses and shops in the Old Town with a total of thirteen high explosive and thirty-nine incendiary bombs. This first raid on Hull killed twenty-five people and wounded forty-five. Unlike the earlier naval bombardments on the east Coast, there was some warning of the impending air raid. Buzzer alarms sounded and the guns of *HMS Adventure*, then in Earl's Yard repair dock, opened fire on L-9. Unscathed, the Zeppelin moved across the Humber to drop more incendiaries on Grimsby. This was to be the first of a series of raids in which Sheffield, Bradford, Beverley, Goole and Hedon, as well as Hull, all suffered damage.

These attacks caused widespread fear and alarm among the people and naturally, they directed their dismay against the government and the armed forces who had failed to protect them from German attacks by sea and air. Less predictable was their open hostility to shopkeepers and neighbours with German-sounding names. Hull, an easily identifiable target at night with Spurn

Blackburn Type L Seaplane, Scalby Mills, Scarborough in September 1914 when it was commandeered for coastal defences.
Bruce/Leslie collection

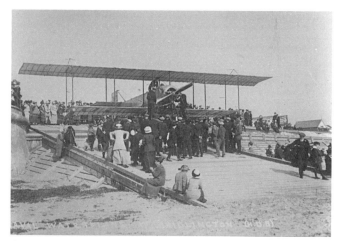

Short S 41 twin float seaplane at Bridlington, September 1914.
Bruce/Leslie collection

acting as a finger beckoning Zeppelins along the Humber, became a hotbed of rumour and protest. After all, it had suffered more casualties and damage than any other city in the United Kingdom and fear of more Zeppelin attacks now encouraged hundreds of families to leave their homes and huddle together on Pearson Park. Thousands more trekked north into the countryside or eastwards to seek shelter in Ferens' capacious stables. There were cases of portly ladies sheltering under rhubarb leaves and trekkers dressed in their Sunday best carrying precious possessions in an attaché case or a Gladstone bag.

This may bring a smile to those who have never experienced sudden air attack. Yet it is a fact that Britain's civilian population was totally unprepared for that kind of war. There were no air raid precautions, no Government advice to help focus civilian minds on effective survival.

People only knew that the Zeppelins were easy to see, frightening to hear and despite the occasional searchlight and naval gunfire, impossible to destroy. Invulnerable, these 'gaseous monsters' were doling out death and destruction to innocent people - for that was how civilians saw themselves in an age that had not conceived the notion of total war. Not unreasonably the people of Yorkshire wanted to know what the government was going to do to protect them from Zeppelin raids. They were not impressed by bland reports that the raid on Hull had simply caused a modest fire in a draper's shop, a timber yard and a row of terraced houses. The raid had been far worse than that and public dissatisfaction fuelled an increasing level of protest and disorder. It was this, rather than the actual Zeppelin attacks, that worried the government and there is little doubt that public sentiment

in Yorkshire, and later on in the rest of the country, reinforced the official view that government could not guarantee to protect its people against air attack. In years to come, government would make contingency plans for dealing with a massive breakdown in *public morale* during any future conflict with a European power.

However, on the night of 9/10 August 1915 two Bristol TB-8s and a Blériot IX did rise from RNAS Atwick and prevented Kptlt Loewe's L-9 from bombing Bridlington. Loewe simply moved westwards and when he thought he was over Hull he dropped his bombs. In fact, he was over Goole and sixteen people died there that night. Loewe returned to Yorkshire via Whitby on 8/9 September and flew up the coast to bomb the benzole works at Skinningrove between Whitby and Saltburn. Despite several direct hits, including a 'dud' that fell on the TNT store, the works enjoyed a lucky escape. Two B.E.2s and

The first air raid on England: Zeppelins L10, L-11, L-12, L-13.

Air Raid Precautions

The Government had begun to issue air raid precautions in the form of posters and one printed late in 1915 gave silhouettes of airships, including Zeppelins, so that people would be able to distinguish these from British airships. Additionally, the Government warned people to take cover on the approach of enemy aircraft and preferably find refuge in a basement. People were urged not to gather in the streets or stand outside watching searchlights and gunfire; and on no account should they touch unexploded bombs.

The main problem confronting people in Yorkshire was the apparent lack of resistance on the parts of the RNAS and RFC and the tardiness in providing anti-aircraft guns during 1915-1916. People had no difficulty in identifying Zeppelins. They took issue with the dilatory attitude of the Government in providing adequate defence.

Certainly, there was little to oppose Viktor Schütze as he loitered over Hull on the night of 5/6 March 1916. He was leaning out of the control gondola, watching the scene below through his binoculars:

> "One hit had a specially far-reaching effect; radiating round the burst more and more houses collapsed and finally showed up, in the snow-covered harbour area, as a black gigantic hole. A similar bigger dark patch in the neighbourhood seemed due to the raid of L-14 . . . with binoculars it was possible to see people running hither and thither in the glare of the fires."

(Quoted A.H.Jones, The War in the Air, Volume III, OUP (1928-1931) p. 69)

Böcker, Commander of L-14

point, the wind-blown L-11 commanded by Victor Schütze appeared over the city and dropped its bombs on terraced houses clustered around the docks. At least eighteen people died and over fifty were injured.

Once more Hull's citizens were incensed. It was nine months since the last attack yet no gun had fired at the Zeppelins on the night of 5/6 March, nor had any British aeroplanes managed to intercept them over the County. Why, they asked, was the important East Coast left so unprotected? Eventually, Hull received a solitary gun and this was mounted high on Blundell's factory for all to see. That it had been sent to keep the natives quiet became apparent when it turned out to have been made of wood! Once this was discovered, political pressure from Hull led to the installation of heavy anti-aircraft guns and searchlights around the city and on the night of 5/6 April 1916 Schütze discovered the new defences. He crossed the coast at Hornsea, salvoed four bombs on Hull then turned tail to escape a furious barrage. Engine trouble forced him to abandon his planned attack on Hartlepool but he was a persistent airship captain and he therefore contented himself with Skinningrove, always a brightly lit target. He dropped nine high explosive bombs and a score of incendiaries but did very little damage to a plant that was showing all the signs

a Caudron G-3 took off from RNAS Redcar but failed to intercept.

B.E.2s were also flying from Appleton-Wiske in North Yorkshire during 1915 but again there were no effective interceptions. Not until early 1916 did the first specially formed Home Defence Squadrons arrive in the County. The first was No 33 Squadron, formed at Filton in January 1916; the second was No 36 Squadron based at Cramlington near Newcastle with B.E.2c detachments at Seaton Carew; and the third was No 47 Squadron, formed at Beverley on 1 March 1916. But the process was far too slow. Germany's Naval Airship Division was on the attack again and Hull was a 'target of opportunity' for L-11 and L-14 on 5/6 March 1916. The Zeppelins' primary objectives were the naval bases at Scapa Flow and the Firth of Forth but gales forced two airships south. Alois Böcker, commanding L-14, identified Beverley and then, further south, the darkened city of Hull outlined by a recent fall of unkind snow. Böcker bombed Beverley and then used his incendiaries to start fires in Hull. At this

Zeppelin L-32.

of having a charmed life. There were no interceptions that night. Fog shrouded several airfields though Squadron Commander C. Draper took off from Scarborough and patrolled the area between Hull and Spurn Head. Three B.E.2c aircraft took off from Cramlington and Beverley and one 36 Squadron pilot, Capt. J. Nichol, died when his bombs exploded after hitting a house in a vain attempt to land in thick fog.

The March raid had spurred the RFC into action. No 33 Squadron moved to Yorkshire that month and set up its headquarters on Beverley racecourse flying B.E.2c and B.E.2d interceptors plus a few Bristol Scouts. These new Home Defence Units had a demanding role: night reconnaissance and airship interception for which their pilots had little or no training. Because of the difficulties of night flying, especially with an obligatory black-out during airship raids, the Squadrons needed numerous landing fields scattered across the County. Most of these were meadows with few permanent buildings and today, for example, there is no trace of the landing ground at South Cave or of the three airstrips at Farsley, Seacroft and Middleton that protected Leeds. No 33 Squadron's B Flight first flew from the Knavesmire racecourse at York where the RFC had built a very effective flare-path. On the night of 2/3 May 1916 Zeppelin L-21 came in over Scarborough, bombed York for ten minutes and departed over Bridlington. Nine people were killed and twenty-seven injured. Local citizens claimed that the airship's accuracy was because it had simply followed the flare-path to the city centre. Popular wrath prevailed and B Flight transferred its B.E.2s to Copmanthorpe though the move did not save York from two more Zeppelin attacks.

On the same night L-23 crossed the Yorkshire coast at Robin Hood's Bay and for some reason dropped an incendiary on Danby High Moor before attacking Skinningrove and Easington. By then the fire raging on Danby Moor had attracted two more Zeppelins: L-17 bombed the blazing heather and Skinningrove; L-13 came south from the fire, turned over Market Weighton and left Yorkshire via Scarborough. Aircraft from Doncaster, Bramham Moor, Cramlington and Beverley took off in search of the intruders as did RNAS interceptors from Whitley Bay, Scarborough and Redcar. F/Lt B.P.H. de Roeper flew for an hour after taking off from Redcar and spotted L-17 when it was briefly held in Skinningrove's searchlights. But he failed to catch it. Nor did he spot another airship, the L-16, that had wandered over North Yorkshire.

★ ★ ★

Now that the threat to arms factories in the northern industrial towns was taken seriously, a fourth Home Defence Squadron, No 57, formed at Copmanthorpe to provide training in night navigation and interception techniques. It was not long before these new skills were put to the test. During the night of 8/9 August 1916 L-24 was part of a fleet of nine airships. Its commander was Kptlt Robert Koch whose forty-four bombs killed ten people and injured eleven in Hull. There was a thick mist that night and the anti-aircraft guns fired off a miserable eight rounds before L-24 turned and flew back over the North Sea. The indefatigable de Roeper had again taken off from Redcar and chased a Zeppelin for twenty miles beyond Flamborough Head. His report bewailed the situation:

"if an effective machine had been available, say a 1½ Strutter or a RAF-engined BE, with a quick climb to 15,000 feet and about 20 knots faster than mine, bombs could have been effectively dropped on the Zeppelin." [1]

On 2/3 September 1916 sixteen airships carried out the biggest raid on Britain. Though it proved an utter failure, two airships operated over the Humber: L-13 and L-22.

B. E. 2c 7216 from No 72 Squadron.

Bruce/Leslie collection

Farman Longhorn N 5750 flying from Redcar.

Bruce/Leslie collection

Sopwith Dolphin, 1918.   *Bruce/Leslie collection*

Avro 504K D2059 crashed at Catterick by Sgt Miles of 49 TDS.
                                        R.C.B.Ashworth via G.S.Leslie

FE 2B A8450 'Leeds' with Lord Desborough in front bay and Captain Pixton as pilot.   *Bruce/Leslie collection*

The latter flew over the Vale of York just to the south of Beverley, dropped a few bombs on Humberston and then flew home via Hornsea. Engine trouble plagued the Yorkshire night-fighters and no interceptions were made.

Now a truly Yorkshire Squadron, No 76, was formed at Ripon racecourse on 15 September 1916. 'A' Flight was at Copmanthorpe, a very busy airfield during 1916-1918; 'B' Flight flew from Helperby and 'C' Flight from Catterick. Its first task was to work up as an efficient night-fighter squadron and the training involved was both demanding and dangerous.

No 57 took its F.E.2s to France in December 1916 and incurred heavy casualties on the Western Front. No 76 remained behind to engage in constant and generally fruitless night patrols in its Avro 504s and 504Ks. Ten days after the formation of No 76 Squadron (25/26 September 1916) L-14, L-16, L-21 and L-22 were tasked to attack industrial areas in Yorkshire and Lancashire. L-14 and L-16 nosed across the coast at Hornsea and L-14 salvoed a few bombs on York before being driven off

by the accurate fire from a newly installed anti-aircraft gun at Acomb. Meanwhile, L-16 was scattering bombs across the Wolds and then appeared to be heading for a major attack on Leeds. At the last minute it bombed the Wetherby area and then turned for home. No Home Defence aircraft managed to intercept the enemy airships. Two other Zeppelins headed inland that night: L-21 flew to the outskirts of Sheffield and then went on to bomb Bolton; L-22 followed a similar but more northerly course and attacked Sheffield. With smoke and flames pouring from its armament factory chimneys, the city must have presented an easy target. Yet though he loitered over Sheffield for over twenty minutes, Martin Dietrich, commander of L-22, failed to hit a single factory though his bombs killed twenty-three people.

None of the northern squadrons experienced the success enjoyed by Lt W. Leefe Robinson who shot down SL-11 at Cuffley, near London, and won the Victoria Cross. But during 27/28 November - the last of the raids of 1916 - the northern squadrons scored a long overdue victory when two groups of airships approached the Yorkshire coast. No 36 Squadron's C Flight was then operating out of Seaton Carew when news came through that L-34, commanded by Max Dietrich, was trying to evade a relentless searchlight at Hutton Henry. Lt Pyott took off in his B.E.2c, stalked L-34 across West Hartlepool (where Dietrich dropped sixteen bombs and killed four people) and then shot the Zeppelin down in flames. This was the only airship destroyed by the northern squadrons, though they had done sterling work during most of the raids and helped prevent concerted airship attacks on the industrial cities inland. Despite Pyott's success that night other Zeppelins penetrated the defences over Spurn and Hornsea and went on to bomb

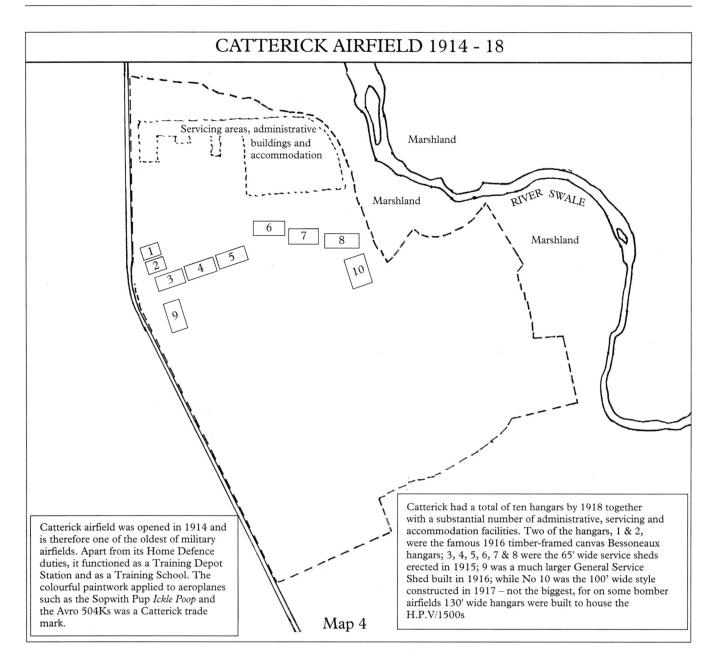

CATTERICK AIRFIELD 1914 - 18

Servicing areas, administrative buildings and accommodation

Marshland

Marshland

RIVER SWALE

Marshland

Catterick airfield was opened in 1914 and is therefore one of the oldest of military airfields. Apart from its Home Defence duties, it functioned as a Training Depot Station and as a Training School. The colourful paintwork applied to aeroplanes such as the Sopwith Pup *Ickle Poop* and the Avro 504Ks was a Catterick trade mark.

Catterick had a total of ten hangars by 1918 together with a substantial number of administrative, servicing and accommodation facilities. Two of the hangars, 1 & 2, were the famous 1916 timber-framed canvas Bessoneaux hangars; 3, 4, 5, 6, 7 & 8 were the 65' wide service sheds erected in 1915; 9 was a much larger General Service Shed built in 1916; while No 10 was the 100' wide style constructed in 1917 – not the biggest, for on some bomber airfields 130' wide hangars were built to house the H.P.V/1500s

Map 4

targets in the East and West Ridings. L-33 salvoed most of its bombs in the fields around Barmby Moor and released the remainder over York where flames and exploding bombs attracted the attention of other Zeppelins. L-16 flew over Barnsley and Wakefield but there were no reports of casualties; and as it returned via York, heavy gunfire from the Acomb defences saved the city from further attack. Anti-aircraft guns tracked this Zeppelin across the Yorkshire Wolds and the last batteries to fire were those at Scarborough. Another Zeppelin, the L-22,

was actually hit by gunfire as it flew back across Flamborough Head; while the Hornsea searchlight illuminated an unidentified airship for several minutes before it climbed away far too rapidly for the old B.E.2Cs that still equipped most of the Home Defence squadrons.

Fortunately for Yorkshire, 1917-18 saw a reduction in airship attacks as the Germans, conscious of the severe operational limitations of hydrogen-filled airships, began using Staaken R-VI and Gotha G-IV aircraft to bomb London. Even so, a few marauding airships continued to

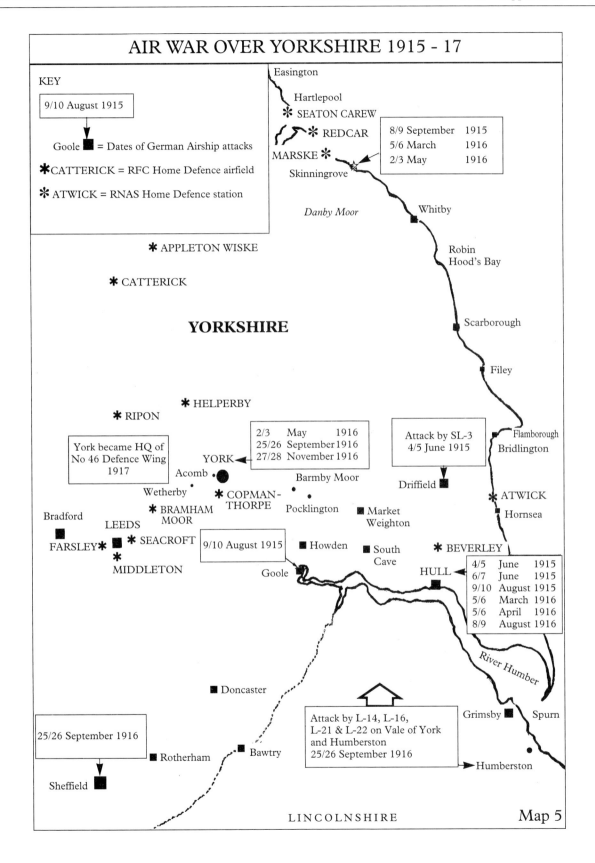

AIR WAR OVER YORKSHIRE 1915 - 17

KEY

| 9/10 August 1915 |

Goole ■ = Dates of German Airship attacks

✱ CATTERICK = RFC Home Defence airfield

✱ ATWICK = RNAS Home Defence station

Easington

Hartlepool

✱ SEATON CAREW

✱ REDCAR

MARSKE ✱

Skinningrove

8/9 September	1915
5/6 March	1916
2/3 May	1916

Danby Moor

Whitby

Robin
Hood's Bay

Scarborough

Filey

✱ APPLETON WISKE

✱ CATTERICK

YORKSHIRE

✱ HELPERBY

✱ RIPON

| York became HQ of
No 46 Defence Wing
1917 |

| 2/3 May 1916 |
| 25/26 September 1916 |
| 27/28 November 1916 |

YORK

Acomb ●

Wetherby

✱ COPMAN-
THORPE

Barmby Moor

Pocklington

Flamborough

Bridlington

| Attack by SL-3
4/5 June 1915 |

Driffield ■

✱ ATWICK

Hornsea

Bradford ■

LEEDS

FARSLEY ✱ ■ ✱ SEACROFT

✱

MIDDLETON

✱ BRAMHAM
MOOR

Market
Weighton

| 9/10 August 1915 |

Howden ■

Goole

South
Cave

✱ BEVERLEY

HULL ■

4/5	June	1915
6/7	June	1915
9/10	August	1915
5/6	March	1916
5/6	April	1916
8/9	August	1916

River Humber

Doncaster ■

| 25/26 September 1916 |

Rotherham ■

Bawtry ■

| Attack by L-14, L-16,
L-21 & L-22 on Vale of York
and Humberston
25/26 September 1916 |

Grimsby ■

Spurn

Humberston

Sheffield ■

LINCOLNSHIRE

Map 5

There was always a cost. Pilot training for Home Defence duties led to many accidents. This FK8 B294 crashed at Beverley.

Bruce/Leslie collection

cross the North Sea to attack England and the favourite entry points remained the Tees, the Humber and the gap between Hornsea and Bridlington. Reports of a Zeppelin on the night of 21/22 August 1917 led to some excitement at Copmanthorpe and Helperby and five aircraft - 4 B.E.2s and a B.E.12 - flew unsuccessful patrols in search of the airship. A Helperby pilot had slightly more success on 25 September 1917. 2/Lt W.W.Cook was on patrol when he spotted the L-55 caught in the beam of the Skinningrove searchlight. At the time Cook did not realise that L-55 was one of ten airships tasked that night to attack coastal convoys and targets of opportunity in Yorkshire. He tried to intercept but his B.E.2e lacked the performance to challenge the German high-fliers. He flew out to sea and glimpsed L-41 glinting in the glare of several searchlights based along the Humber. Again Cook failed to catch her. He reasoned that his best chance of intercepting more airships was to climb on an easterly

course. Choosing an exit point favoured by the Zeppelins, Cook orbited some fifty or sixty miles east of Hornsea until his fuel state became critical. Suddenly he spotted L-42 yet even with his throttle wide open Cook could not catch the Zeppelin so he loosed off as many drums of Lewis gun ammunition as possible before turning for home. Later on the crew of L-42 realised how lucky they had been. On landing they discovered one of L-42's gas cells had been punctured by Cook's bullets. For his exploits that night 2/Lt Cook received a well-deserved Military Cross.

Both the Royal Flying Corps and the Royal Naval Air Service were now coming to terms with the demands of night flying, the prospect of becoming lost over the North Sea and the technical difficulties facing airmen trying to attack a Zeppelin. On 6 March 1917 the RFC formed No 46 Defence Wing at York to co-ordinate Nos 36, 76 and 77 Squadrons for the protection of Northern England; while the need to train aircrew in air combat skills led to the opening of No 4 Auxiliary School of Aerial Gunnery at Marske on 1 November 1917. This used D.H.9s and Sopwith Dolphins for training purposes until it closed on 6 May 1918. On the same day No 2 School of Aerial Fighting and Gunnery formed at Marske and was eventually known as No 2 Fighting School operating Sopwith Camels, D.H.4s and D.H.9s.

By then the war in the air had largely disappeared from the Yorkshire skies and the night of 12/13 March 1918 saw the last major attack on the County. As usual, the F.E.2d crews at Seaton Carew suffered the frustration of having struggled up to 14,500 feet only to see their prey rise 3000 feet higher, out of range of their Pomeroy explosive bullets; while from the German point of view the raid failed due to heavy cloud at 16-18,000 feet and faulty navigation by the Zeppelins. L-61 and L-62 crossed the Yorkshire coast between Hornsea and Bridlington and attempted to bomb Leeds. They misjudged their position and when they finally attacked their bombs fell on Pocklington and Hull. No 76 Squadron's new B.E.12s at Helperby were responsible for the defence of Pocklington and much of the Vale of York but bad weather prevented any sorties until after L-62 had escaped.

Nevertheless, the Helperby aviators liked their new B.E.12b. Said one pilot:

"the machine went well and was still climbing fast at 13,000 feet"[2]

However, it is doubtful if the B.E.12s would have caught the new Zeppelin 'height climbers'. The updated B.E.12 would probably have fared no better than the

F.E.2s though the point remains academic as the B.E.12's value as a night-fighter over Yorkshire was never again tested in combat.[3]

Zeppelins did overfly the County on the following night (13/14 March 1918) and 2/Lt S. Hill took off from Helperby and patrolled Howden in search of Zeppelins. He observed 2/Lt G.W.Wall in another B.E.12 from Companthorpe come under fire from the Howden gunners who later pleaded unfamiliarity with the sound of a B.E.12 engine. There were no interceptions that night nor on 12/13 April 1918 when five of the latest Zeppelins with improved Maybach engines approached the East Coast just to the south of Spurn Head. Though the Zeppelin captains claimed to have delivered telling strikes on Leeds, Sheffield and Hull, most of their bombs fell in open country. The last known reference to a Zeppelin near Yorkshire was on 5/6 August 1918 when the commander of Hull's anti-aircraft batteries reported a Zeppelin flying to the east of Spurn Head.[4]

Yorkshire's defence system throughout the period of Zeppelin attack was seriously hampered by inadequate resources, especially with regard to the quality of aeroplanes supplied to the Home Defence squadrons.

No one has ever disputed the courage and professionalism of the British night-fighter crews or of their opponents who brought their hydrogen filled airships on their perilous voyages across the North Sea. Yet it must be said that the rate of interception by RFC and RNAS aircraft barely improved throughout the war. The introduction of the Bristol Fighter to the northern squadrons took place in the summer of 1918 but of course made no difference to the outcome of the air war over Yorkshire. But had it been more readily available to the three northern squadrons during 1917-1918, the night-fighter techniques constantly advocated by men such as Major T.C.R. Higgins and Major G.W. Murlis Green might have resulted in a higher interception rate and the destruction of more Zeppelins. Higgins strongly advocated the use of the Bristol Fighter for night interceptions; Green proposed a twin-engined night fighter with two upward firing 0.5" machine guns, thus anticipating the Luftwaffe's *schräge Musik* by a quarter of a century. Instead, the British Government took a gamble that Germany would be unable to maintain an intensive Zeppelin penetration of Northern England. Fortunately for Northern England and for Scotland, it was a gamble that paid off.

Chapter Four

The First World War 1914 - 1918

Yorkshire's new strategic role

Defensive operations against Zeppelins were only part of the duties of the RFC and RNAS squadrons based in Yorkshire. From its long coastline facing the U-boat threat in the North Sea, aircraft and airships flew anti-submarine patrols and convoy escort duties from Seaton Carew, Redcar, Kettleness, Atwick, Hornsea and Owthorne. Hornsea Mere provided an inland lake ideal for seaplanes and during 1917 248 and 251 Squadrons RNAS flew Sopwith Baby and Short 184 seaplanes on reconnaissance and bombing patrols. Little survives of their Bessoneaux hangars and the two slipways, though Hornsea Museum treasures an attaché case fashioned from a Sopwith Baby's plywood floats by Gladwin Gelsthorpe, then stationed at the Mere. There is also an unusual alarm bell made from the cylinder block of a u/s Clerget engine and some remnants of a Baby's propeller.

Sub. Lt. Gordon Hyams DFC flew his Baby (N 2078 – the *Jabberwock*) out of Hornsea Mere and on every sortie made sure he had a pigeon in his pocket in case of emergency! He liked the little single-seater seaplane which had an endurance of over two hours and could touch 100 mph at low level when its 130 hp Clerget was on full song. Provided he was well-wrapped up in his Sidcot, scarves and flying helmet, the cockpit was warm even during winter patrols. His routine was to patrol from the Humber to Skinningrove, looking for submarines that preyed on the north-bound convoys leaving Hull. On 26 March 1918 he spotted a U-boat running on the surface in a very heavy sea. about forty miles east of

Scarborough. He flew in low and fast, determined to hit the submarine with his solitary 65lb bomb. However, the lookout saw him and the submarine crash-dived. White foam was everywhere and Hyams had to guess the spot where it had gone under. He bombed but with no tangible result.

His beloved *Jabberwock* did not survive the war as an American pilot crashed it at Hornsea on 22 April 1918. Hyams removed the serial number and name[1] and continued his patrol duties with a replacement seaplane. He helped to rescue the pilot of a downed DH 6 and the American crew of a Curtiss H-1 flying boat that had broken in two during take-off in heavy seas. Mentioned in despatches and awarded the DFC in the King's Birthday Awards 1918, Gordon Hyams was a man who loved flying and whose logbook testifies to his numerous sorties over the U-boat infested War Channel between the Humber and the Tees. In all, Hornsea's 248 Squadron, formed from the Seaplane Flight originally stationed at the Mere, spotted six U-boats, sank one of them and managed to intercept but not destroy one Zeppelin.

Further north, four of the mighty Handley Page HP 0/100 bombers flew from Redcar against the U-boats in 1917. This was the year in which German submarines became the greatest threat to Britain's survival. General Ludendorff, by then the man who wielded most of the military power in Germany, decided on a campaign of

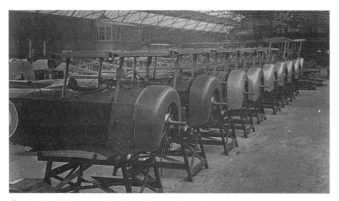

Sopwith Baby production line at Leeds.

B. Robertson via G. S. Leslie

Sopwith Baby B 2099 at Killingholme. This machine was allocated to Seaton Carew on 3 January 1918.

Bruce/Leslie collection

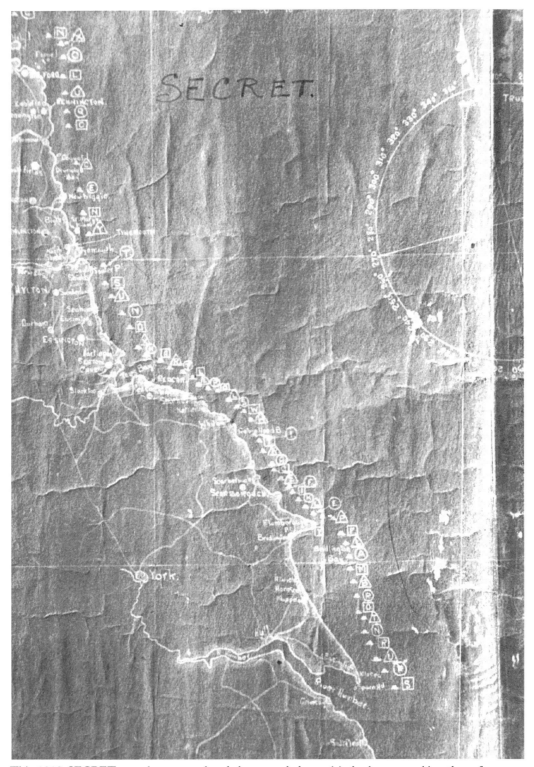

This 1918 SECRET patrol map was hand drawn and shows (a) the buoys marking the safe convoy passage along the Yorkshire coast. (b) the railway lines - so useful for navigation when a pilot was unsure of his position inland.

Stuart Leslie collection

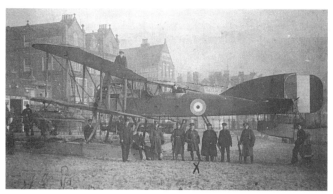

Short 184 N 1225 from Killingholme. Sub. Lt. L. Bassett had to force-land in the sea (19 December 1917) and the aeroplane was towed into Scarborough the next day.

Bruce/Leslie collection

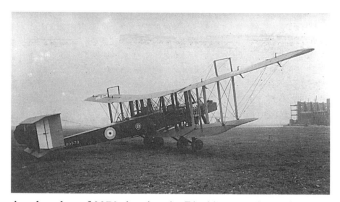

Another shot of 9970 showing the Blackburn trade-mark.

Bruce/Leslie collection

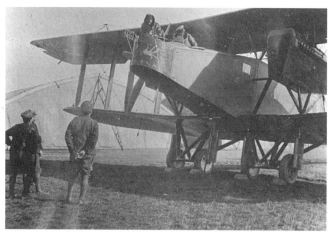

This HP 0/100 was photographed at Redcar in September 1917. It was resting from major ops but still doing some anti-submarine patrols. Its pilot was Lt. Lance de G. Siverking, popularly known as 'Split' – see the device on the nose.

Bruce/Leslie collection

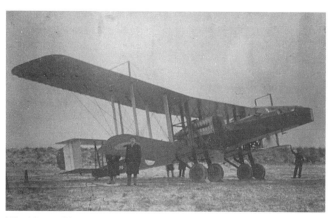

Blackburn Kangaroo 9970 became G-EAOW.

Bruce/Leslie collection

unrestricted submarine warfare to force Britain to sue for peace. As aerial bombing rarely succeeded against submarines the Admiralty decided to fit the Handley Page 0/400s with the new six-pounder Davis gun. As with all heavy armaments in aircraft, the problem was the effect of recoil on the airframe, a difficulty never overcome at Redcar. The blast effect of the recoil damaged the upper wing structure and the 0/400's had to be withdrawn. Much more successful were the Blackburn Kangaroo bombers flying with 246 Squadron from Seaton Carew in 1918. One of these, B 9983, disabled UC-70 as she hid eighty feet down near Runswick Bay. *HMS Ouse* arrived and destroyed the U-boat with depth charges.

Patrol work intensified along the Yorkshire coast during 1917-18. The more powerful F.E.2d and De Havilland D.H. 4s and 6s became a common sight, as were the RNAS airships based at Howden. These airships were of two main types: rigid, where the frame was made of wood or metal, enclosing the hydrogen gas-bags; and non-rigid, where the engines and crew cars were suspended from a cylindrical envelope containing both the hydrogen bags and the deflatable air ballonets for regulating internal pressure. The Admiralty had first commissioned a rigid airship, nicknamed *Mayfly,* in 1908. After an accident wrecked the *Mayfly* in 1911, interest in airships waned for the next two years. However, Admiralty appreciation of the value of airships as observation platforms increased and orders for airships resumed in 1913. During November 1913 all operational airships came under the control of the Naval Wing of the RFC. Then in July 1914 the Naval Wing was redesignated the Royal Naval Air Service (RNAS). After a year of patrols with makeshift SS (Submarine Scout) airships the RNAS decided to establish a chain of 'Coastal Stations' equipped with C (Coastal) non-rigid airships at Pembroke, Pulham, Howden, Longside, Mullion and East Fortune. Howden

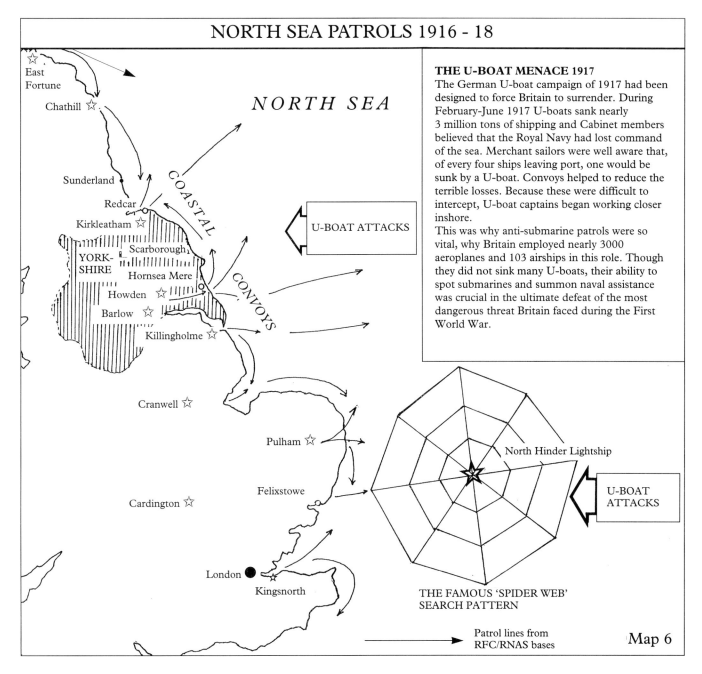

NORTH SEA PATROLS 1916 - 18

NORTH SEA

U-BOAT ATTACKS

East Fortune
Chathill
Sunderland
Redcar
Kirkleatham
Scarborough
YORK-SHIRE
Hornsea Mere
Howden
Barlow
Killingholme
Cranwell
Pulham
Felixstowe
Cardington
London
Kingsnorth

COASTAL

CONVOYS

North Hinder Lightship

U-BOAT ATTACKS

THE FAMOUS 'SPIDER WEB'
SEARCH PATTERN

Patrol lines from
RFC/RNAS bases

Map 6

THE U-BOAT MENACE 1917
The German U-boat campaign of 1917 had been designed to force Britain to surrender. During February-June 1917 U-boats sank nearly 3 million tons of shipping and Cabinet members believed that the Royal Navy had lost command of the sea. Merchant sailors were well aware that, of every four ships leaving port, one would be sunk by a U-boat. Convoys helped to reduce the terrible losses. Because these were difficult to intercept, U-boat captains began working closer inshore.
This was why anti-submarine patrols were so vital, why Britain employed nearly 3000 aeroplanes and 103 airships in this role. Though they did not sink many U-boats, their ability to spot submarines and summon naval assistance was crucial in the ultimate defeat of the most dangerous threat Britain faced during the First World War.

was one of the biggest. It opened in March 1916 as a permanent base with large 'Coastal Sheds' to accommodate new airships. Five Coastals, C-1, C-4, C-11, C-19 and C-21 patrolled the Humber, backed by the unusual non-rigid Parseval P-4 purchased from Germany in 1913.

C-11 had a charmed life. Her first narrow escape took place when she was returning from North Sea patrol on 23 April 1917. It was a murky day and her commander,

F/Lt Hogg Turnour, was trying to locate his precise landfall. As he crossed the coast a hill loomed out of the mist. Emergency use of the elevators proved too late and C-11 dropped her tail and smashed into the ground, shearing off the rear section of the control car. The flight engineer found himself on the ground in company with C-11's engine, watching his airship soar up into the clag. At 3000 feet his three comrades left in the shattered control car tried to operate the gas release. To their

The Howden Group: October 1916
Back row: Hutchinson, Bellamy, Harvey, Playne, Crouch, Turnour (C-11), Scraggs (C-21). *Front row:* Cleverley, V.Case, Robinson, Boothby, Bletherwick, Herron, Booth (C-4), Elmhirst (C-19)

Bruce/Leslie collection

Howden 1917: this is North Sea Airship NS1, ultimately wrecked in a forced-landing.

Bruce/Leslie collection

C-4 flying from Howden on 14 March 1918.

Bruce/Leslie collection

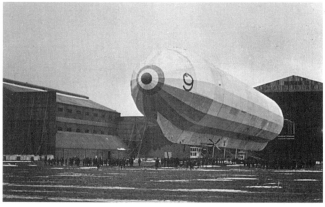

R-9 at Howden on 5 April 1917.

Bruce/Leslie collection

horror, the entire gas bag began to split and once more C-11 crashed to the ground, leaving all three men injured. Meanwhile, the flight engineer discovered he was on Scarborough race-course and walked to the nearest telephone to tell Howden of the disaster. Back in action, C-11 came a cropper over the Humber when on a normal training flight on 21 July 1917. A sudden gas leak caused the airship to descend rapidly. The control car sank below the surface as the gas envelope exploded into flames above it. Four men drowned in this unlucky airship which was again repaired and used for coastal patrols until it was finally struck off charge in March 1918.

At the height of the U-boat menace in 1917 the Humber patrols urgently needed reinforcement from rigid airships. four R-class airships had been ordered in 1915 and Vickers test-flew His Majesty's Airship R-9 in November 1916. However, the Admiralty thought it was too bulky and underpowered.

Vickers promptly fitted it with copies of German lightweight gas-bags and actually installed a Maybach HSLu 240 hp engine salvaged from the wreck of the 'super-Zeppelin' L-33 brought down in England in September. R-9 then flew from Barrow to Howden early on 4 April 1917. Just after she left Barrow R-9 encountered a snow storm and strong winds forced her nose down. Her engineers managed to trim out the airship, release most of the ballast and rise above the storm. She reached Howden safely that afternoon. At Howden, R-9 joined the Rigid Airship Trial Flight where she was used to train crews for the next generation of rigids that came to Howden: R-25, built by Armstrong-Whitworth at Barlow in Yorkshire; R-27, built by Beardmore on the Clyde; and three modified Parsevals. R-26 was a late arrival. Vickers had been so absorbed by

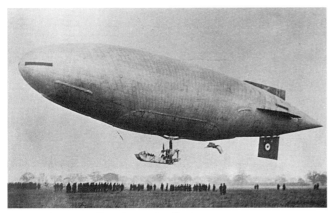

Parseval No 4 at Howden, 5 April 1917.

Bruce/Leslie collection

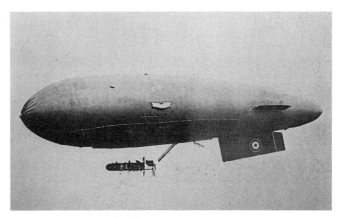

SS P2 at Howden, March 1918.

Bruce/Leslie collection

C Star 1 - the first of its type.

Bruce/Leslie collection

the demands of the R-9 that the completion of R-26 had been deferred until April 1918. R-26 flew several patrols from Howden and actually held the airship endurance record – a flight of 40 hours 40 minutes on 4/5 June 1918.

Many other airships flew from Howden, including three new Sea Scout Z-class airships (SSZ-32, 38 and 58). These undertook regular North Sea patrols, side by side with three updated Coastals known as 'C Star' airships, identified by the Star of David painted on their envelopes. Even Howden, now the biggest coastal station, was now cramped for space. New Rigid hangars, Coastal sheds, barrack blocks for over a thousand personnel and new quarters for the first WRAFs who arrived in 1918 meant that Howden had to expand. Two satellite mooring-out sites at Lowthorpe and Kirkleatham helped to alleviate the problem though airships still jostled dangerously close to one another at Howden Royal Naval Air Station.

The Howden disaster of August 1918 underlined this point. While a US Navy team was attaching a new crew car to the non-rigid SSZ-23, someone managed to spill some petrol and set fire to the airship. Moored nearby were SSZ-38 and SSZ-54. Both went up in flames. Even worse, the fire spread to R-27, then housed in its rigid shed. The airship was destroyed and the shed badly damaged. R-29 had better luck. Built by Armstrong Whitworth at Barlow and commissioned on 20 June 1918 it flew up to East Fortune Royal Naval Air Station. There it helped to destroy U-115 near Sunderland on 29 September 1918. Cruising low over the sea, it spotted an oil patch and dropped a 230lb bomb, disabling the submarine. Two destroyers, *Ouse* and *Star*, arrived and finished off U-115 with depth-charges.

Meanwhile, the Admiralty had been impressed by drawings brought to England by Herman Müller, a Swiss

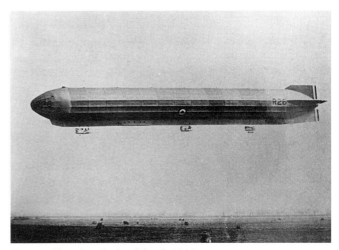

R-26 at Howden during March 1918.

Bruce/Leslie collection

who worked for Schütte-Lanz in Mannheim where he was in charge of the girder construction workshop. Two new rigids, R-31 and R-32, were virtually carbon copies of SL-7. R-31, commissioned on 6 November 1918, lifted off for her flight to East Fortune. Very quickly the wooden girder framework began to break up and the brand-new airship made an emergency landing at Howden where RNAS personnel minutely examined her inside R-27's charred shed. They discovered that moisture had swollen the timbers, weakened the glue and damaged the joints. R-31's crew had had a lucky escape.

Despite these unfortunate episodes there is no doubt that the airship patrols from Howden were a deterrent to U-boat commanders who now found it dangerous to surface for battery recharging. Once an airship spotted a U-boat, especially those that loitered in shallow waters, it could remain overhead and guide the Navy or a seaplane to the target. It is a matter of fact that only one merchant ship was ever torpedoed when airships escorted the convoys. In war the airship proved its value; but when peace came the Admiralty felt disinclined to maintain its airship fleet and dispensed with the patrol force in 1919. The newly formed RAF, however, continued to use airships experimentally until 1927.

★ ★ ★

When war began in August 1914, Yorkshire was a major centre of arms production directly facing the enemy across the North Sea. Its people, its factories and its supply systems were vulnerable to attack by surface vessels, airships and submarines. During 1914-15 it lay defenceless and was the first county to be subjected to both heavy sea and air bombardment. Yet the first moves made to protect Yorkshire, now a favourite entry point for Zeppelins based in occupied Belgium and north-west Germany, were not made until 1916. Then came radical changes as the strategic importance dawned upon Britain's War Cabinet. By 1 April 1918, when the RFC and the RNAS amalgamated to form the Royal Air Force, airships, landplanes and floatplanes patrolled the convoy routes passing Yorkshire's long coastline and harried the U-boats. Home Defence night-fighter units defended the major cities. Sherburn-in-Elmet had grown into a major RAF Acceptance Park and its large flying ground housed an array of specialist factories. In less than three years Yorkshire had been transformed into a region of immense importance for the Royal Air Force. Moreover, it had strong links with the aircraft construction business and in

this industry the Blackburn Aeroplane and Motor Company had achieved national importance.

Robert Blackburn had won the respect of the Admiralty and the War Office before the war began and during May-June 1914 his firm was entrusted with the construction of 111 B.E.2c biplanes. With the large Leeds factory at Olympia and with Soldier's Field on the doorstep, Blackburn was in a strong position both to manufacture under licence and to develop original designs.

His solitary Type L seaplane had a very brief service career. After major modifications at Scalby Mills, where Blackburn had built a large wooden hangar, the Type L was fitted with a machine-gun. Flying the newly-armed machine to the RNAS base at Killingholme, test pilot Rowland Ding hit the cliffs at Speeton and wrote-off the aeroplane in 1915. By then Blackburn had designed the extraordinary Blackburn TB, a large twin-fuselage seaplane. His aim was to create a long range interceptor aircraft that could locate enemy airships and destroy them with Ranken incendiary darts. Lack of proper bracing between the two fuselages, and the subsequent and unwanted flexing that went on, made accurate flying both difficult and exhausting. Though the RNAS accepted four Blackburn TBs for evaluation it was obvious that they were unfitted for aerial combat.

Equally, Blackburn's second attempt to manufacture an effective anti-Zeppelin fighter, the Air Department of the Admiralty A.D. Scout, and its Triplane development, proved a failure. Both aeroplanes were of unorthodox design. The pilot of the A.D.Scout sat high in a nacelle attached to the upper biplane wing. At his feet and below a large windscreen lay a Davis two-pounder quick-fire recoilless gun. Behind him was a 100 hp Gnôme engine driving a pusher airscrew. This arrangement gave the pilot a magnificent view but he lacked the manoeuvrability vital when closing for an attack on a Zeppelin. To overcome this, Blackburn shortened the wingspan and transformed the A.D.Scout into a Triplane. None of the wings carried any dihedral but each had an aileron. Most authorities agree, as Jackson does, that the Blackburn Triplane was "one of the most extraordinary aircraft ever built." Four Scouts,(two built by the Bedfordshire constructor Hewlett & Blondeau) and one Triplane, were delivered to the RNAS but all proved to be overweight and difficult to fly. Eventually, all five were scrapped.

Blackburn now turned to more conventional configurations and built two General Purpose GP twin-engined floatplanes that at first glance anticipate the Heinkel He 59 floatplanes of 1931 vintage. His GP was a tough but graceful aeroplane, the first designed to carry a torpedo and to have wireless-telegraphy as standard equipment. It was an important aeroplane in so far that it exemplified a new policy decision by Blackburn to specialise in the design and manufacture of naval aircraft. To this end, he built a seaplane test centre at Brough Aerodrome on the northern bank of the River Humber. Numbered 1416 and fitted with 190 hp Rolls Royce engines, the second GP underwent its trials during East Yorkshire's bitter winter of 1916. Despite sub-zero temperatures and drift ice on the Humber the machine performed well and it was tragic that after the RNAS accepted it at Yarmouth the Admiralty refused to grant Blackburn a contract. Fortunately, the Kangaroo land version of the GP was an instant success. Ten of the famous Kangaroos, most fitted with 270 hp Rolls Royce Falcon IIIs, served at RAF Seaton Carew during 1918.

Meanwhile the Olympia Works fulfilled other contracts for the Admiralty, contracts that required close co-operation with Sopwith Aviation. Sopwith had designed the Baby seaplane and then subcontracted its manufacture to Fairey Aviation and Blackburns. Olympia Works turned out 186 of the little seaplanes and tested all of these on the Humber at Brough. Then came a second Sopwith contract and to meet this Blackburn built a brand new factory at Sherburn-in-Elmet. Jigs for the T.1 Cuckoo torpedo bomber were set up by February and Blackburn completed a large production run of 132 aeroplanes during 1918. Britain's first aircraft carrier, HMS *Argus*, set sail with a squadron of Cuckoos on board but none saw action during the Great War. Both of these subcontracted models aroused overseas interest: ten Baby seaplanes served with the Norwegian Naval Air service; while six of the Cuckoos went to Japan in 1922 with another Blackburn type, the *Swift*, to assist in updating the aircraft of the Imperial Japanese Navy.

During the last year of the war Blackburn deliberately underpriced a new torpedo bomber design in his desire to win an Admiralty contract for an aeroplane capable of taking off from the deck of the *Argus* armed with the potent Mark VIII torpedo weighing 1423 lb. He named the bomber *Blackburd*, an ancient spelling and un-forgettable for some of the design ideas it incorporated. As the aeroplane had to be able to be able to fly from and land on an aircraft carrier Blackburn decided that his Blackburd would have wheels for take-off but must be able to jettison these before launching the Mark VIII torpedo. Returning to *Argus*, the Blackburd would land on two steel skids. No defensive armament would be carried. Torpedo tests and the subsequent landings must

Interesting shot of *Argus*, the Royal Navy's first flat-top carrier in the Firth of Forth 1918. Note the battleship, balloons and two of the Sopwith Cuckoos built by Blackburns
Bruce/Leslie collection

have been a spectacular sight at Brough during the spring of 1918. Three prototypes emerged from the factory and the third, N-115, actually carried out deck trials aboard *Argus*.

Several other Yorkshire firms besides Blackburn won aviation contracts during 1914-18 and one of them, Charles Portass & Son in Sheffield, shared in the production of Britain's ultimate fighter, the Sopwith Snipe. During 1918 fifty Snipes emerged from the firm's Buttermere Works and were issued to the RAF, together with those built by other sub-contractors. No. 43 Squadron took its Snipes into action on 26 September 1918 and later fitted four 20 lb Cooper bombs to each aeroplane for use in the ground-attack role. Australian pilots liked the sturdy Snipe and No. 2 and No. 4 Squadrons (Australian Flying Corps) fought the last great air battles over the Western Front with these aircraft.

Canadian squadrons also received the Snipe and their most extraordinary combat was fought out between Major Bill Barker and a formation of Fokker D VIIs on 27 October 1918. This highly decorated Canadian pilot had already destroyed forty-six enemy aircraft and was that day flying his personal Snipe E8102 back to England. Unable to resist a final shot at a high-flying Hannoverana[2], he was jumped by no less than fifteen Fokkers. He shot down the Hannoverana and three of the Fokkers. Badly wounded, out of ammunition and with smoke pouring from his battered Bentley engine, he managed to crash-land the Snipe. Major Barker recovered from his wounds and was awarded "one of the best-earned Victoria Crosses in the history of air warfare."[3]

Another Yorkshire manufacturer, P.J. Pybus, Man-aging Director of Bradford's Phoenix Dynamo Company,

MANUFACTURING CENTRES & ACCEPTANCE PARKS IN YORKSHIRE 1914 -18

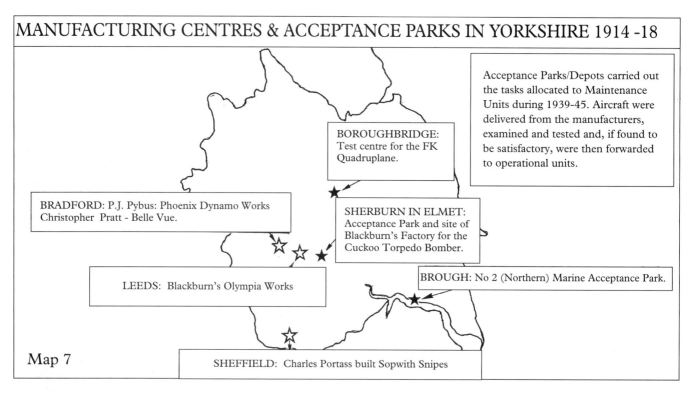

Acceptance Parks/Depots carried out the tasks allocated to Maintenance Units during 1939-45. Aircraft were delivered from the manufacturers, examined and tested and, if found to be satisfactory, were then forwarded to operational units.

BOROUGHBRIDGE: Test centre for the FK Quadruplane.

BRADFORD: P.J. Pybus: Phoenix Dynamo Works Christopher Pratt - Belle Vue.

SHERBURN IN ELMET: Acceptance Park and site of Blackburn's Factory for the Cuckoo Torpedo Bomber.

LEEDS: Blackburn's Olympia Works

BROUGH: No 2 (Northern) Marine Acceptance Park.

Map 7

SHEFFIELD: Charles Portass built Sopwith Snipes

was a man of considerable enterprise and foresight. He had already designed the Phoenix twin-rotor helicopter observation platform. Tethered to a ship and powered by an electric cable running from the ship's generator, it was planned as a replacement for the large and some-what clumsy observation balloons currently in use. Through his efforts, and with the aid of a brilliant design engineer, a Naval Lieutenant named W.O. Manning, Yorkshire became a manufacturing centre for flying boats after Pybus successfully tendered for the erection of twelve

Short 184 seaplanes. The first of these flew in 1916 and these were so successful that contracts for building ten landplane versions of the Short 184 and a production run of Maurice Farman Longhorn trainers flowed into the Bradford firm. Pybus was fortunate that his workforce, mainly women, could readily transfer their skills to the manufacture of complex projects such as the giant Felixstowe flying boats. Helped by the expert cabinet makers employed by Christopher Pratt & Sons at the Belle Vue Drill Hall, Bradford, the workforce produced its first

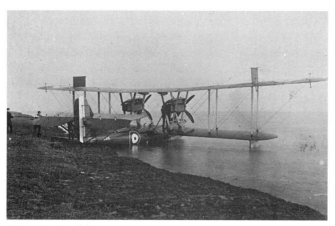

Phoenix Cork N.86 at Brough Marine Acceptance Depot.
Bruce/Leslie collection

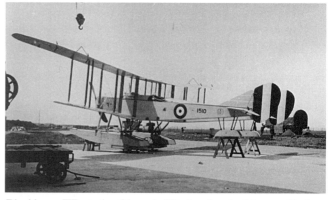

Blackburn TB at the Olympia Works; fitted with two Gnôme Monosoupape engines. Broken up at Killingholme in August 1917.
Bruce/Leslie collection

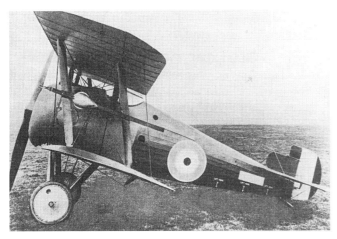

Sopwith Snipe.

The Blackburn AD Scout.
Bruce/Leslie collection

Felixstowe F.3 in 1917. Admittedly, the F.3 was somewhat slower than its famous predecessor, the Felixstowe F.2A[4], but it could carry a bigger bombload and had a greater range.

Bradford-built Felixstowes served on the North Sea Coastal Stations, taking part in the 'Spider Web' patrol system*. This was a complicated octagonal search system devised in April 1917, the centre of which was the North Sea Hinder Light Vessel owned by neutral Holland. A single flying boat cruising at eighty knots could search a quarter of the web in three hours - and the F.3 had an endurance of just over six hours. [5]

Bradford's Phoenix Dynamo Company was the sole manufacturer of the unusual Armstrong Whitworth FK 10 quadruplane. It was about the same size as the Snipe but fitted with four wings. Designed as a two-seat fighter-bomber, N511 test flew at Boroughbridge in April 1917. A few Quadruplanes reached the RNAS that year but they were too slow and had too poor a service ceiling to be effective under combat conditions. As the FK 10 was outclassed in all respects by the brilliant Sopwith 1½ Strutter, the Armstrong Whitworth Quadruplane production line rapidly gave way to Sopwith Snipes, 150 of which were turned out by Phoenix Dynamo.

Armstrong Whitworth was marginally more successful as an airship constructor and leased the airfield at Barlow, south of Selby, in 1917. Construction workers swiftly erected a large airship shed, stores and barrack blocks and the design team and engineers arrived to build the R-25. Fitted with four 250 hp Rolls-Royce engines, it could cruise at over fifty knots and became operational at RNAS Howden on 15 October 1917. Five more airships based on the 23X class[6] were ordered for the RNAS in January

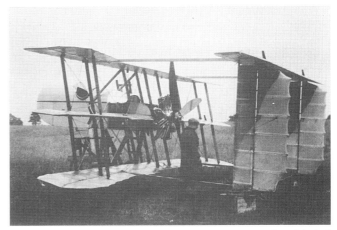

Blackburn Triplane with Clerget engine and four-bladed propeller.
Bruce/Leslie collection

Sopwith Cuckoo built by Blackburn. This is the 5th production model based at Torpedo School at East Fortune. It is shown releasing its torpedo in the Firth of Forth 1919.
Bruce/Leslie collection

* see page 37

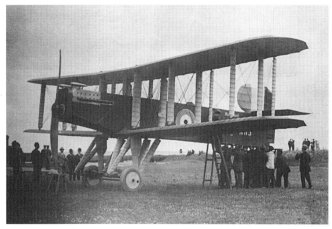

Prototype Blackburn Blackburd, built May 1918. It crashed at Martlesham July 1918.

Bruce/Leslie collection

W.Rowland Ding's Blackburn White Falcon.

Bruce/Leslie collection

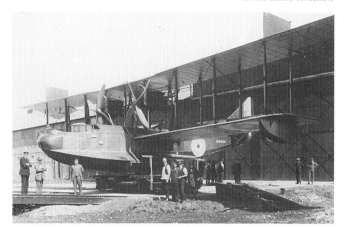

F-3 N4404 at Brough.

Bruce/Leslie collection

1916 and Armstrong Whitworth won two of the contracts - for R-29 and R-30. However, once the wreckage of naval Zeppelin L-33 (forced down by gunfire in Essex 23/24 September 1916) was examined by Admiralty experts it was seen how backward British airship technology really was. Work on several airships including the R-30 was promptly stopped and the Admiralty therafter preferred Felixstowe-type flying boats for its long-distance patrol work. As we have seen earlier, the R-29 was a well-built airship and went on to engage in successful combat with the enemy.

Such changes in Admiralty policy encouraged the Phoenix Dynamo Company to offer a smaller and more powerful flying boat capable of carrying the new 520 lb bombs over one thousand miles. Manning's design team won the contract for two such experimental flying boats and the first Phoenix P.5 Cork test-flew at Brough in 1918. With its seven machine-guns, high speed and rapid rate of climb it was a formidable aeroplane that appeared just too late to see war service. Military contracts were axed and Portass, Vickers and Phoenix saw the demand for service airships and aeroplanes disappear overnight. Manning's brilliance in this specialised area of aeronautical design then spent itself on two unsuccessful projects: the construction of the Fairey Atlanta flying boat and then a modification of the Cork optimistically designed to win *The Daily Mail* £10,000 prize for the first non-stop transatlantic flight.

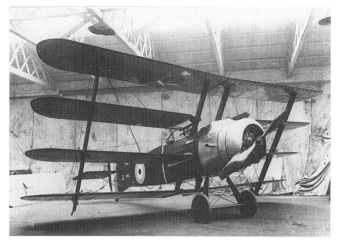

FK 10 Quadruplane.

Bruce/Leslie collection

★ ★ ★

When the Armistice was signed on 11 November 1918 the Royal Air Force was the most powerful in the world. It had

Another shot of White Falcon. Aphra Burley, WRD's daughter, wrote in a letter to the author (23 April 1993):

> *"For me, the most interesting plane in Yorkshire circa 1916 was the 'White Falcon' built by Blackburn - it is said, out of left-overs not required by the factory - for my father's personal use".*

Bruce/Leslie collection

22,000 aircraft, 3330 of which were front-line bombers, fighters and reconnaissance machines serving with 188 front-line squadrons. Within a year demobilisation had more than decimated the Royal Air Force; while the Women's Royal Air Force had all but disappeared. Evelyn Abbott was posted to Killingholme (an American flying-boat station on the Humber), said farewell to the American crews and then organised the demobilisation of all the WRAFs north of the Humber from her headquarters in York's Micklegate. Her final posting was to WRAF Doncaster where she watched the St Leger and then, as the last remaining WRAF, demobilised herself in November 1919. By then a mere twelve operational squadrons remained in the Independent Royal Air Force and only two of these were based in the UK.

Coastal stations closed down, Home Defence landing grounds reverted to pasture, factory production lines came to a standstill. Over the next few years the RAF underwent reorganisation and matters improved a fraction. By the autumn of 1924 squadron strength had crept up to forty-three front-line units though the aircraft they flew were mostly combat-proven machines of

1917-1918 vintage. During the government's long quest for economy and retrenchment the post-war RAF flew its Bristol Fighters, DH 9s and Sopwith Snipes for many years to come. Thus it could not be held that Britain was well-defended in the immediate post-war period. From 1920 to 1922 No. 25 Squadron's Snipes provided the sole fighter defence of the UK and these sturdy little aeroplanes remained in RAF service until 1927.

Of course, aircraft manufacturers - many of whom had prospered during the Great War - recognised the need for change and optimistically looked forward to the rapid expansion of all forms of civil aviation, a mood reflected in Yorkshire. Commercial flying, banned throughout the war, returned on 1 May 1919. After all, flying had been a popular spectator sport in all the Yorkshire towns before the Great War. Surely, argued the manufacturers, people would now be more air-minded than ever before. They would swarm to the air-shows, clamour to travel in airliners and airships or at the very least part with a ten-shilling note for a flight in a converted wartime bomber. So the Twenties began as a decade of high hopes for the future of popular aviation. But the fruit of bitter experience was that if one wished to make a small fortune in flying one must first of all start with a big one. Many an entrepreneur discovered the truth of this in the lean post-war years.

Yet public interest in flying never died and aviation always held a special fascination for the British people. This was partly due to successful government wartime propaganda that had deliberately fostered the adulation of the 'ace' for 'morale-boosting' purposes. In the post-war world of the Twenties the names of great fighter-pilots such as Ball, McCudden, Bishop and Mannock, alongside Immelman, Boelcke, Voss and Richtofen, were well-known and swiftly passed into folklore. It was also a harsh world for most with high unemployment and low incomes. People tended to confine their aeronautical enthusiasms to air shows and to the extensive newspaper coverage of their new heroes and heroines who performed feats of daring by taking tiny aeroplanes to the ends of the earth in truly amazing transoceanic and transcontinental flights.

Chapter Five

Civil Aviation 1919-1939

As early as May 1917 Britain's Air Board[1] had set up a Civil Aerial Transport Committee to assess the needs of post-war commercial aviation. At the time, the Air Board expected that the war against Germany would culminate in intensive strategic bombing operations against Berlin and other cities and that the conflict would not end until well into 1919. Once Germany had been defeated, the Board assumed that in the post-war world air links between Britain and the Empire, particularly India, would have the greatest priority. In February 1918 the Committee recommended that the state should take responsibility for civil aviation and that "Empire route surveys" should begin as soon as possible. In the event, the state was ill-placed to make much impact on civil aviation in the immediate post-war years. Rapid advances on the Western Front and political upheavals in Germany led to an unexpectedly early end to the war in November 1918. A Civil Aviation Department was not formed until February 1919 and on 1 May 1919 the ban on civil flying ended. International civil aviation did not become legal until 14 July 1919.

By then three of the major wartime bomber builders - Vickers, Handley Page and Blackburn had converted their military aircraft to passenger use. Vickers transformed their Vimy bomber - it had never been used operationally - into the Vimy Commercial and the first of these flew at Weybridge in April. Handley Page adapted the 0/400 bombers as airliners at their Cricklewood plant. Thanks to a benevolent government decision to allow flying at a few specified airfields during the Easter Bank Holiday eight hundred passengers paid for joy-rides over London in Handley Page 0/400s. At the same time, George Holt Thomas, owner of Airco (Aircraft Manufacturing Company), was also buying up and converting surplus RAF machines and his firm became the biggest of the post-war civil aviation companies.

In Yorkshire, Blackburn was equally quick off the mark. On 22 April 1919 he founded the North Sea Aerial Navigation Company to exploit the growing importance of Leeds as a manufacturing and professional centre and to connect it with Amsterdam. He decided to use his own aeroplanes for passenger, mail and freight services and on 10 May 1919 bought the RAF's surplus Kangaroo

bombers based at Seaton Carew. His first charter flight was a cargo of ladies' raincoats from Heaton's in Leeds to Amsterdam, an urgent order that was being held up by a Dutch dock strike. Blackburn's main operating problem was that his aircraft had first to fly south to secure customs clearance at Lympne before going on to Amsterdam. So although the Kangaroo was successful as a freight aircraft and logged over 20,000 miles on its North Sea flights, the firm made a loss on the project. It tried to balance the books by offering joy-rides in two Avro 504Ks and these flew from many towns and villages in Yorkshire and County Durham. Avros 504s were easy to modify for air taxi work and there were plans to run such a service between Brough, Harrogate and Scarborough and possibly into County Durham. However, both Avros crashed during 1920 - a far from propitious start for Blackburn's North Sea Aerial and Transport Company.

Surprisingly, Blackburn did not enter the Air Ministry Civil Aeroplane Competition announced in 1920. Civil servants were worried about the safety and reliability of 'bomber conversions', especially with the centre of gravity problems that might emerge once private firms began loading up fuselages with freight and passengers for which the airframes were not designed. £64,000 was on offer in 1921 when the competition took place at the Aeroplane Experimental centre at Martlesham and the Marine Aircraft Experimental Establishment at Felixstowe. There

Joy-riding in the Avro 504K G-EASG at Bridlington. Note the interesting motor-cycle parked by the fence.

Bruce/Leslie collection

were three classes: large aircraft, small aircraft and amphibians. Handley Page's W.8 and the Vickers Vimy Commercial shared second and third place; the judges were unwilling to award a first prize.

However, Blackburn did try to win the prize money offered for the first Britain-Australia flight but Kangaroo G-EAOW force-landed in Crete in December 1919. A second long-distance flight with a Kangaroo to India aborted in May 1920 when the Air Ministry prohibited such flights because of unrest in the Middle East. The final blow to the Kangeroo's commercial future came in 1922 when Blackburn entered two aircraft in the first-ever King's Cup Race. Both had to divert to Manchester and retire from the race. Shortly afterwards Blackburn removed the four highly tuned Falcon III engines and offered them for sale. The rest of the Kangaroos also lost their Falcon IIIs when the RAF needed these engines to keep its force of Bristol Fighters flying. Four Kangaroos remained in Yorkshire and Blackburn reconditioned them as trainers when the RAF Reserve Flying School was set up at Brough in 1924. One Kangaroo crashed in 1925 but the other three, known as Pip, Squeak and Wilfrid, plodded round the Yorkshire skies until they became obsolete in 1926. They met their doom at Sherburn-in-Elmet where they stood in hangars used by the Yorkshire Flying Club before being taken out one at a time to face destruction in the local breaker's yard.

Blackburn had also been one of the few manufacturers to produce a civilian aeroplane in the middle of the Great War. He had built a one-off *White Falcon* for the personal use of Rowland Ding and this aeroplane became a communications aircraft from 1915 onwards. [2] Then in March 1919 Blackburn revealed the little Sidecar aeroplane in a bid to capture a nascent private owner market. Fitted with a 40hp ABC Gnat engine, this tubby little aeroplane aroused a great deal of interest when displayed in Harrod's surrounded by lovely ladies in elegant furs modelling the latest flying fashions. Blackburn's Sidecar had side-by-side seating for two people who peered out of their cramped seat behind twin miniscule windscreens. Blackburn was positive that side-by-side seating was the ideal arrangement for an instructor teaching a pupil to fly. Unfortunately, Blackburn had again built an underpowered aeroplane and, in this form, the Sidecar never flew. [3]

Although the Sidecar was a failure, Blackburn had tried to point the way and answer one problem facing manufacturers in the post-war age: how could one create a widespread interest in private flying and private ownership when cost was always the critical factor?

The Blackburn Sidecar.   *Bruce/Leslie collection*

Thirsty, high-powered engines such as those fitted to wartime aeroplanes were unaffordable and far too heavy. Something light, cheap but equally efficient was essential.

There was to be no immediate solution. In fact, the relatively small numbers of people who were keen to fly seemed to be veering towards glider ownership. As ever, the *Daily Mail* was quick to turn this new sport into a publicity stunt and it soon offered a prize of a thousand pounds to the pilot who could glide the furthest in a flight lasting more than thirty minutes.

This was indeed a challenge. Suddenly Sir George Cayley's ideas became relevant. His papers were read as were all the writings of pioneers such as Lilienthal, Pilcher and the Wrights. After all, it was through their careful experiments with gliders during 1900-1902 that the Wright brothers had been able to make the first powered flight in 1903. Moreover, the Wrights still held the duration record for a glider: ten minutes set up in 1911! These matters were very much in the minds of glider enthusiasts when they assembled in Sussex at Itford Hill during October 1922. The *Daily Mail* competition was a great success. Alexis Maneyrol from France collected the thousand pounds and when everyone left Itford Hill it was in the expectation that gliding would become the popular craze of the Twenties.

It was not to be. Manufacturers were already asking an obvious question: why not fit a small engine to a glider and thus become independent of wind-currents, thermals and launching slopes? Exactly one year after Itford Hill, the first 'Motor Glider Competition' was staged at Lympne in Kent. Twenty-three British competitors took part, including the factory machines sponsored by de Havilland, Avro, Westland, Vickers and Supermarine. There was no entry from Yorkshire and a private venture, Shackleton's *Wee Bee*, won the competition.

The importance of Lympne was that it aroused the interest of Britain's Air Council in light aviation. It now encouraged the design of small, reliable two-seater aeroplanes that would enable people to learn to fly safely and cheaply. At a time of financial stringency what could be better than to induce manufacturers to compete for a cash prize ? The Air Council therefore offered £3000 for an aeroplane that could equip state-sponsored flying clubs. Unfortunately, the Air Council's specification was far too stringent for the technology of the day. Its ideal aeroplane would have folding wings; it would exceed 60 mph but be equally safe at speeds below 45 mph; it would fly for ten hours without servicing apart from essential fuel and oil; it would be capable of short 'getting-off' and 'pulling-up' - the 1924 jargon for take-off and landing; and would achieve all of this on an engine of no more than 1100 cc.

With his experience of deck-landing aircraft Blackburn was well-placed to design a likely winner from Yorkshire and in 1924 the Bluebird I emerged from the Leeds Olympia Works wearing competition number 12 just in time for the two-seater trials at Lympne due to be held from 29 September to 4 October 1924. Once more Blackburn was let down by an inadequate engine. Its 1100cc Blackburne Thrush built by Burney & Blackburne Engines in Bookham, Surrey, lacked sufficient power and Bluebird I never flew at Lympne. Blackburn's experience was not uncommon as engine unreliability plagued many of the competitors who flew at Lympne. There was a strong feeling that the 1100cc engine was just not up to the task prescribed by the Air Council so no-one was surprised when the Air Ministry announced that it could not possibly sponsor any of the Lympne entrants as suitable machines for the new flying clubs.

The Hawker Cygnet.   *Bruce/Leslie collection*

Lympne was the venue for two more light aeroplane competitions in 1925 and 1926 and the Bluebird I, re-engined with the new 60 hp Armstrong Siddeley engine, proved a winner. It captured the Grosvenor Trophy with a speed of almost 85 mph before flying back in triumph to Brough. But it was not the overall winner. Sidney Camm's lightweight Hawker *Cygnet* won first prize. What is interesting about the results of these competitions is that none of the winners of the various Lympne trials became a popular flying club machine. In contrast, Bluebird I aroused a lot of interest especially after it won the Yorkshire Aeroplane Club's 1926 handicap race and then flew across the Channel to Beauvais. The pilot who flew it to France was actually on his honeymoon and Blackburn must have thought the trip propitious as he unashamedly marketed his side-by-side Bluebirds as ideal 'Honeymoon Models' !

Meanwhile the Air Ministry had moved on the matter of sponsored flying clubs. De Havilland's new DH 60 Moth had flown on 25 February 1925 and with its 4500 cc engine it proved to be, as *The Times* put it, 'An Aeroplane for Youth'. Reluctantly - because of the big engine disliked by certain civil servants - the Air Ministry accepted the Moth as a standard aeroplane for the new subsidised flying schools. Most of the credit for the formation of these went to Sir Sefton Branckner, Director of Civil Aviation at the Air Ministry since 1922. His aim was to build through the flying clubs a reserve of British pilots and thus create a national 'air sense' and a 'nation of airmen'. Airwomen should have been included for the first pilot to be trained by the taxpayer was Mrs Sophie Elliott-Lynn. As Lady Heath she would shortly fly solo to South Africa! Sir Sefton Branckner had a keen understanding of the perpetual financial crises faced by flying clubs and he arranged that each of the chosen clubs would receive two Moths and a spare engine (total value £2000), a first-year grant of £1000 and a subsidy of £10 for each pilot trained.

During the autumn of 1925 the first five sponsored clubs - Yorkshire, Lancashire, London, Midland and Newcastle - received their first aeroplanes. Yorkshire had to accept its two Moths at Soldier's Field, Leeds, moving them across to Brough until the new club premises were finished at Sherburn-in-Elmet in 1926. Anxious to meet the flying clubs' urgent requests for reliable aeroplanes, Robert Blackburn built thirteen Bluebird IIs, three of which went to the Yorkshire Aeroplane Club at Sherburn. He had no difficulty in selling Bluebird IIs and IIIs though he retained a couple at Brough for his *North Sea and General Transport Company* operations. The

The surviving B-2 flying low in front of the apron at Brough.
British Aerospace, Brough

Arrow Active I.

A.J. Jackson, British Civil Aircraft 1912-1972,
Vol 1, Putnam, p 286. Flight Photo 12150

last of the Bluebird series was a sleek all-metal aeroplane available with wheels or floats and a wide variety of engines and sold as the Bluebird IV in 1929. All the Yorkshire clubs clamoured for Bluebird IV, especially after S/Ldr Slatter flew the prototype from Brough to Durban, South Africa. Between them, the newly-formed York County Aviation Club at Sherburn (1932), the Hull Aero Club, Sheffield Aero Club and the Reserve Training School at Brough absorbed about twenty of the production aircraft.

Most famous of the Bluebird IVs was G-ABDS. Piloted by Mrs Victor Bruce, this Bluebird was the first light aeroplane to fly round the world (September 1930 - February 1931). By then the light aeroplane had become accepted as a means of international travel, an extraordinary change in public attitude when one remembers that seven years earlier a flight by Bert Hinkler in a light aeroplane over one hundred miles of English countryside was reported as a major aeronautical achievement in the newspapers of 1924.

After the Bluebird IV came the most attractive of biplane trainers ever produced by Brough, the Blackburn B-2. It first flew in December 1931 and as A.J. Jackson has remarked, "All who flew the B-2 were unanimous that Blackburns had produced one of those outstandingly fine aeroplanes which appear too rarely." [4] It was a delight to fly even though novice pilots had to work hard on the big rudder that was perpetually out of balance. Blackburn had predicted that most of the B-2s would go to the RAF he also saw it as a racer and as a club instructional aircraft. But the B-2 had no success as a racer when entered for the 1932 and 1934 King's Cup Air Races

though it did prove itself as a superb aerobatic aeroplane. The Air Ministry liked this and the B-2 became the mainstay of the two Blackburn-controlled *Elementary and Reserve Training Schools* at Brough and Hanworth. B-2s had many adventures and all but one were destined to be written off by 1951. The survivor, G-AEBJ, was lovingly maintained in perfect flying condition by British Aerospace at Brough. On 12 July 1950 the last of the B-2s flew off Filey Sands to commemorate the fiftieth anniversary of Robert Blackburn's first flying school; and there are many who hope that Bravo Juliet will commemorate the hundredth anniversary as well.

Another aerobatic biplane, the Arrow Active, appeared in 1931 from a Leeds manufacturer, Arrow Aircraft Ltd. It was cast in the mould of the attractive fighter biplanes of the Thirties. Two of these tiny all-metal biplanes appeared and the first, the Arrow Active I, competed against the two Blackburn B-2s in the 1932 King's Cup Air Race. Flown by F/Lt E. Edwards, the Active I achieved 132.2 mph against the B-2's creditable average of 114.37.

Alex Henshaw bought the the Active I in 1935 and relates in his *The First Flight of the Mew Gull* its dramatic end. He was flying from Grimsby to Blackburn's factory at Brough, where he hoped to fit the Active with a more powerful engine so that he could carry out an inside loop, then known as a 'bunt'. On the way he decided to try the 'bunt' even though his engine lacked power. In the vertical, he was hanging on top of a stall when the engine backfired and the petrol tank exploded. At this point Alex Henshaw parachuted and the Active I crashed near Covenham. The second aeroplane to emerge from Arrow's workshops was the Actve II G-ABVE and this flew in both the 1932 and 1933 King's Cup Air Races at an average speed of 137 mph. Fortunately, Victor Echo survived the Second World War in storage at Yeadon and

The King's Cup Air Races 1922-1934

Originally the King's Cup Air Race was a race round Britain for seaplanes. Later, it became a two-day race for landplanes around a short course spaced out by pylons. Ideally, the entrant should be a private owner and because most private owners owned light aeroplanes average speeds were usually low. 'Batch' Atcherly's speed of over 150 mph in a Grebe was exceptional. The 1934 race was won by a Monospar - the first time a twin-engined aeroplane had been successful.

Note the Bluebird's triumph in 1931; and a woman pilot's victory in 1930.

Year	Aircraft	Pilot	Average Speed
1922	DH 4a	F.L. Barnard	120.0
1923	Siskin	F.T Courtney	149.0
1924	DH 50	A.J Cobham	106.0
1925	Siskin	F.L Barnard	141.0
1926	D.H. Moth	H.S Broad	90.4
1927	D.H Moth	W.L Hope	92.8
1928	D.H. Moth	W.L. Hope	100.75
1929	**Gloster Grebe**	**R.L.R Atcherley**	**150.3**
1930	**Avro Avian**	**Miss Winifred Brown**	**102.7**
1931	**Bluebird IV**	**E.C. Edwards**	**117.84**
1931	Fox Moth	W.L. Hope	124.25
1933	Leopard Moth	Capt. G. de Havilland	139.51
1934	Monospar ST 10	F/Lt H.J. Schofield	134.16

The Active II came into the hands of Desmond Penrose in 1979. In 1980 he flew her to second place in the King's Cup Air Race "although she was the oldest, open cockpit, non-radio, non wheel brake aircraft entered."
Desmond Penrose

provided most of the entertainment at the pre-war Air Pageants mounted by the newly-formed aero clubs. Sherburn-in-Elmet staged its first display in 1926 where one of the stars of the show was the Moth that had won the 1925 King's Cup race. By 1931-2, when Britain's economy was in an especially parlous condition, the flying clubs had managed to create a reserve of trained pilots, a nation-wide interest in general aviation and a modest number of jobs into the bargain as well. Independent flying clubs mushroomed and in Yorkshire, for example, the Hull Aero Club opened on the old Hedon race-course in October 1929. A copy of its *Air Pageant Souvenir Programme* survives in the Hull Local Studies Library and it records the city's distinction in having the Municipal Aerodrome opened by Prince George, destined to become King George VI in 1937.

During 1934 Yorkshire saw Robert Blackburn's dream of a Hull-Amsterdam air link finally come true - but not with a locally manufactured aeroplane. KLM, the Royal Dutch Air Line, began a daily passenger and mail service between Liverpoool and Amsterdam Schipol via Manchester and Hull using Fokker Trimotor aircraft. Blackburn had to content himself with a regular air ferry service between Hull and Grimsby in 1933 after a little Desoutter I aircraft belonging to National Air Services had pointed the way the previous year. Blackburn's North Sea and Aerial Transport Company operated his new twin-engined monoplane, the Blackburn Segrave I G-ABFR, but Yorkshire and the north of England were not ready for international and local air services in the mid-Thirties and the Blackburn and KLM ventures came to an end in 1934 and 1935 respectively. There was more money in a

was then restored to flying state and placed on the strength of the Tiger Club 1957-8. It was eventually bought by the de Havilland test pilot Capt. Desmond Penrose and in his expert hands the little Active II with its wingspan of 24 ft 0in thrilled the crowds at Elvington's Air Show in August 1992.

It was the Blackburn Bluebirds, together with DH Moths, Avro Avians and Westland Widgeons, that

Apart from the prominently displayed name of the Airport Garage there is little to commemorate the existence of Hull's Municipal Airport at Hedon.

regional link with London and in 1935 Crilly Airways began an air service between Doncaster and Croydon Airport with a DH Dragon and four years later a new airfield to the south-west of the original racecourse landing ground became Doncaster Airport.

As the most prominent aircraft manufacturer in Yorkshire, Robert Blackburn had several irons in the fire. His factory had three prototype twin-engined aircraft under construction: the 1932 CA 15C Monoplane; its Biplane version; and the 1935 B-9 Monoplane. The two CA 15s never flew; while the B-9 emerged from the Brough workshops as a very handsome aeroplane but was doomed never to leave the ground. These disappointments meant Blackburn's final shelving of any hopes of competing for the major Empire air routes. Earlier he had formed the Cobham-Blackburn Air Line by working closely with another great aviation pioneer, Sir Alan Cobham. They had even commissioned a survey of a possible route between Cairo and Nairobi, for their plan had been to design a specialist passenger flying boat, the CB-2 Nile, to transport passengers across Africa. Blackburn must have felt betrayed by the politicians after Sir Philip Sassoon, Under-Secretary of State for Air, had flown to Egypt and back in a Blackburn Iris flying boat. *The Times* had reported his enthusiasm for the aeroplane:

> ". . . he thought travel by flying boat was delightful. There was very little vibration and an extremely good speed could be kept up . . . the whole trip had been a very useful and valuable test of the capabilities of the flying boat."

Yet the government went on to award the African route to British Airways who proceeded to operate a *landplane*! Only the hull of the Nile flying boat had been built and this was tested to destruction at Brough during 1935.

One more Yorkshire air service started that year from a new aerodrome. The Leeds-Bradford Municipal Aerodrome had opened at Yeadon on 17 October 1931. At first it was simply a very large landing ground operated by the Yorkshire Aero Club who had moved there from Sherburn in 1931. But in 1935 North Eastern Airways began charter services to Blackpool using a seven-seater Airspeed Envoy. This was a new design from a brand-new Yorkshire aviation manufacturer, Airspeed Ltd., founded in a disused bus garage in York. Had the money been forthcoming from Hull, Airspeed would have built its factory on the municipal airfield at Hedon.

Among the founders of Airspeed was Nevil Shute Norway who had worked with Barnes Wallis at Howden on the R-100 first as chief stress calculator and then as deputy chief engineer. Together with Hessell Tiltman, a performance calculator who worked for Airco before the firm went into liquidation, they approached Lord Grimethorpe, a wealthy East Riding landowner and keen pilot, for financial support. Lord Grimethorpe became chairman of the new company and Nevil Shute paid tribute to the motives of a man prepared to risk his investment in a new aviation company:

> "In times of depression he felt it to be his duty to hazard money in an effort to create employment in his part of the country . . . he would take satisfaction that through his agency nearly a hundred working men had had employment . . ."[5]

The fourth distinguished member of Airspeed was Sir Alan Cobham who promised that if the firm could manufacture aeroplanes capable of short-field take-offs with ten passengers aboard he would order two of them for £10,000. This was a substantial order for 1931 but an attempt to float shares to secure extra capital was not a great success - even though Amy Johnson bought a few and Capt. Geoffrey de Havilland sent Airspeed his best wishes !

Airspeed's first product was a glider called the *A.S.1 Tern*. Designed for hillside soaring, it was taken to Sherburn and with Nevil Shute at the controls it was towed into the air by the firm's Buick (August 1931). Tern was a comfortable and stable aeroplane and when it flew at Ravenscar, Sutton Bank and local air shows the glider won the firm plenty of publicity. As D.H Middleton has emphasised in his *Airspeed*:

> "In its day Tern held all British records . . . Airspeed had been proved capable of building an aircraft which flew well."[6]

Two Terns were built and then Airspeed went on to construct the attractive Ferry tri-motor biplane designed to have all the qualities of a D.H. Moth *and* the ability to carry ten passengers Transported to Sherburn for its trials and awarded a Certificate of Airworthiness at Martlesham, the prototype Ferry G-ABSI joined Sir Alan Cobham's Flying Circus and eventually carried 159,300 passengers in three years of trouble-free flying. Airspeed's second Ferry G-ABSJ also went to Cobham's Flying Circus in 1932 and was sold in 1934 to an enterprising company called *Himalaya Air Transport and Survey Ltd* who carried pilgrims to holy shrines in the mountains. One more Ferry, G-ACBT, was built at York; the fourth was completed at Airspeed's new Portsmouth factory.

Of course, the tri-motor Ferry was a fairly conservative biplane design, a criticism that could not be levelled at Airspeed's next product - the single-engined *Courier* with a retractable undercarriage. By then Airspeed had moved to Portsmouth and so this was not a Yorkshire first. Airspeed then reformed as *Airspeed (1934) Ltd* and went on to design the *Envoy*, one of which was chosen to fly in the King's Flight; and from the Envoy came the RAF's first twin-engined advanced monoplane trainer, the Airspeed Oxford.

It was in one of these aeroplanes that Yorkshire's most famous woman pilot was to lose her life. Amy Johnson (1903-1941) had thrilled the world with her exploits as a long-distance aviator in the best known of all light aeroplanes, the Gipsy Moth. According to legend, she came to aviation almost by accident, as an impulse during a bus ride that took her past Stag Lane Aerodrome. At the time she was a graduate working for a solicitor's office and could just afford to take her flying lessons at the London Aeroplane Club in Stag Lane. She went solo in April 1929 though her instructors regarded her as a barely average pilot and were always critical of her landings. Later, when contemporaries considered Amy's breath-taking exploits, they were sometimes surprised at the shallowness of her instrument flying skills. Yet Amy Johnson had determination, courage and a more than average dose of 'pressonitis' that rarely leads to the survival of old, bold pilots. Her entry into the male preserve of aircraft engineering was equally extraordinary, considering the times in which she lived. In 1929 she became the first woman to gain a British Ground Engineer's licence; and she went on to take her 'B' Licence and win a Second Class Navigator's Certificate.

Amy Johnson's most remarkable flight was in *Jason*, a two-year old Gipsy Moth G-AAAH. In 1930 she flew the aeroplane solo from Croydon to Darwin, Australia, in nineteen and a half days. After becoming 'Australia's sweetheart' and evading numerous proposals of marriage, Amy returned to Britain courtesy of the *Naldera* and Imperial Airways. After a brief holiday and the award of her CBE, she flew *Jason* up to Hull where, after a rapturous reception, she funded 'The Amy Johnson Cup for Courage' and an *Amy Johnson Scholarship in Aeronautics* at the then University College of Hull. Long-distance flying now became an obsession. In 1931 she decided to follow the Trans-Siberian Railway route to Peking (Beijing) and took off in *Jason III*, another Moth, donated by readers of the *Sunday Graphic* and the *Daily Sketch*. Fifty miles from Warsaw the Gipsy Moth crash-landed in a field of potatoes with dire results for the propeller and undercarriage. When she eventually reached Moscow by train, Lenin's widow praised her as an example to Soviet womanhood.

She married Jim Mollison, the long-distance pilot, in 1932, created several long-distance records and divorced him in 1938. She made good money from her writing and relaxed at the Yorkshire Gliding Club's base at Sutton Bank. Then in the summer of 1939 she achieved the one ambition that had for so long eluded her: a paid job in aviation. After working for *Portsmouth, Southsea and Isle of Wight Aviation Ltd*, she joined Air Transport Auxiliary (ATA) and was lost while ferrying an Airspeed Oxford from Blackpool to Kidlington on 5 January 1941. *HMS Haslemere*, an armed trawler on convoy escort duty in the Thames, steamed towards the spot where the Oxford hit the water and her commanding officer dived in to try to rescue an unidentified survivor. Other crew members thought they saw a woman dragged under the trawler's stern. Amy Johnson was never found; she was ATA's first casualty on active service. Her achievements and the curious circumstances of her death evoke constant interest and she is undoubtedly an important figure in aviation history. Honoured by her native city, Hull, her statue stands in Prospect Street. Sewerby Hall in Bridlington houses her logbooks, trophies and other memorabilia and, thanks to the media of yesterday and today, Amy Johnson remains a household name.

Amy Johnson's connection with gliding highlights the aviation achievements of a third Yorkshire genius, Frederick N. Slingsby. Britain did not enjoy the same level of technical education as did Germany where University and Technical Academic Flying Groups concentrated on glider design. Of course, this emphasis was the result of the 1919 Versailles Treaty that forbade the construction of all aircraft in Germany, a rule relaxed slightly in 1922 when light aircraft, balloons and gliders were permitted.

The Type 6 Kirby Kite 1935

This sailplane was named after the Yorkshire town where Fred Slingsby had established his new factory. During 1935 Slingsby was overwhelmed with orders for Falcons and Grunau Babies and persuaded his work force to concentrate on the Type 6 during the evenings. It was unusual for a factory in Northern Engand during the depression of the mid-Thirties to be working overtime but Slingsby was determined to have his new gull-wing design ready for the gliding competition due to be held at the end of August 1935.

Fred Slingsby carried out the first flight tests but the pilot at Sutton Bank was John C Neilan who won the Wakefield Cup for the longest cross-country flight. Twenty-five Kirby Kites were built up to 1939 and during the war, when most civil/private aeroplanes, gliders and sailplanes were commandeered by the Royal Air Force, Kirby Kites were used for radar detection flight - preparing for the anticipated invasion of Britain by German glider-troops in 1940. After this Kirby Kites were used for glider-pilot training at Ringway. A few Kites went to the Air Training Corps though they were unsuitable for ATC cadets; Kirby Cadets were preferred.

A few Kites have survived and the Museum of Army Flying at Middle Wallop has a superbly restored example that gave a demonstration flight at the 1992 Austers Galore Fly-in.

A German glider launch on the Wasserkuppe.

British glider design was relatively slow to develop, largely due to the popularity of light aircraft during the mid and late Twenties. One or two firms such as Handasyde and de Havilland produced designs, as did gifted individuals such as Cpl Manuel of the RAF who built his *Wren* gliders. But it was Frederick N. Slingsby who transformed the British gliding scene in the Thirties and whose contribution to the history of Yorkshire aviation may be compared with Sir George Cayley and Robert Blackburn - each man, in his own field, an aviation genius. 'Sling' was an RFC veteran, part-owner of a woodworking factory and one of the founders of the short-lived Scarborough Gliding Club in 1930. He built his first glider, a German *Falke*, at his Scarborough base in 1931 and then went on to design and build his own Slingsby Falcon on a new production line in Scarborough's abandoned tramshed. This was not a propitious time for any kind of new business ventures and Scarborough Gliding Club was close to bankruptcy in 1932. Other clubs at Leeds and Bradford were in the same parlous condition and eventually all came together to form the Yorkshire Gliding Club based on a superlative site at Sutton Bank.

In 1933 'Sling' began producing an English version of a Lippisch-designed *Zögling* glider that had already been modified by R.F Dagnall of the RFD Company. Because of its origins the Slingsby Type 3 Primary Glider has always been known as a *Dagling*. It was a single-seater and usually appeared in two forms: a pilot's seat completely open to the elements or a small nacelle that gave the novice a false sense of security. There were many crashes, some of them fatal, and part of Slingsby's prosperity derived from the repair of damaged Daglings. A much sleeker glider, the Hjordis (named after a Norse hero) appeared in 1934 and, probably because it was a 'one-off', did not receive a Slingsby type number. Slingsby Sailplanes needed a two-seater design and so there was great jubilation when the Yorkshire firm was asked to modify a Falcon owned by Espin Hardwick and transform it into a side-by-side glider. This was the Falcon 3 on which work began when the firm moved to its present base at Kirkbymoorside.

Slingsby produced thirteen different types of glider between 1931 and 1939. Some of these such as the Grunau Baby 2 were to German designs.

The Grunau Baby was the most popular glider ever built and estimates of the total number manufactured in Europe before and during the Second World War range between 4-8000. Slingsby's contribution was modest - no more than fifteen - for he was soon involved in the design and production of the Type 6 Kirby Kite, the Type 7 Kadet and the Type 6 Tutor. The Kirby Kadet (later known as the Cadet TX Mk 1) was actually designed by John Stanley Sproule who had been a Vickers' apprentice and helped to build Manuel's Wren gliders. The prototype

A German balloon with an ominous name.

by Geoffrey Stephenson made the first soaring crossing of the English Channel, having flown 127 miles at an average speed of 48 mph.

Yorkshire was marginally associated with that most famous of all international air competitions, the Schneider Trophy. Blackburn had designed an entry in 1923, a year in which Britain was host country for the event. Yorkshire's challenger was the *Pellet*, a small single-seat flying boat. It was unlucky from the start. During its launch at Brough the Pellet's starboard float went under in a fast tide and the aeroplane turned turtle. Salvaged and dried out, the Pellet travelled by rail to Southampton where it over-heated and had to be rescued by motor-boat. As it took off for its second flight the Pellett porpoised, stalled and then nosed under the water. The pilot, R.W Kenworthy, escaped but the Pellet was a wreck. Six years later a rather more successful Schneider Trophy aircraft, the Supermarine S6, arrived in Hull during the city's *Civic and Empire Week* and went on display at the Artillery Barracks in Park Street. The S6 had won the 1929 Schneider Trophy at Spithead with an average speed of 328.63 mph. Flown by S/Ldr Orlebar AFC, the S6 then won the World Speed Record at 357.7 mph.

★ ★ ★

By far the most dramatic event in Yorkshire's post-war aviation history was the R-38 disaster on 24 August 1921. Britain's early rigid airships were inferior to the captured L-33 and the two airships L-64 and L-71 received from Germany as part of Britain's war reparations. Some of the engineering principles employed by German designers were not always understood by their British counterparts at Cardington and the reader will remember that after the R-31 made an emergency landing at Howden in 1918 the airship's girder joints were found to be structurally unsound as moisture had ruined the casein wood glues.

R-38 was the last of the wartime rigids and was still unfinished when the Armistice was signed. Despite R-34's successful transatlantic return flight during July 1919 the government determined to abandon all rigid airship construction unless overseas buyers could be found. As late as March 1921 Winston Churchill, then Secretary of State for Air, was telling the House of Commons that government cut-backs meant that existing airships, their bases and all their equipment would have to be offered for sale to private companies. But at that time there were no private companies with sufficient resources to fund a world-wide airship service, the original government plan.

Kadet appeared in 1936 and was flown at Sutton Bank by Yorkshire Gliding Club and its experiences there led to numerous modifications that turned the Kadet into a first-class primary glider that would initiate many a wartime ATC cadet - including the author - into the delights of first a series of exciting ground slides and then becoming airborne from a winch or, more usually, behind a tow car driven at top speed across the aerodrome.

Britain's entry for the 1937 International Gliding Competitions on the Rhön in Germany included several of Slingsby's designs: the beautiful Gull 1 and his latest King Kite, a most elegant shoulder gull-wing sailplane. The team left Hull in June and performed moderately well on the Wasserkuppe, memorable as the gliders were all launched by uniformed Hitler Youth. Then the Yorkshire firm won a soaring record: in 1939 a Slingsby Gull piloted

So when the United States Navy expressed an interest the government was delighted to negotiate a sale in 1921. R-38 came to Howden to begin its trials and an Anglo-American crew arrived to learn to fly the airship - now given the US designation ZR-2. This crew first worked up on the R-34, veteran of the first flight to Long Island and back. On one training flight R-34 had the misfortune to scrape the top of the Yorkshire Moors near Guisborough and though it managed to reach Howden it showed all the signs of being overstressed. Beyond repair, R-34 was dismantled for scrap. It was not an auspicious start.

On 23 August 1921 the Anglo-American crew lifted off from Howden in R-38 under the command of F/Lt Wann. His intended destination was Pulham but reports from that aerodrome suggested that fog was about to roll in and that a landing would be impossible. R-38 therefore spent the night loitering high above the Yorkshire coast and next morning, in perfect flying conditions, she began her trials at about 2,500 feet. All seemed well when R-38 appeared over Hull in order to practise high-speed turns over the Humber. At a speed of 62.8 mph someone ordered the rudders to be put hard over to port, then to starboard and back to port again. Why such orders were given at so high a speed has never been established as the officers must have understood that such reckless actions could only result in structural failure. Within seconds there came an explosion. Youthful Fred Batte heard it:

> "I was on a Hessle tram going into Hull. We could all see the airship. It wasn't very high but it was lurching to one side. There was a violent bang and as I ran down the gangway to the front of the tram I heard a second bang from the airship. You could see it breaking up and on fire and the front part fell in the river."

Fred Batte had heard two gas cells exploding, causing the airship to break amidships. The flaming nose section fell into the Humber not far from Hull's docks and houses, a narrow escape for the city. The remnant of R-38 was still airborne, dropping quite slowly towards the river. Five crew members, four British and one American, out of the forty-nine men aboard, managed to escape. Wind and tide swept most of the wreckage down the Humber and it eventually sank in deep water.

This disaster did not deter Charles Dennistoun Burney, a man totally dedicated to British-built airships that would provide, as he put it:

> "the keystone of the arch of Imperial communications."

Backed by Vickers and Shell Oil, he had put up a proposal to the Air Council in 1922 for a new 'Airship Guarantee Company'. If it could take over all the existing government-owned airships (R-33, R-36, R-37, R-80, L-64 and L-71) it would build giant airships 760 feet long capable of linking Britain with Canada and India. Sir Samuel Hoare, Secretary of State for Air, accepted Burney's exciting idea on 26 July 1923 and the planning began. Then came the extraordinary general election of 6 December 1923 with the result that Britain's first Labour Government came to power in 1924 with Ramsay MacDonald as Prime Minister. He was impressed by the prestige Britain would enjoy as a great airship power but insisted that the project should begin by building two airships, one by private enterprise and one by government designers. Thus was born the idea of the R-100 and the R-101, the 'capitalist ship' and the 'socialist ship' as they were soon dubbed by the media of the day.

Nevil Shute Norway, better known as Nevil Shute, was an aeronautical stress calculator by day and a novelist by night who later worked on the design of the R-100. In his autobiography [4] he did not mince words, regarding those whom he saw responsible for the R-38 disaster over the Humber. Nevil Shute had no doubt that the civil servants who had designed the R-38 had failed to calculate the crucial forces that would operate against the ship during a high-speed turn. He was quite appalled when Ramsay MacDonald decided to commission another 'government' ship to be built at Cardington but delighted when in 1924 the Airship Guarantee Company bought the old RNAS station at Howden (abandoned in 1921) for £61,000. Shute was working for de Havilland at the time but moved to Vickers as a stress calculator. He undoubtedly shared the Labour Government's enthusiasm for airships as the best mode of international travel; his quarrel was with the designers at Cardington who in his opinion ought to be in jail for manslaughter instead of being given the chance to build another ship, the R-101.

Barnes Neville Wallis (1887-1979) was chief engineer at the Airship Guarantee Company and designer of the R-100. Undoubtedly the outstanding airship designer in Britain, Barnes Wallis hired Shute as his chief calculator and the two men worked together first at Vickers' design office in London and then at Crayford in Kent. By 1926 the refurbished Howden base was ready for building the R-100 and the design team moved to Yorkshire. Howden now became a busy industrial centre providing work and services for hundreds of riggers and machinists drawn from the towns and villages of the East Riding. Business boomed at Faulkner's Dairy with daily deliveries to the airfield; the local stores prospered as it packed up food

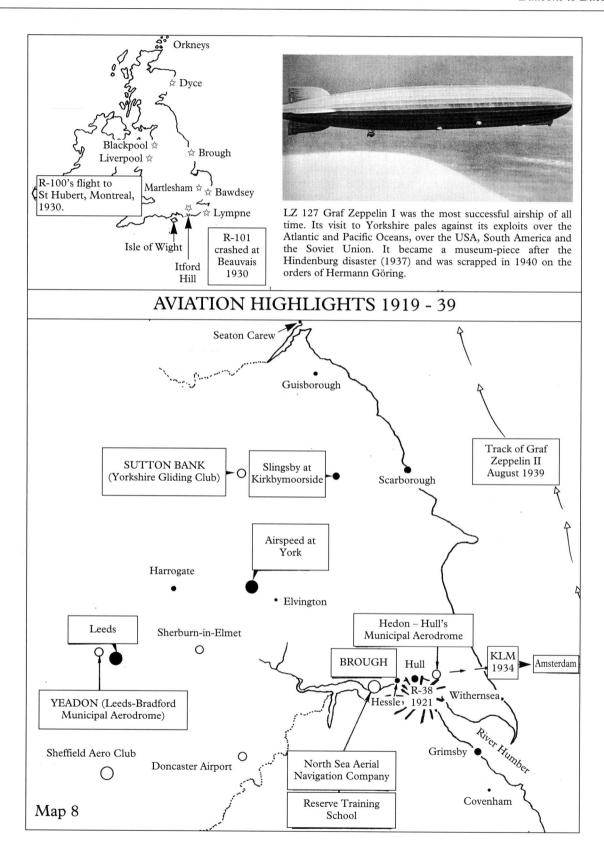

Orkneys

☆ Dyce

Blackpool ☆
Liverpool ☆   ☆ Brough

R-100's flight to
St Hubert, Montreal,   Martlesham ☆
1930.   ☆ Bawdsey
                                  ☆ ☆ Lympne

Isle of Wight   R-101
                       crashed at
Itford   Beauvais
Hill   1930

LZ 127 Graf Zeppelin I was the most successful airship of all time. Its visit to Yorkshire pales against its exploits over the Atlantic and Pacific Oceans, over the USA, South America and the Soviet Union. It became a museum-piece after the Hindenburg disaster (1937) and was scrapped in 1940 on the orders of Hermann Göring.

AVIATION HIGHLIGHTS 1919 - 39

Seaton Carew

Guisborough

Track of Graf
Zeppelin II
August 1939

SUTTON BANK
(Yorkshire Gliding Club)   Slingsby at
                                  Kirkbymoorside   Scarborough

                                  Airspeed at
                                  York

Harrogate
                                  • Elvington

Leeds   Sherburn-in-Elmet   Hedon – Hull's
                                     Municipal Aerodrome

                                     BROUGH   Hull   KLM   Amsterdam
                                                             1934
YEADON (Leeds-Bradford   R-38
Municipal Aerodrome)   Hessle   1921   Withernsea

Sheffield Aero Club   Grimsby   River Humber

        Doncaster Airport   North Sea Aerial
                              Navigation Company
                                                              Covenham
                              Reserve Training
                              School

Map 8

supplies for collection by the airfield 'hack', an ancient de Dion Bouton station-wagon. Travel to the surrounding district was none too easy and most workers had to use the ferry to cross the River Ouse as the bridge was still being built. But it was well-paid work while it lasted, for men and women alike. Riggers and machinists could earn £2.15.0d (£2.75) for a 47 hour week while foremen often took home over £4.00. Many Hull workers rented accommodation in Howden because the cost of a weekly return ticket from Hull Paragon to Howden North (ten shillings or fifty pence) was too expensive. Some Hull workers married Howden girls and at one time the R-100 was known as the Honeymoon Airship.

Barnes Wallis introduced some new construction techniques at Howden, notably a spiral seam machine that could produce helical strips of the light aluminium alloy called duralumin. Eleven miles of duralumin tubing went into the construction of R-100 and all of this was made by men and women machinists working in an adjacent engineering workshop. Barnes Wallis was proving the value of his new 'geodetic' system of strengthening the girders of an airship, a technique that was later to be used in the Vickers Wellesley and Vickers Wellington aircraft. His main problem was to improve the quality and safety of the hydrogen-filled gasbags and he ordered the best he could find from BG Textilwerke GmBH in Berlin. Made of single-ply cotton lined with two layers of gold-beater's skin, the bags had to be varnished and then sprayed with alloy dust. A somewhat officious Berlin representative supervised the inflation of each gasbag. His name was Herr Strobb, corrupted by the Howden workers to 'Here's trouble'.

Fire and water were Barnes Wallis' constant foes. He prohibited all motor-cars within a quarter of a mile of the construction shed. Cigarettes and matches had to be handed in by all workers when they arrived at 0730 for the morning shift. Hob-nailed boots were forbidden and everyone had to wear soft-soled shoes. He found condensation hard to defeat as Howden airfield sat below sea-level and was often water-logged. High humidity meant condensation inside the giant shed and the danger of corrosion in the duralumin tubing was ever-present. Barnes Wallis therefore insisted that every inch of the girders had to be varnished and he employed a team of thirty men for three months on this task alone. Money was in short supply and the staff supplemented funds by acting as guides to the thousands of people who visited Howden, paid their shillings, and watched the R-100 being built.

Completed in November 1929, R-100 had to wait for a fortnight of Yorkshire gales to subside. The socialist

ship R-101 had already been built and had so far completed seven test flights. At Howden the meteorological expert cautiously suggested that still air would arrive on 14 December and next day R-100 was ready to be walked from its shed along the painted centre line in precisely the right weather conditions - a dead calm. Five hundred soldiers from the Yorkshire and Lancashire Regiment bussed in from the barracks at York to make up the handling team under the personal direction of Barnes Wallis. Seven hundred and nine feet long, the airship was almost the same size as the Atlantic liner *Mauretania*. On 16 December 1929 R-100 lifted off. It circled Howden at a thousand feet, carried out turning tests over York and then flew to Cardington.

R-100's great achievement was to fly to Canada and back during July-August 1930. The original plan to fly to India was dropped when it was calculated that the flashpoint of the petrol used in R-100's Rolls-Royce engines would be too dangerous once the airship entered the tropics. R-101 did not need this consideration as she was powered by diesel engines. R-100's arrival over Montreal gripped the imagination of the Canadian people. Their government had built a special mast at St Hubert outside the city and 30,000 Montreal families drove out to the airport to watch the spectacle. Special trains brought 150,000 more to see the airship that had been built in Yorkshire on what was truly "a great day in the history of aviation in Canada." R-100's return flight was uneventful though Neville Shute managed to win one of the daily sweepstakes ($6.75) by calculating the correct number of nautical miles covered.

Shortly after the triumphant return of the capitalist ship, the socialist ship R-101 took off to fly to India. Caught by a storm over Beauvais on 5 October 1930, the crew appeared to lose control. R-101 went into a long dive for some thirty seconds, hit a hill and burst into flames. Of the fifty-four people on board only six survived. The casualty list included the Secretary of State for Air, Lord Thompson of Cardington, and Sir Sefton Branker, who had worked so hard to further the cause of civil aviation in Britain. News of the horrific end of R-101 came as an immense shock to the British people who equated the R-101 disaster with the loss of the *Titanic*.

This second major disaster brought British airship development to an end. Vickers' well-proven R-100 counted for nothing. It never flew again. Dismantled, it was crushed to scrap by the breaker's steam-roller at Cardington. Howden rapidly lost its link with aviation as the design teams dispersed and today little is left at Howden to remind the visitor that from 1916 to 1930 the

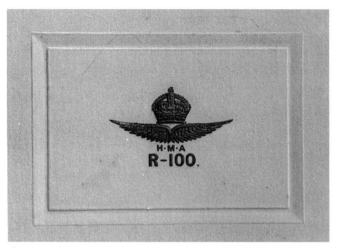

Contemporary greetings card commemorating R-100

airfield played a unique role in the history of aviation in Yorkshire and the world. Fortunately, there is compensation to be found at the Yorkshire Air Museum, Elvington, where the Barnes Wallis Collection is now housed.

Two airships returned to the Yorkshire skies during the 1930s. The first was the remarkable German Graf Zeppelin built in 1928 at Friedrichshafen. Coded D-LZ127 it flew across Hull in 1931 and must have reminded many watchers of those dangerous days in 1915-1916 when the 'silver cigars' rained down death and destruction on the Old Town. It flew along the Yorkshire coast from Withernsea, demonstrating the enviable German reputation for reliability and safety. Eight years later, in May 1939, Graf Zeppelin II (D-LZ130) was readied for a flight over the North Sea, this time with a much more menacing intent. Luftwaffe Generals Milch and Udet had already hinted during a visit to the RAF in 1937 that the Third Reich had developed radio-detection apparatus that was well in advance of anything the British possesed. Graf Zeppelin II's mission in 1939 was to test the effectiveness of the British system of radio-detection, later known as radar. She was specially equipped as an airborne radio interrogation airship with high-frequency receivers and elaborate aerial arrays slung below the gondolas. She flew under the direct command of General Martini, Luftwaffe Director of Signals.

Graf Zeppelin flew from Frankfurt to Bawdsey Research Station near Felixstowe and then moved up the coast to Yorkshire. Britain's Chain Home radars tracked her all the way and when Graf Zeppelin reached the Humber estuary she began her radio interrogation. Directly overhead Hull, the Graf Zeppelin transmitted a position report confirming she was over the North Sea a few miles off the Yorkshire coast. Presumably she was awaiting a correction from British radar to tell her where she really was ! At the time the British operators were actually confused: had Graf Zeppelin made a genuine navigational error or was she tempting the Bawdsey tracking station to report her actual position? So they made no response and the German airship cruised along the Yorkshire coast before turning for home.

Dissatisfied by the experiment, General Martini ordered another test of the 350 feet aerials that were springing up between the Orkneys and the Isle of Wight. On 2 August 1939 Graf Zeppelin began her second interrogation of the British installations. After all, they seemed so different from the secret *Freya* and *Würzburg* radars being developed in Germany that Martini suspected they might be very high-powered radio *transmission* aerials. This time Graf Zeppelin kept well outside the three-mile limit and flew level with the Bawdsey detectors. On this occasion, British radar failed to locate the airship and she was not sighted until she reached Kincardineshire. Two fighters despatched from Dyce managed to intercept her. Graf Zeppelin then returned to Germany having failed to detect any British high frequency signals.

But she had certainly detected the radar installations. They were obvious to all though the general public who had seen them sprout first at Orfordness and then at Bawdsey were convinced by clever RAF propaganda that they all emitted death rays ! What Graf Zeppelin had *failed* to detect was that the British system, no better than its German equivalent, was linked in a most efficient manner to a fighter defence system shortly to be perfected in the first year of war.

Chapter Six

The RAF 1919-1934

Britain's Royal Air Force emerged from the First World War "in power, accomplishment and prestige easily the greatest in the world."[1] Its 188 squadrons were standing-to on all the fighting fronts. In just over four years, they had destroyed 8000 enemy aeroplanes and shot down 200 balloons; dropped 8000 tons of bombs and fired twelve million rounds of ammunition in their ground attack role. 8136 airmen had died; 7245 were wounded. On Armistice Day, 11 November 1918, 30,122 officers and 253,410 other ranks were available to fly and service the 22,647 aeroplanes held on charge. Behind the fighting men throbbed Britain's industrial might and there was very little that British men and women working in the factories and shipyards could not do. As Churchill observed in his capacity as Minister of Munitions, they were actually engaged during 1918 in "executing a plan for 100,000 aeroplanes." Production figures for 1918 up to the end of October exceeded 26,000 aeroplanes and 29,000 aero engines. Such was the capacity of the British people at a time of full employment, intensive government control of industry and immense capital investment.

Within months, all this was to change as the RAF was placed on its peace-time footing. In December 1919 Winston Churchill, Secretary of State for War and Air in Lloyd George's Coalition government, presented the 'new look' RAF. It was a shadow of its former self and in many ways was fortunate even to survive. Lloyd George was not enthusiastic about maintaining the RAF as an independent arm and told Churchill that there would be no separate Minister for Air and he would have to combine it with his responsibilities for the War Department. Churchill decided that most squadrons would have to be based abroad to protect Britain's imperial interests in Egypt, Somaliland, Palestine and India; and when Britain established the brand-new kingdoms of Iraq and Jordan (following the 1921 Cairo Conference) the defence of these new nations depended on the presence of RAF squadrons. The new *political* value of the RAF as well as its current role in the defence of the UK was constantly stressed by its greatest ally, Lord Trenchard. But even he was unable to prevent the massive reductions in RAF bases and manpower in the UK. Politicians argued that there was no evidence that the country faced the threat of

air attack from a potential European enemy: thirty-three RAF Squadrons would be ample to meet Britain's needs at home and overseas. Twenty-one would serve in the Empire, two would be based in Ireland, five in mainland Britain (the 'Inland Area') and five with the Royal Navy (the 'Coastal Area'). Yorkshire was not entirely overlooked: Catterick would remain an air base and its extensive buildings would be preserved. But apart from Catterick, government policy during 1919-20 meant that everything else would close in Yorkshire.

Doncaster's fate was typical. During 1916 its B.E.2s had briefly used the old racecourse, scene of the pre-war air displays, after which the aerodrome became an important Training and Depot Station. SE 5s and Avro 504s were contantly in the circuit. Air Mechanic A. M. Merrix was certainly impressed when he arrived there in 1918. As he walked across the square on his way to report to the Orderly Room an Avro 504 crashed in front of him. It caught fire and no-one could help the pilot for he was trapped in the cross-bracing and burnt to death. Merrix had barely recovered from this experience when another 504 crashed into a tree on the edge of the Doncaster Road. As he later said, "it was quite a sensational start"[2] and he was deeply impressed that this highly organised Flying Training School, equipped with hangars, three Flights and over thirty aeroplanes, could take such matters in its stride. Then, quite dramatically, the entire operation was shut down in 1919.

A similar fate awaited Eastburn (Driffield). A former 33 Squadron landing ground, it became a specialist centre in air combat. No.3 Fighter School moved in during 1918 with an Avro 504 and a little Bristol Monoplane. Permanent buildings arrived in the spring and Eastburn Aerodrome formally opened on 15 July 1918. 217 Squadron brought its D.H.4s back from France and came to Driffield in 1919 in order to disband. No 202 Squadron followed suit in 1920, by which time Eastburn was a well-equipped airfield of over 240 acres.

Despite the recent investment, Driffield was doomed and its new buildings were gradually dismantled. Cuts such as this enabled the the RAF budget to be reduced to £15 million annually - just enough to keep 3280 officers and 25,000 airmen on strength. Churchill gave up his

DH 9A J 827 of No 47 Squadron.

Bruce/Leslie Collection

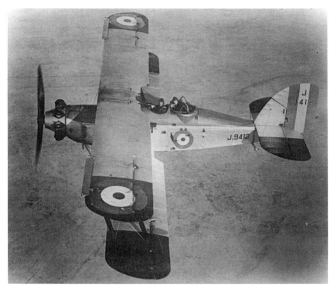

A Wapiti IIA of No 30 Squadron.

Bruce/Leslie Collection

joint War/Air responsibilities on 5 April 1921 and his successor was Captain Frederick Guest who remained as Secretary of State until Lloyd George's government fell from power in 1922. In Stanley Baldwin's first government (May 1923-January 1924) Sir Samuel Hoare became the first Secretary of State for Air.

Meanwhile, public anxiety about these swingeing cuts in Britain's air power surfaced briefly due to a new European crisis. Germany had just defaulted on her reparations payments and on 11 January 1923 elements of the French and Belgian armies entered Essen to begin the systematic occupation of the Ruhr. Britain had formally voted against military action but did nothing to hinder French troop trains crossing the British occupation zone to enter the Ruhr. Overnight the old entente between Britain and France evaporated. People were suddenly anxious about the safety of Britain in the face of an all-powerful French military machine. Had not *The Times*, a year earlier, warned of the serious imbalance between the French *L'Armeé de l'Air* and the RAF ? What was the government going to do about the so-called 'French threat'?

Government had already reacted in 1922 by promising fifteeen new squadrons for the RAF. Only two had materialised by the time the French occupied the Ruhr. In March 1923 a committee chaired by the Marquess of Salisbury recommended that the RAF should have a new Home Defence Force "of sufficient strength adequately to protect us against air attack by the strongest air force within striking distance of this country." [3] This new force

would be called the Air Defence of Great Britain (ADGB), subdivided into one 'fighting area' equipped with fighters and three 'bombing areas' equipped with bombers plus a special Air Defence Group equipped mainly with bombers. In all there would be about six hundred aeroplanes in the new 'Fifty-two Squadron Plan'. The simple philosophy behind this curious arrangement was that the best form of defence was attack: neutralise an enemy by means of a 'knockout blow' against his bases and industrial centres.

Implementation of ADGB was slow but at least a plan had been made, a plan that marginally involved Yorkshire. Thornaby, a small site used by 76 Squadron during the war, expanded during the late Twenties and on 17 March 1930 608 (North Riding) Squadron formed there. It flew Westland Wapitis, a 1927 replacement for the faithful D.H.9s. The Wapiti could carry a 500 lb bomb load and had a range of 360 miles. 608 Squadron's Wapitis formed a part of No.1 Air Defence Group, though no *fighter defence* whatsoever was provided for the County of Yorkshire.

Catterick, one of the oldest of Britain's military air-fields, had survived. During the war numerous squadrons formed at and deployed from Catterick: 76 Squadron, responsible for the defence of Leeds and Sheffield, kept a flight of B.E.2s here during 1916-18; two Canadian Reserve Squadrons (Nos. 83 and 88) began their careers here; and on 1 December 1917 No 115 Squadron formed at Catterick with its Sopwith Pups until it transferred to Netheravon in April 1918. As a Yorkshire-formed

Squadron, one may say that No 115 began the county's connection with a heavy bomber force as it took its Handley Page 0/400s to France. From here it conducted fifteen raids, the first of which was the attack on Metz-Sablon described as the "finest piece of work which has ever been done by a new squadron."[4] Though Catterick basked in the reflected glory of 115 Squadron, it was something of a false dawn. The parent base was not developed for bombers. There was very little flying at Catterick before 11 October 1927 when No. 26 Squadron reformed as an Army Co-operation Squadron. This was the first squadron to receive the Armstrong-Whitworth Atlas specially designed for artillery spotting, signalling and message pick-up work. In 1933 26 Squadron replaced its Atlas aircraft with the Army Co-operation Hawker Audax I, a variant of the Hawker Hart day-bomber.

The years 1932 to 1934 saw a transformation in attitudes towards defence. Young men who had survived the horrors of 1914-1918 and had brought up their families in the Twenties now developed an understandable revulsion against war. There was a growing if misplaced belief in the value of international disarmament and the power of the League of Nations. Yet when the World Disarmament Conference began in Geneva in February 1932 the outlook for world peace looked grim. Japan invaded Manchuria in 1931 and in February 1932, just five days before the Conference began, her bombers and fighters flattened the port of Shanghai. Stanley Baldwin, who served as Lord President in Ramsay MacDonald's two National Governments (1931 and 1931-35), was appalled at the scale of Chinese casualties and quite unrealistically pressed for the end of warfare and the total abolition of all military and naval forces. British intervention managed to arrange a cease-fire in Shanghai but failed to stop the Japanese take-over of Manchuria. Baldwin became increasingly disheartened by the lack of progress at Geneva and in the House of Commons on 10 November 1932 he made his most memorable statement on the subject of air power:

> "I think it is as well for the man in the street to realise that there is no power on earth that can prevent him from being bombed.Whatever people may tell him, the bomber will always get through. The only defence is offence, which means you have to kill more women and children more quickly than the enemy if you want to save yourselves."

On the one hand the government was specifying new aeroplanes so that the RAF could carry out the 'knock-out blow' (Specification P.27/32 led to the the Fairey Battles that would eventually equip fifteen squadrons in Bomber Command); and on the other it advocated the total abolition of military aeroplanes and massive cuts in the defence budget, a programme so disastrously managed that on 15 September 1931 12,000 sailors on five Royal Navy warships based at Invergordon refused to fall in for duties!. It was an incoherent national defence policy heightened by the arrival of Adolf Hitler as Chancellor of Germany in 1933 and by Japan's decision to leave the League of Nations and the Disarmament Conference the same year. Britain was reducing her defence expenditure; the rest of the world was not.

Such were the limitations under which Britain's wretched aircraft manufacturers tried to operate. The Air Ministry simply issued specifications and then invited manufacturers to tender designs for evaluation at the Martlesham Aeroplane and Armament Experimental Establishment that formally opened on 20 March 1924. Scores of different designs, civil as well as military, underwent their tests at Martlesham and among them was a substantial number of Blackburn aeroplanes. Since his successful completion of the Cuckoo contract, Robert Blackburn wanted to produce a rugged torpedo bomber that would drop its weapon accurately without needing to jettison the undercarriage and fold its wings for stowage in the new aircraft carriers such as *Courageous*, *Eagle* and *Furious*. Designed by the brilliant Major Bumpus, the new Blackburn T.1 Swift attracted foreign interest and during 1922 two went to the United States, two to the Imperial Japanese Navy and three to the Spanish Navy. The Royal Navy's requirements were more demanding and a modified form of the Swift, known as the Blackburn T.2 Dart, was in production from 1921 to 1926. Of the 117 Darts built for the Fleet Air Arm, N9804 made history when it became the first aircraft to make a night-landing on an aircraft carrier at sea. It was a safe and reliable aeroplane, with a stalling speed as low as 38 knots. During manoevres off the Isle of Wight in 1930 fifteen Darts made dummy attacks on the battleships *Rodney* and *Nelson* and scored eight hits. Fighter interception proved impossible as the Darts were capable of slow speed evasive action that totally frustrated the fighter pilots. In this way, Fleet Air Arm crews gained invaluable experience in the techniques of accurate torpedo dropping and Darts served aboard the carriers until 1933. Blackburn was so delighted with the Dart's performance that he built three civil two-seater seaplane versions for his civilian flying school at Brough - the only seaplane flying school in Britain. One of these, G-EBKH, flew until 1933 when garage owner Reg Fowler bought it and put it on show at his Hatfield business along the Doncaster Road.

Blackburn Dart at night on HMS Furious (462 Flight)
6 May 1926.

Bruce/Leslie Collection

The Blackburn Blackburn prototype N150.

Bruce/Leslie Collection

Equally successful were the Blackburn R.1 Blackburns built for reconnaissance work and gunnery spotting. Two Flights of Blackburns served with the Fleet Air Arm on *Eagle*, *Argus*, *Furious* and *Courageous*. A few dual-control versions, rejoicing in the unofficial name of the Blackburn Bull, gave pilots the chance to do dummy deck-landing practice at Leuchars No.1 FTS but attempts to convert the Blackburn into a seaplane and into an amphibian trainer were not taken up by the Air Ministry. Production Blackburns were built during 1925-6, two years in which the company managed to interest the Greek government in a modified seaplane version of the Dart. This was the Blackburn T.3 Velos, four of which were built at Leeds and twelve at the Greek National Aircraft Factory at Old Phaleron. Blackburn also produced a long-range version for sale in South America but the solitary demonstrator (the T.3A) failed to win any orders. As a civil aircraft it joined the growing fleet of seaplanes at Brough. Five more Velos appeared during 1929-30 and all but one were sold as scrap in 1932. One survived, registered G-AAAW in the name of Ian Parker. There were high hopes for its preservation when the Shuttleworth Collection paid one guinea for the aeroplane but the needs of older masterpieces took priority. Old Warden's restorers, anxious to use quality aviation timber to preserve their Blériot and Deperdussin machines, dismantled the last of the Velos. All that is left today is its superb Napier Lion engine.

Two impressive experimental aircraft flew from Brough during 1924-5. These were Blackburn T.4 Cubaroos designed to meet the Air Ministry's need for a long-range coastal defence aircraft that could carry either bombs or a 21 inch torpedo. The Cubaroo was a big single-engine aeroplane with a wingspan of 88 feet and a crew that included a pilot and navigator sitting side by side and two gunners in the prone position who fired their weapons from rotating doors close to the lower wing roots. On the top of the rear fuselage was a high gun ring, accessible from the main cabin, to give protection against rear attacks. The two Cubaroos met all the needs of the specification and offered a quite exceptional range of 1,800 miles. But tastes change. In 1925 the Air Ministry decided that coastal patrol aircraft would have to be twin-engined to ensure reliability over the sea. Neither Cubaroo entered service.

Undeterred, the Blackburn design teams used their Cubaroo experience to construct the RB.1 Iris long-range reconnaissance flying boat. Powered by three 650 hp Rolls-Royce engines. Assembly of this big flying boat - it had a wing span of 95 feet 6 inches - took place at Brough where it took off from the Humber on 19 June 1926. Considerably modified as Iris II, it carried out major tours of Scandinavia (1927) and the Middle East (1928). After a fruitless search for a lost submarine, the Iris II was the star of the air show held at Hedon to mark the opening of Hull Municipal Aerodrome in October 1929. Its range and reliability impressed the Air Ministry who ordered three Iris III flying boats. These underwent constant modification to become Iris Vs. One crashed in 1931 but was replaced by a new machine. Famed for their long-distance flights, the Blackburn Iris flying-boats were the biggest aircraft in RAF service. A later development, the R.B.3A Perth, came into service with Coastal Area in 1933. Four of these large flying-boats were built at Brough during 1933-34 and three regularly patrolled the Irish Sea from their Stranraer base. The fourth was held at Felixstowe for experimental work.

A link between the Iris, Aircraftman Shaw and Bridlington

Col T.E. Lawrence, the famed Lawrence of Arabia, joined the RAF after the First World War and took the name of Ross to hide his identity. When reporters discovered who Aircraftman Ross was, he joined the Royal Tank Corps (1923-25) and then transferred into the RAF as 352087 Aircraftman Shaw (he actually changed his name by deed poll during 1927).

Shaw witnessed the crash of the Blackburn Iris (Plymouth Sound 1931) and was concerned by the lack of fast power boat support to rescue flying boat crews.

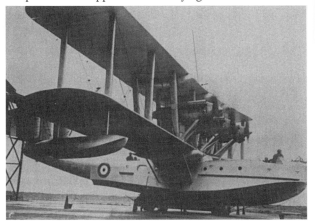

Iris flying boat.   *D. Bell*

From then on he was committed to the design and improvement of RAF launches and in, the opinion of H. Montgomery Hyde, "was one of the prime architects of our Air Sea Rescue Services."* By 1934 Shaw had made a detailed study of launch design and advised on their construction and engine types. He wrote the first procedure manual on Air Sea Rescue techniques (The 200 Class RAF Seaplane Tender). In November 1934 he was posted to the RAF Marine Craft Detachment at Bridlington, then under the control of the Armament School at RAF Catfoss. When he arrived the five armoured boats used for high speed targets on the RAF bombing range at Catfoss and the five seaplane tenders were all out of the water being serviced or awaiting new engines. By January 1935, thanks to AC2 Shaw's energy, his expertise and his extraordinary range of political and service contacts, all ten were operational. During his brief stay at Bridlington (his 1935 discharge from the RAF occurred whilst he was there) he stayed with some of the other airmen at the Hotel Ozone and was much impressed by the RAF's pleasant life-style, a marked contrast with his two years in the Royal Tank Corps.

* H. Montgomery Hyde, Solitary in the Ranks, Constable 1977, p 241.

In complete contrast with the Cubaroo, Iris and Perth designs were Blackburn's various attempts to meet the specialised needs of the RAF: reconnaissance monoplanes, naval trainers, spotter/interceptors, high-level bombers and light-weight fighters. An RAF ferry pilot managed to crash the first Airedale reconnaissance monoplane at Brough (1925); the second, though tested at Martlesham, suffered Air Ministry rejection in 1926. Blackburn was equally unlucky with the 1926 T.R.1 Sprat intermediate naval trainer. An attractive aeroplane that could be easily converted to a seaplane, it failed to impress the Air Ministry who preferred the Vickers Vendace.

A more streamlined design, part-spotter, part-interceptor, was the 2F.1 Nautilus. It was a successful deck-landing aircraft but, having failed to beat the Hawker Naval Hart, the sole RAF Nautilus served out its time as a useful communications aircraft. Blackburn's attempt to impress the Air Ministry with the new B.T.1 Beagle high altitude bomber also failed. Its first Bristol Jupiter VIIIF engine lacked power and Martlesham suggested an uprated engine; but even with the extra 130 hp from the Bristol Jupiter XF it lacked both speed and a desirable service ceiling when carrying bombs or torpedo. Similarly, fighters such as the F.1 Turcock. the F.2 Lincock and the unnamed F.3 fitted with a Rolls-Royce engine did not enter production on any significant scale. The Turcock was a private venture built in Leeds with an eye on the Turkish market. It first flew at Brough on 14 November 1927 but crashed at Martlesham during trials the following year. Nine Lincocks, tiny fighters with a wingspan of 22 feet 6 inches, made a great impression on overseas buyers. Highly aerobatic, they never served with the RAF though Lincock I did carry spurious markings at the 1930 RAF Hendon Air Display. Both The Lincock I and the Lincock II prototype greatly impressed crowds as a display aircraft in the United States and Canada but no orders resulted. Eventually, Blackburn sold two Lincock IIIs to Japan and two to China in 1930; while the Italians built one under licence as the Piaggio P11 fighter trainer that flew in 1932. Blackburn's unusual F.3 never managed to leave the ground. The F.3 was the Yorkshire manufacturer's response to one of the toughest Air Ministry specifications ever issued: the aeroplane had to be fast (250 mph+) with a service ceiling higher than any other fighter, fully equipped for night-fighting and armed with four Vickers machine-guns. No manufacturer could meet this specification and despite the skill and craftsmanship that went into this unusual aeroplane the Blackburn F.3 experienced metal fatigue in its fuselage during protracted taxying tests in 1934.

Blackburn's contribution to the Finnish Air Force (FAF)

The FAF Ripon shown below is the 'pattern' aircraft built at Brough.

R1-121.   *Central Finland Aviation Museum*

Valtion Lentokonetehdas (VL) built twenty-five FAF Ripons at the old Suomenlinna factory: one in 1930, fourteen in 1931 and ten in 1934. The photo of the service Ripons is taken over the Baltic Archipelago near Helsinki.

RI-151 and RI-156.   *Central Finland Aviation Museum*

The FAF made extensive use of the Ripons and during the Second World War (Winter War and Continuation War) they functioned as night reconnaissance aircraft and often served to drop supplies and evacuate wounded in their ambulance role. Occasionally, they operated as light bombers attacking Soviet army camps. The Finnish Navy tested them on torpedo-bombing and smoke-screen trials. During their long careers the Ripons were fitted with a variety of engines: Jupiter IV, liquid cooled Hispano Suiza 12, Armstrong-Siddeley Panther IIa and the Bristol Pegasus .

The last FAF Ripon IIF flew in 1944 and RI-140 still exists, stored in a hangar at Vesivehmaa airfield seventy miles north-east of Helsinki.

Blackburn B-5 Baffin, one of the first two pre-production aircraft, after its successful trials at Martlesham Heath.

British Aerospace

During these years of depression, Blackburn produced one outstanding aeroplane that did yeoman service with the Fleet Air Arm. This was the T.5 Ripon, designed as a replacement for the Dart. It first flew in 1926, impressed Martlesham and won a government contract for the production of the T5A. Ripon IIA. This carried out successful test flights at Brough in 1927 and during 1928 amazed the journalists who gathered to watch its performance at the factory. The demonstration Ripon made a fast approach down the Humber, dropped its torpedo and then pulled up into a loop, an impressive manoeuvre for a biplane with a lower wingspan nearly a foot longer than the upper plane.

Ripon IIAs served on *Glorious*, *Courageous* and *Furious* and five travelled on *Eagle* to take part in a 1931 British sales drive in Buenos Aires. During 1931-32 Blackburns upgraded the IIA into the IIC, featuring improved wing design and construction. History does not record why there was no IIB though the next designation, IIF, stands for 'Finland' where twenty-five aircraft were built under licence by the Finnish National Aircraft Factory. They served in Winter War (1939-40) against Russia; and in the Continuation War (1941-44) when Finland fought as an ally of the Third Reich against the Soviet Union. An alternative design, the Blackburn B-3, featuring a much more powerful Rolls-Royce Buzzard IIIMS, did not go into production; but the B-5 Baffin became the standard Fleet Air Arm torpedo bomber in 1934 and served with 810 Squadron (*Courageous*), 811 Squadron (*Furious*) and 812 Squadron (*Glorious*). Twenty-nine Baffins flew with the Royal New Zealand Air Force. These Yorkshire-built aeroplanes went on active service in 1939 and during the following year one RNZAF Baffin followed a patrol line that led it from South Island, beyond the Antipodes Islands and towards Antarctica.

Such was Blackburn's contribution to the equipment of the Royal Air Force and to Commonwealth and foreign air forces up to the beginning of 1934. Every aeroplane accepted for service was a biplane as the Air Ministry still suffered from monoplane-phobia that had restricted designers since before the First World War. Thirteen Fighter Squadrons formed the Air Defence of Great Britain during 1930-1932, all equipped with biplane Bulldogs, Demons and Furies. In order to be able to carry out Britain's 'knockout blow' the Wessex Bombing Area had ten Bomber Squadrons flying mainly Virginia and Hyderabad aeroplanes plus the Wapiti, Sidestrand, Fox and Gordon; while No 1 Air Defence Group had twelve Bomber Squadrons flying Wapitis, Hyderabads and Horsleys. By 1934 there had been no significant updating of the RAF. Britain preferred to put her faith in the League of Nations and in the outcome of the Disarmament Conference. But the League was moribund and the Conference collapsed in November 1934. Britain had wasted two years and in that time had become

gradually aware that Germany, the nation she had militarily discounted since 1919, was rapidly rearming with modern warships and new types of aeroplane. Though the Luftwaffe was not formally revealed until 1 March 1935, it had already re-equipped during 1931-33 and had secretly formed thirteen Bomber *Staffeln*, five Fighter *Staffeln*, eleven reconnaissance *Staffeln*, four Coastal *Staffeln* and, ominously, one Dive-bomber *Staffel*. All sported innocent names to lull foreign correspondents, none of whom guessed that the 'Hansa Flying School' was really Bomber *Gruppe* Fassberg; and that the 'Forest and Agricultural Experimental Institute' was the cover name for Reconnaissance *Staffel* Prenzlau.

Fortuitously, a senior RAF officer, whose contribution is rarely recognised by historians, became Chief of the Air Staff in 1933. He was Sir Edward Ellington who held office for the next four crucial years. Under his leadership the RAF would be transformed into a truly modern air force.

Foundations of the Luftwaffe

Gerhard Fieseler points the way for future fighter pilot training.

Heinkel He 70.

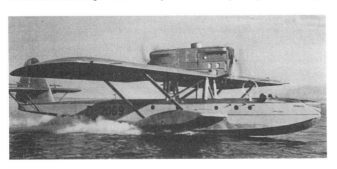
Dornier-Wal.

Dornier Do-X.

Chapter Seven

The RAF 1934-1939 and The Fleet Air Arm 1937-1939

The Royal Air Force

The appointment of Sir Edward Ellington in 1933 was one of those happy political moves that ensures the good fortune of Great Britain in time of unexpected adversity. He was a supreme facilitator and under his leadership common sense, innovation and initiative were given full rein. He was fortunate in the array of intellects that gathered around him in government, in the Royal Air Force, in the civil service and in private enterprise: Lord Swinton, Secretary of State for Air 1935-7; H.E.Wimperis, Director of Scientific Research at the Air Ministry; HT Tizard, ex-RFC pilot and now Chairman of the Aeronautical Research Committee; Air Chief Marshal Sir Hugh Dowding; Barnes Neville Wallis; Robert Watson Watt; Ralph Sorley; Sydney Camm and Reginald Mitchell - to name but a handful of the truly great. Had Ellington been a different kind of man steeped in the misplaced tradition of the RAF's knockout blow or had been insensitive to the dangers posed by Germany's nascent Luftwaffe, it is possible that the genius of Camm and Mitchell would not have been harnessed to that remarkable product of the Rolls-Royce factory in 1933, the Merlin engine[1]; or that he would not have been impressed by Ralph Sorley's calculations on how to destroy a fast, high-flying enemy aircraft in a two-second burst from eight machine-guns. [2]

Happily, the Air Ministry issued Specification F.5/34 that would lead to the production of two types of eight-gun fighters for the RAF: the Hurricane and the Spitfire. Two other innovations that took place within Ellington's tenure of office, for which the nation would be forever grateful, were the issue of two Air Ministry Specifications (B.12/36 and P.13/36) from which came the Stirling, Halifax and Manchester bombers and the creation of the Royal Air Force Volunteer Reserve in 1937.

Equally important, was the slow conversion of Britain's political leadership to the need for rearmament. They could hardly complain they had not been warned. On 29 November 1934 Winston Churchill, then merely MP for Epping, played the role of prophet in the House of Commons:

> "In the present circumstances of the world, the strength of our national defences, and especially of our air defences, is no longer adequate to secure the peace, safety and freedom of your Majesty's faithful subjects . . . What is the new fact that has broken upon us in the last eighteen months? Germany is rearming . . . but what concerns us most of all is the rearmament of Germany in the air . . .
> I therefore assert, first, that Germany already at this moment has a military air force . . . and that this illegal air force is rapidly approaching equality with our own".

He went on to warn the Commons that unless Britain accelerated her own defence preparations, German air power would overtake Britain's:

> "by the end of 1936 the German military air force will be nearly 50% stronger, and in 1937 nearly double."

Ramsay MacDonald, socialist leader of a 'National Government' since 1931, was known as 'the apostle of peace'. A pacifist by inclination, he came to understand the dangers inherent in the failure of the International Disarmament Conference. That was precisely why he permitted the first of several RAF Expansion Schemes to begin in July 1934, though they were not substantial enough to please Churchill. At least 'Expansion' allowed the RAF to complete its 1923 plan for fifty-two home-based Squadrons plus sixteen new Squadrons for the Fleet Air Arm. It also assisted in the partial re-equipment of a Royal Air Force seeking quality rather than quantity and shunning the French policy of building up large stocks of obsolescent aeroplanes. In 1935, the year in which pacifism in Britain reached its height with a 'Peace Ballot' organised by the League of Nations, Ramsay MacDonald resigned from office. One of his last acts was to produce the White Paper *Statement Relating to Defence (1935)* authorising limited rearmament.

Ramsay MacDonald's successor in November 1935 was Prime Minister Stanley Baldwin. He now made public his private views on defence:

> "When you think of the defence of England you no longer think of the chalk cliffs of Dover, you think of the Rhine. That is where our frontier lies."

With Germany as the potential enemy, Ellington had to supervise the reorganization of the RAF to cope with a threat from a distant European power. Pressed hard by Lord Swinton, Government promised Ellington large reserves of manpower and equipment, plus the prospect of a series of 'shadow factories' financed by the taxpayer but operated by existing private aircraft manufacturers. This would guarantee a *constant* output of aircraft: 158 a month in 1938; 800 a month in 1939. This level of production was equal to four months of reserves in a heavy-loss war situation. He had in mind, of course, the likely loss of Battles, Blenheims, Hampdens and Wellingtons in fiercely-contested daylight operations. Even these production levels were insufficient to cope with the needs of essential North Sea and Atlantic patrols against German U-boats and surface raiders. With admirable foresight, Prime Minister Chamberlain's government therefore allocated £25 million in 1938 for the purchase of suitable American aeroplanes. One of the most important acquired in this manner was the military version of the Lockheed 14 named 'Hudson' after the English navigator Henry Hudson.

Ellington's unique command system came into operation during 1936. ADGB vanished. In its place came Fighter Command, Bomber Command, Coastal Command and Training Command. New Commands needed new airfields as well as new aeroplanes and Bomber Command, in particular, required well-placed bases for possible attacks against Germany. Ellington's eyes turned to the four eastern counties whose long coastlines bordered the North Sea: Yorkshire, Lincolnshire, Norfolk and Suffolk. Yet in all of these four counties there was but one base suitable as a bomber station and that was Bircham Newton near King's Lynn in Norfolk. Later on, a satirical writer in Air Historical Branch described the four counties as a 'demilitarised zone' as far as their potential for offensive air warfare was concerned.[3]

It was urgent that matters were put right. Survey teams hastened north of the Wash, looking for sites that were at least fifty feet above mean sea level (to reduce the problem of drainage) and not more than 600 feet above mean sea level (to avoid the low stratus and frets that plagued the Yorkshire countryside). Compulsory land purchase began and before long new bomber bases at Finningley, Linton-on-Ouse, Driffield, Dishforth and Leconfield were under construction by the No.3 (Expansion) Works Area based on Lincoln. Yorkshire had truly become 'bomber country', defended by a new fighter base being built at Church Fenton. There was a common plan to these new airfields: several C type hangars crouched on the ground; around them were the technical sites, messes and domestic buildings, built in a simple mock-Georgian style to blend with the rural surroundings. A watch office or control tower and a water-tower were universal. There was no attempt at dispersal and consequently all the new Expansion airfields were prime targets for the Luftwaffe.

The five Yorkshire Expansion bomber bases soon became operational: Finningley and Driffield in July 1936; Dishforth in September 1936; Leconfield in December 1936 ; Linton in May 1937. Church Fenton opened in June 1937. All were grass airfields and all opened with two squadrons. Yorkshire's skies filled with the roar of Rolls Royce Kestrels as the Handley Page Heyfords flew in from their bases at Boscombe Down and Worthy Down to Finningley, Dishforth and Leconfield. Heyfords were the last of the RAF's biplane heavy bombers, remarkable for a fuselage attached to the upper wing and a lower wing carrying heavily spatted wheels and a 3000lb bomb load in its thick centre section. Six Yorkshire Squadrons were originally equipped with this bomber: Nos 7 and 102 at Finningley, Nos 166 and 97 at Leconfield, Nos 10 and 78 at Dishforth. The first production Heyford had flown in 1933 and so was relatively 'modern' compared with the aircraft flown in by 58 and 215 Squadrons when they took over Driffield in September 1936 with their Vickers Virginias. No 58 Squadron had flown Virginias since 1924 and they had been much modified over the years. The Mark X was a heavy night bomber with a crew of four. Of all-metal construction and fabric covered, it had twin Napier Lions and a bomb-load of 3000lb.

Linton's first aircraft were of a totally different calibre. The base had opened in May 1937 and became the new headquarters for No 4 Group Bomber Command in July

Bombays at Driffield during the A.O.C's. inspection 21 October 1937.   *Yorkshire Air Museum*

77 Squadron Whitley K8960 pranged at Driffield just before the outbreak of war.   *Yorkshire Air Museum*

A visiting Gloster Gauntlet of No 74 ('Tiger') Squadron. Note the "illegal" tiger stripes along the rear fuselage. These black and yellow decorations blocked out the space for the RAF serial number, contravening regulations.   *Yorkshire Air Museum*

1937. Nos 51 and 58 Squadrons took off from Boscombe Down with their new Armstrong Whitworth Whitley Mk I aircraft and arrived at Linton on 28 April 1938. However, No 10 Squadron at Dishforth had already converted to the Whitley Mk I in March 1937 and was the first Squadron in 4 Group to operate this new bomber. It was a notable aeroplane. One of the new generation of RAF monoplane night bombers, the Whitley was the first to be *designed* for night operations, the first to have a retractable undercarriage and the first to have turretted defensive armament, initially with Vickers Gas Operated (VGO) and twin Browning .303 machine guns.[4]

All Whitleys Marks I-III were fitted with twin Armstrong-Siddeley Tigers, not the most reliable of engines. Several Squadrons entered the Second World War equipped with the Tiger Whitleys; but 4 Group rapidly converted to the Mark IV with its more powerful Merlin engines - with an added bonus. These engines had warm-air ducts, much appreciated by the Yorkshire-based crews who took part in the long-distance raids of 1939-40.

Finningley also had a new bomber, entirely different in concept. No 76 Squadron, disbanded at Tadcaster in June 1919, had reformed at Finningley in April 1937. It was the first squadron to receive the Vickers Wellesley. This was a single-engined, two-seat general purpose bomber capable of carrying a 2000 lb bomb load. A great deal of publicity focused on this aeroplane in 1938 when three Wellesleys of the RAF's Long Range Development Flight based at Cranwell achieved a world distance record of 7,157.7 miles that stood until 1946. Valuable though this was, the Wellesley was unfitted for combat operations in Europe and by the time war began in September 1939 only four of these aircraft were still at Finningley. By then most had moved to the Middle East and 76 Squadron had re-equipped with Handley Page Hampdens. Finningley's role was to provide training facilities for squadrons converting to the Hampdens, 212 of which were serving in

Bomber Command by September 1939. No 76 Squadron then moved to Upper Heyford and gradually lost its identity as it merged with No 6 (Training) Group and then disappeared completely to become part of No 16 Operational Training Unit.

On the fighter front, Church Fenton opened in June 1937 and No 72 Squadron and No 213 Squadron soon brought their Gladiators and Gauntlets in from the south of England. No 64 Squadron, equipped with two-seat Hawker Demons, replaced 213's Gauntlets in May 1938. Later that month thousands visited Church Fenton for its Empire Air Day display. This event was graced by the appearance of not just Blenheims and Spitfires but by the Secretary of State for Air, Sir Kingsley Wood, and Ellington's successor as Chief of the Air Staff, Air Chief Marshal Sir Cyril Newall. Detached to Digby during Home Defence exercises in August, No 64 Squadron managed to lose four of its Demons when unexpected fog forced the crews to fly southwards in search of a lucky break in the clag. Low on fuel, they radioed for instructions to Duxford and were told to set their Demons on a course of 225 degrees Magnetic - and then bale out! In December 1938 No 64 exchanged its Demons for the new Bristol Blenheim IF night-fighters. As well as the usual fixed Browning firing forward and a single Vickers K in the dorsal turret, the Blenheims had a specially-made gun-pack of four Brownings slung below the fuselage. No 72 Squadron kept its Gladiators at Church Fenton throughout the 1938 Munich Crisis, when the little biplanes donned 'war camouflage' for the first time. Not until April 1939 did it begin to re-equip with Spitfire Is.

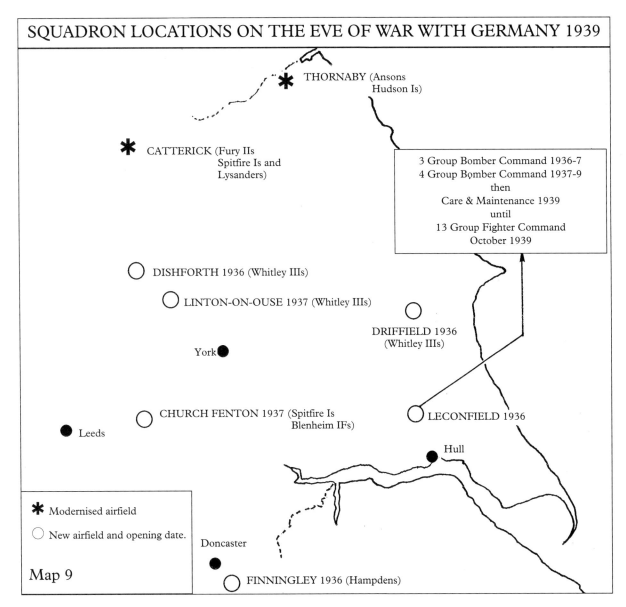

SQUADRON LOCATIONS ON THE EVE OF WAR WITH GERMANY 1939

THORNABY (Ansons
Hudson Is)

CATTERICK (Fury IIs
Spitfire Is and
Lysanders)

3 Group Bomber Command 1936-7
4 Group Bomber Command 1937-9
then
Care & Maintenance 1939
until
13 Group Fighter Command
October 1939

DISHFORTH 1936 (Whitley IIIs)

LINTON-ON-OUSE 1937 (Whitley IIIs)

DRIFFIELD 1936
(Whitley IIIs)

York

CHURCH FENTON 1937 (Spitfire Is
Blenheim IFs)

LECONFIELD 1936

Leeds

Hull

✱ Modernised airfield

◯ New airfield and opening date.

Map 9

Doncaster

FINNINGLEY 1936 (Hampdens)

Further north at Catterick, 'Expansion' meant full-scale modernisation to provide facilities for three operational fighter squadrons. The airfield remained under Army Co-operation Command control until September 1939, when the resident No 26 Squadron took its new Lysander IIs to France. Meanwhile, No 41 Squadron had been based at Catterick since the summer of 1936 and had exchanged its Hawker Demons for the sleek single-seater Fury IIs. In January 1939 it began to receive Spitfire Is but only one flight was fully operational when war began eight months later. On the eve of war No 609 Squadron Spitfire Is transferred from Yeadon to Catterick. 609 had originally formed as an Auxiliary Air Force bomber

squadron at Yeadon (10 February 1936) and converted to Harts and Hinds at the end of 1938. Its Spitfires did not arrive until August 1939 so 609 Squadron was even less well-prepared for combat than 41 Squadron. Catterick's Spitfires were part of No 13 Group, while Church Fenton's squadrons came under No 12 Group command.

Thornaby was the second Yorkshire airfield to be modernised during 1936-38. There had been every intention of converting it into a fighter station but, as the German threat increased, more stress was rightly laid on the need for additional general reconnaissance squadrons. For over three years the 'backbone of Coastal Command' was to be the twin-engined Avro Anson Mk I, some of which were built by A.V.Roe & Co, at Yeadon Aerodrome. Fitted with two 335 hp Armstrong Siddeley Cheetah VI engines, the much-loved 'Annie' was to be a common sight in North Yorkshire. No 608 Squadron had exchanged its day-bomber Wapitis for two-seater Demon fighters in 1937 and it was still technically under Army Co-operation Command until 20 March 1939 when 608 transferred to Coastal Command (No. 18 Group) and began to work up on Ansons at Thornaby.

Three other squadrons that served in Yorkshire (Nos 220, 233 and 244) took part in the mass formation fly-past of Avro Ansons at Hendon in June 1937. No 224 Squadron arrived in July with its new Ansons and became the first to convert to the American-supplied Hudson Is in May 1939. No. 233 Squadron also brought its Ansons to Thornaby in July 1937 and received the first of its Hudson Is in August 1939, two months after it had left Thornaby for a brief spell at Bircham Newton where it had exchanged places with No 220 Squadron. This squadron, destined to distinguish itself in the Norwegian campaign 1940-41, transferred to Thornaby on 21 August 1939.

Such were the airfields and aeroplanes in Yorkshire on the eve of the Second World War. But what of the men that flew the Whitleys and the Ansons, the Blenheims and the Spitfires? All were peace-time volunteers but not all were officers or NCOs as they would be by 27 May 1940. Thousands of air-minded youngsters had wanted to fly but 'Expansion' had called for only 2,500 pilots. Yet there was still a need for an extra 2,069 air-observers, 3,867 wireless operator/air-gunners (WOP/AGs) and 554 specialist air-gunners so lucky boy-entrants might be accepted as tradesmen aircrew. Arrival at Padgate or Cranwell would be followed by recruit training with all its enjoyable anguish, air experience flights in Valencias and Wapitis and handling the machine-guns or primitive wireless-telegraphy (W/T) equipment of the 1930s. Trained as Aircraftmen Gunners or Aircraftmen Wireless Operators, some joined their Yorkshire-based squadrons for flying duties on Whitley bombers, for which they were paid an extra one shilling and sixpence a day - with another sixpence if one qualified as an air gunner and wore the 'winged bullet' badge.

In 4 Group, gunnery training was carried out either at the Group Pool based at Leconfield or on the squadrons. Whitley IIIs, delivered to squadrons August 1938 onwards, had an hydraulically operated ventral 'dustbin' turret with twin .303 Brownings. "A cramped and claustrophobic metal cylinder" was Larry Donnnelly's memory of his new crew position when he joined 10 Squadron at Dishforth in May 1939.[4]

The Fleet Air Arm

Naval aviation suffered the same cut-backs after 1918 as the RAF. The term 'Fleet Air Arm' to describe the carrier aircraft came into use from 1924 and in 1937 the Navy was promised full control of its own air power. This actually happened in May 1939. All Fleet Air Arm (FAA) personnel were naval and the Admiralty had its own naval stations back, having lost them when the old RNAS had been merged into the RAF in 1918. The FAA's role was essentially that of the strike aeroplane launching a torpedo at an enemy ship, a tradition established by Blackburn's Cuckoos and Darts between 1918 and 1933.

To provide a modern torpedo-spotter-reconnaissance aeroplane for carrier operations, Robert Blackburn produced the B-6 Shark as a private-venture response to Air Ministry Specification S.15/33. The last of the Blackburn torpedo biplanes, it boasted a number of innovatory design features. Its mainplanes were braced with rigid slanting struts; its folding wings (with detachable tips) had an hydraulic locking system; it had a tracking tail wheel and deck-arrester hook; it was stressed for catapult launching and was readily converted to a seaplane. The Shark went through its trials at Brough and was then tested at Martlesham and on *Courageous*. To Robert Blackburn's delight, the Shark won its first contract in August 1934. Shark II appeared in FAA service in 1936, powered either by a Tiger VI or a Bristol Pegasus IX engine. Shark III, fitted with a glazed canopy, entered service in 1937.

Altogether, Blackburn supplied the FAA with 238 Sharks, some of which were built at his new factory in Dumbarton. He also produced six Shark IIAs for the Portuguese Navy and spectators at Brough were treated to an impressive display of Shark manoevrability and firepower when Blackburn laid on a demonstration for the Portuguese Naval Mission to Britain (3 March 1936). Seven standard Mark II's entered service with the Royal Canadian Air Force in 1937; and Boeing Aircraft of Canada built seventeen Mark IIIs under licence. Two special Sharks, 525 and 526 [5], went out to help Boeing construct their Pegasus-engined versions, most of which served on Canada's western shoreline. Several of these aircraft were still in service at the end of the Second World War.

During 1933-34 Blackburn inserted the similar B-7 general purpose aeroplane into the Shark production line. As it was not intended for FAA service, its wings did not fold but it was extremely strong and Blackburn hoped it would fill the dive-bomber aspect of Air Ministry

Specification G.4/31. It had all the features of a naval Shark and could carry a torpedo as well as bombs. By the time it reached Martlesham in May 1935 the specification was out of date and the Air Ministry had dropped the idea of a biplane dive-bomber. As the Shark look-alike B-7 had no more value it flew back to Brough to be scrapped.

Four leading aviation manufacturers vied with Blackburn to win orders from Air Ministry Specification 0.27/34. Blackburn's B-24 prototype K5178 was the winner and the Air Ministry chose well to call the first dive-bomber to serve with the Fleet Air Arm the Skua. Built at Brough by Blackburn Aircraft Ltd (the company's latest name), this all metal monoplane with a retractable undercarriage first flew on 9 February 1937. Blackburn's second prototype, K5179 flew at Brough in May 1938 and had the longer nose shrouding its 840hp Bristol Mercury IX radial engine. Its unexpected appearance at Ipswich Aero Club's 1938 Air Display was a bonus for the present writer and other small boys who lined the Nacton Road for a good view of the proceedings. The aeroplane was well-advertised in the aviation press in its dive-bombing role and it quickly captured the public's imagination.

Writers of popular literature featured the Skua in their stories and M.O.W. Miller wrote a 'Long Complete Air Thriller' about the dive-bomber's fictional exploits during the Palestinian Arabs' rebellion in a 1939 edition of *Air Stories*.

Fleet Air Arm's requirements remained urgent and though the Brough factory achieved demanding monthly production targets (of the 190 Skuas made, 154 were delivered before September 1939), the FAA was still short of long-range fighters when war began.[6] At the end of 1938, when Brough airfield was temporarily out of action, Blackburn tested Skua IIs with the more powerful Bristol Perseus XII engines at Leconfield. These soon equipped Nos 800 and 803 Squadrons on board *Ark Royal*; No 801 Squadron flew its Skua IIs from *Furious*; while No 806 Squadron based at Eastleigh was gradually converting to Skua IIs.

Blackburn's Skua was the only monoplane in FAA carrier service on the eve of the Second World War. Its sister aircraft, the Blackburn B-25 Roc two-seat fighter, never flew from a naval carrier. Designed as the FAA's equivalent of the RAF's Boulton Paul Defiant, the Roc featured an electrically operated 4-gun turret located

Blackburn Roc. This example, L3059, crashed on take-off near Blackburn's Dumbarton factory in December 1939.

British Aerospace Military Aircraft Division, Brough

PALESTINE PARTY

One after another, those Skuas dived to the attack . . .

A Story of Air Adventure above the Palestine Coast

J.Drigin's drawing of Skuas diving to the attack in the fictitious yarn 'Palestine Party' (April 1939).

behind the pilot's canopy. Because of this highly specialized fitting, and because the Brough factory was overwhelmed with the demands of producing more

Skuas and tooling up for the new twin-engined B-26 Botha, the Roc was subcontracted to Boulton-Paul Aircraft at Wolverhampton. The first Roc (L3057) flew in December 8, carried out tests at Brough and then flew to Martlesham with two other Rocs (L3058 and L3059) for full-scale trials. L3057 and L3059 then went to Blackburn's Dumbarton factory for converting into seaplanes, by which time Britain was at war with Germany.

* * *

Exactly what Britain would accomplish in the air was uncertain. Hermann Göring had no anxieties, at least not on 9 August 1939 when he made this statement:

"As Reichs Minister for Air, I have convinced myself personally of the measures taken to protect the Reich against air attack. In future I will look after every battery, for we will not expose the Ruhr to a single bomb dropped by enemy aircraft".

Hermann Göring.

Personal conviction was one thing; the reality of war would be another.

Chapter Eight

Year of the Whitley

"This morning the British Ambassador in Berlin handed the German Government a final note stating that, unless we heard from them by 11 o'clock that they were prepared at once to withdraw their troops from Poland, a state of war would exist between us. I have to tell you now that no such undertaking has been received and that consequently this country is at war with Germany."

These were the words of Prime Minister Neville Chamberlain broadcasting to the nation his declaration of war against Germany at 1115 hours on Sunday 3 September 1939. Previously, Chamberlain had been willing to sacrifice the sovereign independence of Czechoslovakia (1938) in an effort to appease the land-grabbing *lebensraum* of Adolf Hitler. When this failed, Chamberlain took a most unusual step in an attempt to stop Nazi aggression: he had guaranteed the sovereign independence of Poland, a country that was palpably beyond the reach of Britain's armed forces. Hitler regarded this guarantee as a political bluff and invaded Poland on 1 September 1939.

On 3 September 1939 Britain demanded that Germany cease her aggression against Poland and immediately withdraw her armed forces. Adolf Hitler made no response and the Prime Minister declared war on Germany.

On that day Yorkshire was essentially a bomber county with 4 Group's Whitley squadrons poised to strike.

ORDER OF BATTLE: 4 GROUP
3 SEPTEMBER 1939

10 Squadron	Dishforth	Whitley IV
78 Squadron	Dishforth	Whitley IV
51 Squadron	Linton-on-Ouse	Whitley III
58 Squadron	Linton-on-Ouse	Whitley III
77 Squadron	Driffield	Whitley III
102 Squadron	Driffield	Whitley III

Two airfields were temporarily non-operational: Leconfield (4 Group Pool) held the Whitleys of No 97 and No 166 Squadrons; Finningley (within 5 Group) was on 'Care and Maintenance'. Two other satellite airfields at Cottam and York were allocated to the Whitley

Squadrons; as were the 'scatter' airfields at Ternhill, Yeadon and Sealand. 78 Squadron at Dishforth was non-operational. Catfoss had hosted the RAF's No 1 Armament Practice Camps and its Fairey Gordons and Hawker Henleys had been towing sleeve targets for most of the spring and summer. P/O Peter Parrott was stationed there but as he said, "On the day war broke out we fled west-wards in the Henleys, reaching Stranraer in the evening and Aldergrove the next day."[1] Yorkshire was now on a war footing with 4 Group ready to strike at the enemy.

Yet, in the opinion of the Official History, Bomber Command simply did not have the training or the equipment to attack German targets in the daytime. As for night bombing, it would be lucky if its crews could even find the target area, let alone the target itself.[2]

This was somewhat unfair to 4 Group, the sole Group in Bomber Command to have carried out systematic night training. As Alastair Revie has rightly observed when describing the RAF's peacetime activities, some RAF bomber squadrons were scrupulous in their attention to working up their night-flying skills. No 58 Squadron, for example, based at Linton-on-Ouse flying Whitley IIIs, spent four nights a week, if weather conditions were suitable, on night-flying exercises.[3]

However, all Bomber Command squadrons were restricted by the pleas of President Roosevelt of the United States. He urged that there should be no air attacks on civilian populations. Britain promptly agreed to this and assured the President that

"unrestricted warfare on civilian populations as such will never form part of our policy."

A fortnight later, the Germans indicated that they accepted Roosevelt's limitations on indiscriminate bombing. Similar pressure came from our own French ally who urged Bomber Command not to attack the German mainland in case it brought retribution down on the heads of the French people. Consequently, the Whitley squadrons were assigned futile night-time Nickel operations - leaflet dropping over German territory.

The first 'bumph-mission' was flown by Nos 51 and 58 squadrons, ten of whose Whitleys moved to Leconfield for their first raid on Germany on the night of

3/4 September 1939. They reported negligible opposition, not surprising for the Germans were neither prepared for such inoffensive raids nor much bothered to prevent them. Air Marshal Harris later commented that as far as he was concerned the only thing that Nickelling accomplished was to provide most of the Continent's toilet paper requirements for the rest of the war.[4]

Those who had to fly the leaflet raids tended to agree in less delicate phraseology, not least because the physical process of dropping the leaflets was itself usually uncomfortable and sometimes hazardous. Large parcels of leaflets wrapped in brown paper had to be loaded into the Whitley and stacked just forward of the ventral turret. After unpacking the parcels to reveal bundles of leaflets held together with elastic bands, two crew members were needed to dispense them to the enemy: one to pass the bundles and the other to shove them down the flare-chute. At 20,000 feet and with only one oxygen-point available this was a cold, uncomfortable and highly strenuous task. Theoretically, the rubber band came off after the leaflet bundle had left the chute. Sometimes it broke and then the chute ejected scores of leaflets inside the fuselage.

Yorkshire's Whitley squadrons carried out ten such raids during September 1939, mainly to the Ruhr, Hamburg, Kiel and Bremen. Normally, the squadron aircraft - rarely more than ten flew in any one night - crossed the coast at Flamborough and, skirting the then neutral countries of Belgium and Holland, set course for their German targets. Occasionally, some aircraft were pre-positioned at Reims as on the night of 9/10 September when the targets included distant Nuremberg. Desultory flak inflicted a certain amount of damage over Germany and several Whitleys crashed in France and Yorkshire.

No 102 Squadron suffered the first losses: on 8/9 September flak shot down a Whitley over Thuringia and all crew members were made prisoners-of-war; another Whitley force-landed at Nivelles and all the crew were interned.[5] On 1/2 October No 10 Squadron made the first leaflet raid on Berlin. Four aircraft reached the German capital; one failed to return, presumably ditched in the North Sea. The winter of 1939-40 was atrocious and kept the leaflet-raiders on the ground for the first fortnight in October. When they resumed, the crews were tasked to carry out reconnaissance as well as drop leaflets. Their observations built up a valuable intelligence bank concerning German defence dispositions during the so-called 'phoney war'. In December Yorkshire's Whitleys carried out daylight security patrols over the German seaplane bases at Borkum and Hornum in the Frisian Islands. The object of these sorties was to deter the Heinkel He 115s from taking off on their mine-laying missions against Britain. They were a constant menace to shipping and their magnetic mines had already claimed many merchant vessels in the river estuaries and along the coasts of Eastern England.

While the Whitleys went about their various 'job-finding' tasks, events involving 3 Group's Wellington bombers were changing the whole strategic purpose of Bomber Command. For years, the RAF had believed that its new daylight bombers, the Blenheims, Hampdens and Wellingtons, would be capable of carrying out the 'Western Air Plan' by taking out specific enemy targets with pinpoint accuracy and thus rapidly reducing the enemy's capacity to fight. With the 'no mainland target' restriction, the RAF concentrated on enemy shipping, particularly units of the German Navy - the Kriegsmarine - in their northwestern German bases. Relatively low-level bombing attacks were favoured and the RAF hoped that their delayed-fuse 500lb bombs would either go straight down the funnels of *Emden* and *Admiral Scheer* or at least penetrate their deck armour.

No. 77 Squadron's Whitleys KN-N, KN-R and KN-L engaged in parachute dropping.

Yorkshire Air Museum

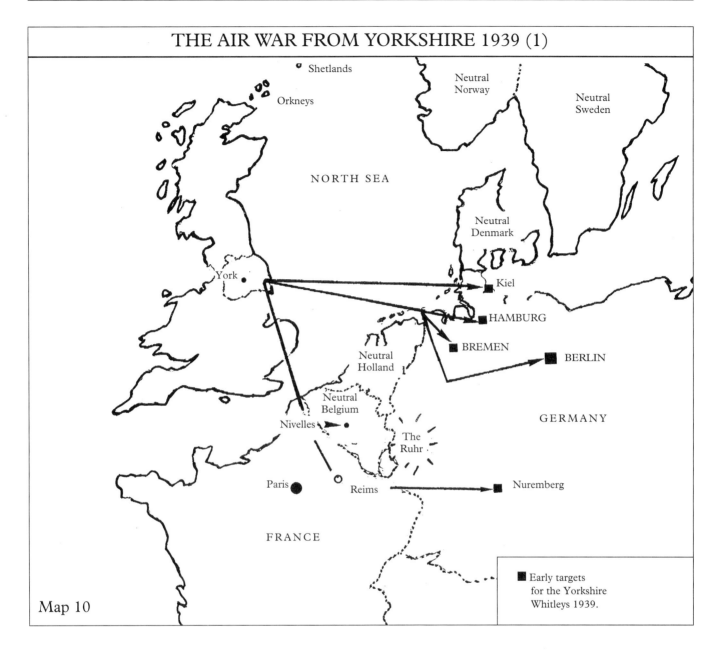

THE AIR WAR FROM YORKSHIRE 1939 (1)

Map 10

Early targets
for the Yorkshire
Whitleys 1939.

Three raids on Wilhelmshaven were disastrous failures. Courageous crews found that their bombs did not always penetrate German armour and some that did failed to explode; that their radios did not work; and that their defensive firepower was useless against high level beam attacks from German fighters. Five Blenheims and two Wellingtons were lost on the second day of the war; and even when the day bombers attacked German destroyers at sea as eleven Hampdens did on 29 September 1939 a 'hornet's nest' of German fighters brought down five of the Hampdens. But the two decisive days came in mid-

December 1939. 14 December saw the biggest RAF operation to date when seven Whitleys, twenty-three Hampdens and twelve Wellingtons flew on a North Sea shipping search. In the Schillig Roads just north of Wilhelmshaven the Wellingtons found a convoy and prepared to attack. Suddenly German fighters appeared and shot down five of the Wellingtons.

Four days later twenty four Wellingtons again tried to bomb ships off Wilhelmshaven but were quickly detected by a new German Freya radar station on Wangerooge Island. The controller vectored German fighters on to the

THE AIR WAR FROM YORKSHIRE 1939 (2)

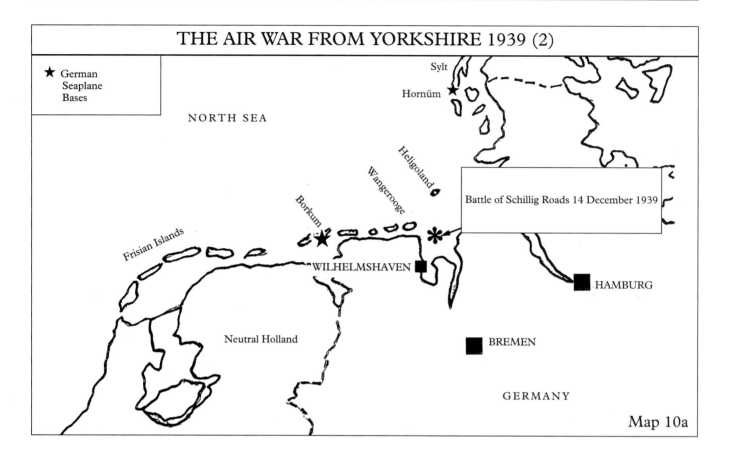

★ German
Seaplane
Bases

NORTH SEA

Sylt

Hornüm ★

Heligoland

Wangerooge

Borkum

Frisian Islands

Battle of Schillig Roads 14 December 1939

WILHELMSHAVEN

HAMBURG

Neutral Holland

BREMEN

GERMANY

Map 10a

formation now somewhat ragged because of the accurate naval flak.

A major air battle now ensued, one of the biggest in the history of aviation up to that time, with over eighty aeroplanes involved. Ten Wellingtons went down in flames, two more had to ditch and three force-landed - a total of fifteen bombers lost out of the twenty-four that began the mission. An appalled Air Ministry promptly suspended daylight attacks and ordered the Hampdens and Wellingtons to join Nickelling sorties in the New Year when the Yorkshire Whitleys resumed their long-range leaflet raids. By March 1940, from their forward base at Villeneuve outside Paris, the Whitley squadrons were visiting targets as far away as Poznan, Vienna and Warsaw.

On 15 March 1940 a 77 Squadron Whitley returning from Warsaw had a remarkable and much-publicised adventure. Low on fuel and a trifle lost, the pilot dropped down to find a land-mark, As dawn was breaking he spotted a large field and decided to land to ask the way. Conversation with the local populace rapidly established that they were in Germany. Despite being encumbered by

heavy boots and Sidcot suits, F/Lt Tomlin's crew broke all records for taking up positions, starting engines and departing German air space.

Four days later the shooting war began in earnest on 19/20 March 1940. Thirty Whitleys from Driffield, Dishforth and Linton joined twenty Hampdens for an attack on Hornum seaplane base on the island of Sylt. This was the RAF's first offensive operation against a land target since war began, specifically ordered by the War Cabinet after German bombers had attacked Scapa Flow on 16 March and killed one civilian and wounded five more. The raid on Hornum lasted six hours. Twenty tons of high explosive and 1,200 incendiary bombs, it was said, hit the target area and crews claimed excellent bombing results. One Whitley from 51 Squadron failed to return and so the Hornum operation appeared to prove that the RAF could carry out a precision night bombing attack with a bearable 2% loss. However, when intelligence officers scanned pictures brought back first by a Blenheim and then by a PR Spitfire on 6 April there was no sign that there had even been a raid on the island! Moreover, the Germans insisted that no damage had been done and that most bomb loads had landed in the sea. To underline their point, the Germans invited a group of Americans to visit the base so that neutral observers could tell the world that RAF bombing was far from accurate. These revelations shattered the earlier euphoria in Bomber Command's Uxbridge Headquarters.

Here, Air Chief Marshal Sir Edgar Ludlow-Hewitt had long been wrestling with the raison d'être of Bomber Command. The heavy losses of daylight bombers contrasted with the comparatively light losses experienced by the Whitleys during their night operations. Inexorably, they pointed to the abolition of Bomber Command's day bombers and to the wisdom of converting them into a night bomber force. Most of the Air Staff now agreed that the self-defending daylight bombers flying in close formation had little future and Bomber Command could not continue to accept the high loss of aircrew and aircraft suffered during the air battles of 1939. Hampdens and Wellington must become night-bombers.

Ludlow-Hewitt analysed the recent night-flying experience of the Whitley crews and understood the vital improvements they demanded: self-sealing petrol tanks, because fabric covered aircaft went up like a torch when spilt petrol ignited; reliable radio equipment and navigational aids to improve target location and provide crews with a better chance of survival when returning to England in low cloud and fog; proper de-icing equipment to replace the miserable compounds smeared on the leading edges; heated flying suits and more accessible oxygen points for crews committed to hours of flying at 20,000 feet; improved air traffic control and better availability of diversionary airfields for aircraft returning with battle damage and dead and wounded on board. He could comprehend the hardships facing his crews for he had built up an immense knowledge of the detailed requirements of airmen in a shooting war. From the first he had begun to retrain his crews and convert several bomber squadrons into Operational Training Units. He had conserved his crews and their aircraft as far as possible, realising from the outbreak of war that it would take time, skill and a great deal of practice before an *effective* bombing force could be assembled. His qualities earned him the admiration of his airmen and thus it came as a shock when the Command heard that their leader was leaving his post. On 3 April 1940 Air Marshal Sir Charles Portal became Air Officer Commander-in-Chief Bomber Command. When Ludlow-Hewitt privately told his friend Arthur Harris, then commander of No 5 Group, that he was going Harris exclaimed, "My God, a disaster, a catastrophe!" Of

course, it was not. Portal stopped the Nickel raids and ordered the Yorkshire Whitleys to engage in the night bombing offensive.

Events overtook this order. On 9 April 1940 German forces invaded Denmark and Norway and, as Churchill would later admit, when explaining British defeat in this Norwegian encounter, the quality of the German infantry, the enterprise of the airborne troops, the novelty of the blitzkrieg, were all beyond the experience of the best of the British Guards Regiments.

Bomber Command was equally baffled. To attack the German supply ships and Hitler's newly-acquired airfields in southern Norway involved a round trip of roughly one thousand miles, entirely over the sea. There was little hope of bomber support for the troops fighting even further away in Narvik.

It was in the context of the unexpected Norwegian campaign that Brough-built Skuas established their value as dive-bombers. 803 Squadron had earlier tried low-level attacks on 14 September 1940 when two of its Skuas bombed a surfaced U-boat. One of their 250lb bombs bounced on the waves, exploded and brought down both of the Skuas whose crews were promptly taken prisoner by the UC-30's submariners. Skua crews changed their tactics when operating over Norway. Skuas from Nos 800 and 803 Squadrons based at Royal Naval Air Station Hatston in the Orkneys made an early morning dive-bombing attack on the German warship *Königsberg*. This 8000 ton cruiser had been badly damaged by Norwegian gunners when it had covered the German landings at Bergen and was now tied up alonside a jetty in Bergen harbour, undergoing repairs. Fully bombed up with a semi-armour piercing 500 pounder, eight 20 pounders and plenty of .303 ammunition, the Skuas were difficult to trim fore and aft and accurate flying by the two squadrons in darkness was a considerable achievement.

The attack on the *Königsberg*.   *FAA Museum Collection*

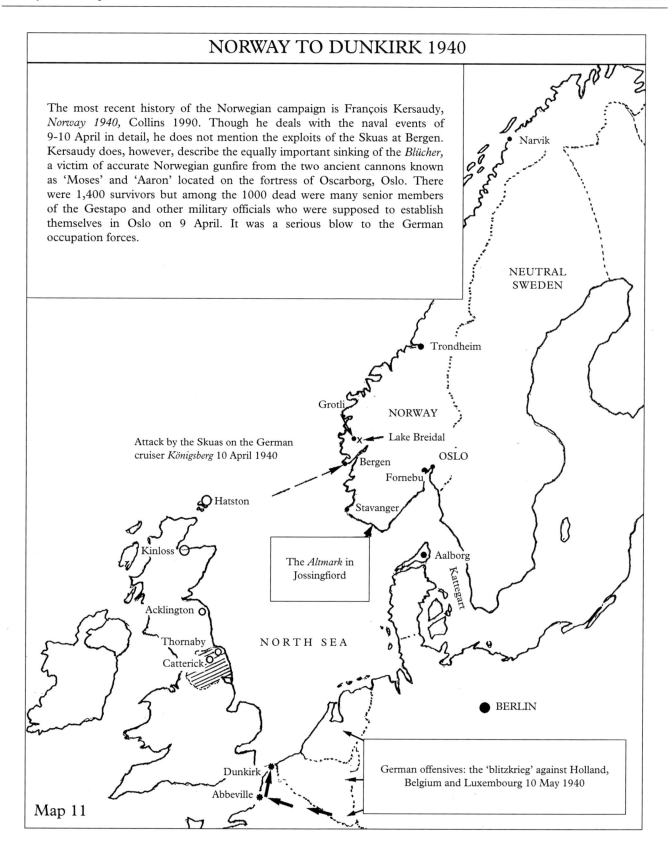

NORWAY TO DUNKIRK 1940

The most recent history of the Norwegian campaign is François Kersaudy, *Norway 1940,* Collins 1990. Though he deals with the naval events of 9-10 April in detail, he does not mention the exploits of the Skuas at Bergen. Kersaudy does, however, describe the equally important sinking of the *Blücher,* a victim of accurate Norwegian gunfire from the two ancient cannons known as 'Moses' and 'Aaron' located on the fortress of Oscarborg, Oslo. There were 1,400 survivors but among the 1000 dead were many senior members of the Gestapo and other military officials who were supposed to establish themselves in Oslo on 9 April. It was a serious blow to the German occupation forces.

Narvik

NEUTRAL SWEDEN

Trondheim

Grotli

NORWAY

x ← Lake Breidal

OSLO

Attack by the Skuas on the German cruiser *Königsberg* 10 April 1940

Bergen

Fornebu

Hatston

Stavanger

Kinloss

Aalborg

The *Altmark* in Jossingfiord

Kattegatt

Acklington

NORTH SEA

Thornaby

Catterick

BERLIN

Dunkirk

Abbeville

German offensives: the 'blitzkrieg' against Holland, Belgium and Luxembourg 10 May 1940

Map 11

Captain R T Partridge, a Royal Marine pilot flying L3025, led 800 Squadron; Lt W P Lucy led 830 Squadron. At 0700 hours on 10 April 1940 the Skuas screamed down from 6000 feet at a diving angle of 65 degrees. At 1800 feet they released their bombs, turned and escaped almost at sea level. On the way home one Skua inexplicably dived at full power into the sea - the sole casualty. Behind them in Bergen the *Königsberg* was on fire and sinking, demonstrating the accuracy of the Skua as a dive-bomber when used against a warship. Its place in the history of naval aviation was assured: it had been the first British aeroplane to shoot down a German aircraft (a Dornier Do 18 on 25 September 1939); and now it had sunk the *Königsberg*. Three weeks later, Captain Partridge and his observer Lt. Bostock, had to force-land on frozen Lake Breidal near Grotli. They set fire to Skua L2940 and then made their way to Andalsnes where they left Norway aboard *HMS Manchester*.

In Yorkshire, the Whitley crews were given two prime targets: shipping in the Norwegian fiords and the Kattegat; and the German airfields at Trondheim, Stavanger, Kjeller, Fornebu and Aalborg. Portal had authorised one last daylight raid (12 April) by a combined force of eighty-three Hampdens, Blenheims and Wellingtons against the mass of German shipping in Stavanger. German resistance was intense and the Hampdens lost six and the Wellingtons three to flak and fighters, though the Germans admitted the loss of five of their own fighters. Night attacks by the Whitleys led to far fewer casualties but were often frustrated by atrocious weather conditions. 'Tail-end Charlie' Larry Donnelly recalled a flight from Dishforth on the night of 11/12 April 1940:

> "on our northerly course, we found the weather deteriorating as the frequency of the storms increased. Ice formed on the wings and chunks flew off the propellers, banging with resounding thuds on the fuselage. Snow swirled into the tail turret and I had to keep moving the breech block of my VGO back and forth to prevent it from freezing up."[6]

To have to ditch under these Arctic conditions was to dice with death, as Squadron Leader Raymond Chance did on the night of 19/20 April. Based at Driffield but flying from Kinloss with 77 Squadron to raid Trondheim, his Whitley's port engine caught fire and the burning aeroplane crashed into the sea just before midnight. His graphic report of how he escaped from the aircraft, almost drowned, listened to the death cries of his navigator, Pilot Officer Hall, and prevented the two non-swimmers in his crew from falling off the rim of the dinghy, is a testament to a man's determination to survive. He didn't realize, throughout the ordeal, that he had broken bones and a hair-line fracture to his skull. Later he was to analyse the reasons for his survival:

> "One may ask how it is possible to survive so long in the water in those latitudes with severe head injuries, a crushed foot and a broken ankle. The answer is really quite simple. You decide quite calmly whether 'to go now', in which case that's it. Or you look at the vast black ocean and say to yourself, "You'll get me sometime, but I'll give you a run for it. You will have to get me. I will never surrender."[7]

He was lucky to be rescued. The destroyer *Basilisk*, herself soon to be sunk at Dunkirk, spotted the dinghy and Ray Chance eventually recovered and, among other things, flew Blenheims with 2 Group.

Between 6 April and 10 May 4 Group's Whitleys carried out fourteen attacks on German airfields in Norway. It is difficult to estimate the value of these raids which cost three bombers, all of which, it is believed, were brought down by one deadly accurate flak unit near Sylling. German engineers were quick to repair any damage to airfields and the Whitley missions in no way hindered the build up of German air strength in Norway or the security of German naval units that, for a time, had robbed Britain of her control of the northern seas. For all concerned, the Norwegian campaign was a débâcle, as the tragic fate of the Skuas at Trondheim underlines.

After the loss of the carrier *Glorious* and her two escorts to the guns of *Scharnhorst* and *Gneisenau*, *HMS Ark Royal* launched her Blackburn Skua IIs against the German warships anchored at Trondheim (12/13 June 1940). One bomb managed to land on the *Scharnhorst* but it failed to explode. Intercepted by German fighters, the Skuas were quickly overwhelmed and half were shot down. Captain Partridge's own Skua was hit by two Me 109s and, with the petrol tank on fire, he baled out to land in a fiord and was eventually taken prisoner. His observer, Robin Bostock, was killed. Thirty-four years later the Naval Air Command Sub-Aqua Club recovered Captain Partridge's Skua II L2940 from the depths of Lake Breidal and its remains were brought back to Britain. It is believed that the last time a Skua was put on show had been in Hull during December 1940. Now Skua 2940, originally delivered from Brough in 1939, resides in the Fleet Air Arm Museum at Royal Naval Air Station, Yeovilton. Evocatively displayed, it is the sole surviving Skua II of the 190 made.[8]

Other Yorkshire squadrons, besides the Whitley bomber forces, had seen action since war began in September 1939. Church Fenton, now in 13 Group, had two squadrons: 72 and 64. No. 72 Squadron had converted to Spitfire Is and these were operating from their sector airfield at Leconfield shortly after war was declared. The first attempt at interception came on 16 October when 64 scrambled to defend East Yorkshire against enemy raiders - but this proved a false alarm. This was not the case on 21 October when two 72 Squadron pilots intercepted a gaggle of 14 Heinkel He 111s and shot two of them into the sea. Catterick had become a sector Station in 13 Group and was host to 41 Squadron's Spitfires. One flight carried out coastal patrols, intercepting a Heinkel 115 floatplane on 17 December 1939 and shooting down a Heinkel He 111 on 3 April 1940. Both engagements took place just off Whitby. It was in the same area that F/Lt Peter Townshend had encountered a He 111 on 3 February 1940. He had been posted from Tangmere when 43 Squadron moved to Acklington, "a bleak, windswept terrain near Newcastle." He was on convoy protection patrols, leading Blue Section and flying at wave-top level. He spotted the Heinkel, opened fire and the German bomber crashlanded in the snow to the west of Whitby. Townshend had scored the first German bomber to be shot down on English soil since 1918.[9]

Not far from Whitby, Thornaby had become part of Coastal Command in September 1939. Here 220 Squadron began to convert to Lockheed Hudsons and flew operational patrols with these aircraft the following month. With its long-range capability, the Hudsons could cruise far out into the North sea and comfortably reach the coast of Norway. One 220 Hudson flying from Leuchars (25/26 November 1939) helped rescue the British submarine *Triad* that had broken down a mile or two off the coast of Norway. Three inquisitive Dornier 18 flying boats appeared but the Hudson's firepower scared them away. Hudsons often encountered German air patrols and had already managed to shoot down two Dornier 18s. With its twin nose guns, the Hudson could operate as a fighter and 'Battle Flights' actively sought out the enemy. Two He 111s encountered on 1 January 1940 were shot down but 220 Squadron lost a Hudson coded NR-T in this combat - its first casualty.

On 15 February Thornaby's Hudsons began to play a crucial role in hunting an elusive German merchant ship. For weeks, the Navy had been searching for the German tanker *Altmark*, known to have refuelled the battleship *Graf Spee* and to have on board Merchant Navy seamen

who had been captured in the Atlantic and Indian Oceans. A 'Battle Flight' of three Hudsons took off to find the *Altmark* though the aircrews had been warned that this mission was to be an 'unostentatious reconnaissance' of the Skagerrak as Norway was still neutral. After more than six hours in the air the Hudsons returned to Thornaby to report clear weather over the Norwegian coast but no sign of the oil tanker. Reports from Norway filtered into Thornaby and there was no doubt that the *Altmark* was shadowing the coast and had already passed Bergen on its way to a German port. Three more Hudsons took off on 16 February and sent back the "enemy first sighting" report for which the Admiralty had been waiting. The motto of 220 Squadron is "We observe unseen" but a low-level run by NR-K had left the German crew under no illusions that Coastal Command had found them. The tanker took evasive action but ran aground on the ice in Jossingfiord. She was a sitting duck when *HMS Cossack* crashed against the *Altmark's* hull. A naval boarding party arrived to shout the words that rang round the world in 1940:

'The Navy's here!'

After releasing the merchant seamen prisoners, the Royal Navy brought them back to port, escorted by Thornaby's Hudsons. Within two months 220's Hudsons were fully engaged in the Norwegian campaign, bombing enemy supply ships in the zone between Holland and southern Norway.

As the Norwegian campaign drew to a close and the Germans seemed to be gaining all of their objectives while the allies secured none of theirs, a major change took place in Britain's political leadership. Disasters in Norway had destroyed Neville Chamberlain's political credibility as Prime Minister and now he toyed with the idea of recommending to King George VI either Lord Halifax or Winston Churchill as his successor. Next day, on 10 May 1940, came the shattering news that Hitler's Panzers and Luftwaffe had attacked Holland and Belgium. Liberal and Labour leaders now agreed to serve in a War Cabinet headed by Winston Churchill and so it was that, after ten years out of office, Churchill became Prime Minister. He now presided over five days of disaster, beginning with a massive Luftwaffe strike against Allied ground and air forces. British Air Forces in France (BAFF) suffered appalling casualties and failed to inflict any significant delay on the enemy. On 15 May Holland surrendered, blasted into submission by the Luftwaffe attack on Rotterdam the previous day. At the time it was said that 30,000 people died in the raid though in fact 980 died as the German bombers totally devastated the city centre. On the same day that Holland surrendered the French Prime Minister, Paul Reynaud, telephoned Churchill to confess that France was beaten. All would be lost, he said, if Britain did not send her reserve fighter squadrons to France. Churchill told him that the RAF wanted to bomb German communication centres, oil plants and factories, that Dowding wanted to conserve his remaining fighter squadrons in the UK and that, if all else failed, Britain would fight Germany alone.

Air power and its appropriate use dominated the Cabinet meeting on that decisive day and the outcome is important as it was to have great impact on Bomber Command in general and Yorkshire in particular. We do not have full minutes of those crucial discussions but it is clear that Dowding, wishing to save his fighter squadrons, supported the RAF's wish to bomb the Ruhr. Churchill was convinced that Dowding was right. The Germans had control of the Dutch airfields and there was a likelihood that the Luftwaffe would use these bases for an attack upon Britain. He therefore reasoned that it would be a good psychological move to hit the Germans where it hurt most, thus disabusing them of the belief that Britain was finished. His words helped to lift the despair in the Cabinet Room on that difficult day, 15 May 1940.

Field Marshal Ironside, Chief of the Imperial General Staff, kept a diary of these tumultuous times. He noted how delighted the RAF offices were when they heard that the government was endorsing raids on German mainland targets – for that is what they had wanted to do ever since the war began. But Ironside was an old enough soldier to reflect upon possible German reprisals and what they might mean for the future. Would the Luftwaffe then bomb mainland Britain? He believed the risk was worth taking. Britain's future clearly depended upon the war in the air.[10]

The chance was taken to begin a strategic air offensive against Germany, though with relatively puny forces. BAFF's commander, Air Marshal Sir Arthur Barratt, had already asked 4 Group to bomb German communication lines in Holland and Whitleys from all of the Group's operational squadrons joined Wellingtons on missions that, on the night of 14/15 May, included Mönchen-Gladbach among the road and rail targets. Then on the night of 15/16 May 1940 the target list covered targets east of the Rhine: Düsseldorf, Gelsenkirchen, Wanne-Eikel were the first to receive 4 Group's attention, a night that was to prove a watershed in the history of Bomber Command.

There were sixteen selected targets in the Ruhr and twenty-four Whitleys, thirty-six Hampdens and thirty-nine Wellingtons constituted the main force. Additionally, six Wellingtons, together with six Whitleys from Dishforth, were sent to attack road and rail targets in Dinant. That night, although six aircraft had to turn back, more than one hundred RAF bombers were over German or German-occupied territory. German defences failed to shoot down a single bomber though one of 115 Squadron's Wellingtons strayed off course and crashed near Rouen. All the crew died.

Despite Cabinet approval for a strategic bombing offensive against Germany, the immediate threat to Britain remained in France where Allied land and air forces were failing in their attempts to stem the German blitzkrieg. 4 Group's Whitleys were immediately returned to the task of bombing German troop concentrations and communication centres and only occasionally carried out strategic attacks. When they did return to Germany the Whitley crews noticed that Gelsenkirchen and Hannover were ringed with heavy and light anti-aircraft defences; moreover, they observed the occasional night-fighter on patrol. During the attack on Hanover on 18/19 May 1940 a 77 Squadron crew destroyed an Me 110.

Navigation aids remained a problem, as Dishforth's Whitleys demonstrated during their attacks on the Ruhr. While F/O Peter Rutter was bringing his 77 Squadron Whitley back from a raid on Krefeld, bad weather forced him to fly on instruments for 2 hours 20 minutes. When the cloud finally broke all he coul see below him was a thick blanket of fog. His WOP/AG failed to to raise a radio fix and Rutter's crew realised they were lost. Down to 2000 ft and with very little fuel remaining Rutter orbited a flashing red beacon and decided to land nearby. On finals, his lights picked out the glint of power cables and he just managed to clear these before touching down in almost nil visibility. Rutter soon discovered he handed landed on the side of a hill; a few yards to port there was another line of power cables; and in the bomb-bay there were still two 500 lb bombs, fused and ready to explode! A lot of luck and superb piloting skill had saved another crew and another aeroplane, the exception rather than the rule. Most crashes occurred when pilots struggled to locate the beacon on their home airfield and came in by guess and by God. Rutter's Whitley had landed on a hillside in North Wales, a long way from Dishforth.[11]

A slightly more embarrassing navigational difficulty came during the Ruhr attacks on 27/28 May when a 10 Squadron Whitley from Dishforth missed its primary target due to a faulty magnetic compass. The crew spotted what they thought was a Luftwaffe airfield in Holland. Having completed their bomb run they then set course for home but failed to find the North Sea. They were already over England and the airfield they had bombed was Bassingbourn in Cambridgeshire.

★ ★ ★

By 21 May 1940 the Seventh Panzer Division commanded by General Erwin Rommel had reached the English Channel, neatly cutting off the British and French armies in the north from their comrades in the south. For the Allies, their sole chance of survival was evacuation by sea, assuming the Panzers did not cut off the escape route to Dunkirk first. Certainly, German field commanders wanted to do this. General Blumentritt, then Chief of Operations, was positive that

> "if the Panzer units had attacked Dunkirk without pause, then the mass of the British troops would not have been able to return to England."

But Hitler, who had once fought in Flanders and was worried about the battle-worthiness of his war-weary Panzers, preferred to listen to Göring. Blumentritt was not impressed:

> "After the great and rapid successes of the Panzers, Marshal Göring too wanted some share of the glory for the Luftwaffe . . . he persuaded Hitler to let the Luftwaffe have the honour of carrying out the blow against the British troops."[12]

But the Luftwaffe failed in its task and its failure was due to the presence of the Royal Air Force, not always, it must be said, within sight and sound of the soldiers lined up on the beaches, on the heavily bombed Mole or up to their necks in a bullet-spattered sea. Admittedly, on two days of the nine-day air battle over Dunkirk, 27 May and 1 June, the Luftwaffe was master of the skies. On these occasions the RAF did appear in force but the time-gaps in its patrols were too great. On 1 June the Luftwaffe slipped in, unmolested by the RAF, and sank thirty-one ships. Frequently, low-flying Heinkels were able to terrorise the beaches with machine-gun fire and the occasional hand-grenade. RAF losses over Dunkirk were severe: 99 aircraft against 132 German machines destroyed. Despite these terrible difficulties, over 338,000 British and allied servicemen made their escape and this itself was a great victory, a victory. as Churchill said, "gained by the Royal Air Force."

Yorkshire's Whitleys and some of Blackburn's aeroplanes contributed to this success. 4 Group unceasingly attacked targets in Germany and France: oil, plants, marshalling yards, key bridges and troop concentrations. Interestingly, 51 Squadron attempted the first 'pathfinding' operation when bombing the oil plant at Hamburg on 2/3 June 1940. Three Whitleys, each carrying thirty flares, flew back and forth over the target, illuminating it for the rest of the Dishforth and Linton bomb-aimers. Distant operations such as these made no impact on the men struggling to get off the Dunkirk beaches though Blackburn Skuas and Blackburn Sharks towed flares to reveal German E-boats edging in-shore to sink ships evacuating troops under cover of darkness.

France had tried and failed to stop the Germans. On 25 June 1940, she accepted an armistice. German forces would take control of northern and western France. For the remainder, Marshal Pétain became the new Head of State on 11 July. He firmly believed that unoccupied France ('Vichy France') would become part of a 'new European order', that Germany would win the war, and that Britain would have her neck wrung 'like a chicken'. Curiously, there was no German plan for the continuation of the war against Britain. Hitler, if we are to believe his words, admired the British Empire and hoped to come to some accommodation with Churchill's government. Göring, however, assumed that there would be an invasion and on 30 June he instructed the Luftwaffe to be ready to create the right conditions by defeating the enemy's air force, "destroying his ground organization, and disrupting his aircraft industry, thus defending Germany's own *Lebensraum*." On 2 July Hitler still hoped for peace with Britain but nevertheless ordered the Wehrmacht and Kriegsmarine leaders to draw up an initial contingency plan for the invasion of Britain.[13]

A fortnight later, on 16 July, Hitler issued *Führer Directive No. 16 On preparations for a landing against England.*

The order stated:

Since England, in spite of her hopeless military situation, shows no sign of being ready to come to an understanding, I have decided to prepare a landing operation against England and, if necessary, to carry it out . . . The aim of this operation will be to eliminate the English homeland as a base for the prosecution of war against Germany and, if necessary, to occupy it immediately.

i)   The landing will be in the form of a surprise crossing on a wide front stretching from about Margate to the area west of the Isle of Wight . . . Preparations for the entire operation must be completed by the middle of August.

ii) The English Air Force must be so reduced morally and physically that it is unable to deliver any significant attack against the German crossing . . .

iii) The invasion will bear the code-name *Seelöwe* (Sealion).

Clearly, Sealion's first requirement was the destruction of RAF Fighter Command. This meant wiping out the British Chain Home radar system and the airfields on which the fifty-two squadrons of Hurricanes, Spitfires, Blenheims and Defiants were based. For this task Hitler assembled three Luftflotten: Luftflotte 5 based in Norway and the main threat to Yorkshire and the north of Britain; Luftflotte 2 located on the captured airfields of the Low Countries and northern France; and Luftflotte 3, whose Stukas and fighter escorts flew from bases scattered between the Cherbourg Peninsula and the River Somme.

Ranged against this mighty force was a British defence system that was under the most stringent control, a control based upon intelligence, observation and crisply guided direction. And it was control not just of Fighter Command, but of Bomber Command and Coastal Command as well, for all three played a significant part in the great event that was looming - the Battle of Britain.

Yorkshire's role in this battle took three distinct forms: the defence of the county against air attack; the use of local airfields for rotating and resting squadrons exhausted by the heat of battle; and undertaking offensive operations against invasion barge assembly areas and the major industrial centres of Germany and Italy. This meant, of course, that Yorkshire's airfields, as well as Fighter Command's front-line bases in the south, would be subjected to regular attention from the Luftwaffe.

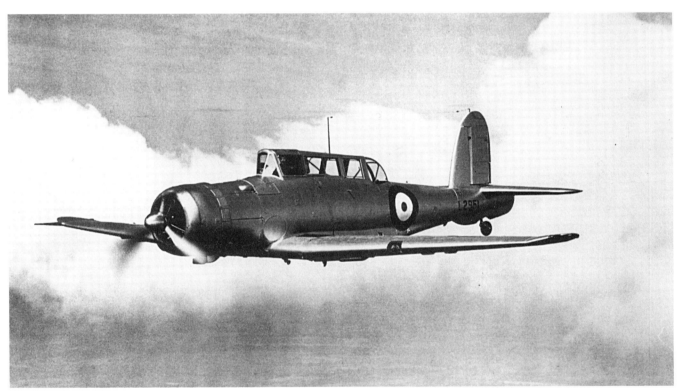

Blackburn Skua L2951 c. 1940.

FAA Museum
Neg. No. SKUA A/4

Chapter Nine

The Battle of Britain
June - October 1940

Bomber Command's Whitleys were now the long-distance element of Britain's sole means of carrying the war directly to the German homeland. Targets were widespread but selected to demonstrate to the German people that no corner of the Third Reich was safe from Armstrong Whitworth's twin-engined bombers. At the same time the Whitleys had to support French units still fighting the Wehrmacht, a difficult task when aircraft had to pinpoint bridges and crossroads in the dead of night, even with the help of flares. A 102 Squadron Whitley flying from Driffield to bomb a bridge at Abbeville on 9/10 June had as its 'second dickey' young Pilot Officer Cheshire on what was for him a "strangely uneventful raid."[(1)]

On 10 June Mussolini declared war on Britain and France and 4 Group had the task of bombing the Fiat aero-engine works at Turin and the Ansaldo factory at Genoa. For this attack on 11/12 June five Yorkshire squadrons (Nos 10, 51, 58, 77 and 102) were first required to fly to aerodromes in the Channel Islands. Here they took on board maximum fuel and then attempted their hairy take-offs from the short grass fields on Guernsey and Jersey. Larry Donnelly's Whitley had to take off from Guernsey where the air strip ended abruptly at the cliff edge:

> "As we taxied out we were slightly, but not fully, reassured when the preceding aircraft got off safely. There had been much bated breath as we watched them disappear over the cliff-edge at the end of the take-off run followed by sighs of relief as they finally appeared flying above the waves of the English Channel."[(2)]

The flight over the Alps to Genoa took six hours and electric storms and lightning strikes added to the stress of a very difficult mission. Thirty-six aircraft had assembled in the Channel Islands. Of these, two Whitleys failed to take off, twenty aborted, one 77 Squadron aircraft crashed in flames near Le Mans and eleven claimed to have bombed more easily recognisable targets such as railway marshalling yards. Officially, the raid was dubbed a success and 4 Group received congratulations from Sir Archibald Sinclair, Secretary of State for Air. On the same night 'Shiny Ten' Squadron lost one of the four Whitleys it sent to Abbeville.

By now Bomber Command's Whitley, Wellington and Hampden squadrons had established their routine of night attacks on a multitude of enemy targets. Oil plants, aircraft factories and aluminium works were high on the list and losses remained gratifyingly low. 51 Squadron's Whitleys attacked Germany on 17/18 June and two were lost; twenty-two Whitleys took off on 19/20 June and only one failed to return; and for the rest of the month only two Whitleys were brought down by enemy fire during eight major raids.

But no flight was without its dangers. Some Whitleys returning from sorties over enemy territory had to contend with trigger-happy defenders in Britain. On 28/29 June a 58 Squadron Whitley flown by F/Lt Frank Aitken had the bad luck to landfall over Newcastle where friendly fire was alarmingly accurate; and to add insult to injury three Spitfires and a Blenheim forced him down at Thornaby. Even the bombs carried in the Whitleys were a source of danger to the crews and none more so than the curious 35lb 'W' bomb (Water Bomb), a mini-mine designed to sink oil barges strung out along the River Rhine. It was a small cylindrical weapon with a fusing system that turned into a nightmare for the Whitley crews. It had a soluble fusing plug that was supposed to dissolve and then arm the bomb a few minutes after the Whitley had dropped it in the river. Unfortunately, the plugs were unstable and the electrical arming system sometimes short-circuited. So the 10 Squadron crews who carried 'W' bombs to the Rhine on 14/15 and 16/17 June were lucky that none exploded in the aircraft. An explosion in the Dishforth bomb dump on 22 June was thought to be due to a temperamental 'W' bomb. Officially described as "a constant source of danger during carriage", 'W' bombs were promptly withdrawn from operational use.

★ ★ ★

Meanwhile, the Luftwaffe crews were coming back from leave. Ground crews were renovating newly captured airfields in the Low Countries, France and Norway in readiness for the air war against Britain. Factory-fresh Ju 88s, He 111s, Do 17s, Me 110s and Me 109s were equipping the highly trained and experienced *Geschwader* By mid-June German aircraft, singly and in small groups, were testing the Yorkshire defences. There were a few brushes with Heinkels over the North Sea and bombs fell near Stillingfleet on 18/19 June. Several German aircraft crossed the coast during July and early August to reconnoitre Yorkshire's airfields and to lay mines in the Humber. On 2 August Catterick experienced a minor raid while extensive mining went on between the Tees and the Humber. The situation, everyone agreed, was ominous.

By August 1940 Fighter Command's Order of Battle in Yorkshire was impressive, indicating that Dowding's foresight ensured a strong fighter presence in the County.

---

13 GROUP

Catterick	219 Squadron	Blenheims
		(with a detachment at nearby Scorton, opened as a satellite field in October 1939)

12 GROUP

Church Fenton	73 Squadron	Hurricanes
	249 Squadron	Hurricanes
Leconfield	616 Squadron	Spitfires

302 Squadron, the first of the Polish squadrons, had formed at Leconfield on 13 July but did not become operational until 19 August.

While the fighters carried out their routine North Sea patrols the Whitley squadrons hammered targets in Italy and Germany. Oil refineries and factories in the Ruhr were not only fire-bombed but 'razzled' as well. 'Razzles' were small incendiary devices made of leaves of gauze and celluloid strips (about 1in x 3in) sandwiching pellets of phosphorus. Another version, called 'Decker', was bigger and filled with latex to increase the burning time. Carried to the target in cans of water and alcohol, they were supposedly harmless until the long-suffering WOP/AG poured them down the flare chute in a futile attempt to destroy the German forests and the ripening harvest by fire. Known in Germany as *Englische Visitenkarte* (the English visiting card), they burst into flames as soon as they dried out. They were universally unpopular with German souvenir hunters and the Whitley crews. When 10 Squadron tried some razzling on 11/12 August, clusters of leaves fluttered from the chute and adhered to the fabric covered elevators. As soon as the leaves dried out in the slipstream the fabric promptly caught fire. That night six Whitleys suffered damage from their own razzles.

On 13/14 August the Whitleys flew from Yorkshire to bases in southern England in order to extend their range. Their targets were Turin and Genoa and one Whitley was hit by an Italian night-fighter.[3] Captained by P/O Pip Parsons, the damaged Whitley cleared the Alps but gradually lost height over France and the English Channel. Pip Parsons and his second pilot died when they ditched a mile from the coast. Fishermen rescued two of the crew but failed to spot WOP/AG Jimmy Marshall still struggling in the water. Peggy Prince saw him from her window. Still clad in her pyjamas she jumped into her canoe, paddled out to sea and hauled Jimmy Marshall on board. For this feat, remarkable even for a physical training instructress, Miss Peggy Prince won the British Empire Medal.

While these Whitley operations were in progress, changes took place in the fighter defence of the County. No 249 Squadron's Hurricanes operated from both Leconfield and Church Fenton and had drawn blood on 3 July by shooting down a Ju 88 off Hornsea. The Squadron departed Yorkshire on 14 August for its new base at Boscombe Down. From here, two days later, F/Lt J.B. Nicolson won Fighter Command's only Victoria Cross when he stayed in his burning Hurricane in order to destroy an Me 110. Fighter Command's first major test came on 15 August when the Luftwaffe began its main offensive against airfields in the south, East Anglia and in north-east Britain. Luftflotte 5 did not expect a highly sophisticated defence in the North and was unaware of the advantages Britain enjoyed with radar, ground-to-air radio contact and - to a lesser extent - the Ultra device for breaking German codes. Moreover, Dowding had always assumed that the Germans would try to stretch his defences to their limits, that his northern squadrons would come under attack from Luftlotte 5 in Norway while the south and east would be the targets for Luftlotten 2 and 3. He had made his plans accordingly.

In Yorkshire, the Chain Home radar gave early warning on the 15 August of the two raids coming in from Aalborg and Stavanger. This was a complex and well-planned attack by 149 German aircraft. Sixty-five He 111s from I and III/KG 26 and the whole of I/ZG 76 (thirty-four Me 110s) were heading for the two Whitley bases at Dishforth and Linton. Suddenly they were intercepted by 13 Group and thrown into total disarray. None of the raiders hit their Yorkshire targets and 13 Group destroyed eight He 111s and seven Me 110s.

Further south the Leconfield pilots were at lunch, irked by the absent Luftwaffe and envious of the high scores being claimed by fighter squadrons defending the

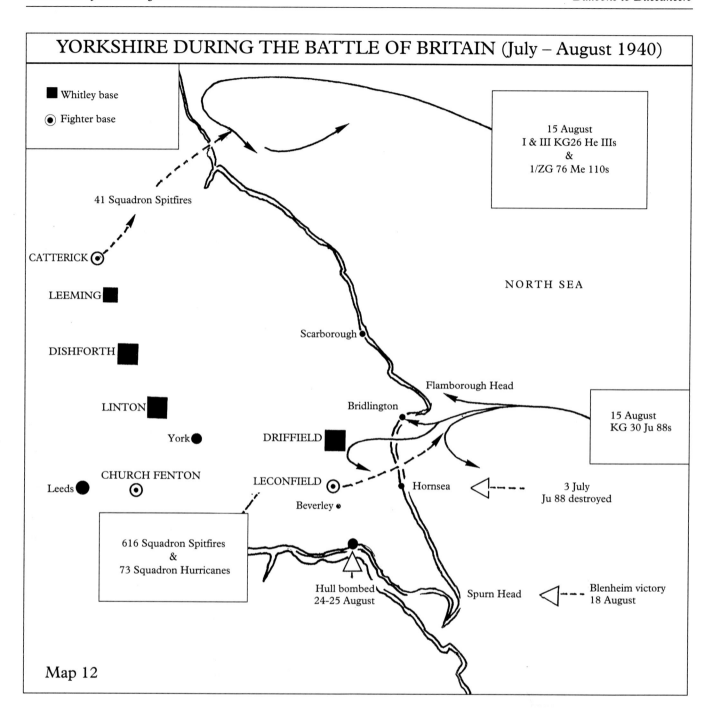

YORKSHIRE DURING THE BATTLE OF BRITAIN (July – August 1940)

■ Whitley base

◉ Fighter base

41 Squadron Spitfires

CATTERICK ◉

LEEMING ■

DISHFORTH ■

LINTON ■

York ●

DRIFFIELD ■

Leeds ●

CHURCH FENTON ◉

LECONFIELD ◉

Beverley ●

NORTH SEA

Scarborough ●

Flamborough Head

Bridlington ●

Hornsea ●

Spurn Head

Hull bombed 24-25 August

15 August
I & III KG26 He IIIs
&
1/ZG 76 Me 110s

15 August
KG 30 Ju 88s

3 July
Ju 88 destroyed

Blenheim victory
18 August

616 Squadron Spitfires
&
73 Squadron Hurricanes

Map 12

embattled south. Suddenly, the urgent voice of the controller came over the Tannoy:

"616 Squadron scramble. 616 Squadron scramble all aircraft."

In his *Flying Start*, Hugh Dundas, a 616 Squadron pilot, remarked on the speed of the Squadron's reaction.

Spitfires roared off the airfield, and without waiting to form into battle flights, headed east towards the enemy. About fifteen miles out, the Leconfield pilots encountered fifty of KG 30's Ju 88s. They were coming in fast and low towards Flamborough Head, splitting into small formations once they saw 616 Squadron's Spitfires backed up by 73 Squadron's Hurricanes. A few Junkers escaped the fighters and concentrated on Bridlington, damaging houses and blowing up an ammunition dump. Others sped towards Driffield, already alerted by the ever-vigilant Observer Corps tracking posts. Here the Luftwaffe's bombing was accurate and effective: ten Whitleys destroyed on the ground (five from 77 and five from 102); four hangars badly damaged; much of the accommodation wrecked. Fifteen airmen died that day at Driffield where the airfield's defences managed to shoot down one of the Ju 88s. Fighters scored five more so the Luftwaffe suffered a 10% loss (sixteen bombers and five fighters) during this major raid on the East Riding of Yorkshire.

Nevertheless, the Ju 88s had hurt 4 Group. The previous night No 77 Squadron had sent twelve Whitleys to bomb St Nazaire with the loss of one aircraft; nine of 102's Whitleys had attacked the Caproni aircraft factory. But the Luftwaffe raid on 15 August forced Driffield to stand down. KG 30 had virtually put the airfield out of action and so could claim that their raid was at least a partial success. Against this the Germans had to weigh Luftflotte 5's losses, high enough to signify that it was "to all intents and purposes finished in the daylight battle . . . ."

Reichsmarschall Göring was still determined to give the British no rest:

> "Our night attacks are essentially dislocation raids made so that enemy defences and population shall be allowed no respite."

Though bombs fell on Beverley that night the next two days of the Battle of Britain were relatively quiet for Yorkshire. Church Fenton, Catterick and Leconfield played only a small part in the fighting on 18 August 1940 when the Luftwaffe tried unsuccessfully to complete its task of destroying all of 11 Group's airfields in the space of one week. There was one significant combat over the County on what has been called "the hardest day" of the battle. P/O Richard Rhodes and Sgt 'Sticks' Gregory were patrolling in a 29 Squadron Blenheim IF bereft of any sophisticated electronic interception equipment. Suddenly Rhodes caught a glimpse of what he took to be cockpit lights and chased an enemy intruder across Yorkshire. As it reached Spurn Head Rhodes opened fire with two eight second bursts from his four forward firing machine-guns - some 2,397 rounds of ammunition. According to his report:

> "The enemy aircraft appeared to be slowed down . . . "

He then drew alongside to allow Sgt Gregory to fire

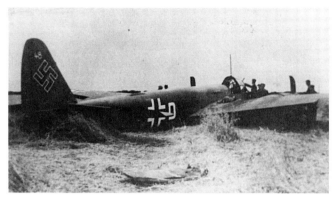

JU88 brought down on the Bridlington - Scarborough Road 15 August 1940.   *Yorkshire Air Museum*

his Vickers. His target, a Ju 88C-2 of 4/NGJ1, caught fire and crash-landed in the sea. None of the German aircrew survived in what was the first of many Luftwaffe intruder flights over Britain.

Meanwhile 302 (Polish) Squadron had become operational and on 19 August its Hurricanes claimed an enemy aircraft destroyed near Hull. When the Squadron flew down to Northolt towards the end of the battle it replaced the Poles of 303 Squadron who came to Leconfield for a hard-earned rest after constant combat over London and Kent. Britain owes a great debt to these Poles. Brilliant and ferocious pilots, the fliers of 302 and 303 Squadrons played a decisive role in the Battle of Britain and between them accounted for 7½% of the total number of German aircraft destroyed by Fighter Command. The second Polish squadron to form in Yorkshire was 306 at Church Fenton (28 August) though it did not see action until after the Battle of Britain ended.

The ubiquitous Whitley, Wellington and Hampden bombers continued to blight the lives of the German populace and their complaints eventually spurred Göring to insist that it was the Luftwaffe's bounden duty to make

> "attacks on the ground organisation of enemy bombers".

So, while the Yorkshire Whitleys went to Milan, Augsburg and Stuttgart on the night of 24/25 August, 170 German aircraft ranged over England attacking eight airfields. Hull was bombed, Driffield suffered fire damage to No. 1 Hangar and the Sergeants' Mess was again hit. This time Nos 77 and 102 Squadrons evacuated the base and 102 went to newly-opened Leeming from which 10 Squadron's Whitley Vs had been operating since July.

On that same night (24/25 August 1940) one or two Luftwaffe crews accidentally bombed London. For Churchill, this was a heaven-sent opportunity. He had already confided his strategy to Lord Beaverbrook, Minister of Aircraft Production:

"... when I look around to see how we can win the war I see there is only one sure path. We have no Continental army which can defeat the German military power ... Hitler ... should he be repulsed here or not try invasion ... will recoil eastward, and we have nothing to stop him. But there is one thing that will bring him back and bring him down and that is an absolutely devastating, exterminating attack by very heavy bombers from this country upon the Nazi homeland. We must be able to overwhelm them by this means, without which I do not see a way through."

(8 July 1940)

After the Luftwaffe's accidental attack on the capital, Churchill had no difficulty in persuading his War Cabinet to order a retaliatory blow against Berlin. Aircraft from 3, 4 and 5 Groups responded on 25/26 August 1940: seventeen Wellingtons, fourteen Whitleys and twelve Hampdens. Despite atrocious weather, one or two 10 Squadron Whitleys flying from Yorkshire reached the Berlin area though most of the bombers that attacked Berlin that night were Hampdens and Wellingtons. German sources indicated that very few of the twenty-two tons of high explosive dropped actually fell on the city. Berliners even managed to make a joke of the whole affair, especially when their radio station announced that the RAF's only success was the destruction of a summer house in the suburb of Rosenthal. Yet this first attack on Berlin, together with the relatively light raids that followed over the next fortnight or so, were to have profound consequences for German aerial strategy and the outcome of the Battle of Britain.

Undoubtedly, the crucial period lay between 24 August and 7 September. During that time, Fighter Command lost 103 pilots killed and 128 seriously wounded - about 25% of 'The Few'. 466 Hurricanes and Spitfires had been destroyed or were out of action. Lord Beaverbrook's aircraft factories and the remarkable civilian repair depôts, plus the efforts of RAF ground crews, could just keep up with the daily fighter losses; the problem of fighter pilot provision was a different matter.

Driffield Whitleys after the raid 1940.

Yorkshire Air Museum

Though 260 ardent young pilots were available, many were still in their training units and unfit for immediate combat. It is a fact that when inexperienced pilots were committed to the battle, the chances of their being killed in their first air combat were very high. Dowding had to remove some of his reserves from less threatened areas - such as Yorkshire. Squadrons had already gone from Church Fenton and Leconfield. On 5 September 504 Squadron, which had recently arrived at Catterick, received orders to move south. Bombay troop carriers ferried key ground staff down to Hendon before lunch; the rest went by train; while the pilots flew their Hurricanes straight to their new base. Within two days they were in action, remembered for Sgt. Holmes and his ramming of a Dornier Do 17 when he was out of ammunition. The Dornier crashed on Victoria Station and Sgt Holmes parachuted into a dustbin.

He was luckier than most. Dowding was running short of pilots and would be hard pressed to defend the whole of southern England if the Luftwaffe continued its deadly attacks against the forward fighter bases. Several were by now in a critical state: Manston and Lympne were out of action for the time being; Biggin Hill could cope with one squadron. Though the Luftwaffe had not won air superiority it was certainly close to parity with the RAF on or about 1 September 1940. Hurricanes and Spitfires were intercepting and destroying a high percentage of the enemy but it was impossible to prevent some Me 110s and 109s slipping through and causing extensive damage to aircraft factories, the Luftwaffe's new target. Scores seemed roughly equal:

	Luftwaffe losses	*Fighter Command losses*
4 September	21	19
5 September	21	22
6 September	35	23

Yet the Luftwaffe crews, outstanding fliers and unquestionably courageous, were themselves growing dispirited. Their tactics were bringing few dividends and many saw the battle as one of total attrition. Jolted by Hitler's furious reaction to the RAF raids on Berlin, Göring decided on a mass daylight attack on London. It would be bigger than any air raid mounted before and he took personal command of the air war against Britain. He hoped the onslaught would be decisive and invigorate his tired young bomber crews who on this occasion would have the advantage of close support from Messerchmitt escorts. Standing on the cliffs at Cap Blanc Nez, Göring felt that this time he would not fail his Führer. Above him nearly a thousand Luftwaffe aircraft were formating at 8000 feet, ready to head for the British capital on Saturday 7 September 1940.

Naturally, it is tempting to see Göring's decision on 7 September to begin daylight raids on London as the salvation of Fighter Command, simply because the move relieved pressure on the front-line airfields. Len Deighton and Max Hastings both believe that though London now bore the brunt of the Luftwaffe attack, Göring had muddled his strategic priorities:

"The diversion of forces against London was one of the greatest blunders of the battle."[4]

Not all historians of the Battle share this view. Alfred Price, for example, states quite categorically that:

"one of the most enduring myths of the Battle of Britain is that the Luftwaffe lost it because of Göring's blunder in switching the weight of the attack from Fighter Command's airfields to London . . ."[5]

Price argues that the size, skill, quality and morale of Fighter Command was so high that, had the Luftwaffe persisted in trying to destroy all the Hurricanes and Spitfires it would have destroyed itself in the process. Therefore, the Luftwaffe could not ever have won the Battle of Britain. Every RAF fighter pilot who died, in one sense, took with him five trained German aircrew. Attacking airfields or attacking London made no difference. The rate of loss was always the same for the Germans. This was certainly the case on the date we celebrate as Battle of Britain Day, 15 September 1940. Radar watched German formations assembling over the French coast; Ultra picked up Göring's precise instructions. Fighter Command had the organisation and resources to react wherever and whenever it was needed. At the end of the day's battle, the Luftwaffe had lost 61 aircraft and the RAF 29, with sixteen pilots killed. One of the most distinguished pilots who fought that day, Douglas Bader, never accepted the low tally of German aircraft brought down and always felt that German losses were much higher.

Wing Commander H.R. Allen[6] stresses other factors that explain why Hitler could never have invaded Britain in the summer and autumn of 1940. He accepts that fighter airfields were sometimes out of action; but there was never at any time a total shortage of flying grounds for RAF fighters. He points out that the only way to destroy RAF airfields in 1940 was for an invading Wehrmacht to occupy them; and how could the Kriegsmarine transport three armies across the English Channel to accomplish this ? Allen believes that the 'Fleet in being' at Scapa Flow was a total deterrent and that the Kriegsmarine had no hope of securing the English Channel long enough to effect a substantial landing on the south coast. First, it had no ships capable of challenging the might of the Royal Navy. At Scapa Flow there were seven battleships, an aircraft-carrier, a dozen cruisers and a score of well-armed destroyers and torpedo boats. The Germans had no capital ships available and how could the lone Hipper class cruiser meet this array of firepower? Only the discredited Stukas could deal with heavy warships, assuming these lacked fighter protection from 11 Group. But there is no evidence that Dowding would have hesitated to bring in his northern squadrons to deal with Ju 87s if an invasion were imminent. Moreover, the Kriegsmarine had not even produced a convincing plan for transporting the three armies allocated by von Rundstedt. German naval opinion favoured the assembly of Rhine barges, capable of three to four knots fully laden, yet unable to withstand the rigours of a rough Channel crossing. This would mean that German troops would have to face wind and tide, perhaps for two hours or more, together with sea and air attack from British forces. Weakened by these experiences, they would then have to assault a coastline where shore batteries would decimate the landing craft and minefields would turn the beaches into death traps. It follows, therefore, that the concept of a seaborne invasion of Britain was seriously flawed, a view supported by Hough and Richards in their *Jubilee History of the Battle of Britain*.[7] In no way does this discredit the achievement of 'The Few' who won the Battle of Britain and as Sir Maurice Dean has remarked:

> ". . . no-one need doubt that the Royal Navy would have done all and indeed much more than men can. Still, the situation did not arise. The Luftwaffe were defeated by the Royal Air Force. That was that." [8]

And though it is not often taken into account, it is significant that, on the same day that Göring decided to attack London, Bomber Command and Coastal Command began the 'Battle of the Barges'. Bombers of all types, including seven Whitleys from Linton and Dishforth, went to the Channel ports and destroyed many of the barges. Undoubtedly, this was Bomber Command's most important role during the Battle of Britain and over the next three weeks the Yorkshire-based Whitleys attacked most of the invasion ports: Antwerp, Ostend, Zeebrugge, Boulogne, Dunkirk, Calais, Le Havre and Brest. At the same time, other formations of Whitleys bombed the *Bismarck* at Hamburg, hit the *Scharnhorst* at Kiel and continued to range over Axis territory as far as Berlin, Lauta, Munich, Regensburg, Turin and Genoa. Göring had no explanation to offer an enraged Führer as to why Bomber Command could roam over German targets and destroy invasion barge assembly areas apparently at will; and why a reportedly 'defeated' Fighter Command could shoot down dozens of Luftwaffe aircraft on 15 September 1940.

Although the British people did not know this at the time, these events forced the German leadership to revise their plans. Göring lost 1733 aircraft between 10 July and 31 October 1940; the RAF lost 915. Yet 451 RAF pilots survived the Battle; and of these 217 had been operational since war had been declared over a year earlier. Göring could not compete with these statistics and yet his duty, insisted the Führer, was to bring the British to heel. Logic forced the Reichsmarschall to adopt Bomber Command's night bombing philosophy because he now confronted exactly the same problem that Churchill had faced during July. The only way to carry the war to the enemy was to bomb their homeland in the full knowledge that, with the aircraft and navigational aids Göring had at his disposal during 1940, the effects would not be decisive and would certainly not lead to the destruction of Fighter Command. Consequently, once the Luftwaffe began its night 'Blitz' on Britain, Adolf Hitler, with his invasion ports wrecked and about 15% of his barges sunk, had no option but to postpone Operation Sealion (12 October 1940).

Chapter Ten

Yorkshire's other roles in 1940

During the Battle of Britain, one of 'Yorkshire's Own' Spitfire squadrons, 616, had distinguished itself in defence of the County. Transferred to 11 Group on 19 August, it flew down to Kenley, an airfield very much in the forefront of the Battle, and for the next fifteen days 616 intercepted Luftwaffe formations coming across the coast towards London. 616 was originally the South Yorkshire Auxiliary Squadron formed at Doncaster in November 1938. Another County squadron, formed at Yeadon in 1936, was 609. Based at Middle Wallop for most of the Battle, it certainly lived up to its motto, 'Tally Ho'. Its Spitfires claimed one hundred enemy aircraft destroyed by 20 October 1940.

A third squadron that had formed in Yorkshire was 608 (North Riding) at Thornaby in 1930. For the first part of the Battle of Britain No 608 flew its Ansons on air-sea rescue and anti-invasion patrols, apart from A Flight which had gone to Silloth to convert to the Blackburn B-26 Botha I. Blackburn had planned the Botha as a three-seat, twin-engined reconnaissance aircraft capable of carrying a torpedo inside the bomb-bay. However, the Air Ministry insisted on a crew of four but refused to allow the installation of engines more powerful than the Bristol Perseus X or XA, both of which were rated at less than 1000 hp. Determined to make this RAF landplane a success (it was the first he had built since the Kangaroo), Blackburn threw the resources of Brough, Olympia and his new factory at Dumbarton into the project and won contracts for a substantial production run of 580 aircraft.

His first production Botha flew at Brough on 28 December 1938 and the RAF equipped No. 1 Operational Training Unit at Silloth with four Bothas to convert the crews from 608's A Flight. Sorties over the North Sea began on 10 August 1940 and despite bad weather conditions the Bothas were rarely grounded. With an endurance of around 4½ hours, the Botha proved a reliable and relatively comfortable patrol aircraft and only one out of the thirty supplied to Thornaby's 608 Squadron went missing on operations, not a bad record for a base notoriously difficult to approach in bad weather. However, Coastal Command regarded the machine as underpowered in its offensive role and withdrew the Botha from operations, replacing it with 608's 'Faithful Annies'.

While Coastal Command was flying its Bothas, Blenheims, Ansons and Hudsons in the north of the County and using Catfoss as its Operational Training Unit, 5 Group had converted Finningley into a training base for its Hampden aircrews. No 106 Squadron's Hampdens had arrived from Cottesmore on 6 October 1939 to be joined briefly by No 98 Squadron flying Fairey Battles. This squadron went to France, suffering heavy losses both in the air and on the sea. Many ground crew, escaping from France on board the *Lancastrian*, drowned when the liner was bombed and sunk on 11 June 1940. No 106 became operational on 8 September 1940 as a mine-laying squadron and its Hampdens later took part in the Battle of the Barges. When 106 moved to Coningsby in February 1941 C Flight remained behind at Finningley to form 25 Operational Training Unit.

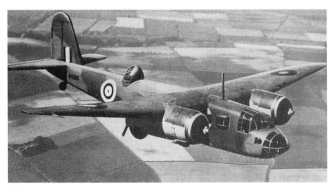

Two fine shots of the Blackburn Botha.
British Aerospace, Military Division, Brough

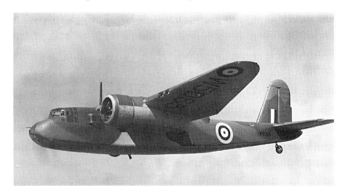

Yorkshire Air Museum

A Finningley Hampden coded ZN-L.

Bruce/Leslie Collection

As the strategic importance of Yorkshire increased, so did the need for new airfields. 4 Group had already moved its Headquarters from Linton to Heslington Hall, York, on 6 April 1940 and in the months that followed a rash of new bomber bases spread across the County: Lindholme and Leeming (June); Tholthorpe (August); Topcliffe (September). Lindholme had opened as an operational 5 Group base on 1 June 1940 and 50 Squadron took its Hampdens from here to Hamburg on 14 July and went on to bomb Berlin and take part in the Battle of the Barges. Leeming had begun its operational career as a night-fighter base and 219 Squadron flew a detachment of its Blenheim 1Fs against intruders during the early stages of the Battle of Britain. 10 Squadron had used Leeming for its Whitley Vs on 20 July. Then on 1 August No 7 Squadron reformed at Leeming and became the first squadron in Bomber Command to operate the new Short Stirling four-engined bomber.

The Stirling represented an important advance in strategic bombing philosophy, not least because it was specifically planned as a four-engined aeroplane. This was in contrast to the Halifax and Lancaster bombers which were designed as twin-engined bombers powered by the Vulture engines.[1] Built to Air Ministry Spec. B. 12/36, which restricted the wingspan to a size capable of being accommodated within a standard RAF hangar, the Stirling had two fundamental design weaknesses: a low aspect ratio shoulder wing that necessitated a complex style of undercarriage; and a fuselage structure that required the division of the bomb bay. This meant that the Stirling could never carry bombs heavier than 4000 lb. Its entry into service suffered some delay when on 15 August and again on 4 September Luftwaffe bombers and the *Freijagd* (hit and run 'freebooter' fighters) targeted Shorts' factory at Rochester. They destroyed at least six completed Stirlings and severely damaged the entire

production run, a deadly accurate raid and a notable Luftwaffe victory. When the first Stirling arrived at Leeming the crews found that the low aspect ratio wing limited the Stirling's service ceiling to about 17,000 feet, even with the thrust provided by four 1650 hp Bristol Hercules XVI engines. Crews concentrated on working up efficiency on long cross-country flights and it was on one of these that the very first production Stirling crashed near Kirkby Lonsdale in September 1940. By October the squadron was ready for operations and moved to 3 Group's Oakington base from which it flew for the remainder of the war.

Whitleys from No 102 Squadron replaced the Stirlings. When these in turn transferred to Linton, No 35 (Madras Presidency) Squadron came to Leeming on 20 November 1940 expressly to receive the RAF's second type of four-engined bomber which would eventually equip every squadron in 4 Group. This was the Handley Page Halifax, destined to play a major role in the strategic bombing offensive against Germany as well as to serve with Coastal Command, with the airborne forces as an assault glider-tug, with SOE (Special Operations in Europe) and as part of 100 Groups's electronic counter-measures activities. Its fame as a fighting aeroplane, with an airframe that could adapt to a variety of uses, was unsung yet unsurpassed among bombers in the Second World War.

At first, No 35 Squadron had only two Halifaxes, L.9486 and the first prototype, L.7244, on loan so that crews could have some handling experience. Squadron Leader Gilchrist enthused about the Mk I, showing trainee pilots that that he could land it 'hands off', controlling the aircraft by using fore and aft trim. Not all the pilots were convinced. At certain power settings the Halifax felt unstable and sometimes it had an unhappy tendency to enter a stall from which recovery proved difficult. One thing that the new bomber did reveal was the need for longer, stronger runways. As yet Leeming did not have these and on 5 December 1940 No 35 Squadron moved into Linton where paved runways had at last been completed. It was on a test flight from Linton that F/O Henry DFC died in the first fatal Halifax crash (11 January 1941). He had been Larry Donnelly's Whitley skipper and had left 'Shiny Ten' in August 1940 to go to 35 Squadron.[2]

Thus it was Yorkshire that saw the entry into service of the first two operational squadrons to fly the RAF's four-engined bombers: 7 Squadron with the Stirling and 35 Squadron with the Halifax. Neither became operational in 1940 and sorties over Germany remained the lot of 4 Group's Whitleys and 5 Group's Hampdens flying regularly from their Yorkshire bases. Their role was largely dictated by the unenviable position in which Britain found herself during the closing months of 1940. Although much comfort was drawn from the fact that the RAF had won the Battle of Britain, the devastating night attacks on British cities showed that the Luftwaffe was not a defeated air force.

What course of action, destructive to the enemy and attractive to the hard-pressed British people, lay within the power of an isolated Britain? Churchill had spoken about the "one sure path" in July. Portal, Commander-in-Chief of Bomber Command, had no doubt that the RAF represented:

"the one directly offensive weapon in the whole of our armoury, the one means by which we can undermine the morale of a large part of the enemy people . . ."

Portal was not an armchair killer, intent on the destruction of the German people. But he did see them as the essential means by which the Nazi war machine was maintained. He believed that if he could disrupt their working lives, destroy their factories, make them cower in their shelters and finally force them to abandon their industrial towns, then Germany would lose the war.

To achieve this aim, the German people would first have to experience the power of Bomber Command and it had to be admitted that, in terms of aircraft numbers during the autumn of 1940, the RAF's raids over Germany were markedly smaller than the Luftwaffe's blitz on Britain. With undiminished ardour, the Whitley squadrons in Yorkshire regrouped their forces and joined the Hampdens from Finningley in a series of raids on Italy, Germany and German-occupied Europe. Between November and December 1940 harsh lessons were learned, lessons that highlighted the two endemic weaknesses of Bomber Command: high losses and poor navigation. Sorties were usually flown against a variety of targets, including oil plants and Berlin, with insignificant results. Yet pilots persevered under the most difficult of conditions as in the case of P/O Leonard Cheshire's experience on the night of 12/13 November 1940. He was captain of Whitley DY-N flying from Linton tasked with an attack on on the Wesserling oil plant near Cologne. Hit by flak in the front turret, he then had the misfortune to have a flare explode inside the fuselage. Cheshire graphically recorded his feeling in his own writings,[3] recalling the pressures on an airman to call it a day and bale out from a blazing aircraft almost impossible to control. But with the support of his young determined

crew he brought the battered Whitley under control, completed his bomb run and returned to Linton. For this exploit Cheshire received his first DSO and his eighteen year old wireless operator, terribly burnt and blinded in the chaos of a badly holed fuselage, received the DFM.

On the following night (14/15 November 1940) eighty-two bombers raided Hamburg and Berlin. There were heavy losses. Ten bombers (four Whitleys, four Hampdens and two Wellingtons) failed to return. Churchill considered this diversity of raids in very adverse weather conditions most unwise and warned that the loss of so many aircraft was "a very grievous disaster at this stage of our bomber development."

This criticism came at a time when the Luftwaffe's destruction of the centre of a British city provoked new thinking in Bomber Command Headquarters. Led by KG 100, the Luftwaffe carried out a precision raid on Coventry on the same night that the RAF visited Berlin, 14/15 November.[4] Later the Luftwaffe 'Coventrated' Southampton (30 November/1 December) and the War Cabinet authorised Portal to carry out a retaliation raid on a German city.

Portal was now able to define German 'industrial centres' within specified cities, rather than individual factories, as legitimate targets. He named this new plan *Operation Abigail*. At least two hundred bombers - the Luftwaffe easily assembled far more than this for their raids on Britain - should attack a single German city. Dusseldorf was the ideal target but meteorological reports caused the raid to be switched to Mannheim on 16/17 December 1940. In imitation of KG 100, eight Wellingtons would fly ahead of the main force and drop large quantities of incendiaries so that there would be no mistake about the aiming point. In the event, only 134 aircraft took off on this operation. The Wellington 'pathfinders' could not find the city centre and most bombs hit residential districts away from the city centre while others fell on the other side of the Rhine at Ludwigshaven. Poor navigation and inadequate target marking had led to scattered bombing so that this first example of a *general* attack on an industrial city by Bomber Command was not a success.

The implication of Operation Abigail was that the the War Cabinet appeared to have accepted the philosophy of 'area bombing'. Yet it still required Bomber Command to attack particularly difficult targets such as the synthetic oil plants at Gelsenkirchen and Merseburg. Several raids in the closing weeks of 1940 reported excellent results but a Photographic Reconnaissance Spitfire

A 35 Squadron Halifax BII Series I W7676 TL-P in mid 1942. This aircraft was lost in the attack on Nuremberg 28/29 August 1942.
Yorkshire Air Museum

brought back incontrovertible evidence that bomb loads were missing their targets by a wide margin. Inaccuracy now had to be added to the twin problems of high losses and poor navigation that beset Bomber Command. And to add to those problems Luftwaffe intruder aircraft began to appear over the Yorkshire airfields of 4 and 5 Groups.

Germany's first night-fighter intruder unit NJG1 (Nachtjagdgeschwader 1) operated from Schipol airfield near Amsterdam. Renamed I/NJG2, the unit transferred to Gilze-Rijen in September 1940. NJG2 flew a few Me 110s and Dornier Do 17 Z-10s but its main equipment was the Ju 88 C-2, one of which had already fallen to the guns of a 29 Squadron Blenheim on 18 August. Linked to the German wireless interception service, 1/NJG2 monitored Bomber Command's radio transmissions day and night so that it would have an approximate idea of the RAF's strength and intentions. For operational purposes 1/NGJ2 divided eastern Britain into three patrol areas or *'Raumen'*. *Raum C* covered Yorkshire and its Ju 88s were active over the County on the night of 20 October 1940. Pilot Officer Brown had just taken off from Linton in his 58 Squadron Whitley, setting course for the Skoda Works in Czechoslovakia. Over Thornaby he encountered Hauptmann Hulshoff's Ju-88. A burst of fire sent the Whitley down and there was only one survivor. Four nights later Linton was again under attack. Just as the Whitleys of 102 Squadron were taking-off for Berlin, Feldwebel Hahn swept over the airfield in his Ju 88 and destroyed a Whitley flown by P/O Davies. On 28 October Leutnant Völker intercepted a 49 Squadron Hampden returning to Lindholme after bombing Hamburg. Völker fired a burst and P/O Bufton and his crew were all killed when their Hampden hit the sea off Skegness.

With the equipment available in 1940 it was difficult to oppose the intruders of 1/NJG2. No 256 Squadron, which had flown flying boats in the First World War, reformed as a night fighter unit at Catterick on 23 November 1940. Though it began training on Boulton Paul Defiants, it never became operational in Yorkshire and the main burden of night interceptions remained with the Blenheims. In order to train crews in radar-assisted night-fighting skills, 54 Operational Training Unit was set up at Church Fenton on 21 December 1940. It was the first of its kind and one of its instructors was none other than Squadron Leader James Nicolson VC, still recovering from his terrible injuries. 54 OTU was the first of its kind and crews underwent training on single-engined Defiants and twin-engined Blenheim Is and Oxfords. During 1941, Church Fenton would win great respect for its night-fighting skills, but at a very high cost because its trainee crews had to risk both the vagaries of Yorkshire weather and the unwelcome attentions of the *Fernnachtjager* intruders from 1/NJG2.

Bad weather hampered daylight operations during November/December 1940 but the night skies witnessed a great deal of air activity. Almost every night, the people of Yorkshire listened to the desynchronised drone of the Heinkel and Dornier bombers en route to targets in the Midlands and the North. Many raiders used the landfalls favoured by their Zeppelin forerunners: the Humber, Spurn Point and Flamborough Head. Generally, Yorkshire had escaped the worst of the blitz and, so far, no city had suffered as Liverpool, Coventry and Birmingham had suffered until the nights of 12 and 15 December when Sheffield experienced a devastating fire-blitz. About 700 people died in these two raids which did a great deal of industrial damage.

Interestingly, the effect on morale was quite different from that which the Air Staff had anticipated and might well have caused them to reflect on what the reaction of German civilians would be in similar circumstances. Once the 'All Clear' sounded, survivors emerged from their Anderson shelters, stared at their battered homes so often scarred by shrapnel if not by bombs, queued up at the mobile canteens and drew water from standpipes to make a cup of tea. They cleaned up as best they could. Soot was everywhere as bomb blast proved highly efficient in bringing it down from most chimneys in a Britain heated by coal-fires. They talked and joked with one another and often surprised themselves at their unexpected sociability. "Reserve between neighbours," it was said at the time, "has been broken down, and even complete strangers have started to talk to each other – something quite unheard of

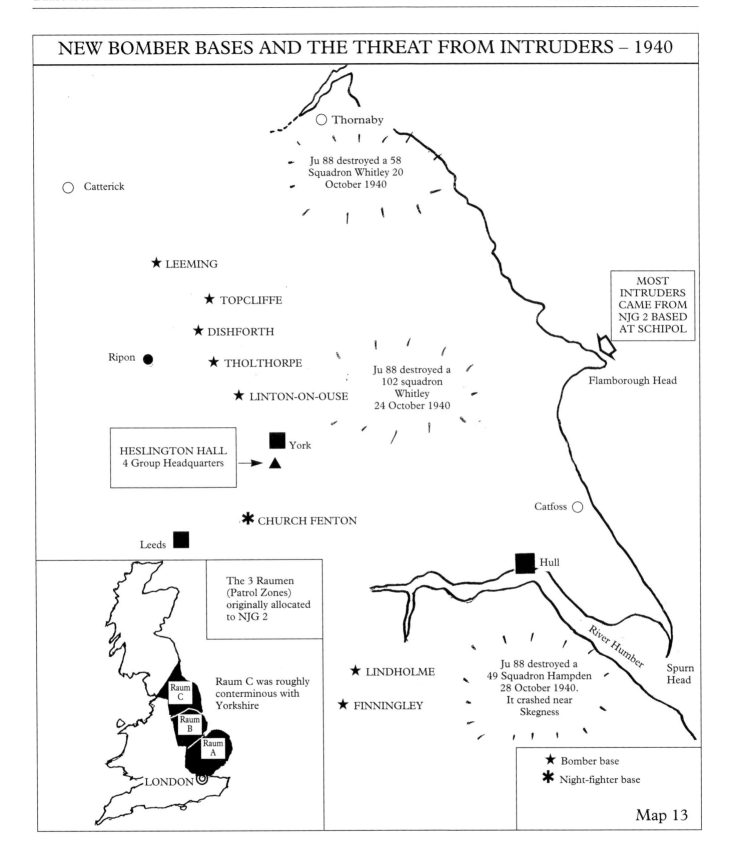

NEW BOMBER BASES AND THE THREAT FROM INTRUDERS – 1940

○ Thornaby

Ju 88 destroyed a 58
Squadron Whitley 20
October 1940

○ Catterick

MOST
INTRUDERS
CAME FROM
NJG 2 BASED
AT SCHIPOL

★ LEEMING

★ TOPCLIFFE

★ DISHFORTH

Ripon ●

★ THOLTHORPE

Ju 88 destroyed a
102 squadron
Whitley
24 October 1940

Flamborough Head

★ LINTON-ON-OUSE

HESLINGTON HALL
4 Group Headquarters →

■ York
▲

✱ CHURCH FENTON

Catfoss ○

Leeds ■

Hull ■

The 3 Raumen
(Patrol Zones)
originally allocated
to NJG 2

Raum
C

Raum
B

River Humber

Raum
A

Spurn
Head

Raum C was roughly
conterminous with
Yorkshire

★ LINDHOLME

Ju 88 destroyed a
49 Squadron Hampden
28 October 1940.
It crashed near
Skegness

★ FINNINGLEY

LONDON ◎

★ Bomber base
✱ Night-fighter base

Map 13

95

in Yorkshire." In the East and North Ridings they became expert at discriminating between the sound of a Merlin-engined Whitley and the rasping roar of the Junkers Jumo radials. "It's one of ours," was perhaps the most comforting statement one could hear in wartime Britain. Another source of satisfaction was that all could see how seriously air raid defence was taken. Barrage balloons certainly deterred some raiders; anti-aircraft guns and searchlights scored occasional successes. Churchill knew that the blazing searchlights and roaring anti-aircraft guns were not particularly effective against the Heinkels and Dorniers. But he also understood that the noise and the light *looked* impressive. Everyone came crowding out of their Anderson shelters to watch the 'fireworks', convinced they were truly 'hitting back'.

This was certainly true of Hull whose time of tribulation would come the following year. Hull's defence chiefs had taken elaborate air raid precautions and the city had a protective ring of barrage balloons, searchlights and batteries of 4.7 and 3.5 anti-aircraft guns. These were put to the test from July 1940 onwards when single raiders dropped high explosives and incendiaries. Saltend was hit on a July afternoon and a ruptured oil tank was in flames all night as Hull's firemen – four of whom won George Medals – laboured to save as much fuel as possible. Parachute mines tended to do more damage than ordinary high explosive bombs and two of these flattened most of Strathmore Avenue in October, sadly an occasion when the defences had been caught napping and no sirens had sounded.

It was also a time for forming fresh squadrons. Already Yorkshire had welcomed the new Polish squadrons. Now the County played host to the American plots of No. 71 Squadron, the first of the famous Eagle Squadrons. Their history began when Charles Sweeney, a wealthy financier, encouraged Americans to abandon their neutrality and fight Nazism. He contacted Air Vice Marshal Billy Bishop, ex-Sopwith Snipe pilot and Canada's greatest World War I ace, who in turn persuaded American aviator Clayton Knight to head a recruitment agency for American citizens keen to serve in either the Royal Canadian Air Force or the RAF. The 'Clayton Knight Committee' processed applications for what Sweeney called 'Eagle Squadrons'. He claimed to have invented the

name and borrowed the Squadron insignia, he said, from the design on the front of his US passport.[5] The first volunteers arrived in Yorkshire in September 1940 to join No. 71 Squadron reforming at Church Fenton. This squadron had begun life in 1917 as a volunteer Australian fighter unit (later renumbered 4 Australian Flying Corps) and destroyed 76 German aircraft on the Western Front. So the first three American pilots who arrived at Church Fenton on 19 September 1940 – Gene Tobin, Andy Mamedoff and Shorty Keough – inherited quite a fighting tradition.

Although the Battle of Britain was still in progress and the American volunteers were already experienced combat pilots, the RAF was slow to make 71 Squadron operational. At first the only aircraft supplied to 71 was an unserviceable Miles Magister trainer and, as the Squadron Record Book attests, all personnel were 'completely browned off'. Out of the blue arrived four American Brewster F2A Buffalo fighters. These tubby little aeroplanes had been acquired by the British Purchasing Commission and the first delivery arrived in the country during July 1940. 71 Squadron pilots, who had all flown Hurricanes and Spitfires, were appalled by its low speed, poor landing characteristics – it tended to float during the approach causing pilots to over-shoot – and lack of spare parts. Walter Churchill, 71 Squadron's British CO, tested out the Buffalo. Parts fell off the machine and he had to make a forced landing at Linton. Eventually, all four Buffaloes were discreetly 'written off' in carefully planned ground loops and replaced by Hurricanes on 7 November 1940. A fortnight later the first Eagle Squadron left Yorkshire for Kirton-in-Lindsey where it became operational on 4 January 1941.

These were splendid developments but the real issue for Yorkshire was whether or not the War Cabinet was convinced of the need to create a strategic bombing force and willing to pour the huge resources into an emergency expansion programme so that the new generation of four-engined heavy bombers could operate safely from concrete runways on well-defended modernised airfields. It was becoming a serious logistical problem and the Prime Minister was showing signs of disquiet.

Chapter Eleven

Diverse Tasks
January - July 1941

As 1940 drew to a close Churchill confided to Portal the deep anxiety he felt regarding the strength of Bomber Command. The Luftwaffe could bomb Coventry with 449 bombers on 14 November and hit London with 413 bombers on 8 December, yet Portal could not approach these figures for RAF raids on Germany:

> "I am deeply concerned at the stagnant condition of our bomber force. The fighters are going ahead well, but the bomber force, particularly crews, is not making the progress hoped for. I consider the rapid expansion of the bomber force one of the greatest military objectives now before us . . ."

Both 4 and 5 Groups were doing their best to remedy this difficult situation. Re-equipment of squadrons with four-engined aircraft such as the Halifax required the creation of Heavy Conversion Units, the upgrading of old airfields and the building of new airfields for heavy bombers. Simultaneously, from the limited number of airfields available, and with their old Whitley, Hampden and Wellington warhorses, Bomber Command had to try to react positively to the various strategic directives issued by the Air Staff. In the first half of 1941 these included the destruction of the German oil industry (an impossible task), the devastation of German industrial centres, the weakening of German morale and, amidst all of this, constant attacks to be directed against German U-boat bases and those harbours where battle-cruisers such as *Scharnhorst* and *Gneisenau* were sheltering. Response in Yorkshire to all these commitments was conspicuous, not least in the opening of new bomber bases: Middleton St. George in January; Driffield the same month[(1)]; Pocklington in June and Snaith in July.

Now that Portal was Chief of the Air Staff, Bomber Command's new leader was Sir Richard Peirse. His immediate task was to implement the very specific directive sent to him on 15 January 1941:

> "the sole primary aim of your bomber offensive, until further orders, should be the destruction of the German synthetic oil plants . . ."

Clearly, the War Cabinet believed that Germany was on the brink of a fuel crisis. If Bomber Command could wipe out the seventeen major oil plants, of which nine were of crucial importance, Germany would have to reduce the scope of her military activities during 1941. Such was the assumption, based upon the scantiest of information, that presented Bomber Command with a most formidable task. The nine main targets included Gelsenkirchen, already the subject of several raids and demonstrably difficult to attack. Synthetic oil plants such as the Nordstern plant at Gelsinkirchen were highly dispersed installations, hard to locate in the heavily polluted haze of the big industrial areas yet relatively easy to repair after incendiary and high explosive bombardment. Nevertheless, Bomber Command flew to these targets, notably to Rotterdam's oil storage tanks on 10/11 February and to the plants at Gelsenkirchen and Homberg on 14/15 February followed by Sterkrade and Homberg again on 15/16 February 1941. Little damage resulted and German military planning was in no way inhibited. Bad weather and reported searchlight glare hindered accurate bombing. Three Short Stirlings made their début over Europe during the Rotterdam raid and unloaded their 500lb bombs on the oil storage areas.

As well as these attacks on the strategic oil targets were the thousands of sorties against U-boat pens, naval bases and industrial centres. For example, six Manchesters - the first time the type saw action - flew with fifty-one other aircraft to attack Brest on 24/25 February. Another 'first' was achieved on 10/11 March when six Halifaxes of No 35 Squadron joined the Blenheims for a raid on Le Havre's harbour installations and the local canal. None of the aircraft was lost to enemy action but tragedy struck Halifax L9489, piloted by Squadron Leader Gilchrist. A British night-fighter intercepted his Halifax as Gilchrist was overflying Surrey on his way home to Linton. The night-fighter pilot, unaccustomed to the sight of a four-engined, twin-tailed aircraft over England, shot the bomber down.

Sir Richard Peirse soon had to reduce his strategic bombing offensive against oil. Churchill now regarded the Kriegsmarine, with its U-boats and surface raiders, as the greatest threat to Britain's survival. Certainly, in February- March 1941, Britain faced a difficult situation. Deprived of all her European allies, she depended upon imports from her Empire and the United States of America. All the food and all the war material had to come in by sea. Consequently, the Battle of the Atlantic became, in the mind of the Prime Minister, the most important single factor in the Second World War. Britain was the last line of defence against Nazi Germany. If the Atlantic supply lines were cut, Britain would succumb.

He therefore urged Bomber Command to do all it could to influence that outcome and on 9 March 1941 Peirse received the Air Ministry directive that, for the next five months, would send his bombers to the those parts of Germany and occupied Europe directly involved in the maritime war. These targets were both widespread and well-defended.

Naturally, the Admiralty wanted to have all factories involved in U-boat production attacked as often as possible. This was not easy as the plants involved in construction and accessory work were widely dispersed: Augsburg and Mannheim made the marine diesel engines; Kiel had three U-boat construction yards, Hamburg had two, Bremen and Vegesack had one each. Big U-boat bases existed at Bordeaux, St. Nazaire and Lorient. And to add to Bomber Command's problems, Admiralty chiefs were worried about the damage caused by Germany's long-range Focke-Wulf FW 200 Condor units based at Bordeaux-Mérignac in France and at Stavanger in Norway. Flying from Mérignac, I/KG 40 had already threatened convoys by dropping 2,200lb mines in the main entrances to harbours and estuaries; and in late August 1940 some of these four-engined bombers had raided Liverpool. Now they were sinking huge tonnages of merchant shipping - I/KG 40 claimed 363,000 tons from August 1940 to February 1941 and 2/KG 40 at Stavanger had even bombed Iceland.

Yorkshire's Whitley Squadrons played an important part in this so-called 'maritime diversion'. Portal was now keen that his main force on each major raid should be divided into two elements: one to concentrate on a specific maritime target such as the U-boat yards in Hamburg; the other to treat the entire city as 'the target'. In this way Portal and his colleagues on the Air Staff moved one more step towards the concept of 'area bombing', the inevitable increase in civilian casualties and the anticipated destruction of German morale. Yorkshire's Whitleys made at least 1800 sorties during the period 12/13 March and 6/7 July, losing fifty-five aircraft in these operations. Their experienced crews - in company with Halifaxes, Manchesters, Hampdens and Wellingtons - targeted the Blohm & Voss U-boat construction yards on 12/13 March and twenty 500lb bombs and hundreds of incendiaries caused extensive damage to the slipways. Next night the Whitleys went back to Gelsenkirchen and helped put the

Hydriewerken Scholven plant out of action for several days. Despite its venerable appearance, the Whitley V maintained its reputation as a Bomber Command workhorse and rarely suffered serious casualties. Exceptions were the Berlin raid on 17/18 April when five Whitleys failed to return to Yorkshire; and the disastrous attempt to hit the U-boat yards at Bremen (27/28 June) when eleven of the thirty-five Whitleys (a 35% loss) fell victim to severe icing, flak and intense night-fighter attacks. Most of the bombers were off course and had attacked Hamburg by mistake. Thirteen aircraft failed to return from this raid, the heaviest night loss of the war so far. It was the shape of things to come.

Supported by an increasing number of Yorkshire-based 4 Group Wellingtons and Halifaxes, and side by side with 5 Group's Hampdens, the Whitley would never again be in the majority on a main force raid. Yet it would still have its moments and in two highly effective heavy raids on Kiel (7/8 and 8/9 April) ninety-three Whitleys flew from Yorkshire to this embattled German port. Sheer weight of numbers did not always spell success in the first half of 1941 simply because reliable navigation aids and effective target marking remained as elusive as ever. Seventy-eight Whitleys went to Bremen on 8/9 May but failed to hit the A.G. Weser submarine yards; and when eighty raided Schwerte on 12/13 June in an attempt to destroy the railway yards, haze prevented accurate bombing.

Whitleys from Yorkshire took part in the first Allied paratroop operation of the war when aircraft from No 51 and No 78 Squadrons at Leeming flew to Italy for 'Operation Colossus'. Dropping from specially converted Whitleys, paratroopers from No 11 Special Air Services Battalion attacked the Tragino Aqueduct in southern Italy on 10/11 February 1941 with marginal success.[2] In addition to these attacks on mainland Europe, some Whitleys were sent to search for U-boats out at sea. For a time No 77 Squadron became part of 19 Group, Coastal Command, based at Chivenor, and one of its Whitleys depth-charged and sank U-705 in the Bay of Biscay.

Back in Yorkshire, as new squadrons and new airfields were becoming operational, men from the Commonwealth countries arrived to play their part in operations against Germany. Canadian, Rhodesian, New Zealander and Australian volunteers had served in the RAF since the beginning of hostilities and thousands more were arriving in the UK every year. They came because patriotism was strong, because in their minds, and in the minds of their families, England was still the Mother Country. To drive this home the media made dramatic appeals to the young men of the Commonwealth, many of whom were just as keen to fly as were their counterparts in the UK.

Typical of the propaganda approach is this sample from a British recruiting film widely shown in Australia:

". . . the need of the hour is desperate. Without the help of the young men of Australia we cannot win this war. The Air Force asks you to do a man's job, to take your place alongside the gallant pilots, observers and air gunners who are now fighting your battle. The Huns were whipped in the first Battle for Britain. We have the finest 'planes in the world to drive them back, to smash them and blast their cities. We want you to fly these planes. Come on, do a man's job."

The Empire Air Training Scheme soon rallied the young men who, as a "cheerfully obedient generation"[3] believed what they were told, that something had to be done and that they were the people to do it. Most wanted to be pilots but, of course, most failed the high standards set in the Empire Air Training units. 'Washed out' they may have been, they still wanted to fly and the Royal Air Force jumped at the chance of remustering them as navigators, wireless operators and gunners. Almost all preferred to be aircrew and that is why so many Canadian, Australian, New Zealander and Rhodesian sergeants appeared in the UK to begin their battle training in Bomber Command. It remains a sad fact that though all were promised commissions on the completion of their first tour of thirty operations, two-thirds of these young men would still be sergeants when they went missing. Despite the high loss rate, the Commonwealth countries had so many volunteers that they were were able to form their own squadrons, many of which served in Yorkshire.

When they completed their training, aircrew went to their Operational Training Units (OTUs). Here, irrespective of their nationality and backgrounds, they were allowed to choose with whom they flew. How men came together to form a five man crew for a Wellington or a seven man crew for a Halifax was left entirely to chance. Perhaps some made the wrong choice, a choice that contributed to disaster on their training flights for Bomber Command casualties exceeded 12,000 dead and wounded in the Operational Training and Heavy Conversion Units alone. But if the crew made the right choice and survived their tour and the war, they formed a bond closer, it was said, than blood brothers.

The first Canadian bomber squadron to form in Yorkshire was No. 405 (Vancouver) Squadron of the Royal Canadian Air Force at Driffield on 23 April 1941.

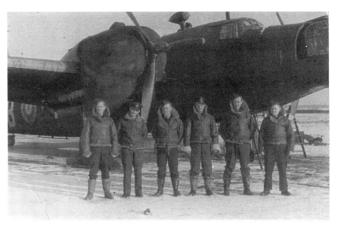

405 Squadron Wellington. 405 was the first RCAF bomber squadron to form overseas and it flew Wellingtons from May 1941 to April 1942. *Yorkshire Air Museum*

Converting to Wellingtons, it moved to Pocklington in June and flew its first bombing attack as part of the raid on Schwerte's marshalling yards in company with the Whitleys on 12/13 June 1941. No 408 (Goose) Squadron RCAF was the second to appear in Yorkshire, having formed at Lindholme on 24 June 1941. No 408 moved to Syerston in July and its Hampdens' first operational sorties were against the Rotterdam dockside on 11/12 August. In contrast, Yorkshire's first Australian squadron had formed in Williamtown, New South Wales on 8 July 1941. Its Yorkshire home was Holme-on-Spalding Moor and it was officially established there as No. 458 Squadron, Royal Australian Air Force, on 25 August 1941. 458's Wellingtons flew their first operation against Germany on 20/21 October 1941.

By then the Wellington was the mainstay of Bomber Command and it became a common sight in the Yorkshire skies. More Wellingtons were built than any other type of British bomber during the Second World War and thanks to the genius of Barnes Wallis and his geodetic system of construction, it was an exceptionally strong and safe aeroplane. It was also highly adaptable and two modified Wellingtons from 3 Group carried the first 4000lb high capacity bombs ('cookies' or 'blockbusters') to Emden on 31 March/1 April 1941. Brand-new Handley Page Halifaxes were beginning to arrive in Yorkshire where No 76 Squadron had a third lease of life, reactivated at Linton on 1 May 1941. It shared the same base and the same problems with No. 35 Squadron, already dogged by a series of hydraulic failures and tailwheel shimmy faults on the Mk I versions. While these were being remedied, the Luftwaffe took an interest in the expanding activities of Linton-on-Ouse and on 12 May attacked the airfield,

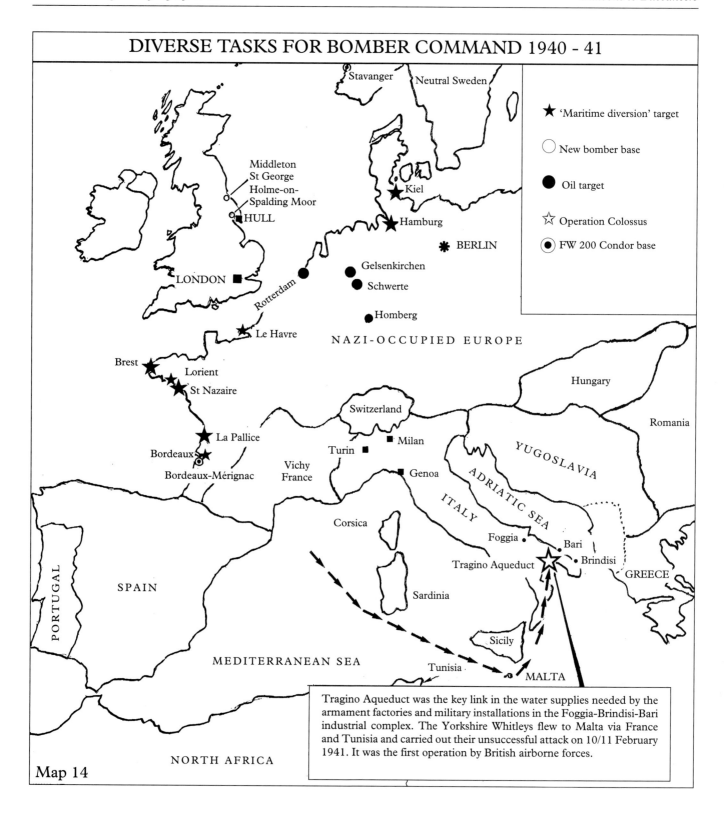

DIVERSE TASKS FOR BOMBER COMMAND 1940 - 41

Legend:
- ★ 'Maritime diversion' target
- ◯ New bomber base
- ● Oil target
- ☆ Operation Colossus
- ◉ FW 200 Condor base

Map labels:
Stavanger · Neutral Sweden · Kiel · Hamburg · BERLIN · Middleton St George · Holme-on-Spalding Moor · HULL · LONDON · Rotterdam · Gelsenkirchen · Schwerte · Homberg · Le Havre · NAZI-OCCUPIED EUROPE · Brest · Lorient · St Nazaire · La Pallice · Bordeaux · Bordeaux-Mérignac · Switzerland · Turin · Milan · Genoa · Vichy France · Corsica · Sardinia · ITALY · ADRIATIC SEA · YUGOSLAVIA · Hungary · Romania · Foggia · Bari · Brindisi · Tragino Aqueduct · GREECE · Sicily · Tunisia · MALTA · PORTUGAL · SPAIN · MEDITERRANEAN SEA · NORTH AFRICA

Tragino Aqueduct was the key link in the water supplies needed by the armament factories and military installations in the Foggia-Brindisi-Bari industrial complex. The Yorkshire Whitleys flew to Malta via France and Tunisia and carried out their unsuccessful attack on 10/11 February 1941. It was the first operation by British airborne forces.

Map 14

damaging two Halifaxes and killing three airmen. Linton's Station Commander, Group Captain Garraway, also died in this raid when he led his fire-fighting teams in an effort to douse the flames caused by incendiary bombs. No. 35 Squadron retaliated on 11 June and set off to bomb Duisburg. Navigational problems led to misidentification of target, a problem shared by other crews flying Wellingtons, Stirlings and Whitleys. They all missed their primary target as Duisburg recorded 'no damage' that night. To the south, Cologne unintentionally suffered death and destruction.

No. 76 Squadron moved from Linton to Middleton St. George in June and three of its aircraft had the distinction of taking part, together with eight 35 Squadron Halifaxes and seven Stirlings, in the first four-engined heavy bomber raid on Germany. The target was the Hüls rubber factory (12/13 June) but only one Halifax managed to bomb successfully. Compared with the Luftwaffe raids experienced in Britain 1940-41 these operations were relatively insignificant. Yet they provided the crews with invaluable operational experience and exposed in combat technical weaknesses in the new four-engined designs. Equally important, they highlighted the growing efficiency of the German night-fighter defences; four-engined heavy bombers were just as vulnerable to interception as were the old Whitleys and Hampdens. No 76 first lost a Halifax to an Me 110 from II/NJG 1 during an unsuccessful raid on the *Tirpitz* (20/21 June); and when No 76 sent a solitary Halifax to hit the *Tirpitz* on 26 June it too encountered an Me 110 and failed to return. One particular Halifax raid mounted from Yorkshire deserves emphasis as it demonstrates the longevity of the dream that day-bombers would be more effective as they could bomb visually from a selected level. Day-bomber exponents pointed to the increased armament carried by the Halifaxes[4] and suggested that a carefully flown 'battle formation' would fend off German fighter attacks. Six No 35 Squadron Halifaxes led by Squadron Leader Tait set off in perfect flying conditions and arrived over Kiel at about 16,000 ft on 30 June 1941. They made two accurate bomb runs, shot down two Messerschmitt 110 fighters and lost one Halifax. This operation delighted the Air Staff and Portal sent No 35 Squadron his congratulations, stating that he looked forward to more devastating *daylight* attacks on German warships.

The next test came on 30 June when No 35 Squadron sent six unescorted Halifaxes to Kiel. Halifax L9499 succumbed to the Messerschmitts but not before it had managed to destroy one of the German fighters. The Yorkshire Halifaxes suffered more serious casualties on

'Tail-end Charlie' of 405 Squadron Wellington. The rear turret doors and the breech of one of his twin .303 machine guns can be seen. The big earphones indicate this is in late 1941 or early 1942.   *Yorkshire Air Museum*

24 July during the raid on La Pallice where *Scharnhorst* had docked for engine repairs. Thirty Whitleys had bombed the harbour area during the previous night and the fires were still smouldering when the Halifaxes began bombing-up with their armour-piercing 250 pounders. Specially positioned at Stanton Harcourt[5], nine No 35 Squadron and six No 76 Squadron Halifaxes flew low under the German radar as far as Ushant and then climbed to 15000 feet for what they hoped would be a surprise attack on *Scharnhorst*. They were unaware that a German destroyer had monitored the track of the low-flying Halifaxes and alerted the defences at La Pallice. Flak shot down one of the leading Halifaxes and as soon as pilots began taking evasive action the defensive formation disintegrated. Five Halifaxes failed to return, three from No 76 Squadron and two from No 35. Five direct hits partially flooded the battle-cruiser and the damage inflicted by the Halifaxes persuaded her captain to

take the *Scharnhorst* from La Pallice to Brest under the cover of a smokescreen the same evening. It was not easy to evaluate this particular daylight operation. Clearly, the Halifax gunners had fought back with great skill and determination and the Air Staff was not yet disabused of the idea that unescorted day-bombers could wreak great havoc on an enemy protected by numerous Me 109 fighters. Still confident, they were determined to bottle up the German battle-cruisers in Brest and two operations codenamed *Veracity 1* and *Veracity 2* were planned for December 1941 by which time the Wehrmacht was at the gates of Moscow and most of the Luftwaffe was fighting in Russia.

Before that happened one Yorkshire city experienced a series of devastating Luftwaffe raids. Kingston-upon-Hull had the unenviable record of enduring eighty-two air raids in the Second World War, the worst of which took place in the period February-May 1941. Many other Yorkshire towns and cities had also suffered, or would suffer, heavy air raids but none so consistently as those inflicted upon Hull. Six serious raids took place in February when Heinkel 111s dropped parachute mines and high explosive bombs on the dockside installations. After its long association with the whaling trade, Hull had developed substantial oil-based manufactures, particularly the paint and cattle-feed industries. Located on or close by the banks of the Humber, their factories and warehouses were easy to find from the air and therefore easy to burn, a beacon light for other bombers streaming across the North Sea. Luftwaffe bomb-loads differed from those of Bomber Command for although the Germans had developed heavy bombs - the Luftwaffe dropped a 5000lb bomb on London in 1940 - the technique by 1941 was to drop canisters of high explosives designed to scatter over a large area. These smaller high-explosive bombs were far more deadly than their British equivalents and, when added to the parachute mines that fell on the city, the resultant blast damage became exceptional in Hull.

Twenty-three parachute mines intensified this blast damage from March onwards. In April one of these devices exploded on top of a public shelter, killing more than fifty people. Hull's ordeal reached a climax in two raids on the nights of 7/8 and 9 May 1941. The first saw incendiaries followed by high-explosive bombs, spreading fires in all directions. For over six hours the raid went on while firefighters were swamped by literally hundreds of blazing buildings. Miles away, the bright red glow of burning Hull was visible to the Whitley crews flying back from Brest to their Yorkshire bases. Next night thousands of people trekked out of the city, fearing the worst. Scores

of bombers began a five-hour attack shortly after midnight and much of the city and its suburbs were devastated by fire. In two nights over 120 tons of high explosive had fallen on Hull plus an unknown number of incendiaries; while nearby towns and villages had also sustained casualties and damage. The city's industrial and commercial base had been largely destroyed and its defences overstretched by the intensity and duration of the attacks. An RAF calibration team posted from the south of England to reset the blast-damaged radar-controlled AA guns, and who had survived the Luftwaffe attacks on front-line airfields during the Battle of Britain, was shocked by the damage. Corporal Ted Rowland, a wireless-operator mechanic/fitter, recalled the scene:

> "Following the great raid and damage at Hull, we were ordered to go to Leconfield and await orders. Our job was to visit various gun-sites to help get the re-calibration done on the G.L's (gunlayers). Devastation was almost everywhere. I was surprised to see Bournemouth Corporation buses running in and around Hull, and was told that the Hull bus depot had suffered a direct hit."[6]

It is permissable to speculate on what might have happened in Hull had the Luftwaffe returned in force for the third night running. The stiff upper lip of 'Britain can take it' was something of a myth at that time and there can be no doubt that constant air attack was having a detrimental effect upon British morale. Much of what had actually happened at Coventry, Portsmouth, Liverpool and Hull was denied the general public in the name of national security. Contemporary evidence from Mass Observation[7] notes the decline of morale in the St Paul's area of Hull and speaks of "helplessness and resignation" among the people but then goes on to stress that, although morale was shattered further by the widespread raid on the city (Tuesday 18 March) and by the double raid in May, the fact that there was no follow-up by the Luftwaffe enabled people to cope. Traumatic events became transformed into 'blitz stories' and people talked out their problems so that "the recovery was phenomenal." Nevertheless, the destruction of so many factories meant that jobs suffered and this problem, plus the terrible blast damage to house property, forced many people to seek help from reception areas. A catalogue of the worst damage shows how Hull's suffering was exceptional, even when compared with Liverpool, Coventry, Southampton and Portsmouth: the east bank of the River Hull flowing into the Humber was a mass of smouldering flour mills; Spillers, Gilboys, Ranks, Ingleby, Lofthouse and many others had disappeared; the famous

Reckitts plant was in ruins; there was no gas during May; while the Holderness Road (which had lost its popular Ritz cinema) boasted the biggest bomb-crater in the north of England. Worried researchers from Home Security came to Hull, recorded that only 6000 of its 93,000 homes had escaped bomb damage and noted in 1942 that Hull and degenerated into a "torpid and apathetic" city.

It is enlightening to note modern historians who, on the one hand, deplore Bomber Command's attacks on German morale as 'wishful thinking' and yet, on the other, quote the "numbed and shattered people of the city" when describing the effect of the Luftwaffe raid on Coventry and suggesting what might have happened if the bombers had returned the next night. In the event, the bombers did not return to Coventry; nor did they come back to Hull for the third night running. There was a respite, a time for people to collect their thoughts, to cope with the horrifying aftermath of unrelenting aerial bombardment. Hull and the British people in general were fortunate that the Luftwaffe preferred to bomb scores of provincial towns and cities rather than concentrate on a prolonged and deliberate destruction of a single strategic objective as Hull undoubtedly was - though it may not have seemed so to Hull's weary population in 1941. There was one other serious air raid on the city but not until 18 July when Hull was again left burning with another 140 people dead. Of course, this was more than two months after the May blitz and as Deighton and Hastings have rightly stressed:

> ". . .any benefits in the morale battle gained by sporadic attacks were far outweighed by the ability of the cities and their civil defence forces to withstand *occasional* battering when they might have cracked under *repeated* bombardment."[8]

This lesson was not lost on the British Air Staff. Very gradually they were clarifying their objective: the systematic destruction of a German industrial city and its workforce in a prolonged series of attacks. There can be little doubt that they wanted this to happen during the first half of 1941; but whatever their desire, they were constrained by the limitations imposed by the type and number of aircraft in Bomber Command at that time. Moreover, despite the roving Blenheims, Hurricanes and Defiants, the RAF was still hard-pressed to intercept enemy aircraft at night. Apart from the Blenheims at Catterick - and desperately few of these had any quality Air Interception (AI) radar - Yorkshire had no major night-fighter base geared to the defence of the County. The problems of 1915 - within the memory of many Yorkshire people - seemed to be returning with a

---

The Atcherley Twins

Richard and David Atcherley were two members of a Yorkshire family who made a profound impact on aviation in the County and beyond. They were cousins of Lt Jack Empson, the pilot killed in the tragic crash at Northallerton described in Chapter 2. Although their mother, Eleanor Atcherley, was determined that neither twin should fly, both had long careers in the RAF, both served in the Second World War as Group Captains and both achieved the rank of Air Vice Marsal - with Sir Richard going on to become Air Marshal.

Richard 'Batchy' Atcherley came to Church Fenton in 1941 to develop a special operational unit training night-fighter pilots. Training was often interrupted by the Luftwaffe and having lost several trainee pilots to intruders, Batchy's typical response was to offer a silver tankard, a cheque for £50 and a 72 hour pass to the first pupil pilot who shot down an intruder. P/O Babbington spotted one and opened fire. The Luftwaffe pilot fled and Babbington had a long weekend pass. Clearly, his student pilots enjoyed their time under Batchy's command. One of his good points was to exploit his proximity to the family home at York. He persuaded his mother to arrange for the daughters of family friends to visit Church Fenton and 'Batchy's Young Ladies' often arrived at the airfield in busloads as partners for the weekend dances. As one converted padre conceded, ". . . never was Church Fenton a happier station than when he was there."*

'Batchy' had achieved distinction through his individuality, inventiveness and constant quest for speed. Originally an engineering apprentice with Robert Blackburn at the Leeds factory, he had won fame first by piloting the Gloster Grebe to win the 1929 King's Cup Air Race (Lord Trenchard told him "it was a great win for the RAF") and then as one of the pilots in the 1929 Schneider Trophy Competition against the Italian team. F/O Waghorn achieved 328.63mph. Atcherley managed 325mph but was disqualified after he lost his goggles (these were open cockpits and at one time his speed touched 370mph), narrowly missing one of the pylons and two of the judges.

During the war, Batchy takes credit for devising the Drem system of airfield lighting (at one time some said that it should have been called the 'Atcherley system'). After the war he became Commandant of the Cadet College at Cranwell where he broke his back demonstrating a new glider.

David was lost when his Meteor crashed in the Eastern Mediterranean (8 June 1952) but Batchy went on to become Air Officer Commanding Flying Training Command and twice visited Church Fenton during 1953 in that capacity. He was perfectly at home in a Meteor jet and flew an F86 Sabre and a CF100 while on secondment to Canada. His last official role in the RAF, in fact a signal honour, was to review the passing-out parade at Cranwell in December 1958 - the first ex-Commandant to take the salute at a function normally restricted to royalty.

A most entertaining account of the careers of the two Atcherley brothers may be found in John Pudney, A Pride of Unicorns, Olbourne Book Co., 1960.

vengeance. Germany's night-fighter force was expanding and was strong enough to maintain intruder operations over Yorkshire, Lincolnshire and East Anglia. On 24 April 1941, for example, Heinz Völker's Ju 88 destroyed a Blenheim from No 54 OTU at Church Fenton where chaos reigned as other Blenheims crashed and 50kg bombs fell from a second intruder. Two nights later Church Fenton's trainee night-fighter crews were bounced by Leutnant Pfeiffer who forced a Defiant, still showing its navigation lights, to fly into the ground. A brief but lively firefight went on over Driffield on 3 May when a No 77 Squadron Whitley was in the circuit. A Ju-88 attacked from behind but the Whitley's rear-gunner opened up and forced the Junkers to break off the action. There is no doubt that I/NJG2 lost numerous aircraft during this period for many a Ju 88 disappeared into the North Sea and one smashed into Skelder Moor near Whitby on 3 June. However, I/NJG2 could still show its teeth. On 13 June a Ju 88 shot down and killed a trainee crew flying their Wellington in the Finningley circuit. Five days later Sgt Neighbour was on his first solo in a Blenheim when intruders appeared in the vicinity of Church Fenton. Circling a beacon, he inadvertently lost height and flew into the ground. By the end of July 1941 intruder sorties over Yorkshire diminished. Most of the action was now restricted to Raum A and Raum B (see Map 13) and gradually this would also come to an end until the last sorties were flown on 12 October 1941. It was Hitler's personal wish that I/NJG2 should desist: RAF 'terror bombers', said the Führer, should not be shot down in Britain. The proper place for night-fighting was over the Third Reich, where *dem Deutschen Volk* could witness their destruction by their own air defences. There would be no more intruder operations over Britain until August 1943.

Daylight raids on Yorkshire had also declined and Fighter Command used the County's fighter airfields at Catterick, Leconfield, Driffield and Church Fenton largely for the formation of new squadrons and the resting and re-equipping of war-weary units. One consequence was that there was a great deal of aircraft exchange going on between squadrons and these well-worn aeroplanes, in the hands of trainee aircrew, often met with tragic accidents. No 256 Squadron reformed at Catterick on 23 November 1940 as a night-fighter squadron. Its Defiants experienced a fairly high accident rate and the Squadron pilots hurriedly scrounged Hurricanes to replace their losses. When 256 moved on, No 68 Squadron reformed at Catterick and flew Blenheim If night-fighters. As soon as it became operational it

converted to Beaufighters and moved to High Ercall in April. Allied pilots also formed new squadrons at Catterick in 1941. Czechs flew war-weary Spitfire Is at Catterick where the third Czechoslovak fighter squadron, No 313, was formed on 10 May 1941. Belgians also flew Spitfire Is at Catterick when 131 Squadron arrived in July, side by side with Norwegians who were forming No 331, the first of their fighter squadrons within the RAF.

Similar frenetic squadron movements took place at the other three sector airfields and though it would be tedious to list every change, Driffield's contribution is worth noting. Its role as a fighter base in 1941 was short but lively. It had re-opened in January 1941 under the control of 13 Group, Fighter Command and No 213 Squadron's Hurricanes rested there and at Leconfield. Driffield also saw the formation of No 485, New Zealand's first fighter squadron, which moved across to Leconfield in April. Most of its daylight patrols were spent escorting convoys hugging the East Coast and several pilots remarked that Merchant Navy gunners ignored the 'colours of the day' and loosed off rounds at any aeroplane in the vicinity. Patrols occasionally encountered a lone raider and on 2 June 1941 No 485's Spitfires destroyed a Junkers 88 attacking a convoy off the Yorkshire coast. When Driffield reverted to Bomber Command (1 April 1941) an important development was the arrival of No 2 BAT (Blind Approach Training) Flight. Bomber captains in 4 Group now spent a week at the airfield flying Whitley Vs, practising on the new radio aids designed to assist landing in difficult weather conditions. Standard Beam Approach (SBA) was first devised and produced by C. Lorenz AG and Telefunken and had been in use on civil aerodromes in Germany since 1935. Britain acquired the rights to this invention in 1936 and managed to extract the vital Lorenz equipment from Holland just as the Wehrmacht had begun the invasion of the Low Countries. The first RAF experiments with the Lorenz system began in October 1940 when bomber crews in Yorkshire depended on rather cumbersome devices to land their aeroplanes in bad weather conditions. At first, the bomber bases adopted the old civil aviation ZZ system: the pilot was guided by his airfield D/F station to bring him overhead for a controlled landing. Later, QGH (controlled descent through cloud) allowed the air controller to talk down the bomber pilot down through cloud so that he was properly positioned for an immediate runaway approach. Once the controller had ordered all the returning bomber pilots to set the same airfield barometric airfield pressure (QFE) on their altimeters, he could stack several bombers at different heights ready to enter finals at his command. An additional aid was the high-powered Chance Light that under some conditions could illuminate long stretches of a runway.

Standard Beam Approach was an improvement on both the ZZ and QGH systems. Its one drawback was the amount of concentration it required from the pilot. As he controlled his aircraft - perhaps unusually demanding because of battle-damage - he had to watch the direction indicator which synchronised his magnetic course with the beam transmitted along the runway centre-line. At the same time he had to listen in his earphones for the continuous buzz that told him he was on that centre line; or a series of dots telling him he was left of centre; or continuous dashes signifying he was right of centre.

An illuminated outer marker emitted a radio tone and showed him when he was two miles away from the threshold. Similarly, an inner marker showed him when he was over the threshold. Keeping on track was a matter of confirming the sound with the instrument reading and remembering that when the needle kicked left he, the pilot, had to steer left. Driffield's BAT Flight also used a Link Trainer to familiarise the pilots with this new navigational technique before letting them fly in bad weather in one of the units seven special Whitleys. Yorkshire's renowned bad weather provided ideal training conditions and this controlled experience of Standard Beam Approach was to prove invaluable for 4 Group's aircrews, destined to be involved in a new strategic bomber offensive against Germany.

Chapter Twelve

A New Offensive
July - November 1941

Profound changes in the strategic objectives of the Air Staff emerged on 9 July 1941. A new directive to Sir Richard Peirse acknowledged that Bomber Command had been unable to inhibit Germany's military activities in Europe, something of an understatement when one bears in mind that the invasion of the Soviet Union had begun on 22 June 1941. It also accepted that it was not within Bomber Command's present competence to destroy Germany's synthetic oil plants. Peirse's new targets, therefore, were to be the cities surrounding the Ruhr. If the rail-links to and from these cities could be cut and kept cut, then Germany's biggest industrial region would be isolated and the strength of the Wehrmacht on the Eastern front would be substantially weakened. Peirse now had a new responsibility: to assist Britain's Soviet ally in every possible way.

To this end, the directive of 9 July 1941 unequivocally sanctioned area bombing:

"... you will direct the main effort of the bomber force, until further instructions, towards dislocating the German transportation system and to destroying the morale of the German civilian population as a whole **and of the industrial workers in particular.**"

Ideally, Peirse would send his Main Force to attack easily identifiable cities, especially those located on the banks of the River Rhine: Duisburg, Dusseldorf and Cologne. On moonless nights, more distant cities would serve as the main target: Mannheim, Frankfurt, Bremen and Hamburg. Meanwhile, Peirse had to continue with precision daylight attacks against the German naval bases, exemplified by the Halifax raids on Kiel, La Pallice and Brest.

These were indeed formidable tasks yet the directive made no mention of how Peirse could achieve them with his fundamental problem unsolved. Bomber production barely kept up replacement needs, let alone the demands made by the training and expansion programmes. New squadrons were often milked to serve in Coastal Command or in the Middle East and this meant that despite the unstinting efforts of RAF ground crews and the civilian repair depots there was always a shortage of serviceable aircraft. Peirse had been promised the new heavy bombers but they were slow to enter squadron service. Avro's Manchester had a superb airframe but its Vulture engines were unreliable; while all sorts of technical problems held up the supply of Stirlings and Halifaxes. Consequently, when Peirse sent his Main Force to attack the Ruhr in the second half of 1941, he had to send predominantly twin-engined Whitleys, Hampdens and Wellingtons that had been operating over Germany for well over a year.

Yorkshire's bomber squadrons were involved in most of the major raids for the rest of 1941. Heavy attacks on Cologne, Münster and Osnabrück on 7/8 July led to optimistic reports from crews that area bombing seemed to have neutralised large parts of each city. Next evening, the Yorkshire squadrons went to Aachen. This was the first time the city had been subjected to any kind of major attack and again the crews reported that the raid had been successful. However, doubts about the extravagant claim made by returning crews were now beginning to emerge. Intelligence data from Germany spoke of inaccurate bomb-aiming and numerous *unexploded* bombs found both within and outside the target areas. Reports such as these caused dismay among the War Cabinet and the Air Staff. Lord Cherwell, Churchill's scientific adviser, was aware that it was current practice to instal bomb-cameras in attacking aircaft and that Bomber Command had built up a substantial library of strike photographs. He decided, without reference to the Air Ministry and without Peirse's knowledge, to have over six hundred photographs analysed by an expert civil servant, D. M. Butt, and the Photographic Interpretation Section. This analysis was then compared with crew reports. Published on 18 August 1941, the 'Butt Report' caused consternation in Bomber Command. In a nutshell, British bombs were not hitting their targets. Faced with Butt's conclusions, not all of which were shared by Portal and the men of Bomber Command, Peirse had to accept that his crews were ineffective against most targets even on clear, moonlit nights. The Osnabrück raid of the 7/8 July, for example, showed that the Whitleys and Wellingtons had missed the railway yards. Three Whitleys had been lost; no Germans were killed; and three minor buildings had been hit. That was all.

Butt's findings had also highlighted the problem of decoy fires, lit by the Germans to mislead the most experienced of crews. In a major raid on Cologne (18/19 August), for example, five out of the seventeen Whitleys despatched failed to return. Later, the Cologne city report mentioned heavy bombing of the *decoy* site: there were no casualties in the city and only one fire. These frustrations were in part balanced by the fact that in August and October 1941 bad weather conditions over Europe caused bomb-aimers to release their loads by dead-reckoning.[1] Consolation may be found in some of the September raids when the weather was generally better. On 7/8 September a raid on Berlin caused heavy damage; but the losses that night were the worst so far. And when Whitleys and Halifaxes went to Nuremberg on 12/13 October, in company with Wellingtons and Stirlings (a total of 152 aircraft), there was only one fatal casualty in the city that night. Almost all the bombers missed the city and rained their high explosives and incendiaries on the village of Lauingen (65 miles from Nuremberg) and the little town of Lauffen (95 miles from Nuremberg). Bomber Command returned to Nuremberg on 14/15 October with eighty aircraft but weather conditions were so bad that only one Whitley, piloted by Squadron Leader A.J.Snow of No 78 Squadron flying from Middleton St George, found the target. There was a growing feeling of frustration in some of the Squadrons, something that had not before been apparent.

Conscious that his Command was about to face the most stringent criticisms, Sir Richard Peirse resolved to impress his superiors and boost the morale of his aircrews with a 'maximum effort' against Berlin. Four Groups, 1, 3, 4 and 5, would supply the bombers for this operation on 7/8 November 1941. Additionally, Peirse ordered

simultaneous attacks on a demanding list of targets: the Ruhr, Mannheim, Norwegian shipping lanes and the Channel ports. A total of 392 aircraft would take part in this complex operation to which Yorkshire's squadrons contributed forty-two Whitleys, ten Wellingtons and nine Halifaxes. This was the biggest bomber force yet despatched from Britain and was probably the maximum number of serviceable aircraft available to Peirse that night. It was something of a desperate decision and because it led to a series of events that put the future of Bomber Command at risk the Berlin raid is worth considering in some detail.

Air Ministry forecasts for the night of 7/8 November 1941 were not good. They warned of thunderstorms, hail and icing with the dreaded cumulo-nimbus cloud-tops towering up to 15,000 feet. There would be a westerly wind which, as usual, would increase fuel consumption on the homeward leg of a round trip of 1,200 miles. Peirse ordered his crews to fly high on the outward leg and low on the homeward, hoping that the bombers, given reasonably moonlit conditions, would be able to avoid the peaks of the high convection clouds. Air Vice-Marshal John Slessor, Commander of 5 Group, took the advice of his senior meteorological officer: it would be unreasonable to send the Hampdens to Berlin in dangerous icing conditions. Slessor therefore decided to abandon Berlin and diverted his Hampdens to alternative targets. Air Vice-Marshal Roderick Carr of 4 Group decided to accept the risks and so his Whitleys, Wellingtons and Halifaxes flew eastwards from Yorkshire across the North Sea for a landfall in Denmark before turning south-east to Berlin. The other two Groups flew direct to the German capital, thus presenting the enemy flak batteries and night-fighters with the challenge of a twin-pronged assault. But it was

Since the end of May 1941 the RAF had dropped a series of propaganda leaflets on German targets. This particular example shows a Whitley about to be bombed up with a new *Bezirksbombe* (blockbuster). This leaflet, the eighth in a series of the RAF's Luftpost, was carried by a 78 Squadron Whitley captained by Harry Woodhatch during the attack on Hamburg on 16/17 July 1941. Since the Aachen raid (9/10 July 1941) the Whitleys, Hampdens and Wellingtons had endured very poor weather conditions and logbooks bear frequent witness to icing and bad visibility during attacks on Cologne (9/10 July), Bremen/Vegesack/Emden (13/14 July) and Hamburg (16/17 July) - factors that contributed to the bombing inaccuracy then under scrutiny by D.M.Butt.

the weather that proved to be the worst enemy that night with winds of 80mph and an outside air temperature of -42C. Surviving logbooks reveal the conditions:

> "Bad. Icing 2-10,000 feet. 10/10 cloud with few breaks. Fuselage temperature -60C. Frost on crews' faces. Thunderstorms. Crew sickness due to turbulence."

Icing proved to be the killer. It built up on the propellers and the leading edges, remoulding the crucial aerofoil shape of the thick Whitley wing, encrusting the perspex and blinding the crews. Flying an aeroplane in these conditions was immensely tiring; and, to add to the stress, it used more petrol and reduced the chance of a safe return. Many crews had to abandon the mission or attack alternatives because of mechanical failure and icing. Only two of the most determined crews from Lindholme, No 304 (Polish) and No 305 (Polish), managed to attack Berlin.[2]

Yorkshire's losses were grim. No 405 (Vancouver) Squadron RCAF lost one aircraft. Six of its Wellingtons managed to return either to Pocklington or Driffield but Sgt Hassan's Wellington disappeared after radioing 'Mission completed'. Flak badly damaged F/Lt Fauquier's aircraft but he brought it home for a crash-landing. Yorkshire's Whitleys suffered the most. Flying low over the North Sea to escape the ice, with giant waves below promising no hope of a successful ditching, the Whitleys gradually succumbed to fuel starvation. Sgt Matthews was at a thousand feet over the sea, steering the course that Topcliffe radio said would bring him home, when he and his crew vanished; P/O Tuckfield was heading for Linton, sixty miles out from Scarborough, when he too was lost; P/O Brown was also on track for Linton when his radio suddenly went silent. Nine Whitleys failed to return to Yorkshire after what was - to date - the most demanding mission of the war. Leeming was lucky. All the Whitleys of No 10 and No 77 Squadrons returned, even though P/O Hacking's aircraft was hit by flak and then struck by lightning. No. 51 Squadron at Dishforth, No. 58 at Linton and No. 78 at Middleton St George each lost two Whitleys; while No. 102 Squadron at Topcliffe lost three.

Two of Yorkshire's Halifax squadrons were on the Berlin raid and with their more powerful engines could climb higher than the Whitleys. Four of No 35 Squadron's Halifaxes attacked Berlin and all returned safely. Two No 76 Squadron aircraft managed to make it to "the Big City", bombed through cloud from 15,000 feet and returned. Despite the safety record of these Halifaxes on the Berlin trip, four others were were lost on 'minor

operations' - one over the Ruhr and three on a 'gardening' (mine-laying) mission to the shipping lanes outside Oslo. Surviving Halifax crews reported that compasses and airspeed indicators had frozen solid. Overall, Bomber Command's loss on 7/8 November 1941 was thirty-seven aircraft (9.4%), a statistic made even more alarming when one appreciates that over a quarter of the bombers that *actually bombed Berlin* failed to return.

The effects of this disaster were felt throughout the Yorkshire squadrons and the whole of Bomber Command. Crews were tired, frozen and sickened by what had happened. They all knew that experienced airmen and valuable aircraft should not be squandered in this fashion. Station commanders were equally furious that their crews had been sent on Bomber Command's biggest mission to date, to one of the most difficult and distant targets, in conditions that were totally unsuitable. Underlining the dangers presented by the weather was the fact that enemy opposition was relatively light: flak was *not* a major problem over Berlin (though it was to aircraft that wandered off track) and there were few known night-fighter interceptions. In his first summary of the Berlin raid, Sir Richard Peirse told Portal that he had expected to lose at least twenty-five aircraft to flak and night-fighters; the additional twelve losses, he said, were due to the exceptional keenness of the crews to press on in dangerous cloud conditions and to excessive petrol consumption when pilots used extra power to counteract icing.

Clearly, the operation was marginal from the outset and the Whitleys and Wellingtons had operated at their maximum limits. Portal was not persuaded by Peirse's arguments and not much impressed by the latter's remark that Group and Station Commanders could have followed Slessor's example and aborted the raid if they had really felt that weather prospects were so menacing that they placed the entire operation in jeopardy. Portal was inclined to believe that the essential failure lay with Peirse who seemed to have misinterpreted the meteorological information. However, although Peirse did modify his original statement to Portal, it was obvious that further recrimination would prove counter-productive and damaging to everyone's morale. It was left to the Prime Minister to resolve the situation. On 11 November, having heard the about the grievous losses on the night of the Berlin raid, Churchill wondered what purpose there was in attacking Berlin in such a hostile environment:

> "There is no need to fight the weather and the enemy at the the same time. It is now the duty of both Fighter and Bomber Command to re-gather their strength for the spring."

So there the matter was left for the rest of the year. Bomber Command continued to attack Germany, but on a much smaller scale. Needless to say, Peirse removed Berlin from his list of targets. At the highest level, the future of Bomber Command was in the melting pot.

★ ★ ★

As a result of Bomber Command's incursions into Germany during 1941 the German defence systems had been radically improved. Even though most Luftwaffe units were committed to the war in Russia, German aircraft production and crew training methods permitted an expansion in the night-fighter force. Hauptman Wolfgang Falk had been the original commander of the first night-fighter Geschwader and in 1940 his Me 110s formed the nucleus of I/NJG 1; II/NJG 1 had Me 109s; III/NJG 1 had Ju 88s. The Geschwader crews recognised the importance of Falk's pioneering work and for the rest of the war all the *Nachtjagdgruppen* carried the diving falcon insignia (Falk = Falcon) on their aircraft.

In July 1941 Oberst Josef Kammhuber took charge of the *Nachtjagdgruppen*. The Me 109s had gone and his crews were now flying twin-engined fighters, mainly Messerschmitt 110s with a few Junkers 88Cs and Dornier Do 17Z Kauz IIs. By August the highly efficient Kammhuber had built up a ground-force dedicated to night-fighter defence and this grew into *Fliegerkorps XII* with himself as *Generalleutnant* in charge. Kammhuber's technique was to divide north-west Europe into three night-fighter zones. Within each zone were two *Würzburg A* radars, one tracking the night-fighter, the other controlling the large 150cm *Flakscheinwerfer* searchlights to illuminate the enemy bombers with their billion candle power beams. This was the *Helle Nachtjagd* (illuminated night-fighting) system that helped his pilots intercept the bombers. At first the radar range was a mere eighteen miles but once the new *Würzburg-Riese* radar became available in the early autumn of 1941 the night-fighters could be vectored on to their targets up to fifty miles away.

Even more sophisticated *Freya* radars enabled Kammhuber to replace the *Helle Nachtjagd* with the *Himmelbett*

A Yorkshire Airfield's link with SOE - Special Operations Executive

An ex-35 Squadron airframe fitter was in 1992 recalling strange goings on at Linton in late 1941: "two Halifaxes parked at a certain spot were loaded with civilians. All very secret! When the Halifaxes returned no civvies came out!" Although he did not know this at the time, Halifaxes were being used at Linton to convert Polish crews to the type. The conversion course was run by S/Ldr Tait and F/Lt Franklin and the object was to use these crews to drop supplies and agents into Poland, beyond the range of a heavily laden Whitley. Several Halifaxes were modified for this work and based at Newmarket. The first SOE operation flown from Linton was *Operation Ruction* (7/8 November 1941). Weapon experts and supplies were parachuted to the Polish Home Army outside Warsaw. It was a difficult and dangerous flight and after the drop the crew had to force-land in Sweden.

Another important role for Linton was on 28/29 December 1941 when F/Lt Ron Hockey took off from Linton in Halifax L9613. His mission was to to take three squads of specialists to Czechoslovakia. He flew via Tangmere probably unaware of the significance of his flight. The first two squads were weapon and radio experts. The third was a team charged with the assassination of Reinhard Heydrich, Chief of the Reich Security Head Office and Protector of Bohemia and Moravia. All three squads parachuted safely and the Halifax returned to base. Why the British, working closely with the Free Czech Government in London, wished to assasinate Heydrich remains an unsolved mystery. They must have been aware of the reprisals that the Germans would take on the Czech civilian population. Perhaps, say some cynics, that was

why the assassination was ordered. Heydrich was having some success in persuading the Czechs to support the Nazi regime. Massive reprisals might cause Czechs to react and form a resistance movement; but if they were seen to co-operate with the Germans, their attitude might have a harmful effect on morale among resistance groups in the rest of Occupied Europe. After some time the agents managed to injure Heydrich with a hand grenade as he was riding in an open motor car in Prague on 27 May 1942. He died in Prague a week later.

No-one could have foreseen the scale of the German reprisals. After a shoot-out in the Church of Chales Borromae in Prague, the Germans captured and shot three men whom they named as the assassins: Sgt Josef Gabcik, Cpl Jan Kublis and Lt Adolf Opalka. The Germans then proceeded on what the Czechs called the 'Massacre of the Innocents'. Many thousands were exterminated over the next few days until the climax was reached with the deliberate razing of two Czech villages, Lidice and Lezacky, and the murder of their entire male populations, the despatch of all women to concentration camps and the distribution of children to unknown areas.

These deeds were officially announced by the Reich Radio Service and described in some detail in German-controlled newspapers and magazines. The hostility of the Czech people towards the Germans was now guaranteed.

(For a contemporary view of these events see the Czech Ministry of Foreign Affairs, *Four Fighting Years*, Hutchinson, 1943, Ch XI The Reign of Terror since 1941.)

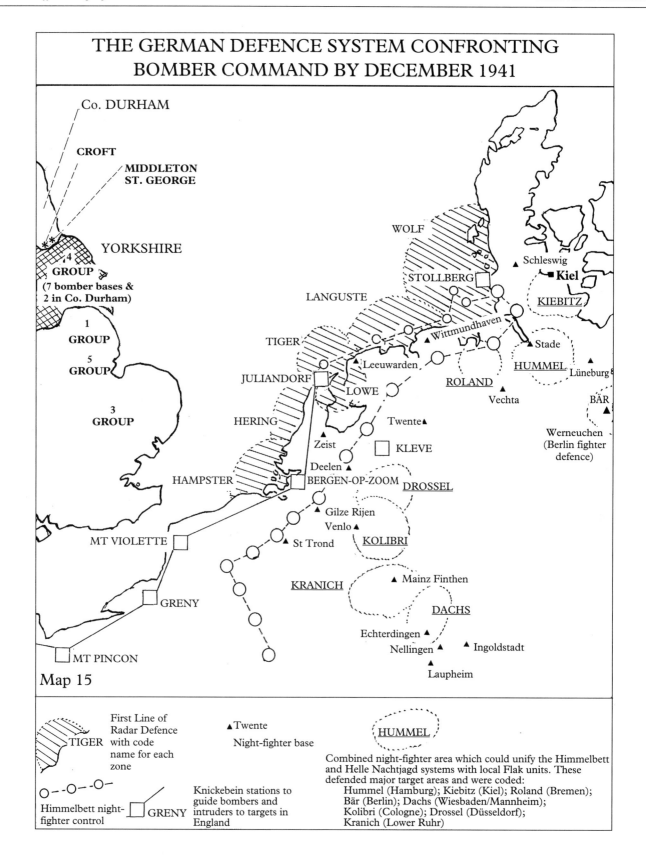

THE GERMAN DEFENCE SYSTEM CONFRONTING
BOMBER COMMAND BY DECEMBER 1941

Map 15

Legend:

First Line of Radar Defence with code name for each zone — TIGER

Himmelbett night-fighter control

▲ Twente — Night-fighter base

Knickebein stations to guide bombers and intruders to targets in England — GRENY

HUMMEL — Combined night-fighter area which could unify the Himmelbett and Helle Nachtjagd systems with local Flak units. These defended major target areas and were coded:
Hummel (Hamburg); Kiebitz (Kiel); Roland (Bremen);
Bär (Berlin); Dachs (Wiesbaden/Mannheim);
Kolibri (Cologne); Drossel (Düsseldorf);
Kranich (Lower Ruhr)

radar-directed system. Freya provided area surveillance while the Würzburg radars shared target-tracking and fighter direction. Each unit, so equipped, formed a *Himmelbett* box and a line of these barred Bomber Command's flight path by the autumn of 1941. RAF crews called it the Himmelbett Line and treated it with considerable respect. Meanwhile, the energetic Kammhuber was soon asking for radar-equipped night-fighters and Telefunken produced its advanced *Lichtenstein* sets, capable of bringing a night-fighter with 200 metres of its target in bad weather. Kammhuber's crews complained that the *Lichtenstein's* massive aerial array would be too heavy and they would be too slow to intercept enemy aircraft. They were soon disabused of this idea after Oberleutnant Ludwig Becker, pilot of the much slower Do 215B, shot down six RAF bombers during August-September 1941 while using an experimental *Lichtenstein* set. Fortunately for Bomber Command, the new radars were slow to appear and did not come into general use until 1942.

Germany's other main form of defence against Bomber Command was the flak arm of the Luftwaffe. Most feared was the 88mm gun which could fire its high explosive shell up to 20,000 feet. Flak batteries were usually of four guns which salvoed their fire to burst inside sixty yards of sky and a skilful battery could fire 10 -12 salvoes per minute. Supplementing these big artillery pieces were the light flak guns that 'hosepiped' the sky with their multicolour tracers, creating a terrifying scenario for the approaching bomber crews.

One offensive weapon that the Luftwaffe failed to use against Bomber Command in the closing months of 1941 was the night-fighter intruder force. Hitler's order had, of course, removed I/NJG2 from its base at Gilze-Rijen and this extraordinary decision enabled the RAF to build new bomber bases with their long, vulnerable concrete runways and to carry on training in the OTUs and HCUs without interruption. There was the occasional raid from a lone Heinkel or Ju 88 but the nagging fear of a fighter in the circuit, waiting to pounce on a Whitley or a Wellington as it turned on finals, had vanished by the end of September. In Yorkshire, Marston Moor became operational in November as 4 Group's Heavy Conversion Unit; Croft was home for No 78 Squadron Whitleys at the end of October; Dalton opened in November to accommodate 102 Squadron's Whitleys so that Topcliffe could be brought up to standard as a heavy bomber base. By the end of December, four Yorkshire squadrons - Nos 10, 35, 76 and 102 - were flying Halifaxes, some of which were the improved B II Series. Across the Humber in Lincolnshire, the first Lancasters were joining their squadrons. There was a promise of Mosquitoes and the hint of new navigational aids. Obediently, Bomber Command was conserving its strength so that it could dole out death and destruction against those targets specified by the War Cabinet. Now that the United States was in the war - the Japanese had attacked Pearl Harbor on 7 December 1941 - aircrews could be not sure what these would be, though they all knew what to expect on the other side of the North Sea: radar-directed night-fighters, radar-controlled flak, blinding searchlights and the prospect of thirty sorties over Germany before their first operational tour was over.

Chapter Thirteen

The Survival of Bomber Command
December 1941- June 1942

While the War Cabinet was deciding the future of Bomber Command, Sir Richard Peirse continued to order the relentless bombardment of German capital ships in Brest. This reached a climax on 18 December 1941 when three Yorkshire squadrons - Nos 10, 35 and 76 - took part in a daylight raid codenamed *Veracity 1* on *Scharnhorst and Gneisenau.* No 10 Squadron had fought throughout 1941 with its Whitley Vs and had just converted to the Halifax B Mk II at Leeming. *Veracity 1* was its first operation with this uprated version of the bomber.[1]

The plan was to use Stirlings and Manchesters as well as the Halifaxes in a precision bombing attack from 10,000 feet, with the Stirlings going in first. Difficulties caused by operating a variety of aircraft types in precisely timed daylight attacks soon appeared. The Halifaxes arrived at the assembly point too early and were forced to orbit. When the Stirlings appeared - there was no sign of the Manchesters - they took the lead with the Halifaxes close behind. Unexpectedly, the Stirlings began to climb, forcing the Halifaxes to bank to starboard. The bomber crews were fortunate that no *Staffel* of Me 109s interrupted these complex manouevres. Once over the target, the Stirlings took the brunt of the flak and fighter opposition. Then came the Halifaxes in perfect battle formation. They bombed and turned just as the Manchesters came in for the attack. Both warships were hit and only one Halifax had to ditch some sixty miles off the English coast. It seemed reluctant to sink and its pilot, Wing Commander Collings, left the dinghy to recover his favourite pipe. Pilot and crew were rescued that evening.

Bomber Command regarded *Veracity 1* as a success and planned a repeat performance, *Veracity 2,* for 30 December 1941. Bad weather closed down the airfields of 3 and 5 Groups, so the operation was carried out solely by the Yorkshire Halifaxes. Escorting Spitfires from No 306 (Polish) Squadron had to turn back just before the Halifaxes reached the French coast so the bomb run was made, unprotected, against heavy German defences. There was no element of surprise and two Halifaxes went down on the initial bomb-run, victims of an accurate flak barrage. The crew of another Halifax lost an engine to flak and then had two more shot to pieces by an Me 109. With a dead rear-gunner and just maintaining flying speed, F/Sgt Whyte had no option but to ditch eighty miles from the English coast and await the arrival of an RAF Air Sea Rescue launch. As all the Halifaxes sustained flak damage the mission underlined again the risk bombers ran, even with partial escort, when they attacked a fiecely defended target in clear weather conditions. 'Salmon' and 'Gluckstein' (aircrews' names for *Scharnhorst* and *Gneisenau*) were to be left alone for the time being and it was almost a month before the Halifaxes were back in action.

★   ★   ★

The New Year began with the dismissal of Sir Richard Peirse as Commander-in-Chief of Bomber Command and the temporary appointment of Air Vice-Marshal Baldwin, commander of 3 Group, in his place. While a question mark hung over the future of Bomber Command, attacks on enemy naval bases continued and particularly on the German warships berthed at Brest. By then both *Scharnhorst* and *Prinz Eugen* were immobilised and still under repair, while Wellingtons from No 1 Group had managed to drop a bomb alongside *Gneisenau,* tearing a twenty foot gash in her hull. Yorkshire's Whitleys were frequently over Brest and also visited St. Nazaire, Emden and Bremen. On 26/27 January some of the Whitleys reverted to Nickelling, the first leaflet-only raids on Germany since the Spring of 1940. On 29/30 January the Halifaxes were back in action as Nos 10 and 76 Squadrons sent their aircraft to attack the latest threat to the Russian convoys sailing from Britain: the 42,900 ton German battleship *Tirpitz* hidden in a fiord near Trondheim.

Prime Minister Churchill said he would regard the destruction of the *Tirpitz* as the "greatest event at sea at the present time." He spoke with deep emotion for the recent weeks had been some of the most disastrous for Britain. Japanese Nell and Sally bombers[2] of the 22nd Air Flotilla, flying from bases near Saigon, had sunk the battlecruiser *Repulse* and the battleship *Prince of Wales* (10 December 1941). The loss of these two ships, known as *Force Z,* was an even greater shock to the British than the totally unexpected destruction of the battlecruiser

Hood during the *Bismarck* chase in May 1941 and the torpedoing of the *Ark Royal* in November 1941. These latest blows in the Far East hit hard at national esteem for not only had the Royal Navy lost control of the Far Eastern war theatre but seemed to have no means of regaining it. That was why Churchill wanted to eliminate the *Tirpitz* threat:

> The entire naval situation throughout the World would be altered and naval command in the Pacific would be regained . . . The whole strategy of the war turns at this period on this ship which is holding four times the number of British capital ships paralysed . . . I regard the matter of the highest urgency and importance.

The Prime Minister was to be disappointed. Seven Stirlings accompanied nine Halifaxes to attack the Tirpitz on 29/30 January. Heavy cloud conditions across the North Sea and over the target meant that none of No 10 Squadron's Halifaxes glimpsed the German battleship though one No 76 Squadron Halifax and a Stirling managed to bomb with no tangible results, the first of many encounters between Yorkshire's Halifax squadrons and the *Tirpitz*.

A few days later came the 'Channel Dash' (12 February 1942) in which the Germans scored a brilliant tactical victory over the British. Endless bombing of Brest had finally convinced the Kriegsmarine that *Scharnhorst* and *Gneisenau* - now joined by the cruiser *Prinz Eugen* - would be safer in Kiel. Though British intelligence had more than a hint that the three German warships would soon try a break-out from Brest, the 'Channel Dash' took the armed services entirely by surprise. Hurriedly, Bomber Command squadrons were ordered to prepare for action and, among many others, the Halifaxes bombed up and flew towards the Channel. Most crews in Nos 10 and 35 Squadrons found that rain and low stratus obscured the target though a sudden cloudbreak enabled S/Ldr Thomson to drop his bombs with no visible effect. Donald Bennett, commander of Leeming's 77 Squadron, was still fighting his war with Whitley Vs and was particularly irate when his bombed-up aircraft were ordered to stand down and play no part in this crucial battle. He was scathing in his commments[3] when he heard that the one action that had been truly pressed home without regard for casualties was the work of 825 Squadron's Swordfish torpedo biplanes led by his friend, Lt Commander Eugene Esmonde - entirely without fighter support.

It was only in the evening, having fended off all the British attacks, that first *Gneisenau* and then *Scharnhorst*

hit mines laid, said the RAF, by Bomber Command. Even so, both ships, together with the undamaged *Prinz Eugen*, reached German ports. Later the War Cabinet was dismayed to learn that the Germans had successfully jammed the British radar during the break-out from Brest.

★   ★   ★

Bomber Command's failure to prevent the 'Channel Dash' - apart from the failure of both Coastal Command and the Royal Navy to meet their own responsibilities - might have marked its end as a strategic bomber force. Churchill now had the details of the tragic Berlin Raid in November 1941 and was only too conscious of the recent failures against *Tirpitz* and the other German capital ships. Some ministers and senior civil servants now pointed to the inadequacies of Bomber Command. Had it not already been found wanting as a strategic force? Had it not discovered in 1939 let alone 1942 that daylight bombing was prohibitively expensive? Even more serious, was it not true that when the Command turned towards night operations the aircrews were unable to hit their targets? Did it not seem that the time was ripe to transform Bomber Command into a Tactical Air Force in support of the Army, rather along the lines of the Luftwaffe's role in the Battle of Poland and France?

It was fortunate that such views did not prevail. Churchill remained true to his belief that the Command represented Britain's sole means of carrying the war to Germany. On 14 February 1942 Bomber Comand received what we we can now see as the definitive directive concerning area bombing:

> "It has been decided that the primary objective of your operation should now be focused on *the morale of the enemy civil population and in particular of the industrial workers.*"

This was a view universally shared by the military for the Joint Chiefs of Staff had already stated in July 1941, after Hitler had invaded the Soviet Union, that the destruction of the German war economy could only be carried out by aerial bombardment. Bombing must be:

> "on a scale undreamt of in the last war" for only then "shall we be able to return to the continent . . . occupy and control portions of his territory and impose our will upon the enemy . . ."

The Chiefs of Staff could not have foreseen the cost of this policy in terms of the effects of a national commitment to a Strategic Bomber Force, to the investment in complex electronic research and to losses in nightly battles on a scale unprecedented in aerial warfare. Yet it was precisely this that was implied in the directive of 14 February 1942 and the man chosen to carry out this awesome task was Air Marshal Arthur T. Harris. He took up his appointment as Commander-in-Chief of Bomber Command on 23 February 1942.

He was pleased that the German warships had left Brest. For some time he had regarded the *Scharnhorst* and *Gneisenau* as an 'incubus', a nightmare for scores of RAF crews who had tried so hard to sink these warships. Relieved of this responsibility, it was a good time to take over Bomber Command.[4]

But he did not neglect the German warships. Six of the Yorkshire Halifaxes took part in a raid on Kiel with forty-three Wellingtons and ten Hampdens on 26/27 February 1942. It was Bomber Command's first victory over the German fleet. A direct hit on *Gneisenau* wrecked her bows and killed many of her crew. Three aircraft, including a Halifax, were lost on this successful operation. Four days later the Whitleys went to Wilhelmshaven to mete out the same punishment to *Scharnhorst* but failed to find her. Three of the Whitleys failed to return. As a climax to the winter raids on the warships, Harris authorised another attack on *Tirpitz*, moored close inshore and well-protected by radar-controlled flak. Thirty-four Halifaxes flew low over the North Sea, well under the German radar, only to find that thick cloud and fog rolling across Aas Fiord completely obscured *Tirpitz*. They loitered as long as they dared - too long in several cases - in the hope that conditions would improve but eventually they had to jettison their loads. Six Halifaxes failed to return, three from 10 Squadron and three from 35 Squadron - a shattering 18% loss.

Better weather conditions prevailed at the end of April and thirty-one Halifaxes with twelve Lancasters set off from forward bases in Scotland for another attack on *Tirpitz* (27/28 April 1942). This time the weapons were different. As the battleship was moored against the steep sides of the fiord, the planners believed that spherical mines dropped on the *land* would roll down and explode under her hull. The operation required a low-level approach through a long Norwegian fiord in which other German vessels equipped with multiple anti-aircraft guns were anchored. It sounded a risky proposition and not all the crews were confident that their briefing was realistic. At Leeming, W/Cdr Donald Bennett's 77 Squadron had just exchanged their Whitleys for Halifaxes and he was none too enthralled with the prospect of carrying out these complex manoeuvres in a four-engined aeroplane loaded

with four 1000lb spherical mines.[5] These weapons were originally naval mines, one hundred of which had been acquired by the RAF. Filled with Amatol explosive and fitted with a special hydrostatic fuse, the mines had lugs attached for carrying inside the Halifax. Bennett noted that with the mines in place the bomb doors would not close properly – though this was possibly the least of his worries[6] It was a clear night as the bombers flew towards Trondheim but once they began their attack they realised that the Germans had contrived a mechanical mist to conceal the main target. Nearby ships opened up on the Halifaxes and four of the bombers plus a single Lancaster were lost. Again, these were grievous losses, bearing in mind that no bombs or mines fell on *Tirpitz*.

Two of the lost Halifaxes and their crews are of special interest. Donald Bennett was piloting his Halifax IIA (W1041) and brought it on course at 200 feet. He saw *Tirpitz* too late to drop his mines and although his starboard wing was on fire, he turned for a second run when flaps and undercarriage began to trail and ever-spreading flames indicated it was time to abandon the aircraft. Bennett managed to climb a little and the crew parachuted, but not before his Flight-engineer, F/Sgt Colgan, had found and clipped Bennett's parachute in position and also rescued the badly wounded tail-gunner.

Bennett jumped just as the starboard wing folded and swiftly made contact with his WOP, Sgt Forbes. They found the escape kits issued to aircrew invaluable and the two men crossed into Sweden with the help of Norwegian families. Two other crew members escaped and the rest became prisoners-of-war. Wing Commander Bennett returned to the UK and was summoned by Harris to form the Command's Pathfinder force.[7]

Halifax W 1048, S-Sugar, was brand-new and on its first operational flight with No 35 Squadron. Flown by P/O Donald McIntyre, it was hit by flak and crash-landed on frozen Lake Hoklingen. All the crew survived, though the flight engineer, Sgt Vic Stevens, had a badly injured foot. When the ice thawed, S-Sugar slid to the bottom of the lake and remained there for thirty-one years. In 1973 an RAF expedition attached oil drums to the remains of the bomber, raised it to the surface and transported it back to the UK. Today it is the sole surviving original Halifax, displayed with pride at the RAF Museum, Hendon.

Handley Page Halifaxes made one more attempt to disable *Tirpitz* before the end of the month. On 28/29 April twenty-three of the bombers plus a solitary Lancaster made another unsuccessful raid on Hitler's giant battleship. Two of No 35 Squadron's Halifaxes were shot down and 10 Squadron almost lost one over the North Sea. P/O Whyte's bomber suffered hydraulic failure through flak damage. His flaps descended and the bomber gradually lost speed until it reached a critical 110 mph. Whyte managed to hold this speed long enough to land on the Shetland Islands.

The last days of April 1942 were significant not just for the Halifax exploits but because they marked the final Bomber Command operations involving 58 Squadron's Armstrong Whitworth Whitleys. No 58 Squadron had been using the Whitley since the first night of the war and on 27/28 April 1942 it sent two of these venerable aeroplanes from Linton-on-Ouse to raid Dunkirk before transferring permanently to Coastal Command and away from Yorkshire. They had been reliable, versatile aeroplanes, having achieved lasting fame on 27/28 February 1942 when 51 Squadron had dropped British paratroopers during the Bruneval raid. Led by W/Cdr P.C.'Percy' Pickard, the Whitleys had been on detachment at Thruxton to take part in special training duties with 'C' Company of 2 Para. Photo-reconnaissance had revealed the presence of a *Würzburg* radar on top of the cliffs at Bruneval and it was the task of 2 Para to overwhelm the German defences and bring back to the UK vital parts of the radar equipment. 2 Para, accompanied by a small team of radar experts led by RAF Sgt C.W.H.Cox, dropped from the Whitleys and carried out an entirely successful mission, providing the 'boffins' with a detailed knowledge of German radar defences.

★ ★ ★

Though he had not yet put *Tirpitz* out of action, Harris had in effect won a significant victory over the Kriegsmarine, something the Royal Navy had not been able to accomplish. He had neutralised two potentially dangerous German warships and no longer had to dissipate his bombers in pointless raids on Brest. Instead, he was able to plan some spectacular raids on targets in Germany and Occupied Europe though the tonnage of bombs dropped was slightly below that achieved in the period February-May 1941. On some of these raids Bomber Command aircraft were able to use a new navigational aid called Gee. For some months scientists had been working on new radio aids and the resultant Gee was in full production by the beginning of 1942. Gee depended on radio transmissions from three ground stations. Their pulses were picked up on a special Gee (for

Grid) set in the bomber. The navigator took a Gee reading and then consulted a Gee map to find his precise position. Range was about 400 miles and the reading was accurate to plus or minus six miles. This was an immense improvement over dead reckoning and enabled crews to ignore decoy sites placed some distance from the primary target. Additionally, Harris insisted that target flares should be dropped by the most experienced crews. Gee and accurate flare-marking might result in low-level precision bombing. To test some of the new techniques the biggest raid of the war to date was launched on 3/4 March against the Renault factory at Boulogne-Billancourt in Paris where lorries destined for the German armed forces were rolling off the production lines.

Bomber Command regarded this attack as one of the most successful to date. It lasted 1 hour and 50 minutes; 235 bombers were despatched; 223 bombed; 234 returned. There were no collisions over the target. Yorkshire's Whitleys and Halifaxes took part and suffered no losses though French civilian casualties were twice as bad as those usually suffered by German cities. In fact, Gee was not used on this attack though the target marking, totally successful, pointed to the shape of things to come. It was certainly a more effective raid than the attack on Essen during 8/9 March 1942. Lead aircraft equipped with Gee were frustrated by dense industrial haze and no hits were registered on the primary target, Krupp's armament factories. Eight aircraft were lost but the ten Yorkshire Halifaxes that went to Essen returned safely. The first successful Gee-led raid was on Cologne (13/14 March) and again the Halifaxes escaped without loss. On this occasion the lead crews carried incendiary bombs as well as marker flares and their illumination of the rubber factories led to accurate bombing.

Decoy fires remained a problem, particularly around Essen and Stuttgart, and to test accurate navigation and fire-raid techniques Bomber Command visited Lübeck on 28/29 March. About 30% of the city was wiped out in what was essentially an incendiary bomb attack on a city centre filled with half-timbered buildings. In April came Rostock's turn. Again, this was a medieval city which had the misfortune to house a Heinkel factory though this was not hit until the third raid. On 26/27 April the fourth Rostock raid virtually finished off the city. German newspapers that had forgotten Warsaw, Rotterdam, London, Coventry, Plymouth and Southampton, reacted with horror and now began calling each attack *'ein Terrorangriff'* - a terror raid. Harris had no illusions about the importance that the Lübeck and Rostock operations had for his crews. For the first time his bomber crews could see the results of their handiwork and their success provided a much needed fillip to the morale of not just the fliers but the ground crew as well during those dark days of 1941. Success at Lübeck and Rostock also heartened the civilian population who were weary of the procession of defeats suffered on land, sea and in the air.[8]

Fire-raids against ill-defended medieval cities were one thing, but could Bomber Command bring off similar success against a well-defended modern industrial city? Surely the Command was too small for the War Cabinet's strategic objectives? And Gee, despite its advantages, was not a magic weapon. Gee had serious limitations. It was not a blind-bombing device. It could not see through the clouds. Gee's value lay in helping the navigator to bring his bomber into the general target area. If the target itself could not be seen by the bomb-aimer, the attack had little chance of success. In the Ruhr, where industrial pollution usually blanketed the ground, it was always difficult to bomb accurately.[9]

Could he create a force of a thousand bombers, guide it to a German city and saturate it with incendiaries and high explosives ?

★   ★   ★

At the time, the people of Yorkshire were more concerned that the Luftwaffe did not seem to be facing the same problem, that it had no difficulty in finding the precise target it had been ordered to attack. This was the certainly the view of the citizens of York, victims of a so-called Baedeker raid on 29 April 1942. Hitler and his Propaganda Minister, Josef Goebbels, were demanding reprisals for the fire-raids on Lübeck and Rostock. Targets would be chosen, it was reported, from the German Baedeker Handbook for Travellers listing buildings bearing the 'three stars' denoting historical and arch-

itectural interest.[10] Luftwaffe sorties against British cities had begun on 23 April and these intensified after the first Rostock raid. Exeter, Bath and Norwich were all hit and then came the turn of York on 29 April 1942.

Marker flares and incendiaries began falling on the city at 0232 hours though the air raid siren was not sounded until some ten minutes later. At first it seemed to be purely an incendiary raid and the local citizens and air raid wardens, together with the soldiers at Lumley Barracks, worked hard to extinguish the flames caused by these phosphorus weapons. Then came the high explosives, aimed with accuracy and effect. Groups of Ju 88s and Dornier 217s had crossed the Yorkshire coast between Flamborough and Hornsea at heights up to 12,000 feet and then dived on the city with the main intention of destroying the railway station and marshalling yards. The Edinburgh-King's Cross train that had just arrived was set on fire and the entire roof and platform system of the southern end of the station was wrecked. Marshalling lines were cratered and one of the famous A4 Pacific class locomotives, the *Sir Ralph Wedgwood*, was badly damaged. Other parts of the city also suffered. Rowntree's factories caught fire, the newly constructed roof of the great Guildhall collapsed and altogether about 30% of York was damaged in this remarkably accurate and well-sustained raid. Precisely how many German bombers bombed York and how many were shot down by the Yorkshire defences remains in dispute. Just one

Damage to '*Sir Ralph Wedgwood*' after the York Baedeker raid 1942.

Dornier 217 coded U5+QP was reported missing from its Soesterberg base.

On patrol that night, and part of a short-lived defence experiment, was a 1459 Flight Douglas Havoc Turbinlite night-fighter equipped with a powerful searchlight in its nose to illuminate enemy bombers. It flew in company with a Hurricane whose pilot would, in theory, pounce on a very surprised German. The Havoc did manage to focus its searchlight on one Dornier 217 but the Hurricane was too slow to engage the bomber which dived away into the darkness.

So it appeared that Hitler's plan to avenge Lübeck and Rostock had some success in York. Air attack had robbed Britain of its oldest surviving medieval Guildhall, reduced St Martin le Grand Church in Coney Street to a smoking ruin and destroyed the Bar Convent School in Nunnery Lane where five nuns had died. On the Nunthorpe Estate three bombs demolished houses in Nunthorpe Grove where several families had no air raid shelters because of the tendency of the area to flood. Approximately eighty people died in York's Baedeker raid and about one-third of the workforce failed to turn up for work at Handley Page's Repair Depot at Clifton although the depot had not been badly damaged during the attack.

This bizarre development in the air war with RAF bombers flying from their Yorkshire bases to set fire to medieval German cities while Luftwaffe aircrews targeted York, Bath, Exeter and Norwich in a deliberate attempt to destroy the cultural heritage of the British people, had entirely opposite effects from those intended. Morale in Germany and Britain did not suffer. Air attack of the kind employed during March-April 1942 actually stiffened civilian attitudes; and there was a near unanimous call for increasing air bombardment of their respective enemies! People proved resilient, capable of with-standing intense but relatively brief bombing raids.

But there was a significant difference between the British and German experience. It lay in the fact that the Luftwaffe, with half of its strength tied up on the Russian front, could not increase its capacity for a sustained air assault on Britain even though it did manage a fierce raid on Norwich on 8/9 May and three consecutive night attacks on Birmingham at the end of July. In the main, the Luftwaffe offensive between August 1942 and January 1944 may be categorised as a series of 'tip and run' raids, deadly and destructive to all who had the misfortune to experience them but not in any sense critical to the survival of the British military and industrial infra-structure. Luftwaffe sorties over Britain were not

comparable with the activities of Bomber Command, a situation that took on a special significance in May 1942 when Air Marshal Harris received Churchill's authority to assault a German city with one thousand aeroplanes.

To assemble a thousand aeroplanes capable of flying to Berlin and back meant using Bomber Command's entire front-line force plus all the aircraft assigned to the Operational Training and Heavy Conversion Units. Few commanders have taken such a calculated risk. But Harris was prepared to throw Britain's entire offensive reserves - for that is what Bomber Command constituted in the Spring of 1942 - into a single attack designed to convince the world at large that the nation's greatest strength lay in the strategic power of an expanding bomber force, a force capable of deciding the outcome of the war. At least, that was the propaganda message. It must be said that Britain's dangerous position in war theatres during early 1942 - notably the Middle East and the Battle of the Atlantic - meant that any new weapon, including the four-engined bomber, was in great demand by Coastal Command and by the military commanders in Egypt. Harris naturally wanted to ensure that most if not all of these bombers came to *his* Command. A dramatic expression of bombing power such as a thousand bomber raid could, he felt, only help his case.

Ironically, production of new bombers was painfully slow during most of 1941-42 so that Bomber Command's true expansion in terms of these new heavy four-engined bombers was not yet a reality. Its mainstay for the rest of the year was the twin-engined Vickers Wellington, a remarkable design updated to tackle bigger bomb loads and carry them deep into intensely defended enemy territory. For the time being the Groups outside Yorkshire had to be content with meagre supplies of the new Avro Lancaster.

Meanwhile, most of 4 Group's Squadrons in York-shire - and a solitary Squadron at Elsham Wold - were converting to the Handley Page Halifax. This became a lengthy process when Squadrons had to be 'screened' or stood down during the conversion process while they awaited new aeroplanes fitted with Gee equipment. Despite this, by the time of *Operation Millennium* the Halifax was the most numerous of the four-engined bombers operating from airfields in Yorkshire that now boasted better runways and standard beam approach system. So when Harris called for a maximum effort from all bomber stations Yorkshire was in a particularly strong position to respond.

Harris launched the thousand bomber raid (code-named *Operation Millennium*) against Cologne on

30/31 May 1942. His original intention was to target Hamburg but weather conditions over North Germany that night were marginal. With an unprecedented number of bombers in the air, Harris needed good visibility in moonlight conditions over the target area and his meteorologists assured him that the skies above Cologne were more predictable than those over Hamburg. Moreover, Cologne was well within the range of Gee. Harris had three objectives: to transit a thousand bombers in a short space of time across the target area, without the risk of collision, in the first systematic attempt to make use of the 'bomber stream'; to saturate the target with incendiaries; and then to use improved varieties of high explosive bombs to spread the fires and destroy the buildings. Seven types of bombers took part in the attack on Cologne and it is instructive to note the preponderance of Wellingtons, whose numbers exceeded the total of all other types:

602 Wellingtons; 131 Halifaxes; 88 Stirlings;

79 Hampdens; 73 Lancasters; 46 Manchesters;

28 Whitleys

Significantly, 365 of these aeroplanes, including most of the Whitleys, came from OTUs while Flying Training Command supplied four of the Wellingtons. A total of 1047 aircraft took off for Cologne and it is believed that 868 actually bombed the target. Churchill expected to lose a hundred aircraft and crews. In fact, forty-one failed to return:

29 Wellingtons; 4 Manchesters; 3 Halifaxes;

2 Stirlings; 1 Lancaster; 1 Whitley; 1 Hampden.

Aircrew were very conscious of the risk of collision and listened intently at their briefings to the emphasis on accurate flying and careful timing. These were crucial if the flak were to be overwhelmed and the chance of a collision avoided. Gunners were urged to avoid shooting at every twin-engined aeroplane for there would be a lot of Whitleys and Hampdens about that night. When questioned on the likelihood of collision, briefing officers were instructed to tell crews that the boffins at the Air Ministry had calculated that only two aircraft would be lost in this manner. Ralph Barker has an amusing reference in his *The Thousand Plan* to the response at one airfield:

"Have the boffins worked out which two aircraft it will be?". . . the briefing officer, judging his audience correctly, replied in similar vein, "I have it on the highest authority that it will be a Tiger Moth and an Anson."[11]

Drawn from fifty-three airfields, the crews displayed a very high standard of airmanship. In ninety minutes the bomber stream destroyed a vast acreage of Cologne mainly by fire and it is thought that within this giant procession of aircraft there was indeed but one collision, a tribute to the tactics, timing and organisation adopted by Harris.

Squadrons flying from their Yorkshire bases had mixed experiences. No 158 Squadron had recently been formed at Driffield and was on the point of converting to Halifaxes. It nevertheless sent nine Wellingtons to Cologne, losing two of them.[12] No 78 Squadron had recently acquired new Halifax BIIs at Croft and had the bad luck to encounter an evil array of cumulo-nimbus clouds packed with thunderstorms on the return flight to Yorkshire. F/O Foers had just let down through cloud when he collided with an OTU Hampden heading for base. Not far away, No 78's new Commanding Officer also had problems in the cu-nims and had to belly-in on Wittering airfield.

No 405 Squadron lost one aircraft in a collision on the first operational sorties from Topcliffe in their brand-new Halifaxes, having converted from Wellingtons in April. Highly experienced squadrons such as No 35 at Linton, No 76 at Middleton and No 102 at Dalton reported intense opposition over the enemy coast and from the defences in the Himmelbett Line. A Halifax BII flying with No 76 Squadron had already made history by dropping the first High Capacity 8000lb bomb on Essen on 10/11 April and on the Cologne raid the squadron plastered the city with nearly 17,000 incendiary bombs. One of Leeming's 10 Squadron Halifaxes - twenty-two of which took off for Cologne - was caught by a night-fighter near Eindhoven and shot down. Perhaps the most extraordinary incident involved a Halifax from 1652 Heavy Conversion Unit at Marston Moor. F/Lt Wright was an experienced pilot and he needed all his skill to survive the accurate fire from a Venlo-based night-fighter. Two bursts shattered part of his control surfaces and set fire to a wing. For a few minutes the Halifax became uncontrollable in a terrifying spiral dive. When Wright pulled the machine out at 6000 feet the bomber went into a loop! Nose high, the Halifax stalled and at this point Wright deemed it wise to bale out.

Low casualties among the Yorkshire squadrons were due in part to the tactics adopted. Harris sent the aircraft across Cologne in three waves. Gee-equipped Halifaxes and Lancasters were in the third wave and their losses were much lighter than those taken by the Gee-equipped Wellingtons and Stirlings in the first wave who had acted as pathfinders and took the brunt of the flak as they dropped their flares and incendiaries. Moreover, crews in

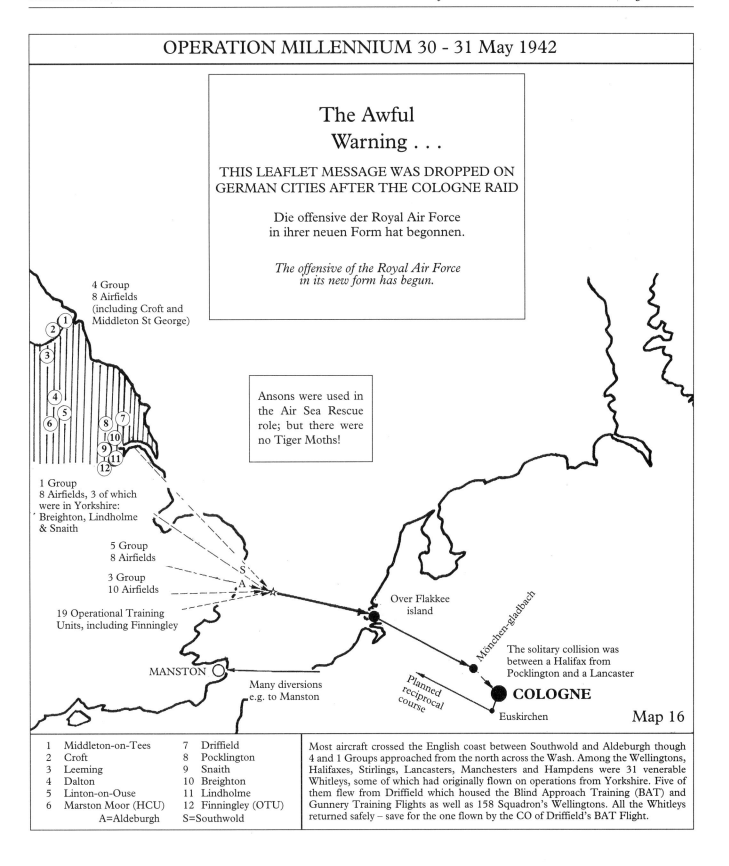

OPERATION MILLENNIUM 30 - 31 May 1942

The Awful Warning . . .

THIS LEAFLET MESSAGE WAS DROPPED ON
GERMAN CITIES AFTER THE COLOGNE RAID

Die offensive der Royal Air Force
in ihrer neuen Form hat begonnen.

*The offensive of the Royal Air Force
in its new form has begun.*

4 Group
8 Airfields
(including Croft and
Middleton St George)

Ansons were used in
the Air Sea Rescue
role; but there were
no Tiger Moths!

1 Group
8 Airfields, 3 of which
were in Yorkshire:
Breighton, Lindholme
& Snaith

5 Group
8 Airfields

3 Group
10 Airfields

19 Operational Training
Units, including Finningley

MANSTON

Many diversions
e.g. to Manston

Over Flakkee
island

Mönchen-gladbach

The solitary collision was
between a Halifax from
Pocklington and a Lancaster

COLOGNE

Planned reciprocal course

Euskirchen

Map 16

1	Middleton-on-Tees	7	Driffield
2	Croft	8	Pocklington
3	Leeming	9	Snaith
4	Dalton	10	Breighton
5	Linton-on-Ouse	11	Lindholme
6	Marston Moor (HCU)	12	Finningley (OTU)
	A=Aldeburgh		S=Southwold

Most aircraft crossed the English coast between Southwold and Aldeburgh though 4 and 1 Groups approached from the north across the Wash. Among the Wellingtons, Halifaxes, Stirlings, Lancasters, Manchesters and Hampdens were 31 venerable Whitleys, some of which had originally flown on operations from Yorkshire. Five of them flew from Driffield which housed the Blind Approach Training (BAT) and Gunnery Training Flights as well as 158 Squadron's Wellingtons. All the Whitleys returned safely – save for the one flown by the CO of Driffield's BAT Flight.

the second and third waves had no difficulty in identifying the target: the glare could be seen for sixty miles on the way in; and on the way back the Halifax rear-gunners reported they could still see Cologne burning one hundred miles distant. By then the city's defences had been overwhelmed.

In Britain the raid was seen as a great success. Sir Frederick Handley Page sent Harris a congratulatory telegram and Harris in reply thanked him for providing Bomber Command with the Halifax. "Such a powerful weapon to wield," was the compliment he sent to Sir Frederick though it would not be long before Harris changed his mind about the aeroplane.

But the most important consequence of *Operation Millennium* was that it finally converted Churchill. The Prime Minister felt that at last there was a chance that his new Chief of Bomber Command could organise a strategic bomber offensive against Germany. He was not alone in his faith in Arthur Harris. General Arnold, commander of the USAAF, sent his tribute, hoping that America's B-17s and B-24s would soon be in the fight against Germany, side by side with Bomber Command. From Moscow came a plaudit from General Golovanov, commander of the Red Army's Long Range Bomber Force, for the "initiation of successful massed blows on Hitlerite Germany."

And for those thousands of young aircrew, plus the even greater number of RAF, RCAF and WAAF personnel who stayed on the ground to keep the aeroplanes flying, Cologne's ordeal was a visible sign that all their sacrifices were now producing results. Harris had ordered his briefing officers to tell the crews that they had the opportunity "to strike a blow at the enemy which will resound, not only throughout Germany, but throughout the world." This they had done and a delighted Churchill signalled Harris:

"I congratulate you and the whole of Bomber Command upon the remarkable feat of organisation which enabled you to despatch over a thousand bombers to the Cologne area in a single night and without confusion to concentrate their action over the target in so short a time as one hour and a half. This proof of the growing power of the British bomber force is also the herald of what Germany will receive, city by city, from now on."

As for the Chief of Bomber Command, he was now the nation's hero. On 10 June 1942 he received a knighthood from King George VI. Five years later, Sir Arthur was able to write:

"My own opinion is that we should never have had a real bomber offensive if it had not been for the 1000 bomber attack on Cologne, an irrefutable demonstration of the power of what was to all intents and purposes a new and untried weapon."[13]

Bomber Command had indeed been saved.

Chapter Fourteen

Grim Preparations and a Crisis Survived
May - December 1942

Mosquitoes brought back the eagerly awaited photographs of Cologne shortly after the thousand bomber raid. These revealed that some six hundred acres of the city had been devastated, evidence that encouraged Harris to repeat his success. After all, he had a thousand bombers ready for action.[1]

He selected Essen as his next target, hoping to put the 'city of Krupps' out of action. He managed to assemble 956 aircraft and these set out on 1/2 June 1942 for the second 'thousand bomber' raid. Weather conditions were good over the North Sea but once over the Ruhr the crews found that industrial haze and cloud obscured the target. Although the Wellington pathfinders did their best to illuminate the city with flares the attack was a failure. No 76 Squadron had briefed seven of its Halifaxes to hit a specific target in the centre of the Krupps complex but the bomb-aimers could not even identify it. Major navigational errors led to the bombing of other towns such as Oberhausen (far more people were killed here than in Essen), Duisburg and Mulheim. Krupps, it transpired, had not been touched. The Wellington force lost fifteen aircraft and eight Halifaxes failed to return. Bomber Command's total loss that night was thirty-one bombers.

Though he had not followed up the great raid on Cologne, Harris was determined to keep hammering Essen. Throughout June he launched four more attacks on this difficult target but none was successful. There was no industrial damage in Essen but fifty-three aircraft failed to return. The chart shows the loss pattern:

Follow-up raids on Essen	Aircraft loss	Number of Halifaxes lost
2/3 June 1942	14	2
5/6 June 1942	12	1
8/9 June 1942	19	7
16/17 June 1942	8	4

Interspersed with these raids were the persistent but unrewarding assaults on Emden and a 'softening-up' attack on Bremen (3/4 June) prior to the third 'thousand bomber' venture.

With the help of Coastal and Army-Co-operation Commands Harris assembled 1067 aircraft for the attack on Bremen (25/26 June 1942). Seven Halifaxes from 76 Squadron were among the target-finder crews who found Bremen obscured by cloud but used their Gee to mark the aiming points. Incendiary bombs created hundreds of fires and these, fanned by strong winds, caused most of the damage that night. On balance, however, the raid was not a success. Losses were the worst to date. Forty-eight aircraft failed to return though the crews from four ditched bombers were rescued. A worrying feature of the raid was the very heavy loss rate among Operational Training Units. Twenty-three warweary Wellingtons and Whitleys crewed by instructors and students were shot down. 124 Halifaxes went on this, the last of the year's thousand bomber raids, and six of these were lost. One from Driffield ran short of fuel and ditched near Scarborough; another fell to the guns of a night-fighter over Holland, now one of the most dangerous stretches of Europe that Bomber Command crews had to cross.

Such massive raids had a salutary effect upon the German defence systems and bomber crews soon found that German resistance had not only stiffened but had grown much more sophisticated. By August 1942 Kammhuber enlisted the help of the powerful *Heinrich* transmitters and these quickly swamped the Gee signals once Bomber Command aircraft were overflying the Continent. Navigators had to rely on one sure fix before crossing the enemy coast. Kammhuber also widened the *Himmelbett* line and brought in the very powerful *Mammut* and *Wasserman* radars that enabled the Luftwaffe to plot the progress of bomber aircraft as soon as they set course from their bases in Yorkshire, Lincolnshire and East Anglia. This meant that the ever-expanding German night-fighter force was always ready and waiting; though all depended on the ability of the Luftwaffe controllers to direct their fighters to the correct part of the sky.

The RAF's new bomber stream tactics presented the Germans with a completely different kind of problem and *Fliegerkorps XII* reformed in May 1942 with three night-fighter divisions, some of which were equipped with the Dornier Do 217J. This modification of the Dornier 217 bomber had first seen service in March that year and its crews found it a rather cumbersome and heavy machine. Nevertheless, those fitted with *FuG 202 Lichtenstein* radar could usually score a success with the force of their massive fire-power: four MG FF cannon and four MG 17 machine-guns located in the nose and in an underbelly forward-firing gunpack.[2] Flak too had intensified as the Germans threw more of their resources into defence of the *Reich* thereby reducing their anti-tank strength on the Russian front.

Such was the opposition during the summer and autumn of 1942 when Bomber Command carried out smaller but more powerful raids on German targets, featuring a greater use of four-engined bombers, heavier incendiary loads plus a number of the new 4000lb and 8000lb Heavy Capacity 'blockbusters'.

★ ★ ★

For the Yorkshire-based squadrons this was the most critical time in the history of 4 Group. Superficially it was a time of gathering strength as more airfields, improved aeroplanes and better bombs became available. For example, during 1942 Melbourne was rebuilt with the now standard heavy bomber runway 'Letter A' configuration: a main concrete runway of 5,500 feet and two alternative runways each of 4000 feet. As construction work was still in progress when 10 Squadron moved in during August their new Halifaxes had to use Pocklington for bombing-up and refuelling. Dalton was also being rebuilt as a heavy bomber airfield with 428 (Ghost) RCAF forming there in November, the same time as 427 (Lion) formed at Croft and 429 (Bison) at East Moor. Rufforth welcomed 158 Squadron from East Moor with its Halifax BIIs,[3] Burn became the base for 431 (Iroquois) and Skipton-on-Swale accommodated 420 (Snowy Owl) with its Wellington Mk IIIs. 4 Group's Wellington and Halifax numbers were swelling rapidly, supplemented by 460 Squadron RAAF at Breighton and 101 Squadron at Holme-on-Spalding Moor. At this time Nos 460 and 101 were in 1 Group and it is interesting that Yorkshire housed the headquarters of 4 Group (York) and 1 Group (Bawtry). No 101 Squadron had enjoyed the distinction of flying its Wellingtons in all three of the thousand bomber raids without losing a single aircraft. It was about to write a new chapter in its history at Holme-on-Spalding Moor as it re-equipped with Lancasters, the first time that substantial numbers of these bombers had been based in Yorkshire.

Elvington became operational in October when No 77 Squadron moved in with its Whitleys, immediately converting to Halifax BIIs. Snaith also became a 4 Group Halifax base in October after 150 Squadron transferred its

Wellington IIIs across the Humber to Kirmington. The replacement squadron at Snaith was No 51, fresh from its tour at Coastal Command and still flying Whitleys. It was delighted to receive its first Halifax BIIs from Elsham Wolds where 103 Squadron was converting to Lancasters. 103 Squadron was equally delighted to part with the Halifaxes. Dr. Robert Henderson, 103 Squadron Medical Officer, had been very concerned by the number of fatal crashes experienced by aircrews during their training sorties. Writing in 1986, he mentioned that the cause was a design weakness in the Halifax's triangular fin and rudder design that sometimes led to 'rudder stall' and a spiral dive into the ground. His crews were already worried by the poor performance of Halifax aircraft on training sorties; what, they wondered, would happen when they flew over enemy territory?[4]

At the time, the 'fin/rudder stall problem' had not been properly diagnosed and criticisms of the Halifax tended to concentrate on rather more obvious shortcomings. For example, in his *Journeys into Night* Don Charlwood describes the shoddiness of finish of the early Halifax series, their heavy all-up weight of twenty-six tons that made aileron turns something of a tussle. He records the joy of 103 Squadron crews when they found they were going to do no more operations on Halifaxes; and their ensuing misery when told they would have to continue training flights on their Halifaxes while awaiting the arrival of new Lancasters.[5]

In fact there was growing alarm at the Halifax loss rate on both sides of the Humber and Handley Page was receptive to the criticism of those who flew the aeroplane in anger, notably W/Cdr Leonard Cheshire. Now CO of No 76 Squadron, holder of two DSOs and a DFC and recognised as the outstanding bombing leader, he could exert influence in the right quarters. He was positive that the lack of any form of ventral defence on the Halifax, its bulbous nose with a near-useless front turret, unnecessary armour plating, clumsy exhaust shrouds, barrage balloon cutters and a permanently locked-down tail-wheel all contributed to a complex problem in which drag, weight and poorly disposed defensive armament were the root causes of the Halifax's unsatisfactory combat performance. No-one could deny that squadron losses were rising in " a distressingly steep curve" during 1942. Moreover, Cheshire believed that the design of the twin triangular fin and rudder was fundamentally unsound and on several occasions - much to the alarm of some of his crew- he tested the consequences of deliberately putting the big bomber into a stall. The spiral dives and spins that resulted required all his strength and airmanship to restore the Halifax to straight and level flight and he would sometimes land nursing damaged rudders caused by the stress of his air test.

Handley Page had been progressively modifying the Halifax since the first of the BI Series I entered service with 35 Squadron at Linton in January 1941. The Series II aircraft had a stronger airframe and twin VGO machine-guns located to fire out of each side of the fuselage; while the Series III incorporated uprated Merlin XXs, a better fuel system and redesigned engine cowlings and exhaust shrouds. The last improvement was an attempt to cure that other Halifax bugbear: engine overheating. When the BII Series came off the production line a bulky Boulton-Paul mid-upper turret replaced the beam guns so that the Halifax now had three power-operated turrets fitted still with the puny .303 machine-guns and no match for the German night-fighter cannon. Other changes followed swiftly. The BII Series I Special had its front turret deleted; while the BII Series Ia had the improved Merlin 22s. Then a shortage of Messier undercarriages led to a contract being awarded to Dowty for a new undercarriage design (1942). Dowty's gear was a godsend

as far as ground handling was concerned and to differentiate this new equipment Dowty Halifaxes became the B Mk V Series. One drawback emerged: Dowty components were castings rather than forgings and these could fail under extreme conditions, particularly at take-off.

Deletion of the front turret and the use of the 'Tollerton fairing' reduced drag though the loss rates did not improve and the fin/rudder stall problem remained unsolved throughout 1942 though highly competent pilots were posted to Yorkshire's Conversion Units to instruct young pilots how to cope with the unusual attitudes sometimes adopted by Halifaxes with the triangular fins and rudders. To add to their problems, the all-up weight of these big bombers increased because the Mk II/V models as supplied to the Yorkshire squadrons were designed to carry the new High Capacity bombs plus the big incendiary canisters. The 4000lb HC bomb was the RAF's first 'blast bomb' and is better known as the 'cookie'. Built as a reaction to the powerful German parachute mines dropped on Britain during the 1940-41 blitz, the 'cookie' could be fitted into the bomb-bays of Halifaxes, Wellingtons and the cavernous Lancasters. Later on the versatile Mosquito harried Berlin with a 4000 lb bomb for this little wooden aeroplanes could take one 'cookie' at very high speed to its target - and that often included the German capital. The 'super cookie' or 8000lb HC bomb also arrived in 1942 to be carried solely by Halifaxes and Lancasters for no other British bomber had an appropriate bomb-bay. This huge weapon was not simply two 4000lb bombs joined together but was actually made of two wide-bodied cylinders each of 4000 lbs fitted with a drum tail to aid stability and accuracy in the free fall.

Twenty-eight of these 'super Cookies' fell on enemy-occupied territory during 1942. Together with the four-pounder 'fire-raiser' and the thirty-pounder incendiary bomb, they were the shape of things to come.

This gives a good close-up view of the Tollerton fairing and the starboard Merlins. This crew called themselves "The Stooges".

Yorkshire Air Museum

From their Yorkshire bases, flying Halifaxes with these fearsome bombloads, the crews of the RAF, RCAF and RAAF squadrons launched their attacks upon Germany, Italy and the Occupied territories. Their losses were consistently high and by the end of August 1942, after carrying out 1770 sorties against enemy targets, 109 Halifaxes had failed to return. This meant that 4 Group was suffering a casualty rate of 6.2% and aircrew could easily calculate the odds. If there were a casualty rate of only 2.5% then the chances of surviving fifty operational flights were slightly better than four to one against. If the rate jumped to 4% it meant that out of every hundred Halifax crews only thirteen would survive the two tours. Yet after the August raids on Duisburg, Osnabrück, Mainz, Saarbrücken and Nuremberg, Halifax losses reached 10.1%. Morale was bound to suffer once it became clear to everyone that there was a very real risk in Yorkshire that 4 Group could be wiped out with little to show for its sacrifice. Sir Arthur Harris was deeply concerned by the problems inherent in the Halifax design and was swiftly losing his earlier enthusiasm for the type. Yet it is undeniable that many crews had formed an affection for their big bomber and had not lost confidence in its battle-worthiness. Squadrons were far more concerned to find ways of dealing with night-fighters.

Their most effective manoeuvre against a stern attack - adopted by the whole of Bomber Command - was 'corkscrewing' the aircraft in a series of banked dives designed to lose a stalking night-fighter. Mid-upper and rear-gunner usually acted as fire-control, shouting instructions to the pilot over the intercom. Flak splinters and bullets ripping into a bomber often cut the intercom and then a gunner would resort to the emergency coloured light call system, as taught at 1652 Conversion Unit based at Marston Moor:

On the red light: series of dots = corkscrew left

On the green light: series of dots = corkscrew right

When it was safe to resume course, three A's in morse were sent on both lights.

If the pilot felt he was losing control or decided he had to ditch, the crew had to be ready to handle any emergency. Using the 'call' light the pilot would signal in morse:

Series of N's	=	send help to gunners
Series of D's	=	stand by to ditch
Series of P's	=	prepare to bale out
Continuous dash	=	BALE OUT !

Because there was no standard ventral armament on any of the Halifaxes entering service during 1942 there was no defence against an unseen night fighter attack from below, particularly from an Me 109 coming up almost vertically. The Luftwaffe pilot would let his fighter hang on its propeller, on the edge of a stall, and pump cannon shells into the bomber's wing-tanks. Crews were desperately worried as they all knew that German fighters preferred to attack from astern and slightly below when the four exhausts showed fiery red and the Halifax was silhouetted against a sky made bright by flares, flak and searchlights. Cheshire was equally anxious to correct this weakness and encouraged Sgt George Coates and LAC Frank Layton to experiment with a ventral gun hatch, later adopted by Canadian and few of 4 Group's Halifax squadrons. Perhaps the only comfort a crew member had at this time was that the rate of survival from a Halifax shot down over Europe was marginally better than that experienced by those who flew Lancasters, Stirlings and Wellingtons.

Such were the thoughts that troubled young aircrew at a time of great difficulty in 4 Group and it was left to Sir Arthur Harris to resolve the problem. He decided that all Halifax aircraft would be screened and essential modifications carried out. For the next three weeks aircrew were to be rested from missions over Germany.

So, at a critical moment in the history of Yorkshire's 4 Group, the seven operational Halifax squadrons - Nos 10, 35, 76, 78, 102, 158, and 405 - all stood down.

Privately, Harris was seeking to rationalise the composition of his Main Force aircraft. He regarded the Stirling as a failure and the Halifax as second best to the Lancaster, essentially because of their slow speed at the limit of their operational ceiling (usually between 12000 and 18000 feet) and their resulting vulnerability to German heavy flak. By December 1942 he was writing to the Secretary of State for Air, Sir Archibald Sinclair, and did not attempt to conceal his feelings:

". . . the Stirling and Halifax are now our major worries. They presage disaster unless solutions are found . . . The Stirling Group has now virtually collapsed . . . There should be wholesale sacking of the incompetents who turned out approximately 50% rogue aircraft from Short and Harlands. . ." [6]

He went on to stress the problem of the Halifax:

". . . nothing whatever ponderable is being done to make this deplorable product worthy for war or fit to meet those jeopardies which confront our gallant crews . . ." [7]

Unaware of their commander's true feelings, the Halifax crews soon recovered from their brief loss of confidence. At least two factors helped in this. The first was the formation of a Pathfinder Force with new navigational and bombing aids that would gradually lead to an improvement in the accuracy of Bomber Command's attacks; the second was a new emphasis upon training.

There had been interest in a 'Target Finding Force' ever since Group Captain S.O. Bufton had used Whitleys to light up 10 Squadron's targets. Bufton believed that this technique should be adopted so that the whole of Bomber Command could benefit and he suggested that the best crews from each squadron - those who could find their targets, bomb accurately and return safely - should come together to form an élite Target Finding Force. Harris was far from enthusiastic. Neither he nor most of his Group Commanders wanted their best men removed from each and every squadron as this would have a damaging effect upon training and leadership. So Bufton decided to ask the same question in a different way: would Sir Arthur allow one squadron from each group to form this urgently needed force? Harris was still reluctant, hoping that new navigational aids such as Oboe and H2S would be available before the end of 1942. But they were not forthcoming and Harris had to acknowledge the wisdom of creating this new force. Although he had no recent combat experience, Harris well understood the problems facing his night-bomber crews. It would be an enormous help if a specialised force could locate and mark their targets ahead of them.[8]

He insisted on christening it the 'Pathfinder Force' and it came into being on 15 August 1942, under the command of the Australian pilot Air Commodore D.C.T. Bennett who had escaped from his crashed Halifax back to Britain via Sweden. Harris had the highest regard for Bennett. He considered the Australian to be an out-standingly courageous pilot and an absolute wizard in long-range navigation – just the man to form and lead the new Path Finding Force.[9]

Harris retained direct control of the Pathfinder Force and insisted that the Groups supplying the original aircraft would be responsible for replacing those lost during pathfinding operations, a ruling that only Air Vice-Marshal Carr's 4 Group accepted without complaint. This Group contributed No 35 Squadron to the new force and the Squadron's Halifaxes transferred from Linton to Graveley in August 1942. Carr consistently supported the Pathfinder Force and never raised objections when asked to supply it with replacement Halifax aircraft. It was no

---

Air Vice-Marshal Sydney Bufton DFC

1908-1993

After surviving Hitler's *blitzkrieg* against the Low Countries and France during 1940, Bufton found himself posted to No 10 Squadron at Leeming. No 10 Squadron was flying Whitleys and Bufton was worried by the fact that the steady rate of losses with these twin-engined bombers was not compensated by a steady destruction of German industry. His concern for the pin-prick effect of Bomber Command's attacks on Germany during 1940 intensified after he heard of his brother's death in an 83 Squadron Hampden. But he had no illusions about survival: "One was attuned to getting the chop..." Nevertheless, if he and his crews had to risk their necks every night it would be preferable to undertake each sortie in a first-class aeroplane, capable of carrying a heavy bombload to distant targets that could be bombed with accuracy and effect.

He was therefore delighted when the chance came to command the re-formed No 76 Squadron flying the new Halifaxes first from Linton-on-Ouse and then from Middleton St George. His experiences with 4 Group convinced him that it was vital to form an élite Target Finding Force in order to mark **ahead** of the Main Force. Bufton was a clever planner and realised that an élite force was anathema to Sir Arthur Harris who was pinning his hopes on the new navigational aids - that was why he suggested that each Group should provide a Squadron to form the new force and then test out the new navigational and target-finding devices over Germany during the autumn of 1942.

Fortunately for Bomber Command and the outcome of the war, Sir Arthur heeded Sydney Bufton's advice. During 1943 Bufton was appointed Director of Bombing Operations at the Air Ministry where he smoothed the way for good relationships between Sir Arthur and the chiefs of the 8th USAAF during 1943-44. The two men worked together closely for the remainder of the war and throughout Bufton remained a loyal supporter of Sir Arthur Harris.

---

coincidence that both Bufton, who had spawned the Pathfinder idea, and Bennett, who provided the leadership, had both served in 4 Group.

Bomber Command operations using the new Pathfinder squadrons began in August 1942 even though no satisfactory target markers yet existed. No 35 Squadron took its Halifaxes on the first Pathfinder operation against Flensburg (18/19 August). Even experts make blunders and faulty navigation led the entire force off course and one of No 35 Squadron's aircraft failed to return. Yorkshire's Halifaxes were back in action for the

Karlsruhe raid (2/3 September) and for the Bremen raid the following night when the Pathfinders introduced their wave system of target marking: a procession of Illuminators, Supporters, Backers-up and Primary Visual Markers, the basis of all future night operations.

The 'Pathfinder Method' depended on reliable navigational aids and the ability of specially briefed crews to carry out precise operations on the approach to and overhead the aiming point.

Illuminators: dropped the initial 33lb 4.5 in Reconnaissance Flare suspended by parachute and fused to burn at a pre-selected height for 3-4 minutes; then added specific markers such as the early Red Blob (a converted 250lb incendiary casing) and the famous 'Pink Pansy' - a 4000lb bomb casing filled with pyrotechnics that exploded on the the ground to create a circle of coloured fires.

Supporters : Came in with bombs to attack flak batteries during the initial finding and illumination of the target.

Backers-up : Renewed the flares and markers as required.

Primary
Visual
Markers: Used when the aiming point had been positively identified and could be seen through the bomb-sight. Then the markers would be dropped precisely and the chances were that the Main Force would saturate the target.

Very slowly, the new navigational and bombing aids appeared. Many of the Pathfinders and some of the Main Force carried Gee but, as we have seen, this was easily jammed by Germany's counter-measures once the bombers crossed the enemy coastline. Another aid, also dependent upon the curvature of the earth, was Oboe, first used in December 1942. A pilot flew along the perimeter of a circle which was calculated at a given point to pass through the middle of the target. Accurate flying was achieved via a radar pulse from a ground station in Britain. This pulse was transformed into a musical note and changes in the note instructed the pilot to adjust his course until he heard the sound first of dots and then dashes signalling the precise moment to release his target markers. Oboe soon proved itself the most accurate aid available and could be used to bomb through cloud and industrial haze - ideal for the Ruhr. It had two

disadvantages: its range was 280 miles, thus excluding many German targets beyond the Ruhr; and it required two ground stations serving one aircraft at a time. High-flying Mosquitoes provided the answer: they could accommodate the Oboe equipment and carry markers to identify targets. These were the aircraft chosen to mark from 28,000 feet on 20 December 1942 when an experimental attack on a coking plant at Lutterade provided encouraging results.

At the same time a new airborne radar scanning device known as 'Stinky' or H2S was under development at the Telecommunication Research Establishment (TRE) at Great Malvern. H2S transmitted its impulses from the aircraft downwards and outwards and its rotating aerial picked up the radar reflections from the ground and transformed them into an image on a cathode ray tube.

Bennett had also devised three procedures for interpreting the target markers. 'Newhaven' meant that Main Force aircraft could bomb the TIs (Target Indicators) they could see on the ground; 'Parramatta' warned that poor visibility required H2S ground marking; 'Wanganui' signified sky-marking when Main Force crews would bomb through flares suspended by parachute.[10] By the beginning of 1943 Bennett could say of his new Pathfinder Force, and perhaps speak for the whole of Bomber Command, that at long last

". . . we had the crews, we had Oboe and H2S, we had the pyrotechnics and we had a little experience . . ."[11]

As far as 4 Group's crews were concerned they were merely told that everyone would benefit from extra training to improve their flying skills. Careful analysis of accidents and combat losses had already highlighted a weakness in pilot experience after completion of the Heavy Conversion Course. For example, a pilot coming from the HCU and who then flew a Halifax as 'second dickey' on less than three operations tended to survive no more than two Main Force operations as aircraft captain. In contrast, those pilots who flew as second dickey for six or more operational sorties tended to have a much better rate of survival. Improved pilot skills, it seemed, was one answer to rising aircraft losses. In between their normal operations over Germany and Italy Yorkshire's squadrons now began intensive practice cross-country flying.

Adding to the crowded skies were aircraft from the growing number of Conversion Units in the County: 1652 at Marston Moor; 1665 at Breighton; 1658 at Riccall; and 1659 at Leeming. Their training sorties were not without their dangers, partly because some aircraft supplied to HCUs were war-weary and often badly maintained. One crew member then flying in Yorkshire, Bill Webb, maintained that conversion training was "far more dangerous than operations over Germany"[12] though the youthful veterans of Bremen, Aachen, Cologne, Hamburg and Mannheim flying their cross-country sorties over Northern England may not have subscribed to this view. However, few would have disputed the statement that Merlin engine overheating was "the dread of all Halifax crews" and Handley Page's engineers busily supervised trials and engine modifications to try to overcome this problem.

★ ★ ★

Halifax performance problems, though crucial to Yorkshire's 4 Group, paled into insignificance against the giant task of defeating the three Axis powers of Germany, Italy and Japan. Loud cries could be heard from armchair strategists echoing demands from the Soviet leader Josef Stalin, to desist from bombing raids and to concentrate instead on the long awaited 'Second Front.' Few - apart from perhaps Harris himself - disagreed with John Ehrman's statement when he said that the Continent must somehow be freed from the clutches of Nazism and that the process of liberation could only begin when the first British or American soldiers advanced up the beaches of Europe.

In fact British and Canadian troops did wade ashore at Dieppe in August 1942. This was the ill-fated *Operation Jubilee* designed to test the German coastal defences and to experience the difficulties of gaining control of a well-defended port area. It is worth noting the preponderance of Canadians who composed the main attack force: the Royal Hamilton Light Infantry, the Queen's Own Cameron Highlanders, the Essex Scottish Regiment, the South Saskatchewan Regiment and the Royal Regiment of Canada. Canadian casualties totalled 3379; all the new Churchill tanks were lost.

If Jubilee taught anything it was the need to defer an invasion of Europe until the Allies were in total command of the air plus the ability to land large forces of infantrymen on the beaches where there were no heavily defended port installations. Moreover, Jubilee had taken place in August 1942 when Halifax bomber losses over Germany had reached a crisis level, demonstrating the extraordinary power and resilience of the German armed forces at this stage of the war. The German defenders at

Dieppe were never seriously worried even when confronted by Royal Marine Commandos, squadrons of brand-new British tanks, and the best of Canadian assault infantry. They did not even need to summon help from a nearby German Panzer division. It is a fact that Germany's armed forces were at their zenith between August 1942 and the Battle of Kursk in July 1943. They were able to sustain their losses at El Alamein (November 1942), Cape Bon (January 1943) and Stalingrad (1942-43) and still maintain in the west, facing Britain, a strategic reserve of four Panzer divisions, three SS Panzer divisions and the superbly equipped Gross Deutschland division. There would be no hope of invading Western Europe in 1942 or even 1943 until such time as the German capacity to resist a seaborne invasion had been significantly reduced. This was the burden that the Allied Combined Chiefs of Staff placed squarely on RAF Bomber Command and the Bomb Groups of the United States 8th Army Air Force.

Thus it was clearly Britain's responsibility to maintain the air war against Germany, using the new weapons and new navigational aids slowly entering squadron use. Exponents of air warfare had much on their side. Had not Japan's first naval defeats at the Battles of the Coral Sea (May 1942) and Midway (June 1942) been accomplished entirely by air power? Was it not air power that enabled US Marines to land on the first Japanese-controlled Pacific atoll at Tarawa in November 1942? Would it not be air power that would one day ensure a successful Allied landing on the beaches of Western Europe?

How exactly this would be accomplished remained a matter of argument in 1942. The Royal Navy suggested that the RAF should somehow defeat the German fighter force and then, in broad daylight and with total control of the skies, bomb the crucially important oil refineries and ball-bearing plants - termed 'panacea targets' by a sarcastic Harris. Sir Dudley Pound, First Sea Lord, deplored the RAF's lack of enthusiasm to take on German day fighters, ignoring the mediocre defensive armament allocated to British heavy bombers. Sir Dudley was, of course, preaching the philosophy of the United States Eighth Army Air Force, now established in the UK, but still unblooded in an attack on a *German* target.

Amidst this sterile debate the Halifaxes and Wellingtons of 4 Group returned to the assault on Germany during the autumn and early winter months of 1942. Weather conditions were appalling and these precluded or limited operations against German and Italian targets. For example, when 4 Group sent twenty-eight Halifaxes to Flensburg on 26/27 September 1942 the entire force had to be recalled. An attack on Krefeld (2/3 October) encountered dense haze; thunderstorms hindered the raid on Aachen (5/6 October) and caused several crashes in the UK. Pathfinders managed to mark Osnabrück accurately on 6/7 October but two big attacks on Kiel (13/14 October) and Cologne (15/16 October) failed because of clever German decoy fires. Of the seventy-one 'cookies' carried to Cologne that night only one landed in the city. Targets changed once Bomber Command undertook operations against Italy to coincide with the new offensives in North Africa following Montgomery's victory at El Alamein and the Allied invasion of North Africa (Operation Torch). Nevertheless, 4 Group's attack on Genoa (23/24 October), in company with 3 Group's Stirlings, was a total failure in that the most of the Main Force missed Genoa and bombed Turin and Savona. However, one Halifax from 76 Squadron dropped down to 6000 feet just below the cloud base and confirmed that some parts of Genoa's port installations were on fire. W/Cdr Cheshire was over Genoa that night and had a running fight with an Italian night-fighter, thought to be a Fiat CR 42 biplane. 4 Group made amends on 7/8 November and 15/16 November with two successful attacks on Genoa's industrial centres.

November 1942 produced even worse weather. Icing and unpredictable winds made operations even to a relatively well-defined target such as Hamburg exceptionally difficult. This was well illustrated on 9/10 November when Pathfinder marking of the huge port area proved inaccurate. As late as the raid on Mannheim (6/7 December) total cloud-cover would defeat the Pathfinders. According to Middlebrook[13], although 272 aircraft were on the Mannheim operation, German sources that night recorded the loss of one wooden building used for storing hay, 29 dead animals and no human casualties whatsoever.

It was as well that Bomber Command remained unaware of the paucity of its achievements in 1942. Most squadrons, and especially those in 4 Group, had taken heavy casualties. The chequered history of No 76 Squadron flying from Linton makes the point: 466 sorties to European targets; 183 sorties chalked up by its Middle East detachment. Total casualties for the 649 sorties were twenty-six crews lost to enemy action and a further nine in accidents. Typical of all squadrons in 4 Group, 76 had

suffered a complete turnover in Halifax bombers in that its establishment at any one time was seventeen aircraft. Yet as its squadron historian records:

> "Morale was high in the squadron and throughout the Command for, during the last few weeks of 1942, a steady increase in trained aircrews had reached the squadrons." [14]

This steady increase had been supplemented, exceptionally in 76 Squadron, by members of the Royal Norwegian Air Force. The first of these were Lieutenants Gunnar Halle, Bjorn Naess and Erik Sandberg who would captain their own Halifax bombers in later operations over the Third Reich and Italy.

The Halifax still presented difficulties: ". . . problems with engine failures would persist throughout the life of the Halifax, despite the skilled attention of those that attended them." [15] But the crews could tolerate this disadvantage provided they could have warning of the stealthy approach of the deadly German night-fighter, defend themselves and have a reasonable chance of completing their tour. TRE had produced two devices to deal with night-fighters and the radar on which they depended: Mandrel and Tinsel. Bomber Command crews had grown accustomed to use their own methods to jam the German night-fighter radar and their usual but ill-advised ploy was to turn on the 'J' (Jamming) switch on their IFF (Identification, Friend or Foe) system. Unfortunately, this also had the effect of breaking their strict radio silence and enabled a well-equipped night-fighter to track the course of the bomber stream.

Mandrel was TRE's answer to this problem. Operated from ground stations in the UK or carried in an aircraft, Mandrel 1 first saw action on 5/6 December 1942. It was jamming device transmitting on the 10 MegaHerz bands used by enemy radars and may be seen as the first stage in Bomber Command's offensive against the Luftwaffe's *Freya*, *Mammut* and *Wassermann* radars - the beginning of RCM or Radio Counter-Measures. Its weakness was that extended Mandrel use encouraged enemy night-fighters to home in on the transmissions. Stage two of the offensive was Tinsel, introduced on 2 December 1942. This was a high frequency radio weapon located inside the bomber. Once the radio-operator picked up the German controller's signals to night-fighters, he would then blot out the German broadcast by transmitting the bomber's engine noise on the same frequency via a small microphone located in an engine nacelle. Tinsel had some success but required constant modification as vibrations from the bomber's engines tended to break up the carbon elements in the microphone. Professor R.V. Jones was distinctly worried by the use of the codeword 'Tinsel'. He thought that it might give the German defences a clue to a new device being prepared to counter the German *Wurzbürg* radars and the night-fighters they controlled - the metallic strips called 'Window'.

However, the secret was well-preserved and as 1942 came to an end the two sides seemed well-matched. Bomber Command now had its Pathfinders equipped with Oboe and H2S, backed up by the Defiants of Fighter Command providing a 'Mandrel screen ' over the North Sea. As the Main Force approached the enemy coast, using Gee up to the last possible moment, so the Mandrel screen flooded the *Freya, Mammut* and *Wasserman* radars while Tinsel's engine noise swamped the German fighter controllers. Ahead of them at the close of 1942 were nearly four hundred German night-fighters, mainly Me 110s, Ju 88s and a few Dornier 217s. Most carried heavy cannon and variants of the combat-proved *Lichtenstein* radar. A new kind of war dependent upon ELINT (Electronic Intelligence) was about to begin.

★ ★ ★

At this stage it is perhaps useful to examine the main duties of the young airmen who composed the crews of Bomber Command's Halifaxes and Lancasters that flew from Yorkshire over the next three years. All were volunteers no matter where they came from for there were no conscripted men in the aircrews of Bomber Command. Both types of heavy bomber flown from Yorkshire typically carried a crew of seven and, unlike the Luftwaffe, the bomber pilot was always the captain or 'skipper' of the aircraft irrespective of whether he was a commissioned officer or an NCO. He was responsible for the lives and well-being of the other six crew members and when the moment of truth arrived, if the aircraft had been fatally hit or fire threatened an imminent explosion, he would stay at the controls until all of his crew had safely baled out.

Because of the array of gauges and the vital responsibility of calculating fuel reserves accurately, each of the four-engined bombers carried a flight-engineer. Most of the Canadian squadrons had RAF flight-engineers who, during 1942-43, converted to Halifaxes and Lancasters either at 1659 Heavy Conversion Unit (at Leeming until it moved to Topcliffe) or at 1652 HCU at Marston Moor. Flight-engineers received elementary pilot training and were familiar with all aspects of bomber tactics, including asymmetrical flight and landing on two

or three engines. They acted as reserve gunners and could take over the bomb-aimer's duties if necessary. Some pilots had the engineer to help with throttles, flaps and under-carriage during take-off and landing but most preferred to handle these controls themselves as they could react quicker in sudden emergencies. This was certainly the experience of one Flight Engineer on 25 June 1943. Sgt Ed Solman RAF had completed seventy-one flying hours by day and sixteen by night at 1659 HCU and then joined 427 RCAF Squadron at Leeming. As flight engineer on Halifax IIs piloted by W/Cdr Burnside DFC, he was in U-Uncle (DK 144) as it thundered down Leeming's runway en route for Gelsenkirchen. Suddenly the aircraft swung and Burnside fought for control. There was nothing a flight engineer could do for seconds later the undercarriage collapsed and the aircraft nosed in. All the crew survived but Halifax DK 144 was a write-off.

The bomb-aimer's major duties were, of course, restricted to the final bomb-run over the target when he took up his prone position behind the complicated bomb-sight controls in the perspex nose of the aircraft. From here he gave course corrections to the pilot, ordered bomb doors open and controlled the bomb run over the target. He announced bombs or markers gone, waited for the camera photo-flash to indicate that a target photograph had been taken and then ordered bomb-doors closed. Operating the bomb doors correctly was crucial as these large metal structures - thirty-five feet long on the Lancaster - vibrated madly in the slipstream. At other times the bomb-aimer would man any nose-guns, drop Window and give assistance to crew members as required.

Navigators had a complex and demanding task by the end of 1942. At the beginning of the war they guided their aircraft by dead reckoning and by using astro sextants to provide a fix over the ground. Now they had to be competent in interpreting a series of new radio and radar navigation aids such as Gee, the main Bomber Command navigation aid throughout the war. The navigator was responsible for working out courses that avoided the main enemy flak defences and fighter beacons and yet ensure that his aircraft arrived over the target at precisely the right moment. Much depended on knowing the correct winds at different altitudes and these were given to him by the wireless operator.

The original WOP/AGs were now wireless operator specialists in their own right, maintaining radio silence throughout a sortie but listening out all the time for the vital Group HQ messages such as broadcast winds, recall signals and important weather changes that might affect route and altitude. Wireless operators helped to dispense Window, operated Tinsel, acted as reserve air gunners and later on monitored the Fishpond radar that gave warning of the proximity of other aircraft.

The four-engined heavy bombers had two gunners in the mid-upper and rear turrets. Isolated from the rest of the crew for eight hours or more, they were responsible for spotting enemy fighters and passing evasive action instructions to the pilot. They underwent an exacting training in the Operational Training Units before transferring to a Heavy Conversion Unit. They had to have good night vision and train themselves not to lose it by gazing too long at fires on the ground or explosions in the air. As they could be jumped by a night-fighter at any time their primary duty was to carry out a constant search of the night sky. They needed quick reactions and the right mental attitude to the cold, cramp and general discomfort caused by sitting on a small pad in the rear turret or balanced on a sling in the mid-upper.

Every night that there was a Main Force raid, literally thousands of these highly motivated and highly skilled young men set out to bomb their targets and face the flak and the night-fighters flown by equally skilled and determined young Luftwaffe crews.

Chapter Fifteen

The Battle of the Ruhr
5/6 March - 24 July 1943

At 0001 hours on 1 January 1943 6 Group, Royal Canadian Air Force, became operational on its Yorkshire airfields. Air Vice-Marshal G.E. Brookes, a Canadian commanding 6 Group, set up his headquarters at Allerton, Yorkshire. Hundreds of Canadians had joined the RAF at the outbreak of the war and by the end of 1942 thousands were in Britain, serving in the RAF and in RCAF squadrons such as No 405 Squadron RCAF (Vancouver) at Topcliffe and No 408 RCAF Squadron (Goose) at Leeming. No 419 Squadron RCAF (Moose) had transferred from 1 Group and finally arrived at Middleton St George via Leeming, Topcliffe and Croft. These three squadrons, all flying Halifaxes, were the precursors of fourteen Yorkshire-based heavy bomber squadrons whose bravery, initiative and skill have had few rivals in the history of aerial warfare. Britain's awareness of its debt of gratitude to 6 Group has been sadly dulled in the second half of the twentieth century and it may surprise some to learn that the cost of operating 6 Group, apart from the pay and allowances of non-Canadian attached personnel, was paid entirely by the Canadian government out of its own taxes. An RCAF Overseas Headquarters had been based in London since 1940 and was responsible for the administrative control of all Canadian personnel overseas, not just in the UK. Moreover, in tribute to the RCAF's contribution to ultimate victory the Royal Air Force has permanently set aside the 6 Group number. It will only be used by the Royal Canadian Air Force "if the need should ever arise again."

Australians and New Zealanders were also represented in Yorkshire's expanding bomber stations during 1942 though they had not formed their own national bomber groups. Thousands of Australians flocked to serve in the Royal Air Force and in November 1941 an Australian Squadron, No. 460, had formed at Molesworth as part of 8 Group. It came to Yorkshire in January 1942 and flew its Wellingtons from Breighton as a 1 Group bomber squadron. Most crews were a mixture of RAAF and RAF personnel and their Wellingtons flew to all major targets during April-August 1942. They stood down to convert to Halifaxes in September but did not fly them operationally as No 460 Squadron was destined to move to Binbrook as a 1 Group Lancaster squadron in May 1943. No 458

Squadron RAAF had settled into Holme-on-Spalding-Moor during 1941 and flew Wellington 1s until it transferred to the Middle East in January 1942. No 466 Squadron RAAF formed at Driffield in October 1942 as part of 4 Group's Wellington force, moved to Leconfield in December but did not begin operations until January 1943.

Wellingtons still outnumbered the Halifaxes in 6 Group as late as March 1943; while 4 Group retained seventy-two Wellingtons and three Whitleys alongside its 138 Halifaxes. Interestingly, in September 1942 No 101 Squadron had transferred from their Suffolk base Stradishall to Holme with their Wellington Is. In October they began their conversion to Lancasters and the East Riding became closely acquainted with Avro's four engined bombers as they roared low over the Wolds and the Vale of York. Accidents were not uncommon even for a fully operational squadron: a diverted Lancaster had the bad luck to touch down at Holme immediately below another aircraft; Sgt Fussell's Lancaster was shot down by friendly Bofors fire near Grangetown; Sgt Hazard CGM hit the beach at Atwick in March 1943, a month after he and his crew had distinguished themselves in combat with a CR 42 over Milan, and P/O Hobday's Lancaster failed to gain sufficient height after take-off and stalled into the woods at South Cliffe within sight of the church on the hill at Holme.

With over twenty operational airfields Yorkshire was already a crowded county. But with more RAF and Commonwealth squadrons joining 4 and 6 Groups, new sites were being surveyed and developed throughout 1942-43 and the latest was at Lissett near Bridlington. It officially opened in February 1943 but it had been occasionally used as a Relief Landing Ground during the previous December/January. Bob Fewlass, whose family had a holiday home near Skipsea, watched its construction with intense interest, especially when the air firing range at Catfoss was in use.

During 1942 and 1943, whilst there was still a road along the cliff top, there was a never ending stream of lorries going to and from Whittow Gap. From the place where the old slipway had been they built a concrete road parallel to the cliffs, about forty yards from the edge, in the direction of Bridlington.

From this road operated the mobile Priestman grabs and sand and gravel from the beach (both, of course, anathema to a builder nowadays because of the salt) were loaded on to the lorries and taken to Lissett and, later on, to Carnaby for runway construction. Each lorry had a pole aft of the cab surmounted by two yellow wooden circles, presumably for identification as the coast was still under strict security guard and we were only allowed back to our bungalow a few times during 1942-4 for purposes of inspection, to see that the roof was still watertight and that the doors and windows were OK.[1]

Despite certain weaknesses of construction, the three main runways at Lissett were ready in the New Year and the Halifaxes of No 158 Squadron flew in from Rufforth.

After the creation of 8 Group as the specialist Pathfinder Force (8 January 1943) and the gradual re-equipment of his Bomber Groups with four-engined aircraft, Harris believed he was ready to start "the real offensive." Certainly, 1943 would witness air warfare on an unprecedented scale. Bomber Command fought four great battles over the Reich: the Battle of the Ruhr (March-July); the Battle of Hamburg (July-August); the Second Battle of the Ruhr (October-November); and the Battle of Berlin which began in November 1943 and lasted until March the following year. This time, Bomber Command would not be the sole force dedicated to the destruction of Nazi Germany. Flying on daylight missions were the aircraft of the United States Eighth Army Air Force. During 1942 B-17 Fortresses and B-24 Liberators had begun flying from British bases to attack targets in Occupied Europe. Then on 27 January 1943 sixty-four B-17s went to Wilhelmshaven, their first raid on a German target. It took the Germans entirely by surprise as they could not conceive that Allied bombers would make the same mistakes the Wellingtons had made in 1939 over Wilhelmshaven and try to bomb without fighter support. But the B-17s did precisely this and shot down seven of the German fighters sent to stop them. This new American threat forced the Luftwaffe to restructure its defence system and before long air battles over the Reich were going on day and night in a vast and unrelenting aerial conflict in which thousands of young men were locked in combat 20,000 feet above the earth.

Harris was anxious to unleash his bombers on German cities but found himself beset by new directives, the first of which, on 14 January, ordered him to devastate the four French towns of Lorient, Brest, La Pallice and St Nazaire. He carried out this order knowing that while he was bombing French towns and killing French civilians he would be unable to neutralise the U-boat shelters. For months the Germans had been building defensive concrete shelters so thick that they were impenetrable by British bombs of 1943 vintage and, understandably, he was furious that his long planned assault on German industry had once more been deferred. The first of eight attacks on Lorient began on 14/15 January with aircraft mainly from Yorkshire's 4 and 6 Groups. Pathfinders marked the target accurately but the bombing was scattered. One of 6 Group's Wellington Mk IIIs failed to return. It was from 426 RCAF (Thunderbird) Squadron that had formed at Dishforth in the previous October and was the first of many casualties to be borne by 6 Group. Bombing French ports had little or no effect on U-boat availability for the war that was raging in the Atlantic even though, during the last attack on Lorient (13/14 February 1943) one thousand tons of bombs fell for the first time on an enemy target, turning this unfortunate French town into a desert. Curiously, the armchair critics of Bomber Command who rail against the policies that led to the destruction of Hamburg, Berlin, Dresden and Pforzheim, and the consequent loss of *German* lives, rarely remember the sacrifice of *French* civilians during 1943-1944.

While the French raids were in progress Harris received a new directive from the Chiefs of Staff at the Casablanca Conference (21 January 1943):

> Your primary object will be the progressive destruction of the German military, industrial and economic system, and the undermining of the morale of the German people to a point where their armed resistance is fatally weakened. Accordingly in order of importance the targets should be German submarine construction yards, the aircraft industry, transportation, oil plants, other targets in war industry.

The directive went on to mention that Harris should also attack objectives 'of great importance' and among these it listed Berlin which should be bombed:

> . . . when conditions are suitable for the attainment of specially valuable results unfavourable to the morale of the enemy or favourable to Russia.

As a result of these directives, Harris was able to use the 'Casablanca criteria' to select targets such as a Ruhr industrial centre, an oil plant or the great sprawling complex of the 'Big City'. Obviously, the War Cabinet and the Chiefs of Staff would leave it to him to evaluate, in terms of weather conditions and availability of bombers, the strategic value of attacking a target at a given time. The 'given time' was usually four nights in any one week, a very high level of demand on the aircrews and aircraft during 1943.

First, the new but untried devices showered upon Bomber Command - Oboe, H2S, sky markers, ground markers and the improved bombsights first issued to Pathfinder aircraft - had to be tested in a Main Force attack. Harris chose to evaluate the new target indicators over the German capital and the raid on 16/17 January was the first since November 1941. Haze defeated the Pathfinders and the following night seventeen Halifaxes joined 170 Lancasters in another effort to hit the city centre. Once more, poor results and heavy losses (11.8%) showed that accuracy both in marking and in bombing still eluded the attackers. No 76 Squadron lost two Halifaxes that night and one of these was captained by Bjorg Naess, the first of thirteen Norwegians who would die flying with this squadron. In contrast, on 27/28 January Oboe Mosquitoes backed up by 8 Group Pathfinders enabled the Main Force Lancasters and Halifaxes to destroy several industrial centres in Düsseldorf.

Yorkshire's bombers did not take part in the first H2S trial against a major target (Hamburg 30/31 January) though a few joined the attack on Cologne on 2/3 February to attempt the co-ordination of sky/ground marking under H2S direction. That night a Pathfinder Stirling crashed in Holland and the Germans recovered an H2S set from the wreckage. They sent it to Telefunken's laboratories in Berlin, where German technicians began working on an electronic counter-measure. When 302 bombers, including eight-six Halifaxes, returned to Berlin on 1/2 March to try to concentrate markers on key targets in the city using H2S, clutter on the cathode screens ruined the operation. However, an unknown aircraft managed to hit the Telefunken works and destroy the test centre where the captured H2S set was located. It was a shortlived success. Within the hour, a Pathfinder Halifax had crashed in Holland and the Germans were delighted that yet another H2S set had fallen from the heavens. Before long they had devised *Naxos*, an airborne radar capable of detecting H2S transmissions.

In February 1943, the month before the formal opening of the Battle of the Ruhr, Bomber Command had sent its Main Force to targets in France, Germany and Italy on no less than fourteen nights. Its success rate was growing fast: the attack on Wilhelmshaven (11/12 February) was a triumph for H2S with excellent results through cloud; at the very end of the month the raid on St Nazaire resulted in the destruction of about 60% of the port. The price was high: eighty-five aircraft

had failed to return. Morale, however, had never been higher and through luck, good training and superb leadership one squadron had survived the month's operations without a single loss. This was Leonard Cheshire's 76 Squadron, whose good fortune was mentioned in the *Daily Telegraph* (9 March 1943) and underlined at Linton by a full squadron parade of officers, men and WAAFs who heard a special message of congratulations from Headquarters, Bomber Command.

The Battle of the Ruhr opened on 5/6 March 1943 with an attack on Essen by 442 aircraft, ninety-four of which were Halifaxes, and may be considered to be the first raid in what Harris termed his 'Main Offensive' against Nazi Germany. The raid had several unusual features: three of the eight Oboe Mosquitoes had to turn back, together with 53 other aircraft; it was the night that saw the 100,000th Bomber Command sortie chalked up; and aircraft attacked in distinct waves according to type, the Halifaxes leading the first wave, lower level Wellingtons and Stirlings in the second and Lancasters in the third.

Accurate navigation led the bomber stream across the North Sea, over Holland and to the turning point marked by yellow flares dropped by the heavy Pathfinders. The first of the Halifaxes turned south at this marker and began their bomb run into Essen, aiming for the red TIs dropped by the Oboe Mosquitoes. For this raid, the agreed tactics were to flood the city with incendiaries and then spread the fires with high explosive, a ploy that for once proved to be successful over Essen. Twenty-two Pathfinders maintained a constant shower of green TIs to supplement the Mosquito reds and in the space of forty minutes very serious damage was inflicted both on the main industrial centres and on 5000 or more houses. Flt Lt K Reynolds, flying a 158 Squadron Halifax from Lissett, painted a vivid picture of the Pathfinders' accuracy:

> "After the first target indicator marker was dropped Essen seemed swamped with Halifaxes. Pathfinder yellow marker was dead on time and the first red target indicator flare burst just after passing the turning point . . . . The target was blazing with incendiaries and the flashes from the HEs lighting up the long buildings. I think Krupps really got a pasting."[2]

Krupps, of course, was the primary target and that night the Main Force severely damaged fifty-six of the major workshops. Accurate bombing wiped out another thirteen - permanently. This meant that 27% of Germany's most important industrial complex was now

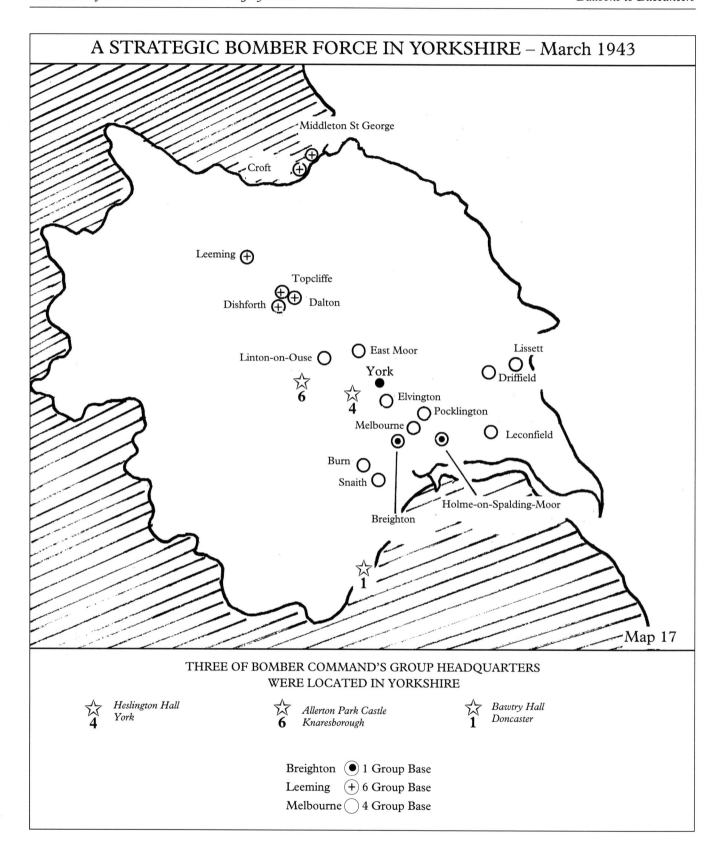

A STRATEGIC BOMBER FORCE IN YORKSHIRE – March 1943

Middleton St George

Croft

Leeming

Topcliffe

Dishforth Dalton

Linton-on-Ouse   East Moor   Lissett

York   Driffield

☆ 6   ☆ 4

Elvington

Pocklington

Melbourne   Leconfield

Burn

Snaith

Holme-on-Spalding-Moor

Breighton

☆ 1

Map 17

THREE OF BOMBER COMMAND'S GROUP HEADQUARTERS
WERE LOCATED IN YORKSHIRE

☆ 4 *Heslington Hall*
York

☆ 6 *Allerton Park Castle*
Knaresborough

☆ 1 *Bawtry Hall*
Doncaster

Breighton ⊙ 1 Group Base
Leeming ⊕ 6 Group Base
Melbourne ◯ 4 Group Base

out of action for the cost of twenty-three crews. German casualty figures vary slightly for the night's raid but if the top figure of 482 is taken as correct it means that more people were killed in Essen that night than in any previous raid on a German city, including the thousand bomber attacks. This sort of statistic underlines the fact that the four-engined bombers, now in the majority, could carry far more bombs and hit much harder than those which flew to Essen in 1942. German reaction endorsed this and Goebbels commented that Essen had suffered an "exceptionally severe raid". He was worried about how the people could react if such devastation continued, knowing that the Luftwaffe was unable to retaliate against British industrial centres in the same way:

> "Reports from the Rhineland indicate that in some cities people are gradually getting rather weak at the knees. That is understandable. For months the working population has had to go into air raid shelters night after night, and when they come out again they see part of their city going up in flames and smoke. The enervating thing about it is that we are not in a position to reply in any kind to the English. Our war in the East has lost us air supremacy in essential sections of Europe and we are completely at the mercy of the English" [3]

Hitler's response was to sanction the manufacture of reprisal weapons against the British. He was now willing to divert crucial German resources towards rocket and jet propulsion; and decided to reduce emphasis upon nuclear weapon research, a significant if then unappreciated consequence of the bomber offensive against Germany. Goebbels was far more realistic about Germany's defences and believed that though the night-fighters had won some notable successes, they were "not sufficient to compel the English to desist from their night attacks." Extra-ordinarily, in view of the damage to Essen, Goebbels was unable to persuade Hitler that an improvement in the night-fighter force was desirable. The Führer preferred not to visit scenes of mass destruction in German cities and had little technical understanding of the best way to counter the bomber stream. Accordingly, much-modified versions of proven aircraft such as the Me 110 F4 and the Ju 88C6 remained in production and little effort was made to accelerate the manufacture of new and faster designs such as the redoubtable Heinkel He 219.

Harris waited a week before returning to Essen as he had no intention of limiting Bomber Command solely to industrial targets in the 'Happy Valley' of the Ruhr. That was why he decided to bomb Nuremberg and Munich that week - to create anxiety in other German cities and to

Bobby Sage's downed Halifax.   *Yorkshire Air Museum*

dilute the Luftwaffe's defences by stretching them as far as possible. Wind blew the markers away from the city centre on the night of the the Munich raid (9/10 March) but there was a bonus in that the BMW aero engine factory was hit and put out of production for over six weeks. One of No 77 Squadron's Halifaxes from Elvington was shot down on the way home. Its pilot was W/Cdr Bobby Sage who, together with his crew, baled out over enemy-occupied territory. W/Cdr Sage might have been a successful evader but a Polish miner betrayed him to the Gestapo and he became a prisoner-of-war. [4]

After a less successful raid on Stuttgart when German decoy 'Target Indicators' managed to mislead most of the Main Force the bombers returned to Essen on 12/13 March and caused chaos and destruction inside the Krupps factory complex. The Oboe Mosquitoes marked superbly on this occasion and the fact that they were becoming indispensable was shown when their non-appearance on 26/27 March 1943 led to the failure of the raid on Duisburg. Five Oboe Mosquitoes had to abort the mission because of mechanical failure and another had the sad distinction of being the first Oboe Mosquito to be shot down. On the next night Harris dispensed with Mosquitoes and sent the Main Force to attack Berlin. Most of the 396 Lancasters, Stirling and Halifaxes missed the target entirely ; about one quarter of the bombs failed to explode; and stray bombs managed to devastate widely separated military establishments such as Tempelhof airfield and the Luftwaffe's radar warehouse at Teltow, some eleven miles away from the Pathfinders' aiming points. A slightly smaller Main Force returned to Berlin on 29/30 March. Weather conditions were bad with icing and strong, variable winds that made navigation a nightmare. 4 Group led the Main Force attack and it despatched sixty-five Halifaxes into a hailstorm that swiftly scoured the de-icing paste from aircraft leading edges and rendered many of the bombers unstable and dangerous to fly. No less than twenty-four Halifaxes had to abort the mission. Linton's No 76 Squadron sent eleven Halifaxes to Berlin and six of these aborted. Altogether, four Halifaxes failed to return that night and two of them were from 76 Squadron. Sgt Cursley needed just one more operational sortie to complete his tour when his Halifax went down. F/Lt Jack Wetherly DFC[5] was on the fifteenth operation of his second tour when his Halifax K-King with an eight man crew encountered a night-fighter over Schleswig-Holstein and crashed at Gaiushorn-Welmbutte. Jack Wetherly and all of his crew died.

Harris sent the Main Force back to Essen on 3/4 April and 30 April/1 May. When Goebbels visited the city in April he was appalled by the damage and the loss of industrial production. After his train arrived at the partially wrecked station, he found he could not drive round the city. There was rubble everywhere. In fact, some Nazi Party officials advised him to move industry out of Essen. Dispersal, they said, would mean that the British would never find their targets. Goebbels disagreed:

> "There would be no purpose in doing this, for the moment Essen is no longer an industrial centre the English will pounce upon the next city, Bochum, Dortmund or Düsseldorf."[6]

Harris was only too willing to prove him correct. City after city in the Ruhr and north-west Germany fell victim to Bomber Command in 1943: Düsseldorf, Bochum, Dortmund, Stuttgart, Cologne, Duisburg, Frankfurt, Mannheim, Remscheid, Hagen, Mulheim and, of course, constant attacks on Essen. More and more of the cleaned-up Halifax B. Mk II Series Ia and I Specials were arriving to reinforce the battle-hardened squadrons and to replace the harsh losses not just above Germany but over Italy and Occupied Europe. Uncertain weather - uncertain in that meteorological forecasts were often unreliable - remained an implacable foe; and no more so than over the icy North Sea where pitot heads often went unserviceable and in the clag of the Vale of York and the mists of the North York Moors where many a Yorkshire-based bomber met its end. Apart from the better aeroplanes, a few of the Yorkshire stations were delighted to greet 'Butch', Air Marshal Harris, who so rarely left his headquarters at High Wycombe or his house at Springfield. But he came to Melbourne in the summer of 1943 when the airfield was still unfinished and renowned as an extremely uncomfortable posting for aircrew, ground crew and WAAFs. He boosted morale at Melbourne, praised No 10 Squadron's record and emphasised its key role in the strategic bombing offensive against Germany.

So despite the icing, the flak and the fighters, the Main Force pressed on night after night. No 76 Squadron flying from Linton was in the thick of the action, destroying factories on the edge of the Kanal Hafen at Dortmund, backing up the Pathfinders at Duisburg and scoring direct hits on the Bochumer Verein steel works at Bochum. Sgt Cousins never forgot the beams at Bochum:

> "Searchlights were everywhere, unbroken walls of them. It was as light as day and the whole of the Ruhr valley seemed to be lit up by the moon and lights. Near the target there must have been fifteen large cones with between thirty and forty beams in each. The lights would wave about until they found somebody, then all the beams in the area would fasten on to that aircraft and shells would be pumped up the cone just like water spurting from a park fountain."[7]

Nor did he forget the flak and the night-fighters for his Halifax was hit by both. Flak removed an elevator and Cousins applied full boost to keep the Halifax in level flight. Then out of the night came the flash of cannon fire from a 7/NGJ 1 night-fighter. Leutnant Augenstein's Ju 88 had raked the faltering bomber and Cousins had to order everyone to bale out. Just before this happened another pilot from 7/NJG 1, Leutnant Rapp, shot down the Halifax flown by F/Sgt Bawden. Luckier than most, another pilot, Sgt Ward, managed to bank his Halifax towards an attacking Ju 88 and accurate fire from mid-upper and rear turrets forced the night-fighter to veer away.

★ ★ ★

Bomber Command's three great successes during this First Battle of the Ruhr were: the massive attack on Dortmund (23/24 May); the destruction of Wuppertal-Barmen (29/30 May), regarded as the most effective of all the Ruhr attacks; and the remarkable neutralisation of Düsseldorf (11/12 June).

Harris sent 826 aircraft to Dortmund on 23/24 May 1943 with the intention of eliminating the important Hoesch steelworks in the northern part of the city. One hundred and ninety-nine Halifaxes from the Yorkshire Squadrons - almost 10% of which failed to return - joined 343 Lancasters, 151 Wellingtons, 120 Stirlings and thirteen Mosquitoes in the biggest attack since the 'Thousand Bomber Raids' the previous year. This was a

Yorkshire's order of Battle on the eve of the first Battle of the Ruhr March 1943		
1 Group		
101 Squadron	Holme-on-Spalding Moor	Lancaster
460 Squadron RAAF	Breighton	Lancaster
(plus 8 more Squadrons across the Humber)		
4 Group		
10 Squadron	Melbourne	Halifax
51 Squadron	Snaith	Halifax
76 Squadron	Linton	Halifax
77 Squadron	Elvington	Halifax
78 Squadron	Linton	Halifax
102 Squadron	Pocklington	Halifax
158 Squadron	Lissett	Halifax
196 Squadron	Leconfield	Wellington
429 Squadron RCAF	East Moor	Wellington
431 Squadron RCAF	Burn	Wellington
466 Squadron RAAF	Leconfield	Wellington
6 Group RCAF		
405 Squadron	Topcliffe	Halifax
408 Squadron	Leeming	Halifax
419 Squadron	Middleton St George	Halifax
420 Squadron	Middleton St George	Wellington
424 Squadron	Topcliffe	Wellington
425 Squadron	Dishforth	Wellington
426 Squadron	Dishforth	Wellington
427 Squadron	Croft	Wellington
428 Squadron	Dalton	Wellington

highly sophisticated operation with clear ground marking in good weather conditions. Flak and night-fighters took a heavy toll (thirty-eight bombers or 4.6% of the raiders) but Hoesch ceased production for months and about 600 people were killed. Much of Dortmund remained derelict after the raid and Harris was able to ignore the city for the next twelve months. However, the defences were not swamped on this occasion and searchlights continued to guide the night-fighters towards the bomber stream. Radar-predicted flak was worryingly accurate and when a 431 Squadron RCAF Wellington from Burn found itself coned extraordinary events followed. The rear-gunner reported the aircraft on fire and several crew members heard the order to bale out. With the pilot gone the bomb-aimer, Sgt Sloan RAF, took command and brought off an impeccable landing at Cranwell. Awarded the Conspicuous Gallantry Medal, Sloan later became a Halifax captain with 158 Squadron at Lissett and survived the war.

The attack on Wuppertal-Barmen 29/30 May was Germany's worst experience to date. Bearing in mind the involvement of 4 and 6 Groups and the overall 4.6% loss, it merits some analysis. Located in the Wupper valley, the two towns of Barmen and Elberfeld had united into one during 1929 and were known in 1943 as Wuppertal-Barmen, now a substantial industrial city of some 360,000 people specialising in the manufacture of ball-bearings and components for the Wehrmacht and the Luftwaffe. It had survived the air war almost untouched and many thousands of munitions workers actually commuted to other Ruhr industrial centres from this reputedly 'safe' city. Harris planned his assault meticulously and, with one or two minor exceptions, his plans worked perfectly. It was to be an Oboe-directed raid governed by eleven Mosquitoes equipped with the latest 'Pink Pansies' released by barometric fuses 3000 feet above the target. Harris planned a bomber stream some 150 miles long, six miles wide and two miles deep composed of five separate bomber waves of about 130 aircraft in each. Distributed among the waves were backers-up to ensure precise timing and marking. At a point thirty-nine miles south-west of Wuppertal yellow markers would indicate where bombers had to turn on a course of 068 degrees, begin their bomb-run and then release on the red markers. As the Pathfinders knew from experience that crews tended to bomb early (there was a natural desire to leave the target as quickly as possible) they decided to allow for the expected 'creep back' by concentrating red TIs in the north-east corner of Barmen. Creep-back would then ensure that the entire target was bombed as the stream was briefed to approach from the south-west.

At 23.00 hours on 29 May 1943 6 Group's 419 Squadron at Middleton St George ran up their engines, followed by 10 Squadron at Melbourne, 102 Squadron at Pocklington and 158 Squadron's seventeen Halifaxes at Lissett. These Halifax squadrons had the furthest to go and were therefore the first to start. Altogether, 185 Halifaxes flew with 292 Lancasters, 118 Stirlings and 113 Wellingtons and by 23.30 hours the Halifax leaders had been picked up by the German *Wassermann* and *Mamut* early-warning radars. These alerted the Arnhem-Deeling fighter control system who scrambled the whole of NJG-1 into their orbiting positions in the Himmelbett Line, barely five minutes after the Lancaster, Wellington and Stirling squadrons south of the Humber had set course for Germany.

Pathfinders dropped their yellow markers by H2S exactly thirty-nine miles south-west of Wuppertal-Barmen. Mosquitoes overtook the bomber stream at 300

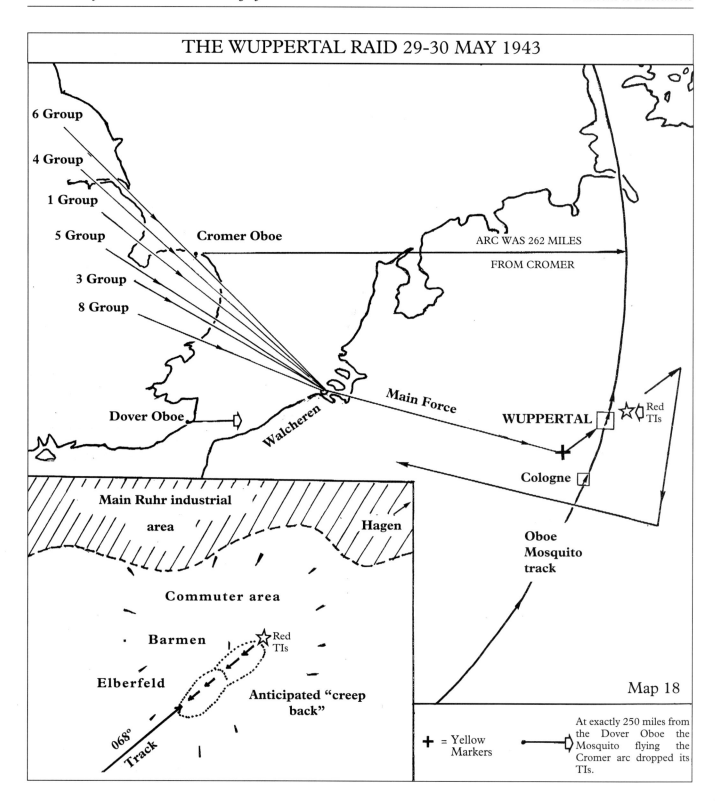

THE WUPPERTAL RAID 29-30 MAY 1943

6 Group

4 Group

1 Group

5 Group

3 Group

8 Group

Cromer Oboe

ARC WAS 262 MILES

FROM CROMER

Dover Oboe

Main Force

Walcheren

WUPPERTAL ☆ 🏳 Red TIs

Cologne

Oboe Mosquito track

Main Ruhr industrial area

Hagen

Commuter area

Barmen

☆ Red TIs

Elberfeld

Anticipated "creep back"

068° Track

Map 18

✚ = Yellow Markers

● ——🏳 At exactly 250 miles from the Dover Oboe the Mosquito flying the Cromer arc dropped its TIs.

knots and turned into the target with their red markers. Exactly 250 miles from the Oboe transmitter at Dover, the Oboe signal instructed the Mosquitoes to drop the TIs. They were not precisely timed but they were perfectly located. This enabled the Main Force to thunder on at heights between 12 and 18000 feet and drop a bombload on Wuppertal every six seconds. Their incendiaries and High Capacity bombs swamped the defenders firing mainly light flak guns that could barely reach the Stirlings, let alone the high-flying bombers. For the Germans, fire-fighting was almost impossible once a fire-storm caught hold on Barmen, causing firemen to suffocate and buildings to explode. Almost four hours passed before emergency fire-crews could get in from nearby Bochum and other towns. By then over 700 acres were devastated - greater than London lost in the entire blitz - and five of the 'big six'' factories were completely gutted. Fire proved the main killer and current estimates suggest that 3,400 people died in the disaster at Wuppertal. Bomber Command lost thirty-three aircraft: ten Halifaxes, eight Stirlings, eight Wellingtons and seven Lancasters. Pathfinders also suffered heavily. For example, four of No 35 Squadron's Halifaxes failed to return that night. Between them, 4 and 6 Groups lost six Halifaxes, 158 Squadron at Lissett losing two of its big bombers after a run of good luck. On balance, Middlebrook regards the Wuppertal raid as "the outstanding success of the Battle of the Ruhr". [8] Even so, Harris sent the Main Force back to this unhappy town on 24/25 June. It cost him thirty-four bombers. 1800 Germans died and 2400 were wounded. By then Elberfeld, in a phrase much used by Hitler back in 1939-40, "had ceased to exist."

On 11/12 June 1943 Harris launched another massive Oboe-controlled raid, this time against Düsseldorf. Two hundred and two Halifaxes, more than any before, joined the 326 Lancasters, 143 Wellingtons, ninety-nine Stirlings and thirteen Oboe Mosquitoes, a total of 783 aircraft. One Oboe Mosquito accidentally released its TIs fourteen miles from Düsseldorf and these clearly misled part of the Main Force. Even so, the majority bombed on target. With over 8000 fires to combat, the emergency services could not endure the deadly accurate high explosive attacks. 140,000 people had nowhere to sleep after this raid and very few of them had anywhere to work next morning as forty-two factories shut down for months and almost as many more could only offer part-time work. Several weeks elapsed before the local services were

properly adminstered as the bombers had destroyed Düsseldorf's Nazi Party headquarters. Casualties on both sides were severe: 1292 Germans killed; thirty-eight Bomber Command aircraft (4.9%) failed to return. There are no entries in Goebbel's diary for June 1943 though he has some illuminating sentences towards the end of May:

> "The English are giving sensational publicity to their successes in the air. They exaggerate a lot but unfortunately much of what they say is true. . . The English wrested air supremacy from us not only as a result of tremendous energy on the part of the RAF and the British aircraft industry but also thanks to certain unfortunate circumstances and our own negligence . . ."[9]

This first Battle of the Ruhr is regarded as a success for the British bomber offensive. If one follows the accepted dating for the battle (5/6 March to 24 July), when 23,401 night sorties against Germany took place, exactly 1000 bombers were lost - an overall loss rate of 4.3%. Over 57,000 tons of bombs were dropped and enormous damage was caused to the productive capacity of Nazi Germany, damage that had a marked effect on the ability of the Third Reich to support its huge battle front against Russia in the east. During these harrowing five months Harris had never lost the trust and affection of the young crews whose heroism had sustained a remarkable and successful bombing offensive against the most heavily defended industrial area in the world. The dry, distant quality of his leadership continued to inspire as young men constantly came forward to join his Command. Britain's Air Training Corps guaranteed tens of thousands of youthful volunteers, supplemented by the legions who came from the Commonwealth. The occasional encounter and the earthy nature of his personal messages - few and far between - may sound banal today but they fired the young men of 1943. When they went to Berlin he told them,

> "Tonight you are going to light a fire in the belly of the enemy"

and after their first attack on Essen he promised they would soon be back,

> "giving it a second barrel without pause."

They did not hesitate to take part in the second great battle against German industry: Operation Gomorrah, the Battle of Hamburg, July-August 1943.

Chapter Sixteen

From Hamburg to Peenemünde
July - August 1943

As the Battle of the Ruhr drew to a close, Sir Arthur Harris was planning his next move. Confident that his new-found target accuracy could now be concentrated with great effect upon a readily identifiable city, he determined to use the might of Bomber Command to wipe out Hamburg, Germany's greatest port. On 27 May 1943 he sent a *Most Secret Operational Order* to six of his Group commanders. This described his intention "to destroy Hamburg", next to Berlin the biggest city in Germany. He considered that the assault merited the status of 'The Battle of Hamburg' and victory in this contest between air power and a great industrial port would require a series of raids not just by Bomber Command but by the American heavy bombers assembling in England. Code-name for the battle was *Operation Gomorrah*, scheduled for the end of July and beginning of August 1943. The attack fitted in neatly with *Pointblank* (10 June 1943), the latest directive issued by the Combined Chiefs of Staff. *Pointblank* listed twenty-two major targets, of which Hamburg was one, that were associated with aircraft production, the manufacture of ball-bearings and the construction of U-boats.

The first raid would have two features that were of the utmost importance to the whole of this battle and to future Bomber Command Operations over Europe. First, the creep-back technique so effectively used at Barmen-Wuppertal would be built into the crucial location of the Aiming Points. Pathfinders were instructed to drop their TIs in the northern sector of the city so that the "fringe merchants" who tended to drop their bombs just before reaching the Aiming Point would in fact unload directly on the target. The second innovation that undoubtedly saved the lives of many aircrew in this and later operations was the use of 'Window'.

Window was a simple device designed to fool the Luftwaffe's radar defences. Metal strips measuring 25 x 5 cm would be dropped by the bombers once they were within range of enemy night-fighters. Because it was cut to the frequency length used by German radar, each strip floating to earth produced a blip on a Würzburg screen. In turn the blip gave the operator the impression he was tracking a British bomber. But as the Main Force would be dropping thousands of these strips a German night-fighter flying through a cloud of Window would find its Lichtenstein screen filled with the image of hundreds of bombers approaching at incredibly high closing speeds. Therefore Window, in conjunction with Mandrel, Tinsel and the new Monica and Boozer radars[1], would confuse the German ground controllers, mislead the Freya operators and compel the Lichtenstein-equipped night-fighters to chase after illusory bombers. Of course, it was not a total answer to the existing night-fighter threat. Major Herrman had already demonstrated during the Battle of the Ruhr the effectiveness of single-engined night-fighters patrolling high above a city picking off enemy bombers silhouetted against the fires, indicators and searchlights from below. These *Wilde Sau*, Wild Boar fighters, were independent of both radar and the twin-engined night-fighters and so presented a constant threat.

Window was not a new idea. Its ability to distort radar images had been known to British and German scientists (who called it *Düppel*) since 1940 when the idea had surfaced in Britain. However, the War Cabinet banned its use in case the Germans copied the idea and wrecked the Chain Home radar system; and as the Germans felt precisely the same way about *Düppel* they had not used it either. Sir Arthur Harris was well acquainted with Window and constantly sought permission to make use of it on operations, stating it was criminal not to use a device calculated to save the lives of hundreds of aircrew. Eventually Churchill gave approval for its use in Operation Gomorrah, a bombing campaign in which he showed special interest.

At squadron level, Intelligence Officers were required to read a standard explanation of the use of Window at briefings and to tell the crews that its careful use would confuse the German defences:

> ". . . . you should have a good chance of getting through unscathed while their attention is being wasted on packets of Window."

To achieve this desirable situation, crews had to understand that "the benefit of Window is a communal one." They had to fly accurately in the bomber stream to take advantage of Window dropped not just by themselves but by all the crews on the way to the target and on the way home as well. Such was the new device awaiting Germany's early warning and defence radar controlling the flak and the night-fighter boxes of the Kammhuber Line.

Saturday 24 July was a glorious summer day in Germany and the short hot night to come indicated that Bomber Command would probably choose a target in the Ruhr rather than risk a costly overland flight to somewhere such as Berlin. There were early hints of intense radio and air activity over Yorkshire, Lincolnshire and East Anglia and the Cuxhaven Freya functioning on top of tall towers was the first to report that a bomber stream was tracking across the North Sea on a course parallel to the German coastline. It could be Lubeck again or even Rostock. Luftwaffe Fighter Control suspected a sudden dog-leg towards Bremen and the five Air Division Command and Control Staffs in their bomb-proof *'Kammhuber Kinemas'* readied themselves to transmit the height and course of the bomber stream and vector their night-fighters into position.

Within the *Kammhuber Kinemas* the *Helferinnen* - the Luftwaffe's WAAFs - sat in banked rows of seats and tracked both bombers and night-fighters with projectors that illuminated a giant frosted glass screen showing a map of Germany overlaid with a grid system. As soon as a Würzburg picked up a bomber so a *Helferin* would locate it on the giant screen. This would be interpreted by all the controllers sitting in the stalls - the flak commanders, met. officers, radar and night-fighter experts - and then it would be up to the Luftwaffe Divisional Commander to scramble his night-fighters and instruct them to orbit their beacons or fly direct to the correct Freya grid reference. Each night-fighter had a transceiver on board and when the Würzburg interrogated this a red neon sign illuminated in the pilot's cockpit. Under radar control, the pilot and his radar operator had voice contact with the ground controllers and could react quickly to instructions. It was a systematic and well-tried procedure and that night it appeared that the bomber stream had gone to some pains to give the defences plenty of warning and was therefore in line for a hot reception.

Suddenly all the blips on the radar seemed to stand still. Flashes of light zig-zagged across the screens in front of amazed controllers. No data was being displayed; there was no way that they could direct their night-fighters. Window was cascading down while Bomber Command's Mandrel aircraft swamped the early warning radar transmissions. German fighter crews on patrol found themselves flying through a snowstorm of shiny paper while their Lichtenstein sets showed traces of targets in all directions. In the Kammhuber Kinemas and the cockpits of Me 110 and Ju 88 nightfighters German defenders who were skilled in voice control techniques and electronic wizardry found themselves helpless. It was at that precise moment that the Illuminators arrived and showered the city with their target indicators. The Battle of Hamburg had begun.

★ ★ ★

The two Yorkshire Groups had left the Yorkshire coast at Hornsea in perfect flying conditions, though fog in southern England prevented most of the Mosquito intruders from joining the battle. One that did fly to Germany was a 25 Squadron Mosquito from Church Fenton and this shot down an unsuspecting Ju 88 just before the Main Force crossed the German coast. However, a cruising night-fighter - possibly a Dornier 217 - destroyed a 76 Squadron Halifax; while a few minutes later a 51 Squadron Halifax flown by a crew on their first 'op' came under attack from a Do 217. A watchful rear-gunner gave it a long burst and the Dornier went down in flames. [2] Over the target the Main Force encountered little opposition from a city reputedly one of the most heavily defended in the Third Reich. The Halifaxes and Wellingtons from the Yorkshire Squadrons were in the second, fourth and fifth waves and their devastating bombloads created immense destruction and contributed to the deaths of 1,500 Germans. Bereft of radar guidance, searchlight beams meandered aimlessly across the sky; while flak gunners reverted to the old box-barrages to keep the bombers as high as possible. Bomber Command's crews were mightily impressed by the effect of Window. One Canadian flying in a 429 Squadron Wellington noted that:

> "the crew hoped to do as many trips as possible in the next few weeks so they would finish their tour before the enemy found a solution." [3]

All the Canadian aircraft returned safely but 4 Group had lost four Halifaxes, one each from 51 Squadron at Snaith, 76 at Holme, 102 at Pocklington and 158 at Lissett. Next day (25 July 1943) the First Bomb Wing of the 8th USAAF dropped 1396 tons of bombs on Hamburg; and on the following day it returned to deliver a similar attack. Harris had sent his Main Force to Essen on the night of 25/26 July in order to exploit the surprise factor of Window. He had hoped to deliver a second blow to Hamburg but a reconnaissance Mosquito came back early with the news that the city was blanketed by smoke. So he decided to defer a second *Goodwood* (maximum effort) on Hamburg and go to Essen instead. As usual, the aim was to neutralise the Krupps armament works and the

705 aircraft despatched achieved a precision night raid that "inflicted more damage on Essen than all the previous attacks put together." [4][10] According to Goebbels:

"the last raid on Essen caused complete stoppage of production in the Krupp Works. Speer is much concerned and worried." [5]

It certainly worried Dr. Gustav Krupp who arrived at his office the following morning, saw the extent of the devastation and collapsed. His subsequent illness and long convalescence removed him as an active director of Krupp's policies. [6]

There was no follow-up raid on Hamburg on 26/27 July as Harris rested his squadrons after their two nights of maximum effort. [7] However, he did keep Hamburg's population awake by sending six Mosquitoes to the beleagured port. In the morning a reconnaissance Mosquito had another look at Hamburg and reported that there was still a lot of haze, signifying that the planned Newhaven marking would not be satisfactory. At the last moment it was decided to mark by Parramatta. This was carried out by Blind Markers and all the TIs were dropped by H2S. Because of the wind they fell a mile or so east of the Aiming Point but this error still placed the yellow markers well within the city at 0055 hrs on 28 July. For the next fifty-five minutes the Main Force of 735 bombers droned over Hamburg dropping over four thousand tons of High Capacity explosive bombs and incendiaries. [8] By 0130 hours it was obvious to the crews in the fourth and fifth waves as they approached the target that the smoke and the fire boiling 20,000 feet below were of an exceptional ferocity. They were watching the beginning of a firestorm that would not reach its terrifying climax until the last of the bombers were on the way home.

Below the bombers was a sight that few aircrew would ever forget. After Sgt W.G. Hart had completed his bomb run in a 51 Squadron Halifax he felt he was looking down on an "active volcano" and that his own contribution was "like putting another shovelful of coal on the furnace." A Breighton airman, F/Lt Forsdike, felt "fascinated but aghast, satisfied yet horrified" by what he saw. F/Sgt Parry, in a Halifax from Holme-on-Spalding Moor, had seen plenty of "firework displays" over other targets but Hamburg, he said, "was the daddy of them all." F/O Lennard, high above the target in a Lissett Halifax, said the impression of the fires at Hamburg "will be remembered all my life."

This was how some of the crews felt during the second raid on Hamburg. They were convinced they had, in the words of Elvington-based Sgt Burger, "pulled off some-

Order of Battle: The Yorkshire Groups Battle of Hamburg 1943					
4 Group AVM Carr Heslington Hall, York			**6 Group** AVM Brookes Allerton Park Castle, Knaresborough		
Squadron	*Airfield*	*Type*	*Squadron*	*Airfield*	*Type*
10	Melbourne	Halifax	408	Leeming	Halifax
51	Snaith	Halifax	419	Middleton St George	Halifax
76	Holme-upon-Spalding Moor	Halifax	427	Leeming	Halifax
77	Elvington	Halifax	428	Middleton	Halifax
78	Breighton	Halifax	429	East Moor	Halifax
102	Pocklington	Halifax	432	Skipton-on-Swale	Wellington
158	Lissett	Halifax			
466 RAAF	Leconfield	Wellington	Non-operational		
			426	Linton-on-Ouse	both converting to Halifaxes
			431	Tholthorpe	
			434	Tholthorpe	Halifax
Fighter Command					
Squadron	*Airfield*	*Type*			
25	Church Fenton	Mosquito			

thing special . . . . that this was a bit more than a run-of-the mill affair." What they did not know was that they had unintentionally created a firestorm, the product of the concentrated bombing and the extraordinary meteorological conditions prevailing in the Hamburg area on that fateful night. As Musgrove emphasises in his *Operation Gomorrah*, "the weather conditions over the city were primed to exaggerate the effects of bombing beyond all belief." [9]

In simple terms, a mass of warm air hung over Hamburg. Much colder air surrounded it, forming a meteorological 'chimney'. Once incendiary bombs fell on the city, the temperature of the warm air rose by 5° or 6°F and travelled up the 'chimney', sucking cold air into its base. As the intensity of the Hamburg fires became greater, so did the speed of the ground level winds being forced into the 'chimney' until it created a firestorm raging at ground level, tearing through buildings and consuming the oxygen in cellars and air raid shelters. *Die Katastrophe*, as the Germans termed that dreadful night, was atmospheric. Estimates of deaths were very approximate, as so many people had been reduced to cinders. Thousands died of carbon monoxide poisoning and total casualties exceeded 40,000 dead and a slightly smaller number injured. It was some three hours later, when the firestorm ended, that the first of 1.2 million survivors abandoned their city centre. They called it the 'Dead Zone'.

Above them flew the German night-fighter pilots, themselves hardly daring to believe their eyes. Wilhelm Johnen was one such pilot, fruitlessly chasing the Window blips on his Lichtenstein screen. Later on he wrote about the suffering that had taken place thousands of feet below his aeroplane:

> The raging fires in a high wind had caused terrific damage and the grievous loss of human life out-stripped any previous raids . . . The fires spread unhindered causing fiery storms which reached heats of 1000° and speeds approaching gale force . . . The fiery winds tore the roofs from houses, uprooted large trees and flung them into the air like blazing torches. The inhabitants took refuge in air raid shelters in which they were later burned to death or suffocated.
>
> The devastating raid on Hamburg had the effect of a red light on all German cities and on the whole German people. Everyone felt it was now high time to capitulate before further damage was done. But the High Command insisted that 'total war' should proceed . . . [10]

Of course, the Bomber Command crews returning to Britain had no knowledge of the extent and nature of the destruction they had helped to cause in Hamburg. All were anxious to return to their bases and none more so than the crew of F/Sgt Elder's Halifax struggling to reach Holme-on-Spalding Moor. It seems that it was the policy of 76 Squadron to require the mid-upper gunner to push the bundles of Window through the flare chute. Consequently, Sgt Smith was not in position when the Halifax came under fire from two night-fighters. Elder was already flying on three engines and control became even more difficult when the rear-gunner called 'Corkscrew to port!' Smith was killed instantly and flight-engineer Berry took his place in the turret. Simultaneously, the intercom became unserviceable and Elder noticed the 'call-light' blinking on his instrument panel.[11] After another bout of evasive action and with a fire blazing in the bomb-bay, Elder finally restored the battered bomber to level flight. Berry fended off the two night-fighters with a prodigious expenditure of .303 ammunition and then climbed down to put out the fire in the bomb bay. Eventually,

the Halifax reached the coast of East Anglia and Elder made a successful wheels-up landing on the runway at Shipdham, home of 'The Flying Eightballs', the B-24 Liberators of the US 44th Heavy Bombardment Group.

Eleven Lancasters, four Halifaxes, a Wellington and a Stirling were lost on the night of the firestorm - 2.2% of the Main Force. Yorkshire's losses totalled five of these: 102 Squadron at Pocklington lost two Halifaxes; F/Sgt Elder's Halifax had crashed-landed at Shipdham; Canada's 6 Group lost a 408 (Goose) Squadron Halifax from Leeming and a 429 (Bison) Wellington from East Moor.

Harris regarded these losses as acceptable, expressed satisfaction at the results so far achieved and ordered two more major attacks, on 29/30 July and 2/3 August. The third Bomber Command attack, on 29/30 July, was as intense as that of the previous raid though, with different meteorological conditions prevailing, the incendiaries did not create a firestorm effect.

Half-way through the Battle of Hamburg, Harris gave his crews a brief rest and then assembled 777 bombers for the third attack on the smoke-covered city. Most of the aircraft were airborne by 2200 hours but before long forty-five of them had turned back because of difficulties with instruments and controls. One of the Yorkshire Halifaxes from 78 Squadron dived out of control into the sea even before the first of the German night-fighters engaged the bomber stream. Another eight, together with a 432 Squadron Wellington from Skipton-on-Swale, were lost to the flak and the night-fighters whose new *Wilde Sau* and *Zahme Sau* 'running commentary' tactics were clearly paying dividends. Intruder Mosquitoes did their best to attack the night-fighter airfields. F/Lt Cooke had taken off from 25 Squadron's base at Church Fenton only to have engine trouble over the North Sea. He turned back but was never heard of again. In Hamburg, the damage was again on a vast scale with most bombs falling in the Barmbek area of the city. Bombloads were roughly the same as those carried on the night of *Die Katastrophe* but because meteorological conditions were not the same there was no firestorm during the third raid. Submarine research and design factories plus important mechanical engineering plants were blasted with high explosives and then set on fire with incendiaries and much damage was done to machinery *inside* the factories. War production in these areas never fully recovered for rest of the war. [12]

The battle was by no means over. Bad weather conditions forced Harris to cancel the fourth raid projected for 30/31 July. His alternative was to send a relatively modest 273 aircraft to bomb the small industrial town of Remscheid. Most historians see this raid as "the true end of the battle of the Ruhr" [13] and certainly it could hardly have been more devastating. Marked by Oboe, the bombing was some of the most accurate to date. Approximately 83% of Remscheid was left a mass of rubble. Most of the factories were hit and full production was never regained. Fifteen Bomber Command aircraft failed to return from a town where 1,120 Germans died and 6,700 were injured. The 'red light' that Johnen had mentioned was indeed shining on German towns.

Harris insisted on a fourth attack on Hamburg, even though a reconnaissance Mosquito warned that the dreaded cumulus-nimbus clouds might reach 30,000 feet with the risk of thunderstorms. Briefing officers discovered that crews were not readily convinced that there was anything left to bomb in Hamburg and meteorological officers were unwilling to say precisely where the thunderstorms might be. Airfields in Yorkshire and Lincolnshire were overcast with a very low cloud-base and constant rain. Most crews expected a recall and were very surprised to be told that the raid would go ahead as planned. At Middleton St George the crews of 428 RCAF Ghost Squadron were relieved to hear that if the weather became too severe they were to drop their bombs and return to base. All the Halifaxes and Wellingtons from 4 and 6 Groups took off without incident and headed for the Main Force assembly point west of Heligoland. The German running commentary had kept up a precise description of the Main Force speed, height and direction and *Zahme Sau* fighters were swarming into the area.

One 10 Squadron Halifax from Melbourne forced a Ju 88 to break off its attack but for the rest there was a very real risk that the night-fighters would pounce on the Main Force before it reached its target. Ahead of them the crews could see thunderstorms streaking the sky with flashes that, at first glance, looked like heavy flak. No pilot likes to fly near the thunderhead of a black cumulus-nimbus where lighting strikes are a constant danger and a sudden upsurge of air can turn an aircraft on its back, twisting it into a spiral dive. The events that followed, known in Bomber Command as "the night of the storm", may be exemplified by the experiences of three aircrew flying from Yorkshire.

Sgt Burger was in a Halifax from Elvington, trying hard to reach a flight level of 20,000 feet.

"The poor old Halifax was now really struggling and, very soon, the whole airframe seemed to be shuddering and everything started to rattle. At around 15,000 feet, the gallant aircraft gave up the ghost and just would not go any higher."

A layer of ice began to alter the wing and elevator surfaces and

"the Hally decided it didn't much like the situation and so it started to come down again rather too quickly . . ." [14]

As in the case of so many other aircraft, the bombs had to be jettisoned before the Halifax returned to straight and level flight. Isolated tail-gunners had an especially unhappy time. Sgt Atkinson, 'tail-end Charlie' in a Holme-on-Spalding Halifax watched the sparks arc across his four Browning machine guns and vowed that "nothing on God's earth would have got me to touch those guns !" [15]

Storm conditions were so bad that the night-fighters found it hard to intercept the straggling bombers. Sgt Troake had the bad luck to encounter no less than three Ju 88s flying parallel on his port beam. Two banked towards him in an attack but as they moved in and Troake began his corkscrew a lightning flash destroyed everyone's night vision. A few minutes later Troake found himself alone - a very lucky escape. [16]

Less than four hundred bombers managed to reach Hamburg or its outskirts that night; the rest bombed other targets of opportunity or simply jettisoned their loads. The most badly damaged target was the little town of Elmshorn where lightning set fire to houses and the flames attracted the Main Force bombers. Half the town was destroyed that night by bombs intended for Hamburg where, at best, the bombing was scattered. There were few casualties and the damage inflicted did not have any significant effect upon the city's war production. The raid itself lasted barely an hour. Tail-winds meant that the first aircraft arrived over the target area shortly before zero hour and the last to bomb was an RAAF Wellington from Leconfield that unloaded its incendiaries at 1255 hours.

The return flight was itself an ordeal as so many aircraft had mechanical damage caused by the storm and by enemy action. One RCAF crew, flying a Halifax from 427 Squadron's base at Leeming, had very real doubts about making it home. P/O 'Van' Vandekerckhove had heavy icing and an unserviceable constant speed unit on his starboard outer engine. Over the Kiel Canal the Halifax was barely at 4000 feet and the crew faced an uncertain flight aross the North Sea. Was this the best place to bale out? With no night-fighter to harass them, they were able to discuss the problem and decided to try for Leeming. They made it and 427 Squadron's Halifaxes all survived 'the night of the storm'. Sadly, Holme and

Snaith both lost a Halifax to fighter attack; Middleton St. George lost a 419 Squadron Halifax to icing and then two of 428 Squadron's Halifaxes, due to a combination of bad weather and enemy action. Just one of 6 Group's Wellingtons failed to return, a 432 Squadron aircraft flying from Skipton-on-Swale.

For the time being, the Battle of Hamburg had ended. The sheer weight of bombardment had been unprecedented: 4,243 tons of high explosives and 4,101 tons of incendiaries had wrecked the second biggest city in Germany where the effects of the Anglo-American attacks were to be felt for the remainder of the war. Despite the fact that Hamburg was given a year to recover - a tactical error on the part of Harris - production never again reached 90% of the pre-July 1943 figures. Approximately 45,000 people had been killed and over a quarter of the surviving population never returned to the city. Many of the gutted industrial centres were simply abandoned. Admittedly, the great submarine yards remained in being but their role changed drastically. Blohm & Voss and Deutsche Wreft, the biggest of the U-boat constructors, could no longer keep up with German losses in the Battle of the Atlantic where the new Allied corvettes and their lethal depth-charge systems, coupled with increased maritime air cover, sounded the death-knell of the previously successful German 'wolf-packs'. Speer's answer was to disperse industry wherever possible but the administrative and transportation problems created by this policy led to a production slow-down in prefabricated submarines and the new U-boat designs were slow to come off the slipways. Hamburg became an assembly plant where, *after* August 1943, it took twice as long to build a U-boat than it had done *before* July 1943.

Bomber Command's losses during the Battle of Hamburg had been relatively low: eighty-seven aircraft (2.8%) shot down by German defences that had made a rapid recovery from the ravages of Window after the first raid. From Yorkshire, 4 Group's Halifaxes and Wellingtons had carried out 656 sorties (more than any other group) for the loss of eighteen aircraft; Canada's 6 Group had despatched 306 aircraft for the loss of eight.

Should Harris and the Americans have repeated without pause this mode of attack, a sequence of heavy night and day raids, on other German cities within range of Oboe or with geographical features easy to detect by H2S? In Britain, there were many who thought they should; in Germany there were many who feared they would. And should the Allies not have taken some

political action at this stage of the war? Certainly, Air Vice-Marshal Bennett of the Pathfinders believed so:

"I tried to convey to the C.-in-C.what I felt about the staggering success of this raid and what it must be doing to the German people and the German High Command . . . . if some appropriate political action had been taken at that time, peace feelers might very well have started to emanate from Germany . . . . Unhappily, nobody seemed to realise that a great victory had been won, and certainly nobody realised its effect on the German people at that time."[17]

There is no doubt that the Nazi leadership believed that the Allies might follow up the Battle of Hamburg with a military operation in northern Germany. That was why substantial numbers of SS patrolled the Hamburg region to stifle expressions of war-weariness among the survivors; and why Wehrmacht units remained on stand-by against a possible invasion for several weeks after the fourth Bomber Command raid. However, the Allied political leadership had no intention of allowing Germany to sue for peace. Similarly, there was no intention of invading German-occupied Europe before the Allies had won air superiority. For the Casablanca Conference of January 1943 had done far more than advocate the heaviest possible air attacks on German towns and cities. It was at this conference that President Roosevelt stated he would accept nothing else but unconditional surrender from both Germany and Japan and that he would make no deals with the enemy. Churchill, it must be said, was surprised when he first heard the words 'unconditional surrender' from the President's lips; so were the Chiefs of Staff who quickly appreciated that the enemy now had no alternative but to fight on. 'Total war !' was the Nazi cry thereafter, constantly demanded by Hitler, Goebbels and the Nazi propaganda machine. Predictably, when the German people were asked whether they supported total war they responded with a mighty 'Ja !' The blinding realisation by the armed forces and the civilian population that they had no hope now of suing for peace terms acted as a prop to national unity, so recently undermined by reaction to the Hamburg firestorm. To that extent, therefore, it was an Allied political decision rather than reaction to their horrifying experiences in the firestorm that persuaded the German people to fight on with even greater determination and intensity. As for the Allies, 'total war' in the air meant that the pitiless attacks on enemy towns and cities would continue; while the Germans placed their hopes on a new form of bombardment, unmanned V-1 and V-2 reprisal weapons.

During the fortnight following 'the night of the storm', Yorkshire's squadrons took part in three major raids on Mannheim, Nuremberg and Milan. These raids, marked by accurate bombing and relatively few aircraft losses were undertaken entirely by four-engined aircraft now that the sturdy Wellington had been taken out of most Main Force operations. [18] In Yorkshire, its replacement was the Lancaster II, built by Armstrong-Whitworth and powered by four Bristol Hercules engines. Three hundred Lancaster IIs entered service and the reason for their radial engines was the fear of a possible shortage of in-line Merlins. Crews were grateful for the extra power from the Hercules on take-off but discovered that both their best cruising speed and operational ceiling were inferior to the performance of the in-line Lancaster. In Yorkshire 426 (Thunderbird) Squadron RCAF was the first to convert to the Lancaster II and its Linton crews were soon to be blooded in Bomber Command's most remarkable Main Force precision attack - the raid on the Peenemünde rocket research station during 17/18 August 1943.

* * *

Frustrated by the limitations imposed by the 1919 Treaty of Versailles, especially in the matter of long-range guns, the German Army was quick to spot the offensive possibilities of the rockets being built by keen amateurs. Many of these pioneer scientists dreamed of space exploration but the German Army, in the person of Reichswehr Captain Walter Dornberger, invited the most brilliant of these amateurs to work at a newly-established Army Test Centre at Kummersdorf-West. This was where Werner von Braun, for example, came to work on the first experimental German rocket known as the Aggregat 1 or A-1 in 1933, the year in which Adolf Hitler came to power. The A-1 never flew, but two examples of the A-2 successfully lifted off to a height of about 8000 feet in 1934. Two years later the German Air Ministry and the new Army Ordnance Board bought part of the peninsula of Peenemünde and its two tiny off-shore islands Ruden and Greifswalder Oie.

By the beginning of 1943 Peenemünde was the biggest rocket research centre in the world with work well advanced on at least three secret weapons: the A-4 supersonic missile, the Fieseler Fi 103 flying bomb and the EMW Wasserfall anti-aircraft 'flak rocket'. Still in the discussion stage was the fantastic 'V-3' project, the plan to construct batteries of guns with barrels 416 feet in length for shelling London. Intelligence reports frequently mentioned German rocket research but the Allied political leadership attached little credibility to these. Perceptive young scientists such as Scientific Intelligence Officer Dr. R.V. Jones who had earlier discovered the threat posed by the giant Würzburg sites, now warned of the dangers of unmanned missiles falling on London and elsewhere, emphasising that there was no known defence against a weapon capable of causing damage and casualties on a scale greater than one of Bomber Command's Main Force raids.

In April 1943, after much discussion, the British government appointed Duncan Sandys MP to investigate all the evidence concerning German long-range rockets. In his *The Mare's Nest* David Irving gives an exciting account of the many intelligence sources that came to Britain's help at this crucial time. This new material led Duncan Sandys to conclude that Peenemünde was indeed a major threat to Britain's security at home; and after the sharp eyes of a WAAF photographic interpreter, Constance Babington Smith, had detected the futuristic outline of an Me 163 rocket fighter, a new threat emerged to the bomber stream over Germany. A meeting of the War Cabinet on 27 June 1943 decided that Bomber Command should attack Peenemünde.

Bomber Command's tactics for this raid, code-name *Hydra,* were unique. First, it was to be a precision attack in *moonlight conditions* by 596 aircraft with three prime objectives: to destroy the experimental station; to wipe out the factory sites; and to kill the German scientific and technical experts who would probably be in their sleeping quarters when the raid took place. Harris emphasised the need for total destruction and called for maximum effort from all the Halifax, Lancaster and Stirling squadrons. In Yorkshire, 4 Group's 145 Halifaxes were in the first wave and had the task of attacking the living and sleeping quarters; 6 Group's Halifaxes and Lancaster IIs were in the third wave with orders to destroy the experimental works and 'incapacitate' as many of the German rocket experts as possible. There was to be no visual bombing. All bombardiers would drop their loads on ground markers . The approach would be from the north, in a straight line from the island of Ruden (it would be marked by a new target indicator called a Red Spot Fire) at a height of 8000 feet, on a precisely calculated 'time and distance' bearing. Most aircraft carried high explosive bombs. For example, only 25% of the Yorkshire Halifax squadrons carried incendiaries; the rest had loads made up of heavy high capacity bombs. There were two other unusual features: a 'master of ceremonies' or 'master bomber' would control the forty minute raid throughout; and Mosquitoes would carry out a 'spoof raid' on Berlin

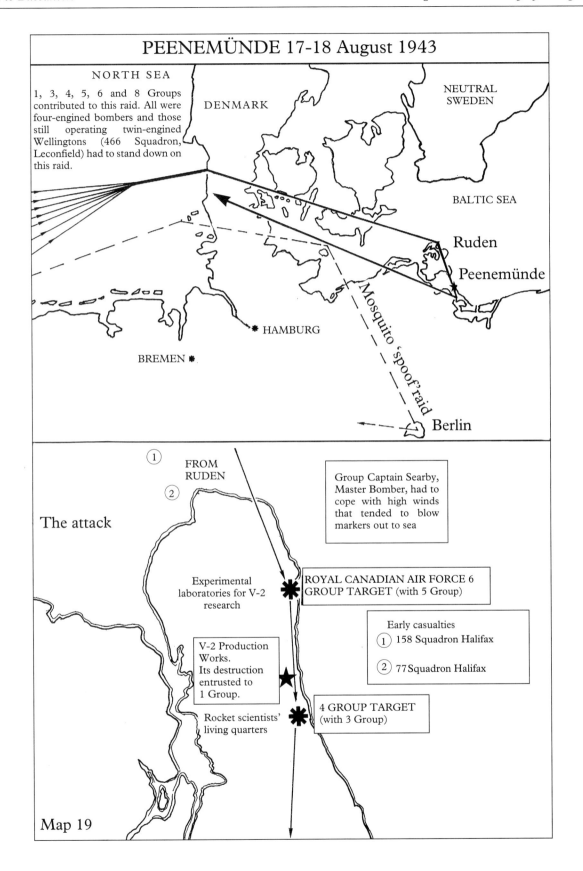

PEENEMÜNDE 17-18 August 1943

NORTH SEA

1, 3, 4, 5, 6 and 8 Groups contributed to this raid. All were four-engined bombers and those still operating twin-engined Wellingtons (466 Squadron, Leconfield) had to stand down on this raid.

DENMARK

NEUTRAL SWEDEN

BALTIC SEA

Ruden

Peenemünde

Mosquito 'spoof' raid

HAMBURG

BREMEN

Berlin

The attack

FROM RUDEN

① ②

Group Captain Searby, Master Bomber, had to cope with high winds that tended to blow markers out to sea

Experimental laboratories for V-2 research

V-2 Production Works. Its destruction entrusted to 1 Group.

Rocket scientists' living quarters

ROYAL CANADIAN AIR FORCE 6 GROUP TARGET (with 5 Group)

Early casualties
① 158 Squadron Halifax
② 77 Squadron Halifax

4 GROUP TARGET (with 3 Group)

Map 19

to persuade the night-fighters that the Main Force was heading for the German capital. For the past few nights, Harris had been careful to send a few Mosquitoes to Berlin. They flew high and fast, always on the same track to Berlin, always over the little peninsula of Peenemünde. Dutifully, each night the sirens sounded the alert at the research centre and each night they were ignored by the rocket experts, taking their ease during those warm August evenings.

August 17th 1943 had already witnessed what was so far the greatest daylight air battle over Germany. That afternoon, the 1st and 4th Bomb Wings of the USAAF made their heroic assault on the German ball-bearing factories at Schweinfurt and the fighter manufacturing centres at Regensnburg. Three hundred and seventy-six B-17s set out to deliver accurate attacks on both targets. As they lacked fighter escort, they lost sixty aircraft in the two raids. By 1600 hours the Battles of Regensburg and Schweinfurt were over and a jubilant Luftwaffe now awaited the anticipated raid from Bomber Command. Two German crews had one small surprise awaiting the bombers. One hundred miles south of Peenemünde was Parchim airfield, home of 5/NJG 5. Two of their Me 110s had been fitted with a pair of upward firing cannons apiece and christened *schräge Musik* (slanting or jazz music). The crews were hoping to use it for the first time that night, insisting that their armourers should not insert tracer in the ammunition as they didn't want the *Tommies* to discover that the new mode of attack would not be from abeam or behind the bombers but *from below*.

In Yorkshire the crews of both Groups had enjoyed a fairly restful week. The Canadians in 408 Squadron based at Linton went on another week's leave and their Halifaxes stood idle. Apart from 431 Squadron at Tholthorpe which was still converting to Halifaxes, the rest of the Group went to war. Security was unusually tight as the crews were briefed for the raid on Peenemünde but they were not told the precise reasons for the attack. Most were led to believe that they were setting out to destroy a new kind of radar. Nevertheless, from the unusual nature of their bomb-loads they understood they were going somewhere special that night.

Thirty Mosquitoes and Beaufighters were tasked with Intruder operations and 141 Squadron from Wittering had the new Serrate equipment on board, enabling its Mosquitoes to pick up radar emissions from German night-fighters. Four of Church Fenton's Mosquitoes flew as Intruders that night and the crew of one of them became prisoners-of-war after being shot down near Westerland. First to attack were the eight 'spoof'

Mosquitoes over Berlin. There the German defenders assumed these were the vanguard of the Main Force and a fierce barrage opened up over the city. Darting over the capital were Hajo Herrman's *Wilde Sau* and one of them brought down a Mosquito to the west of Berlin. All night-fighers were now ordered to patrol the city and there they circled for the next thirty-six minutes while, one hundred miles away, the first of the Lancaster Pathfinders hit Peenemünde at 0010 hours on 19 August 1943. The 'spoof' had been a great success, for the cost of two Mosquitoes.

As the first Halifaxes and Stirlings went in at unusually low levels Peenemünde's accurate flak quickly claimed victims. First to fall was a 158 Squadron Halifax from Lissett, hit at 4000 feet. Next was an Elvington Halifax, blown to pieces by a flak shell with its bomb-bay still full of high explosive. Behind the Halifaxes came the Lancasters from 1 Group, saturating the main production area and some of the flak batteries with 4000lb cookies, followed by the bombers of 5 and 6 Groups. Above them flew the Master Bomber, Group Captain Searby, in a Pathfinder Lancaster. His task was to control the Aiming Point marking and direct the shifters and backers-up. Orbiting over the target, Searby made seven runs across Peenemünde where he had to cope with unexpectedly high winds that blew several of the cascading target markers out to sea. All the crews appreciated his calm, assured directions. One Canadian flying in a 434 Squadron Halifax from Tholthorpe said "it was just as though he was in the room talking to you - absolutely fantastic." Another of 6 Group's pilots, F/O Westland, was a backer-up in a Middleton St. George Halifax. His view was that everybody did "a fantastic job". The raid reminded him, he said, of those fireworks displays back home every 24th of May when they celebrated Queen Victoria's Birthday.[19]

Coinciding with the third wave came the first of the thirty-five night-fighters flying high over Peenemünde. Their arrival presaged trouble for 5 Group's Lancasters and the Canadians. 6 Group's Halifaxes and Lancaster IIs came in low and one pilot from Middleton St.George remarked that the sky was as bright as day over Peenemünde. He could see other bombers around him as though they were attacking in formation. Obviously the German aircrew had no difficulty in spotting them. Suddenly a Halifax flying quite close to him disintegrated. German fighters had dived into the bomber stream and a brief but fierce air battle took place as the Halifaxes and Lancasters, together with one or two of the more tardy Stirlings, began climbing away from their targets. Awed crews watched more aircraft catch fire and explode in mid-air causing them to report that the Germans were firing a new kind of shell called a 'scarecrow' designed to replicate an exploding bomber. Presumably most of these 'scarecrows' were the victims of *schräge Musik*, the existence of which was not suspected until well after the Peenemünde raid. However, most of the forty-six combats recorded that night involved conventionally-equipped night-fighters.

In all, two Mosquitoes and forty four-engined bombers were lost during the Peenemünde raid: twenty-three Lancasters, fifteen Halifaxes and two Stirlings. Proportionately, the Canadian crews from 6 Group suffered the heaviest casualties. Out of the fifty-two Halifaxes and nine Lancaster IIs sent to Peenemünde no less than ten Halifaxes and Lancasters failed to return. All seventeen Halifaxes in 419 Moose Squadron bombed the target but three were shot down. No 426 Thunderbird Squadron lost its commander, Wing Commander Leslie Crooks DSO, DFC, when his engines caught fire. He managed to belly in but the Lancaster II promptly exploded and only the bomb-aimer survived. A second Lancaster II piloted by F/Lt Shuttleworth crashed in flames shortly afterwards. No 427 Lion Squadron was returning to Leeming when a night-fighter shot down P/O Brady's Halifax but Sgt Schmitt, another Leeming pilot, decided to evade the flak and the fighters by going home at zero feet. A persistent Me 109F tried to shoot him down but the Halifax gunners blew it up as it came in on its fourth pass. With all his crew alive, Schmitt brought his battered Halifax into Mildenhall where he wrote it off in a heavy landing. No 428 Ghost Squadron at Middleton St. George and No 434 Bluenose Squadron at Tholthorpe lost three Halifaxes each. No 434 Bluenose was the thirteenth heavy bomber squadron formed to serve in the RCAF overseas and had flown its Halifax Vs in anger only once before - on the Milan raid (12 August 1943). Named after the famous Bluenose schooner depicted on the Canadian ten cent coin, the squadron painted its Merlin spinners bright blue in defiance of current regulations. Ten Bluenose Halifaxes had gone to Peenemünde and the loss of three of these was a hard blow to the squadron commander, Wing Commander Harris. Despite this, morale in the squadron and in all the other Canadian squadrons in 6 Group remained noticeably high.

The same could be said for 4 Group for it lost only three of the Halifaxes that flew to Peenemünde. Four Yorkshire squadrons from Snaith, Breighton, Holme-on-Spalding Moor and Pocklington welcomed back all their bombers safely but Nos 10 and 158 Squadrons stationed at Lissett both lost a Halifax, while Sgt Shefford's crew from 77 Squadron at Elvington had all died when their Halifax exploded in the opening phase of the attack.

Bomber Command deemed their sacrifice to be worthwhile. Rocket research at Peenemünde had been set back at least two months and probably more - and this had been the true object of the exercise. As he later wrote, Harris knew he could never put

> "a complete stop to the use of V-weapons by bombing Peenemünde; we knew very well by then that if the enemy chose to give first priority to the production of anything, a single attack on any plant could only cause a delay of a month or two at most."[20]

Moreover, Dr Thiel, the genius behind the design of the rocket motor and the *Wasserfall* missile was dead, as were over one hundred 'regular German staff'. Blamed for Schweinfurt, Regensburg and Peenemünde in the space of one day and unable to withstand the endless criticism from Hitler and Göring, Generaloberst Hans Jeschonnek, Luftwaffe Chief of Staff, committed suicide. Other lesser known people than this died in the attack and most of these were in the forced labour camp at Trassenheide, accidentally pulverised during the raid. Research and production were dislocated for many more months but Speer had by then relocated much of the rocket testing and production capacity of Peenemünde to more secure sites in the Harz Mountains and in Poland. Peenemünde remained in being for the rest of the war but it was never again visited by Bomber Command.[21]

However, the PR Mosquitoes continued to overfly the battered peninsula and on 28 November 1943 S/Ldr John Merifield brought back a photo of what appeared to be a launching ramp on Peenemünde airfield. The skill of WAAF Constance Babington Smith proved invaluable. She examined the blurred image:

> "I could see that on the ramp there was something that had not been seen there before. A tiny cruciform shape, set exactly on the lower end of a launching ramp - a midget aircraft actually in position for launching."[22]

She had solved the problem of the 'ski-sites' increasingly photographed in France and made sense of the various intelligence reports that pilotless aircraft were being tested in Germany. As she later wrote:

> ". . . the nature of the most imminent cross-Channel threat was at last established beyond doubt. It was going to be a flying bomb."[23]

Chapter Seventeen

The Battle of Berlin: The Bomber Offensive
(1) August to December 1943

The prospect of a sustained battle against the German capital aroused mixed feelings among the aircrews of Bomber Command. Everyone understood that the Big City was the ultimate target, a name they would be proud to write in their logbooks; but they also knew that because Berlin was the centre of national government and housed a major section of the German armaments industry it would be heavily defended by night-fighters, searchlights and flak units. Oboe had enabled Bomber Command to raid the Ruhr with devastating results for Essen and the Rhineland towns; Window had defeated the Germans at Hamburg; a 'spoof' and low-level flying had fooled them on a moonlight night at Peenemünde. But what new device would bring success over Berlin, a distant target notoriously murky and cloud-covered in the harsh winter conditions of northern Europe?

Much faith was placed in H2S, still mainly the preserve of the Pathfinder squadrons. But H2S could not identify individual targets in Berlin: the tempting Alkett tank workshops, the Erkner ball-bearing-plant, the vital BMW, Focke-Wulf, Heinkel and Dornier aircraft factories, the AEG, Lorentz and Siemens electronic firms and the big gun manufacturer, Rheinmetal-Borsig. These were hidden in the midst of the third biggest city in the world, where urban sprawl completely filled the H2S screens. The chances of finding and destroying these depended largely on luck and on a heavy saturation bomb drop.

An even greater problem facing the crews was the speedy German reaction to Window. Drastic changes in policy and command structure led to an unexpected expansion in the German night-fighter force during the autumn and winter of 1943-44. Controllers largely abandoned the Himmelbett box system and perfected their *Wild Sau* (Wild Boar) and *Zahme Sau* (Tame Boar) tactics. Bomber Command's enthusiastic use of diversionary forces and last-minute course changes forced the German controllers to accept that most bombers would penetrate the target area. But once they were there the Wild Boar would range freely above the flak level, pouncing on individual aircraft, while the Tame Boar twin-engined fighters would tend to fight *within* the bomber stream, especially once the Main Force had left the target area. These new tactics cost the lives of many

Bomber Command men: the now widely used *schräge Musik* brought sudden death without warning; the use of decoy aircraft, when a night-fighter showing a light approached a bomber, engaged the attention of the gunners and sat just out of range while his wingman moved in from the opposite quarter and shot the aircraft down. Now the controller relied upon radio contact with his fighters so that his running commentary gave the location, height, speed and course of the Main Force. It was a technique carefully monitored by the RAF's Y Service and gradually methods of jamming or subverting the running commentary were brought into play. But in terms of operations over Germany it could not be denied that within a few weeks after Peenemünde the Luftwaffe had devised an efficient and deadly defence system, one that Bomber Command would fail to overcome during the Battle of Berlin.

Proof of this was forthcoming in the Berlin raid carried out on 23/24 August 1943. Harris hoped that the 727 bombers he had earmarked for this operation would re-create the city-centre destruction achieved at Hamburg, albeit on a smaller scale. For the northern squadrons, it was to be a maximum effort. 4 Group sent 156 bombers, a higher figure than any of the other groups. Moreover, the high level of serviceability enabled Lissett's 158 Squadron to send twenty-eight crews to Berlin; no other squadron would exceed this figure throughout the entire battle. Breighton's 78 Squadron put up an impressive twenty-seven Halifaxes, as did 51 Squadron at Snaith. In contrast with the Lancaster, the Halifax usually had to fit an extra fuel-tank in the bomb-bay for the Berlin trips and this meant it could carry barely half the Mark I and Mark III Lancaster bomb-load to the Big City. Canada's 6 Group were now flying Lancaster IIs from Linton and these 408 and 426 Squadron aircraft had slightly longer bomb-bays so they could carry up to four tons of flares, incendiaries and high-explosives.

The raid highlighted all the difficulties the Command would face during the coming winter. Accidents such as the sudden disintegration of a 102 Squadron Halifax from Pocklington over the North Sea; or unexpectedly early interceptions as in the classic *von unten hinten* (from below and behind) attack by an Me 110 on a 77 Squadron

Halifax, causing it to invert and spin down out of control. Once the Main Force had by-passed Bremen the German controllers realised that there was to be no significant diversion and plumped for Berlin as the most likely target. They immediately vectored their night-fighters towards the city where the first Pathfinders laid the TIs inaccurately. Despite the efforts of the master of ceremonies[1], creep-back was unavoidable and the best that could be said of the bombing was that it was widespread. There were many lucky hits on military targets and at least 850 people were killed. Bomber Command's main deception that night was to swing north-westwards for the return flight and a 102 Squadron Halifax was one of two aircraft to seek refuge in neutral Sweden. Losses were not evenly spread: Nos 78 and 158 Squadrons both lost five aircraft; Nos 10 and 76 Squadrons came through unscathed. One 78 Squadron Halifax with the original triangular fin and rudder survived at least ten fighter attacks but lost two engines and had to wrestle with the challenges of asymmetric flight. With the English coast in sight the pilot finally lost control and the bomber spun into the sea near Cromer.

For those that managed to cross the coast the problems continued to mount. Thick fog blotted out the Vale of York and seven of Melbourne's Halifaxes had to land away. Nearby Breighton was also clamped down and its Halifaxes were diverted to Leconfield where fog had just begun to roll in over the airfield. Milling around the overlapping circuits were aircraft from several Yorkshire stations and before long a 78 Squadron Halifax had collided with another. Both came down on the outskirts of Beverley, a tragedy that underlined the pressing need for well-lit emergency landing grounds (ELGs) close to the Yorkshire moors and in the Vale of York. Work was in hand with the Fog Investigation Dispersal Operation (FIDO) at Woodbridge ELG and other selected Bomber Command stations but none would be available in Yorkshire before the end of 1943. Many a bomber crew would die unnecessarily because of the seemingly low priority given to FIDO and ELG planning in the County of Yorkshire.

The raid on 23/24 August had cost sixty-two bombers, the Command's highest loss to date. Three nights later, Harris sent 674 aircraft to attack Nuremberg (the second time this distant city had been attacked in August) and thirty-three bombers failed to return; plus another 603 aircraft to the two towns of Mönchengladbach and Rheydt on 30/31 August. This was an Oboe-directed raid and produced highly concentrated bombing in exchange for the loss of twenty-five aircraft. Bomber Command's crews

'Bombing up' MP-Y at Holme dispersal 1943. This aircraft swung on take-off prior to the Mönchengladbach raid 30/31 August 1943. A tyre burst and it caught fire.

Yorkshire Air Museum

went back to Berlin on 31 August/1 September, the first time that logbooks record that Ju 88s were marking the Main Force route with large white flares that seemed to hang in the sky from a height of 20,000 feet. It was an unsuccessful raid carried out by tired crews dismayed by the new German marker system and war-weary aircraft that needed a longer period of maintenance work than had been allowed for by Sir Arthur. For example, Melbourne sent ten Halifaxes to Berlin. None was lost but three aborted and another three returned early.

Clearly, 4 Group was in need of rest and recuperation. So were the Canadians in 6 Group who had despatched fifty-eight aircraft; seven were missing and eight had returned early. Harris did not allow 4 Group to participate in the third Berlin raid of this series (3/4 September 1943) and the three 6 Group Lancaster IIs that went to the Big City that night returned safely.

After this there was no Main Force attack on Berlin for the next two months. Harris desperately needed a more reliable form of H2S. He wrote:

"The three attacks on Berlin which we had carried out in September (sic) had altogether failed to hit the centre of the city and until we got the new type of H2S I considered it better to attack other cities which we had a much better chance of destroying . . . . " [2]

He certainly destroyed the next target. All the heavy bomb groups took part in a double attack on Mannheim and Ludwigshafen (5/6 September) where Germnan reports again spoke of 'a catastrophe'. However, other raids on Munich (6/7 September) and Hannover (22/23 and 27/28 September) were far less effective. In fact, the pattern of raids beyond Oboe range was very much a hit and miss affair unless, first of all, the H2S blind markers were correctly placed and, second, the follow-up visual markers were accurately dropped.

The raids on Kassel fulfilled these requirements. Both 4 and 6 Groups were involved in this attack upon this important military and industrial target on 3/4 October and twenty Halifaxes from Holme bombed the green TIs with telling accuracy. Fires spread rapidly to engulf the Henschel works and about fifty FW 190 fighters were burnt out on the Fieseler production line at Bettenhausen. Twenty-four aircraft failed to return from this raid and four of these were from No 76 Squadron at Holme. One Canadian Halifax V, carrying a 4000lb 'cookie' and piloted by F/Lt Laird, was hammered by a *schräge Musik* fighter. Dunmore and Carter give a graphic account of what happened in their history of 6 Group RCAF,

MGM Pictures present the lion to No 427 'Lion' Squadron, Royal Canadian Air Force. One perk for the Canadians at Leeming was that they could now enjoy a free pass when a MGM picture was being shown at a cinema.

Reap the Whirlwind. [3] Two of the crew were killed and Sgt Cardy, the flight engineer, was badly wounded. After several attempts to jettison the cookie it released itself, crashing through the closed bomb doors. Despite his injuries and his frequent lapses into unconsciousness, Cardy monitored the engine instruments with the help of Sgt Corbally, the bomb-aimer. Laird managed to reach Leeming only to discover that the hydraulics had failed and that he he could not lower his undercarriage. Leeming control had no wish to have a Halifax crash landing on the runway and ordered the crew to bale out but Laird knew that he was too low for this and that, anyway, Cardy would never survive a jump. At this point Cardy recovered consciousness in time to solve Laird's dilemma. The wounded flight-engineer supervised the "axe and back-saw operation which finally locked down both wheels" and Laird landed safely. Cardy received the Conspicuous Gallantry Medal; Laird won the DFC.

The second raid on Kassel cost forty-three aircraft but was the most destructive attack carried out on a German city since Hamburg. Concentrated incendiary drops produced the requisite firestorm but, compared with Hamburg's terrible experience, on a far smaller scale. Fire gutted the Henschel works where the majority of the flying-bombs were being made and several authorities, including Middlebrook, believe this attack put back the planned V-1 assault on England by at least two months. So the second bombing of Kassel may be regarded as equal in importance to the Peenemünde raid. Both had succeeded in delaying the V-weapon schedules, a considerable achievement for Bomber Command. Bad

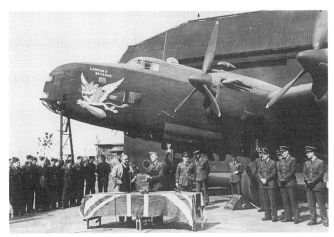

This Halifax V provides an excellent view of Canadian nose art.

weather and severe icing on the way home may have accounted for some of the losses that night. Certainly, F/Sgt Bowly thought so as he piloted his Halifax back to Leeming from which base Nos 427 Lion and 429 Bison had taken part in the Hannover and Kassel raids. As he glanced out of his cockpit he could see "clear ice about a foot thick on the airscrew spinners and about six inches thick on the leading edges of the wings."[4] Yorkshire's losses on the second Kassel raid included three of Melbourne's eleven Halifaxes, four of which had already returned early because of icing problems.

By now Harris was anxious to resume the interrupted assault on Berlin. He hoped the new H2S sets and the improved Mk XIV bombsight, designed by Profesor P Blackett and Dr Braddick, would guarantee greater accuracy over the German capital. One sad chapter in the history of the Mk XIV bombsight was written in Yorkshire. A 23-year old scientist, Dorothy Robson, worked in Farnborough's Instrument and Photographic Department. Part of her duties was to air-test the Mk XIV and she came to Holme to fly with F/Lt Jimmy Steele. It was a hazy afternoon when reports came through that her Halifax had crashed near Market Weighton.[5] It was 3 November 1943.

This was the day on which Harris wrote to Winston Churchill a letter that has become the most widely quoted of all Sir Arthur's correspondence. His letter urged the Prime Minister to give priority to the destruction of Berlin:

"I await promised USAAF aid in this, the greatest of all air battles. But I would not propose to wait for ever, or for long, if the opportunity serves . . . "

He went on to list the other German cities waiting to be attacked by Bomber Command and commented:

"We have not far to go. But we must get the USAAF to wade in with greater force . . . We can wreck Berlin from end to end if the US will come in on it. It will cost us 400-500 bombers. It will cost Germany the war. [6]

Of course, it was unrealistic at the beginning of November 1943 to expect the USAAF to undertake a systematic daylight bomber offensive against Berlin without long-range fighter escort. No doubt Harris had heard about the arrival of the first of the North American P-51B Mustang fighters[7] at Boxted airfield near Colchester. Powered by the Packard version of the Rolls-Royce Merlin 61 engine and with an extra eighty-five gallon tank behind the pilot, the P-51B already had a combat range of 475 miles, far better than any other Allied single-engined fighter. Fitted with a pair of wing-mounted drop-tanks, the combat radius from East Anglian airfields shot up to 650 miles. Berlin was now within range of an American fighter! Unfortunately, these P-51s were only just in production. Every war theatre clamoured for them and the few that arrived in Britain needed several modifications before they were fit to fly on combat missions in the tough weather conditions of north-west Europe. Not until 5 December 1943 did they take part in a daylight escort sortie and this was to a French target. It was another three months before 121 P-51s set out to escort B17s on the first USAAF raid on Berlin (4 March 1944) only to be driven back and suffer heavy losses in bad weather conditions off the Dutch coast.

So it was in their slow-moving box formations, devoid of fighter cover, that the B-17s made their heroic strikes on Regensburg (17 August: 24 bombers lost) and Schweinfurt (17 August: 36 bombers lost; 14 October: 60 bombers lost). Even America's 'Mighty Eighth' could not sustain these losses at such an early stage of its history and that is why Harris undertook the next sixteen raids that made up the main Battle of Berlin - plus another sixteen major assaults on other German cities - without significant American help. He found some comfort in the fact that his American counterpart, General Eaker, would have liked to have attacked the Big City by day had he enjoyed the right resources at the right time.

However, the significance of the American absence was that the vital factor in Harris' recipe for the wrecking of Berlin, the "promised US help" of which he had written to Churchill, did not and could not materialise in 1943. He had no alternative but to increase his own night-bomber capacity through the formation of new squadrons, by maximising the load carried by Lancasters and by ensuring that Bomber Command did not lose the initiative in electronic warfare. It was because he was unwilling to ask his crews, who had enough to remember at the best of times, to engage in constant spoofs and radio counter-measures that he authorised the formation of No 100 Group (Special Duties) on 23 November 1943. Its tasks were: to destroy enemy fighters in the air using Serrate-equipped Mosquitoes; to intrude German air space and attack night-fighter bases; and to use airborne and ground counter-measures to jam German radar and radio transmmissions. This was why 101 Squadron's specially-equipped Lancasters had an extra crew member who could understand German. His task was to monitor enemy fighter control transmissions and then jam them with his ABC (Airborne Cigar) equipment. From October 1943 onwards ABC Lancasters took part in every Main Force raid on Germany.

★ ★ ★

The main Battle of Berlin began on 18/19 November 1943. Twenty-three Lancaster IIs from Canada's 6 Group flew with the Main Force to Berlin while the Halifaxes flew to Mannheim and Ludwigshafen to present the German night defence with the task of coping with two major bomber streams 250 miles apart. Though the ploy proved successful the raid on Berlin was a failure largely due to malfunctioning H2S sets. Very careful preparation went into the next assault on 22/23 November. This time Harris had five Lancasters equipped with the new 3-centimetre H2S and these successfully marked a totally cloud-covered city. At least three small fire-storms were started and shortly after the raid was over smoke from the burning city topped 19,000 feet. German casualties were over 2000 dead and there is no doubt that the Yorkshire squadrons were of crucial importance in what Middlebrook has described as "the most effective raid on Berlin of the war".[8] Snaith and Melbourne both lost two aircraft and one Halifax was missing from each of the Elvington, Lisset and Tholthorpe squadrons. Middleton St George lost one of its Lancaster IIs with an all-Canadian crew and there was a particular tragedy when, on return, an Elvington Halifax collided with a Pocklington bomber and both crashed at Barmby Moor. All the crew members died.

Harris was mainly worried about the poor performance of the Stirlings on this raid. Losses according to type were: Lancasters 2.3%; Halifaxes 4.2%; Stirlings 10%. He therefore decided to bar the Stirling from raids over Germany. Apart from its losses to enemy action, the Stirling's bomb-load did not match that carried by Lancasters and Halifaxes and the number that aborted during the long haul due to mechanical trouble was intolerable. This meant that in addition to the American non-starters Harris had now deprived himself of most of 3 Group's aircraft. Converting these squadrons to his beloved Lancaster would take some time and the fact that he could actually sustain the Lancaster and Halifax losses at their present rate was a tribute to the Avro and Handley Page factories and to the repair centres and ground staff on the operational airfields. On the third and fourth raids (23/24 and 26/27 November) the only northern aircraft to participate were the Lancaster IIs. Linton bore the losses on 23/24 November, including one Lancaster that crashed on return near Malton. The weather was against the bombers on 26/27 November and fog forced Lancasters from other Groups to divert to Yorkshire's airfields. A No 50 Squadron Lancaster made several approaches to Pocklington, then ran out of fuel and crashed at Hayton; a No 103 Squadron Lancaster was on finals at Middleton St George when it hit a Halifax; and a No 619 Squadron Lancaster just failed to reach the threshold at Elvington's main runway.

Having dealt with the Stirling problem, Harris was now reluctant to send the Halifaxes to Berlin at least until the new Mark III version so eagerly awaited by the 4 and 6 Group crews came on squadron strength. Flying below the Lancasters and carrying smaller bomb-loads, the Halifax IIs and Vs were being shot down in increasing numbers. Bomber Command headquarters was always dismayed when the Halifax statistics appeared. When Nos 408 RCAF and 78 Squadrons had first received the Mark V in August 1942 they were concerned by the inability of the Dowty undercarriage to survive heavy landings. For a time Mark Vs were taken off main Force operations but the demands for maximum effort in 1943 meant they were back in action despite severe restrictions being placed on their bomb-loads. There was little ground staffs could do to prevent undercarriage collapse during swings on take-off and landing and the upshot was that the Halifax squadrons took more casualties and had more 'early returners' than did the Lancaster units.

Yet when the Lancasters had to bear the brunt of the first two December raids on Berlin (2/3 and 16/17 December) their losses began to climb towards 9.0%, enough to make their crews fatalistic. That is why most crews at this stage of the Battle of Berlin would have sympathised with the worried rear-gunner at the end of a pseudo-jovial briefing whose response to his commander's cheerful "Good hunting !" was "And Good-bye !"

During the autumn and early winter of 1943 the later production Halifax BIIs and BVs coming to the northern squadrons had the aerodynamically pleasing perspex nose, the new rectangular fins that Cheshire had urged Handley Page to fit and, sometimes, the factory installed H2S radar housed in the ventral bulge. There was no H2S fitting on Halifaxes destined for squadrons experimenting with the use of a mid-under ventral gun bay, a cold and difficult firing position providing a token defence against the *schräge Musik* tactics of the Tame Boar interceptors. Most of these 'new look' Halifaxes took part in raids on major targets other than Berlin before the end of the year: Leverkusen (10/20 November); Frankfurt 25/26 November; the Stuttgart diversion (26/27 November); and the very effective raid on Leipzig (3/4 December).

The tactics adopted on the last two Berlin raids during 1943 were more successful than most. On 22/23 December, when the Halifax squadrons were left out of the Battle of Berlin, the Mosquito diversion at Leipzig completely fooled the German controllers. On 29/30 December, when the Halifaxes were back in action, the Mosquito spoofs were again effective and the German controllers remained unsure where the Main Force would attack. Over Berlin where there was 10/10ths cloud, Window and skymarkers confused the German radar and the flak was generally inaccurate. Even so, it hit a Melbourne Halifax piloted by Sgt Burcher who bombed, lost two engines and then made it back to a FIDO-equipped airfield. Several heavy bomber bases now had powerful sodium lights to guide the bombers to the threshold and, on foggy nights, used the petrol-fed Fog Investigation and Dispersal Operation. Woodbridge Emergency Landing Ground opened on 15 November 1943 and the first of the Yorkshire-based bombers to land there was a Canadian Halifax from 431 Iroquois Squadron returning low on fuel from Ludwigshafen (18/19 November). More than ever before, Yorkshire needed an ELG and, thankfully, work began on the selected site at Carnaby at the end of 1943.

By then the redesigned Halifax B Mk III fitted with four Bristol Hercules radial engines was in full production. Nos 466 RAAF and 433 Porcupine Squadrons were the first in Yorkshire to receive the Mk IIIs and these arrived at Leconfield and Skipton without the H2S scanners, a deficiency put right by a team of experts that travelled around the northern bases in December 1943 fitting radar equipment inside the ventral bulge. Thereafter much of the radar maintenance was carried out by WAAF Radar Mechanics, trained on operational Gee and Radar equipment. The Australians at Leconfield were delighted

with their new Mk IIIs especially after all twelve returned safely from a gardening sortie off the Dutch coast on 1 December 1943. Equally pleased were the Canadians at Skipton's 433 Squadron. They began their operational training on the new Mk IIIs. Gradually, the older Mk IIs and Vs were withdrawn from front line service and passed across to Coastal Command and the heavy Conversion Units. The new Halifaxes had more efficient oil coolers (and from February 1944 some would have extended wingspans), improvements that led to a better operational ceiling en route to the target (about 17.000 feet) and an enhanced rate of climb. 6 Group enthusiastically equipped many of its Mk IIIs with the mid-under gun bay housing a single 0.5 inch machine-gun while the crews at Tholthorpe and Croft sometimes went one better and installed 'twin fifties' rather in the manner of the ball-turretted B-17 Fortresses.

These changes may sound impressive but they did not take place simultaneously or even apply generally by the beginning of the New Year. For example, No 433 Porcupine did not become operational on the Mk IIIs until January 1944; while the three Canadian squadrons who had exchanged the warmth of their Tunisian bases for the vagaries of Britain's northern weather - 420 Snowy Owl, 424 Tiger and 425 Alouette - were not on Main Force strength until February 1944. It was the constant demand for maximum effort that outstripped the supply of B Mk IIIs and squadrons such as No 77 at Elvington, No 428 Ghost at Middleton St George and No 434 Bluenose at Croft had to soldier on with their Merlin-engined IIs and Vs for most of the winter raids that marked the climax of area attacks on Berlin and other German cities.

Another important factor influencing the composition of 4 and 6 Groups was the inexorable loss of experienced crews, a problem confronting the whole of Bomber Command. There was never any shortage of keen young aircrew and in one important sense this never-ending supply compounded the problem Harris had to face. Crews coming off the Operational Training and Heavy Conversion Units were always eager to fly, to take part in the thrills and purposefulness of the Main Force raids on Germany. But by 1944 skilled and experienced leaders were few and far between. Veteran crews were often siphoned off from squadrons to join the Pathfinders; and because Pathfinder losses were so heavy it was not unusual for an able HCU crew to be posted directly to 8 Group before even taking part in an operational sortie over Germany. Shortages frequently forced Squadron Commanders to put themselves on 'ops' and casualties among such fliers were very high. Less experienced men had to fill the gaps and it must be said that in almost every case they met their awesome responsibilities, to which they were so rapidly promoted in their twenties, with competence and understanding. But in the demanding months of January, February and March 1944 few Squadron Commanders could allocate time for the gradual induction of new crews into combat flying. There were fewer second dickeys now and a fledgling crew would find as a matter of course that its first sortie involved a long and complex flight from Yorkshire to Berlin, Augsburg or Schweinfurt.

Flying into battle now meant flying against the most sophisticated night-fighter force in the world. No matter how assiduous they were in dispensing their metal strips of chaff, crews knew that the Ju 88s and Me 110s now had their new SN-2 radar, capable of penetrating the fog of Window. Beset by flak "so thick that you could walk on it" and "walls of searchlights that ruined your night vision", blunders or momentary errors of judgement were all too common among inexperienced crews. It was this lack of experience among new crews over Germany that so often led to fatal consequences as Bomber Command stepped up its remorseless offensive. It is futile for armchair strategists and cosy moralists to rail against the choice of target and manner of bombing employed by the Command during 1943-44. One crucial fact must never be forgotten: the Command had been for years the lonely spearhead of the Allied offensive against Nazi Germany. Bomber Command's aircrews were following in the footsteps of their predecessors who had always seized the initiative and flown their offensive morning patrols over enemy lines on the Western Front in the First World War. By April 1917 they had faced a seemingly omnipotent 'Albatros scourge' and suffered terrible losses until sheer numbers and superior quality overwhelmed an enemy forced on the *defensive*. During 1943-44 the young men who flocked to fly the Halifaxes and Lancasters were playing a similar role. Their heavy losses during the Battle of Berlin were due, as the Official History stresses, to the fact that the Main Force was unable to challenge and destroy the German night-fighters in the air as the Americans were later able to do, after the advent of the Mustang, in their battles against the German day-fighters.

"The heavy bombers possessed neither the armament nor the performance seriously to damage the German Night Fighter force in the air. The best their gunners could do with their small calibre weapons was to provide some deterrent to the less skilled German pilots. Restricted to .303 calibre machine guns they were substantially outshot and completely outranged by their cannon-equipped enemies. Their armour plating was progressively removed, until little remained, to increase their bomb lifting capacity. Belching smoke from their exhausts as well as radar emissions from their navigational and fighter warning apparatus made them all too apparent to those who hunted them. Once engaged in combat, they had little chance of victory and not much of escape, whilst the large quantities of petrol, incendiary bombs, high explosives and oxygen with which they were filled often gave spectacular evidence of their destruction . . . in a generally highly inflammable and explosive condition, these black monsters presented an ideal target . . ."[9]

Convincing though this may sound, it must be remembered that the Lancasters and Halifaxes were never designed "seriously to damage the German Night Fighter force in the air". They did not deliberately seek out the night-fighters; their aim was to confuse and mislead the enemy rather than engage him in air-to-air firefights. As more and more heavy bombers thundered over the Third Reich it was to be expected that a people as resourceful as the Germans would devise ways of finding and shooting down enemy aircraft at night. That is why the Luftwaffe increased its *defensive* night-fighter force to around 250 aircraft though, because of Hitler's insistence on the continued manufacture of offensive bombers, fewer resources were allocated to defence than the desperate situation really demanded. Expert German pilots destroyed five or six bombers during a single sortie and some built up impressive scores especially when using their *schräge Musik* guns. But the technical advances brought in by the Luftwaffe never stopped the bombers coming back to attack; and in those attacks the vast majority of the 'black monsters' survived their sorties into Germany and carried out devastating raids upon cities, arms centres and key communication points. Moreover, they sustained their losses even when spoofs, diversions and thick, concealing clouds were not on their side.

Bomber Command had spent four years dictating a particular style of war, a war in which the Luftwaffe was compelled to react to the limit of its allocated resources. Had the Halifaxes and Lancasters devoted their attention in the winter of 1943-44 to ball bearing plants and synthetic oil refineries, assuming the Pathfinders could have found them, the Germans would surely have moved their flak, radio beacons and night-fighters to defend these 'panacea' targets. The Command would have still taken heavy losses while the Ruhr and Berlin flourished. Secondly, had the armament of Bomber Command's Main Force been uprated with American-style 0.5" machine guns and had each bomber carried eight or ten of these weapons plus large reserves of ammunition in order to seek out and engage the the enemy, the speed of the aircraft would have been seriously reduced, possibly by as much as sixty miles per hour. This would have delighted German fighter crews who often commented that

Lancasters and the later Halifaxes were very slippery aeroplanes to catch once they had dropped their bombs and begun their rapid departure from the target area. True precision bombing, which meant flying under conditions relatively free from constant enemy attack, would elude the Main Force of Bomber Command until the Allies enjoyed air superiority over the Third Reich.

The truth of this statement would have harsh illustration in the attacks on Berlin in 1944 and on the 'Long Leg' to Nuremberg (30/31 March 1944).

Chapter Eighteen

The Battle of Berlin: The Bomber Offensive
(2) January to March 1944

Yorkshire's Halifax squadrons were rested on New Year's Day while thirty-one Canadian Lancasters joined the other Groups slogging their way to Berlin. Although all the Canadians returned safely, twenty-eight bombers were lost that night, most of them to the up-rated Ju 88s with their SN-2 radar and *schräge Musik* guns. Next day, after a heavy fall of snow, the same groups readied themselves for yet another raid in which the northern Lancaster squadrons were to play their part. 6 Group despatched twenty-eight Lancaster IIs and all three squadrons - Nos 408, 426 and 432 - lost a Lancaster apiece. Icing might have claimed more but for the sort of "misinterpretation of orders" described in this extract from J. Douglas Harvey's *Boys, Bombs and Brussels Sprouts* when his crew reacted to the problem of a failing Mark II Lancaster carrying an excess of ice at 17,000 feet. They had been briefed at No 408 Squadron's base at Linton, where it was already snowing hard, and warned that icing would be a severe problem.

Doug Harvey remembered that his CO had urged crews to bomb from 18000 feet. If they could not achieve this they should resort to the old trick of dropping a small part of their bomb-load – the CO thought a few cans of incendiary bombs would be appropriate – and thus reduce the strain on the four thundering Bristol Hercules engines that powered the Lancaster II.

En route to the target, Doug Harvey found himself flying in solid cloud and the crew could see the ice building up on the wings. Even with the throttles pushed hard forward, the Lancaster was making little headway and there was a very real risk that she would stall and fall away. As he was just about to cross the Dutch coast Doug Harvey had to make a swift decision if he had any hope of avoiding the German flak and searchlights ringing the Zuider Zee. He was well aware that although his Lancaster II had reliable engines whose reduced exhaust glow helped hide the bomber from the German night-fighters, ultimate crew safety would depend on gaining altitude.

His bomb-load that night comprised one 4000lb blockbuster or 'cookie' and a variety of incendiary bombs. The 'cookie' was the more important – regarded by the RAF and the RCAF as the most effective weapon for area

targets. The incendiary bombs were usually thirty pounders or the tried and tested four pounders. By 1944 these were packed in 'Cluster Projectile No. 14s' – 'cans' of 106 x 4lb incendiaries, each can weighing a total of 500lbs. Doug Harvey decided he would drop three of these and called up his bomb-aimer on the intercom, instructing him to select and drop three, a total of 1500 lbs. He then opened the bomb doors – extra large on the Lancaster II – and sensed their vibrations in the icy slipstream. When the bomb-aimer released, Doug Harvey felt the Lancaster surge upwards, the usual result of dropping a 'cookie'. He quickly retrimmed the aircraft for level flight, heard the bomb-aimer confirm 'Bombs gone' and then closed the bomb doors.

From that moment onwards Doug Harvey was able to keep the Lancaster climbing until it reached Berlin at a height of 24,000 feet, well above the flak and the fighters! In splendid isolation, the Lancaster made its approach to the target. The bomb-aimer called for bomb-doors open, carefully passing minute heading changes to the pilot. Once more it was 'Bombs gone' – but the Lancaster did not surge upwards as it should have done. Everyone knew that the bomb-aimer had nothing to drop on the German capital. But the bombing process was solemnly completed, the bomb doors closed and Doug Harvey's Lancaster II made it back to Linton that night.[1]

Other Lancasters had a much harder time. A No 432 Squadron Lancaster experienced constant icing and hydraulic problems on the way to the Big City and the pilot began his bomb run with a u/s altimeter and air speed indicator. F/O MacIntosh later stated that "I continued climbing and bombed from at least 23,000 feet."[2] Despite his height a night-fighter sent a burst into the Lancaster's fuselage and though the gunners shot down the fighter the Lancaster went into a near vertical dive, pulling out at 10,000 feet. Unfortunately, the bomb doors had fallen open and this extra drag, coupled with declining power from over-stressed engines, meant McIntosh was losing height. Over the North Sea the crew had to throw out everything that moved, including the guns, to help maintain flying speed and McIntosh was able to bring his Lancaster into Woodbridge ELG. The aircraft was a total write-off.

New squadrons were now flying from Yorkshire. No 640 formed at Leconfield on 7 January with B Mk III Halifaxes; No 578, also with the new Halifaxes, began a distinguished bombing career at Snaith on 20 January when Berlin was the target; while 433 Porcupine at Skipton-on-Swale began operations as part of 6 Group on 2/3 January when three of its Mk III Halifaxes took part in a gardening sortie off the Frisian Islands.

The eleventh raid on Berlin (20/21 January 1944) was the heaviest so far: 769 Lancasters and Halifaxes plus the usual 'spoof' Mosquitoes. Meteorological forecasts were optimistic that there would be total cloud cover all the way to Berlin; and to fool the German controllers a brand-new route had been chosen to ensure safe passage to the Big City. In the event, the cloud level was at some 12,000 feet above Berlin and the searchlights played their beams along its base, throwing the Main Stream Halifaxes and Lancasters into silhouette. This was graphically reported by the crew of a Mosquito flying at over 35,000 feet. They could see the German night-fighters some 5000 feet below them; and below them was the Main Force, clearly visible to the enemy.

Cloud and icing levels were critical and the conditions they created and the effects they had on visibility were not at that stage of the war fully appreciated by Meteorological Officers at Bomber Command Headquarters. About one hundred German night-fighters operated in the vicinity of Berlin that night and there were some fierce air-to-air combats in which the Junkers and Messerchmitts were not always invincible. A 578 Squadron Halifax from Snaith forced down one Ju 88; a 640 Squadron Halifax drove off another; and the rear-gunner of a 102 Squadron Halifax from Pocklington sent a Messerchmitt down in flames. But these were limited successes to be balanced by Bomber Command's heavy losses, particularly in the two Yorkshire Groups. Twenty-two Halifaxes and thirteen Lancasters failed to return. No 102 Squadron was the hardest hit as its relatively low-flying Halifax B IIs proved exceptionally vulnerable to flak as well as to Tame Boar night-fighter attack. It had sent sixteen Halifaxes to Berlin and of these five were shot down over or near the target and two were lost over England: O-Orange crash-landed near Norwich; P-Peter ran out of fuel and the crew baled out over Driffield. The "Queen of the Wolds" received a number of parachutists that night. F/Sgt Johnson was flying a flak-riddled 434 Bluenose Halifax with no rudder controls, no ailerons and most of the electrical wiring out of action. Somehow, he managed to bring his bomber back to Yorkshire before he and his crew baled out over Driffield. Another Canadian pilot, F/Sgt Cozens in a 427

Lion Halifax B11 was out of fuel over Norfolk and after three approaches into Coltishall had the misfortune to hit a high tension cable.

Such were the problems facing the Yorkshire crews valiantly trying to return to their northern climes and still without benefit of an Emergency Landing Ground north of Woodbridge. Altogether, 4 Group lost sixteen aircraft and 6 Group lost eleven in a raid that appeared to cause widespread damage in Berlin. In his *Bombers over Berlin* Alan Cooper is quite specific about the nature and precise tonnage of the bombs dropped on the city plus the damage caused to industrial plants and the vital public services. Martin Middlebrook, however, notes the absence of German media reaction towards this raid and suggests two possibilities: there may have been "some order issued to conceal the extent of the damage"; or perhaps "the entire raid missed Berlin."[3] Though Bomber Command's losses over Berlin were serious, the unsuccessful raid on Magdeburg during the following night caused an even worse 15.6% loss among the Halifax squadrons. Thirty-five of the Mark IIs and IIIs were missing, most of them falling to the guns of the German night-fighters. Four of the lost Halifaxes came from Pocklington's 102 Squadron, bitter testimony to the growing sophistication of the voice-controlled system of Tame Boar interceptions.

For the next assault on Berlin, Harris had to accept that 4 Group had had enough. It needed time to replace its lost aircraft and train its new crews. Yorkshire's contribution on the night of 27/28 January was therefore restricted to the three Lancaster II squadrons in Canada's 6 Group. Of the forty-eight despatched to Berlin, 426 Thunderbird Squadron lost four of its bombers; three of 408's Lancasters failed to return; and 432 lost a Lancaster captained by F/O Patterson. The Luftwaffe had been out in force and crew reports suggested that Me 210s were active, alongside Me 110s and FW 190s, over Frankfurt; while the Ju 88s and Me 109s were mainly encountered over the Big City. Again, widespread bombing hit many vital targets and Berlin reeled under the strain of incessant air attack. But the intensity of the bombing achieved at Hamburg and Wuppertal was lacking in Berlin. Inadequate numbers of aircraft were reaching the city and when the Main Force did arrive the bombing was generally scattered. Undoubtedly, the fierce winds encountered during those stormy January nights blew the sky-markers away from the aiming points. For Harris, the only solution was to increase the number of bombers taking part in each operation and that is why, on 28 January, he ordered a maximum effort from all Groups against the German capital.

Bomber Command managed to despatch 432 Lancasters, 241 Halifaxes and five Mosquitoes, a remarkable effort in view of the recent aircrew losses and the pressure imposed on the ground crews who had to work day and night to keep the squadron aircraft serviceable. Diversionary sweeps and the long northern route over the top of Denmark split the German night-fighter force though their controllers managed to assemble sufficient Luftwaffe crews to wreak destruction on the bomber stream over Berlin. The raid caused enormous damage within the German capital and official reports from the city archives speak of "mountains of rubble." But the cost to Bomber Command was high. Twenty Lancasters were shot down; twenty-six Halifaxes failed to return. In 4 Group, 10 Squadron at Melbourne and 77 Squadron at Elvington were shattered to discover that both had four Halifaxes missing from this operation; while Snaith, Pocklington and Lissett each mourned a missing bomber. Australia's 466 Squadron at Leconfield lost a Mk III Halifax. Nine aircraft from 6 Group failed to return: 431 Iroquois and 434 Bluenose lost three Halifaxes apiece; 419 Moose lost a BII; while 429 Bison had two of its Mk II Halifaxes missing. But this was not the full extent of the casualties. The long diversion had used up precious fuel reserves and many bombers, especially those that had suffered minor damage to their fuel lines, were running short of petrol when they reached the North Sea. Three Halifaxes from 433 Porcupine Squadron at Skipton-on-Swale failed to regain the safety of their base. One crashed at Catfoss, another ditched (fortunately all the crew were saved) and a third managed to cross the coast so that the crew could bale out near Thirsk. One of the Bluenose Halifaxes ran out of fuel over Scarborough and all but one of the crew baled out safely; but three of the crew of an Iroquois Halifax died when the pilot had to ditch. It was no mean a feat to ditch a giant bomber such as the Halifax, perhaps struggling on two engines and with damaged flight controls, in rough seas with a thirty-knot wind driving huge waves across a hundred-foot swell. F/Sgt Pugh attempted it in his 102 Squadron Halifax when he ran out of fuel seventy miles east of Dundee. His crew scrambled into the dinghy but when this overturned the intense cold prevented three men from climbing aboard. One by one they sank while the rest gazed helplessly at a Lindholme lifeboat dropped out of their reach by a deep-search Air Sea Rescue Warwick. Eventually, four men were pulled aboard an Air

Sea Rescue launch from Tayport but of these only three would reach dry land alive.

Harris allowed his crews no respite. From Bomber Command headquarters the order to attack Berlin again flashed to the Groups on the morning of 30 January 1944 - the fourteenth anniversary of Adolf Hitler's accession to power as Chancellor of Germany. Berlin's citizens expected a raid on that particular anniversary and steeled themselves for the event. Harris was unwilling to miss the opportunity. The weather forecast was promising; there were more than four hundred Lancasters still serviceable while Yorkshire's 4 and 6 Groups could, between them, provide an additional 106 aircraft. This relatively small number was due to the fact that Harris at last recognised the risks inherent in sending the Yorkshire squadrons still equipped with the Mk II and Mk V Halifaxes on long-distance operations across the heavily defended areas of northern Germany. Mark IIIs only would be allowed to operate over Berlin.

In spite of the enforced absence of the older Halifaxes and the heavy losses suffered during this costly January offensive, Bomber Command was still able to inflict substantial damage on a city that was truly under siege from the air. Most women and children had by now been evacuated from Berlin; a large proportion of the city's electrical and aircraft manufacturing plant was out of action for weeks at a time; while public transport facilities and main-line railway stations were often at a stand-still. Fire raged in Berlin during the night of 30/31 January 1944 though little of the havoc caused below was visible to the crews flying at 20,000 feet above the cloud-covered city. Thirty-two Lancasters were missing from this operation. Yorkshire lost a solitary Halifax from the RCAF base at Skipton-on-Swale. This was the last of the four January raids against Berlin. Each had been successful and the last one had led to particularly extensive damage, destroying Goebbels' Propaganda HQ and putting much of the city's U-Bahn out of action. It was also significant that, for the first time, a Mosquito escort fighter equipped with Serrate search radar flew with the bombers and scored a victory over a German night-fighter; while some remarkably cheerful bomber crews reported on their return that there didn't seem to be so much flak or so many fighters about as usual. Was German resistance beginning to weaken at last?

They would not know the answer to this until the middle of February. Harris stood his squadrons down for a brief rest. Heavy snowfalls turned this rest into a fortnight's leave for most of the aircrew; while the ground crews brought newly arrived aircraft up to operational standards. Harris intended to launch his next attack on Berlin on 13 February but bad weather conditions pushed the date back to 15/16 February 1944. All the Groups took part, a total of 891 aircraft of which 177 came from 4 Group and 150 from 6 Group. Harris wished to create widespread fires in the German capital and of the total bomb tonnage carried by the Main Force (2.643 tons), incendiaries accounted for 1,413 tons. Harris adopted some novel tactics in the hope of confusing the German defences. He sent a a formation of Mosquitoes ahead of the Main Force to drop TIs, flares and a few bombs to persuade the German controllers that this was a 'spoof' raid. Simultaneously, a picked force of H2S Lancasters flew beyond Berlin to Frankfurt-on-Oder masquerading as Pathfinders marking the 'target for tonight'. On the whole, these diversions met with little success. As soon as German radar picked up the Main Force over the North Sea, the Luftwaffe's reaction was to vector the Tame Boars to the track followed by the bomber stream as far as the edge of Berlin where the flak was sending up barrages to a height of 24,000 feet. Quite unexpectedly, there was a running fight between Bomber Command's gunners and the Tame Boar night-fighters from Denmark to Berlin and back again, a wearying and dangerous experience for the bomber crews.. Surprisingly, flak proved less deadly than expected and it is believed that only three bombers fell over the city.

The raid did not achieve the success that was intended, even though more bombs fell on or around Berlin than on Hamburg at the time of the 1943 firestorm. It had lasted barely twenty minutes and the concentration of aircraft (estimated at just under forty per minute) was a tribute to the accurate flying and precision-timing now characteristic of Bomber Command. Some 3000 separate fires caused immense damage and high-explosives killed an estimated 640 people, though some of these died in towns and villages twenty or thirty miles away from the main aiming point. Those Yorkshire crews going to war in their new Mk III Halifaxes were pleased to be able to fly faster and higher; "height means safety" was a maxim never denied by Halifax men. P/O Foster had brought his new Halifax from Snaith and bombed Berlin from a relatively safe 23,400 feet. For his crew it was a quiet ride and later, when he wrote home, he commented:

> On the whole I shall say Berlin had a rather rough night with the heaviest attack ever. We were almost first in before they got organised. Every-

thing indicated that Berlin is finished and I think we will probably be in at the death. That will be a fitting finish just as Hamburg was a fitting start.[4]

Forty-four years later this former 51 Squadron pilot had to admit that he had been wrong but, as he said, back in 1944 lots of other people were wrong as well.

Twenty-five Lancasters and seventeen Halifaxes failed to return from Berlin that night. In 4 Group, Elvington's 77 Squadron suffered the greatest loss. Three of its Halifaxes were shot down and tragically all the crew members were killed. Holme-on-Spalding's 76 Squadron sent nine of its older Halifaxes to Berlin and lost a B.V to the cannon-fire of a Ju 88 night-fighter near Schweinfurt. No 102 Squadron at Pocklington and No 158 at Lissett both lost two Halifaxes, as did Australia's 466 Squadron based at Leconfield. F/O Clarke and his crew flying in a 10 Squadron Halifax from Melbourne all died when their bomber exploded over Berlin. Four of the Canadian Squadrons in 6 Group - Nos 419, 424, 426 and 434 - each lost one bomber on this Berlin raid. Again, there were tragedies on the return to Yorkshire where the northern part of the County was covered in mist. A 640 Squadron Halifax piloted by F/Sgt Vicary was on low fuel and searching for Leconfield. Even though the crew realised they were well to the north of their base they decided to bale out as soon as they crossed the coast and their Halifax crashed near Coxwold. A second Halifax from 640 Squadron, captained by by F/O Barkley, was less fortunate. He was probably also running short of fuel and looking for somewhere to land when his bomber hit a hill near Scarborough, killing all the crew. At Tholthorpe an RCAF Halifax from 420 Snowy Owl Squadron crashed after several attempts to land. If only there had been an Emergency Landing Ground in Yorkshire. It was almost ready: Carnaby would open on 26 March 1944, one day after the last Bomber Command raid on Berlin.

★ ★ ★

By mid-February 1944 the Battle of Berlin had virtually come to an end. The Americans had not joined in; Germany had not been forced to surrender. Nevertheless, Air Chief Marshal Harris was determined that Bomber Command would make a last raid on the German capital before handing over Berlin to the 8th USAAF as a primary target on 1 April 1944, the date designated for the end of the Combined Bomber Offensive POINTBLANK.

Dramatic changes overtook the Yorkshire squadrons in the month preceding the final assault on Berlin. On

19 February 1944 they were briefed for a major attack upon Leipzig. In Merrick's words, it was "an ill-fated operation from the outset". A total of 823 aircraft, including 255 Halifaxes, set out to attack this distant city that stood high on the primary target list. The previous major raid on Leipzig, an important manufacturer of Ju 88 interceptors, was on 3/4 December 1943 when it had been well marked and accurately bombed by the 527-strong Main Force. However, on the night of 19/20 February 1944 it was a much bigger raid and Harris had ordered some complex diversions including a large Window force on gardening sorties over Kiel and spoof raids by Mosquitoes dropping Window and bombs over Berlin. These did not mislead the German controllers who assembled night-fighters along the entire route of the bomber stream over Holland and Germany. To compound the problem, the Main Force had much higher tail-winds than had been forecast - perhaps the first night when the phenomenon known as the 'jetstream' had been encountered at 18-25,000 feet. The jetstream caused many aircraft to arrive over Leipzig ahead of the Pathfinders and the German flak gunners, after recovering from their astonishment at the sight of scores of Lancasters and Halifaxes orbiting the target area, proceeded to knock twenty of the bombers out of the sky. Another four bombers were lost in collisions and a total of forty-four Lancasters (7.8%) and thirty-four Halifaxes (13.3%) failed to return.

The RCAF's 6 Group in Yorkshire sustained the heaviest loss: eighteen of the 129 aircraft despatched to Leipzig failed to return, a 14% loss. Overall, it was to be the second heaviest Bomber Command loss of the war and placed a serious and unexpected burden on the broad shoulders of Air Chief Marshal Harris. He was actively contemplating changes in Bomber Command's tactics and the Leipzig casualties forced a decision concerning the composition of his Main Force.

During January and February 1944, the casualties inflicted on the Halifax Squadrons in Nos 4 and 6 Groups - Mk III Halifaxes as well as the older Mk II and Mk V models - were alarming by any standards. Reviewing this increasingly gloomy picture, Harris was most concerned by the *cumulative* losses experienced by the Yorkshire Squadrons during January and February 1944, now well over 10%, and though he knew that it was impossible to re-equip *every* squadron with Mk IIIs over the next few weeks he nevertheless decreed that no more of the Merlin-engined Mark II and Mk V Halifaxes would take part in raids over Germany.

Martin Middlebrook neatly sums up the reaction to this news by quoting a 10 Squadron pilot who said:

"I should think that the sigh of relief could be heard all over Yorkshire." [5]

He goes on to observe that Harris had now been forced to withdraw both the Short Stirling and the Merlin-engined Handley Page Halifax from the Battle of Berlin. Both, in their different ways, had been found wanting when faced with the growing power of the German flak and night-fighter force and Harris, as a responsible military commander, had taken the proper decisions in this matter.

Middlebrook also makes the point that it also meant a reduction of 30% of the Command's bomb load and the immediate disappearance of ten Yorkshire Squadrons from the Command's Order of Battle. But as Merrick emphasises, the restriction was limited to No 10 Squadron at Melbourne (for two weeks), No 77 at Elvington (until June), No 102 at Pocklington (until May) and to Canada's 419 Squadron at Middleton St George which converted to the Lancaster Mk X in April. All the other Halifax squadrons in Yorkshire were re-equipped with the Mark III version and contributed to the very heavy raids over southern Germany beginning *immediately* after Leipzig. The Lancaster and Halifax losses incurred during these raids are shown in brackets; discrepancies in total are accounted for by the numbers of Mosquitoes flying with the Main Force heavy bombers.

Date	Target	Main Force	Lancasters	Halifaxes
20/21 February	Stuttgart	598	460 (7)	126 (2)
24/25 February	Schweinfurt	734	554 (26)	169 (7)
25/26 February	Augsburg	594	461 (16)	123 (5)
1/2 March	Stuttgart	557	415 (3)	129 (1)
15/16 March	Stuttgart	863	617 (27)	230 (10)
18/19 March	Frankfurt	846	620 (10)	209 (12)
22/23 March	Frankfurt	816	620 (26)	184 (7)

On 24 March the 1st Bomb Division of the 8th USAAF pulverized Frankfurt for the third time. One more German city had virtually ceased to exist. On the same day, orders reached Bomber Command for yet another attack upon the 'Big City', one more 'maximum effort'. Harris had planned the operation for the night of 21/22 and, unusually, Harris had composed a special message for the crews. It was read out in all the briefing rooms:

Although successful blind bombing attacks on Berlin have destroyed large areas of it, there is still a substantial section of this vital city more or less intact. To write this off, it is of great importance that tonight's attack should be closely concentrated on the aiming point. You must not think that

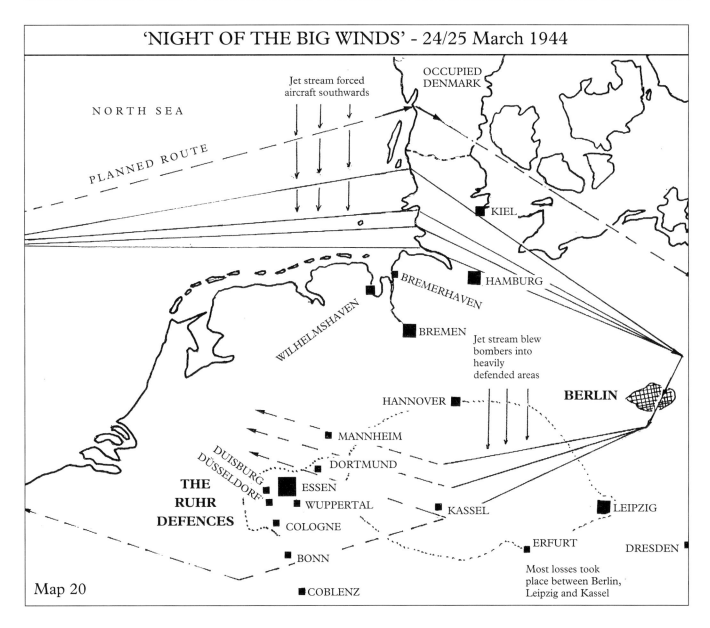

'NIGHT OF THE BIG WINDS' - 24/25 March 1944

Map 20

the size of Berlin makes accurate bombing un-important. There is no point in dropping bombs on the devastated areas in the west and south-west. Weather over the target should be good. Go in and do the job.

Weather conditions over northern Germany had forced Harris to postpone the raid until the night of 24/25 March and by then he was fairly optimistic about his chances of success though with the forecast of mist and fog over Eastern England at around 0200-0300 hours on 25 March it might prove difficult to recover Main Force aircraft to their home airfields. Ground crews sweated all

day to rehabilitate damaged bombers and by the early evening, despite the losses taken during the recent attacks on southern Germany, Harris was able to put 577 Lancasters, 216 Halifaxes and eighteen Mosquitoes into this final assault on Berlin. Strong northerly winds were expected and Harris had introduced a new tactic: a movable 'Zero Hour'. This was to deal with the problem of strong winds and to re-arrange times for the whole Main Force as well as the Pathfinders. Changes in Zero Hour were by means of codes added to the 'broadcast winds' transmitted from Bomber Command Head-quarters to all Main Force and Pathfinder aircraft at regular intervals during an operation. Command HQ received data from specially selected navigators (called 'windfinders') en route to Germany, processed it as rapidly as possible and then broadcast it back to the attackers.

Precise timing was vital as the entire operation was to be carried out with five waves of bombers at the rate of forty bombers per minute over target, a closely-packed force protected as far as possible by showers of Window. Yorkshire's squadrons were present in all five waves with 4 Group flying between 19-24,000 feet and 6 Group at 19-23,000 feet. However, the northerly winds actually encountered across northern Europe and over the target were far in excess of the speeds *broadcast* during the operation. Navigators from the Yorkshire airfields discovered that, after they had set course from Hull, crossed the North Sea and reached the Danish coast, the actual windspeed was 92 mph, over twice the forecast strength. Over northern Germany the jetstream reached 130-140 mph, far in excess of the broadcast winds from Command Headquarters where incredulous meteorological officers deliberately reduced the data received and thus passed inaccurate wind strengths back to the Main Force crews. Six hundred miles away, the navigators in these crews then began to doubt the reliability of their H2S sets once they discovered they were so far south of track. Some Halifaxes were achieving a ground speed of over 300 mph !

These unexpected conditions meant that the Main Force was soon spread out over a wide front and flying ahead of schedule. Two master bombers, in a Mosquito and a Lancaster, did their best to concentrate the far-flung aircraft and revised the Zero Hour from 1030 to 1025 so that early arrivals would not have to wait quite so long for those flying up from the south. Even so, some of the Yorkshire aircraft, well ahead of schedule, wished the Zero Hour had been retimed to 1020. In the event, over 70% of the bombers managed to attack Berlin within their allotted times.

The raid was one of the least successful in this long series of attacks. It went down in Bomber Command history as the 'night of the strong winds' but not as a raid that inflicted significant damage on Berlin except in those already devastated south-west areas of the city that Harris had hoped to avoid. German ground observers noted the scattered nature of the bombing due, undoubtedly, to the inability of Pathfinders to identify specific targets visually. Parramatta blind ground marking (using H2S) and Wanganui sky markers were wind-blown; while the few TIs dropped on the ground were often obscured by cloud

- especially during the first seven minutes of the attack. Blind Backers-Up kept the ground marking going but, as P/O Ollson flying his 426 Squadron Halifax from Lissett observed, results were "difficult to assess because of cloud".[6] There were plenty of fires and the all-NCO crew of Halifax LW371 from 10 Squadron on the way home to Melbourne said they could see Berlin burning 140 miles away.

It was during the return flight from Berlin that Bomber Command sustained very heavy losses. Seventy-two bombers, forty-four Lancasters and twenty-eight Halifaxes, plus one Serrate Mosquito failed to return. Twenty-one of these were shot down by flak on the return flight to England. In truth. this heavy toll was really exacted by the weather: the northerly winds blew many bombers south into heavy flak concentrations over Magdeburg, Leipzig, Kassel and the Ruhr. Churchill had once exhorted Harris not to fight the enemy and the weather at the same time yet Sir Arthur had no option but to fight both in this the great winter offensive against Berlin. Of course, German night-fighters were similarly dispersed by the wind and found that intercepting Halifaxes and Lancasters in the hurly-burly of that night sky was a daunting task. Their deadly *schräge Musik* guns persuaded them to make seventy-seven claims, and it is likely that fifty-six of these were valid, a remarkable achievement by the Tame Boar units, especially the crack night-fighter units NJG-1, NJG-2, NJG3 and NJG-5. Their success was not recognised in Bomber Command's evaluation of this raid and the official report credited flak with the majority of the lost bombers. Coupled with the light losses the following night when, to the total surprise of the German defences, 705 aircraft attacked the Oboe-marked city of Essen in the Ruhr, there was unjustified euphoria about the decline of the German night fighter force. Four nights later, that euphoria would be exploded on the way to Nuremberg.

But the casualties on the last Berlin raid were serious enough with seventy-two aircraft missing. Yorkshire's losses were extensive: fifteen Halifaxes from 4 Group ; and thirteen Halifaxes from 6 Group. In 4 Group, Breighton's 78 Squadron was the hardest hit when it discovered that of the twenty Halifaxes it had sent to Berlin no less than five were missing. Another, piloted by F/O Wimberley, nearly made it back to safety but on the approach into Cranfield his one remaining engine cut out and the Halifax crashed, killing all the crew. Snaith's 102 Squadron lost two Halifaxes piloted by F/Lt Curtis and F/O McPherson. From Lissett, F/Sgt Van Skyke's Halifax failed to return but there was hope that P/O Simpson

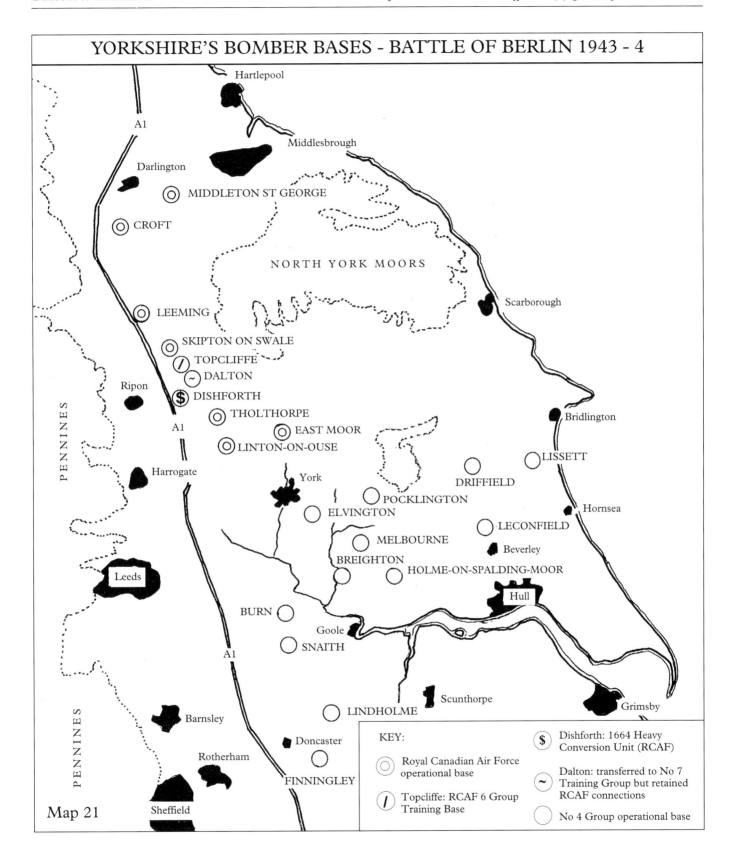

YORKSHIRE'S BOMBER BASES - BATTLE OF BERLIN 1943 - 4

Hartlepool

A1

Middlesbrough

Darlington

◎ MIDDLETON ST GEORGE

◎ CROFT

NORTH YORK MOORS

Scarborough

◎ LEEMING

◎ SKIPTON ON SWALE

/ ◎ TOPCLIFFE

~ DALTON

Ripon

$ ◎ DISHFORTH

◎ THOLTHORPE

A1

◎ EAST MOOR

◎ LINTON-ON-OUSE

Bridlington

○·LISSETT

Harrogate

York

DRIFFIELD

○ POCKLINGTON

·Hornsea

○ ELVINGTON

○·LECONFIELD

○ MELBOURNE

▪ Beverley

BREIGHTON

○ HOLME-ON-SPALDING-MOOR

Leeds

Hull

BURN ○

Goole

○ SNAITH

A1

Scunthorpe

○ LINDHOLME

Grimsby

Barnsley

Doncaster

Rotherham

○

FINNINGLEY

Map 21

Sheffield

KEY:

◎ Royal Canadian Air Force operational base

/ Topcliffe: RCAF 6 Group Training Base

$ Dishforth: 1664 Heavy Conversion Unit (RCAF)

~ Dalton: transferred to No 7 Training Group but retained RCAF connections

○ No 4 Group operational base

Air and Ground Crew Halifax BIII Z-Zebra, 640 Squadron, Leconfield. Holding the motor car horn is the pilot, F/Lt R.W.H. Goorrum.　　*Yorkshire Air Museum*

The table below analyses the heavy price paid by the two Yorkshire-based Groups during the Battle of Berlin.

Bomber Command's Yorkshire Squadrons
Casualties suffered during the Berlin Raids
1943-44

4 Group Royal Air Force (Halifaxes IIs, IIIs and Vs)

Squad-ron	Base	Sorties	Losses	As a %	Men killed
10	Melbourne	133	10	7.5	58
51	Snaith	150	9	6.0	33
76	Holme	146	5	3.4	19
77	Elvington	134	15	11.2	96
78	Breighton	144	12	8.3	56
158	Lissett	136	15	11.0	71
466	(Australian)/ Leconfield	93	7	7.5	31
578	Burn	59	4	6.8	22
640	Leconfield	66	2	3.0	27

6 Group Royal Canadian Air Force (Halifaxes IIs, IIIs and Vs; Lancaster IIs)

Squadron	Base	Sorties	Losses	As a %	Men killed
408	Linton	205	8	3.9	57*
419	Middleton	112	9	8.0	34
420	Tholthorpe	24	1	4.0	2
424	Skipton	20	2	10.0	14
425	Tholthorpe	14	2	14.3	14
426	Linton	210	13	6.2	88*
427	Leeming	111	7	6.3	44
428	Middleton	106	5	4.7	18
429	Leeming	87	7	8.0	34
431	Tholthorpe/ Croft	70	5	7.1	26
432	Skipton/ East Moor	127†	4	3.9	29**
433	Skipton	57	4	7.0	18
434	Tholthorpe/ Croft	77	12	15.6	21†

NOTES:

★ These squadrons flew Lancaster IIs.

★★ 432 Squadron operated three types of aircraft during the Battle of Berlin, if one includes the earlier August raids: Wellington (to October 1943), Lancaster II (until January 1944); Halifax III thereafter.

† This Squadron flew Halifax Vs during the battle and suffered proportionately the highest FTR ('failed to return') in all the Yorkshire Squadrons.

would be able to cross the North Sea. He had radioed that he had lost an engine on port and starboard sides and was losing height just as the Norfolk coast was coming into sight. Unwilling to ditch, he tried a landing on the beach at Ingham where mines had been buried to deter a German invasion back in 1940. Simpson's Halifax exploded, killing him and the rest of his crew. Three of Burn's Halifaxes failed to return, the Australians at Leconfield lost two of their Halifaxes while No 76 at Holme and No 640 at Leconfield each had a crew missing.

6 Group had two recently formed Squadrons on the raid: no 420 at Tholthorpe and No 424 at Skipton-on-Swale. One Tholthorpe crew was shot down but all survived. F/O Kramp flying from Skipton crashed at Olfen with one survivor. All the other Canadian Halifax squadrons took casualties on the final raid: No 425 at Tholthorpe, No 427 at Leeming, No 428 at Middleton St George and No 433 at Skipton all lost two aircraft; No 432 flying from East Moor lost a single Halifax; while No 429 at Leeming had the heaviest loss with three of its Halifaxes missing.

One Squadron in each Group came through the raid without losing an aircraft to the German defences. All of Shiny Ten's Halifaxes returned to base and there was an extra Halifax on the dispersal that night after a 1658 Heavy Conversion Unit aircraft from Riccall took advantage of Melbourne's excellent landing aids. In 6 Group 408 Squadron sent nine of its Lancaster IIs to Berlin without loss to enemy action though one flown by WO2 Kasper had to be abandoned.

Chapter Nineteen

The End of the Main Offensive: The Nuremberg Raid
30/31 March 1944

Prior to the handing of Bomber Command over to the Supreme Allied Commander, General Eisenhower, Air Chief Marshal Sir Arthur Harris completed his main offensive against Berlin and other major industrial cities with an attack upon Nuremberg. As the raid made little or no impact upon Nuremberg's industrial productivity but did result in Bomber Command's biggest loss for the entire war, it is worthwhile considering its planning and execution. The raid has been the subject of considerable historical controversy and a book published by Anthony Cave Brown in 1975 suggested that the target, the route and the tactics had all been leaked to the Luftwaffe.[1] The text had a very wide circulation on both sides of the Atlantic and there was also a German edition. However, when Martin Middlebrook published his second edition of *The Nuremberg Raid* in 1980[2] he was able to demonstrate that there was absolutely no evidence for Cave Brown's suggestions and that the Nuremberg raid was a normally planned operation that went drastically wrong for other very specific reasons.

It was a 'maximum effort' raid designed to inflict great damage on an important industrial city. Most of the northern squadrons were involved in the overall plan and, as usual, all aircrews were given a thorough briefing on the reasons for visiting this particular target. The following re-enactment of the Nuremberg briefing is based on a lecture given in South Africa by S/Ldr Frank Lord DFC and F/Lt P. Fox and the author is indebted to them for permission to reproduce some of the text verbatim.[3] S/Ldr Lord sets the scene, emphasising the security characteristic of a pre-operational briefing:

"We ask you to go back in time to Thursday March 30th 1944 and to imagine you are aircrew sitting in a large Nissen hut on a wartime bomber station in Yorkshire. There would be about 180 of you sitting there, representing the crews; seven men to each of 25 aircraft, plus a few supernumeraries who will be flying with experienced crews to gain experience. The remaining aircraft of the squadron are either out on simulated bombing practice, cross-country navigational exercises, or undergoing overhauls. Their crews are not here.

Facing you are the Station Commander, the Officer i/c Flying, Navigation Leader, Signals and Gunnery Leaders, the Intelligence Officer and the Meteorological Officer. Outside the closed doors and shuttered windows, armed RAF Police stand. You are isolated from the rest of the station for the time being, and the station itself is isolated from the outside world . . ."

Station Commander

"Very shortly you will be called upon to support the invasion of Europe and Sir Arthur Harris is anxious to strike at one last major target before this happens. It is a target he knows is very dear to Churchill's heart."

It had been the Station Commander's responsibility to ensure total security once the teleprinter at High Wycombe had clacked out the target code-name *Grayling*. He had immediately blocked all outgoing phone calls and intercepted all incoming calls. Now the station was totally cut off from the outside world as preparations for the raid began. It was unlikely that he had any inkling of the arguments that had preceded the route selected for Nuremberg. Unlike the Berlin raids, the bomber stream was unable to dog-leg over relatively safe stretches of water such as the Baltic Sea. The plan for Nuremberg was to change course over Belgium and then fly the 'Long Leg' before turning south towards Nuremberg. It was important both to miss the flak defences at Mannheim and Frankfurt and to reduce the flying time as much as possible.

The problem of flying time was felt most keenly by the northern squadrons who, on operations over southern Germany, had further to fly than the Merlin-engined Lancasters in the other Groups. Yet the Yorkshire Groups were equally anxious to secure maximum protection by confusing the defences as far as possible. On the whole the Yorkshire squadrons preferred several dog-legs rather than a long, straight run. So there were objections to the plan: from Pathfinder Leader Bennett; from Carr at 4 Group who was sending

Halifaxes with lighter incendiary loads; and from McEwen at 6 Group with two bomber types (Halifax and Lancaster) in his squadrons. Nevertheless, the Lancaster Groups with the heavier bomb-loads and the faster aircraft had the final say: it would be straight in an out of Nuremberg, as fast as possible.

Of course, the Station Commander sensed that, by choosing this particular route, all sorts of problems might emerge; but he preferred to leave such matters to his technical officers.

Officer i/c Flying

The target tonight is Nuremberg on the River Pegnitz some ninety miles to the north of Munich. As a military target, Nuremberg is an important industrial city with a population of 350,000 (a little larger than Leeds) and a centre for general and electrical engineering. The famous M.A.N. Works produce armaments of all kinds there and, since their large factory in Berlin was bombed, Siemens plant in Nuremberg has stepped up production of its electric motors, searchlights and firing devices for mines.

You've already disproved, on many occasions, Göring's earlier boast that no bombs would ever fall on the Fatherland. Now you'll have the opportunity to dissuade the Nazis from holding further mass rallies in the city most favoured for these. Nuremberg deserves a maximum efort and that is what it will now get. Ten Squadrons of No 1 Group, eight Squadrons from No 3 Group, seven Squadrons from No 4, twelve from No 5, nine from No 6 and 12 Squadrons from No 8 Pathfinder Force Group will participate - altogether 820 Lancasters and Halifaxes will take part. In addition 15 Mosquitoes will adopt an intruder role to seek out night-fighters and destroy them. So you'll have plenty of company and it behoves everyone to keep a good lookout at the turning points to avoid collisions.

H-hour is 0105 through to 0122 (17 minutes). After the PFF has marked the target, the Main Force will bomb from H-hour + 5 for the remaining 12 minutes.

Our time on target is set for H-hour + 9 minutes between the bands of 20,000 to 20,500 feet. Take-off time is 22.00 hrs. Good luck: have a good trip!

Navigation Leader

Navigators have already been briefed and have prepared their charts and captain's maps.

To minimise enemy radar detection, the Main Force will maintain a height of no more than 2000 ft across country and the coast, with navigation lights on to the first turning point at 51° 50 North and 2° 30 East. Please keep a sharp look-out, captains and gunners.

At this point you will start a steady climb, switching off all lights when the turn is completed on to your south-easterly course of 130°. The Belgian coast will be crossed at 8000 feet just to the east of Bruges to the next turning point at 50° 30 North 4° 36 East, just short of Charleroi; there you will alter course to port, gradually climb to your bombing height and reach the last turning point before the target, at Fulda 50° 32 North 10° 36 East, and then on to the target . . . Indicated air speeds will be 172 mph to the first turning point. Then climb at 150 across the coast to the next turning point and hold on to the target. If it is necessary to make a second run on the target, orbit left to avoid others in the Main Force coming up behind you.

On leaving the target, increase speed to 182 and hold this, gradually losing height to cross the coast at 4000 feet. Corrected winds will be broadcast to the Main Force every half-hour between 23.40 and 03.40.

Bombing Leader

Your all-up weight tonight is just short of 65,000lbs. Bomb load is just over 7000lbs with 4 x 1000lb HEs and 3000lb of incendiaries. You have six tanks of petrol - altogether 2200 gallons - more than sufficient for the trip tonight.

Including this squadrons's contribution, altogether 3000 tons of bombs will fall on the target tonight. There are three main concentrations for your attack . . . and, depending on what cloud cover there may be, Pathfinder Force will employ either Wanganui sky flares if the target is completely obscured, Parramatta markers, dropped on H2S, if there is broken cloud partially obscuring the target; or Newhaven ground markers dropped on visual identification, aided by H2S. Night maps should be marked accordingly. Initially red markers and incendiaries will be dropped, then green markers turning yellow; then these will be further fed by red markers, with target illuminators, from 0109 to 0122. Met will tell you that a fairly stiff crosswind can be expected on target, so bomb-aimers will need to be pretty snappy with their bombing. On the other hand they must be careful to avoid the tendency to 'creep-back' with their bombs and miss the vital areas. Make a good job of it, chaps. We don't want to go back again. Window: one parcel a minute over the coast and up to the first turning point over Charleroi. At your next turning point - Fulda - release Window at the rate of two parcels a minute for 5 minutes and at the rate of one a minute after leaving the target . . .

Met (Meteorological Officer)

Warm air is overtaking the cold air forming a warm front which is moving northward over NE Yorkshire and SW Scotland . . . There is a cold front now over Ireland and approaching the western side of England. It may lead to cu-nim (cumulus-nimbus), although we do not expect this to be continuous.

What is forecast is broken but fairly good cloud cover for you all the way to the target and back, and with some low cloud and precipitation in coastal areas. Winds will be moderate 40/50 at 18000 feet and generally blowing SW or W. There may be some low cloud and poor visibility down to 2000 yards at base on return. To sum up then: for the outward flight, broken cloud can be expected everywhere except Southern Germany where it is expected to be layered. Winds WSW 40/50, veering 50/60 over target. Light industrial smog in Groups 4 and 6 areas with valley fog towards dawn . . .

Intelligence Officer

The distance involved (pointing at the Long Leg) precludes wasting time and fuel on too many dog-legs and the route suggests a number of perhaps more vulnerable targets to the German defences, thus persuading them to disperse and thin out fighter concentrations. *The sheer simplicity of the route will surprise the Germans and keep them off balance sufficiently long for you to complete the operation without too much trouble.* I think you deserve this explanation and it may help to dispel any misgivings you may have about the direct route laid down.

As a further encouragement, I can tell you that just ahead of you when you cross the coast, Mosquitoes will open the night's proceedings with low-level attacks on the known night-fighter fields in Holland at Leeuwarden, Twente, Deelen and Venlo in a bid to keep them on the ground until you are well past.

At the same time off Texel and the Heligoland Bight, a force of fifty Halifaxes will start dropping mines as a diversionary move to keep the German ground controllers confused

Additional to this, and a while before the Main Force reaches the target, Mosquitoes will make a feint attack on Cologne between 2335 and 0007 hours. A further force of twenty Mosquitoes will also drop fighter flares, markers and Window on Kassel between 26 and 28 minutes after midnight in an attempt to spoof the German controllers into believing that the main attack is to be the Ruhr, and thus lead them to send the bulk of their fighters there.

So far as the ground defences are concerned, we've tried to route you over the coast both going and coming back where flak and searchlights are believed to be thin and the use of Window here will help to blur the picture from the ground.

Again, the route takes you across the southern end of the heavy Ruhr defensive area. Obviously, much depends on the accuracy of your course-keeping and your ability to maintain a well bunched-together pattern and no straying away from the main stream.

Night-fighters can as usual be expected, *but with cloud cover and Mosquito attacks to keep them grounded, the danger from these, we believe, will be minimised.* Keep a sharp lookout for them, however, and wireless operators, make sure your Fishpond [4] is working at all times.

From twenty-two airfields in the north of England 4 and 6 Groups Halifaxes and Lancasters took off into a dark, rainswept sky. Harris had earlier received reports via a weather Mosquito that the fair weather cumulus cloud presently over Germany would probably disappear during the evening; so there was no chance of cloud cover and the moon would therefore be bright that night. Despite this new information, Harris did not choose to cancel the operation though many of his colleagues at High Wycombe anticipated that he would. Harris was convinced that the gamble was worthwhile and the operations plan remained unchanged.

It was not long before the leaders of the bomber stream encountered two totally unexpected problems. Erratic winds were forcing them off track. Even worse, as they reached their cruising height over Germany they emerged into a sky lit by a brilliant half-moon. Here they encountered exceptionally cold air that caused their engine exhausts to form condensation trails or 'contrails' stretching far behind each bomber. Many crews were struck by the uniqueness of the situation and the sight reminded some of the giant American box formations leaving contrails high in the sky by day. On both sides of the main stream German Illuminators were dropping fighter flares and so bright was the night sky that crews could see Lancasters and Halifaxes cruising nearby, some so close that they could read their dulled red squadron codes by moonlight.

Moving against this armada of 786 heavy bombers were 246 German night-fighters and on the Long Leg towards Nuremberg there was fought the greatest air battle of all time. The German controllers assessed the size of the Halifax mining operation and the Mosquito spoofs and rightly decided they were merely Bomber Command diversions. The clear night sky and the lines of contrails, accurately reported by German observer posts below the Main Force route, convinced them that a southern city was the target. Accordingly, they moved their night-fighters into orbit over Ida and Otto beacons and awaited the Main Force, now reduced to 712 aircraft. Bomber losses began over Belgium where a 550 Squadron Lancaster was the first to fall, a victim of the flak at Liège. Reduction in the size of the Main Force was also caused by the 'early returners', fifty-two of whom had turned back mainly because of engine trouble. The Main Force had limited protection from Mosquitoes. Nineteen of the "Wooden Wonders" had set out on Serrate sorties though their sets could not home in on the latest German SN-2 radar. There were another thirty-three Mosquitoes on Intruder operations, shooting up the German airfields in a vain attempt to ground the night-fighter force.

So that night the German fighter crews had every advantage and could hardly believe their luck. Many had *schräge Musik* and unjammed SN-2 radar; they had plenty of fuel in their tanks; the sky was clear and the Main Force position was precisely marked by contrails. Moreover, they did not have to fly in search of their prey; Bomber Command was coming towards them. Once the carnage started the discipline of the Main Force tactics began to fail. The required cruising height - 19 to 20,000 feet - was fatal because it was here that the contrails formed and here that the Tame Boars flew under their

prey and blasted the bombers out of the sky. In self-preservation some pilots jettisoned part of their loads to secure height; others, especially crews flying some brand new Halifax IIIs from Holme on Spalding, found they could steadily gain height using the power of their uprated Hercules engines. Those who could reach 22,000 feet were relatively safe from the fighters and had a ringside seat from which to watch the massacre that was taking place below.

Some of the Canadian Halifaxes that had replaced the H2S blister with a 0.5" machine gun were at least able to deter the Ju 88s and Me 110s that crept below them. But for those who had no such protection the story was too often the same. Sudden deafening explosions, gaping holes in the fuselage, crew members dead or bleeding from cannon shell hits, flickerng flames in the fuel tanks and then the explosion that blasted dead or unconscious airmen into a sky rent by searchlights, coloured flares, tracer streams and flak bursts. Miraculously, a few of the crews who were catapulted into the night survived to become prisoners of war in a matter of minutes. Not all were so fortunate. S/Ldr Clack was flying a 76 Squadron Halifax from Holme and in the words of the Squadron historian, he

"along with six of his crew died when their Halifax exploded in a pulsating ball of flame. Clack, not yet twenty-one years of age, had barely time to shout 'Prepare to bale out!' when the end came. As the Halifax tore itself apart, F/Sgt Edwards, the mid-upper gunner, realised he was being propelled through a gap opening before him in the fuselage side. For some inexplicable reason he survived . . .'[5]

Experienced fliers with previous operations over Germany to their credit later remarked that they had never before seen parachutes descending at night. Moreover, height did not always spell safety in those exceptional meteorological conditions. Three of 76 Squadron's Halifaxes - including S/Ldr Clack's - fell to *schräge Musik* guns, a fate typical of most of the forty-one Lancasters and eighteen Halifaxes shot down on the Long Leg to Nuremberg.

The prevailing weather conditions also helped the German defenders. Already the bomber force had been misled by a breakdown in the windfinding system and some navigators were basing their calculations on inaccurate information. Now, to compound the problems, the weather over Nuremberg had begun to change. An occluded front, impossible to forecast, had created huge clouds with strong winds blowing across the city. Some Pathfinders were tracking several degrees off course and when they released their skymarkers these tended to drift away to the east. Pathfinders found no flak and no fighters. Nuremberg was keeping quiet under its protective cloud cover and, extraordinarily, when the Pathfinders left there was no Main Force behind them. Most had turned too far north and were now several minutes late for their bomb runs over the city. Twenty of the Backers-Up had survived the main battle and were in a position to renew the markers. But because of the wind, who could tell which of the original markers were accurately placed ? Unknown to the crews, most markers had pinpointed the town of Lauf (its radar image was similar to Nuremberg's) and although some Backers-Up corrected this error the Main Force crews could see in front of them an array of markers that in fact spread from the centre of Nuremberg eastwards to Lauf, a distance of ten miles. With a wide choice of markers and the usual "creep-back" the bombing was, as one crew from Leconfield's 640 Squadron said, "a bit of a shambles".

All of the nine bombers shot down on the final bomb run crashed at spots well to the east of the planned track, mute evidence of the effect of the weather on the final stages of this disastrous operation. But the failure of the Main Force to devastate Nuremberg, the intention of the raid, was also partly due to the fact that an estimated 119 Halifaxes and Lancasters wrongly identified their target and actually bombed nearby Schweinfurt causing modest damage to each of the ball-bearing factories! At first, some crews were reluctant to bomb because of the absence of markers. They orbited the area until they were forced to a decision. W/Cdr McKay, flying a Leaside Squadron Halifax from Croft, spent nineteen minutes over the 'target' before finally dropping his incendiaries on Schweinfurt.

As the bombers turned for home they encountered the thick cloud that had been promised for the outward flight. Some chose to fly 'on top' and risk the contrails now that the moon was waning. Technical problems abounded and none more so than the difficulties facing F/O Dubeski trying to nurse his badly damaged Halifax back to 427's base at Leeming. Both his inner and outer port engines were out of action and he could barely maintain height. As he struggled with the controls his crew reported that a Ju 88 was formating alongside. It stayed next to the Halifax as far as the French coast and then dived away. A chivalrous foe? Humanity amidst the slaughter? It was not the only bomber to be deliberately left alone by a

night-fighter on that extraordinary night. However, two bombers that strayed across Stuttgart received no mercy from the flak and a 51 Squadron Halifax flown by S/L Hill DFC was shot down here. A Canadian Halifax flown by S/L Laird DFC collided with a Lancaster from 622 Squadron and all but one of the fourteen crew members died when the two aircraft fell in Belgium.

There were more sagas as returning aircraft crossed the Channel or took short cuts home across the North Sea. A 429 Bison Halifax had been hit by a night-fighter near Stuttgart but the ventral 0.5" gun had forced the German to break off the encounter. After a violent corkscrew F/O Wilson discovered that his hydraulics were damaged, causing his flaps and undercarriage to drop down. In this condition his fuel would not take him to England and the crew decided to ditch in the Channel. All but the pilot survived and were picked up by Air Sea Rescue launches.

Most 4 and 6 Group aircraft made it safely back to an airfield - even if it was not their home base - but a 578 Squadron Halifax flown by P/O Cyril Barton was not so lucky. A fighter had damaged the Halifax during the 'Long Leg' and amidst the chaos caused by shell-fire and violent evasive action three of Barton's crew misunderstood orders and baled out. Although he now lacked a bomb-aimer, navigator and wireless operator, Barton flew on, bombed Nuremberg and used his captain's map to set a compass course for home. With one of his engines out and low on fuel, Barton brought his bomber across the North Sea and reached the darkened English coast at barely 1500 feet. As he approached the little village of Ryehope, two more engines stopped. He put the nose down and searched for a landing space. Looming in front of him was a row of houses and he lifted the nose to clear these, sacrificing the last of his flying speed. With his three remaining crew members bracing themselves behind the mainspar, Barton came in for his forced landing at Ryhope Colliery, County Durham. One wing hit the end of another row of houses and the battered Halifax slithered to a stop in the colliery yard. Barton was fatally injured in the crash though he lived for thirty minutes after rescuers pulled him from the wreckage. All four men were decorated. Cyril Barton was awarded a posthumous VC, the only VC in the Battle of Berlin and the sole Halifax crew member ever to receive this award. Sgt Trousdale, the flight engineer, received the DFM as did the two gunners, Sgt Brice and Sgt Wood.

At first the debriefing officers had no hint of the disaster that had befallen Bomber Command. The first crews to come in were in some cases those who had bombed Schweinfurt by mistake or who had been in the

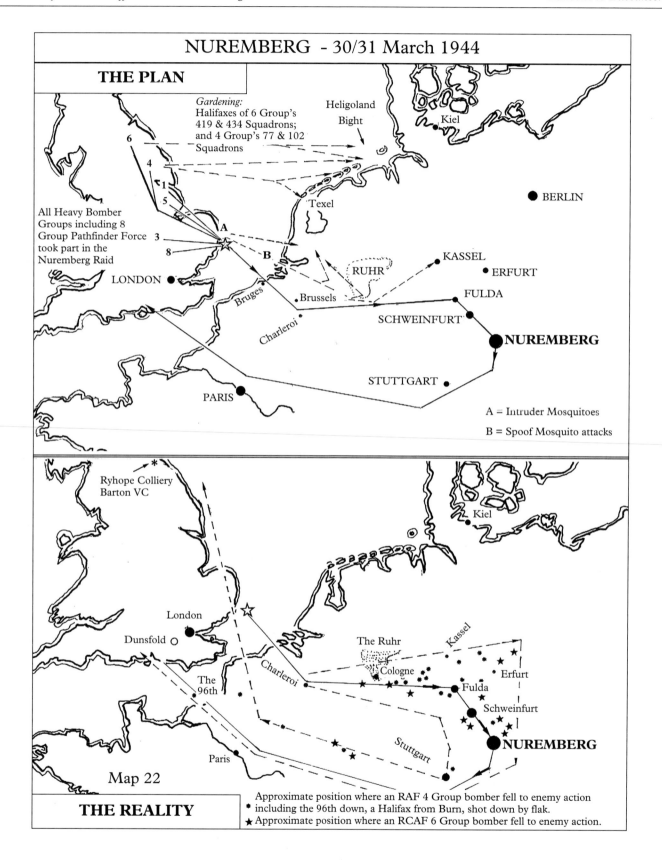

NUREMBERG - 30/31 March 1944

THE PLAN

Gardening:
Halifaxes of 6 Group's
419 & 434 Squadrons;
and 4 Group's 77 & 102
Squadrons

Heligoland
Bight

Kiel

Texel

BERLIN

All Heavy Bomber
Groups including 8
Group Pathfinder Force
took part in the
Nuremberg Raid

A

B

RUHR

KASSEL

ERFURT

FULDA

SCHWEINFURT

NUREMBERG

LONDON

Bruges

Brussels

Charleroi

STUTTGART

PARIS

A = Intruder Mosquitoes
B = Spoof Mosquito attacks

Ryhope Colliery
Barton VC

Kiel

London

Dunsfold

The Ruhr

Kassel

Cologne

Erfurt

Charleroi

The
96th

Fulda

Schweinfurt

Stuttgart

NUREMBERG

Paris

Map 22

THE REALITY

Approximate position where an RAF 4 Group bomber fell to enemy action
* including the 96th down, a Halifax from Burn, shot down by flak.
★ Approximate position where an RCAF 6 Group bomber fell to enemy action.

The Nuremberg Raid 30/31 March 1944

The Yorkshire Squadrons' Order of Battle

4 Group Air Vice-Marshal C.R Carr

Squadron	Base	Aircraft type and number despatched	Comment
10	Melbourne	Halifax (13)	
51	Snaith	Halifax (17)	
76	Holme	Halifax (14)	
77	Elvington	Halifax (10)	Mining force
78	Breighton	Halifax (16)	
102	Pocklington	Halifax (10)	Mining force
158	Lissett	Halifax (16)	
466 RAAF	Leconfield	Halifax (16)	
578	Burn	Halifax (11)	
640	Leconfield	Halifax (16)	

6 Group (RCAF) Air Vice-Marshal C.M. McEwen

Squadron	Base	Aircraft type and number despatched	Comment
408 Goose	Linton	Lancaster (12)	
419 Moose	Middleton	Halifax/ Lancaster	With 428, sent a total of 22 Halifaxes on the mining force
420 Snowy/Owl	Tholthorpe	Halifax (14)	
424 Tiger	Skipton	Halifax (12)	
425 Alouette	Tholthorpe	Halifax (12)	
426 Thunderbird	Linton	Lancaster (13)	
427 Lion	Leeming	Halifax (16)	
428 Ghost	Middleton	Halifax	See above: mining force
429 Bison	Leeming	Halifax (13)	
431 Iroquois	Croft	Halifax	Converting to Halifax BIII in March 1944
432 Leaside	East Moor	Halifax (14)	
433 Porcupine	Skipton	Halifax (12)	
434 Bluenose	Croft	Halifax (7)	Mining force

van of the action. Not every aircraft had been attacked by a vengeful night-fighter or been ripped open by flak. After all, over five hundred of the bombers flew to the Nuremberg area, bombed and returned home without incident. Some of these crews described their flight of eight or more hours as a "quiet ride". This was certainly the opinion of Sgt Ed Solman, an RAF Flight Engineer serving with Canada's 427 Squadron at Leeming. He had been flying operations since the Wuppertal raid (29/30 May 1943) on Halifax Vs piloted by W/C Burnside DFC and then saw plenty of action with F/O Phil Shannon DFC over Magdeburg, Stuttgart, Essen and two trips to Berlin on Halifax BIIIs. The Nuremberg raid was his fifteenth operation and his comments below offer an aviator's overview of the first 'half' of a long tour of thirty-eight operations.

"Phil Shannon was a brilliant pilot, blind as a bat but with different spectacles to correct long-range and close-up vision. Our most worrying problem on these long trips - Berlin and Nuremberg especially - was that the long-range tank on the Halifax III didn't always work correctly.On the Stuttgart trip we were getting quite low coming home but did a small sum and decided we could make it. We did - just - into Dunsfold of all places. We were sqwawking Darkie - that's the emergency call one down from Mayday - and every searchlight in the south of England pointed towards Dunsfold. Not a bad system. We were running on vapour by then and one engine stopped when the tail came down.

Surely, Berlin was always the worst but that was because it was such a long way, not because it was so heavily defended. You were up longer and therefore had a greater chance of being clobbered. Flak was always frightening, but the fighters were worse. On the way home you were lighter, of course, but the fighters had plenty of warning by then. Best to come back over France if you had enough fuel and that was the one good thing about the planned route for the Nuremberg op.

We were lucky there, though. Saw a lot of other aeroplanes. Ours mainly. It was like daylight at 18,000 feet but we weren't troubled by anyone. Phil Shannon liked to come back low in moonlight, ground buzzing, and we all kept our eyes open for pylons when he did this. France was always safer and we tried to come in as far south as possible that night. For us, Nuremberg was the quietest ride of the war."[6]

When the debriefing officers heard similar reports about the Nuremberg operation from highly experienced crews they could not believe the tales told by other aircrew, of numerous aircraft exploding in mid-air or twisting down in a mass of flames to disintegrate on the ground. P/O J. Whiteman was one of a Halifax crew that returned safely to No 10 Squadron's base at Melbourne where they were questioned not only by the station and squadron commanders but by Air Vice-Marshal Carr, commander of 4 Group. When these senior officers asked Whiteman's pilot for a summary of the sortie, he replied:

"I did not think we were going to reach the bloody target, let alone return to base." [7]

Unimpressed by the fervent agreement of the rest of the crew, debriefing officers consoled themselves with the fact that fog over England had caused dozens to divert elsewhere. But by noon next day, when the exact number of bombers that had crashed in the UK or diverted to other airfields was known, the awful truth became apparent. Ninety-five of the four-engined bombers that had set out for Nuremberg had been lost to enemy action.

Over one third of these came from the northern Squadrons. Yorkshire's 4 Group had despatched 119 Halifaxes and twenty of these were missing, a loss rate of 16.8%. No 51 Squadron at Snaith had put up seventeen Halifaxes and lost five with thirty-five men killed, the most severe blow suffered by any of the Yorkshire squadrons. Lissett's 158 Squadron lost four Halifaxes; 76, 78 and 640 each had three bombers missing; while both Nos 10 and 578 Squadrons lost a Halifax.

Canada's 6 group had sent ninety-three Halifaxes. Eleven of these were missing, a loss rate of 11.8%. Leeming's 427 Squadron had despatched sixteen Halifaxes of which three went missing. Two of these fell to the guns of night-fighters while the third had collided with a 622 Squadron Lancaster over Belgium. Only one man survived in these three crews. Nos 424, 429 and 432 Squadrons each lost two Halifaxes; while 433 Squadron at Skipton lost a highly experienced crew in the Halifax piloted by P/O Nielson. Three of the twenty-five Lancaster IIs that had taken off from Linton failed to return: two from 426 Squadron and one from 408 Squadron. This represented a 12% loss rate among the Lancaster IIs bringing the Canadian total to 11.9%, Bomber Command's appalling average on that ghastly night.

Clearly, Bomber Command could not sustain casualties on that scale and it was as well that Nuremberg was the official end to the campaign known to history as the Battle of Berlin. The winter of 1943-1944 had cost the Command 1128 bombers and their crews in an unsuccessful attempt to destroy the enemy's capacity to make war by smashing his major cities. By the end of March 1944, despite Bomber Command's herculean efforts, it was clear that insufficient damage had been inflicted on Berlin and the other industrial centres to force a German surrender. Of course, Harris was despatching far smaller numbers of bombers than the four thousand he had originally demanded for the successful execution of his plan: at no time during the Battle of Berlin did his Main Force ever exceed 875 Halifaxes and Lancasters.

Nuremberg proved a hard task-master and harsh lessons had been learnt. In order to attack a distant German city, on a clear and hostile moonlit night when the German night-fighter force was at the peak of its skill and efficiency, it was necessary to take a calculated risk based on the element of surprise. But there was no surprise factor and in the execution of the plan the bomber stream over Germany had been subjected to the longest running aerial battle in history. The city had not been destroyed and 545 aircrew had lost their lives. Never again would Bomber Command fly in a single stream on a moonlit night against a distant German target. A Nuremberg-style operation was one that could never be repeated until the German night-fighter menace had been reduced; but had Harris ordered Bomber Command to return the following night there is no reason to doubt that his crews would have gone without a murmur.

Next day, on 1 April 1944, Bomber Command came under the direct control of the Supreme Allied Commander, General Eisenhower. For the next six months, Air Marshal Harris employed his strategic bomber force primarily to attack marshalling yards, bridges, flying-bomb sites and gun-emplacements as required by the planners of the Allied invasion of Europe, code-named *Operation Overlord*. Both 4 and 6 Groups would make a major contribution to the preparations for the invasion of Europe and Bomber Command, its depleted ranks soon filled with fresh young crews, new aircraft and, in the case of Yorkshire, even new squadrons, would fly no less than 24,060 sorties before D-Day on 6 June 1944.

Chapter Twenty

Bombing for Overlord

Calls for a 'Second Front Now!' had been made by Russia and by strident demagogues in Britain since 1942. Yet as far as Germany was concerned a second front had been in existence for a very long time. This was the front where, since 1942, Bomber Command had fought a relentless war against the heart of German industry, forcing the Nazi war machine to go on the defensive. Bomber Command's aerial 'second front', climaxing during 1943-1944, was of immense importance because it had coincided with the Red Army's defeat of von Paulus' Sixth Army at Stalingrad (2 February 1943), the destruction of Hitler's gigantic armoured counter-attack at Kursk (July 1943) and the gradual liberation of the Russian homeland from Nazi tyranny prior to the advance on eastern Poland. The thousands of guns, searchlights, fighter aircraft and soldiers assembled to combat Bomber Command's Main Force operations over the Third Reich had deprived the Wehrmacht fighting on the Eastern Front of vital troops and weaponry, notably the 21,000 88mm guns committed to fire at British bombers rather than at Russian tanks.

Yet Hitler could still draw sustenance from the gigantic army of slave workers conscripted in Europe and Russia and from the widespread industrial base still present in the occupied territories, not to mention the iron ore and specialist ball and roller bearings slipping in from neutral Switzerland and Sweden. Though bedevilled by man-power shortages, Hitler mobilised ever-younger year groups in Germany and recruited for the Waffen-SS and 'anti-Bolshevik' armies in occupied territories such as Holland, France, Denmark, Norway, Croatia and the Ukraine. In this way he reinforced or replaced his battered divisions on the Eastern Front, and as far as possible maintained his powerful infantry and armoured units along the Atlantic Wall facing the North Sea and English Channel. Through the organisational genius of Albert Speer, Germany increased war production in the hundreds of industrial centres scattered across the Third Reich. This surge in tank, gun, fighter and ammunition production was possible even under heavy Allied air bombardment by placing a previously 'relaxed' German economy on a more efficient war footing. Impressive though it was, German war production was never as great as it might have been. The bombers had caused most of Germany's industrial cities to crumble into ruin and, as Sir Maurice Dean stresses in his penetrating text *The Royal Air Force and Two World Wars*:

> "The labour in Germany diverted to deal with bomb damage ran into millions of men and women...diverted from the munitions industry, from the armed forces and from the work on the Atlantic Wall. The vast German investment in guns, radar and electronics of all kinds was at the direct cost of other German forces."[1]

This was encouraging for the Allied forces planning a seaborne invasion of Western Europe, scene of the abortive Dieppe raid in 1942. The lesson then had been that a successful landing on an enemy-defended coastline required a protective umbrella of total surprise coupled with air supremacy. Bomber Command would play a key role in ensuring that both essential factors would prevail on D-Day. More immediately, the task was to fulfil the planners' demands to accomplish their 'Transportation Plan' and 'Oil Plan', designed to deprive the German armed forces of fuel and mobility.

Harris had never been enthusiastic about Overlord and was none too keen to allow his strategic bombers to be turned into a tactical air force in support of ground troops. Throughout the preparations for Overlord, he ensured that Bomber Command had the capacity to maintain the offensive against the heart of Germany. Contrary to the fashionable view during the post-war years put about by historians that Bomber Command had not only been defeated during the Battle of Berlin but brought to a 'full stop', his squadrons were able to combine tactical operations against key logistical targets in Occupied Europe with a sustained offensive against the heart of Nazi power, the German industrial centres. Yorkshire's two Heavy Bomb Groups played a full part in the *strategic operations* that preceded D-Day on 6 June 1944 as well as in the tactical requirements stipulated by General Eisenhower.

A summary of 4 and 6 Group participation in the attacks that constituted a renewal of the strategic offensive appears below.

Date	Target	Groups	Comment
20/21 April	Cologne	6	357 Lancasters, 22 from 6 Group
22/23 April	Düsseldorff	4 & 6	All Groups except 5 Group took part; 16 Halifaxes and 13 Lancasters (8 from 6 Group) lost
24/25 April	Karlsruhe	4 & 6	All Groups except 5. Eight Halifaxes and eleven Lancasters failed to return
26/27 April	Essen	4 & 6	All Groups except 5. Six Lancasters and a Halifax lost

After receiving his orders on 4 March 1944, some four weeks before the Nuremberg raid, Harris began the careful planning that preceded the systematic attacks on the railway links feeding not only Normandy (where the five invasion beaches had already been chosen) but also into the 'spoof' area around the Pas de Calais where the activities of Bomber Command were designed to deceive Hitler into believing that the invasion forces would land there. This meant that Bomber Command had to attack as many deception targets in Belgium and the north of France as it did in and around Normandy. This 'Transportation Plan' involved numerous raids on French and Belgian towns and villages and Harris was tasked with pinpointing these precisely without causing horrendous casualties among the civilians who had the misfortune to live there. It was a terrifying balance to achieve: on the one hand there was the desire to deny the Germans the use of the railway system which they would need when reinforcing their troops in the invasion zone; on the other, there were the lives of the very people the Allies were seeking to liberate from Nazi rule, the civilians who had the misfortune to live close to the marshalling yards, repair works and railway stations. This was the task facing the crews of 4 and 6 Groups, veterans of massive area attacks on German cities, now charged with a new kind of precision bombing.

The two northern Groups had already cut their teeth in a precision raid on Meulan-les-Meureaux when 117 Halifaxes accompanied by six Pathfinder Mosquitoes pinpointed the SNCA aircraft factory some fifteen miles outside Paris on 2/3 March 1944. It was an effective raid, marked by Oboe and all of the aircraft returned safely. But the SNCA workshops represented a large factory site separate from the local civilian population. How would the bombers fare when they attacked the first railway yards?

On 6/7 March 1944 the two northern Groups despatched 261 Halifaxes, again with six Pathfinder Mosquitoes, on the first of the pre-invasion operations to the railway yards at Trappes. Visibility was good and the bomb-aimers could see their bombs exploding in the middle of the marshalling yards. Once more, all aircraft returned safely. On the following night, the railway target chosen was Le Mans - an 'English city' at least once a year in the days when the Lagondas, Aston Martins, Jaguars and Bentleys had competed in the Twenty-Four Hours race. Would it still be so after the raid? Again it was Oboe marked through thick cloud by Pathfinder Mosquitoes from 8 Group though they arrived rather late to the dismay of the Main Force. Most of the bombers came from 4 and 6 Group squadrons, with the Canadians providing 124 of the heavies. On the whole their bombs fell squarely on the marshalling yards, inflicting very heavy damage. Just a few fell outside and thirty-one French people died. No bombers were lost but next morning anti-British slogans were daubed on the walls in Le Mans. Such protest was short-lived and there is still a local suspicion in Le Mans that it may have been engineered by the Germans. There was little opposition on these raids though a 10 Squadron Halifax V, one of eight that flew from Melbourne, claimed to have shot down a Ju 88 on the first Le Mans operation.

Bad weather over the next few days prevented a follow-up attack but on 13/14 March, 216 Halifaxes returned to Le Mans to complete the destruction. Maroc station was devastated; locomotives and goods-wagons were ripped apart in another precision attack. A few bombs fell wide and killed forty-eight civilians but the local population bore their loss stoically. The complex Amiens system was the target for 15/16 March, the night when most of the northern squadrons flew their Halifaxes to Stuttgart; and again the next night when forty-one Stirlings joined the Halifaxes for a successful raid on the marshalling yards. Estimates suggest that thirty-six French civilians died in these two raids during which a German ammunition train exploded. Concern for civilian casualties was well shown on 23/24 March, the night before the last attack on Berlin. The target was Laon, with its impressive cathedral high on the hill. Though the railway lines were clearly visible, both the target marking and the bombing went seriously astray

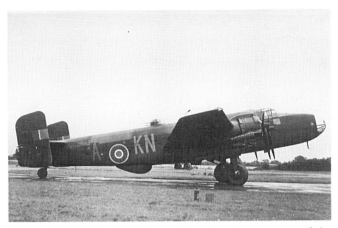

Halifax BIII KN-A Full Sutton. Note that the presence of the H2S ventral blister prevents the crew from fitting downward firing machine-guns.   *Yorkshire Air Museum*

Halifax BIII KN-G near Full Sutton. Note the two trains below.
Yorkshire Air Museum

and after a few minutes the Master Bomber stopped the attack. Unexpectedly, very few French people were killed. Presumably many of Laon's citizens had shown great prudence and moved well away from the railway.

By now the crews of the 4 and 6 Group Halifaxes were becoming expert in their new style of warfare, though they all realised that the main responsibilty was borne by the Pathfinder Mosquitoes. Before March had ended the railway systems at Aulnoye, Courtrai and Vaires had all been attacked and the Germans now had a constant repair problem on their hands. With their usual efficiency they were able to bring the lines back into service and it took them a mere three days to do this after the raid on Courtrai on 26/27 March. But the pattern was set. Relatively small forces of heavy bombers carried out regular attacks on railway targets marked as far as possible by Oboe Mosquitoes. Most raids were conducted from medium levels with minimum enemy opposition and the aim throughout was to concentrate bombing as intensely as possible on the indicated target to minimise civilian casualties. Unfortunately, not all of the bombing was accurate and although great destruction was wrought on the railway yards and the permanent way, French and Belgian civilian casualties were indeed heavy. During the two attacks on the Lille-Délivrance freight yard and the Villeneuve-St-Georges marshalling area (10/11 April) French casualties were similar to those suffered by Germans during area attacks on their cities for 549 people died that night. In contrast, both the Yorkshire-based groups came through these operations unscathed.

But there was to be no respite. Five separate attacks were launched the following night on Tours, Laon, Ghent and Tergnier. 4 Group had unexpectedly heavy casualties, losing ten of its Halifaxes on the Tergnier operation. Twenty-four Canadian Lancasters also flew to Laon though 6 Group's main effort that night was to send 122 Halifaxes to bomb the Belgian Merelbeke-Melle rail complex at Ghent. There was little opposition and great damage was done, albeit at the cost of 428 Belgians who died when several bomb loads exploded in nearby residential areas

Both of the Yorkshire-based Groups were fully involved in the growing crescendo of air attack on railways, flying bomb sites, radio stations, radar sites and gun emplacements. To deter the German repair works, squadrons began using delayed action bombs and the ones dropped by 6 Group at Noisy-le-Sec on 18/19 April were still exploding a fortnight later. Night-fighters were no longer quite the terror they had been during the Battle of Berlin. Some raids on France and Belgium were now carried out without loss though, occasionally, the bombers tangled with Ju 88s and Me 110s. For example, six Halifaxes were lost on the second Tergnier raid (18/19 April) and fourteen during the attack on Montzen (27/28 April). The Canadians lost ten of the fifty-five aircraft they sent to Montzen and attributed this disaster not just to enemy opposition but to the sheer inexperience of the young crews joining the squadrons. There was some compensation for 4 Group at the very end of April when its Halifaxes roared low over Achères, blew up the marshalling yards and departed unscathed having caused no civilian casualties. Gradually, targets were assigned to Groups individually and throughout May the marshalling yards around Paris, Brussels, Hasselt in Belgium and at Boulogne, Louvain and Orleans were put out of action by the heavy bombers. As June approached,

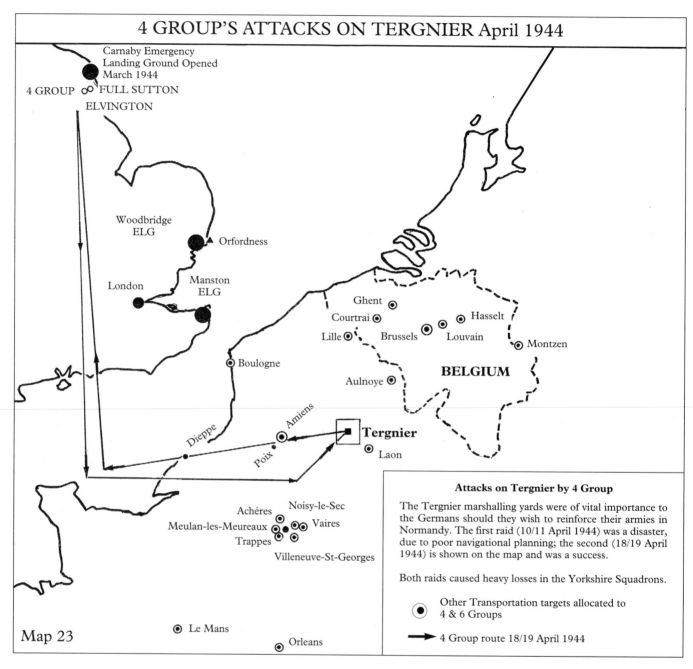

4 GROUP'S ATTACKS ON TERGNIER April 1944

Carnaby Emergency
Landing Ground Opened
March 1944

4 GROUP   FULL SUTTON
ELVINGTON

Woodbridge
ELG

Orfordness

London   Manston
ELG

Boulogne

Ghent

Courtrai

Lille   Brussels   Louvain

Hasselt

Montzen

BELGIUM

Aulnoye

Dieppe   Poix   Amiens

Tergnier

Laon

Achéres   Noisy-le-Sec

Meulan-les-Meureaux   Vaires

Trappes

Villeneuve-St-Georges

Attacks on Tergnier by 4 Group

The Tergnier marshalling yards were of vital importance to the Germans should they wish to reinforce their armies in Normandy. The first raid (10/11 April 1944) was a disaster, due to poor navigational planning; the second (18/19 April 1944) is shown on the map and was a success.

Both raids caused heavy losses in the Yorkshire Squadrons.

    Other Transportation targets allocated to
    4 & 6 Groups

    4 Group route 18/19 April 1944

Le Mans

Map 23

Orleans

the bombers attacked even more precise targets: heavy gun positions on the Normandy coast at Berneval, Trouville and Beaumont; the huge Panzer camp at Bourg Leopold near Antwerp where Tigers, Panthers and Mark IVs were blasted by high explosive and their vital fuel dumps set ablaze. It was a costly operation that night (27/28 May) and nine Halifaxes failed to return.

When 4 Group was tasked to destroy the key German radio-listening station at Ferme-d'Urville on 1/2 June, a newly-formed squadron joined in the operation. This was 346 (Guyenne) Squadron which formed at Elvington on 16 May 1944, the first French Air Force bomber squadron based here and flying Halifax Vs. Its arrival at Elvington had been preceded by 77 Squadron's move to the newly-built base at Full Sutton in May where it completed its conversion to Halifax B IIIs. Both 77 Squadron and 346 Guyenne were part of the 101-strong Halifax force that attempted to wipe out the German Intelligence Signals

Squadron losses during the two attacks on Tergnier

10/11 April 1944

Squadron	Aircraft	Pilot
10	Halifax III ZA-J	F/Lt Barnes
51	Halifax III MH-C	F/Sgt Hall
78	Halifax III LV877	P/O Tait
158	Halifax III NP-G	F/Sgt Sims
158	Halifax III NP-X	W/O Gibson
158	Halifax III NP-Y	S/Ldr Dredge
158	Halifax III NP-Z	F/Sgt Couchman
466	Halifax III LV875	F/Sgt Bond
640	Halifax III C8-T	P/O Axton

18/19 April 1944

Squadron	Aircraft	Pilot
51	Halifax III MH-J	F/Sgt Shackleton
51	Halifax III MH-Y	F/Sgt Sarjantson
158	Halifax III NP-K	F/O Hughes
158	Halifax III NP-Q	P/O Kettles-Roy
466	Halifax III LV956	F/Sgt Casey
640	Halifax III C8-S	F/Lt Boulton

Squadron losses during the Second Raid on Bourg Leopold

For this raid, aircraft were drawn from 6 Group RCAF and 4 Group. 6 Group sent 32 Lancasters and 117 Halifaxes; 4 Group despatched 150 Halifax IIIs/VIs. The Yorkshire Groups were supported by 101 Squadron's ABC Lancasters and 8 Group's PFF Mosquitoes and Lancasters. Nine Halifaxes were lost and a 101 Squadron Lancaster failed to return *.

Squadron	Aircraft	Pilot
RAF		
*101	Lancaster SR-K	P/O Allen
102	Halifax DY-Y	F/O Hughes
640	Halifax C8-O	F/O Williams
RCAF		
420 Snowy Owl	Halifax PT-U	S/L Beall
424 Tiger	Halifax QB-B	F/Lt Mallett
427 Lion	Halifax ZL-P	P/O Devereaux
427 Lion	Halifax LW365	P/O Scobie
429 Bison	Halifax AL-Y	P/O Ross
432 Leaside	Halifax QO-N	F/Sgt Menzies
RAAF		
466	Halifax HD-U	P/O Page

Centre at Ferme-d'Urville where unexpected cloud cover robbed them of success.

4 Group's next operation was the raid on Trappes just outside Paris on the night of 2/3 June 1944, D-Day minus four. At first it seemed no different from any of the previous attacks. As 76 Squadron's historian noted, the

"TIs cascaded on time and the familiar pattern of the attack commenced . . . the swish and roar given off by the high explosive bombs, followed by the slap of disturbed air as the blast effects rippled across the open yards. Rail lines were twisted and broken, sidings cratered and freight sheds reduced to heaps of smouldering rubble . . ."[2]

As the bombers left, they were jumped by night-fighters and fifteen crews were lost that night. Three crews failed to return to Holme-on-Spalding and only one man survived to become a prisoner of war. Even worse, five crews were lost from Lissett's 158 Squadron and Halifaxes were also missing from Melbourne and Leconfield. On the eve of D-Day, Bomber Command was still taking heavy casualties in its effort to smooth the path for the ground forces.

Then on D-Day minus one, after completing their final deception raids against the Pas de Calais gun emplacements and the neutralisation of radio listening posts and radar stations on the Normandy coast, the crews

of 4 and 6 Groups assembled in their briefing rooms to discover where the final targets would be just before the troops hit the Normandy beaches. All of Bomber Command's Groups had their special targets and Yorkshire's are listed below:

4 Group	Maisy	106 Halifaxes
	Mont Fleury	114 Halifaxes
6 Group	Houlgate	106 Halifaxes
	Merville Franceville	86 Halifaxes
		13 Lancasters
	Longues-sur-Mer	25 Lancasters

In all, General Eisenhower required Bomber Command to provide 1132 aircraft to support Operation Overlord on 5/6 June 1944. It was an incredible achievement, a great credit to Sir Arthur Harris and a tribute to the target finding skills and precision bombing techniques developed by experienced bomber crews after thousands of sorties over Germany.

Sgt Ed Solman was again flying with F/Lt Shannon from Leeming en route to 427 Squadron's target at Merville Franceville. His logbook recorded the fact that it was his 29th operation and lasted 5 hrs 45 minutes. Below it was the laconic entry:

'Brown types go in.'

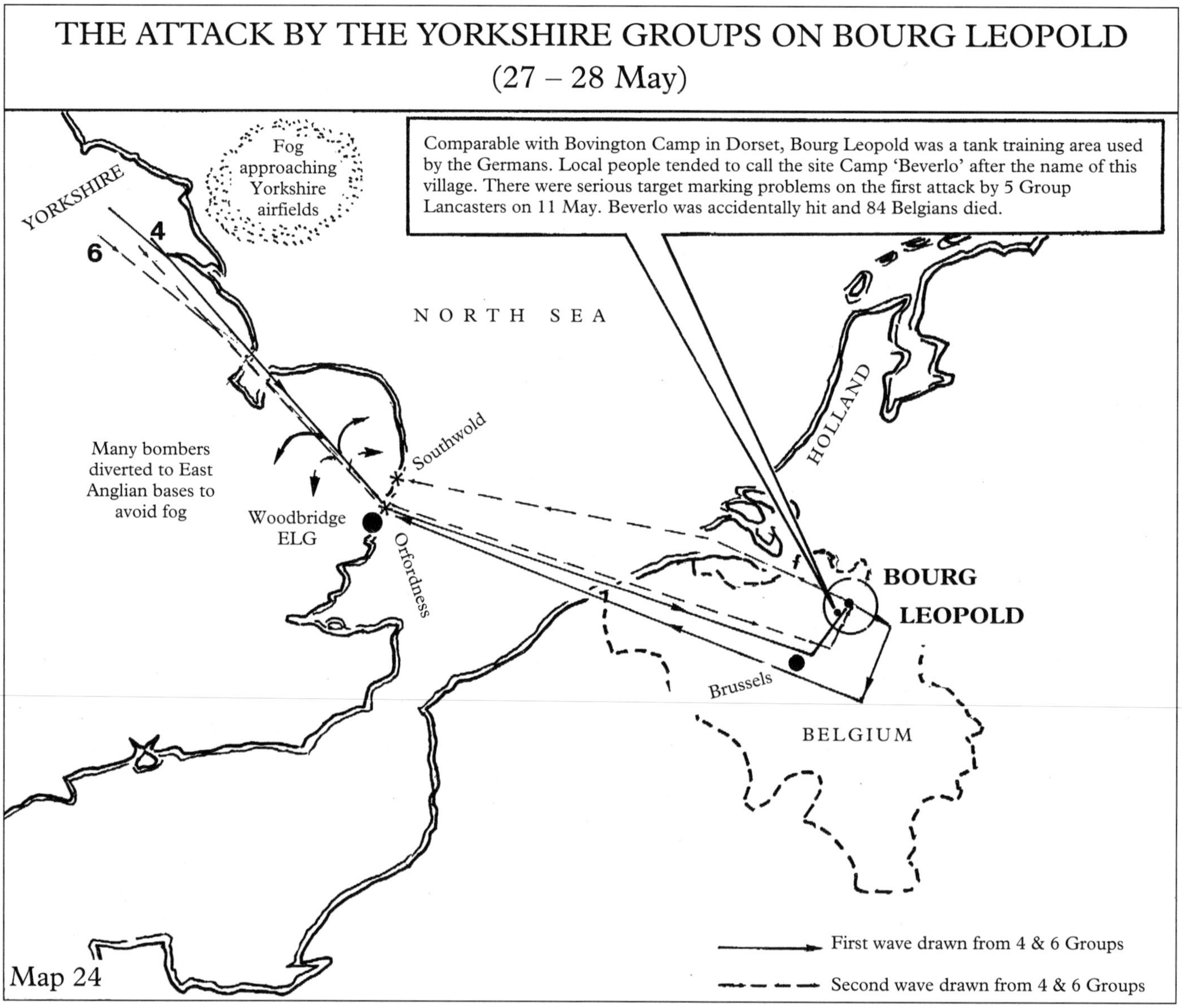

THE ATTACK BY THE YORKSHIRE GROUPS ON BOURG LEOPOLD
(27 – 28 May)

Fog approaching Yorkshire airfields

Comparable with Bovington Camp in Dorset, Bourg Leopold was a tank training area used by the Germans. Local people tended to call the site Camp 'Beverlo' after the name of this village. There were serious target marking problems on the first attack by 5 Group Lancasters on 11 May. Beverlo was accidentally hit and 84 Belgians died.

YORKSHIRE

6   4

NORTH SEA

Many bombers diverted to East Anglian bases to avoid fog

Southwold

Woodbridge ELG

Orfordness

HOLLAND

BOURG LEOPOLD

Brussels

BELGIUM

First wave drawn from 4 & 6 Groups

Second wave drawn from 4 & 6 Groups

Map 24

Allied troops had landed on Gold, Juno, Sword, Omaha and Utah, five beaches along the Normandy coast. Under an umbrella of total air supremacy, the assault troops successfully established themselves in ctheir Normandy bridgehead. A jubilant General Eisenhower could now use Bomber Command to attack any target that was likely to aid the advance of the ground troops facing a determined and well-equipped enemy in Normandy. In company with the US Eighth Air Force and the Tactical Air Forces,[3] Bomber Command's deadly raids on German lines of communications, on airfields, troop concentrations,

village strongpoints and E-boat bases were decisive, so much so that General Sir Brian Horrocks later conceded:

> "In my view the continuous Allied strategic air offensive was the most important operation of the war. Apart from the devastation caused, its effect on Allied morale was great. The air power at our command made it almost impossible for German reinforcements to move into Normandy by day, and I am firmly convinced that the airmen did more to defeat the German armies than any action that was fought on the ground."[4]

So strong was Bomber Command that it also had the resources to turn its attention to two other types of targets that won priority after D-Day: the V-1 flying bomb sites and the German synthetic oil plants. But the Command's strength alone was not the major factor in underwriting the success of these new and varied operations. Since March 1944 the 8th USAAF had been truly earning its title 'The Mighty Eighth'. Now it was taking the war to Germany, challenging the Luftwaffe's day-fighter force in a fight to the death. Escorted by the new P-51 Mustangs and the uprated P-47 Thunderbolts and P-38 Lightnings, the American Bomb Groups deliberately set out to destroy the German fighter force in the true spirit of Pointblank, something that Bomber Command was never equipped to do. On 1 January 1944 General Arnold had exhorted his crews to

> "destroy the Enemy Air Force wherever you find them, in the air, on the ground and in the factories."

By the spring of 1944, the Americans at last had the right kind of fighter aircraft and better located defensive weaponry in their bombers. Superior tactics, bigger numbers and immense firepower effectively destroyed the Luftwaffe's ability to defend Germany and the rest of Occupied Europe. Between February and May 1944 the Eighth Air Force dealt crippling blows on the German aircraft factories and then provoked the fighters to battle by attacking Berlin. For example, on 6 March it sent 730 Flying Fortresses and Liberators, protected by 801 fighters, to the German capital. Sixty-nine bombers were lost; but ninety-two enemy fighters were destroyed, including a number of night-fighters. [5] On 8 April the Eighth Air Force attacked Luftwaffe airfields. The Germans lost eight-eight fighters in the air and forty-nine on the ground, a total of 137 aeroplanes or more than equivalent to an entire Jagdgeschwader! During May, when the strategic bombers were attacking German oil targets, the American fighters were so numerous that they ranged across Germany strafing aircraft and shooting up the German transportation system. On 21 May they destroyed 102 fighters on the ground and by the end of the month the total since February registered:

1550   German aircraft destroyed

900   Locomotives destroyed.

This destruction of front-line fighter strength, even though underground German factories made valiant efforts to replace the losses, gave Bomber Command a partial respite as it sought out every target selected by the staff of the Supreme Commander. On 9/10 June the Yorkshire Squadrons hit enemy airfields at Laval, Rennes, Flers and Le Mans. These attacks were designed to stop the Germans flying in reinforcements now the French resistance and the Tactical Air Forces were cutting more and more rail links and were very successful. Nevertheless, some losses could still be expected. For example, when Bomber Command attacked communications targets on 12/13 June seventeen Halifaxes and six Lancasters were lost, all of them from 4 and 6 Group Squadrons.

It was during this raid that 6 Group's solitary Victoria Cross was won, awarded posthumously to P/O Andy Mynarski, a mid-upper gunner flying in a 419 Squadron Lancaster from Middleton St George. Heading for Arras, the Lancaster came under attack from a Ju 88 and immediately caught fire. The aircraft lost flying speed and an explosion was imminent as it dropped to barely a thousand feet. Holding the bomber's nose up, the pilot tapped out the bale-out order on the emergency light system and then jumped through the nose door exit. But his rear-gunner, Pat Brophy, was still trapped in his turret. He had a parachute but could neither exit into the fuselage nor fall backwards out of his turret. He was resigned to death when Andy Mynarski appeared, axe in hand, in a desperate attempt to break open Brophy's jammed doors. But the flames were too fierce. Gasping for breath and with his clothing on fire, he saw Brophy's hand urgently waving him away. Ignoring the inferno, Mynarski stood to attention, saluted Brophy and then baled out with his uniform and parachute streaming flames. He fell in a French swamp and died shortly afterwards. The bomb-laden Lancaster swooped to earth, skidded and shuddered along the ground, still on an even keel. Unbelievably, the rear fuselage broke away before the bombs exploded and a bewildered Brophy stood up on the green grass of France. He had survived and so had the rest of the crew apart from Andy Mynarski. It was Brophy's account of the brave mid-upper gunner from Winnipeg that led to the posthumous award of the VC.

Night-fighter opposition was equally intense on 16/17 June when 321 aircraft attacked the Sterkrade/Holten synthetic oil refinery. The target required precision bombing but thick cloud rendered the operation a failure. Sadly, the return leg from the oil plant took the bombers close to the night-fighter beacon at Bocholt. Although a bigger Bomber Command force (405 aircraft, many drawn from 4 and 6 Groups) was engaged in Oboe-marked raids on V-1 sites in the Pas de Calais, the night-fighters concentrated on the oil plant raiders and shot twenty-one out of the sky. Flak brought down another ten

214. FSN. 25·6·44 // 8" 17400' → 110° 0930.
MONTORGUEIL. E1. 15 x 500 GP. C 34 SEC. ̴ LORD. U.77

Daylight accuracy. Halifax IIIs smother the V-bomb site at Montorgueil on 25 June 1944. Two other sites were attacked that day and altogether 323 aircraft were involved, including No 617 Squadron whose attack was marked by Wing Commander Leonard Cheshire in a low-flying P-51 Mustang borrowed from the 'Mighty Eighth'.　　　　　　*Frank Lord*

and out of the 162 Halifaxes despatched no less than twenty-two failed to return. This represented a 13.6% loss, bad enough for the Command. But for No 77 Squadron, flying its brand-new Halifax IIIs from its brand-new base at Full Sutton, the night was a disaster. No less than seven Halifaxes failed to return to Full Sutton, one of the worst casualty rates ever experienced by an RAF heavy bomber squadron. There was the occasional Halifax victory, such as the one earned by P/O Sargeant's crew. They had the misfortune to come under attack from three German night-fighters and were hit by an FW 190 and a Ju 88. When the third unidentified fighter moved in the Halifax gunners shot it down. 6 Group lost twelve aircraft, four of which belonged to 432 Leaside at East Moor. At least two Ju 88s fell to the guns of a 408 Squadron Lancaster II and a 432 Squadron Halifax III.

For the next two and half months 4 and 6 Groups attacked the V-1 sites by day and by night, usually without heavy loss. East Moor's historian rejoices that between 17 June and 29 August:

"432 Squadron operated against forty-one targets, of which twenty-three were Crossbow objectives.

The entire campaign of 'Doodle Bug' extermination did not cost the Squadron a single life or aircraft."[6]

So Yorkshire's two Heavy Bomb Groups played an important part in the success of *Operation Crossbow* which, with the anti-Diver (flying-bomb) patrols carried out by Mosquitoes, Spitfires, Mustangs and Tempests, plus the huge array of anti-aircraft guns assembled on the south coast of England, led to the destruction of many of the unmanned missiles. The first V-1s to fall arrived on the night of 12/13 June and about 8,600 would be aimed mainly at London and Southampton by the end of August when most sites were captured by the Allied armies. Bombs would continue to reach the UK but these were usually air-launched from He 111s.

In addition to the V-1 sites, tactical support of the armies and the constant harassing of communications, the two groups were increasingly sent to bomb those most elusive of targets, the synthetic oil plants. During July Harris sent 6 Group to Wesseling and Bottrop while 4 Group attacked Donges. On 23/24 July Harris returned to more distant targets with a raid on Kiel and then on three nights (24/25, 25/26, 28/29 July) his bombers systematically destroyed Stuttgart. At the same time as the final attack on Stuttgart Harris ordered an additional strike on Hamburg, a city that had in part recovered from the devastating firestorm of 1943. In this raid 6 Group lost eighteen of its 187 Halifaxes and 431 Squadron at Croft had five of its seventeen bombers missing. In a massive night's operation on 12/13 August, Harris despatched 1,167 aircraft on such diverse attacks as an experimental H2S raid on Brunswick which dispensed with Pathfinders and, incidentally, with bombing accuracy, a partially successful raid on the Opel works at Rüsselsheim, the relentless assaults on flying bomb sites, tactical strikes on German troop positions near Falaise and minelaying sorties in the Bay of Biscay.

The Command was flexing its muscles, preparing for a return to area bombing in Germany. To insure itself against the huge losses of 1943-44, Bomber Command decided first to mount a major attack on the Luftwaffe's night-fighter airfields in Holland and Belgium. On 15 August 1004 aircraft battered every known air base and while the Command was saturating its most deadly foe with bombs the Allied armies were on the verge of breaking out of Normandy and a new invasion of southern France was taking place.

★ ★ ★

As Bomber Command was about to reach its operational climax it is perhaps appropriate to consider the expansion of the northern squadrons, now approaching their maximum in strength and numbers. The second French Air Force Squadron to form at Elvington was 347 Tunisie on 20 June 1944. It became operational on 27/28 June when it sent eleven of its Halifax Vs to bomb a V-1 site at Mount Cadon. During July both 346 and 347 Squadrons converted to Halifax BIIIs and became fully committed to a wide range of targets in France and Germany. A feature of the two French squadrons in No 4 Group was that the senior officer in the crew - not necessarily the pilot as was the practice in RAF Bomber Command - acted as captain of each Halifax bomber.

During August 1944 the invasion of southern France had encouraged numerous uprisings among the French resistance and the Germans had wreaked their vengeance on many helpless French civilians. Any tourist who wanders off the autoroutes today to explore the charm of French villages must be struck by the ubiquitous memorials to *les braves*, those shot by the retreating German soldiers, not all of them members of the SS Einsatzkommando. Old and young alike were pulled from their homes and executed in the village *place*, in front of the local church or school. This was why the French crews had no compunction about bombing German targets within their homeland and why they perhaps took greater risks, as Dutch and Norwegian crews certainly did, when they flew from Yorkshire.

A new Canadian squadron was also operating from Yorkshire, new in that it had just transferred from a period of distinguished service with Coastal Command. This was 415 Swordfish Squadron RCAF which came to East Moor in July, rapidly converted to Halifax BIIIs and then bombed Hamburg (with the loss of one aircraft) before the month was out. 415 Swordfish Squadron shared East Moor with 432 Leaside which had exchanged its Lancaster IIs for Halifax IIIs in the previous February.

The third non-RAF squadron to arrive in Yorkshire during the summer of 1944 was 462 Squadron Royal Australian Air Force. It formed at Driffield on 14 August, sharing the base with 466 Squadron RAAF which had moved from Leconfield in the previous June. 462 had been the first to fly Halifaxes in the Middle East and by 1944 it was proficient in the use of H2S and the new Mk XIV bombsight. Suddenly it was re-numbered 614 Squadron RAF with the intention of forming it into

a specialist Pathfinder unit. After some five months it reverted to its original RAAF status and reformed as part of 4 Group where it would remain until 22 December 1944. It was then screened from operations and transferred into 100 Bomber Support Group. However, its presence in August 1944 brought the operational strength of the two Yorkshire Groups to twenty-seven squadrons, thirteen in 4 Group and fourteen in 6 Group. With their full complement of squadrons, an Emergency Landing Ground with FIDO under the direct control of 4 Group at Carnaby since June 1944 and a FIDO-equipped airfield at Melbourne, the two Yorkshire Groups were stronger and better equipped than at any previous stage in their history.

Victims of Nazism - French memorial.

This massive build-up in striking power created a complex military infrastructure in the County making it, with its high-powered industrial base centering on Leeds, Bradford, Halifax, York and Sheffield, almost an independent fighting force. As far as the media was concerned, it might well have been this. Little attention was paid to the effort and resources poured into the strategic bomber offensive launched from Yorkshire. This was possibly because neither 4 nor 6 Group had any 'special squadrons' to catch the public interest as, for example, Lincolnshire had with its well-known 617 Squadron of 'dam-buster' fame. [7] The exploits of the British, Commonwealth and European crews who flew from Yorkshire during 1944 in support of the the assault on German military power from D-Day to the 'Battle of the Bulge' in December were, on the whole, overlooked.

Chapter Twenty One

The Assault on Germany
from D-Day to the Ardennes 1944

While Allied troops were establishing themselves in the Normandy bridgehead and preparing for the 'break-out', the composition of Bomber Command had become more sophisticated. The two Yorkshire-based Groups, in company with 1 Group's Lancasters and 8 Group's Pathfinders, were now the core of the Main Force. More often than not, 5 Group acted as a specialist force, a near independent arm of Bomber Command and in the same category as 3 Group now that it had parted with its Stirlings and re-equipped with Lancasters, some of which had the new blind-bombing G-H device. Canadian-built Lancaster Xs were coming into service with 6 Group and the first of these, the much publicised *Ruhr Express*, was serving with 419 Squadron at Middleton St George. [1]

In June 1944 4 and 6 Groups took delivery of the first of the 'wide-span' Halifax VIIs. These new aircraft, together with the remaining Lancaster IIs and the well-proven Halifax BIIIs, represented a major striking force. But because there was ill-founded optimism that the German armed forces were on the verge of defeat, there was some controversy as how best to use it.

Since 14 April 1944 Portal, Chief of the Air Staff, had been subordinate to General Eisenhower and the American leader had been responsible for deciding where and when Bomber Command should strike. Though personally opposed to a major seaborne invasion of Europe, Harris had wholeheartedly committed Bomber Command to the needs of Overlord and had struck up a friendly, professional working relationship with the Supreme Commander. Now, as a result of agreement between the Chiefs of Staff at the 1944 Quebec Conference, control of the Strategic Air Forces returned to Portal and his American opposite number, General Spaatz. Both men understood the value of saturating the German-controlled road and rail systems in Western Europe (the Army's tactical requirement) and the importance of the cumulative effect of area bombing (the Harris technique) but were equally eager to attack the synthetic oil targets, targets that in their view now represented the Achilles' heel of Nazi Germany.

Accordingly, Portal told Harris on 25 September that, amidst the usual requirements to destroy and dislocate the German military, industrial and economic systems, plus the need to support the land and naval forces, there were now new priorities. The first of these was the German oil industry; the second was the rail and canal system and the factories producing armoured fighting vehicles. Harris was not much impressed by the idea of concentrating his Main Force against hard-to-hit oil targets. There were at least one hundred known manufacturing and storage sites and possibly more, for Harris was convinced that others were tucked away in secret locations of which Allied intelligence knew little. All had been widely dispersed and cleverly planned so they could be easily repaired after an air raid. To put these out of commission - permanently - would require a constant round of attacks in the teeth of deadly accurate flak now the German defenders commonly used radar-controlled gun-laying. Of course, Harris could not deny that by September these synthetic oil plants were meeting almost 80% of Germany's needs and that all would come within range of Bomber Command once the long winter nights began. [2] This did not stop Harris from reminding Churchill on 30 September that over the previous five months, while he had been devoting most of his Main Force to the successful support of Overlord and the destruction of the the oil plants, Bomber Command had been forced to neglect the main assault on German industrial cities. Now there was a real and present danger that the long respite had enabled Germany to "reconstitute all her essential war industry." [3]

Concentration on oil, he warned the Prime Minister, would increase that danger. Moreover, had not the Americans already begun to demolish the German oil industry in heavy daylight raids at enormous cost? By September 1944 synthetic oil production had plummeted to a bare 25% of the May figures largely due to the attentions of the Eighth Air Force in the UK and the Fifteenth in Italy. Moreover, German oil stocks were well below the 1.4 million tons held in May. So why devote the strategic night bomber force to the same oil targets so difficult to locate in darkness?

Churchill was impressed but he did not fully accept Sir Arthur's cogent argument. But he assured Harris that he was in favour of "cracking everything in now on to Germany", everything, that is, that could be spared from helping the troops fighting in Europe. This satisfied Harris who now had a very clear picture of what he could achieve with Bomber Command. Coincidental with the required attacks on oil targets he had the strength to mount yet another offensive against the German cities, yet another 'Battle of the Ruhr'. This was why the Yorkshire Groups found themselves maids of all work for the rest of 1944. As a crucial element in the Main Force they were not only going back to Germany by day and night. They were also ferrying petrol to Allied armies in Belgium, bombing U-boats in Bergen and forcing German port garrisons still holding out along the Channel coast to surrender.

There were some compensations during the post-August period as the Luftwaffe was a partially spent force and Bomber Command casualties would never again approach those suffered in the Battle of Berlin. Daylight raids benefited from fighter escort; night operations involved more Intruder and Serrate Mosquitoes dedicated to the reduction of the night-fighter menace via interception of German aircraft in the air and the destruction of their home airfields. There was the prospect of better bombing accuracy now that Gee and Oboe installations were operating from liberated areas of Western Europe; while outward and return flights to and from Germany would, in part, be over friendly territory, thus giving a damaged bomber a good chance of landing on an Allied airfield in Europe.

Some of the raids in which 4 and 6 Groups engaged were historic and one, at least, on 14 August 1944, is remembered with intense sadness. It was the first in which the Main Force, bombing in close proximity to Allied positions, accidentally killed their own soldiers. The Army had asked Harris to bomb seven distinct targets in the Quesnay-Tassilly region, a key German defence area protecting the Caen-Falaise front. It was not the sort of raid that Harris relished, although two similar efforts on 7 July and 18 July, in which the Yorkshire Groups participated, had been totally successful.

Bomber Command's planning for this operation seemed meticulous. It allocated to each target an Oboe Mosquito and ground markers, backers-up, a Master Bomber and a deputy. Over eight hundred aircraft were involved and the various attacks proceeded smoothly until confusion arose over the precise location of 'Aiming Point 21'. Gunners of the 12th Canadian Field Regiment and Polish support troops were encamped in and around a large quarry at Haut Mesnil when they were appalled to see heavy bombers with open bomb doors approaching their position. They immediately lit their yellow recognition flares, the accepted identification colour for all Allied soldiers in the European theatre. Above them the crews in the Halifaxes and Lancasters from both the Yorkshire Groups saw yellow smoke drifting from a quarry. Was this a decayed Target Indicator? The Pathfinders were using yellow TIs that day. Unsure, some crews decided to obey orders and bomb on the approved elapsed time after crossing the coast to the target. They would bomb when their stopwatches told them to and not before. Others, hearing a Master Bomber order 'Bomb on Yellow TIs', decided to attack. Nine 6 Group and four 4 Group aircraft bombed the 'wrong fires'. Then a Lancaster acting as a backer-up put down more markers and this encouraged a second wave of Canadian bombers to attack the quarry. Sixty-five Canadian soldiers died in this sad example of 'friendly fire' and many more succumbed to their wounds. The Polish units nearby also suffered casualties. Naturally, there had to be a scapegoat and the authorities chose to blame the air crews and in particular the Pathfinders who had to hand in their treasured Eagle badges.

On 27 August there was an historic raid on the Rheinpreussen synthetic oil plant at Homberg, the first big raid carried out in daylight on a German target since Blenheims tried to destroy Cologne's power stations on 12 August 1941. Apart from the Pathfinders, this was an all-Halifax attack and 216 bombers set out on a fairly direct route across the North Sea, over Holland and Belgium (still occupied by the Germans) and on to the Ruhr where the Halifaxes came over in tight formations. F/Sgt Jack Espie, RAAF, was piloting a 76 Squadron Halifax from Holme and later remarked on the unusual scene with scores of black painted Halifaxes visible from the cockpit:

"To me it looked like mile upon mile of aircraft, those in the distance like motionless insects."[4]

Through gaps in the clouds he could see the red and green markers dropped by Oboe and around him the black bursts of flak, inspiring all the wireless operators to shovel Window through the chutes in the hope of confusing the radar-predicted guns. Cloud masked many a bomb-run but some damage was done to the oil plant, though not enough to put it out of action. A solitary Me 110 appeared to challenge the escorting Spitfires and then wisely fled the scene. There were a few crises such as the one that befell F/O Lane, pilot of a 462 Squadron RAAF Halifax III from Driffield. This was the Australian Squadron's first raid on Germany and when Lane's port outer engine failed he must have wondered if he had a hope of reaching Homberg. He found the Rhine when another engine misfired after being hit by flak. At very low altitude, Lane's position was doubly dangerous for he ran the risk of being shot down

Australian Bob Tyers returns to Yorkshire 1991 to reacquaint himself with his old 'office' in Yorkshire Air Museum's Halifax.

Halifax III Crew: Leconfield 1944. *Back row*: F/Sgt Bob Tyers, Melbourne, Rear Gunner; F/O John Todd, Queensland, Bomb aimer; F/Lt Len Plasto, Sydney, Skipper; F/O John Moran, Queensland, Navigator; *Front Row*: F/Sgt Cyril Russell, England; Wireless Operator; F/Sgt Paddy Deveraux, Ireland, Mid Upper Gunner; F/Sgt Paddy ?, Argentina & Scotland, Flight Engineer.

Bob Tyers

by light flak and of being hit by bombs from the Halifaxes above. He found a target of opportunity when a gap in the clouds revealed some dockside berths on the Rhine and then banked away to make a safe flight back to Yorkshire.

Morale was high on the raid - after all, it *was* a *daylight* op to the Ruhr - and all the bombers returned safely even though a few landed away. Sgt Bob Tyers, rear gunner in a Halifax BIII from 466 Squadron RAAF, Driffield, recalled that his pilot, F/O Plasto, was having engine and hydraulic problems and put down at Carnaby. As the Emergency Landing Ground lacked any accommodation facilities the aeroplane was soon made airworthy and a ten minute flight took them back to Driffield's comforts later that evening.

Canada's 6 Group was not idle that day either. Two hundred of its Halifaxes and Lancasters hit the big V-1 site at Mimoyecques, again without loss, a feat equalled by 5 Group's Lancasters with direct hits on two ships in Brest harbour. So that day there were 494 sorties against a variety of vital targets- an oil plant, a flying bomb site and enemy shipping - and not a single bomber was lost to enemy action.

A week later on 3 September, the fifth anniversary of Britain's declaration of war on Germany, there was a daylight raid remembered for more pleasurable incidents. Enemy airfields in southern Holland still threatened the bomber streams and Harris decided to saturate the six most important bases. 6 Group concentrated on Volkel while 4 Group bombed Venlo, losing one Halifax during the attack. The raid was deemed successful but weather conditions forced many aircraft to land away. No 77 Squadron's Halifaxes based at Full Sutton received a BFX (a radio code signal directing crews to land away) to Old Buckenham[(5)] One Halifax arriving rather late was confused by the array of lights shining from the densely packed airfields in Norfolk and put down at the adjacent air base of Hethel, home of the 389th Bombardment Group, then equipped with B-24 Liberators. That night the Americans took 'their crew' out to meet the rest of the 77 Squadron crews, one of whom had an even sorrier Halifax to display. A 'friendly' bomb had passed right through the fuselage - a not uncommon event in Bomber Command operations. As a port engine on the Hethel

No 462 Squadron Royal Australian Air Force. One of No 462 Squadron's Halifax IIIs Z5-E based at Driffield. Z5-E was fitted with a ventral turret, details of which were removed by the censor. This aeroplane was lost in a collision over Essen during October 1944.   *RAAF*

despatched actually bombed the target and returned safely.

At this stage of the war, the British 21st Army Group under Montgomery, comprising the Canadian First Army and the British Second Army, had advanced on the so-called 'Great Swan' up the Channel coast, through the battlefields of the First World War and into Belgium. Montgomery now urged Eisenhower to back a daring plan. He should drop airborne troops tasked to capture the bridges between the Dutch frontier and the Neder Rijn river and thus create a "springboard for a powerful full-blooded thrust to the heart of Germany" and end the war before Christmas. This was *Operation Market Garden*, doomed to fail at Arnhem because the paratroopers and glider-borne soldiers were

Halifax was unserviceable, a replacement came down by road from Full Sutton, accompanied by 77 Squadron riggers. For the next ten days both air and ground crew were the guests of 'The Sky Scorpions'.[6] Wide-eyed RAF types were plied with roast chicken and ice cream, fresh fruit and all the American cigarettes they wanted. Col Potts, the new CO, deputed Major Walter Andrews to look after the unexpected guests and the pilot repaid his hosts by giving the Liberator crews, none of whom had flown over Germany at night, a lecture on 77 Squadron's nocturnal sorties.

It fell to 6 Group to carry out another historic daylight raid on 6 September when its Halifaxes and Lancasters carried out Bomber Command's last attack against Emden. This was the Canadian Group's first mass daylight attack on a German target and the raid was a complete success. The Luftwaffe made no effort to intercept the bombers though the flak was intense. Bombing was accurate: shipping moored in the harbour received direct hits; the U-boat constructor Nordsee Werke and big ship-building yard belonging to Berkamer Kleinbohn were completely wrecked. Emden was "a mass of flames"[7] and although flak killed the Deputy Master Bomber every one of the 139 Canadian aircraft

outnumbered and eventually outfought by the German defenders. As their General Bittrich said: "Almost before the British had touched the ground we were ready to defeat them." Yorkshire's contribution to the advance was two-fold. First, both 4 and 6 Groups bombed the German garrisons at Le Havre, Boulogne and Calais, forcing their surrender to British and Canadian troops (12-30 September). Secondly, for over a week, 4 Group mustered its aircraft to supply the overstretched Allied armour and transport with petrol. 4 Group Squadrons ferried hundreds of jerricans daily non-stop from their Yorkshire bases to the airfield complex at Brussels Airport (Evere/Melsbroek) from 23 September to 2 October. Some idea of the arduous nature of the flying can be gauged from the logbook of Sgt R Harvey, air-gunner on a 102 Squadron Halifax III flown by F/O Lightbody from its Pocklington base during the autumn of 1944.

Date	Hour	Aircraft	Remarks	Flying Time Day
26/9/44	0945	Halifax III 'G'	Base - Brussels Airport	1-50
26/9/44	1300	Halifax III G'	Brussels Airport - Base	2-10

27/9/44	1105	Halifax III 'B'	Base - Brussels Airport	1-45
27/9/44	1420	Halifax III 'B'	Brussels Airport - Base	2-10
9/9/44	1120	Halifax III 'G'	Base - Brussels Airport	1-50
29/9/44	1420	Halifax III 'G'	Brussels Airport - Base	2-45
30/9/44	0635	Halifax III 'F'	Base - Brussels Airport	1-40
30/9/44	1010	Halifax III 'F'	Brussels Airport - Base	1-50
1/10/44	1335	Halifax III 'G'	Base - Brussels Airport	1-45
1/10/44	1625	Halifax III 'G'	Brussels Airport - Base	1-55

The turn-round and maintenance times for each aircraft show how hard the ground crews worked. The aircrews were given a day's rest when the petrol ferrying was over and then assigned forty-five minutes of practice bombing to make sure they were "on their toes" for their delayed visit to the Ruhr.

It had been a difficult and hazardous operation for the Halifax crews for the Army's petrol was contained in jerricans packed into the aircraft fuselage with barely enough room for the crews to squeeze past and take up their stations. Once they were aboard, the ground crews filled that space with more jerricans and then closed the main hatch. Each Halifax was therefore "an airborne petrol-bowser" and once they landed the airmen had to wait until the ground-crews who had been ferried out from their Yorkshire bases to Evere/Melsbroek managed to unseal the hatches before they could get out of the aircraft. Landings and take-offs were unusually dangerous operation as the Evere/Melsbroek runways had been heavily bombed in the past and the roughly filled craters stressed the tyres and under-carriages of the Yorkshire Halifaxes, making life especially arduous for the hard-pressed ground crews.

As the petrol airlift wound down, so preparations for the return to the Ruhr began and the next 'Battle' opened on 6/7 October with a devastating raid on Dortmund. 4 Group did not participate in this opening attack as its Halifaxes had spent the day bombing the synthetic oil plants at Sterkrade and Scholven/Buer, losing four aircraft to enemy action. In contrast Canada's 6 Group put up its biggest effort of the war that night. No less than 293 Canadian aircraft (248 Halifaxes and 45 Lancasters) joined the 202 Lancasters and twenty Mosquitoes from 3 and 8 Groups to attack Dortmund in four waves. A few German fighters intercepted the bombers near the target. A 428 Squadron Lancaster X drove off one of the new Me 410s; a Halifax VII from 408 Squadron shot down an Me 109. Two Halifaxes were lost, one from 426 Squadron and the other from 433. As usual there was fog over north-east England and most of 424 Squadron Halifaxes were BFX'd to Mendlesham, home of the American 34th Bomb Group, recently re-equipped with B-17G Flying Fortresses.[8] Such was the beginning of another Battle of the Ruhr by what was now the most powerful bombing force in the world capable, on the same night, of sending 246 Lancasters to Bremen to

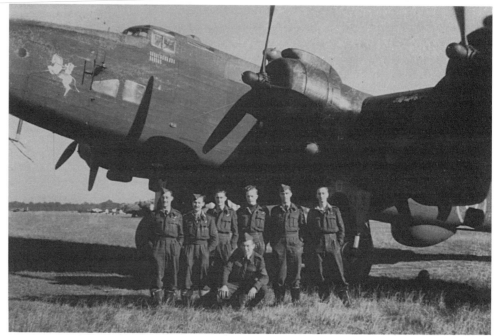

The solitary Halifax at Hethel, September 1944. Tucked away on the flight-line behind the 77 Squadron Halifax III is a B-24D, a Norseman, and a fairly rare Beech AT-7 (possibly General Eaker's personal aircraft). On the left is a B-24J with its distinctive vertical white stripe on a black fin and rudder.

Frank Lord

destroy its electrical industries, the shipyards and both the factories making Focke-Wulf aircraft. So great was the damage at Bremen that Bomber Command never bothered to visit it again.

The next major operation involving the two northern groups was the raid on Duisburg. Over two days was spent in the preparation for this assault, a daylight raid involving 1013 aircraft escorted by fighters throughout the entire mission. The reason for this colossal raid was the Air Staff directive for Operation Hurricane. It ordered Harris to attack Duisburg with maximum forces; while Spaatz was to send 1251 bombers escorted by 749 fighters to Cologne.

Hurricane was designed

"to demonstrate to the enemy . . . the over-whelming superiority of the Allied Air Forces."

It was thought that the best way of doing this was

"to apply within the shortest practical period the maximum effort of . . . Bomber Command and the Eighth US Bomber Command against the densely populated Ruhr."

A solitary Luftwaffe aircraft rose to challenge this gigantic force but fled when it saw squadron after squadron of RAF fighter escorts. Flak remained a problem in the Ruhr. The Germans were depending much more on heavy calibre 105mm and 128mm anti-aircraft guns mounted on railway cars, together with mobile 88mm Grille 10 guns mounted on Pzkw IV chassis, supplemented by 37mm Flak 43 and 20mm Flak 38 mounted on a variety of towed trailers, tank chassis and armoured personnel carriers. These could dodge about a city under attack, though on 14 October 1944 the deluge of bombs was so great that Duisburg's flak defences were saturated and ultimately rendered useless. This was overwhelmingly a high explosive attack and it shattered the city. The weary citizens of Duisburg had no sleep that night. Bomber Command returned to the attack with over a thousand aircraft and an even greater bomb tonnage. Industry in Duisburg stopped; "all mines and coke ovens lay silent."(9)

The sheer capacity to devastate the targets belies the oft-repeated statement that Bomber Command could not destroy German industry. It certainly could - when it could find it. On the very same night that Harris sent over one thousand bombers to Duisburg he still had all of 5 Group in reserve. He sent this Lancaster Group to Brunswick and this specialist force of 240 aircraft was so deadly accurate that the people of Brunswick were quite convinced the following morning that their great city had been wiped out by at least a thousand bombers.

Throughout the autumn and early winter months of 1944, Bomber Command continued its destructive attacks on German industrial and military targets. The extraordinary bomb tonnage dropped on Duisburg and Bremen (14/15 October 1944) would never be repeated by Bomber Command though the next raids on Essen proved to be the heaviest that industrial city ever experienced. On 23/24 October a huge force of 463 Halifaxes took part in an operation which saw a total of 1055 aircraft despatched to the target; and on 25 October the two northern groups helped to deliver the *coup de grâce* to Krupp's famous Borbeck pig-iron plant. Essen had virtually ceased to exist as an important industrial city since most of its manufacturing plant had been dispersed to more remote parts of the Third Reich - though Krupp's surviving workshops in Essen were still able to produce limited quantities of weapons during 1945.

The urgent need to open up the River Scheldt to Allied shipping as a supply route for the British and Canadian armies in Belgium meant a succession of sorties to Walcheren, the island that guarded the entrance to the river and the port of Antwerp. Earlier Lancaster attacks had breached Walcheren's sea wall either side of Flushing, flooding most of the island. However, it still housed eight batteries of German artillery and Bomber Command, including 4 and 6 Groups, flew hundreds of sorties in an attempt to wipe them out prior to an amphibious assault by Scottish and Canadian troops.These air attacks were only marginally successful and fighting went on in Walcheren until 8 November, the German guns having sunk at least nine of the Allied landing craft.

The Halifaxes and Lancasters continued to batter Cologne on 30/31 October and 31 October/1 November, Düsseldorf on 2/3 November and Bochum on 4/5 November. Though much of Bochum's industry was destroyed that night, the raid took an unexpectedly heavy toll of the Yorkshire squadrons. In particular, 346 Guyenne Squadron lost five of its sixteen Halifaxes that night, its worst loss since the two French Air Force Squadrons based at Elvington had begun operating with 4 Group.

Prior to the raid on Bochum (4/5 November 1944) the two French squadrons at Elvington had carried out sixty-three operations against enemy targets, including the massive raids on Duisburg, Essen and Cologne. Between them, 346 Guyenne and 347 Tunisie FAF had also carried 165,725 gallons of petrol to the British Second Army at Brussels Airport during the famous 4 Group airlift September/October 1944. But it was the sixty-

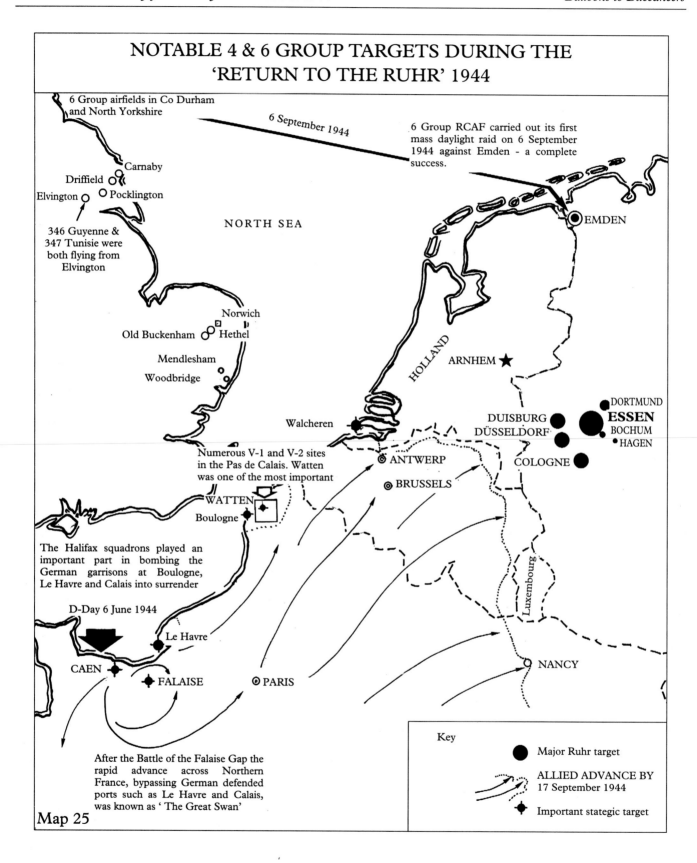

NOTABLE 4 & 6 GROUP TARGETS DURING THE 'RETURN TO THE RUHR' 1944

6 Group airfields in Co Durham and North Yorkshire

6 September 1944

6 Group RCAF carried out its first mass daylight raid on 6 September 1944 against Emden - a complete success.

Carnaby

Driffield

Elvington · O Pocklington

NORTH SEA

346 Guyenne & 347 Tunisie were both flying from Elvington

EMDEN

Norwich

Old Buckenham · Hethel

Mendlesham

Woodbridge

HOLLAND

ARNHEM ★

DORTMUND

DUISBURG · ESSEN

DÜSSELDORF · BOCHUM · HAGEN

Walcheren

ANTWERP

COLOGNE

Numerous V-1 and V-2 sites in the Pas de Calais. Watten was one of the most important

BRUSSELS

WATTEN

Boulogne

The Halifax squadrons played an important part in bombing the German garrisons at Boulogne, Le Havre and Calais into surrender

Luxembourg

D-Day 6 June 1944

Le Havre

CAEN

FALAISE · PARIS

NANCY

After the Battle of the Falaise Gap the rapid advance across Northern France, bypassing German defended ports such as Le Havre and Calais, was known as ' The Great Swan'

Key

● Major Ruhr target

ALLIED ADVANCE BY 17 September 1944

◆ Important stategic target

Map 25

190

fourth French Air Force operation on 4/5 November that resulted in Guyenne's greatest loss and the deaths of twenty-three French aircrew.

On that Saturday night sixteen 346 Guyenne and eleven 347 Tunisie Halifax IIIs took off from Elvington for the attack on Bochum. First to leave was Capt. Robert Baron in his 346 Squadron Halifax III coded H7-J. A highly experienced pilot who had logged 4,500 hours, he was much admired in Bomber Command for his skill, nerve and quite exceptional leadership qualities. Despite his age - he was over forty - he carried on flying operations and Bochum was his twenty-sixth operation. The last of Guyenne's aircraft was airborne by 1800 hours and the squadron rapidly climbed above the clouds to eight thousand feet. There they loosely joined up with the main stream composed of Tunisie's aircraft, another 368 Halifaxes, 336 Lancasters and twenty-nine Mosquitoes. Gunners began nervously scanning the sky to avoid the collision hazard that always stalked these big operations as the heavily loaded bombers began their slow climb to 20,000 feet. On course, high above above the green markers, they reached the red TIs on time. Many fighters intercepted and gunners observed that the Me 109s, FW 190s and Ju 88s were firing tracer and some new air-to-air rocket missiles that left great streaks of orange flame behind them as they curved towards the Halifaxes. From 1946 hours onwards each Halifax dropped its four tons of bombs while above them the Lancasters added seven tons apiece. Flames began to engulf Bochum and crews could see the flash of bomb bursts multiplying amidst the thickening smoke. For many crews there was a strong visual sensation that the black roads of Bochum were gradually rising towards them above the mass of red flames in the furnace below. As one pilot said:

"Elle flamme, cette ville, toute entière."[10]

Capt. Baron's Halifax had been hit and was now heading home on three engines. Around them the crew could see aircraft falling in flames, victims of night-fighters that had taken the stream by surprise. An Me 109 darted in, then another, grievously wounding Baron. Both his mid-upper gunner, Sgt Petitjean and the navigator, Lt. Truche, were wounded but when Baron ordered the crew to bale out these two managed to parachute to safety. The rest died when Halifax H7-J smashed into the ground south of Jülich.[11]

Bomber Command paid a heavy price for this raid, with most of the casualties borne by the two Yorkshire Groups. All the bombers from 347 Tunisie returned from the operation though one aircraft wrecked its undercarriage on landing so that the survivors of

346 Guyenne had to be diverted to Pocklington and Full Sutton. Altogether, twenty-eight Halifaxes and five Lancasters were lost that night, mostly victims of a highly successful fighter interception. It could have been far worse without the Mosquitoes of 100 Group. They claimed to have shot down two Me 110s and four Ju 88s - their most successful escort mission of the war. Shiny Ten at Melbourne commented on the unexpectedly high number of fighter combats and though the Squadron lost Halifax ZA-A two other crews claimed to have shot down Ju 88s. Other Squadrons reported attacks by Me 262 jet fighters, three of which were claimed by the air gunners. One of 4 Group's Halifax Squadrons, 578 at Burn, had not taken part in the raid though its twenty-three Halifaxes were bombed up and ready to go. Unusually high crosswinds hit the airfield at departure time and Burn's Halifaxes were unable to take-off with their maximum bomb weights on board.

Five of the 214 bombers from Canada's 6 Group also failed to return from Bochum. A 433 Squadron Halifax flying from Skipton went down to a fighter attack although none of the crew, all of whom survived, ever saw the enemy machine. The crew assumed they had been yet one more victim of the deadly *schräge Musik* guns. A 425 Squadron Halifax from Tholthorpe, with its starboard wing aflame after a direct hit from flak, suddenly exploded. The RAF flight engineer, Sgt Clowes, was already dead from a shell splinter but the rest of the crew came to as they were hurtling through space and managed to pull their ripcords. F/O Donald Smith, the pilot, fell 15,000 feet before his parachute opened.

The Bochum raid highlighted the conditions in which Bomber Command fought this final Battle of the Ruhr in the closing months of 1944. German night fighters, not so numerous as they had been during the Battle of Berlin, still posed a very real threat to operations at night. There were many reports during November that Me 262 jets fitted with Lichtenstein radar and heavy cannon were attacking the bomber stream and there is at least one claim from the gunners of a 427 Lion Halifax that they had identified and destroyed a rocket-powered Me 163 during the Düsseldorf operation on 2/3 November.

During daylight hours, when the bombers had strong fighter protection, the Halifaxes and Lancasters were always ready to answer calls for help from the Allied armies, now held up by fierce German resistance. However, tactical bombing in support of troops did not always allow ground troops to advance with impunity. All depended on the ability of Allied troops to mop up German defenders who frequently survived the daytime bomb attacks. The massive raid on the three German towns of Jülich, Düren and Heinsburg (16 November 1944) was a case in point. Spearheaded by 76 Squadron from Holme, 413 Halifaxes and 78 Lancasters bombed Jülich without loss and reduced the town to rubble. But the raid had no real tactical or strategic value as American ground forces were unable to advance.

Air support operations in the bad weather conditions of November-December 1944 produced few dividends and Harris concentrated on the synthetic oil plants at Wanne-Eickel, Homberg, Sterkrade and Gelsenkirchen. Most of the precision attacks were carried out by the Lancaster groups. However, 6 Group sent 230 bombers to the Castrop-Rauxel oil refinery on 21/22 November, losing four of its Halifaxes; and on the same night 4 Group sent 232 Halifaxes to the synthetic oil plant at Sterkrade in a very successful raid. A week later the Canadians went to Neuss for a traditional area raid without loss and then on the last day of November they joined 1 and 4 Groups in an attack on Duisburg when it was covered by ten-tenths cloud. The Canadians lost two Halifaxes and one of these was a 429 Squadron Halifax III from Leeming, in collision with a 578 Squadron Halifax from Burn. The two aircraft collided over Holland and all the crew members lost their lives.

On 2/3 December 1944 the Yorkshire squadrons combined with 1 and 8 groups in one of the most effective raids on a German industrial centre. The target was Hagen, an industrial city that had largely escaped attention of Bomber Command. This was predominantly a Halifax raid and the two northern groups sent 394 of these bombers plus eighty-seven Lancasters, some of which came from 1 Group. Aided by twenty Mosquitoes, the force carried out an accurate raid on the main industrial centres most of which were put out of action until March 1945. The outstanding result was the total destruction of the factory that produced the special accumulators for the new types of U-boat such as the Type XXI electro boat with its special hull designed to accommodate batteries of treble the usual capacity. These were the prefabricated U-boats that Speer had been mass-producing in widely-dispersed and skilfully hidden factories. The longer the delay before they were commissioned and worked up to operational efficiency in the Baltic the greater the chance of maintaining Allied supremacy at sea. So this was a classic example of the strategic value of concentrated attacks upon centres of German industry at a stage in the war when hopes of a rapid victory were constantly frustrated by the resourcefulness and determination of

the German people committed to the total defence of their homeland.

The extent of this determination was not well interpreted by the Allied leadership despite the advantages they believed Ultra gave them. Detection of German intentions, German dispositions and German reserves was unsatisfactory during the period after the breakout from Normandy and the advance towards the Rhine. Most radio communication between the German High Command and their field units was by landlines and this defied interception by Ultra. In fact, Allied intelligence had a singularly bad record from September to December 1944, unhappily illustrated by the choice of Arnhem as a target for unsupported airborne troops[12] and the light defence allocated to the front line in the Ardennes. The twin assumptions on which these two military scenarios were based - that the Paras and Glider Units could take and hold the bridge at Arnhem and that the Ardennes were impassable to armoured fighting vehicles and could therefore be held by exhausted combat troops requiring rest and refitting - brought near disaster on the Allied cause.[13]

The bad weather of December 1944, so effectively used by the Germans to shroud the assembly of their brand-new armoured forces prior to the 'Battle of the Bulge', restricted the operations of 4 and 6 groups. Both groups went to Karlsruhe on 4/5 December and carried out another telling attack on German industry, with the total destruction of the Durlacher machine-tool factories; while the raid on 5/6 December shattered the railway marshalling yards at Soest for the cost of two Canadian Halifaxes. Osnabrück on 6/7 December was not quite so successful. The town had enjoyed something of a charmed life for well over two years during which time the Teuto-Metallwerke munitions factory had been in full production. Teuto-Metallwerke received direct hits, as did other munitions factories. Eight aircraft - a Lancaster and seven Halifaxes - failed to return and the Canadian 6 Group bore half the casualties. The two groups were now gaining something of a reputation for their bombing accuracy and this was well illustrated when 4 Group went back to Essen after a five-day stand-down on the night of 12/13 December. The Yorkshire squadrons despatched 163 Halifaxes in company with 349 Lancasters and twenty-eight Mosquitoes from 1 and 8 Groups. Albert Speer, desperately trying to maintain both production and distribution of war material in the face of Allied air superiority, was beginning to despair at the accuracy of the night attacks. In fact, he was convinced that Bomber Command had some new navigational device for the Essen attack, so precise was the bomb pattern. In the event, this was the last night attack by Bomber Command on Essen though it went back by day on two more occasions in 1945. On 15/16 6 Group's Lancasters took part in a raid on Ludwigshafen with 1 and 8 Groups. I.G. Farben had its chemical factories here some of which manufactured synthetic oil. Much of the oil plant went up in flames that night and Middlebrook comments that:

> "It would be difficult to find a Bomber Command night raid which caused so much industrial damage but so little in civilian housing areas."[14]

As 6 Group's Lancasters returned to their bases in the early hours of 16 December 1944 the totally unexpected German offensive began in the west. Allied intelligence had no hint of the fact that Hitler had assembled a new Army Group 200,000 strong. Commanded by Field Marshal Model, it comprised the VI SS Panzer Army (Sepp Dietrich), the V Panzer Army (Manteuffel) and the VII Army (Brandenberger). The offensive smashed through the Ardennes, shattering the weakly held US front, heading for the port of Antwerp and the vast petrol dumps built up after 4 Group's remarkable airlift.

Because of the weather conditions, Allied air power played no part in stemming the rapid German advance. Credit for this must go to the American soldiers who, as it turned out, fought the biggest battle in America's military history. Though Oboe and H2S were useless against German tanks and artillery hiding beneath cloud and mist on a snow-covered terrain, they were still effective against German industrial targets, especially those on which the German Army depended for the supply of war material. Duisburg was such a target on 17/18 December but little or no information is available on the extent of industrial damage that took place in the city. Eight Halifaxes were lost that night, one of them possibly due to collision with a 420 Squadron Halifax that managed to reach Manston Emergency Landing Ground on three engines. After Duisburg, the Yorkshire squadrons concentrated on the German Army's main railway yards at Nippes (21/22 December) and Bingen (22/23 December) and there is no doubt about the success of these attacks. Nippes lost its important repair shops while Bingen was neutralised and its goods trains never again took supplies to the German Army in the Ardennes. Ironically, one 578 Squadron Halifax from Burn that was lost to fighter attack that night had an under-belly gun to help protect it from *schräge Musik* cannon fire. Unusually, the German night-fighter that shot it down did so in a head-on pass. At the end of

the return flight fog still shrouded many of the Yorkshire airfields and there were many diversions. Aircrew had good reason to bless the FIDO-equipped airfields at Carnaby and Melbourne and the latter's FIDO permitted all of 10 Squadron's aircraft to land safely, together with a 78 Squadron Halifax unable to find Breighton.

Next day, Christmas Eve, saw the arrival of a high pressure system over Western Europe. As the clouds began to lift the two northern Groups were detailed to attack German airfields at Lohausen (Düsseldorff) and Mülheim (Essen) just in case the Germans were tempted to ferry in reinforcements by air. For the Americans, Christmas Eve was a 'maximum effort' to destroy enemy airfields and communication centres and was in fact the biggest *American* air strike operation of the entire war with 2046 bombers and 853 escort fighters despatched. Freezing fog conditions still prevailed and the Americans lost several aircraft in take-off accidents. In Yorkshire, Holme-on-Spalding's runway was sheet ice and this, plus the fog, meant the operation had to be cancelled for 76 Squadron. A total of 248 Halifaxes and seventy-nine Lancasters managed to take off and the two key airfields were thoroughly cratered. Six aircraft were lost in these raids and those that returned to Yorkshire found landing hazardous as Melbourne's FIDO had become unserviceable. Fortunately, Leconfield, Driffield and the fighter base at Hutton Cranswick were able to accept many of the diversions.

Direct intervention in the 'Battle of the Bulge' had to wait until Boxing Day when all the Groups in Bomber Command (apart from 100 Group) sent aircraft to attack German troop positions in and around the town of St Vith. Fog still lay across the Vale of York, the Channel and northern France but this time fifteen of Holme's aircraft managed an instrument take-off before clag closed down the airfield entirely. Allied counter-attacks had already forced the German Army to retreat and many of the Tiger and Panther tanks tried to protect themselves from air attack by sheltering in and around St Vith. As the Halifaxes came in low over the target the crews could see the tell-tale tank tracks in the snow and soon picked out the main concentrations of German armour. Bombs showered down on this luckless Belgian town. There were very heavy casualties among civilians and the German defenders. Flak was intense and one lucky shot removed the entire nose section of a 76 Squadron Halifax piloted by F/O Woolf RCAF. F/Sgt Mason RCAF was the solitary crew member who managed to parachute and become a prisoner-of-war. The second Halifax that failed to return from this operation

THE BOMBERS' CONTRIBUTION TO THE DEFEAT OF THE GERMAN ARMIES IN THE ARDENNES 1944 - 5

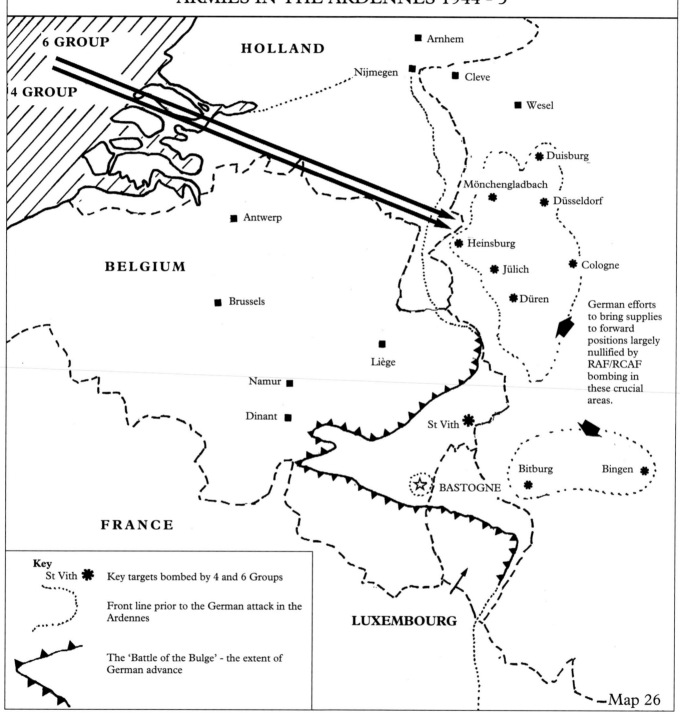

6 GROUP

4 GROUP

HOLLAND

■ Arnhem

Nijmegen ■

■ Cleve

■ Wesel

✳ Duisburg

Mönchengladbach ✳

✳ Düsseldorf

■ Antwerp

BELGIUM

✳ Heinsburg

✳ Jülich   ✳ Cologne

■ Brussels

✳ Düren

German efforts to bring supplies to forward positions largely nullified by RAF/RCAF bombing in these crucial areas.

■ Liège

Namur ■

Dinant ■

St Vith ✳

Bitburg   Bingen ✳
✳

☆ BASTOGNE

FRANCE

LUXEMBOURG

Key
St Vith ✳   Key targets bombed by 4 and 6 Groups

Front line prior to the German attack in the Ardennes

The 'Battle of the Bulge' - the extent of German advance

Map 26

was Melbourne's ZA-Y which ditched in the Channel with the loss of the entire crew.

Because the media of the day concentrated on stories of the Battle of the Bulge, supersonic V-2 rockets and pilotless V-1s released from HE 111s, little credit was given to the achievements of the two Yorkshire Groups. They carried on with their unsung operations amidst the fog, ice and snow showers that made flying conditions difficult and ground crew maintenance a frozen ordeal. Yet there was not much respite for any of the squadrons unless impossibly bad weather forced the planners to cancel an operation. Because the railway yards at Opladen, Mönchengladbach, Koblenz and Troisdorf were still supplying the remnants of the Ardennes front they served as the main targets during 27-29 December). Fortunately, Bomber Command's casualties were light though the Canadians lost the two Lancasters that were shot down on the Opladen raid plus two more when, side by side with 1 Group, they battered the big oil refinery at Scholven/Buer on 29/30 December 1944.

Speer had visited the front at the end of December and listened to Sepp Dietrich's complaints that troops were running out of ammunition now that the rail links on which he depended had been cut by Allied air power. Both men blamed Hitler for the quandary in which the German armed forces presently found themselves. Later Speer referred to that night when he wrote a reluctant tribute to the vital part played by Bomber Command in defeating the German Army in the Ardennes battles.

"As if to illustrate our helplessness, our nocturnal talk was interrupted by a low-level attack from huge four-motored bomber formations. Howling and exploding bombs, clouds illuminated in red and yellow hues, droning motors and no defence anywhere - I was stunned by this scene of military impotence which Hitler's military miscalculations had given such a grotesque setting."[15]

The year ended with a Lancaster and Halifax raid on the Kalk-Nord railway yards and the *autobahnen* at Cologne, symbolising the vital work being carried out by the Yorkshire Squadrons: the steady destruction of the German transportation and communication systems designed to bring about the German collapse in the west. It was not an easy task, especially when coupled with attacks on the oil industry, gardening, area raids and Operation Thunderclap's assault on key cities such as Chemnitz and Dresden that lay in the path of the advancing Russians. The air war that took place from, and sometimes over, Yorkshire would be bitterly contested and it may be helpful to pause at this point to consider the experience of a 'county at war' after its bitter experiences during the blitz of 1940-41.

Yorkshire: The County at War 1942-45

Immense organisation and logistical commitment went into the creation and maintenance of the twenty-seven heavy bomber squadrons in Yorkshire, the four fighter bases, the seven Heavy Conversion Units, the Air Gunnery School at Catfoss and the vital Emergency Landing Ground at Carnaby. The construction of the airfields had been part of the biggest single civil engineering project the County had known and the supply of aircraft, petrol, bombs, flares and other pyrotechnics drew heavily on the industrial resources of the entire nation. Additionally, the training and welfare of the thousands of airman and WAAFs (and the RCAF Women's Division) living and working on airfields in conditions that were often acutely uncomfortable required a sensitivity for which the armed services had not been renowned prior to the Second World War.

By day and by night the Yorkshire skies were filled with training aircraft as well as those engaged upon more deadly tasks. Aircrew who had received their basic flying training in Canada, the USA, Rhodesia and South Africa, now attended their 'finishing schools' in the relatively harsh climate of northern England alongside trainee pilots still undergoing their initial air experience in Tiger Moths and Blackburn B-2s flying out of the airfield at Brough. Accidents were numerous, especially during cross-country

flights in aeroplanes that can at best be described as 'war-weary' and not always up to the RAF's operational standard of 1943-45. Many factors played their part, including the vaguely understood problem of metal fatigue. Venerable Halifaxes in the Heavy Conversion Units tended to shed their propellers with fatal results for the crews and this led several HCUs to fit four-bladed propellers in the hope of breathing more life, reliability and power into the hard-worked Merlin engines.

The aim of the HCUs was to give aircrew the most realistic and up-to-date training possible so that they would have the technical and flying skills to engage the enemy, bomb the target and return to base intact. In the main, the training programme was eminently successful but it was as well that instructors and trainee crews remained unaware that the Luftwaffe had precise details of their codes, pathfinding and aiming techniques, even the names and occupations of their parents! During 1944 instructors at Marston Moor insisted that all trainee crews marked their notes on 'PFF' (Path Finder Force) procedures 'Very Secret' and the act of doing this must have given everyone a great deal of confidence. They had no idea that the Luftwaffe knew precisely the significance of the Parramatta, Wanganui and Newhaven marking techniques; the exact role of supporters and of blind and

Halifax with four-bladed propellers at Marston Moor 1944.

OTUs and HCUs

In his *The British Airman* (Arms & Armour, 1989, p 18), Roger Freeman has two stories that sum up the dangers inherent in Operational Training and Heavy Conversion Units. Undoubtedly, these were due as much to the unserviceability of the aircraft as to the lack of experience on the part of the crews.

The first comes from Eddie Wheeler, then an instructor at 18 OTU at Finningley, who was watching a pupil crew taking off in a Wellington on their first solo.

> "As the plane lifted off the end of the runway, the port engine cut out and the aircraft struggled to gain height. One of the pilot instructors near me said, 'For God's sake, don't turn into the dead engine!' At about 1,000 feet that is exactly what the pupil did and one officer exclaimed, 'He's had it!' As the Wimpy turned, probably in the hope that he could get on to the end of the runway and land, the plane flipped on its back and dropped like a stone. There was a thud followed by an explosion and a huge pall of black smoke. Six young men with high hopes would never see their first operation."

Gerry Hart was posted to Wombleton's HCU for training on Halifaxes. He was far more worried about this than the prospect of going on operations.

> "Having found the billet I'd been allocated, I walked in, chucked my kit bag on the bed and then noticed a bloke sitting on the next bed looking miserable. In an effort to be sociable I joked, 'What's the matter, mate? It can't be that bad.' 'You're new here, aren't you?' 'Yeah,' I replied. He said: 'I've done three bloody cross-country's and come back by train each time. On three consecutive trips I've baled out, ditched and crash-landed.' The bloke was right. It was positively hairy there. The chop rate was pretty high. There were probably other reasons for the high casualty rate, but the state of the aircraft was the main one in my opinion."

visual backers up; the precise equipment of the Pathfinder Mosquitoes; and how Monica and Fishpond were used inside the bombers for aural and visual identification (via cathode ray tubes) of German night-fighters. This information was circulated to all German night-fighter units and to the radar, searchlight and flak defences during 1943-44.

In contrast, flight training at Brough was of marginal interest to the Germans. It was now the home of No 4 Elementary Flight Training School and, in the days before the 600 foot high Humber Bridge and Capper Pass chimney loomed out of the Humber fret just before the threshold of runway 030, a fairly safe airfield for the training of pilots. At least, most thought so, though trainee pilot Gordon Chapman was left with a different impression in 1945:

> "On a late night train I arrived at Brough, hiding in the gloom of a blackout still in force. The railway footbridge was whipped by a chilly March wind that carried a salty tang, a hint of the river close by. Daylight revealed the Blackburn factory. I and the other new arrivals made our way with the early shift workers to the airfield and breakfast. The first days were spent in classrooms where we were introduced to the flying programme and some of the potential hazards. Temptation to fly between the brickworks' chimneys at Gilberdyke would mean a quick end to our flying activities . . . With patient instruction I at last began to learn to fly the wonderfully sensitive Moth. And to get it back safely on the ground without subjecting it to the unkind thump of a landing from twenty feet.

> Going solo was the high point. After about six hours in the air I was handed over to the Squadron Leader for my solo check. This fearsome individual could have been the model for the aircrew 'type'. Dashing manner, handle-bar moustache on a lively face crowned with a silver painted helmet!

> I managed a text-book take-off and felt reasonably pleased with my performance as I flew the downwind leg of the circuit over the river. Without warning, the stick was grabbed from my hand and the aircraft tipped on its side. Though strapped in, I had the impression that the Squadron Leader had gone mad and was trying to tip me out of the aircraft. A thought confirmed, for he gesticulated towards the river below. Above the roar of the wind and the engine I heard the words 'Tidal bore!' Sure enough, there on the wide river was the wave of the bore running on the surface. In other circumstances I might have enjoyed sighting this phenomenon but not at this critical moment . . . I must have completed the rest of the circuit in competent fashion as he left the aircraft after we landed and gave me the thumbs up to take the aircraft up on my own."[1]

Blackburn's factory was busy throughout the war. After the last Bothas were built in 1943 the factory tooled up for the production of Fairey Barracuda torpedo bombers and 635 of these rather ungainly looking aeroplanes emerged from Brough. The factory also repaired damaged aircraft and began designing modifications of US Navy aircraft such as the Wildcat so these could be operated by the Royal Navy. Naval aviation

LS 326 Swordfish built by Blackburn at Sherburn in Elmet. Yorkshire.
Yorkshire Air Museum

Brough's Barracudas

While the Fairey Swordfish was being built at Sherburn, Brough was constructing 535 Fairey Barracuda strike aircraft for the Royal Navy. Powered by a single 1640 hp Roll-Royce Merlin 32 with a four-bladed propeller, the Barracuda was a torpedo/dive-bomber of unusual design. It was the Royal Navy's first monoplane torpedo bomber and the aeroplane was unusual in that it had a shoulder wing and a high mounted tailplane to avoid turbulence from the large Fowler-Youngman flaps that were lowered in the dive-bombing role.

A newly-built Barracuda on test at Brough.
Bruce/Leslie collection

Though it first flew in 1940 the desperate need to manufacture Spitfires, Hurricanes and the early marks of four-engined bombers hindered production of the Mk II until late 1942 when Boulton Paul's factory at Wolverhampton and Westland at Yeovil joined Brough in helping to mass-produce an aeroplane urgently needed by aircraft carriers operating in the Atlantic and Pacific war theatres. The Barracuda's achievements included: the remarkable mass attack on *Tirpitz* at anchor in Kaafiord, Norway (3 April 1944); and the deadly dive-bombing attacks on Sabang submarine base between 16/21 April 1944.

at Brough was but one facet of the Blackburn war contribution: a large workforce at the Sherburn in Elmet factory produced 1,700 Fairy Swordfish (known as the 'Blackfish'); the Dumbarton factory built 250 Short Sunderlands; and in 1942 a Blackburn team set up a British Modification centre in the USA to carry out Royal Navy modifications on the Corsair, Avenger and Hellcat aircraft. This kind of experience encouraged Blackburn to design a new naval fighter known as the Firebrand, and the prototype flew in 1942. When fitted with a 2,520 hp Bristol Centaurus[2] and carrying a torpedo, this powerful aircraft met the Royal Navy's specification for a strike aircraft. Too late to see war service, the Firebrands equipped No 813 squadron in September 1945.

To this variety of aircraft types seen in the Yorkshire skies must be added the Mustangs, Thunderbolts, Spitfires and Martinet drogue-towers that flew from Catfoss Central Gunnery School 1944-45. Prior to those dates Catfoss had seen the Spitfires of 616 Squadron plus the Blenheims, Ansons and Beaufighters from No 2 Operational Training Unit. When 2 OTU disbanded in 1944 Catfoss became the home of the Central Gunnery School dedicated to the improvement of fighter pilots' gunnery skills, a wartime equivalent to the modern 'Top Gun' at Miramar. British and American fighter aces - these included G/Capt 'Sailor' Malan (Commanding Officer 1944-45) and 'Screwball' Beurling - lectured at Catfoss, taught their skills side by side with ballistic experts from Frazer-Nash and Boulton Paul.

Less dramatic was the work being carried out at Kirkbymoorside where, inspired by the successes enjoyed by German airborne troops during the invasion of Holland and Belgium in 1940, Slingsby Sailplanes developed the Hengist paratroop glider. As would be expected from a firm of Slingsby's skill and experience the Hengist was

aerodynamically superb. It was an all-wooden glider (wooden ribs with a stressed plywood skin), a wingspan of 80 feet and accommodation for fifteen fully equipped paratroops who would exit from doors on both sides of the fuselage. But by the time the first Hengist flew at Dishforth behind a Whitley tug (January 1942), the need for a paratroop glider had disappeared. Airborne forces required bigger gliders capable of carrying arms, equipment, vehicles as well as troops and these soon arrived in the form of the Airspeed Horsa and the American Waco Hadrian. Nevertheless, the Airborne Forces Experimental Establishment at Sherburn-in-Elmet continued to test-fly the Hengist and improved versions were manufactured during 1943-44 at Kirkbymoorside in conditions of great secrecy. Unwittingly, its production provided an income for small boys.

David Wall, a National Service pilot after the war, recalls:

"In 1942-3 I lived on a farm at Hutton le Hole, a good place for evacuees and well away from the war except for the army exercises through the village and over the surrounding moors. Pocket money was hard to come by for an eleven year old and therefore supplemented by farming piecework, hoeing turnips at 1d. a row and 'tatty scratting' at 1d a bucket.

Intelligence reported a new source of income from Slingsby's at nearby Kirkbymoorside. This involved collecting a bundle of wooden strips and a bag of nails from their stores, brief instructions and a promise to return the finished goods by next week. "What's it for?" "It's for the WAR EFFORT" or "It's SECRET war work" was all we could obtain. The mundane task was to start some 25 nails into each three foot strip of wooden lath and repeat the process until all hundred strips were completed; then return the now larger bundle to Slingsby's stores and collect the pay. So kneeling on the wooden floor of an empty hen house, I hammered the nails to a working rhyme:

"The stars at night, are big and bright, deep in the heart of Texas."

We never found exactly what these nailed lathes were for but rumour has it they were used to tack plywood skins on to the gliders that were built there for training and troop transport."[3]

Although the Hengist was a delight to fly it was decided not to proceed with mass production of the type and the last ten incomplete Hengists were moved from Kirkbymoorside to be stored first at Sherburn in Elmet and then at Rawcliffe Paper Mills before being scrapped in 1946.

Slingsby Sailplanes had large, unexpected orders for the mass-production of the Type 7 Kirby Kadet. These derived from the formation of the Air Training Corps in 1942 and the decision by the Air Ministry to offer cadets primary flight experience at weekends and summer camps. Gliding instructors were initially trained at Kirkbymoorside where the first ATC Gliding School was opened in 1942. Slingsby Sailplanes had orders for two hundred Kadets and other woodworking firms soon

This is a Grumman Martlet - the name used by the Royal Navy for the Grumman Wildcat fighter up to January 1944 when it was changed to conform with the US Navy's name.

Martlets were serving with No 804 Squadron in 1940 and two of them encountered a Ju 88 over Scapa Flow. They shot down the Ju 88 - notching up the first victory over the Luftwaffe by an American fighter serving with British forces in World War II.

The last surviving 'British' Martlet is in the FAA Museum at Yeovilton.

produced their quota for ATC Gliding Schools that opened on many RAF aerodromes. Dagling gliders were also used and during 1943 an improved automatic release 'Ottfur hook' was fitted to the nose of ATC gliders to improve flight safety. By then winches similar to those used for barrage balloons were available and the Ottfur hook automatically released the launch cable if the trainee pilot approached the dangerous stall position during launch. Thousands of ATC cadets began their flight training in this way and some progressed from ground slides and hops to airfield circuits in their gliders - invaluable for those who went on to the RAF's Elementary Flying Schools to train on Tiger Moths. Many former cadets remembered with some affection the camouflaged and often battered Kirby gliders whose name was changed for patriotic reasons from Kadet to *Cadet TX Mk 1*.

★ ★ ★

Besides the Blackburn factories at Sherburn and Brough and Slingsby Sailplanes at Kirkbymoorside, two other very important factories existed in Yorkshire. Yeadon Aerodrome had since 1941 been the home of No 20 Elementary Flying School equipped with Tiger Moths and when this was disbanded in early 1942 the site was handed over to the Ministry of Aircraft Production. A. V. Roe and Company developed the site into what was probably the most ingeniously planned and camouflaged example of an aircraft factory in England. It was certainly

Glider Construction and Testing in Yorkshire
1939-1945

SLINGSBY TYPE 6 KIRBY KITE
Produced for use with No 1 Glider Squadron (Haddenham).

GAL HOTSPUR Mk I
After the first specification for a military assault glider was issued by the Ministry of Aircraft Production in 1940, General Aircraft Company designed the GAL Hotspur Military Assault Glider. Twenty-four of these were built and Slingsby manufactured thirteen of these at Kirkbymoorside.

SLINGSBY TYPE 18: THE HENGIST I
This was Slingsby's response to a specification for a military transport glider. It had a wingspan of 80 feet, not much shorter than the Airspeed Horsa.

SLINGSBY TYPE 7 KADET/CADET TX Mk 1
Manufactured mainly for ATC Gliding Schools.

GAL 49/50 HAMILCAR
The prototype DP 206 was built at Feltham but then taken 200 miles by road to Snaith bomber base for testing on the 2000 yard tarmac runway. This was also home to No 150 Squadron who in 1942 were fighting the war with their Wellington IIIs from this particularly uncomfortable snowbound site in perhaps the most dismal period of the Second World War. Despite these adverse conditions and after a delay occasioned by the necessary fact that the operational Wellingtons always had runway priority, Charles Hughesdon piloted the Hamilcar in a successful flight behind a Stirling on 27 March 1942. After further tests at e.g. Newmarket and Chelveston, the Hamilcar went into production as a tank-carrying glider.

WACO CG-4A HADRIAN
Hadrian NP 664 was test-flown by the Airborne Forces Experimental Unit (AFEU) at Sherburn in Elmet during 1943.

BAYNES CARRIER WING GLIDER
Slingsby Sailplanes constructed a one-third scale model of this tail-less glider designed to transport a tank into battle. It performed well but never went into production. It was later used at Farnborough for research into tail-less aircraft design.

SLINGSBY TYPE 23
This was a modified Type 6 Kirby Kite developed in 1945. It first flew in December 1945 and was eventually sold to the USA.

one of the biggest and at its peak employed over 11,000 workers, more than half of them women. Housing estates mushroomed around Yeadon Aerodrome, billetting officers scoured the area for further accommodation and buses shuttled the shift-workers from their homes to the factory and back again. They built Avro Ansons by the thousand and then turned their hands to the Avro Lancaster, specialising in the production of those going to the Pathfinding squadrons. As the finished Lancasters emerged (from April 1942 onwards) they were towed along a causeway linking the factory to the runways. Once they were tested and certified as suitable for operations, the Lancasters were usually sent to Maintenance Squadrons before being flown to their operational units by Air Transport Auxiliary pilots.[4]

To the surprise of many RAF types these pilots were sometimes women. Lettice Curtis was the first woman to be checked out as a four-engined pilot (25 February 1943), ferried her first Halifax two days later and over the next two and a half years delivered scores of Lancasters, Halifaxes, Stirlings and Liberators to their squadrons.[5] Of these she considered the Halifax to be the "heaviest of the three British wartime four-engined bombers to handle." When faced with male prejudice - that it was too heavy for a woman to fly - she would always respond by saying that there were few flying incidents, including abnormal attitudes, that could be averted simply by the use of brute strength. She laid far more stress on foresight and good anticipation. Her three-point landing techniques were eventually much admired when ATA pilots delivered the Halifax IIIs to Yorkshire bases in exchange for the in-line varieties. Delivery trips to Pocklington, Driffield and Middleton St George; to Skipton-on-Swale and to Holme-on-Spalding-Moor became at this time almost a daily task for Lettice and her colleagues.

The other major factory, a repair depot, opened at Rawcliffe (Clifton), York, in 1941. Yorkshire was already the graveyard of many a crashed bomber - Whitleys, Wellingtons, He 111s, Ju 88s and Halifaxes - and the RAF had formed in late 1939 the specialist 60 Maintenance Unit on the village green at Tollerton near Linton to recover aircraft wreckage. During the war 60 Maintenance Unit recovered over three thousand crashed aeroplanes and some of these were refurbished at Clifton.

Clifton's grass airfield was first used by Army Co-operation Lysanders but in 1941 the resident No 48 Maintenance Unit began repairing Halifax bombers and therefore needed extensive metalled runways for testing aircraft. The new runways were built on Clifton Common

60 MU towing away the remains of a Heinkel He III. Note that the Queen Mary trailer has a single axle for this mamoth task.

Yorkshire Air Museum

and the first of the Handley Page repair teams arrived in July though one team had already been savouring Yorkshire life since March when they had come to repair a Halifax that had bellied in at Linton and seemed worthy of repair. Although a few rogue Halifaxes reached the squadrons, tribute must be paid to the remarkably accurate production methods adopted by the workers who built the bombers in the first instance: parts were readily interchangeable no matter whether a Halifax had been constructed by Rootes Securities at Speke, by Handley Page at Cricklewood or by Fairey at Errwood Park.

Ian Robinson, a senior test flight engineer at Clifton, air tested these Halifaxes before they were repainted and confirmed that a Halifax might have night camouflage on its Bomber Command 'bits' and Coastal Command whites and greys on the rest, depending on how the Halifax had been reassembled:

"and a sorry sight they were . . . We carried colours of the day but still used to have everything from Black Widows, Spitfires, Mosquitoes, Mustangs and the whole of Nos 4 and 6 Group Halifaxes looking suspiciously at the odd Halifaxes from Clifton."[6]

The Repair Depot also modified and updated Halifaxes as well as repairing nearly 170 of the bombers, while total rebuilds provided Bomber Command with an extra 320 Halifaxes.

* * *

Amidst this extraordinary array of activities, the two Group Headquarters at Heslington Hall, York (4 Group) and Allerton Park Castle (6 Group) had the task of controlling the offensive arm of Bomber Command in Yorkshire. Each day they received their orders from Sir

The Importance of Blackburn's Role in the Modification and Repair of Aircraft

1940-1945

Brough's first contact with US-manufactured naval carrier aircraft was in the summer of 1940 when a Grumman Martlet arrived in the East Riding for modification to Royal Navy combat specifications. Under the generous war-time Lease-Lend Agreement the Americans transferred many different types of aircraft to Yorkshire for up-dating to British standards. First Wildcats (the British name for the Martlet) and then Corsairs, Hellcats, Avengers and Helldivers arrived as deck-cargo on the Atlantic convoys for reassembly at Speke (Liverpool) and Renfrew (Glasgow). American factory drawings and design data were put on microfilm and flown ahead to Britain. Before long Blackburns had so many committments that Brough could not cope. Modification centres were set up at Sherburn, Kirkbymoorside, Leeds, Dumbarton, Keighley and Hammersmith. Jack Hall went across to the States to become the company's Chief Engineer at the new British Modification Centre at Roosevelt Field where he supervised specialist modification of the Hellcats and Corsairs. He also helped transform the Avenger, an aeroplane that urgently needed stronger wings to carry anti-shipping rockets plus better accommodation for the navigator.

Since May 1940 Blackburn had also functioned as a major repair centre for British as well as American designs. It repaired 1,215 aircraft and restored them to operational squadrons. The most important repair centre was at Sherburn-in-Elmet under the supervision of Chief Engineer Tom Bancroft. In February 1944, for example, the Blackburn Repair Organisation returned sixty-one aircraft to the Royal Navy: forty-five Barracudas, a Bermuda, four Swordfish, four Wildcats, three Rocs and four Skuas- no small contribution to the British war effort.

Arthur Harris at his High Wycombe headquarters and in turn passed on their specific requirements to the station commanders. Harris, of course, shaped his instructions according to his understanding of the floods of policy directives that controlled his operations, in particular the January 1943 Casablanca directive that defined his primary object as "the progressive destruction and dislocation of the German military, industrial and economic system . . . " and the June 1943 Pointblank directive that required him to give priority to "the general disorganisation of German industry" connected with aircraft production.

That he was proceeding according to plan was confirmed by a signal from Sir Charles Portal, Chief of the Air Staff, on 30 December 1943:

"As we approach the end of another year I would ask you to accept for yourself and pass on to those serving under you an expression of my heartfelt appreciation of the magnificent achievements of Bomber Command in 1943. I know very well the weight of responsibility which you and your Group Commanders bear so well in devising and directing these great operations. I appreciate too the efficiency and devotion of your Staffs and the willing response of all who work on the ground to the frequent calls made upon them for long hours of hours of hard and heavy work, often under most trying conditions. Above all, I regard with heart-felt admiration and thankfulness the unswerving courage and the constant skill of your crews . . . it is widely recognised that a large share of the successes of Allied arms on all German fronts this year is due to the destruction wrought in the heart of Germany by Bomber Command . . . "[7]

These sentiments, passed on to the crews by Station Commanders, did much to maintain morale in the air and on the ground during the ferocious Battle of Berlin. Life on the bomber airfields in Yorkshire was a unique experience for all. It was isolated for much of the time though relieved by Squadron dances and vaudeville shows, trips to the cinemas and dances in Northallerton, York, Beverley and Hull. More often it was a night in the pub in the local village, the chance of a twenty-four or forty-eight hour pass during a 'stand-down' and, for aircrew, a seven or fourteen day leave at the end of six operations. Dick Cowl, a Halifax bomb-aimer, remembered that:

". . . luxury used to be a night at the Station Hotel in Hull, bed and breakfast for 14/6d. with a hot bath thrown in. No-one ever needed to go without a drink for lack of money, and socially there was plenty of activity to choose from every free evening, from Betty's Bar in York, the Londesborough Arms at both Market Weighton and Selby, to the New Inn at Holme. In reality, there were too few free evenings in the week."[8]

Bill Townshend CGM, DFM recalls the life of a bomber pilot. Life was led, he said:

". . . at two completely contrasting levels: the warmth, conviviality and relative comfort of one's Base; and the long, cold periods of discomfort of operational flights, invariably punctuated with spells of intense and often quite frightening activity, Through six years of sustained aerial warfare, tens of thousands of Aircrew lived these contrasting life-styles."[9]

Some aircrew failed to cope with the stress and strain of 'ops' over Germany and had to be taken off operations, usually at their own request. As all aircrew were volunteers, Air Ministry policy was to deter such a request before the end of a tour. When it did occur official policy was to attach stigma to the man. Aircrew who could not cope with the demands of operational flying were branded 'Lack of Moral Fibre' (LMF), stripped of rank and required to carry out menial duties. That this was uncommon is undoubtedly due to the *esprit de corps* of the Squadron, of being part of a team and unwilling to let down one's friends. And there was always the sensation, as Townshend puts it, that:

"In the heat of battles, as it were, one tends to remain optimistic."

There was also a half-humorous, half-cynical release from stress in their youthful attempts at song and verse, sheltering their fears of collision, flak and night-fighters. Well-known in most of Yorkshire's Halifax squadrons was

THE REAPER

The aircraft droning up above
The aircrew dozing in it
Can all become a tangled wreck
In less than half a minute

'But, how?' you ask and well you may
You who stay upon the ground
The answer to the question is
THE REAPER is around.

He plods the lonely skies at night
His black beard dangling low
His beetled eye-brows, long thin nose
His eyes a fiery glow.

Then suddenly he stops - he laughs
An ugly sinful laugh
And swings his scythe along the skies
As though 'twere cutting chaff.

He hurries where his victim drones
'A Halifax !' he cries.
'I'd sooner prang a Halifax
Than anything that flies.'

He creeps behind, his scythe aloft
His evil lips drawn tight
And with a cry of 'Die you dogs !'
He'll swing with all his might.

So aircrew take this warning
Look out and search the skies
Remember - perhaps it's your turn next
To hear THE REAPER'S cries.[10]

The presence of WAAFs on all the airfields and on numerous barrage balloon sites and petrol dumps ensured a sense of excitement and anticipation among air and ground crews at a time of intense abnormality. By 1942-43 WAAFs had been admitted to most trades in the Royal Air Force and they proved indispensable as plotters, parachute packers, engine fitters, drivers, radar mechanics, cooks, waitresses, and in every station and Group headquarters as typists, telephonists and, in the most confidential areas of work, as WAAF Special Duties. Amy Bridson was possibly the first WAAF to qualify as a radar mechanic and she served first at Linton-on-Ouse (January 1943), winning the first feminist victory for battle dress to replace the issue skirt hardly appropriate for working on a Halifax bomber.

As she said:

> "It might have done a great deal for the morale of the fellows working on the flights to view us jumping in and out of aircraft and clambering over barriers in tunic and skirt, but we felt that this would be carrying patriotism a little too far."[11]

Amy Bridson then moved to Holme-on-Spalding Moor (June 1943), won equality in the NAAFI queue and a rum ration when working in Halifaxes on cold winter days. Holme's 76 Radar Section had a high reputation, an established watering-hole at North Cave's Wembley Café, and the WAAFs were regarded as professional mechanics skilled in the advanced electronics of a modern bomber. Expert in the fitting and maintenance of IFF (Identification Friend or Foe), Gee, Aural and Visual Monica, H2S and finally Loran and Rebecca,[12] they were proud to be serving under their Station Commander, Wing Commander Leonard Cheshire DSO, until he moved to Marston Moor on 22 January 1944.

Group Captain Leonard Cheshire
VC, DSO AND BARS, DFC

His Yorkshire Squadrons

No 102 Squadron

9 June 1940	P/O Cheshire took off from Driffield on his first operation.
15 August 1940	Luftwaffe raid on Driffield: squadron moves to Aldergrove. Returns to Linton in October.
6 Nov. 1940	Attacked target in the Ruhr.
12 Nov. 1940	Direct hit from flak over Cologne. Awarded DSO: "Showing great coolness". . . and . . . "Although the aircraft was only partially answering the controls Pilot Officer Cheshire succeeded in returning to his aerodrame." AVM Coningham, i/c 4 Group noted that Cheshire was "the first junior officer in Bomber Command to be so decorated after fifteen months of war."

No 35 Squadron

	Having completed his first tour Cheshire was posted to Linton-on Ouse (Halifaxes) where he completed his second tour and won a second bar to his DSO and the DFC.
22 Jan. 1942	Screened from operations, he was appointed to No 35 Squadron's 1652 HCU at Marston Moor.

No 76 Squadron

August 1942	Appointed Wing Commander to lead No 76 Squadron at Linton-on-Ouse where G/Captain John Whitley was Station Commander (shot down in April 1943 when acting as second dickey in a raid on Frankfurt). Cheshire won a bar to his DSO (completed 60 operations) and was much loved by ground and aircrew for the quality of his leadership and the care he displayed for all personnel. "It was a sad day," said WAAF Amy Bridson, "when he completed his second tour and left Linton for pastures new at Marston Moor."
April 1943	Promoted to Group Captain and Station Commander at Marston Moor. He left Marston Moor to take command of No 617 Squadron in October 1943 and to become the most extraordinary of Bomber Command's 'master bombers' and low-level target markers flying Lancasters, Mosquitoes and finally a Mustang. His VC (awarded September 1944) was, in part, recognition of his service with 4 Group in Yorkshire.

The WAAFs knew, only too briefly in most cases, all the bomber crews on the base. Every WAAF driver understood only too well that when she drove them in a crew-bus to a waiting Halifax or Lancaster she might be the last woman they ever saw. The casualty rate and the uncertainty of the times in which they lived did not encourage many serious liasons until the later stages of the war when losses in the two Yorkshire groups markedly declined. More casual liaisons sometimes resulted in pregnancies and most stations had a regular WAAF departure due to this. One Squadron historian faithfully recorded these occasions, always adding the words 'Not Guilty' in brackets.

Aircrew morale was also borne up by the availability of Carnaby Emergency Landing Ground and the efficiency of the Air Sea Rescue Service. Yorkshire's role is of interest in that two important rescue devices were invented and developed at County bases. The first was the Thornaby Bag dropped from Lysanders borrowed from Army Co-operation Command. This contained survival kit and special buoyancy bags to help a crewman floating in his Mae West lifejacket. The second was the Lindhholme Gear devised by G/Capt Waring, then Station Commander at Lindholme (1940). This was an eight man dinghy linked to four supply packs by means of a floating rope. This basic equipment was constantly upgraded and it has been reported that Churchill suggested the inclusion of playing cards for the "maintenance of morale."[13] Though G/Capt Waring had designed the Lindholme Gear for his Hampden bombers, the equipment could be carried by most twin engined aircraft. Then in July 1941 three Walrus amphibians were assigned to Air Sea Rescue and before long four specialist squadrons were in operation. Once Lockheed Hudsons entered the Air Sea Rescue service they were fitted with a full-size Airborne Lifeboat Mk 1, as were the later Vickers Warwicks. For a crew floating in their eight-man dinghy the arrival of one of these lifeboats meant they could set course for England with confidence and in relative comfort. Most crews, however, were happy to be rescued from their dinghies and airborne lifeboats by the RAF's High Speed Launches.

This was the experience of Halifax DY-V of 102 Squadron returning to Pocklington on two engines after being hit by flak over Dortmund (5 May 1943). The crew ditched fifty miles from Spurn Point and about three hours later was found by Hudsons. When one carefully dropped its Airborne Lifeboat the bomber crew thought "that the bottom of the Hudson had fallen off."[14]

Supported by three parachutes, the lifeboat landed safely. The bomber crew climbed on board and the Halifax Flight Engineer started the engines while a Hudson helpfully flashed a magnetic bearing so the navigator could set course for home. Eventually RAF High Speed Launch No 2579 arrived, picked up the crew and landed at Grimsby, one of hundreds of bomber crews who owed their lives to the Air Sea Rescue Squadrons, three of which were based in Yorkshire.

Air Sea Rescue Squadrons
Flights based in Yorkshire
1942 - 1945

278 Squadron	Hutton Cranswick	Lysander, Walrus, Anson	1942-45
279 Squadron	Thornaby	Hudson, Warwick	1944-45
281 Squadron	Thornaby	Warwick	1943-44

Equally important was the giant emergency airfield at Carnaby which shared with nearby Lissett the task of receiving and caring for crews whose aircraft were low on fuel or seriously damaged. Carnaby was reserved for pressing emergencies; clear weather diversions, especially during the day-time, were often to operational airfields. When the American 448th Bomb Group returned from its mission to Aachen on 16 November 1944, low haze and fog over East Anglia caused such a diversion to Lissett. G/Capt Tom Sawyer DFC, Station Commander at Lissett, described the twenty-four Liberators as they came in over the Yorkshire countryside:

"... they arrived, and in good order landed one after the other in quick time and without any assistance from our flying control. Their circuit and landing drill and discipline were perfect."[15]

They were just in time as fog rolled in from the sea, clamping down North and East Yorkshire and most of the East Coast for the next forty-eight hours. Lissett therefore had to cope with the presence of over two hundred American aircrew.

"We had enough spare beds and blankets in the stores and luckily more barrack huts too ... for the next three days our cook-houses were going full-blast most of the time, the camp cinema was opened for morning and afternoon sessions as well as for the evening ones and special aircrew buses ran an almost non-stop shuttle service to and from Bridlington for their extra entertainment ... The whole of my station personnel rose magnificently to the occasion . . . I was immensely proud of them all . . . and told them so in a Tannoy broadcast when it was all over."[16]

Carnaby did not have these facilities though it did have over five hundred personnel capable of dealing with the horrors of crashed and burning aeroplanes and with the dreadful injuries sustained by so many crews. Over 1500 emergency landings took place at Carnaby and one of the most remarkable occurred on the night of 8/9 April 1945 involving a No 58 Squadron Halifax III skippered by F/Lt Ronald Lawson. After bombing a merchant ship close to the Norwegian coast an explosion had left a gaping hole in the bottom of the fuselage. The Halifax was now difficult to fly and the DR compass was out of action.

When the smoked cleared, Lawson checked the crew members and discovered that their WOP/AG Sgt Frank Smith was missing. Part of a parachute canopy was wrapped round the mid-upper turret legs but there was no sign of 'Smithy'. Everyone assumed that he had fallen through the hole in the fuselage. They set up the astro compass on Polaris and headed for Carnaby, hoping for the best as below them the world was now shrouded in 10/10th cloud. When they calculated they were near the Yorkshire coast they called up Carnaby only to be told that total fog covered the airfield, not much else was about and could they go elsewhere. When Lawson reported that fuel gauges were on zero Carnaby relented and turned on FIDO for the solitary Halifax. With no flaps, an approach speed of 140 knots and flanked by jets of burning petrol they touched down in the middle of the 3,500 yard runway and braked hard. As they did this, all the flames went out and for a few minutes they sat lost in Carnaby's fog until a patrolling jeep found them. They followed the jeep to a hardstanding, shut down and clambered out of the battered bomber.

There was a sudden shout - Smithy was still there ! He was suspended under the aircraft, arms and legs wound round damaged fuselage spars, held in place face downwards by a dinghy D-ring on his parachute harness. This had providentially hooked round a lug in the bomb bay framing exposed by the force of the explosion. His face had been saved by his oxygen mask, wiped smooth as it grazed along the runway during the landing. He had been under the fuselage for over three hours and could still smile when they released him and removed the mask from his face. [17]

Frank Smith explained what had happened:
"We had bombed the ship and our photoflash bomb exploded immediately under the aircraft,

"And still smiling" Sgt Frank Smith in 1991.

destroying the H2S and leaving a twelve foot hole. But I didn't know that as I was blinded by the photoflash. I pulled out my intercom and made my way to the back of the aircraft and that's when I fell through the hole. I was very lucky that the D-ring hooked on a lug and lasted the next three hours. When we landed that D-ring had elongated by 50% !"[18]

Of course, not all returning crews reached any kind of airfield after they crossed the English coast and had to crash-land and sometimes die in remote, inhospitable parts of the UK. Those who survived were required to make their way back to base as best they could and the appearance of airmen, in full flying kit, on the railways or on the London Tube, usually aroused sympathy and interest plus the offer of free beer. As aircrew did not take the coin of the realm with them on operations, lack of funds when trying to return to base by train or bus sometimes proved embarrassing. One crew that crash-landed in the south of England managed to get as far as Beverley and when they asked the station-master if they might use the phone to contact Leconfield for transport the gentleman first asked them for tuppence.

★ ★ ★

The defence of the County, sorely tested during 1941-42, was relatively relaxed after the summer of 1942. By then the Luftwaffe had switched most of its bombers from Western Europe to the East to support Hitler's *Operation Barbarossa*, the code-name for the invasion of Russia that had begun on 22 June 1941. At a time of respite home defence was improved and updated in terms of anti-aircraft guns, barrage balloon allocation, radar

THE ATTACK ON CHRISTMAS EVE 1944

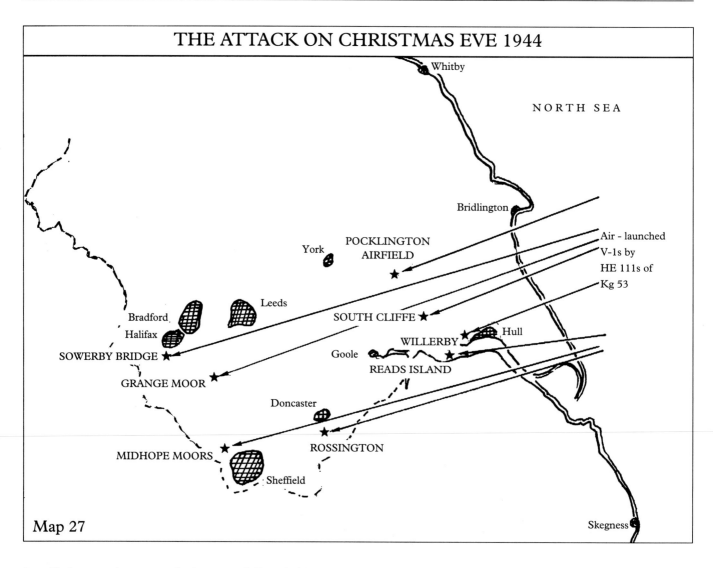

Map 27

installations and a properly integrated Royal Observer Corps (ROC). In Yorkshire there were numerous but ever-changing day and night-fighter squadrons and carefully dispersed decoy fires and decoy airfields to tempt enemy bomb-aimers. Full-size wooden mock-up aircraft were generously distributed over these decoy fields, examples of which are listed below:

Operational base	Decoy airfield	Decoy aircraft type
Church Fenton	Menthorpe	Hurricane
Dishforth	Cold Kirby	Whitley
Driffield	Skipsea	Whitley
Finningley	Owston Ferry	Whitley
Linton	Bossall	Whitley
Thornaby	Grangetown	Blenheim

All but Skipsea and Bossall were fitted with dummy flarepaths and usually termed 'Q' sites.

John Bushby's *Air Defence of Great Britain* has a chapter entitled *Practice to Deceive* and diagrams of the kits used to build a decoy Blenheim and a decoy Hurricane.

From August 1941 onwards concentrations of searchlights were used to dazzle enemy aircrew. Over Hull, for example, this often led to the random bombing of the docks, city and outlying villages by frustrated Luftwaffe crews. All these devices had some success though the two main objects were: to create *gun defence areas* to deter enemy aircraft from making low level raids; and *killer zones* in which searchlights would home in on a target so that it could be intercepted by a night-fighter. This required close co-operation between Ground Controlled Interception radar (GCI) and the Royal

Observer Corps, happily achieved during 1943-1944 when the GCI stations were netted in with ROC Operations Rooms.

The Royal Observer Corps took responsibility for plotting aircraft movements from ground to 5000 feet, the zone in which GCI was ineffective. The country was divided into 'areas' and Yorkshire was part of the ROC Midland area. An area was in turn subdivided into 'groups' and the local group headquarters was in York. The reader will recall that when enemy aircraft appeared over York on 29 April 1942 during the Baedeker raid, the air raid warning did not sound until after the first bombs fell. Quite unfairly, this delay was attributed to York's ROC Centre even though it did not have responsibility for sounding alerts. [19] The Baedeker raids and those that followed were undertaken by faster German bombers such as the Dornier Do 217, the Ju 88 and the Me 410 and they appeared over Yorkshire using marker flares, high explosive bombs filled with the much more deadly 'England mixture', new types of incendiaries and 'butterfly bombs' designed to kill the curious. [20]

Their main objective in Yorkshire was the port of Hull, already battered during the blitz of 1941. During 1942-43 it was the 'north-east coast town' so frequently mentioned in news bulletins and a favourite target for Dornier 217s from KG2, KG 40 and KG 66 operating mainly from Soesterberg and Deelen during 1942-43. Some of these Dornier 217s had already joined in with the Ju 88s for the Baedeker raid on York and now, in the early winter of 1942, they began mining operations in the Humber estuary that lasted from 15 November to 13 December

1942. In the same month the Dorniers launched a heavy raid on Hull. Anti-aircraft fire was always intense on either side of the Humber estuary and the guns managed to inflict serious damage on several Do 217s. At least one low-flying Dornier 217 crashed on the Yorkshire Moors during this period and the German bomber groups lost many more due to collisions and accidents. It was KG 66 that carried out the major raid on Hull (13 July 1943) and gunfire from the city defences caused flak damage to at least three of the German bombers. The guns were even more successful on 25 July when they helped to drive off fifty of the raiders. By then Mosquito IIs from 25 Squadron at Church Fenton and Beaufighter VIs from 604 Squadron at Scorton patrolled the Yorkshire coast aided by the GCI stations at Patrington and Staythorpe. Scorton had been a night-fighter base since February 1942 when two RCAF Squadrons, 406 Lynx and 410 Cougar, had served consecutively on this North Yorkshire airfield. and on 17/18 August 1943, during a another raid on Hull, F/Lt Lomas of 604 Squadron shot down a Dornier 217 and claimed one more as a 'probable'.

Hull's ordeal was still not over and during one of his leaves S/Ldr A. J. Brown, an expatriate Yorkshireman, crossed the Humber in the *Tattershall Castle* ("First-class only 5½d. extra") to visit Hull and recorded his impressions of the heavily bombed city. He noted the packed shipping in the estuary and the rows of barrage balloon barges and the elaborate arrays of anti-aircraft guns.

"But Hull is a stricken city. The narrow streets near the docks which used to be full of curious

---

Bomb HC 4000lb Mk IV 'Cookie'

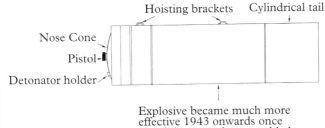

Nose Cone
Pistol
Detonator holder
Hoisting brackets   Cylindrical tail

Explosive became much more effective 1943 onwards once aluminium powder was added to form Minol.

The 4000 lb High Capacity bomb, universally known as a 'Cookie', had a relatively light casing of cylindrical shape. When filled with Minol explosive, its blast effect was massive. Combined with incendiary bombs, devastation by

blast and fire reached maximum levels – a fate endured by Darmstadt on 11/12 September 1944 when 200 Cookies and well over a quarter of a million incendiaries fell on this unfortunate city.

Experience showed that stability and accuracy increased when the Cookie was fitted with a cylindrical tail conforming to the shape of the bomb itself. The nose plate was slightly domed and contained the pistol for detonating the bomb.

For a useful technical treatment of British air-dropped weapons, see Wing Commander John A. MacBean and Major Arthur S. Hogben, Bombs Gone, PSL 1990.

In the opinion of these authors, the 4000 lb Cookie was "probably the RAF's most effective weapon."

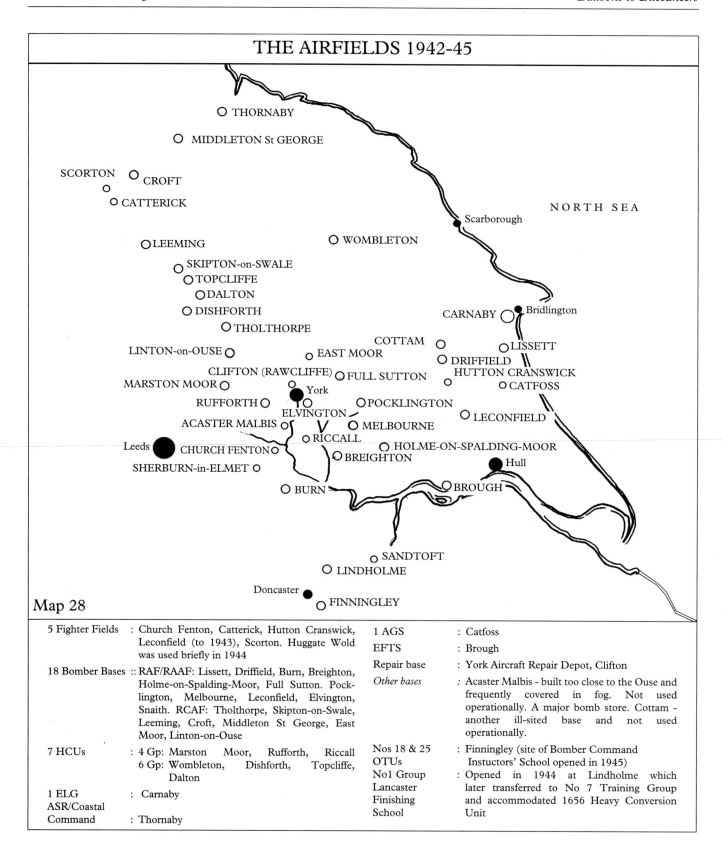

THE AIRFIELDS 1942-45

Map 28

5 Fighter Fields	: Church Fenton, Catterick, Hutton Cranswick, Leconfield (to 1943), Scorton. Huggate Wold was used briefly in 1944	1 AGS	: Catfoss
		EFTS	: Brough
		Repair base	: York Aircraft Repair Depot, Clifton
18 Bomber Bases	: RAF/RAAF: Lissett, Driffield, Burn, Breighton, Holme-on-Spalding-Moor, Full Sutton. Pocklington, Melbourne, Leconfield, Elvington, Snaith. RCAF: Tholthorpe, Skipton-on-Swale, Leeming, Croft, Middleton St George, East Moor, Linton-on-Ouse	*Other bases*	: Acaster Malbis - built too close to the Ouse and frequently covered in fog. Not used operationally. A major bomb store. Cottam - another ill-sited base and not used operationally.
7 HCUs	: 4 Gp: Marston Moor, Rufforth, Riccall 6 Gp: Wombleton, Dishforth, Topcliffe, Dalton	Nos 18 & 25 OTUs	: Finningley (site of Bomber Command Instuctors' School opened in 1945)
1 ELG	: Carnaby	No1 Group Lancaster Finishing School	: Opened in 1944 at Lindholme which later transferred to No 7 Training Group and accommodated 1656 Heavy Conversion Unit
ASR/Coastal Command	: Thornaby		

little shops and sailors' eating houses are gone. The taverns, too have been torn down and there are gaping spaces where the little houses used to be . . . the City Hall and many of the best buildings have been hit. The damage seemed to me to be more scattered than in Coventry and Plymouth but none the less severe, and Hull has had less than its share of public sympathy for its sufferings . . . I passed whole streets of shattered houses, miles from the docks, and somehow it is the little houses that affect one most - not the great buildings."[21]

During November 1943 Hitler demanded that the Luftwaffe should carry out retaliatory raids on Britain as reprisals for the area bombing of Germany currently reaching a peak in the Battle of Berlin. Germany had one operational four-engined strategic bomber and this was the notoriously unreliable Heinkel He 177. Outwardly, its four engines appeared as two. Each nacelle held *two* engines driving one four bladed propeller via a gearbox and a common shaft. These engines had a tendency to catch fire but Hitler, Göring and Goebbels placed great faith in the ability of the He 177 to carry large high-explosive bombs filled with Trialen and Hexogen - the so-called 'England mixture'. *Operation Steinbock* (code-name for the new offensive) was deferred until mid-January 1944 and by that time the Luftwaffe had equipped Ju 88s

as path-finders, using Bomber Command's techniques as their model. During *Steinbock* it was customary for the German crews flying special Ju 88S-1s and S-3s to drop flares as markers and to eject large quantities of *Düppel* - the Luftwaffe's version of Window.

Hull suffered *Steinbock* attacks during March and April 1944 and there is no doubt that the intensity of the attacks in Yorkshire and in London and southern England took the British air defence system by surprise. People in general were not expecting any more air raids and were quite 'jittery' once the *Steinbock* attacks, characterised by heavy calibre bombs causing immense blast damage, hit targets such as Hull, Bristol, the south coast 'invasion ports' and London. Luftwaffe casualties were approximately one aeroplane and four trained crew for every five British civilians killed and the Luftwaffe could no longer sustain these losses, particularly among the Soesterberg-based Dornier 217s. Attacks ended in May 1944 and from that moment onwards the Germans concentrated on bringing their V-1 and V-2 reprisal weapons into operation.

That these were not available in time to cause havoc during the D-Day operation on 6 June 1944 was, of course, due to the unrelenting attacks on V-1 sites by Bomber Command. No V-2 rockets fell in Yorkshire but air-launched V-1 doodlebugs overflew the county during 1944-45. These were all released by venerable

---

Fieseler Fi 103 (V-1)

A tiny airscrew measured the pre-set distance after which the servo mechanism operated the elevators and the bomb dived to the ground.

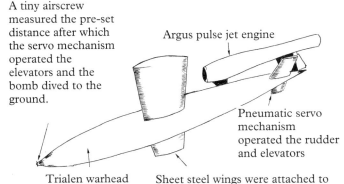

Argus pulse jet engine

Pneumatic servo mechanism operated the rudder and elevators

Trialen warhead

Sheet steel wings were attached to the fuselage at the launching site

Mercifully, few of the V-1 flying bombs fell on Yorkshire. Each one was only 25'11" long with a wingspan of 17'6" yet it could carry a ton of explosive and about half a ton of fuel (low grade aviation mixture) for 250 miles at between 300 and 420 mph. The airframe was made by Fieseler and the 66 pound thrust

pulse jet engine incorporated the highly efficient Argus duct. The entire bomb could be manufactured for roughly £125 in the money values of 1944. During 1944-45 about 10,500 V-1s were fired at Britain – nearly 9000 from catapult ramps and the rest from Heinkel He 111s. The 'V-1' stood for *Vergeltungswaffe 1* or reprisal weapon No.1. Many of the flying bombs that reached Britain carried a warhead filled with *Trialen* explosive. It had exceptional blast power. In fact, the warhead was comparable with the 4000 lb 'cookie' or 'blockbuster' carried by Wellingtons, Halifaxes, Lancasters and Mosquitoes. German designers had never intended the pulse jet motor to cut out when the V-1 began its final dive to earth. It was the sudden end to the distinctive note of the pulse jet – caused when the diving angle starved the fuel lines – that warned people to take cover, thus saving thousands of lives.

For an account of the German secret weapons campaign and the British attempts at counter-measures, see David Irving's brilliant "The Mare's Nest", William Kimber, 1964.

Heinkel He 111s based in Holland at Venlo and Gilze-Rijen until they were forced to pull out during September-October 1944. They reformed as *Kampfgeschwader 53* during November 1944 but had to reduce operations because of a general shortage of aviation fuel. About fifty of KG 53's Heinkels made a mass attack on Manchester during Christmas Eve 1944 and completely fooled the British defences. The Heinkels loosed off their V-1s just off the Yorkshire coast and though some nose-dived into the sea about thirty bombs sped over the county south of Bridlington. They arrived at locations stretching from the Yorkshire coast to Brindle in Cheshire. A lucky shot hit Pocklington airfield and damaged a Halifax parked on dispersal. A second exploded on Read's Island in the River Humber, another dived into Willerby and a fourth landed at South Cliffe. Many sped on beyond the East Riding and four more landed in Yorkshire at Grange Moor, Midhope Moor, Sowerby Bridge and Rossington. Manchester, the target, was lucky and escaped with two bombs crashing on the outskirts of the city.

Further attacks were expected and Anti-Aircraft Command began transferring guns from the south to the coastline between Filey and Skegness. But apart from the events during the night of *Operation Gisela* described

below Yorkshire's air space suffered no more enemy incursions. It is possible that Arado 234 jet bombers may have overflown the Humber estuary between October 1944 and March 1945 but as these were specifically photographing air bases they were able to fly at 33,000 feet at speeds exceeding 450 mph. Mosquito fighters equipped with radar and heavy cannons would be hard-pressed to intercept bombers such as these. Official policy was to ignore the jets as there was little that could be done to oppose them. The Americans flying their new P-61 Black Widow night-fighters from Scorton were not called on to challenge these intruders. Nor were the Mosquito XXXs of 456 Squadron Royal New Zealand Air Force and the Mosquito XIIIs of 264 Squadron, both of which were based at Church Fenton during the closing stages of the war.

The decline of manned Luftwaffe attack upon the prime military and industrial targets that littered the map of Yorkshire was conclusive evidence of the inability of the Luftwaffe to maintain any kind of strategic bombing offensive against Britain during 1944-45, in total contrast with the operations of 4 Group and 6 Group that were about to reach a crescendo of destruction over Germany.

Chapter Twenty Three

Press on Regardless

Back in 1942 Harris had observed that the Germans had sown the wind and would one day reap the whirlwind. His threat was now coming true with a vengeance. Though he had only 1,300 effective four-engined bombers instead of the 4000 he had once anticipated, the air supremacy won by the US Eighth Air Force over Europe meant that Bomber Command could now devastate any German target in accordance with the ever-changing priorities presented to him by the Chiefs of Staff. Harris still had to contend with the uncertain weather conditions prevailing in early 1945 and with the enterprise of the Luftwaffe.

In an attempt to pre-empt Allied air strikes on German ground troops in January, the Luftwaffe carried out its *Unternehmen Bodenplatte* (Operation Baseplate) on New Year's Day 1945.[1] Some 900 Luftwaffe fighters made a mass low-level attack on Allied air bases in Belgium, Holland and France. FW 190s and Me 109s strafed the airfields, so recently vacated by the Luftwaffe and now a welcome refuge for damaged 4 and 6 Group bombers returning from raids on Germany and unable to reach Yorkshire. Most of the airfield defences were taken by surprise and 465 Allied aircraft were knocked out on the ground. But the Luftwaffe paid a very high price for this temporary success: 300 aircraft shot down or badly damaged; 151 pilots killed or missing; 53 captured. It was the biggest single loss ever suffered by the Luftwaffe fighters and an untimely waste of precious fuel and even more precious pilots. *Bodenplatte* certainly weakened the ability of the German fighter defences to oppose Bomber Command's operations over Germany in 1945.

From Yorkshire, operations carried on in routine fashion. On 1/2 January 105 Halifaxes from 4 Group attacked the benzol plant at Dortmund. Although Speer always claimed that the Ruhr's benzol plants were easy to hit - few of Bomber Command crews ever agreed with him - it was cloud cover that prevented a successful attack on this occasion and the factory and its installations suffered no production loss. However, while 6 Group was helping to hammer Nuremberg on 2/3 January 4 Group's Halifaxes professionally wiped out I.G. Farben's factories at Ludwigshafen and Oppau. In the New Year's first three raids from Yorkshire the only aeroplane that failed to return to base was a Halifax that crashed in France.

In total contrast was the area attack on Hannover on 5/6 January when Bomber Command lost twenty-three Halifaxes and eight Lancasters, many of them to German night-fighters that were active over the target and all the way back to the Dutch coast. Ten Canadian Halifaxes failed to return and 425 Alouette at Tholthorpe lost three of its bombers that night. Collision claimed two of the Halifaxes. One of them was Burn's LK-O and its crew fought to regain control when they found themselves in a spiral dive with broken aileron controls and a damaged hydraulic system that had lowered the flaps to 30°! F/Lt Sledge brought the Halifax back to level flight, nursed it across the Allied lines and everyone parachuted

"Chico" - A Halifax BIII at Holme-upon-Spalding-Moor 3 September 1944 - 19 March 1945. *Left to right:* Slim Summerville - *Rear Gunner;* Roy Dare - *W/OP;* Mick ? - *Bomb Aimer;* Bob Hutchinson - *Pilot;* John Stewart - *Navigator;* Bill Walton - *Mid-upper Gunner;* Mike Hallett - *Flight Engineer.*

Yorkshire Air Museum

to safety near Ghent. He received the immediate award of the Distinguished Flying Cross.

Ice, snow and poor visibility at the airfields reduced Yorkshire's contribution to the air war in mid-January although 6 Group managed to take part in the last major area attack on Munich (7/8 January). Poor weather conditions did not stop the Yorkshire squadrons from carrying out their routine gardening sorties to the Dutch coast, Kiel, Norway and the Baltic Sea. The airborne sea mines had been much improved during 1944 and the standard 1500lb A Mk I-IV was now supplemented by the 2000lb A Mk V mine. Its steel cylindrical casings were filled with Amatol or Minol with the parachute and its shroud lines packed in the rear container. These were dropped by static line, usually at 14-15000 ft, and had a variety of hydrostatic water pressure safety switches, depending on whether they were delayed action high explosive, acoustic or magnetic. S/Ldr Frank Lord flew a gardening mission from Full Sutton to Kiel Bay in the Baltic on the night of 12 January 1945 and his description of the sortie highlights the kind of problems encountered by many crews.[2]

The precise target-point was in Kiel Bay (54° 33.6'; 10° 15.5'E) and H-hour was 2030 hrs. Flying H for Harry (Halifax III RG348) that night our start-up time at the hard standing was 1700 hrs, taxi 1722, take-off 1727 and set course 1755 hrs. Experienced crews sometimes took supernumeraries aboard on 'ops' - a newly-arrived pilot for battle experience and the members of aircrew who had been engaged on ground-duties and needed to top-up their total of ops. They were expected to use their eyes and nothing else, unless invited to do so. On that basis they were not altogether regarded as a nuisance though, possibly, as an additional obstruction should the order 'Jump-Jump' be given. That night we had two extra bodies on board: F/Lt Ninian, the Squadron's engineering section leader; and P/O Bell, a wireless operator returned to duty from sick leave. Both were anxious to build on their operational backgrounds. We were to be grateful for their presence later that evening.

Leaving Flamborough Head behind we slowly climbed to 14,000 ft - a height we were told to hold all the way to the target, on the briefed north-easterly course meant to mislead enemy watchers that our intended target lay in Norwegian waters.

At a point short of the Danish coast a 90° change of course southwards was made and we

crossed Denmark safely between known well-defended regions, with our wireless-operator paying out the customary bundles of WINDOW as a protective screen. So far so good. Although there was no moon and it was pitch dark outside, our H2S was giving us excellent pictures of the coastlines with easily recognisable landmarks. We began our timed run to the dropping point where the new U-boats began their sea trials.

Steady, straight and level until the bomb-aimer gave the welcome shout: 'Bombs gone!' The release of more than 4 tons of metal normally gave a very noticeable uplift to the aircraft; this time, flying attitude unchanged, we continued to plod onward.

'Something's gone wrong, Skip,' said the bomb-aimer. Instructed to investigate, the flight engineer reported back that condensation around his bomb-release hasps had turned to solid ice which he and his fellow-engineer (Ninian) were trying to hack away with screwdrivers. We made a large circular tour of the spot and started the run-up again.

And again there was no response when the bomb-aimer pressed his button. Meanwhile the scene outside was beginning to brighten from the interest shown by the defences below and our own radio man, assisted by his companion, redoubled his efforts. A sky flare had been lit and German fighters were no doubt watching our antics with some curiosity without actually being able to pinpoint us in the cloud of metal-strips that were being furiously fed into the sky.

'How are you getting on?' I enquired of the engineeers. 'Still working on it, Skip,' was the reply. 'Please don't go round again,' someone called. The situation outside was getting rather hairy. 'We're not taking these sodding things back !' was my response, 'So keep at it!'

More fighter flares were now lighting the sky around us. For the third time we made our measured approach. The feverish - and breathless, for they were both sharing the same oxygen point - efforts of the two engineers had finally paid off.

'Bombs gone, Skip, thank God!' with more truth in it this time from the bomb-aimer. Perhaps the Halibag looked more like a version of Halley's comet on the German radar screens as we sped our way home. There were others from the Squadron who did not get home that night; they probably had the same icing troubles but did not have the advantage of our extra hands to deal with it. You could not circle an area for 15-20 minutes, abounding in fighters and flak, without attracting attention from one or the other, or both.

Frank Lord's crew, in common with most others, regarded mine-laying as lacking in job satisfaction. There was no observable splash, fireworks or explosion. Inevitably, some crews wondered if it contributed much to the war effort. Frank Weber, a Danish historian who has researched the air war over Denmark 1940-45, is positive that it was, especially in the shallow waters around Denmark where it was very effective against German shipping. Weber estimates that nearly 7000 mines were laid by Bomber Command in Danish waters and the German minesweepers could only destroy 1,038 of these. Moreover, airborne sea mining had an important indirect effect in that the everpresent danger of striking British mines caused important harbours such as Frederikshavn, Aalborg and Aarhus to be closed for long periods. Furthermore, as Weber has emphasised[3], the Germans were forced to devote large numbers of minesweepers, equipment and men to the unending, intensely demanding task of minesweeping.

On the battlefields of north-west Europe the weather still dominated operations in mid-January 1945 and it was impossible for Bomber Command to do more than offer strategic support to the ground troops. Accordingly, on 13/14 January the two Yorkshire Groups sent 242 Halifaxes to bomb the marshalling yards at Saarbrücken, a crucial supply route for German troops still holding out in the Bulge. No aircraft was lost on this operation though Halifax Y-Yorker of 51 Squadron at Snaith collided with another bomber and lost the front nine feet of its nose. The navigator and bomb-aimer were not wearing parachutes and both fell to their deaths from the Halifax. Despite the icy gale howling through the open fuselage F/O Wilson somehow managed to keep control of the truncated bomber and brought the aeroplane safely back to England.

"Seldom, if ever, during World War 2," comments Philip Moyes, "did an RAF bomber land on an English airfield with more damage."[4]

6 Group repeated their success at Saarbrücken with an attack on the railway yards at Grevenbroich (14/15 January) while 4 Group's Halifaxes searched for but failed to hit the Luftwaffe's big fuel storage depot at Dülmen, losing one of Burn's Halifaxes over the target.

These raids had seen little night-fighter activity but the situation changed with a vengeance on 16/17 January when four major targets came under attack from Bomber Command. 6 Group bombed the oil plant at Zeitz with the loss of only one Lancaster but the Halifax crews encountered many night-fighters when they carried out an area raid on Magdeburg. Seventeen Halifaxes failed to return (5.3%) demonstrating the fact that the Luftwaffe could still be very dangerous. Eighteen of No 76 Squadron's Halifaxes carried out an unusually dangerous task that night when they acted as bait for the night-fighters *ahead* of the Pathfinder force, an operation they accomplished without loss.

Area raids were always allocated specific targets and aiming points but the extent of cloud cover during January and early February 1945 forced most Master Bombers to order crews to bomb on sky markers, the least accurate of all the Pathfinding aids. This was well illustrated on 28/29 January when the Yorkshire Groups attempted to destroy the Hirth jet engine factories and Kornwestheim marshalling yards in the Stuttgart area. Two heavy attacks failed to produce concentrated bombing and little damage was done to the enemy's installations. Accurate flak accounted for most of the four Halifaxes and six Lancasters lost in this raid. Cloud cover similarly marred the raid on Mainz on 1/2 February where the object was to destroy as much of the city as possible prior to a ground attack by Allied forces. It was not easy to use Bomber Command simultaneously as both a tactical and strategic force. The Army naturally wanted the bombers to inhibit German rail and road supplies; and at the same time to 'take out' any town that threatened to hold up an Allied advance.

Sometimes the Lancasters and Halifaxes could give the ground troops direct support during an assault on enemy positions. Montgomery's 21st Army Group wished to neutralise the two towns of Kleve and Goch, now part of a strong German defence line blocking the northern sector of the Allied advance to the Rhine. The Yorkshire squadrons were allocated Goch but on arrival the 292 Halifaxes and 156 Lancasters found the target was cloud-covered. The Master Bomber then took a calculated risk: he ordered the Main Force below the cloud base - at roughly 5000 feet - and directed accurate bombing from that height. Smoke billowed upwards and the raid had to be stopped because even at this low bombing level little could be seen of the enemy's defences. Two Halifaxes were lost, one from Elvington and the other, in circumstances described below, from Pocklington. A third, a Halifax III from 640 Squadron at Leconfield, came under attack from an Me 262 jet night-fighter. Its cannon shells raked the Halifax but the pilot managed to

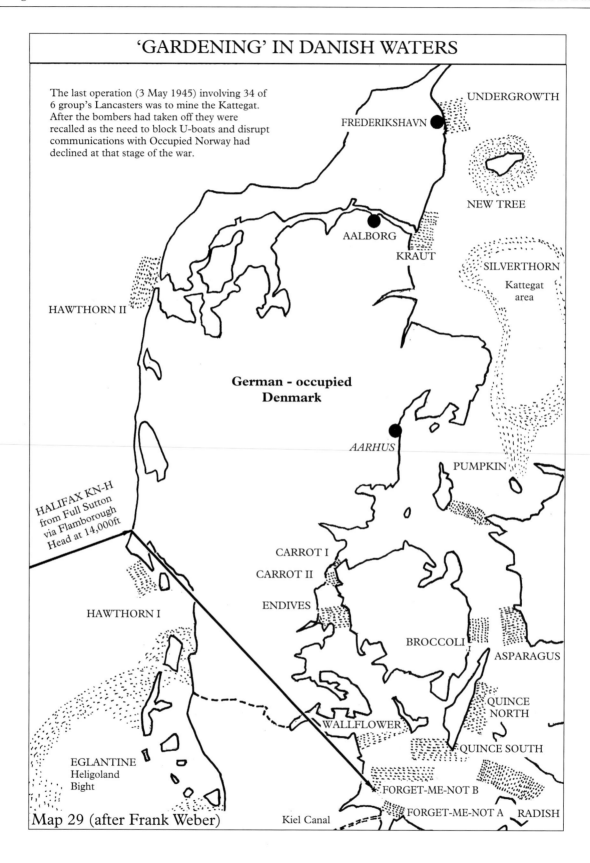

'GARDENING' IN DANISH WATERS

The last operation (3 May 1945) involving 34 of 6 group's Lancasters was to mine the Kattegat. After the bombers had taken off they were recalled as the need to block U-boats and disrupt communications with Occupied Norway had declined at that stage of the war.

UNDERGROWTH

FREDERIKSHAVN

NEW TREE

AALBORG

KRAUT

SILVERTHORN

Kattegat area

HAWTHORN II

German - occupied Denmark

AARHUS

PUMPKIN

HALIFAX KN-H from Full Sutton via Flamborough Head at 14,000ft

CARROT I

CARROT II

ENDIVES

HAWTHORN I

BROCCOLI

ASPARAGUS

QUINCE NORTH

WALLFLOWER

QUINCE SOUTH

EGLANTINE Heligoland Bight

FORGET-ME-NOT B

Map 29 (after Frank Weber)

Kiel Canal

FORGET-ME-NOT A   RADISH

land the aircraft at Woodbridge ELG. Gunners in a 466 Australian Squadron Halifax from Driffield sent an Me 410 plunging down in flames.

One unsavoury incident during the raid on Goch took place after a Ju 88 disabled a 102 Squadron Halifax from Pocklington and then began firing its machine guns at the crew as they parachuted from their bomber. An enraged rear-gunner, Sgt Peckham, was the last to bale out and stayed at his post until he had fired every round of ammunition at the offending Ju 88. Peckham's fire was accurate and the Ju 88 was forced to crash-land on a railway line where the pilot was hit and killed by the next train. The efforts of 4 Group at Goch proved to be in vain. German resistance at Kleve and Goch survived both the bombing and the subsequent 'Alamein-style' bombard-ment by one thousand guns. Allied troops had to fight for every village and take-out every self-propelled gun during a rapid thaw that turned the roads and fields into a mass of glutinous mud. British and Canadian soldiers fighting in the brutal slogging match of the Reichswald battles of 1945 found very little evidence that Germany was beaten. Wehrmacht and SS troops were still receiving supplies from the nearby Ruhr valley where battalions of German engineers and thousands of slave workers were repairing battered marshalling yards so that trains steaming through the long winter nights could shuttle tanks and infantry weapons across the Rhine. Germany's armed forces were far from beaten and Allied soldiers learned the hard way not to underestimate their battle skills. Eisenhower still had to win control of the left bank of the Rhine and then somehow cross it in order to attack the German heartland; while in the east the Soviet soldiers pouring across the Oder faced a Wehrmacht prepared to fight, as their Führer always demanded, to the last bullet and to the last man. At the beginning of 1945 there was every justification for intensive bombing raids on all targets that contributed to the German war effort.

In February 1945 Churchill, Stalin and Roosevelt attended the Yalta Conference in the Crimea. Discussions among the Chiefs of Staff present revealed a Russian interest in British and American strategic attacks on those German cities in the east that were currently functioning as key communication points, refugee centres and dispersal areas for German industry evacuated from the Ruhr two years earlier. The Russians indicated that a line from Berlin, through Chemnitz and Leipzig, would represent the most beneficial target areas as far as the Red Army was concerned and that intensive bombing of Berlin and Leipzig in particular was desirable.

This fitted in neatly with *Operation Thunderclap*, a contingency plan drawn up the previous autumn and now seen to be of great importance in bringing about the defeat of Nazi Germany. Churchill's War Cabinet and the Chiefs of Staff had every reason to try to force a rapid end to the war. German resilience and, in particular, German technological brilliance, produced unexpected threats to the Allied cause. In terms of speed, Me 262 jet fighters and Me 163 rocket interceptors outclassed all Allied fighters; the V-2 defied Allied counter-measures; V-1s were still being released by He 111s flying low under the British radar screen; and if the new U-boats with their 'schnorkel breathing' equipment appeared in substantial numbers they might tip the balance in the Battle of the Atlantic. That was certainly the hope constantly expressed by Josef Goebbels in his daily record of the crises facing the Third Reich.[5]

Even more alarming was the uncertainty surrounding German atomic weapon research. Were the German nuclear scientists really on the verge of building an A-bomb? All that was certain was that somewhere inside the Third Reich the Germans were building an exper-imental nuclear pile. There was every possibility that it might go critical in the very near future, if this had not happened already. In November 1944 photo-reconnaissance suggested that the nuclear pile might be at Hechingen and there was a short-lived crisis until it was shown that the site was in fact a series of German test-drills in search of oil shale to supplement their dwindling fuel reserves.[6] Another terrible thought was that Nazi Germany's research into radiological weapons designed to for use against the *civilian* population of the United States might also be reaching fruition. Although British intelligence knew that work on the the two-stage intercontinental rocket planned to carry radiological uranium bombs to the United States had been halted in favour of concentrating on the V-2, the futuristic A-9 second stage fitted with small wings had already com-pleted a test flight. Moreover, intelligence had discovered that its projected cargo of uranium bombs were stored in a monster underground factory built in the side of Kohnstein Mountain at Niedersachswerfen.[7] This giant factory operated mainly by forced labour drawn from all over Occupied Europe was immune to Allied air attack. Any kind of warhead would, of course, be useless unless the Germans were able to construct reliable long-range rockets capable of delivering bombs to the United States. The Germans did not lack *inventiveness*; in this respect they were in advance of the Allies. Their problem was one of *production* - and there was no certainty that under endless Allied air attack Nazi Germany would be able to find salvation in a series of war-winning secret weapons. But at the beginning of 1945, no-one could be sure.

It was therefore both appropriate and urgent to deliver cataclysmic blows on key German cities such as Berlin, Chemnitz, Leipzig and Dresden in the hope that such attacks might force a general surrender before German scientists produced a war winning weapon of their own. This was the essence of the proposed *Operation Thunderclap* which the Americans, deeply involved in their own top secret Manhattan Project and still unsure whether they had progressed far enough to control the release of atomic energy under combat conditions, positively supported. In Britain, Prime Minister Churchill was determined to exploit to the full this particular use of air power. He reminded Sir Archibald Sinclair, the Air Minister, that he urgently needed *precise* details of the East German cities that Bomber Command could hit *before* he met Stalin and Roosevelt in the Crimea for the Yalta talks beginning on 4 February:

> ". . . I asked whether Berlin, and no doubt other large cities in Eastern Germany, should not now be considered especially attractive targets. I am glad that this is 'under examination'. Pray report to me tomorrow what is going to be done."

Sir Norman Bottomley, Deputy Chief of the Air Staff, had already telephoned Sir Arthur Harris and gathered that the Commander-in-Chief would be willing, subject to favourable weather conditions and a suitable plan for diverting the German night-fighter force, to attack cities defined as 'major communications centres'. This enabled Sinclair to tell Churchill on 27 January that:

> ". . . subject to the overriding claims of attacks on enemy oil production and other approved target systems within the current directive, available effort should be directed against Berlin, Dresden, Chemnitz and Leipzig or other cities where severe bombing would not only destroy communications vital to the evacuation from the East but also hamper the movement of troops from the West."[8]

Sinclair went on to assure the Prime Minister that Sir Arthur Harris would undertake this task once the moon had waned and favourable weather conditions permitted the despatch of heavy bombers to these distant targets. Sinclair thought it unlikely that Bomber Command would be able to begin *Thunderclap* by 4 February. Portal was opposed to a Bomber Command 'Thunderclap-style' raid on Berlin though the German capital was the target for a massive attack by the Eighth Air Force on 3 February

1945. It was because he felt that the *Thunderclap* plan might detract from the present campaign against the synthetic oil targets that Portal gave only reluctant approval to raids on cities where "a severe blitz will not only cause confusion in the evacuation from the East but will also hamper the movement of troops from the West."[9]

The 'Mighty Eighth' intended to begin *Thunderclap* with an attack on Dresden (13 February) but bad weather conditions led to the mission's cancellation. Although Harris had contacted Bottomley (and may also have telephoned the Prime Minister) to express his doubts first, about the tactical advantage of a raid on Dresden at the extreme limits of the Lancaster's range and second, about the possible losses that might be levied by the German night-fighter force[10], he was ordered to go ahead with the attack.

Winston Churchill needed to destroy those eastern German cities still functioning with a degree of efficiency, even though they were the most distant targets that heavily-laden Lancasters could attack. His motives were both military and political. They were based on a fear of Nazi Germany's scientific potential; the possibility of prolonged resistance by the German armies in the west; and a wish to help the Red Army by inhibiting the movement of German reserves to the Eastern Front. Overlaying this was another fear: that an unexpectedly rapid advance by Russian forces across the North German Plain might give Stalin certain post-war advantages in Western Europe that the Allies were unwilling to concede. So for a variety of reasons, time was of the essence. For the Allies, an early crossing of the Rhine and the penetration of the heart of Germany were vital if their armies were to meet the Russians at the agreed line of demarcation along the Elbe.

This was the context of *Thunderclap*, often underestimated by writers who misleadingly shaped public opinion after the Second World War in their efforts to denigrate Sir Arthur Harris and to condemn the war-winning campaigns of Bomber Command. Many have tried to blame Sir Arthur for the decisions that politicians took in 1945. No senior officer in any of the armed forces ever takes *strategic* decisions; these are always the province of his political masters. Harris did not *decide* to attack the East German cities; he was ordered to do so by the Prime Minister. That is why Sir Arthur Harris began planning *conventional* area attacks upon selected East German cities.

Bomber Command assigned 796 Lancasters and nine Mosquitoes for the first of the *Thunderclap* attacks, the raid

THUNDERCLAP! Quest for a quick victory . . .

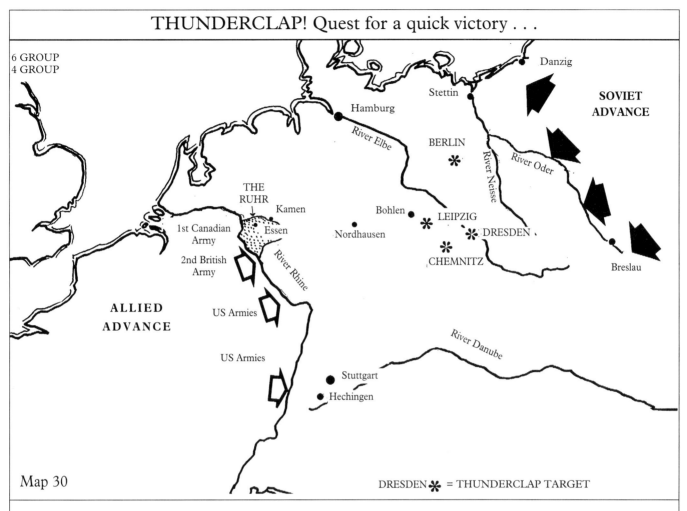

6 GROUP
4 GROUP

SOVIET ADVANCE

Danzig

Stettin

Hamburg

River Elbe

BERLIN ✳

River Oder

River Neisse

THE RUHR

Kamen

Bohlen ●   ✳ LEIPZIG

✳ DRESDEN

1st Canadian Army

Essen

Nordhausen ●

✳ CHEMNITZ

Breslau

2nd British Army

River Rhine

ALLIED ADVANCE

US Armies

River Danube

US Armies

Stuttgart ●
Hechingen ●

Map 30

DRESDEN ✳ = THUNDERCLAP TARGET

The Context of Thunderclap - February 1945

1. After the Battle of the Ardennes (December 1944 - January 1945), the Allies were forced to regroup.

2. German resistance stiffened in an effort to prevent the crossing of the Rhine, especially in the sector west of the vital Ruhr industries, the zone facing the Canadian First Army and the British Second Army.

3. During January/February 1945 the Russians had made startling advances in the east and their armies under Zhukov and Konev had reached the River Oder. It was in the interest of the west to prevent German reinforcement of their threatened Eastern Front.

4. At the same time, Churchill was fearful that these Russian Marshals would soon cross the Oder and head north and south of Berlin via the North German Plain and establish themselves beyond the Elbe even before the Western armies had crossed the Rhine.

5. Equally worrying was the state of German secret weapon research and development. A war-winning blow must be delivered as quickly as possible.

on Dresden (13/14 February 1945) and 786 Lancasters actually bombed the city. Crew briefings emphasised specific objectives: to disrupt "an important engineering, chemical and communications centre and marshalling yards feeding the Nazi's eastern front." In particular, Dresden was a described as a major freshwater port on the Elbe and a centre of specialist manufactures, often located in small workshops where precision electrical instruments for U-boats and lenses for periscopes, machine tools, small calibre flak guns and radio equipment were manufactured. There were also two larger factories reconditioning airframes and aero engines for the Luftwaffe. There was no question about the legitimacy of Dresden as a target and crews were urged to bomb accurately on the markers as the Germans had set up three prisoner-of-war camps in the vicinity of Dresden. Bomb-loads were normal with high-explosive content marginally *greater* than incendiary.

The raid was carried out two waves. First came 5 Group's Lancasters, flying at low-level so their markers would have pinpoint accuracy. Then came the Lancasters of 1, 3, 6 and 8 Groups. None of Yorkshire's 4 Group aircraft was involved in the Dresden raid for they had been given other things to do. Over Germany, meteorological conditions were against the citizens of Dresden then coping with the influx of thousands of refugees fleeing from the Red Army. As in Hamburg during July-August 1943 and later at Pforzheim on 22/23 February, there was a terrible firestorm which engulfed the city in which at least 25,000 people died. Many more were missing and though some of these were evacuees who had already fled to the west, most were never found. It is likely, therefore, that the final death toll was greater than the Hamburg total though far less than the hysterical figures bandied about in the 1960s and finally retracted. [11]

6 Group's contribution to the raid was relatively small. Sixty-seven Canadian Lancasters flew to Dresden and these were drawn from five RCAF Squadrons: No 419 (Middleton St George), No 424 (Skipton-on-Swale), No 428 (Middleton St George), No 431 (Croft) and No 434 (Croft). Although six Lancasters were lost at Dresden, the Canadian crews all returned to base. On the same night 115 Canadian Halifaxes joined 211 of 4 Group's aircraft in a massive diversionary raid on Böhlen's synthetic oil plant near Leipzig. Conditions over Böhlen were very bad with total cloud cover and severe icing as high as 14/15,000 feet. Bombing was erratic and one Halifax failed to return, the sole Yorkshire loss in this first phase of *Thunderclap*.

The next phase against Chemnitz on the following night was, in contrast with the Dresden raid, totally unsuccessful. Bomber Command sent 717 Lancasters and Halifaxes to Chemnitz to destroy its industry and render it helpless in the face of an expected Russian advance. Total cloud cover meant that crews had to rely on wind-blown sky markers and it is thought that most of the bomb loads fell in open country. Five of the 218 Halifaxes that set out for Chemnitz failed to

return. After two nights of concentrated attacks, fresh priorities were accorded to Bomber Command and Thunderclap was put into temporary abeyance until 5/6 March. Thunderclap had not succeeded in forcing a German surrender and Bomber Command returned to attacks on German industrial centres.

Poor weather conditions prevailed both in Yorkshire and over much of the Third Reich and a raid by the two northern Groups on Wesel (17 February) had to be stopped when clouds prevented accurate marking. P/O Oleynik RCAF from Holme on Spalding was one of eight pilots who did not hear the radio recall signal and bombed Wesel on a Gee fix. Another 76 Squadron pilot, S/Ldr Whitty, crashed his Halifax near Brough while making his approach into Holme. Three nights later, Canadian Lancasters delivered the *coup de grâce* to Dortmund's industries while 4 Group's Halifaxes brought synthetic oil production at the Rhenania Ossag plant in Düsseldorf to a standstill. Four of the Yorkshire Halifaxes were lost on this raid. Inexorably, German urban life in general and industry in particular was being systematically shattered. Duisburg and Worms had the similar treatment on 21/22 February. Canadian Lancasters helped to carry out the last area attack on

A conference at Base (shown here) followed immediately details were received from Bomber Command via Group HQ of an intended operation. Target, route, height, defences etc were discussed and courses of each leg, turning-points, timing and other relevant matters were calculated by the officers here who then communicated this information to the various squadrons within their 'clutch' by scrambled phone-link. Seen here during this conference are (l. to r.) S/Ldr Dodd (a flight CO); S/Ldr Savoury (Base Intelligence officer); W/Co Bannard (Sqdn CO); Air Chief Marshal Sir Gus Walker (Base CO); W/Co Cassell (Air staff officer); S/Ldr MacNeil (1st Base Navigation Officer); F/O Arthur Farmer (2nd Base Navigation Officer).

Frank Lord

Duisburg while 4 Group's Halifaxes demolished 40% of Worms, wiping out the one factory in Germany that specialised in the production of sprocket wheels for armoured fighting vehicles. Ten Halifaxes were lost, most of them to night-fighters. Six Canadian bombers went down and three of these came from 432 Squadron based at East Moor. Essen also came under attack from both the northern Groups in a daylight raid on 23 February and then during the night Lancasters of 1 and 6 Groups carried out what is thought to have been the third most devastating raid of the war. The unlucky town was Pforzheim where well over three-quarters of the built-up area was destroyed in a firestorm and 17.600 people died. None of the Canadian Lancasters was lost in the attack on Pforzheim.

For the next week the two northern groups concentrated their attention by night and day on the major synthetic oil plant at Bergkamen (to the north of Kamen) and the two major cities now within range of the Allied Tactical Air Forces - Mannheim and Cologne. The first raid on Bergkamen (24 February) caused a great deal of damage but cloud conditions prevented proper assessment of the condition of the oil plant; while the attacks on Mannheim (1 March) and Cologne (2 March) were devastatingly efficient and did not require the return of the Main Force to these two cities. This must have given Sir Arthur Harris considerable satisfaction for it was against Cologne that he had launched his historic thousand bomber raid at the end of May 1942. Nearly three years later, on 5/6 March 1945, American troops occupied that battered city on the west bank of the Rhine.

It fell to 4 Group on the 2000th night of the war to return to Kamen (3/4 March) where the Halifaxes carried out one of the war's most accurate attacks on a synthetic oil refinery. Pathfinder Oboe Mosquitoes came in high to mark the target precisely with red TIs; Pathfinder Lancasters followed these with green markers and the oil plant was perfectly illuminated. Normally so difficult to hit, the plant was battered with ninety-eight tons of high explosive, including the 2000 lb cookies that created a such a wide radius of blast damage. It was a total success and all production at Bergkamen came to an end. No Halifax was shot down and elated crews turned away to set course for their return to Yorkshire.

The remarkable security enjoyed by the 201 Halifaxes flying from Yorkshire to Kamen was partly explained by the protection afforded by the Pathfinders of 8 Group and the sophisticated ECM (electronic counter-measures) equipment now carried by the aircraft of 100 Group in its new 'Bomber Support campaign'. Perhaps the most

elaborate was *Jostle* carried in the bomb-bays of RAF Fortress BIIs and Liberator BVIs. *Jostle* effectively jammed the eneny night-fighter R/T transmmissions and helped to ensure that over Kamen no Halifax fell to the guns of the *Tame Boar*. Similarly, *Piperack* could jam the FuG 220 AI radars fitted to Ju 88s, Me 110s, He 219s and Me 410s and thus reduced the number of enemy interceptions to zero during the Kamen raid. Another aid was *Carpet*, much used by 8 Group to jam the Würzburg GCI radars and thus useful to a Pathfinder Lancaster or Halifax flying some distance away from the Main Force. Such aircraft were known as *Carpet Sweepers*, invaluable on the night of 3/4 March 1945.

It is also important to record the growing importance of Fighter Command's Intruders and that night twenty-nine Mosquitoes flew with or close to the bomber stream to intercept the German night-fighters. 4 Group was not the only force out that night: the Lancasters of 5 Group bombed the Ladbergen aqueduct on the Dortmund-Ems canal so the Mosquito Mk XXXs had two Main Forces to protect. Their Mk X AI equipment enabled them to intercept and destroy two Ju 88 night-fighters. The raids on both Kamen and Ladbergen were over well before midnight and when the two main bomber streams began their return flights they were quite unaware that the Luftwaffe intended to exact retribution for Bomber Command's attacks on their oil supplies. *Operation Gisela*, a new German intruder threat, had already begun.

★ ★ ★

Though German intruders had been operating over Britain during 1944 and had brought down thirty-eight Allied aircraft for the loss of thirteen Me 410s between March - June 1944, there had been no successful intruder operations over Yorkshire. Throughout that period Yorkshire's solitary loss to German intruders had been a 76 Squadron Halifax III from Holme, shot down over Norfolk on 25 April 1944. Nevertheless, in 1945 the Luftwaffe interceptor crews were still keen to attack Bomber Command aircraft over their own airfields in eastern England and on the night of the Kamen-Ladbergen raids the Luftwaffe decided to mount a mass intruder operation, Operation Gisela.

Late on 3 March 1945 aircraft from seven German night-fighter units took off for England's East Coast and according to German sources 142 Ju 88Gs were involved in *Operation Gisela*. To stay under British radar the Ju 88 pilots trimmed their aeroplanes nose-up and then pushed hard down on their sticks to keep their aircraft at exactly fifty feet above the waves. As the night-fighters roared through driving rain towards the English coast, everyone on board put their faith in the accuracy of their FuG 101 radio altimeters and quite soon that faith was rewarded with sight of the English coast marked by searchlights guiding in the heavy bombers and their fighter escorts. At the same moment the weather began to clear, visibility improved and the Ju 88s split into small attack groups to cover the airfields between the Vale of York and the River Blackwater.

It was just after midnight when the Ju 88s scored their first success over Yorkshire. A burst of fire riddled a 158 Squadron Halifax, causing it to dive out of control and explode on the ground near Sledmere Grange. At Driffield 466 Squadron Halifaxes had already joined the landing pattern when P/O Schrank had to put on a tight bank and pull hard on the controls to avoid tracers from a Ju 88. As he did this the landing lights at Driffield were doused and Schrank decided to climb out of trouble. But he was unable to shake off the fighter and at 6000 feet he gave the order to bale out and put the Halifax on automatic pilot. The unmanned Halifax flew on as far as Friskney where it crashed. More Ju 88s then entered the circuit at Holme-on-Spalding and forced the airfield to shut down its lighting system. The sudden disappearance of the Drem lights[12] dismayed crews already in the circuit. Some were were low on fuel and needed to land within a matter of minutes. P/O Oleynik, veteran of the Wesel raid, came under sudden fire and lost his mid-upper gunner, F/Sgt Maltby, who was killed instantly. Oleynik diverted to Carnaby, survived yet another Ju 88 attack, and managed to land on the ELG. Even this was not without incident as his port tyre went flat and the bomber ground-looped, ending its eventful night by crashing into a stationary Halifax. Not far away, Lissett's Halifaxes were still being strafed though one Halifax badly damaged by cannon fire managed a safe touch-down amidst streams of tracers, coloured flares and winking identity lights.

Carnage and confusion reigned throughout the Vale of York as Halifaxes sought diversionary airfields, a task made more complex by the Heavy Conversion Unit aircraft out on practice cross-country flights. Two Halifaxes from 1664 HCU were in the circuit at Dishforth where the beacon was clearly flashing its identity code 'DH'. A Ju 88 pilot, Leutnant Arnold Döring, had already spotted the morse and was waiting for the Halifaxes to appear in his sights. He set fire to ZU-R with his *schräge Musik* and forced the crew to bale out. Döring then lined up on ZU-S, raked its wing tanks and then watched it explode on the ground. This was the scene at several airfields in the Vale of York as more and more Halifaxes

approached their bases. An Australian Halifax from 466 Squadron was on finals at Driffield when the Drem lights went out. F/O Shelton had little fuel left so he put the Halifax into a climb to gain enough height to bale out. As he crossed Pocklington a Ju 88 put a burst of fire into Shelton's port wing and the Halifax crashed at Elvington. S/Ldr Terrien in a 347 FAF Halifax saw it go down and warned his crew to watch out for Ju 88s. Though they scanned the sky in all directions no-one even saw the night-fighter that shot out their starboard engines. For a few precious moments Terrien held the Halifax straight and level while the crew baled out - all except Terrien who died at the controls. A second 347 Squadron crew on their first mission had been unable to release their bombs over Kamen and jettisoned them in the Wash. They heard a radio message that 'bandits' were operating over Yorkshire and began to divert to Long Marston. They too came under attack from a Ju 88 and managed to bale out of the Halifax just before it exploded over Croft. A 10 Squadron Halifax made three attempts to land at Melbourne, then diverted to Dishforth where the Ju 88s were still attacking aircraft in the circuit. As they made their approach a Ju 88's *schräge Musik* guns ripped into the Halifax which crashed in flames killing five of the crew.

One 76 Squadron crew had a grandstand view of the carnage for they had been flying for nearly an hour over Yorkshire and Lincolnshire, unable to get permission to land at a diversionary airfield. Suddenly they heard their call-sign summoning them to land at Holme. On the way in *schräge Musik* cannon-fire set fire to their starboard wing tanks and one more blazing Halifax dived into the ground.

Operation Gisela certainly surprised the British defences and on this night they were found wanting. Both the ROC and the Mosquito night-fighter squadrons were fooled by the the mass approach under the radar screen. It is thought that thirty-four RAF aircraft were lost to intruder action during *Gisela* and of these at least twelve were from Yorkshire's squadrons and Heavy Conversion Units. German losses have also been put at thirty-four [13] though many of the aeroplanes involved either disappeared into the North Sea or crash-landed at bases in Holland or Germany. The Ju 88 that flew into the ground at Elvington at 0200 hours on 4 March 1945 is recorded as the last German aircraft to crash in Britain during the Second World War.

On the same night several Yorkshire Halifaxes were 'gardening' in the Heligoland Bight, dropping mines above clouds from 15-16,000 feet using their H2S in a

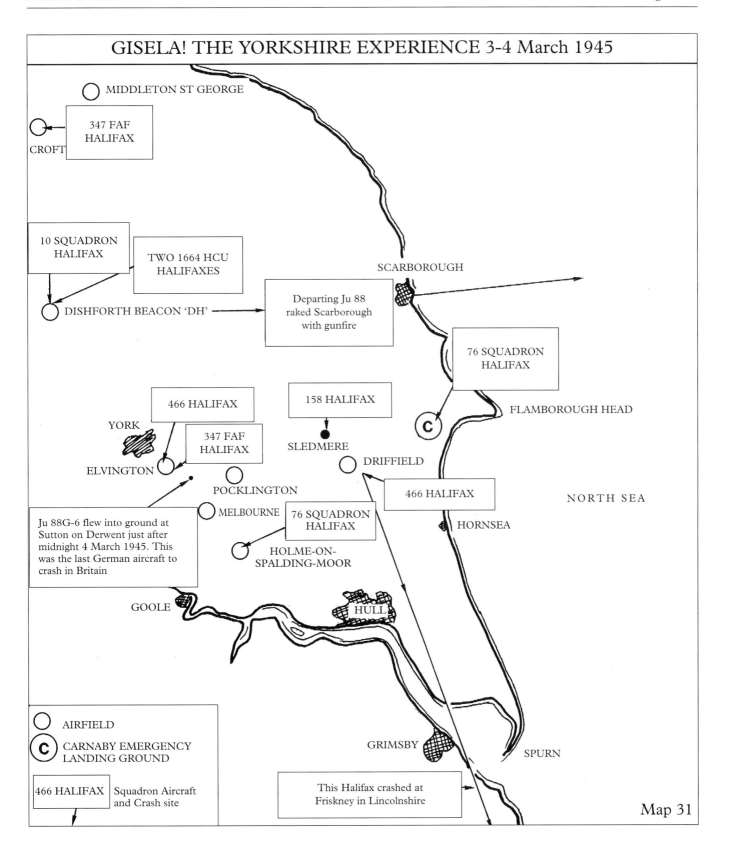

GISELA! THE YORKSHIRE EXPERIENCE 3-4 March 1945

MIDDLETON ST GEORGE

347 FAF
HALIFAX

CROFT

10 SQUADRON
HALIFAX

TWO 1664 HCU
HALIFAXES

DISHFORTH BEACON 'DH'

Departing Ju 88
raked Scarborough
with gunfire

SCARBOROUGH

76 SQUADRON
HALIFAX

FLAMBOROUGH HEAD

466 HALIFAX

158 HALIFAX

YORK

347 FAF
HALIFAX

SLEDMERE

DRIFFIELD

C

ELVINGTON

POCKLINGTON

466 HALIFAX

NORTH SEA

Ju 88G-6 flew into ground at
Sutton on Derwent just after
midnight 4 March 1945. This
was the last German aircraft to
crash in Britain

MELBOURNE

76 SQUADRON
HALIFAX

HORNSEA

HOLME-ON-
SPALDING-MOOR

GOOLE

HULL

AIRFIELD

C CARNABY EMERGENCY
LANDING GROUND

GRIMSBY

SPURN

466 HALIFAX Squadron Aircraft
and Crash site

This Halifax crashed at
Friskney in Lincolnshire

Map 31

Ju 88

The G-6 was a modification of the G-1 apart from its BMW 801G engines and special radio kit. It also had additional internal fuel tanks(usually an extra 81 gallons) and the twin *schräge Musik* cannon.

———

The RAF Museum, Hendon, has on show a very good example of the Junkers Ju 88, often visited by surviving Ju 88 night-fighter crews.

There is not much doubt that this aeroplane, more than any other German type, caused the most casualities suffered by Bomber Command crews. In fact, some authorities go further and believe that there were times during 1943-44 when the successs rate of this night-fighter caused losses that were difficult to sustain.

lengthy operation that did not finish until around midnight. On the return flight to Yorkshire both F/O Giles and F/Lt Scott, flying No 10 Squadron Halifaxes, received diversion signals because of the presence of intruders over the Vale of York. They were lucky. By the time their Halifaxes neared the coast the Ju 88s had fled for home and all diversions were cancelled.

Intruder attacks did not end with *Gisela*. Ten Ju 88s overflew the East Coast on 4/5 March 1945 and one piloted by Feldwebel Rudi Morenz followed a Halifax blithely tracking homewards on Pocklington's beacon. This night the British defences were ready and Morenz had to swing his Ju 88 away from the airfield flak and then turn for home with a Mosquito on his tail. No Yorkshire-based aircraft were shot down on 4/5 March but an intruder forced a Lancaster from No 550 Squadron to crash in the Humber estuary on 17 March 1945.[14] *Gisela* showed that if Hitler had not restricted the use of Luftwaffe interceptors to the territories and coastal waters of the Third Reich during the 1944-45 bomber offensive, the mayhem created on the night of 3/4 March 1945 over Yorkshire might have been repeated on many occasions. Comparable losses of thirty to forty heavy bombers *over their bases* might then have proved unacceptable. As it was, apart from the night of *Operation Gisela*, the departure from and return to the Yorkshire bomber bases by thousands of Halifaxes and Lancasters was accomplished almost without interruption from enemy aircraft.

Chapter Twenty Four

A Decisive Contribution

Bomber Command's *Operation Thunderclap* against key cities in Eastern Germany resumed on the night of 5/6 March 1945 when Chemnitz was selected as the main target. Some three weeks earlier, the Halifaxes and Lancasters of the two northern groups had taken part in a relatively unsuccessful attack on this important city. Now their mission was to ensure the destruction of:

"enemy communications nearest to the Russian Front in the vicinity of Dresden".[1]

It was a bitterly cold evening when fourteen 426 Squadron *Thunderbird* Halifaxes took off from Linton-on-Ouse, climbing away into a dark sky layered with strato-cumulus cloud. They headed south from Linton (the route plan was Base - Reading - English coast) and on into the Continent. Almost immediately they encountered a very dark cloud some ten miles wide that spread south beyond Tholthorpe. Somewhere in the vicinity of this cloud the Halifaxes encountered sudden and very severe icing problems. Ice formed on wings and elevators so rapidly that some of the bombers seemed to fall out of the sky. It is possible that one uncontrollable Halifax from Linton struck a 425 *Alouett*e Halifax from Tholthorpe for both bombers crashed at the same time and place. Shortly afterwards F/Lt Emerson's Halifax from Linton killed several civilians when it came down in Nunthorpe Grove, scene of some of the worst casualties during York's 1942 Baedeker raid. Two 420 *Snowy Owl* Halifaxes crashed on take-off; 419 *Moose*, 428 *Ghost* and 429 *Bison* each lost an aircraft to icing.

Though 4 Group airfields were spared this tragedy, crew reports stress how cold the operation was all the way to Chemnitz which, to their chagrin, was covered by 10/10ths cloud. The raid - by 498 Lancasters, 256 Halifaxes and six Mosquitoes - was directed by a Master Bomber and he told incoming crews that the skymarkers had been blown off course and this would mean an overshoot by twelve seconds on the red and green markers still glowing on the cloud tops. Most of the attackers bombed from 15-16,000 feet without incident though a few night-fighters intercepted the bomber stream and P/O O'Ryan, the Australian captain of a Melbourne Halifax, reported that a Ju 88 had damaged his mid-upper turret. *Schräge Musik* attacks declined that night, possibly because more of the Halifaxes were fitted with ventral gun positions. Overall, the attack was successful with major damage inflicted on railways, roads and industrial plants, some of which, such as the important Siegmar factory making tank engines, were totally destroyed. Fourteen Lancasters and eight Halifaxes failed to return from this second major Chemnitz attack. Conditions in Yorkshire caused major diversions on return and most of Shiny Ten's Halifaxes, for example, landed at Manston.

One that did not was Halifax III MZ 948 'E' captained by F/Lt Desmonde Moss. He had taken off from Melbourne on his thirty-fifth operation at 1708 hours on 5 March 1945. The Squadron Operations Book records:

Aircraft missing: nothing heard from a/c after take-off.

F/Lt Moss DFC was destined to survive after some quite extraordinary adventures which he has documented at length.

"We went to Chemnitz on the night of 5/6 March 1945 - a long, cold journey, cloudy conditions and only a little better over the target area. Our incendiaries were dropped over the target indicators but the 2000lb 'cookie' would not release. We circled and tried to release it in the target area but nothing happened so we set off to return. Our Air Bomber 'Buz' and Flight Engineer 'Jimmy' inspected the bomb release mechanism as closely and carefully as possible. It is no joke peering through a nine-inch hole with a torch in the face of an icy 200mph blast trying to pry loose a ton of freezing steel and high explosive with frost bitten fingers, knowing that if you are successful the numb fingers will probably go with the bomb, and they reported that the release mechanism appeared to be OK but just didn't work; probably ice had formed inside the mechanism.

I decided to descend below cloud into warmer air and try again. Several minutes later we levelled off about 2000 feet above the sleeping countryside and the boys tried again. Again 'It looks OK!' so the bomb doors were opened and the button pressed - with no result! I tried the jettison release - nothing doing! Jimmy tried again with a screwdriver and fire axe but after five minutes could only report that the bomb and the bomb slips were working in the air flow. I warned everybody to hold on tight and threw the Halifax around a bit. Eventually there was a crack and a shout of 'Hurray, it's gone!' Bomb doors were closed and then there was a flash from the ground and we were thrown about a bit more; we had got rather low down in the last few minutes. I opened to climbing power and we went up through the clouds again into clearer air.

We levelled off a few hundred feet above the clouds and got back to normal routine. There was shout from Steve in the rear turret - 'Night-fighter attacking!' and I saw tracers curving away from below and behind us to starboard. I started corkscrewing as violently as I could but it was soon obvious that we had been badly hit. The fuselage filled with smoke and I could no longer hear instructions from the rear gunner. Jimmy was trying to draw my attention to something and I realised that although we were on fire amidships the emergency signal light was flashing. Good for Steve! He was doing his job and shot down a Ju 88. By this time our port inner engine was blazing and out of control; the starboard one was also on fire as was the rest-position area of the fuselage. I could get no reply from any of the gunners - we had one in the mid-under blister on this trip [2] - and we were losing height and unable to bring the flames under control. I decided we had better get out whilst I could still keep the Halifax reasonably steady and ordered 'Bale-Out' on the intercom and also tapped out the letter 'P' several times on the emergency signal light circuit in the hope that the gunners would see it and be able to get out in time. I saw Jimmy pass my seat, wearing his chest type 'chute and disappear past the blackout curtain to the front escape hatch." [3]

At this point F/Lt Moss had opened the canopy above his head and was standing up with his face in the slipstream to avoid the flames that had already singed his forehead and eyebrows. His seat harness impeded his movements and he struggled with a jammed release so that he could follow Jimmy. A sudden explosion tore the Halifax apart and Moss must have tumbled out of the shattered fuselage for he woke up to find himself dangling in his parachute harness a few feet from the ground. Once he had patched up his burns his first thought was to escape - preferably by commandeering an enemy aeroplane. After making an attempt to fly off from

Crew of Halifax MZ 948. *Back row left to right:* F. Fearnley, *M/U*; J. Tasker, *F/E*; L. Webster, *A/B*; R. Fowler, *WOP; front row left to right:* S. Hodgson, *Rear;* F.D. Moss, *Pilot;* R. Devenport, *Navigator.*   *Desmonde Moss DFC*

German airfields first in a wingless Junkers W-34[4] and then in an FW 190, he was captured and taken to Oberursel Interrogation Centre near Frankfurt. He eventually escaped during an air raid, was recaptured, ordered to face a firing squad, escaped again and finally made his way back to Allied lines and Melbourne airfield in Yorkshire. Desmonde Moss then had to suffer the anguish of all pilots who wonder whether they might have accomplished more in the last minutes of their bomber's travail to ensure that their crew had a better chance of living on - for only he and two others survived that raid on Chemnitz in March 1945.[5]

On 7/8 March the Lancasters of 6 Group took part in a Thunderclap raid on Dessau in Eastern Germany while its Halifaxes joined 4 Group in what proved to be a mediocre attack on the oil refinery at Hemmingstedt. Heavy flak followed the bombers over Esbjerg and the Kiel Canal and two Halifaxes fell to night-fighters before reaching the target. There were very mixed feelings about the raid and the general inaccuracy that characterised it. Large-scale oil refineries were notoriously difficult to hit in cloud conditions as they gave a very poor H2S image and the presence of night-fighters alarmed many in-experienced crews. Most damaging was the loss of the Master Bomber early on in the attack for his TIs burnt fiecely for some ten minutes several miles from the target. As one Canadian pilot flying a 420 Squadron Halifax put it:

"It was probably the most unsatisfactory trip of my tour . . . It all went wrong when the Master

French Air Force Halifax BIII at Elvington.
Yorkshire Air Museum

Bomber was shot down . . . Most of the crews bombed on the wreckage of his aircraft. Hardly any damage was done to the oil refinery." [6]

Losses barely justified the effort made. No 578 Squadron from Burn lost two Halifaxes: one was carrying a ventral gunner and crashed next to the Kiel Canal; the other was presumably lost at sea as there were no survivors. The Squadron historian records that "French conversation was heard" during the raid and this

presumably came from Elvington's Guyenne and Tunisie squadrons which sent eleven and ten Halifaxes respectively to Hemmingstedt without loss. The other two missing Halifaxes came from Canada's 408 and 425 Squadrons. Two other Canadian Squadrons lost Lancasters on the Dessau raid - two from 424 Tiger and one from 419 Moose.

From now on the northern groups were contributing both to the overall strategy of destroying U-boat manufacturing centres (witness the raid on the Type XXI *Schnorkel* U-boat yards at Hamburg on 8/9 March), to the 'oil plan' and to the further destruction of the Ruhr and its surviving centres of production and communication. Three major daylight raids on the Ruhr began with a huge assault on Essen (11 March 1945) that permanently paralysed the city. Every Group in Bomber Command sent aircraft to swell the maximum number of sorties to this target that had suffered so much destruction at the hands of the RAF and RCAF. A total of 1079 Halifaxes, Lancasters and Mosquitoes roared over the ruins from which over half the population had long been evacuated but where slave workers still laboured and trains still moved at night loaded with arms and ammunition to ensure that resistance could continue. Though the RAF and RCAF never returned to Essen they paid a price: three Lancasters were lost that day, two of them from Canada's 6 Group. However, Essen's ordeal was not the biggest

F/Lt Maxie Baer (RCAF) "buzzes" Burn control tower at the end of his tour. Note the vehicles - including the car on the roof with a beer barrel on top.
Yorkshire Air Museum

attack on a German target during this period. Bomber Command's ultimate blow fell on the unfortunate city of Dortmund where 1,108 aircraft, including Halifaxes and Lancasters from the two northern groups, finally brought this industrial city's productivity to an end (12 March 1945).

Goebbels' diary entries for early March 1945 reveal something of the anguish of the German people though he does speak of some optimism that the new U-boats "will tear great holes in enemy tonnage" and the mistaken belief that "our V-weapons are still causing considerable destruction in the British capital." He also records the view, much publicised on the Nazi State Radio, that "a new amphibious operation will be necessary since the Rhine is as great an obstacle to military operations as the Channel was . . ."[7] But it is his references to the air war during the second week of March 1945 that are significant. Of course, he does not differentiate between the work of the US 8th/15th Air Forces and Bomber Command when he says:

> "During the last twenty-four hours the air war has raged over Reich territory with devastating effect. The greater part of Dessau is a sheet of flame and totally destroyed, yet another German city that has been flattened . . . Chemnitz in particular makes one's hair grow grey . . . we have no defence worth mentioning with which to oppose the enemy air war . . . "[8]

He does not hide the effect that this was having upon the German people; and, those members of the Air Staff who were once so certain that civilian morale could be broken by air attack would have drawn comfort from his words:

> "The air terror which rages uninterruptedly over German home territory makes people thoroughly despondent. One feels so impotent against it that no-one can see a way out of the dilemma. The total paralysis of transport in West Germany also contributes to the mood of increasing pessimism among the German people . . ."[9]

The power of Bomber Command's 4 and 6 Groups reached its peak with a daylight precision attack upon Wuppertal/Barmen (13 March 1945). Not a single bomber loss was recorded. Wuppertal's marshalling yards disintegrated under a hail of relatively small bombs for some squadrons were carrying nothing heavier than 500 pounders. It was also a day on which a Yorkshire Squadron disbanded. This was 578 Squadron at Burn whose last operation was to send fourteen Halifax IIIs to

Wuppertal. It had lived up to its motto *Accuracy* and in a brief but distinguished career had received 109 Halifax aircraft and lost seventy-two of these on active service. Now its personnel dispersed to serve with other units while the remaining squadrons in 4 and 6 Groups continued their assault on targets decreed by the Chiefs of Staff: a daylight raid on Zweibrücken (14/15 March) to prevent the transit of German troops to the front; a devastating area attack on Hagen (15/16 March) to destroy oil and communication targets; an area attack on Witten's steelworks (18/19 March); and the return of 6 Group to wipe out the oil refinery at Hemmingstedt (20/21 March). During the three great assaults on the Ruhr and in the mixture of tactical and strategic raids that followed German fighters could still damage the bomber stream. Canadian losses on the Hagen, Witten and Hemmingstedt operations demonstrate this: a 425 Squadron Halifax over Hagen, three aircraft over Witten; two Lancasters lost at Hemmingstedt.

With near total command of the sky, the Allies could now prepare for the crossing of the River Rhine, symbol of German national strength and a crucial psychological barrier for German and Allied leaders alike. Bomber Command's preparation for the crossing was vital: on 23/24 March while Bomber Command were destroying the town of Wesel, the point selected for the amphibious operation, British Commandos paddled across the river to occupy the ruins and secure a bridgehead.[10] 1500 Allied bombers attacked local airfields to dishearten the Luftwaffe further and Yorkshire's Halifaxes flew to bomb the marshalling yards and Wehrmacht assembly areas in Sterkrade and Gladbeck. Lt Col Wythe, then a young Signals subaltern, waited opposite Wesel to cross the Rhine and watched a display of aerial power unprecedented in warfare. Just before 1000 hours on 24 March 1945 he saw :

> "the thousand bombers, with glider forces following, help the Army across."

The sight would forever impress him, as it did every wide-eyed soldier present on that historic day. Altogether, 21,680 infantry soldiers packed inside two thousand gliders and hundreds of transport aircraft crossed the Rhine by air in a matter of minutes. To back them up came 240 B-24 Liberators carrying nearly six hundred tons of ammunition and equipment. High above the airborne troops a thousand fighters went in search of brave but foolhardy Luftwaffe pilots; or flew low down to strafe airfields, roads and locomotives. All day long over three thousand heavy and medium bombers were criss-crossing the skies ready to pounce on any town or city where German troops, exhausted but still very dangerous, might be reforming.

Next day 4 and 6 Group aircraft were directed to Hannover, Münster and Osnabrück and then enjoyed a few days of rest and relaxation before renewing attacks on U-boat construction yards and oil plants. Two hundred Canadian bombers from 6 Group flew in daylight to Hamburg on 31 March and began their bomb run in their version of the 'gaggle formation' orginally devised by Leonard Cheshire VC. Unfortunately, the Canadians arrived over the target some ten minutes late and their RAF Mustang escorts had temporarily left the area. Suddenly the Canadians came under attack from Me 262 jets emerging from the clouds below. Equipped with four 3cm Mk 108 cannon, sometimes supplemented with twin racks of R4M 5cm rockets firing explosive shells, they could be deadly against a close formation of bombers that had neither the space nor time to take evasive action. As Galland later commented, "a single hit from one of these was enough to bring down a multi-engined bomber."[11] The Me 262s weaved through the Canadian formations and shot down four Lancasters and two Halifax IIIs. No 433 Squadron's Lancaster B1s came under especially heavy attack during which S/Ldr Holmes' gunners sent down an Me 262 trailing smoke. The two squadrons from Leeming, 427 Lion and 429 Bison, were flying Lancaster BIs and BIIIs and both scored an Me 262 apiece while the rear-gunner on F/O Heaven's Lancaster X was so accurate that an attacking Me 262 exploded under his withering fire.[12] All of this happened within the space of a few minutes, the first major contest between Yorkshire-based piston-engined bombers designed for night operations- and unescorted at the time - and the first generation of subsonic twin-jet interceptors. The Canadians were under no illusions about the deadly threat posed by the Me 262. As F/O Saunders, who piloted a Skipton Lancaster B1 to Hamburg that day, later remarked:

> "Our bombing operations would not have been as successful if the Germans had had the Me 262 at an earlier date."[13]

Adolf Galland was in total agreement:

> "It does not bear thinking about that we could have had these jet fighters, these 3cm quick-firing cannons, and these 5cm rockets years ago, before our war potential had been smashed and indescribable misery had come over Germany through these Allied air raids."[14]

Most of Bomber Command's targets after the Hamburg raid were, as Middlebrook remarks, "strictly

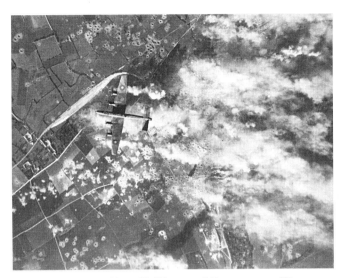

The effects of bombing: Halifax over Mimoyecques (V weapon sites)   *Yorkshire Air Museum*

military ones."[15] 'Area targets' were rapidly disappearing as the British First Army Group under Montgomery and the US 12th Army Group under Bradley successfully encircled the Ruhr and began to strike out towards Bremen, Hannover, Kassel, Erfurt, Nuremberg and Munich - familiar names to the men of Bomber Command. The Yorkshire-based squadrons concentrated on Hamburg's construction yards on 8/9 April and on the following day carried out an accurate daylight attack on Leipzig's railway system. Long-range attacks on Nuremberg and Bayreuth involved 129 Halifaxes from 4 Group in a precision raid on local marshalling yards with great effect and no losses - a far cry from that night in 1944 when ninety-five Bomber Command aircraft failed to return from Nuremberg. 6 Group took part in raids on Kiel (13/14 April) and Schwandorf (16/17 April) with little result and the next two mass attacks on Heligoland (18 April) and Bremen (22 April) were designed to discourage German resistance with Allied forces so close. Over Bremen the cloud and smoke completely covered the target and the Master Bomber ordered 4 Group's Halifaxes not to bomb. On this occasion the Yorkshire squadrons brought their bomb-loads back.

They were able to use them on 25 April when 4 and 6 Groups were tasked with the destruction of German guns on the Frisian Island of Wangerooge. These heavy batteries controlled the sea approaches to Bremen and Wilhelmshaven and this operation proved to be the last of the war for the two northern groups. A vast number of bombs fell on Wangerooge but the guns themselves were

The effects of bombing: The devastation of Heligoland
(542 Squadron 19 April 1945).
Yorkshire Air Museum

346 Squadron's Halifax VI bombers. These aircraft were delivered between 18 March and 31 October 1945 and transferred
to the French Air Force on 31 October 1945. An evocative
photograph of Elvington's misty dispersals flanked by silver
birch trees.
Yorkshire Air Museum

barely damaged and all were in action after the Yorkshire
squadrons had departed. As it was a daylight operation the
Lancasters and Halifaxes flew in loose gaggle formations
and the presence of 482 aircraft in close proximity to one
another heightened the risk of collision, most feared after
the twin threats of fighters and flak. Wangerooge's flak
had damaged a few aircraft but all seemed well until
a No 76 Squadron Halifax hit another's propeller wash
and touched the wing of a third Halifax. Warrant Officer
Lawson, a pilot, was the sole survivor of the collision.
Worse was to come. Two Halifaxes from Leeming, one
from 408 and the other from 426 Squadron, touched and
fell into the sea. The same fate overtook two Lancasters
from 431 Squadron and altogether twenty-eight
Canadians and thirteen RAF aircrew died in these
collisions. Only Lawson lived to tell the tale. One other
Halifax was lost to flak on the Wangerooge operation.
This was a 347 Tunisie aircraft from Elvington, piloted
by Capitaine Hautecoeure.[16]

* * *

As far as 4 and 6 Groups were concerned, this was the end
of the air war in Europe and there is no doubt that for
many newly arrived aircrew it came as a distinct anti-
climax. More brand-new Lancaster Xs and Halifax VIs
had entered Squadron service and some crews who had
just left the Heavy Conversion Units wanted to have at
least one 'op' in their logbooks. But it was not to be.

On the same day that the Germans surrendered
(7 May 1945) 4 Group was made redundant as a strategic
bomber force and most squadrons transferred to
Transport Command. Apart from the two FAF squadrons
at Elvington and 446 RAAF at Driffield (re-equipped with
Halifax BVIs and later on with Liberators) the Group soon
had to part with its Halifaxes. No 640 Squadron at
Leconfield was disbanded on 7 May; No 158 Squadron at
Lissett went to Transport Command though its most
famous Halifax, Friday the 13th, was put on display next
to a Beaufighter for the admiring British people to inspect
in London's Oxford Street. No 51 Squadron was destined
to exchange its Halifaxes for Stirling transports; Shiny
Ten at Melbourne, No 76 Squadron at Holme and
No 77 Squadron at Full Sutton were to fly Dakotas in
India; 102 Squadron at Pocklington would join them,
flying Liberators; No 78 Squadron at Breighton would
operate Dakotas in the Middle East.

The vast majority of Halifax bombers were flown to
Clifton and High Ercall where they awaited sale, civil
conversion or - as in the case of most of these illustrious
aircraft - an unhappy fate in a breaker's yard. Dakotas of

Transport Command took their place on Yorkshire's airfields and former bomber crews began to convert to the joys of this slow but reliable workhorse that had made its own special contribution to victory in Europe. Even new squadrons arrived : No 512 came to Holme-on-Spalding-Moor and No 575 was based at Melbourne (7 August 1945).

There was talk of a 'Tiger Force' to serve in the Pacific and some of 6 Group's squadrons were ordered to return to Canada for training: 405 (transferred from the Pathfinding Force), 419, 420, 428, 431 and 434 plus 408 and 425 who would exchange their Halifaxes for Lancaster Xs.

Sir Arthur Harris came to Middleton St George to see them off. 6 Group had certainly earned his accolade:

"You leave this country, after all you have done, with a reputation that is equal to any and surpassed by none.[17]

Not all the Canadians joined Tiger Force. Almost immediately, 415 Swordfish disbanded at Skipton-on-Swale and 432 Leaside disbanded at East Moor. Three other squadrons, 424 Tiger, 429 Bison and 433 Porcupine, spent some weeks bringing home prisoners-of-war from Germany and then took part in Operation Dodge, transporting troops home from Italy. The Thunderbirds of 426 Squadron converted to Liberators and took part in trooping operations from India before returning to Driffield for disbanding.

One chore carried out by the two French Air Force squadrons at Elvington was to fill their Halifaxes with surplus bombs and dump them in the North Sea. Another was to detach flights to France to help in POW and troop transporting. When these tasks were finished, the British government indicated that 346 and 347 Squadrons should have the privilege of taking their Yorkshire-based Halifaxes to France as an outright gift to the French people. One more Yorkshire airfield saw its squadrons depart, a moment marked by the visit (25 October 1945) of the chief of Bomber Command, not the beloved Sir Arthur Harris for he had now retired, but by Air Chief Marshal Sir Hugh Bottomley. He emphasised the quality of leadership and the courage of the French crews in the bombing offensive against Germany. Sir Hugh went on to say:

". . . at this moment, we think particularly of the brave fliers who have given their lives for the Allied cause. They died not only for France but for all the Allied peoples, for those who have suffered from enemy oppression and aggression.

A 346 Squadron Halifax flying home to France 1945.

Yorkshire Air Museum

We will never forget them. Their sacrifice and their names will forever be part of the History of the Royal Air Force.

We thank you with all our hearts.
Au revoir ! Vive la France ![18]

It would be good to record that the all the crews now climbed into their Halifaxes and roared off to Bordeaux. Indeed the whole of Guyenne took off without incident. Tunisie was due to leave four days later on 29 October but the day was marred when Halifax L8-Q lost an engine on take-off and crashed just beyond Elvington. The pilot and four other crew members survived but Sous-Lieutenant Vellard and Sgt Prades were killed, the last of Bomber Command's 4 Group crewmen still flying a Squadron Halifax to be buried in Harrogate cemetery.

★　★　★

The Yorkshire heavy bomber squadrons had played a major role in almost every aspect of the bombing offensive against Germany. They had built up a reputation for deadly accuracy and throughout the years of warfare consistently lived up to the motto on Bomber Command's badge

"Strike hard, strike sure".

After 1945 there were some who chose to denigrate Sir Arthur Harris and the achievements of his devoted crews in Bomber Command. They made astounding claims, suggesting that the Command was misused throughout 1943-1945 and that if the Command had concentrated on ball bearing factories and synthetic oil plants to the exclusion of Germany's industrial cities the war would have been over much more quickly. They manipulated German statistics, quoted selectively from Speer and

No 6 (RCAF) Group Memorial at Elvington.

No 76 Squadron Memorial, Holme-on-Spalding-Moor with Leonard Cheshire.

Goebbels, and believed that because German war production actually increased while under Bomber Command's unrelenting offensive, the Command should have had different objectives. In short, they argued that Bomber Command should not have carried out its area attacks and not fought the Battles of the Ruhr, Hamburg and Berlin. Britain's proper investment, some suggested, should have met two priorities: the destruction of U-boats in the Battle of the Atlantic and closer co-operation with Allied land forces. Had the British followed these policies the Allies might well have invaded Western Europe in 1943 and saved the world a whole year of warfare.[19]

How these critics acquired omniscience - except through the luxury of hindsight - is never made clear though their conclusions, because they appear devastatingly simple to the ill-informed, received unquestioning publicity in the media and in textbooks and memoirs that abounded after 1945. More recently they surfaced during the 1991 furore over the privately-subscribed statue to the memory of Sir Arthur Harris.

Because, by implication, the critics included No 4 Group of the Royal Air Force and No 6 Group of the Royal Canadian Air Force some consideration of these hostile views is relevant to Yorkshire's role during this controversial period in the history of aviation.

Regrettably, the British government missed its one opportunity to undertake a systematic study of the true effect of consistent air attack on Nazi Germany's ability to wage war. This was in direct contrast to the resolve of the United States government for, with the full support of President Roosevelt, the Americans established their Bombing Survey Unit in Europe (September 1944) with a staff of one thousand. Portal and Sinclair were both anxious to set up a British equivalent under the leadership of an impartial civilian director. They arranged for the RAF element of the Commission to be headed by Air Commodore C.B.N. Pelly and then approached Churchill for his approval in early January 1945. The reader will remember that this was shortly before Churchill decided on the implementation of Thunderclap and before he asked Sinclair to provide precise data on how and when these attacks on East German cities could begin. It therefore came as a surprise to Sinclair to learn on 5 January that Churchill was unwilling to use manpower and brainpower on the American scale just to set up a British Bombing Research Mission. Instead, he offered "twenty or thirty persons" provided "there is a reasonable prospect of getting results soon enough to be of material assistance in the war against Japan . . ."[20]

Portal was appalled and urged his fellow Chiefs of Staff to press the Prime Minister on the matter:

"I look on the British Mission as a means of providing the Government with indispensable data, relevant to future defence policy, about the effect on an industrialised country of direct attack on its war economy."[21]

The Chiefs of Staff supported Portal but again the Prime Minister remained obdurate, repeating his offer of "thirty persons" to constitute a British Bombing Research Commission. So there was never a properly constituted

British inquiry into the effects of the strategic bomber offensive. Pelly's small RAF team soon told Portal of the opportunity that was being missed. Pelly said that photographs and descriptions could not convey the extent of destruction by the RAF:

> "At the vast Krupp works at Essen, a tangle of steel beams and twisted machinery is superimposed on the stratum of rubble which one soon comes to regard as normal in this part of Germany. The RAF's great achievement in rendering the biggest armament works in the world incapable of producing a hairpin is brought home very forcibly, even during a cursory inspection."[22]

Pelly also warned that one could not rely on German industrial records and accounts which he suspected were often falsified. Tax returns and labour records, he warned, must not be taken at face value but must be rigorously checked by experts.

Portal therefore agreed to set up a British Bombing Survey Unit headed by Air Commodore Pelly. Inadequately funded and staffed it depended heavily upon American research. Its findings were never published but the American Strategic Bombing Survey became generally available and formed part of the evidence examined by Webster and Frankland prior to the publication of their *The Strategic Air Offensive against Germany*.[23]

Certain findings are unequivocal. Area bombing did not destroy German morale so this factor by itself did not have a permanent effect upon production. However, morale was hardly an issue by 1944 when most industrial workers were in fact slave workers who were not permitted such emotional luxuries. The German economy was by no means overstretched between 1939 and 1942 and there was 'plenty of slack' that could be turned to the production of war materials between 1943 and the beginning of 1945. The under-employment of German women as 'war-workers', in direct contrast with the situation in Britain, underlines this point. The most effective bombing attacks were on transport, communication and oil targets and upon the experimental V-weapon station at Peënemunde and the V1/V2/V3 sites in France. Germany's most impressive industrial achievement - the high production of day and night-fighters during 1943-1944 - was nullified by their eventual destruction at the hands of American fighter escorts in the great daylight battles over Germany and by the inadequate supplies of aviation fuel available after *Operation Baseplate* due to the effective Allied bombing of oil, transport and communications targets.

So what of the area attacks? What is the historical importance and strategic achievement of Bomber Command's crews and their leader, Sir Arthur Harris? It is this: *on the orders of the politicians*, they created a decisive, war-winning 'Second Front' over Europe long before D-Day 1944. These are almost exactly the words of Albert Speer, economic dictator of Nazi Germany, for he deplored the enormous quantities of guns, ammunition and manpower being diverted to the defence of Germany. So it was through their determination and sacrifice that Harris and his bomber crews forced Germany into a defensive posture from which she never recovered, even though there were Luftwaffe bomber bases within striking distance of Britain. Germany was never capable of launching a continuous offensive bombing strategy after her failure in the Battle of Britain and the subsequent blitz of 1940-41 because she had to divert resources to building fighter aircraft to *defend* the Third Reich against the strategic air offensive launched by Harris during 1942-45, supported by the US Army Air Forces in Britain and Italy (1943-45). It was because the RAF and the RCAF had been on the offensive *throughout* the war, had fought their great battles over the Ruhr, Hamburg and Berlin, *before* the Americans (to whom Sir Arthur Harris always gave 50% of the credit) made their great contribution, that two crucial events were made possible: first, the transformation of Britain into the biggest 'aircraft carrier', arms dump and manpower resource in the world; and second, the Allied invasion of Western Europe. Both were accomplished without significant intervention from a Luftwaffe deprived of its *offensive* arm.

These were the foundations of victory, especially when combined with Bomber Command's other stupendous achievements against the German Navy (gardening, U-boat destruction, sinking *Tirpitz*, *Admiral Scheer*, *Admiral Hipper* and *Lutzow*) and against the German Army (e.g. Caen, Le Havre, Walcheren, the Ardennes and the Rhine). There can be no doubt that Bomber Command's constant war against the German heartland and its contribution to the successful invasion of Occupied Europe saved the lives of tens of thousands of Allied soldiers who, on the whole, were spared the horrors of endless infantry campaigns against well-entrenched German defences. This is in stark contrast with the experience of the Soviet Union which failed to undertake a major strategic bombing offensive against Nazi Germany, preferring instead to concentrate its air power on close ground support for its troops. Russian casualties during the offensives on the Eastern Front after Kursk in 1943 ran into millions of dead and wounded infantrymen and women. Of course, critics of Bomber Command may argue that mistakes were made and that operations took place in the wrong order or at the wrong time or in the wrong place. That tends to be a characteristic of war in any century for war is an imperfect science. The fact remains that Bomber Command carried out with great precision every strategic and tactical task assigned it by the politicians and the Chiefs of Staff.

Great damage was done to the reputation and achievements of Bomber Command by Winston Churchill's ill-advised minute to Lord Ismay, his Chief Staff Officer, on 28 March 1945. No doubt the Prime Minister was protecting his own political future when he penned the following words:

> "It seems to me that the moment has come when the question of bombing German cities simply for the sake of increasing the terror, though under other pretexts, should be reviewed . . . The destruction of Dresden remains a serious query against the conduct of Allied bombing."

For the Prime Minister to use this kind of language to describe a bombing policy that he himself instigated must mean he was seeking a scapegoat to bear the weight of possible criticisms of government strategy at the end of the war. Whatever his motive, he so infuriated Sir Arthur Harris that the Chief of Bomber Command called the minute

> "an insult both to the bombing policy of the Air Ministry and to the manner in which that policy has been executed by Bomber Command."

Churchill had gone too far and he knew it. He replaced the offending minute with another on 1 April and this document mildly indicated that Bomber Command should cease area bombing as the occupation and administration of "an entirely ruined land" would not be to Britain's advantage. After conferring with Harris, Portal agreed that area bombing of industrial cities was now redundant though such bombing of targets vital to the enemy's military dispositions might be necessary to bring about his defeat.

Portal was writing this on 4 April and, as we have seen, the bombing operations after that date were designed to take out specific military objectives such as the shipyards at Hamburg (8/9 April), the U-boats at Kiel (13/14 April) and German troop positions at Bremen (22 April). But by then the damage to Bomber Command's reputation had already been done and the notion of 'terror raids', fuelled first by American journalists and later by books such as David Irving's *Destruction of Dresden* (1963) did unjust harm to historical accuracy and to the feelings of families

who had lost their loved ones in Bomber Command operations throughout the war.

Bomber Command faced further criticism because some said it was immoral to bomb towns and cities where women and children lived - though it is noticeable that few criticisms were uttered when, regrettably and without intent, Bomber Command killed French, Dutch, Belgian, Norwegian and Danish civilians during raids on military targets in Occupied Europe. The German people had enthusiastically supported Adolf Hitler, rejoiced when his armies proved all-victorious in 1939-40, gleefully accepted millions of domestic servants and slave labourers from Occupied Europe, worked with skill and dedication in the armament factories, lived off the produce of Denmark, France and Norway and studiously ignored the genocide of six million Jews. The presence of German workers in and their commitment to the armament centres of Germany automatically placed themselves and their families in grave personal danger and the German authorities took pains to provide air raid shelters just as, in similar circumstances, the British government provided shelters for its own civilian population. For Bomber Command not to have attacked Germany's armament and communication centres would have certainly risked losing the war against the Nazis and that, as Dr. Noble Frankland has pointed out elsewhere, would have been a "greater immorality" than the air offensive that actually took place.[24]

Moreover, one must never forget the feelings of the British people and the nature of the enemy facing them during the Second World War. There was no sympathy whatsoever for the suffering of the German people after the experiences of the blitz, the 'doodle-bugs' and the V-2 rockets; no love for a people who carried out such barbaric exesses against the Polish people, Russian prisoners-of-war and resistance fighters. They were entitled to assume that the Nazis might be equally vicious in the treatment of the British people if Germany won the war.

Richard Walter Darré, German Minister of Agriculture[25] in 1942, is credited with the following horrifying forecast:

> As soon as we beat England we shall make an end of you Englishmen once and for all. Able-bodied men and women will be exported as slaves to the Continent. The old and the weak will be exterminated. All men remaining in Britain as slaves will be sterilised; a million or two of young women of the Nordic type will be segregated in a number of studfarms where, with the assistance of picked German sires, during a period of ten or

twelve years they will produce annually a series of Nordic infants to be brought up in every way as Germans. These infants will form the future population of Britain . . . Thus in a generation or two the British will disappear."

This may seem unthinkable today but in 1942-43 these words were "chillingly real"[26] to civilians and Bomber Command crews alike. Men did not fly to Germany filled with passion and a determination to kill and maim. They flew as volunteers, coping with the complexities of taking a huge bomber on a long-distance flight into strongly defended enemy territory, and with much deeper purposes in mind. F/Lt Ralph Jeffrey, a Lancaster pilot, described this in his letter to the *Sunday Telegraph* (13 October 1991):

"I lived in Croydon throughout the Battle of Britain, the 1941 blitzes and the 'buzz-bomb' raids of 1944, all of which were totally indiscriminate, killing or maiming mainly civilians and razing many fine buildings. My father wasted his youth in the trenches from 1914 to 1918, only to see the Reich rise stronger and more virulent in 1938/9.

My Jewish navigator enlightened me about the terrible things his people had endured during the 1930s so my feelings in 1945 were twofold: that we had to smash the ever-resurgent German war machine for good, and that just retribution was due."

It was to smash the German war-machine that Bomber Command flew to Germany when the Command was the sole offensive weapon that Britain possessed. Yorkshire's Squadrons at their maximum strength constituted over 26% of Bomber Command's strategic bomber force and so they may be proud to share the final accolade bestowed by Webster and Frankland in their *Official History of the Strategic Air Offensive against Germany*: that Bomber Command played the **major** part in the almost complete destruction of the German oil industry and the near total dislocation of the German transportation system; that the area attacks made city and town life almost unbearable and certainly unmanageable.

Cumulatively, the strategic bombers:

"made a contribution to victory which was decisive. Those who claim that Bomber Command's contribution to the war was less are factually in error."[27]

NP-F, a Halifax III of 158 Squadron, on show in Oxford Street in the summer of 1945. It is this aeroplane, which completed 128 operations by VE-Day, that has been replicated by Yorkshire Air Museum.

Crown copyright

Chapter Twenty Five

The Search for Security 1945-1963

On 4 June 1945, after the end of the war in Europe but before the Japanese surrender, Winston Churchill made perhaps the most damaging speech of his career. Broadcasting to the nation, he warned the people of the dangers of voting for a socialist government and stated that socialist policies were "abhorrent to British ideas of freedom"; that, once in power, the socialists would resort to a political police force, a kind of Gestapo, because their policies were "inseparably interwoven with totalitarianism". For the mass of the British people, especially the men and women in uniform at home and overseas, these were not the words they wished to hear. They had been excited by the Beveridge Report and wanted the promise of a Welfare State to come true. They went to the polls between 5 and 26 July 1945 and gave Clement Attlee's Labour Party a landslide victory: 394 seats for Labour; 212 for the Conservatives and an overall majority against all the opposition parties of 148. When Attlee and his wife went to Buckingham Palace to tell King George VI that he was able to form a government he drove in a little Standard 10 motor car. The age of the common man seemed to have arrived and with him, it was expected, the cut back on military expenditure and an increase in government spending on urgently needed social services.

Cuts in military expenditure were self-evident in Yorkshire where the great bomber bases were shut down with scant regard for the bravery and sacrifice made by the British, Commonwealth and European aircrews during six years of aerial warfare against Germany. Airfields that once resounded with the roar of Whitleys, Wellingtons, Halifaxes and Lancasters were abandoned during 1945-46: Lissett, Marston Moor, Burn, Riccall, Skipton, Sherburn, Tholthorpe, Wombleton, Holme, Breighton, and Dalton all closed in 1945; Melbourne, Pocklington, Snaith, Carnaby and Croft suffered the same fate in 1946. Of course, the Royal Air Force had to be run down and the vast majority of aircrew demobilised. Between 1945 and 1950 the RAF's strength declined from well over one million to around 182,000, sustained at that level by the 1947 National Service Act that called up men aged eighteen (still without the vote) to serve in the Armed Forces.

Maintenance Command had the problem of coping with unwanted RAF stores and equipment in Yorkshire. It decided to collect surplus material from the airfields and store it on the most capacious bomber base in the county - and the base that it chose was Marston Moor with its seven hangars and this was where No 268 Maintenance Unit opened shop in 1946. As Guy Jefferson recalled:

"Everything, from bomb trolleys to bacon slicers and bed-pans, was sent to Marston Moor, sometimes all mixed up in the same consignment. The logistics were phenomenal . . . over 100 lorry loads were received each day and just where to store the items became a nightmare . . . a whole building was allocated for fire extinguishers but this soon filled to capacity so they had to be turfed out into the open (eventually filling two aircraft dispersal points) to make way for more delicate electrical tools such as several thousand soldering irons and electric drills piled high to the ceiling . . . Bicycles were a big headache and these occupied one half of a T2 hangar, stacked right up to the roofgirders, over 20,000 in all."[1]

Much of the material was stored on overflow airfields at Wombleton and Holme-on-Spalding Moor and the three sites were not cleared until 1950. Surplus bombs presented one of the most dangerous items and many of these were stacked on the abandoned runways at Acaster Malbis, Scorton, Cottam and Dalton. Some were still on these airfields as late as 1951-52 and the previously secret mustard gas pits at Escrick were not considered harmless until thirty years later!

In truth, the axe that fell during 1945-46 was not quite so drastic as the one that had reduced the youthful RAF to impotence after the First World War. Unlike 1918-19, there was a real fear during 1945-6 that yet another war would have to be fought, this time against a Soviet Union which appeared to be threatening the peace and stability of the post-war world. In a change from the typical left-wing attitudes of the Thirties, a firm defence policy was now a priority for the newly-elected Labour Government. Three new factors now dominated air warfare: air-dropped nuclear weapons, unmanned rocket missiles

THE FATE OF YORKSHIRE'S AIRFIELDS 1945 - 6

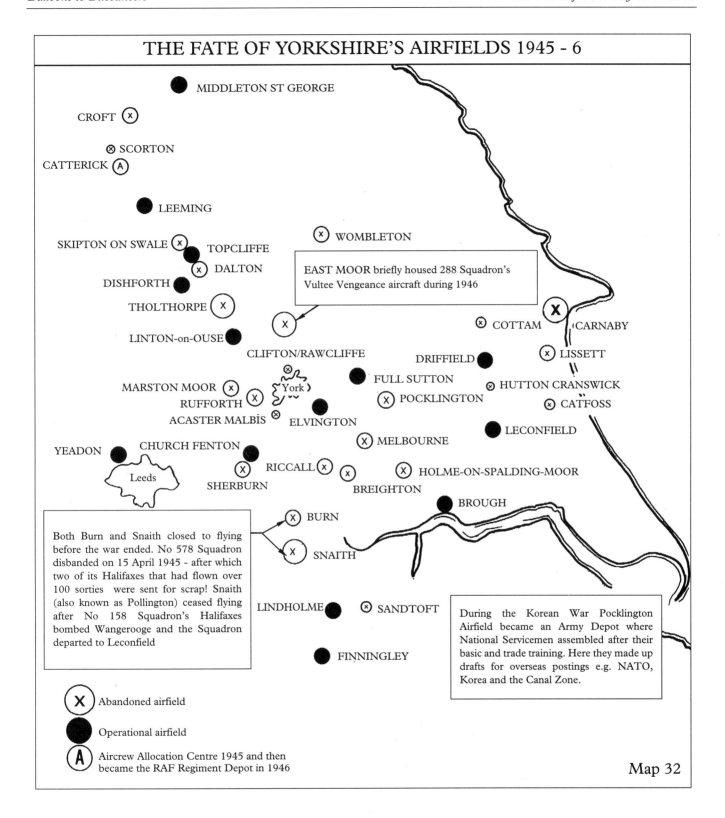

● MIDDLETON ST GEORGE

CROFT ⊗

⊗ SCORTON

CATTERICK Ⓐ

● LEEMING

SKIPTON ON SWALE ⊗

TOPCLIFFE

⊗ DALTON

DISHFORTH ●

THOLTHORPE ⊗

LINTON-on-OUSE ●

⊗ WOMBLETON

EAST MOOR briefly housed 288 Squadron's Vultee Vengeance aircraft during 1946

⊗

⊗ COTTAM

Ⓧ CARNABY

⊗ LISSETT

CLIFTON/RAWCLIFFE

DRIFFIELD ●

MARSTON MOOR ⊗

⊗ York

FULL SUTTON ●

RUFFORTH ⊗

⊗ POCKLINGTON

⊗ HUTTON CRANSWICK

ACASTER MALBIS ⊗

ELVINGTON

⊗ CATFOSS

LECONFIELD ●

YEADON ●

CHURCH FENTON ●

⊗ MELBOURNE

Leeds

RICCALL ⊗ ⊗

⊗ HOLME-ON-SPALDING-MOOR

SHERBURN ⊗

BREIGHTON

BROUGH ●

Both Burn and Snaith closed to flying before the war ended. No 578 Squadron disbanded on 15 April 1945 - after which two of its Halifaxes that had flown over 100 sorties were sent for scrap! Snaith (also known as Pollington) ceased flying after No 158 Squadron's Halifaxes bombed Wangerooge and the Squadron departed to Leconfield

⊗ BURN

⊗ SNAITH

LINDHOLME ●

⊗ SANDTOFT

During the Korean War Pocklington Airfield became an Army Depot where National Servicemen assembled after their basic and trade training. Here they made up drafts for overseas postings e.g. NATO, Korea and the Canal Zone.

● FINNINGLEY

Ⓧ Abandoned airfield

● Operational airfield

Ⓐ Aircrew Allocation Centre 1945 and then became the RAF Regiment Depot in 1946

Map 32

and jet-propelled aircraft. Together, these required a total reshaping of the nation's defences.

This began in 1946 when Britain was divided into six sectors for the control of fighter scrambles against an incoming attacker: the Northern, Eastern, Southern, Western, Caledonian and Metropolitan Sectors. Once the controller had ordered a sector scramble a Ground Control Interception (GCI) station would direct the fighters to their target. The Northern Sector Operations Centre (SOC) was at Patrington where the Sector Controller would scramble his fighters once the enemy was detected on the Chain Home radar and then fight his own air battle through his GCI stations. Britain's two surviving Fighter Groups, Nos 11 and 12, were logistically responsible for the Air Defence of Great Britain but no longer retained control of the *overall* battle.

Yorkshire's fighter bases in the immediate post-war period (1945-47) were at Finningley, Church Fenton, Linton and Yeadon. No 609 Auxiliary Air Force Squadron reformed at Yeadon in 1946 equipped with Mosquito night-fighters. Finningley and Linton were both former bomber bases but their proximity to northern Europe made them important as part of the county's fighter defence against possible Soviet attack. At Linton Nos 64 and 65 Squadrons operated Hornets for three years before converting to Meteor F8s in 1951. Finningley was now the home of No 616 (South Yorkshire) Squadron, Royal Auxiliary Air Force, reformed on 31 July 1946 and equipped with Mosquito NF 30s before returning to its wartime mount, the Gloster Meteor. Another bomber base, Middleton St George, just across the county border in Durham, housed the Mosquitoes of No 13 Operational Training Unit together with the revived No 608 (North Riding) Royal Auxiliary Air Force that had reformed at Thornaby in July 1946. No 264 Squadron flew its Mosquito NF 36 aircraft and was the most frequent visitor to Yorkshire's night-fighter base at Church Fenton, one of the first bases to receive Gloster Meteor jets (Nos 263 and 257 Squadrons).

So among the interesting fighters that now screamed across the Yorkshire skies was the Gloster Meteor, the first jet fighter to enter RAF operational service. It had been in action against V-1 flying bombs during 1944 and had flown sorties in Europe as part of the 2nd Tactical Air Force during April 1945. Its stablemate in Yorkshire was the de Havilland Hornet, flown by Linton's squadrons and by No 19 Squadron when it reformed at Church Fenton in 1946. Both aeroplanes carried 4 x 20 mm guns in the fuselage nose though the Hornet had the armament edge in that it could carry rocket projectiles or bombs

under its wings. The Meteor had a slightly higher service ceiling but before the Meteor F.4s entered service in 1948 there was not much to choose in terms of interceptor capability between the RAF's fastest piston-engined aircraft and the first of its operational jets.[2]

This emphasis upon fighters had created something of a 'bomber gap' during the late 1940s and as Lord Tedder stated in his speech to the Royal Empire Society in 1949:

"We would never win a match with eleven goalkeepers; so we must not forget that it was the bomber that would push the air battle from our skies."[3]

In 1949 bombers were woefully thin on the ground in Yorkshire. The Lancaster remained in limited service with Bomber Command and was soon replaced by the Avro Lincoln and though it eventually equipped twenty-one RAF squadrons it was in essence an aeroplane designed for the Second World War and hardly suitable for the kind of combat envisaged for the future. Its best cruising speed was 215mph at a height of 20,000 feet, no real advance on the Lancaster. Even with its maximum armament of 'twin fifties' in nose, tail and dorsal turrets, supplemented by two 20mm guns in a new ventral position, it would have been hard pressed to survive determined attacks by aircraft with the punch of a 1945-vintage Me 262, let alone the post-1945 jet interceptors. A.V Roe's factory at Yeadon produced six Lincolns (two B Mk 1s and four B Mk IIs) and examples of the type equipped Nos 57 and 100 Squadrons based briefly at Lindholme during 1946.[4] But Yorkshire, a key bomber county during the Second World War, saw very few of Avro's latest four-engined Merlin-powered bombers in the immediate post-war years. Yet the 'Cold War' had reached a threatening level in 1949 - the height of the Berlin Air Lift and the year in which the Chinese Communist Party overthrew Chiang Kai-Shek - and the lack of an offensive arm for the RAF in Yorkshire was disturbing.

In fact, compared with the growing strength of the Soviet Air Force Britain's long-range strike capability was relatively weaker than it been for ten years.[5] The existence of a number of 'cocooned' B-29 Superfortresses attracted an indigent Labour government and the first of these (named the *Washington* in RAF service) arrived on loan from the United States during 1950. Interestingly, the Russian copy of this was the Tupolev Tu-4, already flying with the Red Air Force. Though the American bombers helped to beef up Bomber Command, the B-29s and Lincolns remained "a somewhat fragile bulwark"[6] against the Communist Air Forces and aroused the anger of Harold Macmillan, then the Shadow Defence Minister.

He urged the pressing need for a powerful air striking force that reflected the 'state of the art' in aviation technology. This was not entirely the view of the Labour government which favoured defence against atomic attack rather than offensive initiative by bombers, an attitude that encouraged the Defence Committee in 1950 to recommend that Britain should have an air defence system based on surface-to-air missiles (SAMs). The Committee held the view that SAMs deserved the same priority enjoyed by the relatively slow and defenceless bombers.

Handley Page, Avro and Vickers were all alive to the situation and Handley Page in particular was anxious to persuade the Labour government to interest itself in buying a jet-propelled bomber capable of carrying a nuclear weapon to strategic targets in the Soviet Union. Such an idea naturally met with some political resistance for the Labour government had already sold examples of Britain's latest jet-engine technology to Russia.[7] However, the potential of Handley-Page's new project, termed the HP-80, made great appeal: it would have a crescent wing, carry twice as much as a wartime Lancaster and fly at 50,000 feet at a speed of 520mph. Once the Air Ministry approved the idea Handley-Page asked Robert Blackburn to design and manufacture at his Brough factory in Yorkshire a scaled down model of the proposed bomber, to be known as the HP-88. This emerged as a Supermarine Attacker fighter, VX 330, fitted with a Rolls-Royce Nene jet engine, and mated to a crescent wing. Painted in a glossy blue finish, VX 330 appeared in the Yorkshire skies on 21 June 1951 when 'Sailor' Parker carried out a successful five minute test flight from the old ELG runway at Carnaby. The aeroplane disintegrated over the Stansted runway later in the year, killing Handley Page's chief test pilot, D.J.P. Broomfield. This was after the Labour government had taken the plunge, ordering twenty-five Vickers Valiant jet bombers "off the drawing board" and approving further research into nuclear weaponry, a major slice of a very large defence cake in 1951. By then British forces were increasingly involved in the Korean War which bit deep into the budget with a consequent decline in social services spending. It was this that helped to lose Prime Minister Attlee a great deal of support and he failed to win the 1951 General Election.

★ ★ ★

When the Conservatives returned to power in 1951 Sir Winston Churchill had to admit that Labour stewardship of the armed services had been both responsible and extensive. Fighter Command was

equipping with jet aircraft; research into a nuclear deterrent was at an advanced stage; and the new prototype weapon carriers - the Vickers Valiant, the delta wing Avro Vulcan and the crescent wing Handley Page Victor - all flew between 1951 and 1952. Yorkshire's connection with the 'V-bombers' (Churchill's phrase) was limited to the training facilities offered by Finningley. Designated a dispersal V-bomber base in 1957, Finningley provided Bomber Command's specialist Bombing School and, with a brand-new runway, housed No 101 Squadron's first Vulcans in 1957 and No 18's Valiants the following year.

Elvington also received a new runway but not primarily for use by the RAF. The United States Air Force was seeking a British base for its highly versatile reconnaissance bombers, the Douglas RB-66 Destroyers. These were fast twin jet aircraft featuring a rear gun position. At the time they were seen as useful aircraft to ensure that the USA maintained an air superiority role in Europe, part of America's responsibilities under the North Atlantic Treaty Organisation (NATO) set up in 1949. Elvington was allocated to the USAF in 1953 as a Strategic Air Command base, one of nineteen scheduled to be built on English soil. US engineers moved in to begin the new runway construction during January 1954. The Americans spent £750,000 on a 9,800 ft runway and the huge concrete apron on which the Destroyers would be dispersed. Similarly, the Americans began to recondition the runway at Holme-on-Spalding-Moor where, because of the demands of the Korean War, pilot training had begun in 1952 with North American Harvards and Percival Prentices. Holme was seen as a stop-gap airfield, to be used by American aircraft while the long runway at

RB-66 Destroyer.   *Yorkshire Air Museum*

Elvington was under construction, and the Americans left the base in 1957.

They were also interested in Full Sutton and the 3390th Air Base Squadron moved in during 1955-57; and for a time (1958) the 3916th Air Base Squadron looked after certain technical stores assembled at Lindholme. The presence of large numbers of US engineers did much to enliven the social life of Hull, York, Beverley and Bawtry but little to underpin the NATO defence system. Within four years the Destroyers were redundant and the need for major US bases in Yorkshire diminished. All the Americans had left by the end of 1958 and for virtually no expense the RAF had acquired at Elvington one of the longest runways in the United Kingdom. But the RAF no longer regarded Yorkshire as as a suitable location for V-bomber bases and Elvington quickly fell into disuse apart from a limited function as a Relief Landing Ground for aircraft from Lindholme and Church Fenton, a role that remained unchanged up to 1992 when the RAF vacated the airfield.

Meanwhile, the Air Defence of Great Britain had become more sophisticated as a result of Operation Rotorplan 1951-53. The Chain Home radar system was phased out and in its place came the new Type 80 radar based at selected GCI stations. Yorkshire's Type 80 was positioned at Spurn Head and the new Northern SOC moved to Shipton, near York. At great expense, both the new radar and the SOC went underground into nuclear-proof bunkers and from these the controllers directed a new generation of jet interceptors. Upgraded versions of the Meteor and the De Havilland Venom were outclassed on exercises when the twin-jet English Electric Canberra acted as the incoming 'enemy' bomber. The Canberras came in fast and high over the North Sea and were usually on the other side of the Pennines before being intercepted.

Once more the government had to rethink the defence system and Yorkshire figured as a key element in its new plans. First it had to pay a heavy price. All three Royal Auxiliary Air Force Squadrons were axed in 1957: 609 at Church Fenton (Meteor F8s), 616 at Finningley (Meteor F8s) and 608 at Middleton St George (Vampire FB5s). Shipton was declared redundant and the radar controllers were placed in charge of the fighters now operating as close to the coast as possible. This explains both the constant migration of Yorkshire's fighter squadrons to Leconfield, Leeming and Middleton St George and the decision to end the fighter tradition at Church Fenton and Linton-on-Ouse. Until now, the 'Linton Wing' of North American Sabres had been the solitary Sabre Wing in RAF Fighter Command. These elegant aeroplanes flown by

Yorkshire Squadrons: Order of Battle		
June 1950		
No 12 GROUP		
	Squadron	*Aircraft*
Church Fenton	No 19	Meteor F4
	No 23	Mosquito NF 36
	No 141	Mosquito NF 36
	No 41	Hornet F3
Linton-on-Ouse	No 64	Hornet F3
	No 65	Hornet F3
	No 66	Meteor F4
	No 92	Meteor F4
Finningley	No 616	Meteor F4
Yeadon	No 609	Spitfire LF 16e
Middleton St George	No 608	Spitfire F22

No 92 Squadron (1954-56) had their red and yellow check markings flanking the fuselage roundel and, additionally, painted round the lip of the air imntake. Their supersonic booms over the Vale of York were so frequent that official action had to be taken to curb their enthusiastic pilots. Even more elegant were their Hunter F.6s to which No 92 converted in 1957. Their blue-painted F.6s were the Blue Diamonds, darling of the air shows and the official RAF aerobatic team in 1961. Defence policy changes had forced them to leave Linton by then and they eventually converted to Lightnings at Leconfield in April 1963.

Similarly, Church Fenton's Meteors were outpaced by the Canberras and V-bombers and in July 1959 the airfield passed to Flying Training Command. Nos 19 and 72 Squadrons moved across to Leconfield with their Hunters and Gloster Javelins and their arrival began the transformation of Leconfield into a major Air Defence of Great Britain base. Leeming enjoyed the same sort of interceptor role and No 33 Squadron reformed here in 1957 with Meteor NF 14s though it soon moved to Middleton St George (July 1958) to fly its new Javelin FAW.7s. Because Leeming had a newly built runway that could scramble relatively high performance Javelins it now housed 228 Operational Conversion Unit (the Javelin Mobile Conversion Unit) responsible for training crews for the RAF's first and only twin jet delta-winged fighter. As the Javelin was an all-weather fighter, crews did most of their sorties on the FAW 5 until the dual-control Javelin T3 became available. No 228 OCU came to an untimely end in 1961 even though Javelins continued in front-line service until the late Sixties.

If in fact, by 1958, "Britain's air defence system was at a peak of its efficiency"[8] it was to reach literally new heights after 1960 when a new and powerful jet interceptor entered squadron service. This was the English Electric Lightning, the first single-seat supersonic fighter capable of exceeding Mach 2 in level flight and rocketing vertically to a service ceiling of 60,000 feet. With its advanced Ferranti radar and on-board computers the pilot could locate, track and destroy any manned aircraft within the Soviet armoury during 1960-63. No 92 Squadron and No 19 Squadron began flying their Lightning F2s at Leconfield in 1961 and their superb formations were much admired over Yorkshire's East Riding. Brilliant though the design of the Lightning was it had one major disadvantage: a short operational range.

Middleton St George lost its Javelins in 1962 and then during 1963-64 temporarily housed 226 OCU Lightning Conversion Squadron[9] So by 1963 Yorkshire boasted a solitary front-line fighter base at Leconfield; and of the bomber bases not one was left occupied by a manned bomber squadron after No 101 Squadron transferred its Avro Vulcans from Finningley to Waddington in 1961.

Yet Yorkshire retained its vital strategic role in the defence of the United Kingdom, a role governed by the complex international and political problems arising from the Suez War of 1956. Prime Minister Harold Macmillan had succeeded Anthony Eden in 1957 and he met President Eisenhower in Bermuda (March 1957) and Washington (October 1957) in an attempt to heal the rift in the special relationship between the UK and the USA following the Anglo-French-Israeli attack on Egypt the previous year. Eisenhower's greatest concern was to upgrade the American nuclear deterrent by placing Thor missiles on British bases so that they could hit key targets inside the Soviet Union.

Macmillan was delighted to agree. He saw great advantages in basing American Thor rockets in Britain. Britain had no hope of developing its own rocket deterrent in the immediate future and the Prime Minister saw obvious advantages in acquiring the Douglas Thor. It would give RAF personnel the chance to become familiar with the technology of surface-to-surface ballistic missiles.[10]

A less publicised attraction was that it would be cheap, as the Americans would supply the missiles and the warheads free of charge. In the history of the Cold War it was a time of chilling anxiety as the Russians had just surprised the world with the launch of the Sputnik I satellite (4 October 1957). This success indicated the lead Russia had achieved with her Intercontinental Ballistic Missile (ICBM) known to NATO as *Sapwood* . Thor was a single stage Intermediate Range Ballistic Missile (IRBM) and could be carried by America's Heavy Lift aircraft, the C-124 Globemaster.

The Thor missiles arrived in Britain by Globemaster during 1959-60 when sixty were deployed on RAF airfields, all organised in the same style. The northern complex was in East Yorkshire and had its headquarters at Driffield with four satellite sites at Breighton (No 240 Squadron SM) - the SM suffix stood for 'Strategic Missile' - Full Sutton (No 102 Squadron SM), Catfoss (No 226 Squadron SM) and Carnaby (No 150 Squadron SM), each with three launching pads. The presence of the Thor missiles aroused some alarm in the rural East Riding

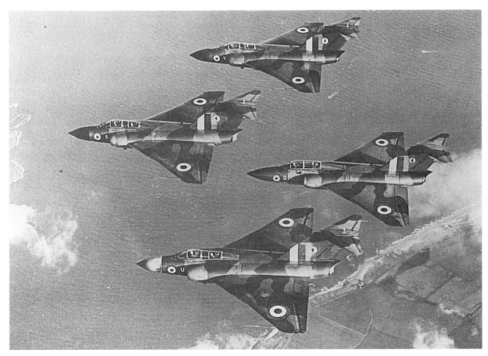

A tight formation of Javelins   *Yorkshire Air Museum*

THE THOR SITES

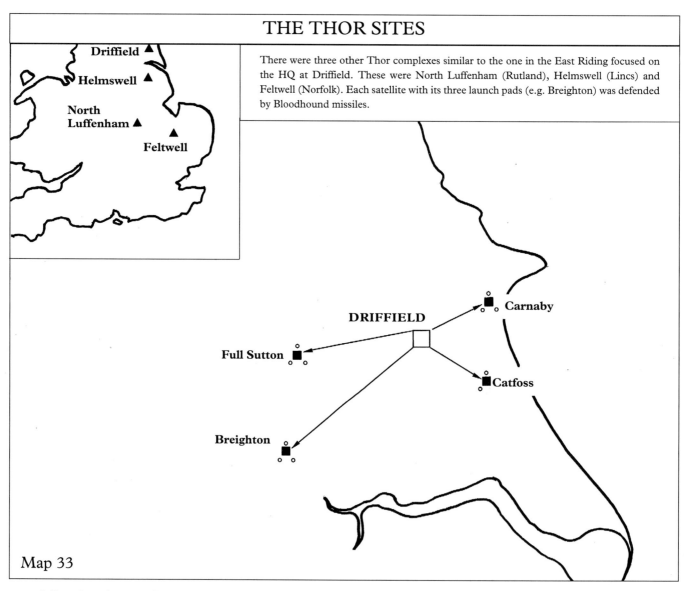

There were three other Thor complexes similar to the one in the East Riding focused on the HQ at Driffield. These were North Luffenham (Rutland), Helmswell (Lincs) and Feltwell (Norfolk). Each satellite with its three launch pads (e.g. Breighton) was defended by Bloodhound missiles.

Map 33

especially when it was discovered that each Thor was under the command of a US officer and that he alone had the power to arm Thor's nuclear warhead. This meant that Bomber Command could not launch an IRBM at the Soviet Union wthout the approval of the American President. However, unilateral nuclear action by Britain was difficult to contemplate and when the Conservative Minister of Defence, Harold Watkinson, assured the nation in 1961 that:

> ". . . As it stands ready at this moment, Bomber Command is capable, by itself, of crippling the industrial power of any aggressor nation."

he was primarily referring to the 140 Valiants, Vulcans and Victors, all of which went on stand-by during the 1962 Cuban crisis. Yorkshire had an unexpected significance in the events of 1962 as the publication of Cabinet Papers in 1993 revealed. Harold Macmillan was prepared to offer a *quid pro quo* to Chairman Khrushchev of the Soviet Union: remove your missiles from Cuba and we will remove our Thor rockets from Britain. To be on the safe side, the RAF arranged in the event of nuclear attack to disperse the V-bombers to widely scattered airfields between Lossiemouth and St Mawgan, including Leconfield, Elvington, Leeming and Middleton St George. Fortunately for world peace, Chairman Khrushchev removed the missiles from Cuba at the behest of President Kennedy during that unforgettable autumn of 1962.

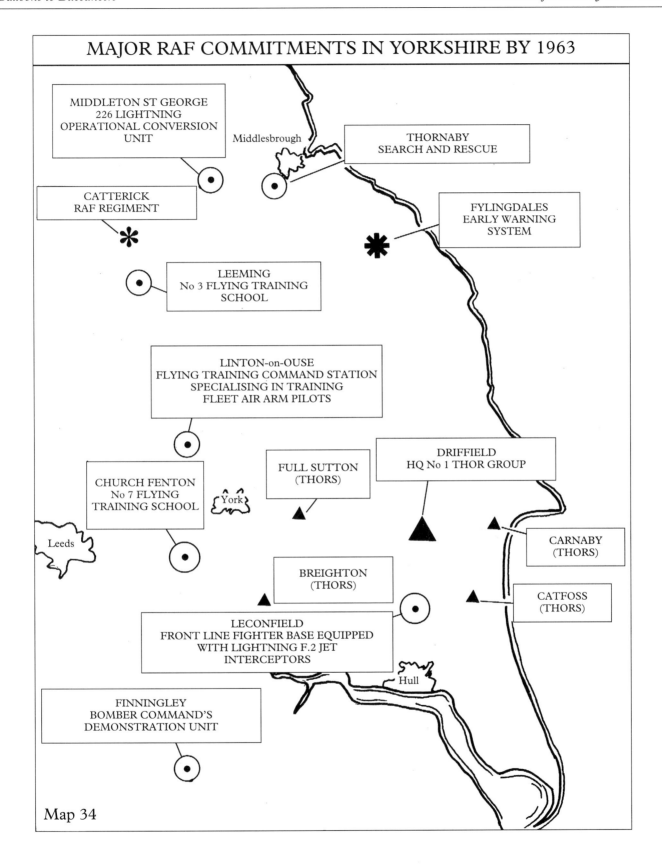

MAJOR RAF COMMITMENTS IN YORKSHIRE BY 1963

MIDDLETON ST GEORGE
226 LIGHTNING
OPERATIONAL CONVERSION
UNIT

Middlesbrough

THORNABY
SEARCH AND RESCUE

CATTERICK
RAF REGIMENT

FYLINGDALES
EARLY WARNING
SYSTEM

LEEMING
No 3 FLYING TRAINING
SCHOOL

LINTON-on-OUSE
FLYING TRAINING COMMAND STATION
SPECIALISING IN TRAINING
FLEET AIR ARM PILOTS

FULL SUTTON
(THORS)

DRIFFIELD
HQ No 1 THOR GROUP

CHURCH FENTON
No 7 FLYING
TRAINING SCHOOL

York

CARNABY
(THORS)

Leeds

BREIGHTON
(THORS)

CATFOSS
(THORS)

LECONFIELD
FRONT LINE FIGHTER BASE EQUIPPED
WITH LIGHTNING F.2 JET
INTERCEPTORS

Hull

FINNINGLEY
BOMBER COMMAND'S
DEMONSTRATION UNIT

Map 34

For the time being the sixty-five foot Thor missiles remained Britain's sole surface-to-surface ballistic missiles with a range of over 1700 miles. By 1963, when Prime Minister Macmillan agreed with President Kennedy to buy American Polaris submarine-launched ballistic missiles and to equip the V-bomber force with new 'stand-off' flying bombs, the Thor missile sites had become redundant. Thor was phased out of RAF service and the five base stations in Yorkshire closed down.

At the same time (17 September 1963), Fylingdales on the North York Moors filled the eastern gap that existed in NATO's Ballistic Missile Early Warning System (BMEWS) since 1958. One BMEWS site existed at Thule (Greenland); another at Clear (Alaska). Fylingdales provided the third and its three radar antennae were hidden inside the three highly visible 140ft-diameter spheres made of fibreglass and resin-impregnated paper. As any pre-emptive Soviet strike was assumed to be directed at the V-bomber bases, Fylingdales' task was to provide Bomber Command with a four-minute warning of the approach of enemy rocket missiles. This was sufficient time for the duty crew on 'Quick Reaction Alert' in each of the V-bomber squadrons to scramble and be in a position to deliver its Blue Steel stand-off H-bomb at low level on an enemy target. Bomber Command was now highly optimistic about its ability to penetrate Soviet air space. In fact, at the beginning of 1964 the new Chief of Bomber Command, Air Marshal Sir John Grandy, assured the British people that:

> "Penetration by aircraft of Bomber Command of areas covered by the most modern and sophisticated air-defence systems could not be successfully prevented."[11]

★ ★ ★

Yorkshire's last remaining RAF role was as a centre of excellence for the training of aircrew and the RAF Regiment. Driffield had been under Care and Maintenance during 1945-46 but then reopened as No 10 Air Navigation School of Flying Training Command. When this disbanded in 1948 Driffield was chosen to host the RAF's first jet training school using two-seat Meteor T7s though this role ended in 1955 when it became the base for the Venom night-fighters equipping Nos 219 and 3 Squadrons. During 1957-58 the Fighter Weapons School transferred from Leconfield to Driffield until it became the Headquarters of the Thor complex described above.

Finningley had been in Flying Training Command since 1947 and by 1960, after housing No 18 Squadron's Vickers Valiants, the base was chosen to be the central

Bomber Command Development Unit tasked with training Canberra, Valiant and Vulcan crews. Leeming's Javelin Mobile Conversion Unit has already been noted and once this closed the airfield turned to initial training with Bulldogs and Jet Provosts and also instructed on Jetstreams for familiarising pilots on multi-engined aircraft. Lindholme was of vital importance as the centre for Bomber Command's top Bombing School and the base eventually became the Radar Centre for training all V-bomber navigators. Immediately after the war Topcliffe had been selected for No 5 Air Navigation School but its training role with Wellington Xs and Ansons was interrupted by the need to convert crews four-engined aircraft so they could fly Hastings transports along the German air corridors during the Berlin Air Lift (1948-9). When its Transport Command role ceased in 1953 Coastal Command used the base for its long-range Lockheed Neptune patrol bombers flown by No 36 and No 203 Squadrons. Four of the Neptunes in 'Vanguard Flight' (1453 Flight) were specially modified as early-warning aircraft for Fighter Command and these regularly left Yorkshire for patrols as far as the northern coast of Norway. When the Neptune squadrons disbanded in 1957 No 1 Air Navigation School reformed at Topcliffe with Varsity, Valletta, Vampire and Marathon aircraft and operated here for five years before moving to Stradishall in 1962.

Constant overflying of the North Sea by Yorkshire-based squadrons, coupled with the ravages of sea and tide along the County's dangerous coastline, encouraged the survival of the Air Sea Rescue Flights. No 275 Squadron at Thornaby had flown Sycamore helicopters in the Search and Rescue role until just before the airfield closed in 1958. The Squadron then moved to Leconfield where it was renumbered 228 (in 1959) and then 202 (1964) when it was flying Whirlwind helicopters.

The closure of so many bases in Yorkshire had not diminished the importance one other branch of the Royal Air Force in the County. This was the RAF Regiment which in 1946 established its depot at Catterick. As with all other branches of the services the RAF Regiment had to reduce its numbers drastically from their wartime peak of over 90,000 men but by 1963 it was still able to fulfil its primary role of defending air bases in the UK and in Germany against enemy attack. Over the next twenty-five years, the Soviet and Eastern bloc Air Forces equipped with new aircraft and missiles and developed new modes of attack. To meet this bid for aerial supremacy the RAF introduced different types of warplanes, weaponry and tactics during the Seventies and Eighties. In meeting this challenge two aviation manufactures in Yorkshire made their own very special contribution.

Chapter Twenty Six

Design and Production of Military Aircraft in Yorkshire since 1945

While battle-weary Halifaxes were being reduced to scrap at Clifton, designers in Robert Blackburn's factory at Brough were hard at work on new aeronautical designs. Blackburn was anxious to preserve his close connection with naval aviation and was proud to see one of his Firebrand F4s take part in the 1946 Victory fly-past over London. In 1947 No 813 Squadron F4s joined HMS *Illustrious* and later served on *Implacable*. Slightly modifed TF5s took part in air races: G/Capt Flood achieved second place in the 1947 High Speed Handicap and in 1949 Peter G. Lawrence won the Air League Challenge Cup at Elmdon. Peter Lawrence later put up an impressive performance at Sherburn-in-Elmet with the one and only Firebrand TF 5A fitted with an injected Bristol Centaurus 57. G/Capt Flood, Peter Lawrence (ex-Royal Navy) and Dick Chandler (ex-RAF) were the test pilots for the Firebrand development and Dick Chandler remembers it as :

> "a good solid aeroplane, responsive to controls, docile with good low-speed characteristics and a normal approach speed. Couldn't see anything on the approach, of course, even though you sat up high behind that big radial engine. All right for someone brought up on Spitfires, though, no problem keeping straight."

The Navy issued No 827 Squadron with Firebrand TF 5s in 1951 and these flew in *Illustrious* and *Eagle* until they were replaced by Westland Wyverns during 1953-55.[(1)] Blackburn's efforts to persuade the Navy to adopt a successor to the Firebrand took the form of the Blackburn B-48, unofficially named the Firecrest. This was single-seat strike aircraft fitted with a Bristol Centaurus driving a five-bladed Rotol airscrew, an impressive looking aeroplane with a pronounced gull-wing reminiscent of the Corsair. Two of the three prototypes actually took to the air. The first was RT 651, hauled to Leconfield by road for its first flight on 1 April 1947. Despite its military potential, the Navy was not keen to adopt piston-engined aircraft for use on carriers[(2)] and the Firecrest failed to win any orders.

Blackburn's next project was therefore designed to be fitted with either the Rolls-Royce Griffon piston engine or the Armstrong Siddeley Double Mamba turbine. The Navy was phasing out torpedo-bombers such as the B-48 in favour of a carrier-borne anti-submarine force. It had therefore issued a specification in 1947 for such an aeroplane and the Blackburn design team produced the B-54/B-88 prototypes, the last of which (alternatively known as the Y.B.1) had the Double Mamba driving a six-bladed contra-rotating airscrew. It was an important aeroplane in that it was the first propeller-turbine design produced in Yorkshire. It allowed the pilot of the Y.B.1 to shut down one engine, feather an airscrew and increase his operational range - invaluable when his radar operators lowered their large radome and began hunting for the elusive schnorkel of an enemy submarine. However, the Y.B.1 had the same wing design as the ill-fated Firecrest and the pronounced anhedral on the inner wing led to to handling problems. Roy Boot, who had just joined the Brough design team from Airspeed, was convinced that a pilot on finals with full flap might easily induce a stall - a terrifying prospect when approaching a carrier in an Atlantic swell. Certainly, tests at Boscombe Down suggested that this would be the case and the Navy turned down the Y.B.1 in favour of the Fairey Gannet (1951) which went on to become the Navy's front-line carrier-borne anti-submarine aircraft between 1955 and 1960.

Blackburn B-46 Firebrand. This aircraft, EK 726, was converted to the T.F.Mk 5. *BAe Military Aircraft, Brough*

The failure of the B-48 and Y.B.1 projects were a great disappointment to Robert Blackburn who was now devoid of any contracts for the Royal Navy. Fortunately, he had other irons in the fire. He closed down his factories in Leeds and Sherburn and concentrated aircraft production at Brough where he had contracts for building Boulton Paul Balliol and Percival Prentice trainers for the RAF. He had also bought out General Aircraft Ltd in 1948 and gained control of all of this company's contracts and designs. Blackburn's purchase also sparked an influx of experienced aviation engineers from General Aircraft who came to work in Brough and made their homes in East Yorkshire. On 1 January 1949 Blackburn and General Aircraft Limited became the driving force in Yorkshire's design and manufacture of military aircraft.

General Aircraft's legacy included a government contract for a very large military freighter, a sign of the respect with which the government held this company. During the war General Aircraft had designed the Hotspur glider and then had gone on in 1942 to produce the remarkable GAL 49 Hamilcar, the largest wooden glider to be built during the Second World War. The Hamilcar carried jeeps or light tanks such as Tetrach and Locust, plus their crews, as part of 6th Airborne Division. They saw action on D-Day (1944) and in the Crossing of the Rhine (1945). After the war one Hamilcar squadron remained in being at Fairford. Thus it was possible, despite the wholsale scrapping of redundant military aircraft, for Blackburn to examine both the Hamilcar glider and its powered version, the Hamilcar 10 fitted with two Bristol Mercury engines. General Aircraft had already carried out feasibility studies for a large four-engined cargo carrying aircraft based on the Hamilcar and so was well-placed when the government issued its 1946 specification for just such an aeroplane. This was how the GAL 60 Universal Freighter Mk 1 was born and it was being built at Feltham when Blackburn bought the Company in 1948. The prototype was finished in 1949 but because the local airfield at Hanworth was too small for a test flight the Freighter was dismantled and taken by road to Brough. Blackburn had a spacious production line at in his North Sea Erection Hall but even this could barely accommodate the huge Freighter, forcing him to employ special framing to hold the aeroplane in a nose-up attitude so that fitters had enough head-room to service the giant slab-sided tail fins.

Bearing the serial WF 320, the 'Blackburn and General Aircraft Universal Freighter Mk 1' flew from Brough on 12 June 1950 with Capt.'Tim' Wood and D.G Brade at the controls. Stories about this first flight are legion and best remembered was Tim Wood's remark to his co-pilot during the landing: 'My side's down; how about yours?' In size it was overshadowed only by the Bristol Brabazon that had flown at Filton on 4 September 1949. During 1950 Capt Wood, with Ed Solman - whom we last met as a Flight Engineer aboard a Canadian Halifax - as Air Test Observer, took WF 320 to Farnborough, pausing en route at Cranfield due to appalling weather. WF 320's short field handling qualities, its amazing braking capacity on the eight main wheels plus its spectacular ability to taxi backwards thanks to its de Havilland reverse-pitch propellers made it one of the stars of the 1950 Society of British Aircraft Constructors' show.

The general acclaim encouraged Blackburn to construct the Universal Mk 2 during 1951-52 while WF 320 carried out a series of exhaustive tests in the skies above East Yorkshire. Ed Solman flew as Flight Test Observer with most of Blackburn's test pilots involved in the Freighter's development: Capt. Wood, F/Lt Parker, Capt. Dick Chandler and Lt. Lawrence, using (during 1950-51) the old wartime bases of Full Sutton and Carnaby. At the end of 1951 Blackburn was operating out of Holme-on-Spalding Moor and some of Ed Solman's log-book entries are interesting:

10.8 .50	Wood/Parker	Flap buffeting investigation.
13.8. 50	Wood/ Chandler	Flaps - Abortive. Weather duff.
11.10.50	Parker/Lawrence	Full Sutton. Vibration and tailplane investigation.
21.3. 51	Parker	Full Sutton. Climb to 20,000 feet.
2. 5. 51	Parker/Chandler	Full Sutton. Circuits and Bumps.
10.5. 51	Parker/Chandler	Carnaby. Handling Flight: door and ramps off.
26.8. 51	Parker/Chandler	Carnaby. Flap stuck down port side.
18.5. 52	Wood	Holme - Carnaby - Holme. Engine cut at take-off.
14.8. 52	Wood	Figheldean Drop Zone. Heavy Supply Dropping - 4000lb Pallet.
28.8. 52	Wood	Figheldean. Drop Zone. Very Heavy Supply Dropping -10,000lb Pallet.
1.10. 52	Wood	Touch down on Humber River bank - 3 tyres damaged.

During 1952 Blackburn received an order for twenty Freighters for RAF Transport Command. The type name now became the Blackburn Beverley C.1 and the first of these flew on 29 January 1955. The second Beverley XB260, designated the Blackburn Universal and awarded a civil registration G-AOEK, flew from Brough to Umm Said via Holme-on-Spalding Moor, Lyneham, Tunis and Beirut as part of a joint venture by Blackburn and Hunting-Clan Air Transport. Piloted in turn by G/Capt Hockey, DSO, DFC, Blackburn test pilot Dick Chandler and Capt Greensted MBE, XB260 then carried out a spectacular airlift of heavy oil drilling equipment on behalf of the Iraq Petroleum Company between Umm Said and Fahoud. In all, XB260 lifted 129 tons of equipment and its potential military value was underlined by Marshal of the Royal Air Force Sir John Slessor:

> "We have got to have a highly mobile reserve of land forces ready to move from A to B with their bulky equipment as quickly as possible, which in my belief is another way of saying 'Beverley'."

The Beverley went on to have a distinguished career in RAF service with five Squadrons: Nos. 47, 53, 30, 84 and 34. No 47 Squadron regularly flew its Beverleys from Abingdon to RAF Wildenrath and was quite accustomed to deliver dismantled Sycamore and Whirlwind helicopters to the British Army of the Rhine. The Beverley became the work-horse of No 1 Parachuting School and thousands of trainee parachutists made their jumps from either the tail boom or the freight bay. Beverleys flew the relief supplies to Vienna during the 1956 Hungarian Uprising and serviced British ground forces operating in the Yemen during 1957. During 1958-9 there were so many nationalist demonstrations and uprisings in 'hostile' areas 'east of Suez' that it was necessary to send 24 Brigade to brand-new barracks at Kawaha in Kenya and expand the RAF bases at Eastleigh, Khormaksar and Bahrein.

24 Brigade formed the spearhead of British reinforcements that would rush to any 'trouble spot' in Africa and the Middle East. Its most important responsibility was to secure British oil supplies in the Persian Gulf. As its most pressing need was for air support to carry out such operations it was the Beverley that was picked to do the job. Part of the Middle East saga actually began at Dishforth in Yorkshire during November 1959. Dishforth had been a Transport Command base since 1945, flying Liberators and Yorks and converting former bomber crews to fly Hastings on the Berlin Air Lift. From 1951 onwards 242 Operational Conversion Unit provided

Blackburn advertisement from *Flight*, 25 November 1955.

trained aircrew and No 30 Squadron based its Beverleys there in 1959. That November the squadron flew six Beverleys to Eastleigh while 84 Squadron operated with Beverleys at Khormaksar. Between them the two squadrons provided 24 Brigade with the vital air support it needed. The Beverleys, though slow, could transform the process of supplying ground forces faced with sudden attack in remote areas. They could fly into small poorly-surfaced strips with reinforcements, radios, generators, food, artillery, ammunition and medical supplies. When 24 Group needed to send troops to Aden the Beverleys could take them from Eastleigh; when British forces at Nizwa in Oman urgently needed a squadron of Ferret armoured cars it was the Beverleys that delivered them in a single airlift. If beleagured soldiers were located where no landing was possible the Beverley could supply them with supplies lashed on its stress dropping platform. Air Chief Marshal Sir David Lee was unstinting in his praise

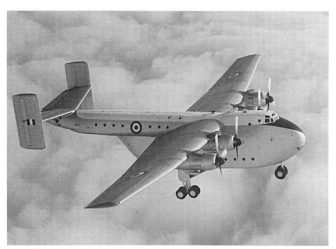

Blackburn XH123. This aircraft served with both No 30 and No 47 Squadrons
BAe Military Aircraft, Brough

The last Beverley, resting at Paull Airfield, then home of Hull Aero Club.

of this remarkable aeroplane produced by the Brough work-force:

> "Many were the indignities heaped upon the Beverley by virtue of its huge size and somewhat ungainly appearance: some alluded to it as the 'furniture van'; others, less polite, called it a 'loosely assembled collection of spare parts', but the fact

remains that it rapidly became indispensable in the Arabian Peninsula."[3]

With the appearance of the Lockheed C-130 Hercules and the RAF's decision to buy sixty-six of these aircraft as a replacement for the 'furniture van' the Beverley's days were numbered, a harsh fact that deeply saddened the Brough work-force who had delivered every one of the

Gathering of the Giants. Beverley aircraft destined for Royal Air Force Transport Command assembled on the apron at Brough. In the centre a diminutive Miles Messenger has just fired-up ready to go. It gives a good idea of the sheer scale of the Beverley.

The NA. 39 XK 486. This was one of the two 'non-folding' prototypes and is seen on test flight 1 August 1958.
BAe Military Aircraft, Brough

Buccaneer S.2B. The bulged bomb-bay may be clearly seen in this shot.
BAe Military Aircraft, Brough

forty-seven Beverleys precisely on schedule. All efforts to change the RAF's mind with the B-107 Military Freighter (a 1956 design to be fitted with four Rolls-Royce Tyne propeller turbines) failedas did the attempts to sell the Beverley to civilian operators. 'Tim' Wood's extra-ordinary heavy drop by parachute over Arras in the East Riding when he released a load of thirteen tons of steel plate from 1500ft entered the record books but won no further orders. Yet the Beverley had, for a heavy lift aircraft of its day, an unparalleled record of safety and reliability due to its rugged construction and exhaustive flight testing by its company pilots and engineers. It was able to take-off on three engines on one flight from Abingdon to Brough, no mean feat with a failed No 4 engine and the task of wrestling with asymmetrical thrust on such a huge aircraft. It survived 300 hours of endurance flying involving thirteen hour sorties simulating a wide range of flight profiles with crews flying in shifts - all without any major servicing requirements. Its performance in severe turbulence, and for a time the pilots actually hunted cu-nims to test this, was outstandingly reliable.

But there was no interest in civil aviation circles and the last flight by a Beverley was on 30 March 1974 when S/Ldr Peter Sedgwick landed XB259 on Paull Airfield, then the home of the Hull Aero Club. It had been purchased by North Country Breweries Ltd who offered it to Hull Aero Club for use as a possible club house in return for the aircraft's careful preservation. Hull Aero Club members maintained the Beverley in excellent condition but matters were taken out of their hands when

the lease on Paull Airfield expired. There was talk of selling the Beverley for scrap when Francis Daly, a Hull businessman, intervened, bought it and presented it to the Museum of Army Transport at Beverley where it is superbly preserved in a non-flying condition.

★　★　★

Though maintenance and the manufacture of spare parts employed Brough factory for several years after the last Beverley had been delivered (WZ889 in May 1958) there had been up to the summer of 1955 a sense of uncertainty about the future as Blackburn had apparently failed in his attempts to design and manufacture an acceptable aeroplane for the Royal Navy. Then Robert Blackburn made a guarded but exciting announcement during his annual report in August 1955.

> "I am very happy to be able to inform you that an important and challenging aircraft development contract, for which a number of other major firms in the industry competed, is being placed with your Company."

He was referring to an Admiralty specification issued in 1953 (Naval Staff Requirement NA.39) for an aeroplane capable of carrying Green Cheese (a guided anti-shipping bomb) or a nuclear weapon and penetrating enemy defences at low level but at high sub-sonic speed. These exacting specifications had engaged the attention of Blackburn's top design team headed by Barry P. Laight and the Blackburn B-103 was the result. The Admiralty was impressed and ordered twenty pre-production models. Blackburn promptly leased the old 4 Group airfield at Holme-on-Spalding Moor and brought its 6000 feet runway up to a high standard that included the installation of arrester gear. Sadly, Robert Blackburn was not destined to see his new aeroplane take to the skies for he died in 1955.

The prototype (XK486), always known to the work-force as NA.39, rolled off the production line in February 1958 and ran up its engines on the apron at Brough. But its test flight would not be held in Yorkshire as Holme-on-Spalding was thought to be inadequate for a such an advanced and expensive aeroplane. So XK486 was dismantled and taken by road to RAE Bedford.

Derek Whitehead's first taxi-run at Bedford was disastrous. The brakes caught fire and a high presssure tyre burst causing damage to the starboard wing. Repairs were rushed through and the first flight took place on schedule (30 April 1958). Whitehead tried the airbrakes for the first time but omitted to tell the pilot of the chase Meteor that he would do this and the efficiency of the Blackburn design was shown when the Meteor overshot at high speed. XK486 stole the show at the Farnborough Display in September as it was the only new aeroplane to be shown. For the next two years XK486 took part in numerous aerodynamic tests and was finally lost in a crash at Little Weighton on 5 October 1960. Both 'Sailor' Parker and his observer managed to eject.

The second aircraft was XK487 and for its first flight (26 August 1958) it was towed from Brough to Holme-on-Spalding Moor, a distance of eighteen miles, and now the centre of the Buccaneer high speed and flight profile trials.[4] Carrier trials were completed by January 1960 and NA.39 at last received its official name: Buccaneer S.1. The Navy's first operational squadron to receive Blackburn Buccaneers was No 801 and they flew from *Ark Royal* in February 1963 before transferring to *Victorious*. The second Buccaneer squadron was No 809 but this remained shore-based at Lossiemouth and eventually reformed as No 736 Squadron responsible for the Buccaneer Operational Training School.

Not all the Navy pilots, used to the Rolls-Royce Avon turbojets fitted to the new Sea Vixens and Scimitars, were impressed. Some suspected that the Buccaneer was a trifle underpowered for its operational task for the first engines fitted to the production Mk 1 aircraft were de Havilland Gyron Junior turbo-jets that developed far less thrust than the twin Avons. This was remedied in the Buccaneer S. Mk 2, fitted with twin Rolls-Royce Speys. A re-engined Mk 1 joined two Mk 2s on board the carrier USS *Lexington* in 1965 and XN974, one of the Mk 2s, flew

home from Goose Bay, Labrador, to its base at Lossiemouth - the first time a Fleet Air Arm aeroplane had made a non-stop crossing of the North Atlantic. [5]

Blackburns made several attempts to interest the Germans in the Buccaneer. In 1961 two Luftwaffe Noratlas freighters carrying ground crews from Holme flew to Fürstenfeldbruck in company with a demonstration Buccaneer; and in April-May 1962 another Buccaneer took part in the Hannover Air Show. No German orders resulted but on 11 September 1962 the South African government ordered sixteen Buccaneers. These Buccaneer S. Mk 50s were not fitted with folding wings as the South Africans wanted land-based aeroplanes. The first S.50s flew at Holme-on-Spalding-Moor in January 1965 and because the South Africans

The all-yellow Hunting H. 126 Jet Flap aeroplane being tested by a Brough research team at NASA's wind tunnel at Ames near San Francisco, 1969.   *BAe, Brough*

Other manufacturers called on Brough's experience with the Buccaneer to test new ideas related to Blackburn's pioneer work (in conjunction with Plannair Ltd) in blowing air tapped from the engine manifolds surrounding the original de Havilland Gyron Junior engines. Air blown through slits or fishtails over the wings (ailerons and flaps) resulted in much better lift and greater stability at low level/low speed – enormous advantages for carrier-based aircraft.

One example was the Hunting Jet Flap experimental aeroplane that first flew at Bedford on 26 March 1963. It had a conventional aerofoil wing but had blown flaps and ailerons using the hot engine gases emitted **directly** from the Bristol Siddeley Orpheus jet pipes. This aeroplane was eventually taken to the USA to undergo testing - under the supervision of a contracted team of Brough engineers - at America's National Aeronautics and Space Administration.

wanted extra boost for take-off this version of the Buccaneer had twin rocket motors located behind the air brakes to provide the extra thrust.[6] Rocket-assisted take-off trials were carried out on the American-built runway at Elvington.

By that time there was considerable political opposition in Britain to the sale of arms to the South Africa. Accordingly, the British Labour government permitted the export of the first sixteen aeroplanes but refused to sell South Africa any more. South African Air Force crews arrived at Lossiemouth, converted to the Buccaneer S.50 and the first eight flew to South African October 1965. One crashed south of the Canary Islands but its crew was saved. The remaining eight S.50s were towed from Holme to Brough, cocooned in salt-resisting plastic, and then towed to Hull Docks for shipping to South Africa during 1966. Here the S.50s were flown by No 24 Squadron SAAF crews from their base at Waterkloof, officially in the role of naval strike/interdiction aircraft.

The Fleet Air Arm received its S.2 Buccaneers in 1965 and No 801 Squadron took these aboard *Victorious* for a Far East tour 1965-67. While they were away Buccaneer S.2s equipped No 809 Squadron *(Hermes)* and No 800 Squadron *(Eagle)*; and a mixture of S.1s and S.2s were used by No. 736 Squadron, the new Buccaneer training squadron, at Lossiemouth. Most of their deck-landing practice sorties were flown from *Ark Royal*. Training was thoroughly enlived by the *Torrey Canyon* saga during March 1967. This giant tanker had grounded on rocks off Land's End and was steadily polluting the sea and Cornwall's beaches with its crude oil slick. Buccaneers flew down from Lossiemouth to Brawdy and from here carried out bomb runs on the *Torrey Canyon*. Some three months later No 803 Squadron received its Buccaneer S.2s and by the end of 1968 Brough had delivered eighty-four aircraft to the Fleet Air Arm, every one of them precisely on schedule.

Then came another defence review in which the Labour government led by Harold Wilson decided to scrap the plans inherited from the Conservatives to build 'super carriers' in the style of the American CVA-01 carriers (1966). Wilson's Defence Minister, Denis Healey, also cancelled the RAF's TSR-2 project and decreed that the Royal Navy should abandon its large aircraft carriers by the end of 1971, scrapping *Victorious* in 1967. Three years later Wilson lost the 1970 General Election but the new Heath government showed no inclination to restore a 'big carrier' programme. Large, expensive carriers were ideal targets for money-conscious Defence Ministers even though *Ark Royal* came in useful during 1972 when she

Refurbished Phantom XT 899 on the apron at Brough
BAe Military Aircraft, Brough

took her Buccaneers to deal with a new trouble spot in Central America. Guatemalans had ambitions to take over British Honduras (Belize) and two Buccaneers flew low over Belize City to 'show the flag'. The exercise demonstrated the value of the presence of a large carrier equipped with aeroplanes of the calibre of the Buccaneer, a view the Americans have justifiably sustained during their operations in the Gulf (1990-91) and off Somalia (1992-3).

But British governments preferred not to see long-term value in either a long-range strike force or a Heavy Lift Capacity for the British Army. The still-born Brough idea for a Blackburn turbo-prop pressurised replacement for the Beverley had been taken over by Shorts. Their design team transformed this into the Shorts Belfast, the largest aircraft to serve in the RAF and the biggest to be equipped with a fully automatic landing system. Belfasts were flown by No 53 Squadron which was unwisely disbanded in 1976 as part of the second round of Labour defence cuts. Meanwhile, *Hermes* converted to a Commando carrier and *Ark Royal* and *Eagle* went to the scrapyard in 1978. Now Britain had no carrier fleet capable of launching long-range strike aircraft and no Heavy Lift capacity for the rapid movement of quick-reaction ground forces. Such deficiences were to be highlighted in the 1982 Falkands War when Britain had to cobble together a Task Force composed of untried lightweight warships, merchant marine freighters and the *Canberra* in order to transport troops and the indispensable Harriers to the South Atlantic.

These decisions eventually worked to the advantage of the Brough work-force (Blackburns had become part of the Hawker-Siddeley Group in 1959) in that the anticipated American F-111 purchase for the RAF was also cancelled, leading to an order for twenty-six new Buccaneers (July 1968). The loss of the big carriers meant that sixty-two Royal Navy Buccaneers would also require modification at Brough for service with the RAF. One optimistic research and design project, that the RAF would now accept a supersonic Buccaneer (the P.150 Project) to replace the lost TSR-2s and F-111Ks, did not materialise. It would have been fitted with reheated Spey 25R engines (as was the Phantom), thin non-folding wings, a longer fuselage and a new tail unit. With a speed in excess of Mach 1.8 it would have provided the RAF with an outstanding strike/interdiction fighter by 1975.

It was not to be. RAF crews began converting to the subsonic Buccaneer first with 736 Squadron at Lossiemouth and then with the RAF's Buccaneer conversion unit (237 OCU) based at Honington. In October 1969 the RAF Buccaneers took up their role as maritime strike aircraft with 12 Squadron; and within a year Buccaneers had become front-line low-level strike aircraft serving with 15 Squadron at Laarbruch (RAF Germany). No 15 Squadron was the nucleus of a new Buccaneer Wing, created from the pool of ex-Navy S.2s and from the production aircraft turned out from Brough. The RAF's last Buccaneers arrived in 1977 and these aircraft served in Germany until the advent of the Tornado in 1983. Some were deployed to Cyprus when Britain tried to solve the problems of the Lebanon in 1983 but roof-top buzzes Belize-style made little or no impression on Beirut and so the Buccaneers were brought home.

Test-flying the Buccaneers went on at Holme-on-Spalding-Moor until 1983 by which time Hawker-Siddeley was part of British Aerospace (briefly nationalised between 1977 and 1981). The last Buccaneer to lift off from an airfield that had seen thousands of Halifax departures was XV350 (7 December 1983) and the carefully maintained runway was then ripped to pieces by the bull-dozers and sold off as an industrial site.[7] Fortunately, Brough had received contracts beginning in 1968 to service and test McDonnell Phantoms (the RAF had 170 of these on its strength) in its Operations Hangar adjacent to the dispersal apron. It is important not to underestimate Brough's role in updating the Phantoms. In the words of Capt Ken Hickson RN, in charge of the support services for the Navy's Phantoms, Brough was to enjoy the status of a 'sister design firm':

PC-9 for the Royal Saudi Air Force on test over the East Riding.
BAe Military Aircraft, Brough

"To provide the same level of support in all aspects after delivery of Phantoms to the United Kingdom as would have been provided if the aircraft had been designed and built a Brough."[8]

Up to 1990 over one thousand Phantom modifications had been carried out at Brough representing, as Roy Boot has commented, "good business for Brough" and all the aeroplanes had to be shipped in and out by road now that high speed flying tests centred on Scampton. Fortunately, the Humber Bridge provided a relatively quick route between Brough and Scampton and the aircraft were towed back and forth as required, a process that continued until the Phantoms were finally replaced by Tornadoes in RAF service.[9] Brough airfield was still used for military test flying and runway 30/12 was expensively resurfaced not just to benefit the the Company's Jetstream and Seneca and the Cessnas belonging to the Police Flying Club and Hull Aero Club but also the PC-9s manufactured by the Swiss Pilatus Company. The RAF expressed great interest in the PC-9 as a suitable replacement for the Jet Provost and British Aerospace tendered to supply 130 of these aeroplanes. The Ministry of Defence then invited British Aerospace and Shorts, who offered a derivative of the Embraer EMB-312 Tucano, to restructure their tenders in the form of their 'best and final offers'. Then on 13 March 1985 the Ministry of Defence required the two companies to revise their prices downward and imposed a curious deadline: 14 March 1985. Shorts' response was an instantaneous £125 million. British Aerospace took five days longer but wanted less: £120 million. Despite a lower price from BAe Michael Heseltine awarded the contract to Shorts of Belfast, a decision presumably prompted by political considerations.

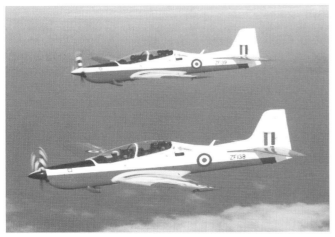

Shorts Tucano trainers in RAF colours.

Shorts of Belfast

Sea Harrier FRS51 in service with No 300 (White Tiger) Squadron of the Indian Navy. These export Harriers fly from *INS Vikrant* (formerly *HMS Majestic*) and *INS Viraat* (formerly *HMS Hermes*).

BAe Military Aircraft, Kingston

T45 Goshawks.

BAe Military Aircraft Division, Warton

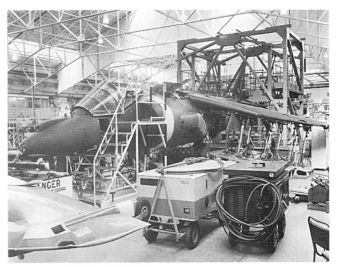

Harrier production line.

BAe Military Aircraft, Dunsfold

Harrier ski jump.

BAe Military Aircraft, Kingston

Harrier update - lower aircraft is the GR5.

BAe Military Aircraft, Dunsfold

Hawk Mk 63 Abu Dhabi Air Force.
BAe Military Aircraft Division, Warton

Hawk 200.
BAe Military Aircraft Division, Warton

Hawk 100.   *BAe Military Aircraft Division, Warton*

Brough's partnership with Pilatus did not end there and for six years the work-force carried out development work on the PC-9 for the Royal Saudi Air Force. Swiss law did not permit the addition of military stores to their exports so this work, together with numerous modifications, went on at Brough - and the only hiccough concerned the pilots' air conditioning of this otherwise superb training aeroplane. The Pilatus project ended in 1991 when the skies of Yorkshire began to echo to the whistle of Tucanos rather than PC-9s as the new trainers joined the last of the Jet Provosts at Church Fenton.[10] It also spelt the doom of British Aerospace Flight Operations at Brough because from 31 December 1992 these too came to an end. The airfield was still manned for the arrival and departure of other aircraft; as were the safety and fire services on an 'as required' basis. But the manufacture and testing of BAe aeroplanes had gradually come to an end - apart from the superbly restored Fairey Swordfish Mk II (Blackfish W5856) that test-flew on 12 May 1993. There was also a shadow cast on the future location of the lone Blackburn B-2 whose survival had owed so much to the skill of generations of Brough experts.

Not all of Brough's design and production work for military aviation emerged as complete aeroplanes though Harrier wings and fuselages were mated on the production line during the late Seventies. Other important sub-contracts maintained some contact with Blackburn's naval tradition: one was for the Nimrod's wingtip pods; and another for the Harrier variants. The latter has meant that Yorkshire has had a role in the manufacture of wings and fuselages for this unique VSTOL aircraft now serving with the RAF, the Royal Navy, the US Marine Corps and the Spanish Navy. It is generally accepted that the presence of Navy and RAF Harriers in the Falklands was indispensable to victory in 1982 and it is pleasant to agree with Brough's own Company historian that:

". . . it is fair to say that the factory again is playing a major part in supplying the Royal

Harriers in action: the South Atlantic 1982.

BAe Aircraft Group, Kingston-upon Thames

A beautiful flying shot of Sea Harrier MLU XZ497. This is the third FRS 2, showing fuselage plug behind the nozzles, just in front of air brake.   *BAe Military Aircraft Division, Dunsfold Aerodrome*

Navy with its latest aircraft . . . work is under way in the Technical Department, supporting Kingston, on a proposed mid-life update for Sea Harrier."[11]

More recently, Brough has concentrated on the remarkable Hawk 60, 100 and 200 series now largely built at the former Blackburn factory, though the final assembly and testing are carried out at British Aerospace (BAe) Warton. The Hawk 60 is a two seat light trainer/attack aircraft ordered by Zimbabwe, Dubai, Kuwait, Abu Dhabi, Saudi Arabia and Switzerland. Rather more rugged is the Hawk 100 which possesses, in the words of BAe's John Weston (Managing Director of BAe Military Aircraft):

> "formidable combat capability, mainly in the ground attack role. It is an advanced jet trainer, but it packs a formidable punch. We know of no other family of aircraft which can span such a range of roles as this unique British product."

The Hawk 200 attracted nations such as Malaysia, Oman and Abu Dhabi who require a light air superiority fighter, cheap to buy and easy to maintain.

> "It is uniquely suited to the export market where small fleets of light but highly potent aircraft are the requirement."

This is why John Weston regarded the Hawk as "an amazingly successful aircraft" originally developed to satisfy an RAF demand for 175 trainers but which has now been sold to thirteen countries around the world. The

first of approximately three hundred examples of the T-45A Goshawk have gone to the US Navy and the production run is expected to last until 1999. BAe produce the Goshawk in collaboration with McDonnell Douglas and the final assembly and testing is carried out in the United States. Another 350 Goshawks will be exported to those nations mentioned above and these orders will generate over £5 billion of exports and appear to guarantee employment in the Brough factory now organised as British Aerospace Defence Ltd, Military Aircraft Division.

★ ★ ★

One other military manufacturer in Yorkshire survived into the 1990s: Slingsby Aviation of Kirkbymoorside. After 1945 the firm had produced T-21 Sedbergh and T-31 Cadet gliders purchased by the RAF to give ATC cadets their introduction to air experience. High performance gliders such as the Swallow, Skylark and Dart went into production and the beautiful Type 34 Sky sailplane won the 1952 World Championships. An unusual run of replica aeroplanes included a Sopwith Camel and a flight of SE-5As for filmcom-panies. Fred Slingsby retired in 1964 but from the 1960s onwards his company manufactured the Type 21B Sedberghs and the Type 31B Cadet TX Mk 3s plus Venture powered gliders for both the RAF and ATC. Its most recent project was to design and develop a military trainer of note.

Civil-registered T67 Firefly G-SFTZ coyly sheltered from the elements at Compton Abbas in 1993.

This was the T67M Firefly two seat primary trainer offering side-by-side seating. Slingsby adapted the design of the wooden Fournier RF.6B and the first T67 flew with a wooden fuselage in May 1981. Slingsby then redesigned the airframe in GRP (glass reinforced plastic) and the military version T67-M200 first flew on 16 May 1985. It was not just the first GRP fully aerobatic aeroplane to fly in Yorkshire - it was the first in the world. An outstanding design with airframe safety one of its main selling points, it is described as having a 'safe life' of 18000 hours, far more than most military trainers. However, it did not at first manage to dislodge the RAF's Bulldogs. Overseas sales were relatively slow though exports have gone, for example, to Japan, New Zealand, Holland and Norway. Orders slipped badly during 1990 but the production line was rescued by a Canadian bid for twelve Fireflies during 1991.

At the same time David Holt, Slingsby Aviation's Managing Director, was in negotiation with Northrop Worldwide Air Services Inc. for the manufacture of up to 113 T67-260M training aircraft for the USAF's Enhanced Flight Screener programme. It would be known as the T-3A and the aeroplane - much admired for its spin entry and recovery qualities - would replace the Cessna T-41 Mescalero which did not have inverted flight capabilities. All parts were to be manufactured in Kirkbymoorside, shipped to the USA and assembled by Northrop Worldwide Services Inc at its Hondo plant in Texas. The Firefly's importance to American military pilot training can be shown by the deployment of the aircraft: fifty-seven Fireflies to be based at Air Training Command, Hondo, Texas; fifty-six Fireflies to equip the Air Force Academy in Colorado Springs. Such an order, combined with Slingsby's other civil aviation projects[12], underpinned both the future of the factory and the reputation of Yorkshire as a centre of excellence in military design and production. It was certainly enough to impress other air forces. The RAF and Canadian Air Force both decided to use Slingsby Fireflies flown by civilians to train their pilots up to basic Private Pilot Licence standard. During 1993 Hunting used twenty civil-registered Firefly 2s to teach RAF and Fleet Air Arm aircrew to fly. The base from which they operated was RAF Topcliffe, Yorkshire.

Chapter Twenty Seven

Aspects of Civil and General Aviation since 1945

Robert Blackburn recalled the difficulties facing civil aviation after the First World War and was determined to make his aerial ventures after 1945 pay their way. He had already formed the North Sea Air Transport Company (28 August 1944), his post-war equivalent of the old North Sea Aerial and Transport Company and this began its charter flights in 1946 with four aircraft, an Auster, a Messenger, a de Havilland Rapide and a Percival Proctor. Significantly, there were no Blackburn designs present though the company monitored the performance of these four aeroplanes very closely in order to profit from the experience of the first charter flights and build this experience into brand new designs for the civil aviation market. Blackburn was delighted by the profits made by these aircraft - though he lost the Proctor in Switzerland after leasing it to another charter company. He replaced it with two more Rapides and then in 1947 bought a Miles Aerovan that sadly crashed after taking off from Croydon.

Between 1947 and 1950 Blackburn ran a very successful civil aviation operation and the North Sea Air Transport Company eventually expanded into the fast short-haul market with two Lockheed 12A/14H transports, another Aerovan and a pair of modified Proctor Vs. These aircraft and in particular the two Lockheeds meant higher maintenance costs and profits from the North Sea Air Transport Company declined in 1950-51. Most of the aircraft were sold though one Rapide was kept at Brough to serve as a communications aircraft after 1958. In 1958 the company bought the first post-war civil aviation design - a de Havilland Dove. This operated from Brough for the next nine years before being replaced by a Dove 8A G-ARBE flown by Dick Chandler, the company's executive pilot. This survived into the 1980s until replaced by the Jetstream and Seneca but was still to be seen flying from Compton Abbas in 1991.

Blackburn/ Hawker Siddeley enjoyed a unique position in Yorkshire as its North Sea Air Transport operations were to some extent cushioned by its manufacturing contracts. This was not the case for other entrepreneurs in Yorkshire after the Second World War where their sole advantage lay in the rapid closure of most of Yorkshire's RAF bases which left the rest of the County with a superfluity of runways and a chance to exploit them for long-overdue civil aviation projects. There was talk of Catfoss as a Municipal Airport for Hull, of flying boat services on the Humber and a regional airport to serve Leeds and Bradford at Yeadon. Initially the new Labour Ministry of Civil Aviation appeared enthusiastic, suggesting that forty-three airfields in the UK might be taken over by the Ministry to meet the needs of airline passengers and freight cargo operators. Official optimism soon evaporated amidst the harsh realities of post-war austerity and in Yorkshire Yeadon was the solitary civil airfield open in 1947. RAF aircraft were still in residence and the modest civil presence took the form of the Lancashire Aircraft Corporation's de Havilland Rapides and Airspeed Consuls flying passengers to the Isle of Man. Once the Berlin Airlift began in 1948 their main business

G-ARBE at the Paris Show.

G-ARBE at Compton Abbas 1991.

turned to the servicing and modification of tired transport aircraft flying down the corridors to the former German capital. Apart from this, civil aviation had made little impact upon post-war Yorkshire and the hopes aroused in 1950 by the prospect of passengers leaving Brough's slipway to board a Hythe flying-boat for Belfast Lough or Southampton Water proved misplaced.

When the Ministry decided to abandon Yeadon in 1953 civil aviation seemed set to decline. Confidence returned after the end of the Korean War (1953) and Yeadon Aviation Ltd took charge of the airfield and encouraged private pilots to join its flying club. BKS Aviation Ltd began offering scheduled services from Yeadon to Belfast, Jersey, Ostend and Düsseldorff during 1955-6 and this attracted the presence of HM Customs, winning limited recognition for Yeadon as a small but growing international airport. Unfortunately, BKS operated too many scheduled flights and began losing money; even its Yeadon-London service provided by rather uncomfortable Dakotas failed to show a profit. Clearly, if the the airfield were to succeed it required better aeroplanes, better control and runway facilities, modern navigational aids and a great deal of investment.

This was the challenge that faced the Leeds and Bradford Airport Committee when it took over in 1959, six years after the Ministry had abandoned the site. Its most urgent need was to build a longer runway and the Committee engaged in a lengthy battle with the Planning Officers of West Riding County Council until a public enquiry decided in its favour. As a result, Leeds Bradford Airport was able to bring its new 5,400 ft runway into use during 1965. Meanwhile, BKS had at last made its new London service pay, Starways was one of the first companies to operate the new Vickers Viscount turbo-prop aircraft and Aer Lingus introduced a Dublin service to begin its long association with Leeds Bradford. Yorkshire Light Aircraft was now the airport's major servicing agent and Northair Aviation provided a Cessna taxi service from Yeadon. However, ever changing aircraft design and passengers' preferences meant that the 5,400 feet runway was not ideal for regular schedule flights by the new generation of wide-bodied passenger jets. Although unsympathetic planners denied Leeds Bradford its extra 2000 feet of runway, Aer Lingus operated Boeing 737s and BAC 1-11s in the Seventies while Air Anglia was flying F27 Fokker Friendships from Leeds Bradford in 1978. One other major draw-back with which Leeds Bradford had to contend has been the ban on night flying that persisted until its reversal on 19 January 1994 and hampered the

Humber Airways Islander G-AXRN.

development of profitable airlines such as the newly-established Yorkshire European Airways operating 18-seat quiet turbo-prop Bandeirantes. The problems experienced by Leeds Bradford faced every Yorkshire entrepreneur hoping to develop some aspect of civil aviation in the Sixties and the Seventies. Autair, for example, managed to persuade Hawker Siddeley to let them to operate scheduled pasenger flights to Luton from Brough in 1966. Within four years Capper Pass won planning permission to build a 600 ft high chimney on the approach to runway 30 and as this represented a very real danger to regular services Autair ended its services from Brough.

Even more galling were the difficulties faced by Humber Airways Ltd which made a brave effort to diversify air operations from its Yorkshire base. The company had originated in Lincolnshire as Humber Air Link operating a Piper Aztec out of Wickenby. Its role was to provide a fast connection between the then prosperous fishing community of Grimsby and London and it offered passengers flights between Wickenby and London plus the luxury of a fast radio-controlled Jaguar car at each end of the journey. Ellerman Wilson Line bought Humber Air Link, renamed it Humber Airways Ltd, and began passenger and charter flights with two Aztecs out of Brough and Kirmington (a wartime Lancaster base in Lincolnshire). Full of optimism, it then bought two Britten-Norman Islanders but efforts to expand the service into a 'triangular route' to Hawarden (following the departure of Cambrian Airways) failed and, before long, when the Capper Pass chimney reached a height of 200 ft, the passenger licence was finally revoked at Brough.

Humber Airways continued with its charter flights and then moved to Leconfield though as Bob Fewlass, one of its directors, observed:

"... it was never viable because of the distance from Hull and the psychological aspect of 'going further away' before setting out for London."[1]

Humber Airways now turned its attention to North Sea oil operations with plans to secure commercial helicopter licences[2], air cargo companies in Heath Row and Paisley and to establish charter links with Aberdeen, the Shetlands and Stavanger. Bob Fewlass decided to "test the temperature of the water" and bought four 1944-vintage Dakotas from Macedonian Airways at Southend-on-Sea to see if the routes were viable with older aeroplanes before buying new aircraft. At that moment, 3 January 1975, Ellerman Wilson decided to pull out of the aviation business entirely.

"The Dakotas never got off the ground. The 'Humberside Airways Limited' and the HAL logo were only partly painted when the axe struck. As a result they were never christened and the aircraft were disposed of during early 1975."[3]

Such was the end of civil aviation in the East Riding - apart from the manufacturing work carried out at Brough for Trident cockpits and forward fuselages plus component orders for the BAe 146 short haul jet air-liner and about 25% of the wings of the A300 Airbus.[4] In the West Riding, Leeds Bradford Airport flourished and civil aviation celebrated its Diamond Jubilee in 1991 on the old Yeadon site. By then Sabena was flying to Brussels, Loganair to Glasgow, Jersey European to Belfast and the Channel Islands, while British Midlands linked Yorkshire with Heathrow by Douglas DC-9 as well as by Boeing 737. Air UK was also offering scheduled flights and Aer Lingus bought the Saab 340B as a replacement for the Shorts 360 on its Dublin route. Leeds Bradford had undoubtedly proved itself as the County's international airport.

Local boundary changes dating from 1974 - unpopular with many residents in Yorkshire - had transferred the East Riding of Yorkshire and part of North Lincolnshire to a new authority called Humberside. South of the River Humber the authority selected the old Lancaster base at Kirmington where Humber Airways had built its hangars. Here it constructed a well-equipped runway that was extended in the late 1980s to accommodate passenger jets for the tourist industry. Though it is not located within the post-1974 boundaries of Yorkshire, Humberside Airport, together with Manchester Airport, competes with Leeds Bradford to meet regional demand for national and international passenger and air freight.

Both Leeds Bradford and Humberside Airports house aero clubs that may use runways specifically licensed by the Civil Aviation Authority (CAA) for use by pilots under training. Private pilot training is no longer supported by any form of government grant: the old subsidy on aviation fuel for private pilots was removed in 1955 while the cost of training and the charges made by the CAA for the compulsory examinations, medicals and the issue of licences has escalated. Despite the financial hurdles, the demand for private pilot qualifications was never higher than in the post-war years and flying clubs mushroomed in Yorkshire.

Blackburn re-opened his Flying Club in 1946, housed it in the most splendid buildings on the airfield and offered his technicians the chance to learn to fly on RAF-surplus Tiger Moths, Austers, a Swallow and the ast of the B-2s. Blackburn held the enlightened view that those who manufactured aeroplanes should also be able to fly them. After an optimistic start, factory support for flying training ended in 1950. All the surviving clubs in Yorkshire now operate on a sociable but strictly commercial basis.

The Yorkshire Aeroplane Club trains on Cessnas and PA-28s at Leeds Bradford where Northern Helicopters (Leeds) Ltd provides tuition on Robinson R-22s and Jetrangers. Hull Aero Club's Cessnas have tended to migrate around the East Riding rather more than most and, having left Brough, can now be found at Linley Hill, near Leven.

Cessna 150 Aerobat G-AZID, then operated by Hull Aero Club, over the Humber in 1984.

G-TAFF at Breighton.

Leeds-Bradford housed G-RAND Aviation's Grumman Traveller and Knight Air Flying School which in addition to its range of Cessnas and a Cherokee sports a beautiful Beech Duchess twin.

The old 4 Group Base at Breighton became the headquarters of Deltaflight Ltd with its Cheetah and a fairly rare aerobatic Bellanca Decathlon; while the Real Aeroplane Club cossets vintage aircraft in its Breighton hangars, encourages aerobatic flying and, at the end of 1991, housed G-TAFF, the lovely yellow Bucker Jungmann that flew from Australia to the UK.

Aerobatic flying is the speciality of Firefly Aerial Promotions Aerobatic School at Kirkbymoorside Aerodrome. This School offers training in the civilian version of the Firefly T67M-160 and 200 versions and tempts the pilot who yearns for 'Top Gun' aerial combat training. Sherburn Aero Club at Sherburn-in-Elmet Aerodrome also sports a Slingsby T67M. Its Aztec and four Piper Cadets add spice of variety to the usual Cessnas; as do the Hughes 300, R-22s and JetRanger helicopters belonging to Heliyorks Flight Training. Doncaster Airport, now closed, had the resident Yorkshire Helicopter Centre with its R-22s and a Jetranger; and Doncaster Aero Club offered training on a Seneca as well as its Cessnas. Yorkshire Helicopter Centre flies its JetRangers and R-22s from Doncaster Heliport and Leeds-Bradford.

Sandtoft Air Services (1985) Ltd flies from Sandtoft Aerodrome which during 1944-45 was a satellite for

Two Heliyorks R-22s over Castle Howard. Heliyorks is professionally committed to the training of rotary wing pilots.

Heliyorks

Lindholme's 1667 Heavy Conversion Unit. It was from here that war-weary Halifaxes and Lancasters did their circuits and bumps and cross-country flights. Less dramatic are Sandtoft Air Services' Cessnas, Senecas and the Piper Tomahawk, Warrior and Archer trainers operated by this flourishing club; and the six Cessna 152s and the solitary 172 flying with The Aviators' Centre there in 1993. Bagby Aero Club near Thirsk provided tailwheel conversions on its Super Cub.

By 1993 - one hundred and forty years after the 'new flyer' had been launched at Brompton Dale - there were eight flying clubs in Yorkshire offering fixed wing flight training and five clubs for trainee helicopter pilots. Humberside Airport's contribution was equally impressive: four clubs provided private pilot training up to instrument rating and apart from the usual Cessna 150s and 172s their aeroplanes included Cessna 310s, a Cessna 172RG, Cherokee 140s and a Cherokee 6, an Archer, a Tiger and a Seminole.

As was appropriate for a County that produced the genius of Sir George Cayley and Fred Slingsby, gliding

The Real Aeroplane Club, Breighton, with some of its 'goodies' on display, including the superbly restored Miles Magister, at the 1993 Air Show.

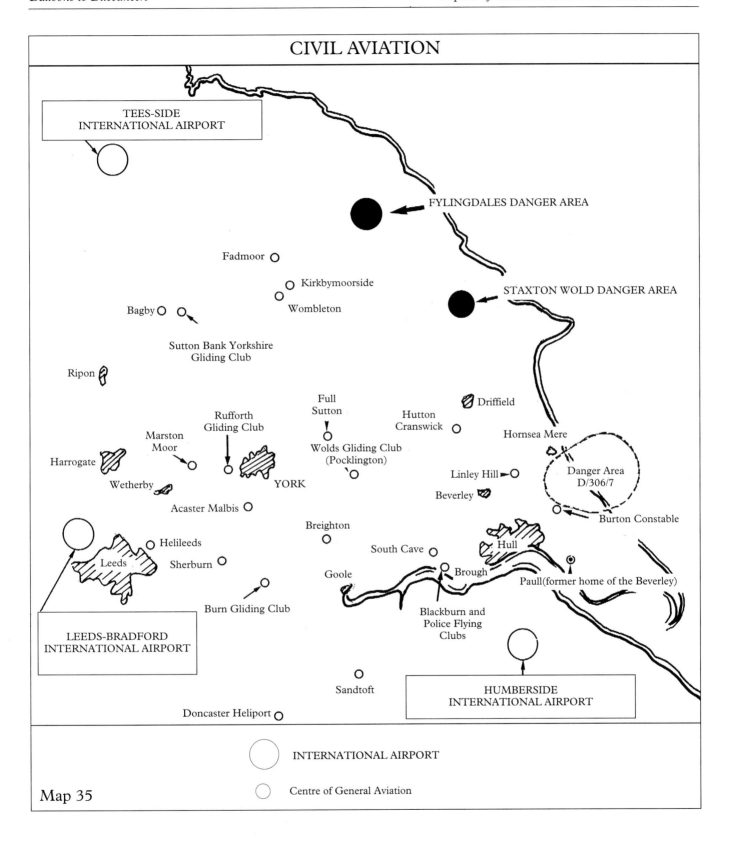

CIVIL AVIATION

TEES-SIDE
INTERNATIONAL AIRPORT

FYLINGDALES DANGER AREA

STAXTON WOLD DANGER AREA

Fadmoor

Kirkbymoorside

Wombleton

Bagby

Sutton Bank Yorkshire
Gliding Club

Ripon

Full
Sutton

Driffield

Rufforth
Gliding Club

Hutton
Cranswick

Hornsea Mere

Marston
Moor

Wolds Gliding Club
(Pocklington)

Danger Area
D/306/7

Harrogate

Linley Hill

Wetherby

YORK

Beverley

Burton Constable

Acaster Malbis

Breighton

Helileeds

South Cave

Hull

Leeds

Sherburn

Goole

Brough

Paull(former home of the Beverley)

Burn Gliding Club

Blackburn and
Police Flying
Clubs

LEEDS-BRADFORD
INTERNATIONAL AIRPORT

Sandtoft

HUMBERSIDE
INTERNATIONAL AIRPORT

Doncaster Heliport

INTERNATIONAL AIRPORT

Centre of General Aviation

Map 35

Hot air balloon passing over the Wolds at North Newbald.

D-600 glider over Yorkshire Gliding Club's centre at Sutton Bank.

Aerial view of the old 4 Group base at Burn.

A hard-working Cessna Pawnee glider tug at the Wolds Gliding Club, Pocklington Airfield.

was a well-supported leisure sport. Yorkshire Gliding Club - recognised as one of Europe's leading clubs - provides a dramatic spectacle when it launches its gliders on the edge of the escarpment at Sutton Bank near Thirsk. Three tug aircraft - a Super Cub and two Piper Pawnees - provide the aero tows. The Wolds Gliding Club at Pocklington maintains the aviation tradition on this former 4 Group Halifax airfield; Rufforth Airfield's houses the York Gliding Centre whose equipment included a Schiebe SF27C motor glider. A variety of gliders, hang-gliders and microlights are often launched from Wombleton and sometimes from Burn; while hot air balloons may ascend from any convenient field. Several companies such as the Flying Horse Balloon Club at Huddersfield offered instructional courses; and local businesses were quick to take advantage of the advertising potential of the giant, colourful hot air balloon. Enthusiasm for most aspects of civil and general aviation - an enthusiasm that had its roots in the eighteenth century - had by no means diminished in Yorkshire.

Chapter Twenty Eight

Service Aviation in Yorkshire 1963 - 1992

By 1963 the surviving RAF stations in Yorkshire were dedicated to the training role; and the tradition of locating combat squadrons in the County had been deliberately terminated. Yet this had taken place at precisely the time when the Warsaw Pact countries[1] were equipping with new aeroplanes and planning new tactics in the event of a war against the West. Most dangerous in the 1962-63 context was the emergence of the Tupolev Tu-95 turbine-engined intercontinental bomber, designated the Tu-20 in Soviet service and known in the West by its NATO code 'Bear'[2]. It was a unique design deriving from the three B-29 Superfortresses that had force-landed in the Soviet Union during the war and from Josef Stalin's 1949 directive that Soviet design teams should concentrate on the development of turbine-engined strategic bombers. The Tu-95 was first seen at the Tushino Air Display in 1955 and western observers were puzzled that a turbo-powered aeroplane of such gigantic size required a swept-wing configuration.

At the time there was little awareness of the sheer power and performance that the four turboprop engines made by Kuznetsov could generate: nearly 60,000hp; a speed of 572mph (Mach 0.82) at 25,000 feet; 520mph (Mach 0.785) at 41,000 feet; a range 9,200 miles with a 25,000lb bomb load. Each of the four engines has twin four-bladed propellers electronically-controlled to maintain a fairly coarse pitch. This ensures that the propeller tip speed is barely supersonic, the aircraft can fly high and fast (at typical jet airliner speeds) and therefore had to have sweptback wings and tailplanes. And if it seems curious to be using the present tense for an aeroplane first displayed in 1955 it is because the mighty Bear is currently (1993) still in service, much modified, up-dated and still capable of fulfilling a remarkable range of military functions. It had the capacity to operate with nuclear weapons in any part of the Northern Hemisphere and was often intercepted over the North Sea or on the 'milk run' from the Kola Peninsula down to Cuba prior to the demise of the Soviet Union and the ending of the Cold War.[3]

Despite its long service record, the Bear was originally a stop-gap aeroplane to be employed for as long as Russia was without a jet-propelled nuclear bomber. The gap was partially filled by another Andrei Tupolev design, the Tu-16 Badger. This was powered by two large turbo-jets buried in the wing-roots and had a performance not dissimilar from the Strategic Air Command's B-47 Stratofortress and the RAF's Vickers Valiant. Its most potent threat was as a carrier of AS-5 Kelt and AS-6 Kipper anti-shipping missiles and was frequently intercepted over the Baltic, the North Sea, the Mediterranean and the Atlantic Ocean. As in the case of the Tu-20 Bear, the Badger was noted for its longevity and astounding array of variants. Each one is identified alphabetically so, for example, Badger F was identified in 1963 as a dedicated intelligence gathering aircraft while Badger-G was a maritime attack aircraft usually seen equipped with advanced radar guidance for a Mach 1.2 Kelt missile with a range of 200 miles.

This was why, for something over thirty-five years, generations of NATO pilots - and quite a few Swedish aircrew - learnt their intercepting techniques with the Bears and the Badgers on their Viggens, F-102s, Lightnings and Phantoms. No 43 Squadron was the first to fly Phantoms in the UK defence role (1969) and was based at Leuchars. This airfield became home to the Leuchars Wing charged with the interception of Soviet bombers which, by 1970, included well over two hundred Tu-20 Bears and nearly two thousand Badgers. 'Treble One' became operational with Phantoms there during 1975 and from 1967 to 1975 No 23 Squadron was part of the Leuchars Wing equipped with the ultimate Lightning, the F.6. As John Rawlings has remarked, this Squadron had

> "more than its share of Soviet Air Force interceptions over the North Sea"[4]

before disbanding in 1975 and reforming with Phantoms. By then the newly structured Royal Air Force of the Seventies had allocated four major fighter defence bases to share the interception role: Leuchars, Binbrook, Coningsby and Wattisham.

The reorganisation of Bomber and Fighter Commands took place on 30 April 1968 when they were merged into Strike Command with its headquarters at High Wycombe. No 11 Group became responsible for Air Defence, Ground Defence and Airborne Early Warning and had its headquarters at Bentley Priory. Here the RAF was confident that the 'quick reaction' performance of the Lightning and Phantom squadrons was adequate for the interception of Bears and Badgers though rumours of a new generation of supersonic Soviet bombers during the Seventies proved most disquieting to Strike Command and to the rest of the NATO air forces. Intelligence reports referred in particular to a new Tupolev 'Backfire' bomber, reputed to have a Mach 2.5 capability and a combat radius of well over 1500 miles. Could the Phantoms and Lightnings cope with such an adversary? John Bushby was convinced in 1973 that even with the best early warning system in the world and an array of surface-to-air missiles:

> "there is not in Allied service at the time of writing any defensive fighter aircraft which can reasonably be considered an effective counter-weapon to such as the Russian 'Backfire'"[5]

Later identified as the Tupolev Tu-22 M-3, the 'Backfire' began its maritime sorties in 1975. Its appearance prompted a re-evaluation of defence strategy and convinced the RAF that it would certainly require the new multi-role combat aircraft ordered by those NATO countries keen to replace the Lockheed 104-G Starfighter. The concept of a new strike/attack aircraft for NATO had been thrashed out in 1968-9 and four European aircraft companies(BAC - now BAe; Fokker, MBB and Fiat - now Aeritalia) were committed to its production and formed the Panavia Aircraft GmbH in Munich on 26 March 1968. Though Fokker pulled out of the deal in 1969 Panavia began the development and construction programme of the aeroplane that was to become the Tornado.

Conscious of the growing threat from supersonic bombers equipped with cruise missiles and the possibility that these aircraft might be joined by the new Sukhoi Su-24 Fencer nuclear strike aircraft and the even newer Sukhoi Su-27 Flanker air superiority fighter[6], the RAF decided to order two versions of the Tornado - the Ground attack/Reconnaissance GR Mk 1 and the Air Defence Vehicle (ADV) F3 interceptor that would be capable of dealing

with Backfires, Flankers and Fencers. Britain had already confirmed in 1976 that 165 of the 385 Tornadoes on order would be the F3 ADV version and the first of these were destined to equip the RAF in August 1981.

These decisions were of the greatest importance to Yorkshire in that the strategic reappraisal had revealed a serious gap in UK Defences between the Humber and the Forth. Reaction time was of the essence and a well-equipped front-line airfield was urgently needed to meet the problem of the 'Humber-Forth Gap'. In 1979 the choice fell upon RAF Leeming in North Yorkshire and the plan was to transform the existing airfield into a base capable of handling up to three squadrons of Tornadoes by 1988. The time scale seemed feasible in 1979 but years of delays meant that work did not begin until 1986. The RAF resurfaced the main 2,300 metre runway, the manoevring areas and taxyways; and built a brand new air control tower irreverently known as the 'Happy Eater'.

Leeming's refurbishment included the 'hardening' of essential facilities. Two hardened aircraft shelters (HAS) can accommodate a total of four Tornadoes; all personnel, briefing and command centres are also hardened against nuclear and conventional attack. G/Cpt John Rooum, Station Commander, had to work up Leeming as an efficient front-line base at the same time as establishing three squadrons equipped with the Tornado F3. This aeroplane was significantly different from the Tornado GR Mk 1 now classified as an an IDS (Interdictor/Strike)

Photographed at Leeming are a No 31 Squadron Tornado GR1 and a No 152 Squadron Meteor NF14. The Meteor became Leeming's 'gate guardian' and is now at the Yorkshire Air Museum. In the background is Leeming's famous 'Happy Eater'!

Yorkshire Air Museum

XS903 at Yorkshire Air Museum, Elvington.

Yorkshire Air Museum

aircraft. Its twin Turbo-Union RB.199-3AR Mk 104 turbofans had the extended afterburner nozzles fitted to improve thrust and reduce drag at low level - one reason why it could storm low-level across Yorkshire's AIAA(Area of Intense Aerial Activity) at up to 800 knots. However, the F3's main function was to intercept at altitude far away from the Yorkshire coast and for this it depended on constant refuelling from tankers such as the VC-10 C1K/K4s and Victor K2s. With a slightly longer fuselage than the GR 1 it could comfortably accommodate four of BAE's Skyflash radar guided air-to-air missiles. The F3 could also carry four AIM-9L Sidewinders under

the inner wing pylons, reserving the outer pylons for other stores. Unlike the Phantom, the F3 carried a single 27mm revolver cannon in the lower starboard fuselage. Crews professed the greatest admiration for the punch and speed characteristic of the F3 though there was comment that more power would be welcome at altitude.

Leeming formally reopened on 11 January 1988 when W/Cdr Kit Smith landed his Tornado on the new runway. The first Tornado squadron was No XI led by W/Cdr David Hamilton, charged with a maritime defence commitment. Its 'twin eagles' badge worn on the Tornado's fin commemorated the fact the Squadron originally flew Vickers FB 5s two-seaters with a gunner in the nose when it first formed in 1915 - especially relevant for its present mount, the two-seat Tornado F3. The Squadron had been the last to fly the Lightning interceptor and the previous Officer Commanding No XI Squadron, W/Cdr 'Jake' Jarron, had made the last flight in his personal aeroplane XS903 into Yorkshire Air Museum at Elvington in May 1988.

No 23 Squadron, commanded by W/Cdr Neil Taylor, became operational on 1 August 1989 in the air defence role. His original Tornado ZE 809 was specially painted in 1990 with the 'Red Eagles' badge on a blue and red fin and the words '23 Squadron - 75th Anniversary 1 September 1990' along the fuselage spine. No 25 Squadron, also in the air defence role, was formerly a Bloodhound missile unit. and was officially redesignated a Tornado F3 Squadron on 1 October 1989. Led by W/Cdr 'Mick' Martin, the Squadron had Tornado ZE 858 on strength at Leeming in December 1988 and by July there were six of No 23 Squadron's Tornadoes on the airfield. However, the operational date for 25 Squadron was 1 January 1990 and this may be taken as the date when the Leeming Wing equipped with Tornado F3s became effective as a key element in the air defence of the United Kingdom.

But before this happened the world was shocked by the news of the explosion of a Boeing 747 over the little town of Lockerbie, just north of Carlisle, on 28 December 1988.

ZE 837 emerging from one of Leeming's HAS.

RAF Leeming

Diamond formation of nine Tornado F3 aircraft from Leeming, three from XI, 23 and 25 Squadrons. This was on the occasion of the visit of HRH The Princess Margaret to RAF Leeming on 25 June 1991.
Via F/Lt Maggie Pleasant, RAF Leeming

On the flight line. The tails of ten Tornadoes of No XI Squadron.
RAF Leeming

A terrorist had placed a bomb in the baggage hold and there were no survivors. Leeming's Mountain Rescue Team departed for Lockerbie in less than an hour after the news of the tragedy came through and over the next two days, together with other personnel from Leeming who travelled either by Chinook helicopter or by road, they carried out the macabre task of recovering bodies from the far-flung wreckage.

★ ★ ★

The first live interception of an intruder in United Kingdom Air Defence Region (UKADR) by a Leeming Squadron was on 10 November 1989. A stand-by Quick Reaction Alert crew from No 23 Squadron scrambled and intercepted two Soviet Maritime Reconnaissance Bear Ds that had overflown the Norwegian Sea. During 1990 Leeming underwent several evaluations to test whether the three squadrons could sustain their air interception role under battle conditions and then they felt they were ready to take part as a key element in a major NATO exercise.

To test the efficiency of Britain's air defence, a mock air battle was fought over the UK during 23-27 April 1990. This was 'Elder Forest 90', held every two years. The exercise required the aircraft of eight nations to carry out over a thousand high and low level attacks on British airfields, bases, radar stations and missile sites. Leeming's two HAS were singled out on 25 April and as two Royal Danish Air Force F-16s came in low and fast the airfield's RAF Regiment ground defenders were on stand-by. Clad in full NBC suits and equipped with automatic weapons

and Rapier missiles they were ready to defend the base against land and air attack. Leeming's Tornadoes were actively involved in interceptions and one of them coded ZE 811 had neatly transformed this into its squadron number: ZE 8XI. Unwanted realism occurred off the Yorkshire coast on 26 April when an F-15C from the USAF 32nd Tactical Wing went into the sea off Flamborough Head. The pilot ejected safely and was rescued by a No 22 Squadron Wessex from E Flight at Coltishall and ferried to the American hospital at Lakenheath.

★ ★ ★

In Yorkshire the bright yellow Whirlwind, Wessex and Sea King helicopters in their Search and Rescue role have been welcome sights for many years.Operated primarily for the rescue of military aviators, their record over the years shows that about 90% of their rescues involve civilians. The Whirlwind Mk Xs carried out over 2000 sorties from Leconfield until they were replaced by the Wessex Mk IIs that have performed yeoman service in the County. With two Rolls-Royce Gnome gas turbines, each of 730hp, and with 308 gallons of kerosene, the Wessex has a top speed of 120 knots and an endurance of about 2½ hours. It is a big aircraft with a length of 65' 10" and a rotor diameter of 56' - an important consideration when hovering next to the windswept cliffs of Yorkshire.

Two episodes during 1984 highlight the crucial importance of maintaining the Search and Rescue (SAR) Flight at Leconfield. The first, on 26 January 1984, took place when the Fleetwood trawler *Navana*,

MALM Dave Allen.

RAF Leeming

Sea King Radar cabin, showing East Yorkshire overlay.

RAF Leconfield

on passage from Aberdeen to the Humber, sank. At the time the stand-by Wessex of No 22 Squadron D Flight at Leconfield was crewed by F/Lt Hugh Pierce (pilot), F/Lt Graham Clark(navigator) and Master Air Load-master (MALM) Dave Allen as winchman. Skilful piloting and dedicated winch operation by Dave Allen resulted in the rescue of the crew of the *Navana*, a feat rewarded by a presentation to the helicopter crew - and to F/Sgt John Lovelace representing the ground crew at Leconfield - at the Savoy Hotel, London.[7]

The second rescue took place on 7 May 1984 when there occurred "the worst fishing tragedy on the Yorkshire coast for more than a decade."[8] About mid-day the fishing coble *Carole Sandra* was hit by a large wave that sank the vessel even before the crew had a chance to make a Mayday call. Four were feared drowned but people on the cliffs at Flamborough Head could see survivors struggling in the waves. A Wessex helicopter from 22 Squadron's D Flight at Leconfield soon arrived to

join the RNLI lifeboats and a small fleet of fishing vessels now taking part in the search for survivors. As the rescue operation went on, tragedy struck again. At 1545 hrs another coble, the *North Wind*, suddenly capsized and all seven men were thrown into the sea. There was an inshore wind of about 25 knots and the ebb-tide was running round Flamborough Head. Three were feared lost but the Wessex hovered close inshore.

> "At times the helicopter blades were only a few feet from the overhang of the cliff and the wind was threatening to dash them against it. There is no doubt that their lives were in danger."[9]

MALM David Allen rescued four people before he was crushed against the side of the Filey lifeboat and suffered injuries to his spine and ribs. He was transferred to hospital and replaced by Sgt Barney Barnes as winchman on board the Leconfield Wessex crewed by S/Ldr Chris Paish and Master Navigator Ron Dedman. A second Wessex, crewed by F/Lt Hugh Pierce, F/Lt Jim Prentice

Westland Whirlwind Mk 10.   *Westland Group*

Westland Wessex.   *Westland Group*

Westland Sea King Mk 3.   *Westland Group*

and MALM Eric Ainstie, joined in the search but seven people were drowned in this twin tragedy. Later the Leconfield crew were honoured by the Shipwrecked Fishermen and Mariners' Benevolent Society and presented with the prestigious *Edward and Maisie Lewis Award* for outstanding air-sea rescue.

Since 1988 the Leconfield Flight has been operating the much wider and more capacious Sea King helicopter with an endurance exceeding six hours and a maximum speed of 130 mph. Shorter than the Wessex (its length is 54' 9"), the Sea King has a bigger rotor diameter of 62'. Its range is well over six hundred miles and it can carry nineteen survivors and more at a pinch. Sea King equipment includes 'state of the art' avionics and this, as well as the two pilots and winchman, requires a radar operator with his own radar cabin. There is the usual VOR, DME, ADF, ILS, radio altimeter and Doppler fit. Additionally, it has Decca Mk 19 and new ground stabilised radar fed by the TANS computer. This enables the radar scope with its relevant overlay to give a constant read-out of the aircraft's position and relative bearing of small objects in the sea. There is a Flight Control System that can take the Sea King down to automatic hover at fifty feet or less in day or night conditions. Crews can switch off all lights and approach the deck wearing night vision goggles of the type regularly used in Northern Ireland. When in the hover the winchman can operate a small joystick to the left of the main cabin door in order to bring the helicopter into a precise position - so vital in air sea rescues.

Nos 22 and 202 Squadrons have frequently exchanged aircraft and personnel and by the end of the 1980s No 202 Squadron had converted to Sea Kings with its head-quarters at RAF Finningly and Flights flying from Boulmer (A Flight), Brawdy (B Flight), Manston (C Flight, Lossiemouth(D Flight) and Leconfield (E Flight). Originally there were fifteen air-sea rescue centres ranging from Sumburgh in the north to Culdrose in the south but savage defence cuts in October 1992 knocked out Brawdy, Manston (its Sea Kings then moved to Wattisham), Coltishall and Leuchars as far as the air-sea rescue role was concerned. Then in December the RAF closed down its repair and servicing facility at Finningley and began moving the Squadron headquarters to Boulmer. As the last Sea King emerged from the repair hangar it was a poignant moment for ground crew and air test crew alike. S/Ldr John Dungate remarked:

"I've been here now for seven years, operating out of here, air testing, collecting and delivery. It will be strange . . ."

Leconfield rescue.

Via MALM Dave Allen

Finningley Flankers.

Sea King XZ 583 then took off to mark the end of an era for RAF Finningley. Leconfield's Flight survived and 202 Squadron continued its vital 'mercy missions' over the mist-shrouded Yorkshire landscape and the storms of the cruel North Sea.

So by the end of 1992 much had changed in the skies above Yorkshire. The whine of the turboprop engines of the graceful PC-9s had vanished. Tornadoes were a little less evident in their low-level role after their 1991 Gulf War experiences[7] and the tank-busting A-10 Thunderbolt IIs seemed less inclined to blast the villages of North Cave, Hotham, Rowley and North Newbald (seemingly cast as carbon copies of East German targets on the A-10 hit list) with the distinctive scream of their twin General Electric turbofans. Gradually, the A-10 Thunderbolts were leaving their bases at RAF Woodbridge and RAF Bentwaters and on 23 March 1993 the last one took off for its new home at Spangdahlem, Germany. F-111s were readying to depart from RAF Upper Heyford and RAF Lakenheath, from which the 48th TFW had carried out a retaliatory raid against Libya in 1986.

At the same time the Northern Group of Forces (formerly the Soviet 37th Air Army) of the Commonwealth of Independent States (CIS) were leaving their bases in Hungary and Czechoslovakia. Relocation of Su-24 Fencers (interdiction and strike aircraft, the equivalent of the F-111) was also taking place in Poland and the tardy disappearance of CIS airpower from former East Germany was only because Chancellor Kohl had generously guaranteed financial compensation for the cost of relocation from the newly united Federal Republic to the CIS.

All of this was an outward and visible sign of the 'peace dividend' following the end of the Cold War and the demise of the Soviet Union, at least in its image as the prime source of the "communist threat to the Free World". Whether the CIS under Yeltsin[10] and his successors would be able to contribute to a stable and peaceful world remained to be seen. But what was evident in this new and unexpected world scenario was a willingness to open the skies and inventory of the CIS to the gaze of fascinated western observers; and to show eagerness to send the latest Tupolev, MiG and Sukhoi designs to Farnborough and elsewhere. At least in the world of aviation *glasnost* had become a reality and nowhere more obviously so than at the September 1991 Finningley Air Show where the incredibly agile and accurately flown Su-27 Flankers held a full-capacity crowd quite breathless.

★ ★ ★

Flying training did not decline in Yorkshire during these years. Perhaps the most dramatic change occurred in July 1989 when, following the Royal Navy's decision to allow women to serve at sea, the RAF decided to train women as pilots. This was due partly to the shortfall in recruits for aircrew training and partly to the professional competence women had demonstrated as aircrew members in other air forces and in commercial flying. Yorkshire University Air Squadron claimed to have been the first UAS to recruit girls and the first to send a girl pilot solo in a Bulldog in 1987. But it was F/Lt Sally Cox and F/Lt Julie Gibson, both of whom had logged 70-90 hours of private flying, who were the first to join No 1 Flying Training School at RAF Linton-on-Ouse in February 1990 and began training on Jet Provosts. Both went solo on 10 May 1990. The RAF anticipated that up to 10% of

BAC Jet Provost

The prototype Jet Provost first flew in 1954 and the first RAF pupil pilot soloed on this jet trainer in 1955. The Jet Provost T.3 began equipping Flying Training Command during 1959 and the aeroplane was soon a common sight in the Yorkshire skies flying from bases at Leeming, Linton-on-Ouse and Church Fenton.

Jet Provost flying low over Holme-on-Spalding-Moor.

Though it had been replaced by the turbo-prop Shorts Tucano, examples of this high performance, reliable and superbly aerobatic jet trainer still hurtled across the Vale of York during 1993 - flown by instructors and RAF pilots on refresher courses.

its annual intake of around 230 trainee aircrew will be women though there were no plans to post them to front-line combat aircraft. F/O Anne-Marie Dawe was the first woman aircrew member to receive the coveted navigator's brevet at RAF Finningley (1 March 1991). F/Lt Julie Gibson was the first woman to receive pilot's wings on 14 June 1991. She had successfully completed her flying training at Linton and was then posted to Finningley's Advanced Flying Training Squadron of the Multi-Engine Training Wing. When Air Marshal C.J. Thompson pinned the wings on her the RAF was signalling the beginning of the end of discrimination against women in service aviation.

At No 7 Flying Training School at Church Fenton the Shorts Tucano proved a great success and F/O Nigel Williams was the first student pilot to solo on this type in January 1990. Four months later the last course of student pilots to train on the Jet Provost graduated at Church Fenton, though a few Jet Provost T5s could still be seen in Yorkshire skies to provide refresher courses for

experienced pilots - but not for long. No 7 FTS at Church Fenton began to disperse its Tucanos to another Yorkshire FTS at Linton-on-Ouse (No 1FTS); while others went to No 3 FTS at Cranwell. These moves were to herald the closure of Church Fenton, once one of the UK's most distinguished fighter bases. As well as the demise of the Jet Provosts, one of Slingsby's most successful air experience gliders disappeared during 1990. This was the motorised Venture which had given yeoman service in the Gliding Schools and was now replaced by the new Grob 109B Vigilant motorised gliders during 1990-91.

⋆ ⋆ ⋆

One other airfield still maintained some contact with military aviation though its flying role with the RAF ended in 1972. This was RAF Topcliffe - now Alanwood Barracks - which was transferred to the Army and occupied by 24 Brigade in 1973. No 666 Aviation Squadron, part of 3 Div. Aviation Regiment, had arrived at Topcliffe in July 1971 to give air support to the Brigade. Fresh from emergency duties in Northern Ireland, 'Treble Six' Squadron flew Scout and Sioux helicopters at Topcliffe between 1971 and 1976 before being posted to BAOR. Appropriately for Topcliffe's wartime connection with the RCAF, Treble Six had a history dating back to March 1945 when it first formed as 666 (Royal Canadian Air Force) Air Observation Post Squadron, flying Austers in support of the 1st Canadian Army.

There were certain drawbacks with the Sioux and Scout generation of helicopters: the Sioux was too light and too fragile for battlefield use while the Scout was too expensive and complicated. That largely explains the Army's decision to standardise on two types of liaison and tactical helicopter: the light five-seater and the transport capable of carrying ten combat-equipped soldiers to the battlefield. A new generation of helicopters - Gazelle, Puma and Lynx - equipped the Army Air Corps (AAC) and the last of these, the Lynx, was often seen in Yorkshire skies flying from the Dishforth base used by the AAC's No 9 Regiment. Dishforth had been rarely used for operational flying after 1961 but it reopened as an Army Air Corps base on 21 February 1991. No 673 Squadron received two of the new AH Lynx Mk 9s in November 1991 and with the temporary posting of 672 Sqadron to Dishforth the revived airfield became the major Lynx helicopter base in the north of England, a status underlined when No 654 Squadron was transferred there from its base at Detmold, Germany, at the end of 1992.

Westland Scouts serving with the Army Air Corps.

Westland Group

AH Mk IX Lynx.

Westland Group

This last posting was a further sign of the times as the peace dividend led to the decline of Detmold and several other military bases in Western Europe. Understandably, during 1989-1990 NATO countries were tempted to reduce radically their expenditure on defence. Yet it must never be forgotten that the prime duty of the British government is to secure the defence of the United Kingdom. Associated with this is the responsibility of meeting both its commitments under the North Atlantic Treaty Organisation and under the sanctions imposed by the United Nations Organisation. False economy was shown up in the Falklands during 1982 and there is never any justification in failing to equip the armed forces of the nation to deal with possible threats to national security and world peace.

Events during 1990-1991 emphasised the validity of this view when the aggressive policies of Iraq's President Saddam Hussein became clear. For many years western nations as well as members of the Soviet bloc had unwisely poured arms and equipment into Iraq in the hope that Saddam would be a bastion against the fundamentalist Islamic government of Iran. This was how Iraq was able to assemble the fourth largest army in the world; how Saddam was able to collect some of the latest air superiority fighters from France and the Soviet Union and equip his bombing force with the well-proven Badger. When the long Gulf War between Iran and Iraq ended in the 1988 cease-fire there were signs that war-weariness would not lead to peace but would help create even greater instability among the oil-rich states of the Gulf.

Few envisaged that in 1990 the United Nations would mobilise the largest international force to see action since 1945 in order to deal with aggression by Saddam Hussein. This multinational force won a rapid victory in Desert Storm, a conflict in which aeroplanes made by Blackburn's factory in Yorkshire played a distinguished and decisive role.

Chapter Twenty Nine

Operations in the Gulf 1990 - 1991

It was entirely unexpected that Tornado F3s based in Yorkshire and Buccaneers built in Brough would both have key roles to play in the Gulf during 1990-91. That they did was due to the Iraqi invasion of oil-rich Kuwait on 2 August 1990, a somewhat embarrassing development for Britain in the light of her past colonial history. As a controlling power in the League of Nations, Britain had created the state of Iraq and placed it under a British mandate (1920). At the time, Britain had maximum regard for the potential oil wealth of the region and paid scant heed to the national aspirations of people now confined within the arbitrary frontiers of the mandate: Mosul, Basra and Baghdad, all occupied by victorious British and Imperial armies during 1918. Admittedly, the peoples of Basra and Baghdad had much in common; but there was no love lost as far as the Kurds of Mosul were concerned. Their ambition was to form a Kurdish national state but, as Britain's motive was to control this strategically and economically valuable region, Kurdish protests tended to be drowned by exploding bombs dropped by RAF aeroplanes sent to police Iraq during the Twenties and Thirties.

Iraq was a monarchy until 1958 when the Revolutionary Command Council created presidential government. Under President Saddam Hussein, Iraq attacked Iran in 1980 and sparked off a war that lasted until the 1988 ceasefire. President Saddam coveted the oil wealth of Kuwait, another Middle East state created by Britain in 1961. As the United Nations had never intervened in hostilities in the Gulf 1980-88, but had merely been useful in arranging the 1988 cease-fire, Saddam felt confident that his invasion and annexation of Kuwait two years later would go unchallenged.

But the world in which he was operating was very different from the world of ten years earlier. Then, neither superpower would have welcomed a massive intervention in the Gulf. But the disappearance of the Soviet Union and its replacement by the CIS meant that Security Council decisions within the United Nations were now more likely to be implemented with the approval of both the USA and the CIS. Certainly, the UN was now in a better position to speak with a single voice than it had ever been before. Possibly, Saddam did not understand this.

"Iraq's battle," he said, "would extend to the whole world."

To prevent this and to secure the liberation of Kuwait the United Nations reacted against Iraqi brutality in Kuwait and the maltreatment of hostages in a series of resolutions. UN Resolutions 661 and 662 imposed sanctions on Iraq and reaffirmed the independence of Kuwait. When Saudi Arabia, fearful of an Iraqi attack, turned to America and the UN for help the United Nations permitted the build-up of a multi-national force both on the soil of Saudi Arabia and on numerous ships in the Gulf. For this extraordinary build-up of 'coalition forces' against Iraq - far bigger than in any other campaign since the end of the Second World War - the Americans chose the code-name *Desert Shield*. Britain's equivalent was *Operation Granby*.[1]

America's opening move was dramatic. Forty-eight F-15 Eagles of the 1st Tactical Fighter Wing took off from Langley Air Force Base in Virginia and flew non-stop to Saudi Arabia, refuelling from air tankers en route. They were in position on 7 August and ready to defend the Saudi oilfields against any Iraqi attack from the air. Two days later the British government announced it would send twelve Tornado F3s and twelve Jaguar GR 1As to the Gulf. RAF policy was to form 'Composite Squadrons' drawn from ground and air crews in the UK and Germany rather than switch entire squadrons to the Gulf. This had the advantage of diffusing losses and casualties among several squadrons rather than hitting hard at the fliers and families of one squadron. First to go were the Tornadoes of No 5 and No 29 Squadrons already at armament practice camp at Akrotiri in Cyprus. They arrived at Dhahran on 10 August and were relieved by the first of Leeming's Tornado F3s on 29 August. The Leeming aircraft joined No XI 'Composite' Squadron and Leeming's station commander, G/Capt Rick Peacock-Evans, established the fighter base at Dhahran. He found his Tornadoes were easy to service and maintain as the Saudis, who also flew F3s, had exactly the same support infrastructure as he had at Leeming. Leeming's crews spent some four months tracking Iraqi aircraft on radar along the Saudi frontier, wondering how their aeroplanes would react if they encountered the new MiG-29s that

Saddam had bought from the Soviet Union as a counterpart to the Tornado ADV. In fact there were no confrontations and most Leeming personnel, including XI Squadron's W/Cdr David Hamilton sporting a 'Desert Eagles' badge, returned to Yorkshire before Desert Shield exploded into Desert Storm.

Thirty or so Leeming personnel were still in Dhahran when the deadline set by the UN for Saddam's forces to quit Kuwait expired on Wednesday 16 January 1991 at 0500 GMT. Cruise missiles fired from US warships in the Gulf signalled the attack at 2150 GMT and this was followed up by waves of bombing strikes on Iraqi airfields as it was believed Iraq's array of front-line aircraft represented the major threat to the Coalition forces. Much publicity attended the Tornado GR 1s who were given the toughest task of all: eliminating the huge Iraqi air bases with their JP233 airfield denial bomb system. These weapons, some sixty SG 357 cratering bombs and 430 HB 876 mines, were carried in twin pods. Together they weighed over 10,000lbs, a much heavier load than Main Force Lancasters and Halifaxes customarily took to Germany in the Second World War. The Tornadoes had to run the gauntlet of intense ground fire, just as the P-51 Mustangs did when they shot up German airfields in 1945. Five Tornadoes were lost in the first week of the war but only one was lost when flying a JP233 sortie straight and low over the enemy airfields.[2]

Later reconnaissance showed that the task of denying the enemy his huge airfields equipped with multiple parallel runways was unproductive. This was because of the devastating effect the coalition allies had on the Iraqi Air Force during the first week of sustained air attack, reminiscent of Israeli air efficiency during the Six Day War of 1967. Most of Iraq's Tu-16 Badgers were destroyed on the ground before the Russian-built bombers could be despatched against Saudi targets; and twenty of Saddam's front-line interceptors fled to Iran on 27 January 1991 after two American F-15Cs had destroyed three Iraqi MiG-23s and a Mirage F1 with their Air Interception AIM-7 and AIM-9 Sidewinder missiles.[3]

Relatively few Iraqi fighters were met in combat by Coalition aircraft and the sole contact between Tornado F3s and Iraqi Mirage F1s (18 January 1991) resulted in the escape of the Mirages due to their superior speed.[4] Consequently, no F3 saw action in Desert Storm and the last routine four-hour combat patrols over northern Saudi Arabia ended on 8 March 1991.

The Tornado GR-1 sorties against airfields and other infrastructure targets were, of course, not flown by aircraft from the Yorkshire squadrons. Nevertheless, the problems

encountered by the Tornadoes in this their first wartime role are relevant. The GR-1s were based at Tabuk and Dhahran in Saudi Arabia and at Muharraq on Bahrain and initially were tasked with systematic airfield denial. After three nights of JP233 attacks the losses (though much lower than had been feared) were sufficient to force a change in tactics. Tornadoes were now loaded with 8 x 1000lb bombs to attack targets from a height of 20,000 feet with effect from 20 January 1991. So despite the high-technology characteristic of the rest of the war the Tornadoes were now adopting the same free-fall bombing methods used by Bomber Command fifty years earlier. Not surprisingly, scattering bombs from this height proved unproductive against Desert Storm targets and in search of accuracy the Tornadoes turned to dive-bombing attacks from a height of 24,000 feet. Accuracy could not be guaranteed because the Tornadoes terminated their dives at 16,000 feet in order to stay above the Triple A fire and the deadly heat-seeking SAMs.

Even this method was not without its hazards and the fifth Tornado was lost on 23 January when a bomb exploded prematurely on release and detonated the rest of the bombs still attached to the aircraft. Dive-bombing with Tornadoes did not guarantee accuracy and the RAF called for help from its two Brough-built Blackburn Buccaneer squadrons based at Lossiemouth. Writing in World Air Power's brilliant Gulf Air War Debrief, Paul Jackson remarked that

> "Of all the RAF elements in Desert Storm, the Buccaneer force proved the most vital and the fastest to respond . . ."[5]

The Buccaneer had been originally ordered as a Wyvern replacement for attacking Russian cruisers and coastal targets such as oil refineries though it was a design that remained well in advance of its specification. It remained a subsonic aeroplane but had advanced features such as boundary layer control systems and through-the-canopy ejection later adopted for Harriers and Tornadoes.[6] In the 1980s its primary role at Lossiemouth was to attack enemy warships with Sea Eagle missiles; its secondary role was to secure absolute accuracy with laser bombs. This accuracy was achieved by the navigator in the rear cockpit firing a laser beam at the target and the laser-guidance system in the bomb would sense the reflected laser energy and home in on its target. The weapon control system fitted to the Lossiemouth Buccaneers S.Mk. 2Bs was a Westinghouse AN/ASQ-153 Pave-Spike installation located within a pod on the port inner wing.

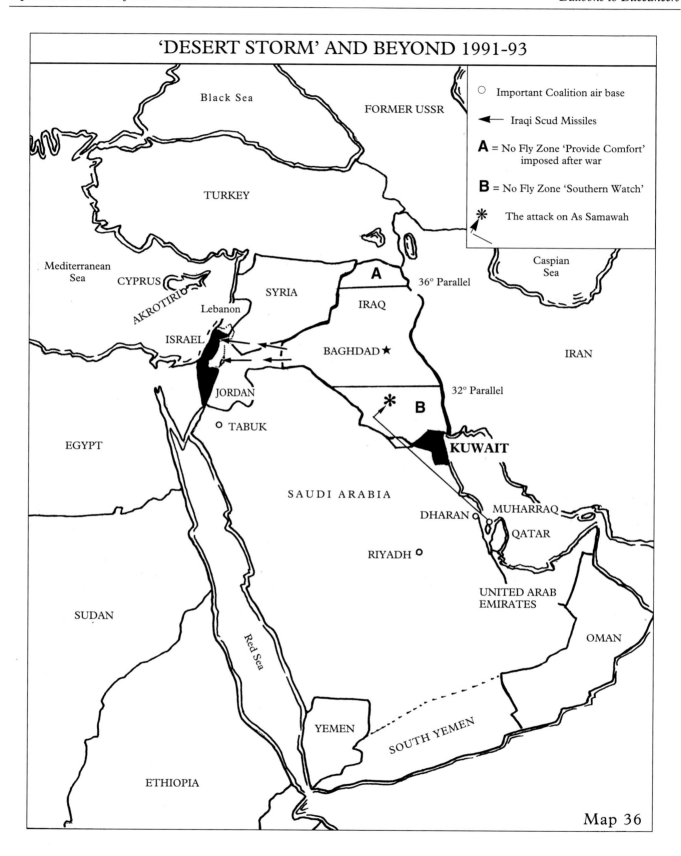

'DESERT STORM' AND BEYOND 1991-93

Black Sea

FORMER USSR

○　Important Coalition air base

←　Iraqi Scud Missiles

A = No Fly Zone 'Provide Comfort' imposed after war

B = No Fly Zone 'Southern Watch'

＊　The attack on As Samawah

TURKEY

Mediterranean Sea

CYPRUS

AKROTIRI

Lebanon

SYRIA

A　　36° Parallel

IRAQ

Caspian Sea

ISRAEL

BAGHDAD ★

IRAN

JORDAN

32° Parallel

○ TABUK

EGYPT

＊ **B**

KUWAIT

SAUDI ARABIA

DHARAN ○

MUHARRAQ

QATAR

RIYADH ○

UNITED ARAB EMIRATES

SUDAN

Red Sea

OMAN

YEMEN

SOUTH YEMEN

ETHIOPIA

Map 36

The Tiger Moth Floatplane taking off from Welton Waters in the East Riding of Yorkshire.

In Scotland and under tight security the Buccaneers had already begun to work up their laser-designation skills, awaiting the call from the RAF throughout most of January 1991. When it came (23 January 1991) the RAF asked for the twelve most experienced crews to go to war in the Gulf. No-one had more experience than S/Ldr R. Phillips who had been with the RAF for twenty-four years and had logged over 3000 hours on Buccaneers. More than one colleague had remarked "that he must live in them". Nor was he a stranger to Yorkshire where he was one of a select band of pilots who flew the little red Tiger Moth floatplane off Welton Waters next to the British Aerospace factory at Brough.

His navigator was S/Ldr Hislop who had seven years experience on Buccaneers, five of them flying behind Phillips. Their Buccaneer, in common with the others of No 12 and No 208 Squadrons, plus No 237 Operational Conversion Unit, was readied with upgraded radios and avionics, painted Desert Pink, and equipped with a single Sidewinder just in case of trouble on the way to the Gulf. The big weapons bay was fitted with extra fuel tanks and this meant that the Buccaneers needed barely three refuels en route to Muharraq via Egypt, the Nile, the Red Sea and Saudi Arabia. The first Buccaneers landed at night (26 January) and next day began their theatre work-up in earnest under the direction of W/Cdr W. Cope.

Smoke from burning oil-wells in Kuwait often interfered with the sorties and as S/Ldr Phillips commented:

". . . there was no chance of a tan as the light was quite dusky even at high noon. In the air we had gin-clear days at 20,000 feet but could not see the ground because of the smoke. We always tried to

attack down wind but even so the smoke and dust caused several aborts."

The first sortie from Muharraq was on 2 February with two Buccaneers accompanying four Tornadoes to hit the As Samawah road bridge across the Euphrates. They attacked in 'cell' formations, each cell being made up of two Tornadoes and one Buccaneer, with a gap of up to two minutes between each cell. It was an entirely successful operation and one of the Buccaneers was piloted by Yorkshire-born F/Lt Gary Mason who had trained at Church Fenton. His navigator was Norman Brown, related to Lt Arthur Whitten Brown of Alcock and Brown fame, the men who made the first flight across the Atlantic in 1919. F/Lt Mason's sister-in-law later commented that it was appropriate for a Yorkshire pilot to captain a Yorkshire-built aircraft on its first flight in anger. There was plenty of protection to be had from the Americans. F-15s escorted each cell; all around them 'Wild Weasels' were hunting for SAM sites; and pairs of F-14 Tomcats were 'on the deck' dealing with the dangerous task of suppressing Triple A sites. As S/Ldr Phillips said:

"We always went in the big package."

However, the 'big package' could not save the sixth Tornado shot down on 14 February during a 'double mission' by four cells against Al Taqaddum. The pilot, F/Lt Rupert Clark, survived two strikes by SAMs though his navigator, F/Lt Stephen Hicks, died. After this loss the RAF reverted to the well-tried twin-cell formation though bad weather caused several 'mission aborts'. From 21 February onwards the Buccaneers swapped their Sidewinders for a pair of laser-guided bombs and worked up a new dive-bombing manoeuvre for self-designated laser attacks. RAF service limits for a Buccaneer dive was 40° but some of the crews discovered that to ensure their bombs landed on target (i.e. within a 1000ft 'basket') a 60° dive was much more effective. After the Tornadoes had bombed their targets, the Buccaneers carried out precision attacks on bridges and, where they could find them, Antonov An-12 Cub transports parked in the open. On the last day of the war (27 February 1991) the Buccaneers attacked a large hangar on an airfield in Iraq. S/Ldr Phillips observed that "it had been missed by all the Tornadoes so we hit it."[7] Despite their brief tour of combat (2-28 February 1991) the twelve Buccaneers based at Muharraq proved indispensable to the Tornado squadrons in the Gulf. They had restored accuracy to the Tornado attacks and were ideal for operations in the desert conditions of the Gulf. They performed well at high level, had a very useful turn of speed and with their

**The twelve Buccaneers from
208 and 12 Squadrons and 237 OCU,
RAF Lossiemouth, that saw combat
in the Gulf during February 1991**

(All carried the name of a Scotch whisky)
Total missions

XV352	U Tamdu	10	
XV863	S Tamnavoulin	6	
XW530	E Glenmoranagie	12	
XW533	A Glenfarclas	11	
XW547	R The Macallan	11	
XX885	L Famous Grouse	7	Destroyed a Cub transport
XX889	T Longmom	14	
XX892	I Glen Lossie		
XX894	O Aberlour	7	
XX895	G Glenfiddich	5	
XX899	P Linkwood	7 ?	
XX901	N Glen Elgin	9	Destroyed a Cub transport

weapons bay fuel tanks possessed a very impressive range. Altogether. the Buccaneers flew 216 sorties and dropped forty-eight bombs in the war to liberate Kuwait and defeat Iraq. Unscathed, they returned to Lossiemouth in March 1991.

Although Leeming-based Tornadoes flew to Gioia del Colle airfield, Italy, in April 1993 to prepare for combat air patrols over Bosnia's air exclusion zones, Kuwait and Desert Storm appeared to be the swansong for the Buccaneer squadrons at Lossiemouth. Both No 12 and No 208 were scheduled to lose the SB-2s when the Buccaneers were finally retired from operational service in 1994. No 208 would disband completely; while No 12 would convert to the Tornado GR1. Simultaneously, the last of the Buccaneer Mk 50s of No 24 Squadron South African Air Force flew their last operational sorties from Waterkloof air base. Four of the remaining five Mk 50s were

earmarked for museum/gate guardian duty and the fifth would be used for systems testing.

During its years of front-line service the Buccaneer had won praise from all who had been connected with its development and operation. Roy Boot, Senior Designer of the detailed development of the Buccaneer, quotes a Central Trials and Tactical Organisation official in 1982: "The Buccaneer may be an old aeroplane in design terms, but it still outperforms many of its more sophisticated juniors in both speed and range. Perhaps future designers should turn towards this excellent aircraft for their model . . ."[7]

These words were specially poignant during 1982, the year of the Falklands campaign in which Britain found herself without a fixed wing aircraft carrier and no means of employing a strike aircraft such as the Buccaneer in the South Atlantic. Of course, the ship-borne VSTOL Harriers proved a godsend on that occasion but they were deemed inadequate to defend the islands against a second Argentinian attack. An air superiority fighter in the Falklands was vital and it was decided to deploy Phantoms from the UK to the South Atlantic. But as Phantoms normally required something longer than Stanley's 4,100ft runway it was obvious that crews would have to use braking parachutes and arrester gear until Stanley's airfield was lengthened. That was why, before leaving the UK, the Phantom crews undertook short-field landing approaches on Brough's 4000ft runway 30/12, the only

Buccaneer in Desert Pink XV352 'U' refuelling from a Victor K2.

BAe Military Aircraft Division

strip of the right length available. So it was that Phantoms of No 29 Squadron came to East Yorkshire before embarking on their transoceanic flight to the Falklands after the war ended, "one of the longest non-stop fighter transit flights in the RAF's history . . ."[8]

Though the Buccaneer did not serve in the South Atlantic, some two years after the fighting ended the Officer Commanding an RAF Buccaneer Squadron in Germany was positive that:

> "So far as I can tell, everyone who's flown the Buccaneer has always ended up with a great love for the aircraft and it has its own personality which endears itself to everyone. It is well liked because of its inherent stability at low level, where it is a sheer delight to fly . . . at one hundred feet it has scored over many other types."[9]

Of course, these were peacetime evaluations. In time of war the front-line pilot will be critical of all combat types and the unequivocal comment of the Desert Storm aviators speak for themselves. S/Ldr Phillips thought that "out there in the Gulf we had the best aeroplane there was." An F-15 jockey, gazing at the venerable but potent lines of Robert Blackburn's masterpiece at it stood on the hardstand at Muharraq in 1991, was heard to remark,

> "You say that airplane's a Buccaneer? Well, I'll have me some of that."

Robert Blackburn (1885-1955) would have been

The last Buccaneer to be handed over at Brough.

BAe Military Aircraft Division

proud. This quiet, retiring genius, whose sole honour was an OBE bestowed in grudging recognition of his remarkable contribution before, during and after two World Wars, never saw the Buccaneer fly. Yet his "important and challenging aircraft" made a much more significant contribution to the history of aviation than he could have ever imagined.

★ ★ ★

Last of a long line of Blackburn aeroplanes to be designed, manufactured and tested in Yorkshire, it was fitting that in 1991 one should have given its final aerobatic display over the County before landing to become part of the permanent exhibition at Yorkshire Air Museum, Elvington. Even more spectacular was the low level pass across the Wolds of the East Riding by twenty of the survivors on 8 June 1993 when they flew in salute over the plane-makers at Brough.

Gradually, the Buccaneers became redundant as the Royal Air Force dispensed with this long-serving aeroplane during 1993-94. Some were scrapped; one was sent to the museum at RAF Cosford; another became Lossiemouth's gate guardian. Then, on 15 October 1993

Buccaneer low over East Riding.

BAe Military Aircraft Division

XV168 hooks the portable arrester gear at Brough 15 October 1993.

British Aerospace, Brough

Hauled away to its hardstanding at Elvington, the Buccaneer's dive-brakes are clearly displayed.

XV168 made the first and last landing by a Buccaneer at its birthplace, Brough, to become the factory's gate guardian. Crewed by S/Ldr Rick Phillips and his navigator G/Capt Nigel Maddox, XV168 hooked the portable arrester gear specially installed for the occasion on Runway 30/12. It was an emotional moment for all the 'Buccaneer men', past and present, at British Aerospace, Brough, and guaranteed that at Yorkshire Air Museum, Elvington, and at Robert Blackburn's famous factory on the edge of the Humber, there would be two examples of this remarkable aeroplane to delight future generations.

About to retire: The last low pass over Elvington before landing.

Buccaneer men at Elvington: Bernard Reuben centre, Dick Chandler behind him.

Losses: RAF and Commonwealth Air Forces 1939 - 1945

From 3 September 1939 to 8 May 1945 the aircraft of Bomber Command carried out 364,514 operational sorties. Many of these sorties were not directed against German cities. They included a vast number of attacks on:

(a) strategic and tactical targets in Occupied Europe

and

(b) minelaying operations ('gardening') throughout the six years of warfare

As a result of direct military action 8,325 aircraft were lost. 47,268 men were killed on these operations; 4,200 were wounded or crippled by their experiences; another 8,300 men died in the 'non-operational' activities (e.g. Training) of Bomber Command.

In the air operations over Germany some 90% of bombers were not intercepted by enemy night-fighters. But when the other 10% were attacked by night-fighters, about half of the bombers were shot down. It therefore follows that many bombers intercepted by Tame and Wild Boar fighters were able to give a very good account of themselves.

Two combat records involving 6 Group aircraft illustrate the point.

W/O J Coulombe, piloting a 426 Thunderbird Lancaster II from was coned by 50 searchlights in the Berlin attack of 2 December 1943. He survived four attacks by Ju 88s and claimed the fifth as a probable when it banked away and accidentally forced a *Wilde Sau* FW 190 coming in for the kill to abandon the combat! Similarly, when F/Sgt S. Puskas was over Essen on 26 March 1944 in a 429 Bison Squadron Halifax from Leeming, he came under attack from three single-engined night-fighters for some twenty-five minutes. This Lancaster had a twin .50" under-belly blister whose gunner, aided by the rear-gunner and a WOP/AG in the mid-upper, shot down two of the attackers.*

The highest levels of casualties in the RAF and Commonwealth Air Forces were during the years 1942 to 1944 (3 September - 2 September in each case) and the extent of the sacrifice in all parts of the world conflict may be gauged from these gross figures relating to the British and Commonwealth Air Forces.

Gross RAF casualties	**Flying (Battle)**			**All causes**		
	Killed in action	Missing	Prisoner of War	Killed in action	Missing	Prisoner of War
Sep 42-Sep 43	10950	950	2145	17367	1356	5180
Sep 43-Sep 44	14336	1752	2780	18968	1882	3256
Royal Canadian Air Force casualties						
Sep 42-Sep 43	2882	280	643	3692	308	654
Sep 43-Sep 44	3920	742	937	5009	771	942
Royal Australian Air Force casualties						
Sep 42-Sep 43	1062	112	199	1495	131	2434
Sep 43-Sep 44	2064	244	362	2537	254	371
Royal New Zealand Air Force casualties						
Sep 42-Sep 43	635	83	142	834	91	163
Sep 43-Sep 44	554	64	98	699	67	109
Royal South African Air Force casualties						
Sep 42-Sep 43	137	34	43	256	37	43
Sep 43-Sep 44	429	95	74	573	116	95

WAAF casualties

Sep 42-Sep 43   33 were killed, including 11 killed in ground battle

Sep 43-Sep 44   71 were killed, 9 of whom died in flying accidents and 25 in ground battle.**

---

*   Excellent accounts of these incidents, together with a valuable description of clashes *in daylight* between RAF heavy bombers and Me 262 jet fighters, may be found in Chaz Bowyer's *Gunner in the Sky* (Dent 1971, Corgi 1981).

**   Source: Royal Air Force Association Anniversary Supplement 1993.

"Straight and True"
RAF Leeming's Tornado Squadrons to 1994

Recent Government defence cuts resulted in radical decline in all three of the Armed Services. Though the cuts led to the demise of several Yorkshire airfields, Leeming survived as the most important air base for the defence of the United Kingdom up to 1994 with its three Tornado-equipped Squadrons, Nos XI, 23 and 25. Leeming was also home to No 15 Squadron Royal Air Force Regiment, responsible for the defence of the airfield with its Rapier Surface-to-Air Missile System.

No 15 Squadron

This Squadron formed in 1946 as No 2700 Light Anti-Aircraft (LAA) Squadron at RAF Nethertown equipped with L40/60 Bofors guns. Renamed No 15 (Field Squadron) in October 1958 it deployed its flight to RAF Gan and RAF Changi (1959-60) and took part in the Indonesian Confrontation (1962-65). After this No 15 Squadron had a distinguished history at RAF Luqa (until the RAF withdrew from Malta in 1973) and at RAF Akrotiri after the Turks invaded Cyprus in 1974. Equipped with tracked Reconnaissance Vehicles (CVRTs), it went on stand-by during the Falklands War (1982). 'C' Flight served in Ascension Island, after which the Squadron was operational as a Light Armour Unit. It then undertook successful security tours at Greenham Common (Operation Roust), in Northern Ireland and in Cyprus. The Squadron disbanded in 1990 but was resurrected in August 1990 for the defence of RAF Leeming.

No XI Squadron

Formed at Netheravon on 28 November 1914, it was the first RFC fighter squadron to serve in the British Expeditionary Force (July 1915). Its first kill with the Vickers Gunbus was on 5 September 1915. In November 1915 2/Lt G S M Insall won the Victoria Cross in combat with an Aviatik. The Squadron converted to Nieuport Scouts in 1916 (Captain Albert Ball won his MC with XI Squadron) and then reverted to two-seaters (FE 2Bs and Bristol Fighters). It disbanded on Christmas Eve 1919 and then reformed on DH 9As and then on Fairey Fawns, Hawker Horsleys and Westland Wapitis.

From 1928 No XI Squadron served overseas, mainly in the Middle East, India and the Far East. It flew

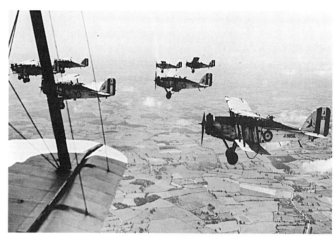

Westland Wapitis.

Westland Aviation

Hurricane IIcs in support of the 14th Army in Burma and was converting to Spitfire XIVs when the war ended. Thereafter it remained abroad for the next twenty years, flying Mosquitoes, Venoms and Meteor NF11s. It disbanded once more and then re-emerged at Leuchars before moving south to Binbrook to fly Lightning F6s. On 1 July 1988 it reformed at Leeming with Panavia Tornado F3s armed with Skyflash and Sidewinder AAMs and a 27mm cannon, part of Strike Command's No 11 Group.

Following Iraq's invasion of Kuwait, No XI Squadron Tornadoes deployed to Dharan in Saudi Arabia until December 1991. When, in 1993, NATO implemented Operation Deny Flight over the former Yugoslavia, No XI Squadron sent its Tornado F3s from Leeming to Gioia del Colle air base near Brindisi (19 April). From here they flew CAP (Combat Air Patrols) over Bosnia.

No 23 Squadron

Formed on 1 September 1915 at Gosport, one of its pilots - 2/Lt J C Slessor - attempted the first night interception of a Zeppelin (L-15) on 13 October 1915. In France the Squadron flew Spad VIIs, switching in March 1918 to Sopwith Dolphins. It disbanded in 1919 but reformed with Sopwith Snipes in 1925 before converting to the RAF's first Gloster Gamecocks. Before 1939 No 23 Squadron flew Bulldogs and Hawker Harts (Demons) and at the outbreak of war it was equipped with Bristol Blenheims.

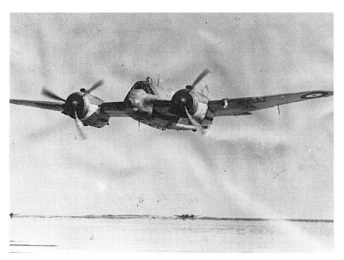

The Beaufighter in its element.

Frank Southern

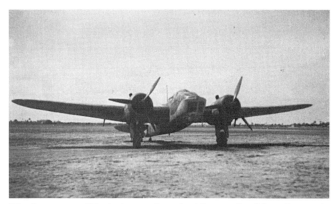

The long-nose Blenheim equipped with a pack of four forward-firing machine-guns. Two examples of this aeroplane have been restored at the Imperial War Museum, Duxford. The first crashed after its restoration; the second, WM-Z, was flying in 1993.

Frank Southern

Before long the Squadron had built a reputation for night-intruder work and its Havocs, Bostons and Beaufighters caused mayhem over German-occupied airfields. It moved to the Mediterranean theatre in 1942 and then came back to the UK to fly night escort sorties with its Serrate-equipped Mosquitoes on Bomber Command raids.

After the war No 23 Squadron flew Mosquitoes NF 30s and NF 36s, Vampire NF 10s, Venoms, Javelins and Lightning F3s. In 1975 the Squadron reformed with Phantoms and took these to Stanley in the Falkland Islands in April 1983, acting as the main deterrent force for the next five years. It then reformed at Leeming in 1988 to fly the Panavia Tornado F3. Within years the opportunities of intercepting a Russian Bear declined dramatically and the last recorded unannounced penetration of UK air space by a CIS aeroplane was on 6 September 1991. For this reason, and partly in the quest for economy, the Conservative government decided to reduce Leeming's operational strength from three to two Tornado Squadrons. No 23 Squadron was to be disbanded in April 1994.

No 25 Squadron

Formed at Montrose in 1915, it took its FE 2bs to France to serve with 1st Brigade. On 18 June 1916 Lt McCubbin and Cpl Waller shot down the German ace Max Immelmann. During 1917-1918 the Squadron operated its DH 4s as bombers and ground attack aircraft and then disbanded in January 1920. It reformed in March 1920 and was for two years in the unique position of being the sole fighter squadron in the UK.

Britain's air defence depended on No 25 Squadron's Sopwith Snipes!

With the arrival of the agile Grebes and Siskins the Squadron became famous for its aerobatic displays, perfecting these in the 1930s with the most elegant of biplane fighter designs, the Hawker Fury. After a brief period with Gladiators and Demons the Squadron converted to the long-nose Blenheims in 1938.

After exchanging these for Beaufighters, the Squadron shot down a Ju 88 in April 1941. In May 1942 No 25 Squadron arrived at Church Fenton, charged with the twin tasks of defending Yorkshire's industrial cities against Luftwaffe attack and carrying out intruder patrols over Germany. The Squadron transferred to Coltishall in February 1944 and became adept at destroying the V-1 'doodlebugs' air-launched by Heinkel He 111s.

No 25 Squadron retained its night-fighter role after the war and was disbanded twice - in 1953 and 1962. When it reformed in 1963 it was equipped not with aeroplanes but with Bristol/Ferranti Bloodhound Mk II weapon systems. Between 1970 and 1982 its three Flights helped defend RAF Bruggen, RAF Wildenrath and RAF Laarbruch. After the Falklands conflict the Flights returned to the UK and reformed at Leeming as No 25 Fighter Squadron after nearly twenty-seven years as a Bloodhound SAM Squadron. Equipped with Panavia Tornadoes, its first task in 1990 was to take over the Northern Quick Reaction Alert (QRA) Interceptor role in the UK Air Defence Region. Nine Squadron crews went to Dharan after the Iraqi invasion of Kuwait and all returned safely prior to Desert Storm.

Aircraft Preservation and Restoration
The work of The Northern Aeroplane Workshop and The Yorkshire Air Museum

The systematic destruction of civil and military aeroplanes for their scrap value is a universal problem for aviation enthusiasts and it is a sad fact that relatively few Yorkshire-built aeroplanes have survived. The nation is grateful that the pioneer Shuttleworth Collection was sufficiently well-endowed to preserve the Blackburn Monoplane; and that British Aerospace, the residual legatee of so many great aviation manufacturers, had a sufficient sense of history to keep the B-2 flying. But the Snipes were scrapped, the majestic Iris flying boats disappeared, Brough's Barracudas vanished and the mighty Halifaxes were all written off.

Then in 1973 began the endeavour to recreate one of the most attractive of all the First World War's aeroplanes, the Sopwith Triplane. This was G-BOCK, the inspiration of John Langham, constructed by the Northern Aeroplane Workshops over a period of seventeen years 1973-1990. Thanks to financial support from the Shuttleworth Collection, the volunteer construction team began work first in Heckmondwike and then in Dewsbury. Because the Triplane was to be a flying display machine, the team decided to finish it in the colourful markings of N6290 *Dixie II*, a No 8 (Naval) Squadron aeroplane, lost on 9 August 1917 during the Battle of Passchendaele. It was taken by BAe transporter to Old Warden and under the careful supervision of Trevor Foreman and Chris Page the brand new Sopwith Triplane was made ready for its first and highly successful sortie. This took place on 10 April 1992 with BAe test pilot, John Lewis, at the controls - a tribute to the skill and dedication of members of the Northern Aeroplane Workshop volunteers.

An even more ambitious project began in 1982 when Rachel Semlyen was inspired to turn the derelict six-acre Elvington site (still boasting its adjacent American-built RAF relief runway) into "a living museum and a lasting memorial". Elvington's long and honourable history had begun in 1940 as a grass airfield, rebuilt during 1941-2 to house first the Whitleys and then the Halifaxes of No 77 Squadron. In 1944 Elvington became home to the Halifaxes of No 346 *Guyenne* and No 347 *Tunisie* Squadrons whose exploits are described in the text. Elvington's long association with the Halifax prompted Chairman Ian Robinson to plan and execute the

replication of a Mark III LV907 named *Friday the Thirteenth* in honour of 158 Squadron's NP-F. This was the bomber that had flown from Lissett, logging 128 operational sorties before being consigned to the scrap merchants. No Halifax III had survived into the 1980s. Pieces of Handley Page aeroplanes existed: a nose section in the Imperial War Museum, a rear fuselage in the Isle of Lewis, some wings from a written-off Hastings, flak damaged engines in Germany. Not all were available to the Museum but the skill and dedication of another band of volunteers, plus generous funds from British Aerospace, from Victor Bingham's royalties*, aircrew associations, local businesses and councils, made the project viable.

Accordingly, an RAF Chinook obligingly airlifted the remains of a No 58 Squadron (Coastal Command) Halifax fuselage (then a hen house belonging to Robert Mackenzie) from the Hebrides to Stornoway. Caledonian McBraynes ferried it by sea and Fry's Metals by land and in this way the nucleus of a new NP-F arrived at Elvington. Michael Edwards, then General Manager at BAe Brough, ensured that his apprentices restored the fuselage as part of their training; and it was BAe that restored the mid-upper gun turret. The splendid four-gun rear turret, a Boulton Paul product presented by the Cotswold Recovery Group, was then fettled by Bernard Jefferson who, after a thousand hours of dedicated labour,

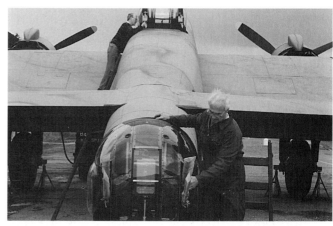

Volunteers working on the turrets of *Friday the Thirteenth*.
Yorkshire Air Museum

brought it up to a standard that convinces many a 4 Group rear gunner that it is the real thing. The RAF parted with the inner wing sections from its Hastings TG536 at Catterick and the main wheels from St Athan; the French Air Force presented the four Hercules engines; and the RAFA acquired the outer wing sections.

Appropriately, the replica of NP-F was wheeled out (less its outer engines and nose section) on 13 August 1993 - the only example of a Halifax III bomber in the world.

Another major restoration project at the Museum is the sole example of a 1941 Mosquito NF II (VI-C H1711). This aeroplane flew from Church Fenton in defence of Yorkshire against the Luftwaffe. Tony Agar acquired the ruined cockpit and fuselage in 1969 and spent many years restoring the aeroplane before moving to Yorkshire Air Museum where his work was marked by the presentation of the Mike Twite Award by *Flypast* magazine in 1992. The quality of Tony Agar's restoration is such that the NF II could take to the air in the years to come. The arrival of Mosquito HT-E on a visit to Elvington boosted the hope an ultimate sortie but the financial prospects of bringing the Mosquito's twin Merlin engines up to operational pitch remained as daunting as ever.

Many other restorations await the enthusiast at Yorkshire Air Museum: a Canberra bomber, a Hawker Hunter - representative of the many that flew from Yorkshire airfields - a very attractive T-33, a Vampire and a Jet Provost. For those who prefer to have "a fan up front", the tireless Dave Tappin acquired an Avro Anson for restoration during 1993. An example of a Mignet *Flying Flea* (reputedly built in Yorkshire during the carefree Thirties) is housed under cover as are superb examples of an English Electric Lightning and Blackburn Buccaneer, both of which flew into Elvington. Last of the preservation aircraft to land in 1993 (on 25 November) was the Handley Page Victor K2 XL231 - the famous

Lusty Linda no doubt grateful for Elvington's 9,800 foot runway. *Lusty Linda* had flown No 55 Squadron's last operational sorties in October 1993 and her battle honours included the Falklands War (1982) and the Gulf War (1991). The Museum is the thus the only place where one can see two generations of Handley Page four-engined bombers.

Yorkshire's connections with Handley Page were closest during the Second World War when almost every bomber airfield in the County housed, at some time, a squadron of Halifax bombers. No 10 Squadron served in Yorkshire at Dishforth, Leeming and Melbourne (1937-45) and in 1958, at Cottesmore, became the first Handley Page Victor Squadron. The reader will recall that the Handley Page HP 88 *test* aircraft equipped with the crescent wing was assembled at Brough and first flown from the old Emergency Landing Ground at Carnaby in June 1951.

In fact, Yorkshire's association with the crescent wing goes back to Rowland Ding's spectacular flights from the Harrogate Stray and Northallerton during 1914 in the Handley Page G 100 biplane. The connection continued after the First World War when the Blackburn Aeroplane & Motor Company married a De Havilland DH 6 fuselage and tail unit to a 200hp Bentley BR 2 rotary engine at the Sherburn works in 1920. To this was added the extraordinary Alula high lift wing as modified by A.A. Holle. The crescent-winged parasol aeroplane that resulted was known as the Holle Wing Blackburn Monoplane among the Brough and Sherburn work force. Its accepted designation is the Alula DH 6 and the solitary example, G-EAWG flew in January 1921 before being exported to France. A second experimental crescent wing-aircraft adapted by Blackburn was the Alula Semiquaver, a Martinsyde Semiquaver G-EAPX fitted with with a high-lift wing and a 800hp Hispano-Suiza engine. Designed to attack the world speed record, it was flown at Northolt by R.W. Kenworthy in 1921.

Tony Agar's Mosquito rebuild.

Yorkshire Air Museum

HT-E's visit to Elvington.

Yorkshire Air Museum

The Holle Wing Blackburn Monoplane/Alula DH 6.

Harry Flinton

Elvington's long runway and generous apron permitted all types of visiting aircraft to land and disperse. Without it, attractions such as Dr Helena Hamilton's beautiful Hornet Moth and an ever-welcome Spitfire would be lost to the thousands of spectators who flock to the Museum each year.

Fortunately, the Museum site itself has a long-term future. Through the sympathetic and supportive co-operation of the owner, Jack Birch of Wm. Birch & Sons, the Museum was able to purchase the site. Deeds were handed over to the Founder Chairman, Rachel Semlyen, in July 1993.

* Victor Bingham, *Halifax - Second to None*, Airlife Publishing Ltd., 1986

Visiting Spitfire.

Yorkshire Air Museum

Hornet Moth.

Aerial view of Yorkshire Air Museum, Elvington. The Canberra and other display aircraft may be seen parked on the old perimeter track in front of the restored Second World War control tower.

Yorkshire Air Museum

Chapter 1 - Sir George Cayley, Gliders and Balloons

1. C. H. Gibbs-Smith, Sir George Cayley's Aeronautics 1796-1855, HMSO, 1962: see International Tributes to Sir George Cayley, p.ix; and Conclusions, pp 199-210.
2. Gerard Fairlie & Elizabeth Cayley, The Life of A Genius, Hodder & Stoughton, 1965, p. 36.
3. C.H.Gibbs, *op.cit.*, p. 43.
4. L.T.C.Rolt, The Aeronauts, Longmans, 1966, p. 75
5. Rev. R.W.B.Hornby's Scrapbook, MS ADD 91 relating to Mr Weller's Balloon Flight, York Minster Library Archives, by permission of Canon J. Toy and M.S. Dorrington.
6. Fairlie & Cayley, *op.cit.*, p. 157.
7. *ibid* p. 157

Chapter 2 - Magnificent Men, Magnificent Women and their Flying Machines

1. Henri Farman had fitted ailerons to a Voisin machine in 1908 and made the world's first cross-country flight. He went on to design his own biplanes, thereafter known as Farmans. For an account of Cody's exploits see Arthur Gould Lee, The Flying Cathedral, Methuen 1965.
2. The aeroplane was designed by Levavasseur but built by the Antoinette Company. One well-known Antoinette pilot was Hubert Latham who tried to fly across the Channel on 19 July 1909 - before Blériot's famous flight later that year. There is a photograph of Latham's Antoinette nose-down in the Channel in Charles Gibbs-Smith, Early Flying Machines, Eyre Methuen, 1975/BCA 1976, pp 54-55.
3. For a discussion of this point see A.J Jackson, Blackburn Aircraft since 1909, Putnam new edition 1989, pp 78-80, 554-555.
4. A.J Jackson, Avro Aircraft since 1908, Putnam, 1990 edition, pp 53-4.

Chapter 3 - The First World War 1914-1918 (i) Zeppelins over Yorkshire

1. Christopher Cole & E.F.Cheesman, The Air Defence of Great Britain 1914-1918, Putnam, 1984, p. 146.
2. Cole & Cheesman, *op.cit.*, p. 408
3. The B.E.12s of No 50 Squadron at Bekesbourne were in action against Gothas, Giants and Rumplers in the last aeroplane raid on Britain 19/20 May 1918.
4. Lt Watt patrolled the Humber area in a 76 Squadron B.E.12b (C3094) during the last Zeppelin raid on Britain (5/6 August 1918) and attracted gunfire from the batteries at Hull and Flamborough. This may well be the cause of the report of a 'Zeppelin' approaching the Yorkshire coast that night.

Chapter 4 - The First World War 1914-1918 (ii) Offensive patrols from Yorkshire

1. These are stored in the Fleet Air Arm Museum, Yeovilton, where a superb replica of Hyams' Sopwith Baby is on display.
2. 'Hannoverana' was the RFC term for the Hannover CL II, III and IIIa. They were two-seat escort and close support fighters, strongly built and capable of absorbing a great deal of punishment. RFC pilots, including Major J.B McCudden VC, DSO, MC, MM, had a great deal of respect for them.
3. Robert Jackson, Aces' Twilight, Sphere Books, 1988, p 152.
4. The Felixstowe F2A may be regarded as the World War I equivalent of Coastal Command's Sunderland. It served during 1917-18 at the height of the German submarine campaign, replacing/supplementing the American Curtiss H.4 and H.12 Large America flying boats. Four F2As and a Curtiss H.12 fought fourteen German seaplanes and shot down eight in June 1918. Another F2A from Killingholme destroyed L-62 over the Heligoland minefields in May 1918.
5. Extra fuel cans aboard F2As boosted their endurance to over nine hours.
6. The 23X Class was part of the programme to lighten airships and at the same time increase their disposable loads. Four were planned. Two were built: the R-27 and the R-29. R-27 was burnt out at Howden; R-29 helped to sink the U-115 (29 September 1918).

Chapter 5 - Civil Aviation 1919-1935

1. After the Naval Wing separated from the RFC in July 1914 to become the RNAS, both services experienced supply difficulties for their different types of aircraft and the spare parts required. A Joint Air Committee (February 1916) proved ineffective. This was followed by the Curzon Air Board (May 1916) and the Cowdray Air Board (February 1917). These were advisory bodies but exerted great influence on military and civil aviation affairs. The Civil Aviation department of the Air Ministry was set up in February 1919. The first Director was AVM Sir F.H.Sykes. He was succeeded by AVM Sir Sefton Brancker who died in the crash of the R-101 (1930).
2. A.J. Jackson, Blackburn Aircraft since 1909, Putnam 1989, pp 102-105.
3. According to A.J. Jackson, *op.cit.*, it was re-engined with a 100hp Anzani in 1921.
4. A.J. Jackson, *op.cit.*, p.331.
5. Nevil Shute, Slide Rule, Heinemann, 1954, pp 156-7.
6. D.H Middleton, Airspeed: the Company and its Aeroplanes, Terence Dalton, 1982, p.15.

Chapter 6 - The RAF 1919-1934

1. S/L C.G.Burge, Encyclopaedia of Aviation, Pitman, 1935, pp 550-559.
2. Quoted Fred Adkin, From the Ground up: A History of RAF Groundcrew, Airlife 1983, pp 89-90.
3. S/L Burge, *op.cit.*, p.568.
4. Quoted Philip Moyes, Bomber Squadrons of the RAF and their Aircraft, Macdonald & Jane's/PBS 1976, p.161.

Chapter 7 - The RAF 1934-39 and the Fleet Air Arm 1937-1939

1 Bill Gunston, World Encyclopaedia of Aero Engines, PSL, 1986, pp 135-137.

2 John Terraine, The Right of the Line, Hodder & Stoughton, 1985, p. 18.

3 Quoted Terraine, *op.cit.*, p. 37.

4 G.L 'Larry' Donnelly, The Whitley Boys, Air Research Publications, 1991, p. 27.

5 Boeing had established a factory in Canada (Sea Island Airport, Vancouver). For details of the Sharks built for the RCAF see A.J Jackson, Blackburn Aircraft since 1909, Putnam, 1989, p. 382.

6 The Admiralty ordered the eight-gun Fairey Fulmar straight off the drawing board. The prototype first flew in January 1940 and its existence was kept secret until September. The prototype is displayed in the FAA Museum, Yeovilton.

Chapter 8 - Year of the Whitley

1 Quoted Bill Gunston, So Few, W.H.Smith Ltd, 1992, p.209.

2 Sir Charles Webster & Noble Frankland, The Strategic Air Offensive against Germany (abbreviated as OH = Official History in later notes), HMSO, 1961, vol I, p.125.

3 Alastair Revie, The Lost Command, PBS, 1971, pp 7-8.

4 Sir Arthur Harris, Bomber Offensive, Collins, 1947, p. 36.

5 Donnelly, *op.cit.*, p. 42. The Whitley was forced down by two Belgian Fairey Fox interceptors. Belgium was still neutral.

6 Donnelly, *op.cit.*, p. 87.

7 Ed. Laddie Lucas, Out of the Blue, Hutchinson, 1985, pp 31-32.

8 R.T. Partridge, Operation Skua, FAA Museum, 1983, pp 143-150.

9 Peter Townsend, Time and Chance, Collins 1978, pp 105-6.

10 Ed. Roderick Macleod & Denis Kelly, The Ironside Diaries 1937-1940, Constable, 1962, p. 309.

11 Occasionally crews would make serious navigational blunders and cross England and Wales and ditch in the Irish Sea or in the Atlantic Ocean, their precise fate unknown.

12 In correspondence with the author 1964-65.

13 Hitler was particularly interested in the glider designs that might be suitable for transporting assault troops and equipment across the Channel.

Chapter 9 - The Battle of Britain June - October 1940

1 Andrew Boyle, No Passing Glory, Collins, 1955, p.98.

2 Donnelly, *op.cit.*, p.133.

3 Probably a CR 42 converted to Caccia Nocturna (night-fighter) standards. Piero Vergnano gives a brief account of the CN Falco in his I Caccia Fiat, Intyrama 1968, pp 35-36.

4 Len Deighton & Max Hastings, Battle of Britain, Michael Joseph , 1990, p. 166.

5 Alfred Price, Blitz on Britain 1939-1945, Ian Allan, 1977, analyses the Battle of Britain in his chapter entitled Fight For Survival pp 55-87.The quotation comes from his *The Hardest Day*, Arms and Armour Press 1988, p.167.

6 Wing Commander Allen developed his ideas in his Who Won the Battle of Britain? (Arthur Barker Ltd 1974); and in his article in *THE TIMES* (14 September 1974).

7 Richard Hough and Denis Richards, The Battle of Britain, Hodder & Stoughton, 1989, pp 327-328.

8 Sir Maurice Dean, The Royal Air Force in Two World Wars, Cassell, 1979, p. 147.

Chapter 10 - Yorkshire's Other Roles in 1940.

1 The Vulture engine was hurriedly designed and manufactured. There were serious teething problems - A. J. Jackson mentions fatigue failures on connecting rod bolts in his *Avro Aircraft since 1908* (Putnam 1990); Bill Gunston notes "inflight fires and other snags made the Vulture unpopular" (World Encyclopaedia of Aero Engines, PSL, 1986). Harald Penrose gives an interesting account of the Vulture engine in Chapters 11 and 12 of his *Architect of Wings* (Airlife 1985) and on p. 190 quotes the view of Sgt Bob Story DFM, a Manchester gunner, who remembered that during the First Thousand Bomber Raid "the Vultures gave trouble and on return a blind approach had to be made to Finningley, Doncaster."

Only 508 Vulture engines were produced for operational use and all of these were fitted to Manchesters. Other Rolls-Royce Vulture engines powered experimental and prototype aircraft such as the Hawker 'R' Type fighter later named the Tornado. Two prototypes were built before Rolls-Royce ceased manufacturing the Vulture.

2 Donnelly, *op.cit.*, p.177.

3 Leonard Cheshire, Bomber Pilot, Goodall Publications, 1979, Ch.6. See also the biographical accounts by: (i) Andrew Boyle, No Passing Glory, Collins, 1957, Ch. 5. (ii) Russell Braddon, Cheshire VC, CBC, 1956, pp 70-78.

4 Much controversy surrounds this raid, the extent of Ultra intercepts, and Churchill's foreknowledge of the event. Evidence is conflicting though it is interesting to speculate why certain Bofors units were rushed to the outskirts of the city the day before the raid.

5 Vern Haugland, The Eagle Squadrons, David & Charles, 1980, p.13.

Chapter 11 - Diverse Tasks : January - July 1941

1 Driffield had been repaired after the devastating Luftwaffe raid on 15 August 1940. Dummy Whitleys were scattered around the base when No 213 Squadron Hurricanes arrived, followed by No 1 Squadron RCAF and No 485 Squadron RNZAF Spitfires. 4 Group did not regain control of Driffield until 1 April 1941 when No 104 Squadron reformed here with Wellingtons, followed two days later by Canada's first overseas Bomber Squadron, No 405 Vancouver RCAF.

2 The paratroopers dropped on target but one Whitley carrying key members of the demolition team plus most of the explosives failed to find the drop zone. This meant that the paratroopers could not destroy Tragino Aqueduct though they did cause considerable damage to the structure All the paratroopers were captured when the submarine *Triumph* was unable to keep its 'pick-up' rendezvous.

3 One of Don Charlwood's phrases during interview.

4 Halifax B1 beam armament originally included twin .303 VGOs mounted on pillars on each side of the fuselage.

Each position had 1000 rounds of ammunition. There was no mid-upper gun turret. Nose defence comprised twin .303 Brownings in a Boulton Paul C Mk II turret plus 2000 rounds; rear defence had a Bolton Paul E Mk I turret with four .303 Brownings and 6,800 rounds.

5   Stanton Harcourt in Oxfordshire had itself been attacked on 16 August 1940 when Wimpey, the construction firm, was building the new runways.

6   In interview with the author at Swinton, North Yorkshire, September 1992.

7   Tom Harrison, Living through the Blitz, Schocken Books/New York and Collins UK, 1976, p.269.

8   Deighton & Hastings, *op.cit.*, p. 203.

Chapter 12 - A New Offensive July - November 1941

1   Dead reckoning made great demands on the pilot or navigator. It required (a) calculating the course, (b) track and (c) ground speed of an aircraft in flight from a knowledge of the true airspeed and wind velocity.

Fixes en route were determined by reference to observation and plotting outside objects (e.g. stars or headlands) and/or by radio aids. Course, track and estimated wind had to be constantly recorded At all times the navigator had to record the following data on what the RAF originally called the Bigsworth Board and, during the war, on 'Navigational Computor Mk III': the exact course steered, the air distance flown and the drift. His calculation of position or 'fix' from this data is called 'dead reckoning'.

This was taught and practised in great detail at Navigational Schools The basic text was Air Navigation, HMSO A.P.1234, 1941. Interestingly, the last example of practical navigation describes the return from Emden to the mythical bomber base of 'Mudbury' in Yorkshire via Flamborough Head.

2   No 304 (Silesian) and No 305 (Ziemia Wielkopolska) were two Polish Squadrons that had formed at Bramcote, Warwickshire, in August 1940. In Yorkshire, as part of 1 Group, they flew Wellingtons until 1942 when No 304 transferred to Coastal Command (7 May) and No 305 moved to Hemswell in Lincolnshire in July.

Chapter 13 - The Survival of Bomber Command December 1941 - June 1942

1   The Halifax B II's most noticeable difference was the addition of the bulky Boulton Paul C Mk II mid-upper turret. The very useful Boulton Paul K Mk I ventral turret (fitted to L9485) was not adopted on aircraft sent to Nos 35, 76 and 10 Squadrons during October-December 1941.

2   Nell was the Mitsubishi G3M Navy Type 96. Betty was the Mitsubishi G4M Navy Type 1. Twenty-seven of these twin-engined bombers had been based in Indo-China in preparation for attacks on American forces in the Philippines. For further details consult René J. Francillon, Japanese Aircraft of the Pacific War, Putnam, 1979.

3   D.C.T Bennett, Pathfinder, Goodall Publications, 1983, pp 135-137.

4   Harris, *op.cit.*, p. 68.

5   Bennett, *op.cit.*, pp 141 - 142.

6   *ibid*, p. 142.

7   The crew of his Halifax W1041 was:

Pilot	Bennett	Escaped
2nd Pilot	Sgt Walmsley	Escaped
Navigator	Sgt Eyles	POW
WOP	Sgt C.R.S Forbes	Escaped
Flight Engineer	F/Sgt Colgan	Escaped
M/U Gunner	Sgt Murray	POW
R/Gunner	F/Lt How	Wounded, POW

8   Harris, *op.cit.*, pp 107-108.

9   *ibid*, Chapter Six, Getting the Weapons.

10. On 27 April 1941 Baron Gustav Braun von Stumm, Deputy Head of Information, gave a press conference in which he said: "Now the Luftwaffe will go for every building which is marked with three stars in Baedeker." See Niall Rothnie, The Baedeker Blitz, Ian Allan, 1992, who gives a thorough survey of the raids and describes the origin of the term 'Baedeker' on p. 131.

11. Ralph Barker, The Thousand Plan, Airlife, 1992, p.25

12. W.R.Chorley, In Brave Company, P.A. Chorley, 1990, pp 17 - 18.

13. Harris, *op.cit.*, p. 113.

Chapter 14 - Grim Preparations and a Crisis Survived: May- December 1942

1   Harris, *op.cit.*, p 120.

2   Some Do 217s had FuG 202 and 'Spanner' equipment and this detected heat radiation from bomber exhausts. See Manfred Griehl, Do 217-317-417, Airlife, 1991, Chapter 5.

3   No 158 Squadron had gone to East Moor to convert to Halifaxes after the Thousand Raid. See Chorley, *op.cit.*, Chapter 2.

4   Quoted Charlwood, *op.cit.*, p 101.

5   *ibid*, p 107.

6   Quoted Dudley Saward, 'Bomber' Harris 1985, pp 246.

7   Quoted Saward *op.cit.*, p 246.

8   Harris, op. cit. p 128.

9   *ibid*, pp 129-130.

10 Bennett, *op.cit.*, has a wonderful story on p. 187 explaining how the three names Wanganui, Parramatta and Newhaven were chosen during a discussion in his office between himself, S/Ldr Ashworth and his WAAF Corporal Ralph.

11 *ibid*, p 138.

12 Quoted by Brian J Rapier, Halifax at War , Ian Allan, 1987, p 30.

13 Martin Middlebrook & Chris Everitt, Bomber Command War Diaries, Viking, 1985, p 329.

14 W. R Chorley, To See the Dawn Breaking, Self-published, 1981, p 58.

15 Merrick, *op.cit.*, Chapter 4: Modifications .

Chapter 15 - The Battle of the Ruhr 5/6 March - 24 July 1942

1   In interviews with the author.

2   Quoted Merrick, *op.cit.*, p 43-43.

3   The Goebbels Diaries (translated and edited by Louis P. Kochner), Hamish Hamilton, 1948, p.208.

4   The Polish miner was executed by the Resistance.

5   Christopher Jary, Portrait of a Bomber Pilot, Sydney Jary, 1990, p 2.

6   Goebbels *op.cit.,* p 249.

7   Chorley, *op.cit.,* p.69.

8   Middlebrook & Everitt, *op.cit.,* p. 394.

9   Goebbels *op.cit.,* pp 316-317.

Chapter 16 - From Hamburg to Peenemünde: July - August 1943

1   *Aural Monica* was fitted inside the tail of the bomber and warned via bleeps in crews' headphones of approaching aircraft. This was disliked as it picked up other bombers in the stream far more often than German night-fighters

     Visual Monica (Fishpond) was a cathode ray tube displaying echoes from other aircraft and operated by the Wireless Operator. It gave range and location of nearby aircraft and was very popular until German night-fighters used *Flensburg* homer equipment to detect Monica radiations and thus locate the bomber. Note the importance of the captured Ju 88 (13 July 1944) described in Alfred Price, Instruments of Darkness, Granada, 1979, pp 246-250.

     Boozer reacted to the gun-laying/night-fighter frequencies of *Würzburg* and *Lichtenstein*. The pilot would see an orange light on his instrument panel when Boozer picked up gun radars or an approaching night-fighter However, if the night-fighter switched of its radar the orange light went out!

2   Possibly this was the Do 217 that had just shot down the 76 Squadron Halifax.

3   Spencer Dunmore & William Carter, Reap the Whirlwind, McClelland & Stewart Inc (Canada), 1991, p 125.

4   Moyes, *op.cit.,* p 348.

5   Goebbels, *op.cit.,* p 332.

6   No doubt his severe artiosclerosis explains why he escaped the death penalty when put on trial at Nuremberg as one of the 22 war criminals. See translator's note in Goebbels, *op.cit.,* p 249.

7   Thirty-eight aircraft had been lost on the two raids, Hamburg and Essen.

8   The Halifaxes and Stirlings carried more incendiaries than usual in order to lighten their bomb loads. According to Martin Middlebrook in his The Battle of Hamburg, Penguin, 1984, p. 235, this brought the incendiary load up to a total of 1,200 tons (940 tons were used on the previous Hamburg raid).

9   Gordon Musgrove, Operation Gomorrah, 1981, Chapter 6, The Firestorm Phenomenon.

10.   Quoted Gavin Lyall, The War in the Air, Hutchinson, 1978, pp 297-300.

11   The call-light system is described in Chapter 14, p 124.

12   Musgrove, *op.cit.,* pp 143-144.

13   One of the best known raids in the Battle of the Ruhr was the attack by 617 Squadron on the Möhne and Eder Dams (16/17 May 1943). The raid caused the deaths (mostly by drowning) of 1294 people, a total that far exceeded

the death toll during the Dortmund raid (693) on 4/5 May 1943.

14   Quoted Middlebrook, The Battle of Hamburg, p 310.

15   Quoted Chorley, *op.cit.,* p 82.

16   *ibid*, p 82.

17   Bennett, *op.cit.,* pp 199-200.

18   The Wellington was still used for raids on Occupied Europe.

19   Quoted Martin Middlebrook, The Peenemünde Raid, Penguin 1988, p 130.

20   Harris, *op.cit.,* pp 184-185.

21   But it was visited by the Americans three times in 1944: 18 July, 4 August and 25 August.

22   Constance Babington Smith, Evidence in Camera, Penguin 1961, p 206

23   *ibid*, p 207.

Chapter 17 - The Battle of Berlin (i): the Bomber Offensive August - December 1943

1   This term was often used as a synonym for 'master bomber',

2   Harris, *op.cit.,* p. 186.

3   Dunmore & Carter, *op.cit.,* pp 174-175.

4   Bruce Barrymore Halpenny, Action Stations 4: Military Airfields of Yorkshire, PSL, 1982, p. 109.

5   Chorley, *op.cit.,* pp 93-94.

6   Quoted Saward, *op.cit.,* p. 285.

7   Harris had served in the United States as a member of the British Purchasing Commission and was well aware of the significance of America's supplies of aircraft to Commands other than his own e.g. Hudson, Catalina, Dakota, Liberator, B-17 C Fortress, the Harvard and the Allison-engined Mustang I. Douglas Bostons began flying with 2 Group Bomber Command in October 1941; North American Mitchells served in 2 Group from September 1942 onwards.

8   Middlebrook & Everitt, *op.cit.,* p 453.

9   OH (Webster & Frankland), *op.cit.,* Vol ii, pp 201-202.

Chapter 18 - The Battle of Berlin (2): The Bomber Offensive January-March 1944

1   J. Douglas Harvey, Boys, Bombs and Brussels Sprouts, Goodread Biographies, McClelland & Stewart Ltd (Canada), 1981, pp 125-126.

2   Dunmore & Carter, *op.cit.,* p. 201.

3   Alan W.Cooper, Bombers over Berlin, PSL, 1989, pp 146-148; and Middlebrook & Everitt, *op.cit.,* pp 465-466.

4   Quoted Cooper. *op.cit.,* p. 181.

5   Martin Middlebrook, The Berlin Raids, Penguin , 1990, p. 272.

6   Quoted John Searby, The Bomber Battle for Berlin, Airlife, 1991, p. 145.

Chapter 19 - The End of the Main Offensive: the Nuremberg Raid 30/31 March 1944.

1   Anthony Cave Brown, Bodyguard of Lies, Allen & Co., 1976.

2　Martin Middlebrook, The Nuremberg Raid (Revised Edition), Allen Lane, 1980.

3　This lecture was delivered to the Johannesburg Branch of the South African Military History Society on 9 June 1977. Both authors flew with Bomber Command during the Second World War and are anxious to emphasise that the text is not a literal transcript of a briefing for the Nuremberg raid but is very close to those given on Yorkshire bomber bases in March 1944.

4　*Fishpond* was the customary name for Visual Monica. It was a tail warning device connected to H2S and scanned the area covered by H2S to pick up aircraft approaching behind/below the fuselage. The scan showed up such aircraft as blips on a cathode ray tube. Monitoring *Fishpond* was part of the WOP's duties

5　Chorley, *op.cit.*, p. 141.

6　Interview with the author 1991.

7　Quoted Middlebrook, Nuremberg Raid, *op.cit.*, p. 250

Chapter 20 - Bombing for Overlord

1　Dean, *op.cit.*, p 276.

2　Chorley, *op.cit.*, p 148.

3　Terraine, *op.cit.*, has an excellent summary of the work of the Tactical Air Forces in 73. *Air supremacy; interdiction, Tactical Air Forces; 'Bodyguard'*.

4　Quoted Eric Taylor, Operation Millennium, Hale, 1987, p.17.

5　For a detailed treatment of this raid see Jeffrey Ethell & Alfred Price, Target Berlin - Mission 250; 6 March 1944, Jane's Publishing, 1981.

6　I. D. Foster, East Moor History, Yorkshire Air Museum Publications, 1990, p 17.

7　For pure excitement, Paul Brickhill's The Dam Busters, Evans 1951/Pan 1954 remains a classic.

Chapter 21 - The Assault on Germany: from D-Day to the Ardennes 1944.

1　For a brief description of the history of Ruhr Express see Dunmore & Carter, *op.cit.*, p. 343.

2　Ploesti had been overrun by the Red Army during August 1944.

3　Quoted Saward, *op.cit.*, p. 347.

4　Quoted Chorley, *op.cit.*, p. 157.

5　James Stewart, the film star, was then serving as Operations Officer with the 435th Bomb Group at Old Buckenham, near Attleborough, Norfolk.

6　The 389th Bomb Group.

7　Quoted Dumore & Carter, *op.cit.*, p. 319.

8　The 34th had been flying B-24H/J Liberators (23 May - 24 August). It then re-equipped with B17G Fortresses and used these on operations until 20 April 1945, the date of its last mission.

9　Middlebrook & Everitt, *op.cit.*, p. 602.

10　Louis Bourgain, Nuits de Feu sur l'Allemagne, L'Imprimerie Panda, 9130 Noisy-le-Sec, 1991, p 157.

11　Bourgain, *op.cit.*, pp 158-159.

12　Ist Airborne Army HQ and 21st Army Group chose to disregard intelligence reports (and Dutch Resistance information) that at least two SS Panzer Divisions (IX Hohestaufen and XX Frundsberg) were in the Arnhem area.

13　For all sorts of reasons, 30 Corps failed to reach Arnhem; and most of the supplies dropped to the 4th Parachute Brigade fell into German hands. 8,905 airborne soldiers and 1,100 glider pilots had landed around Oosterbeek and of these only 2,163 escaped death or capture. For the Ardennes, the German effort was total. The German call-up age was down to sixteen; Hitler replaced his lost mobile reserves and sent eighteen divisions from the Eastern to the Western Front. Facing them in the Ardennes along an 85 mile front were the US 99 Infantry Division, 900 men of the 1st Cavalry, the 106th Infantry - all mostly unblooded troops - and the battle-weary 28th Division that had already lost over 6000 men in the previous battles and was resting in the Ardennes. The Allies had no idea that Germany still had the power to launch yet another strike in the classic blitzkrieg style.

14　Middlebrook & Everitt, *op.cit.*, p. 632.

15　Albert Speer, Inside the Third Reich, Weidenfeld & Nicolson, 1970, p 418.

Chapter 22 - Yorkshire: the County at War 1942-1945

1　Correspondence/interview with author 14 April 1992.

2　The first nineteen production Firebrands Mk I and Mk II were fitted with in-line engines. The strike fighter Firebrand IIIs had the Bristol Centaurus radials and four-bladed propellers. The Firebrand TF IV first flew in May 1945 and it was this version that equipped 813 Squadron Fleet Air Arm.

3　Letter to the author 19 June 1992.

4　Maintenance and Ferry Command pilots as well as ATA pilots flew the Halifaxes. Lettice Curtis gave her views on flying the Halifax in Geoffrey Jones, Raider - the Halifax and its Flyers, William Kimber, 1978, pp 39-40.

5　ATA civilian pilots saved the RAF thousands of aircrew hours. They converted to Halifax bombers via a special course based at Pocklington, East Yorkshire.

6　Quoted Merrick, *op.cit.*, p. 104.

7　Quoted Saward, *op.cit.*, pp 295-296.

8　Via J. Rotherham, August 1992.

9　Via J. Rotherham, September 1992.

10　Via J. Rotherham, October 1992.

11　Amy J. Bridson, From Needles-Sewing to Irons-Soldering, Merlin Books, 1989, pp 16-17.

12　Loran was the American equivalent of Gee but inaccurate over short distances. Rebecca was also American and was used from 1942 onwards (e.g. when the Halifaxes took the Horsa gliders to Norway in Operation Freshman) to ensure accurate drops of agents or airborne supplies.

13　John Chartres, Fly for their Lives, Airlife, 1988, p 9.

14　Coastal Command Review, 1943, quoted by Chartres, *op.cit.*, p 39.

15　Sawyer, *op.cit.*, p 179.

16　Sawyer, *op.cit.,* p 180.

17　I am grateful to F/Lt Ronald N. Lawson for providing me with these details. Others are available in his privately published *Flying and Other Logs,* copyright Angela Mary Lawson (1989), and available from 14 Woodlands Court, Timperley, Altrincham, Cheshire, WA15 7QQ.

18　In interview with the author, 1991.

19　For a full description of the work of the Royal Observer Corps see T. E Winslow, Forewarned is Forearmed, William Hodge & Co (1948) and especially Ch. VI : *The Air Raid Warning System.*

20　For an account of these SD-2 bombs see Alfred Price, Blitz on Britain 1939-45, PBS, 1977, pp 151-152.

21　A.J. Brown, Ground Staff, Eyre & Spotiswoode, 1943, p 134.

Chapter 23 - Press on Regardless

1　For a recent survey of the event see Donald L. Caldwell, JG26 -Top Guns of the Luftwaffe, Orion Books, 1991, Chapter 13.

2　I am grateful for sight of S/Ldr Lord's captain's map and pencilled notes thereon; and for his kindness in granting me three interviews at his home in Bideford, Devon.

3　In letters to the author, 1992-3, and in:

(i) Bomber Command Newsletter , No 13, February 1990, Bomber Command Minelaying in Danish Waters.

(ii) Vestallierede Luftangreb i Danmark under 2. verdenskrig, published by Aarhus Universitesforlag, 1988, with Henrik Skov Kristensen and Claus Kofoed.

4　Moyes, *op.cit.,* p 79.

5　See Goebbels' final entries in The Goebbels Diaries: The Last Days, ed Hugh-Trevor Roper, Secker & Warburg, 1978.

6　When Allied scientists entered Germany hard on the heels of the advancing troops they found the partly built atomic pile and the German nuclear scientists at Haigerloch, 50km south-west of Stuttgart.

7　Described in Geoffrey Brooks, Hitler's Nuclear Weapons, Leo Cooper, 1992.

8　Quoted Saward, *op.cit.,* p 373.

9　Quoted Saward, *op.cit.,* p 371. Curiously, Denis Richards in his Portal of Hungerford, Heinemann, 1977, does not treat in any detail the Thunderclap issue, though he does examine (as does Dudley Saward op. cit.) the extraordinary correspondence between Portal and Harris during 1944-45.

10　This point was made most strongly by the RAF Chaplain in Chief at the Harris Statue Dedication in 1992 (See *Wingspan* magazine, September 1992). In a letter to The Daily Telegraph (27 May 1952), S/Ldr P. Tomlinson, notes that he tape-recorded an interview with Sir Arthur Harris in South Africa after the war. Sir Arthur stated that the order to bomb Dresden actually came from General Eisenhower, the Supreme Allied Commander. After receiving this order Sir Arthur checked with the Air Ministry ". . . it was to be bombed. It was bombed and thereafter they all turned their backs on it."

11　David Irving wrote to *The Times* (7 July 1966) concerning the casualty figures quoted in his *The Destruction of Dresden* (1963) in which he had originally estimated deaths as between 35,000 and 220,000. He stated that he had fresh information that lowered the death toll to 25,000, in line with the British and Russian estimates issued in 1945. These revised figures have been ignored by certain authors on the grounds that they "appear too low". For example, on p.180 of their *Target: Hitler's Oil* (William Kimber, 1985) Ronald C. Cooke and Roy Conyers Nesbit prefer to deny post-war East German estimates of 35,000 dead and speak of a "revised estimate" by David Irving of "100,000" as the "most acceptable figure". Apart from a mention of unspecified "important circumstantial evidence", they do not explain why, on what grounds, or to whom this figure becomes "acceptable".

12　See Index references to Air Marshal 'Batchy' Atcherley and his tour at Church Fenton, Yorkshire. Officially, Drem lights were developed at Drem airfield for No 602 Squadron Spitfires on night patrols. On runway approach, the Spitfire's forward vision was always poor and exhaust flames at night made matters worse. Drem developed a system of perimeter lights along the lines of those installed at Church Fenton that helped the pilot as he made his curving approach. The idea was adopted and refined and became 'Airfield Lighting Mk I' but the system was usually termed 'Drem Lighting' during the war.

13.　I have followed the figures collected by Simon W. Parry in his *Intruders over Britain: the Luftwaffe Night Fighter Offensive 1940-1945*, Air Research Publications, 1987.

14.　The last British bomber to fall to the guns of a German intruder was probably a 1665 Heavy Conversion Unit Halifax, then based at Saltby, shot down near Wittering on 20 March 1995.

Chapter 24 - A Decisive Contribution

1　As related to the No 10 Squadron Halifax crews during their briefing at Melbourne.

2　"A very brave fellow" was the comment made by F/Lt Desmonde Moss DFC about his mid-under gunner, F/Sgt L.L. Hall.

3　By permission of F/Lt Desmonde Moss DFC.

4　F/Lt Moss was convinced at the time that it was a single-engined 'Ju 52'; he agreed that it might have been a Ju W-34; or it could have been the remains of a Ju 52 lacking two wings and two engines.

5　The crew list that night was:

F/Lt D. Moss	Captain Bombing	- 'Des' survived
F/Sgt Davenport	Navigator	
WO L.A. Webster	Air Bomber	
F/Sgt R. Fowler	Wireless Operator-	'Jock' survived
F/Sgt L.L. Hall	Mid-Under Gunner	
Sgt H. Tasker	Flight Engineer	
F/Sgt S.T. Hodgson	Tail Gunner	- 'Steve' survived
F/Sgt Fearnley	Mid-Upper Gunner	

6　Dunmore & Carter, *op.cit.,* pp 352-353.

7　Goebbels, *op.cit.,* pp 56-57.

8   Goebbels, *op.cit.,* p. 78.

9   Goebbels, *op.cit.,* p. 113.

10 Wesel was a mass of rubble and German resistance went on amidst the ruins until dawn 25 March 1945.

11 Adolf Galland, The First and the Last, Methuen, 1955, p. 355.

12 This was a 431 Squadron Lancaster. Both F/O Heaven and his tail gunner F/Sgt Kutchna were decorated for this action.

13 Quoted Dumore & Carter, *op.cit.,* p 355.

14 Galland, *op.cit.,* p. 356.

15 Middlebrook & Everitt, *op.cit.,* p. 644.

16 Bourgain, *op.cit.,* La Dernière Mission, pp 184-187.

17 Quoted Carter & Dunmore, *op.cit.,* p. 362.

18 Bourgain, *op.cit.,* pp 268-269.

19 These views took no heed of the sheer power of the German armed forces on land, sea and in the air during 1943. One of the most succinct accounts of German strength in the spring and summer of 1943 appeared in The Times (19 April 1990) when Alan Clark noted :

(a) the relative *inactivity* on the Eastern Front between March and July.

(b) the remarkable German victory over the Russians at Kharkov after the Battle of Kursk and

(c) the presence of a huge reserve in the West: five Panzer divisions, 3rd, 6th, 7th, 11th and 19th; three SS: Das Reich, Liebstandart andTotenkopf; and the best equipped division in the entire German army, Gross Deutschland.

At a time when the Allies did not have air supremacy, this was the size of the reserve Hitler committed in the west during 1943 in case the Allies invaded; for it would be in the West, said the Führer, that the battles to decide the outcome of the war would be fought.

20 Quoted Richards, *op.cit.,* p. 333.

21 *ibid*, p. 334.

22 *ibid*, p. 335.

23 The Official History in four volumes.

24 *"The greater immorality open to us in 1940 and 1941 was to lose the war against Hitler's Germany. To have abandoned the only means of direct attack which we had at our disposal would have been a long step in that direction."* From Dr Noble Frankland's speech at the Royal United Services Institution, December 1961.

25 S/Ldr Beryl E. Escott uses this quotation as a chapter heading in her Women in Air Force Blue, PSL, 1989. Darré was found guilty of black market frauds and disgraced in 1942. He survived, presumably because of his long personal friendship with Hitler. Imprisoned by the Allies for five years after the war, Darré died in 1953.

26 Escott, *op.cit.,* p. 231.

27 OH Webster & Frankland, *op.cit.,* Vol III, p. 310.

Chapter 25 - The search for security 1945-1963

1   In correspondence with the author 12 November 1992.

2   The Hornet served in Fighter Command 1946-1951; and against the Malayan Communist Party guerrillas up to 1955.

3   Quoted Andrew Brooks, V-Force, Jane's, 1987, p 32.

4   I am grateful to Guy Jefferson for this information.

5   See Alexander Boyd, The Soviet Air Force, Purnell, 1977, and especially Chapter 13, *The Day of the MiG-15.*

6   A.J. Jackson, Handley Page Aircraft since 1907, Putnam 2nd ed. 1987, p 502.

7   In 1946 a benevolent Labour government sold to the Soviet Union twenty-five Rolls-Royce Nene 2 and thirty Derwent 5 centrifugal flow turbojet engines. The MiG-15 jet fighter fitted with copies of these engines flew in 1947 and was then the world's lightest and fastest jet fighter and a positive threat to the United Nations' forces in Korea (1950-53). Critics of weapon sales today should reflect on past actions.

8   Bushby, op. cit, p 193.

9   The OCU transferred to Coltishall in 1964 when the RAF decided to vacate Middleton St George. This former RAF base became Teeside Civil Airport and officially opened in 1966.

10 For his evolving views on defence see Harold Macmillan, Riding the Storm, Macmillan, 1971.

11 Quoted Brooks, *op.cit.,* p 136.

Chapter 26 - Design and production of military aircraft in Yorkshire since 1945

1   No 830 Squadron flew its Wyverns at Suez in November 1956.

2   The advent of turbine and jet propelled aeroplanes meant that the Royal Navy was now reluctant to store highly volatile petrol aboard aircraft carriers.

3   Air Chief Marshal Sir David Lee, Flight from the Middle East, HMSO, 1980, p 155. For a detailed acount of Beverley operations see Bill Overton, Blackburn Beverley, Midland Counties Publications, 1990 and A.J Jackson, Blackburn Aircraft since 1909, Putnam, 1989, pp 463-479.

4   It travelled on its own wheels as did all the aircraft tested at Holme.

5   It was not refuelled en route. When it landed at Lossiemouth it had sufficient fuel left for another thirty minutes of flying.

6   Most South African air bases were located on high ground where temperatures were equally high. These conditions dictated the need for extra boost.

7   It must be stressed that several firms, notably J. Rotherham Masonry, have made every effort to preserve the buildings at Holme and to erect memorials to the Squadrons who flew from Holme during 1939-45. J. Rotherham Masonry is held in high regard by the survivors of No 458 Squadron RAAF, No 101 Squadron RAF and No 76 Squadron RAF, for a time commanded by G/Capt Leonard Cheshire. Several reunions have been held at the old airfield and 76 Squadron marched past there in September 1987 when G/Capt Cheshire took the salute.

8   Quoted Roy Boot, From Spitfire to Eurofighter, Airlife, 1990, p 185.

9   The last Phantoms supplied to the RAF were ex-US Navy F4Js, modified and serviced at Brough after 1985.

10 The first Tucano delivery was to Central Flying School, RAF Scampton, on 1 September 1988.

11 From Blackburn to British Aerospace 1909-1985, British Aerospace plc, 1985, p. 51.

12 Slingsby specialised in various structures and components made from composite materials e.g. airship gondolas for Airship Industries, now taken over by Slingsby.

Chapter 27 - Aspects of Civil and General Aviation since 1945

1 In correspondence with the author, 14 November 1991 and 6 February 1992.

2 Humber Airways were negotiating with North Sea Helicopters/Management Aviation of Bourn (Cambridge) who held one of the three helicopter licences. The other two licence holders were Bristow and British European Airways.

3 Interviews with author, July and November 1992.

Chapter 28. - Service Aviation in Yorkshire

1 The Warsaw Pact countries were the Union of Soviet Socialist Republics, Poland, East Germany, Czechoslovakia, Hungary, Romania and Bulgaria. They formed the military alliance known as the Warsaw Pact in 1955, the Soviet equivalent of the western allies' North Atlantic Treaty Organisation (NATO) formed in 1949. In service terminology, the Warsaw Pact was frequently abbreviated to 'Warpac'.

2 The term 'Bear' was also adopted by the Soviet aircrews.

3 The Bear is still encountered and two were picked up by the RAF's new Boeing E3-D Sentry AEW-1 on 10 June 1991. Tornado F3s from No 25 Squadron at Leeming, Yorkshire intercepted and one took a picture of a Bear-D (depicted on p.10 of RAF Yearbook 1992).

4 John Rawlings, Fighter Squadrons of the RAF and their Aircraft, PBS New Edition, 1976, p.564.

5 John R. Bushby, Air Defence of Great Britain, Ian Allan, 1973, p. 197.

6 The Sukhoi Su-24 Fencer strike aircraft has not been widely seen in the West. It is an interdiction 'frontal bomber' and at least three Regiments were stationed in East Germany during the 1990s. The 1992 Flanker strength totalled 800+ aircraft. The Su-27 Flanker is well-known in the west and is a long-range interceptor equipped with very advanced 'dog-fighting' AA-11 'Archer' missiles. Polish-based Flankers had the range to escort Fencer strike aircraft as far as Yorkshire   Russia agreed by treaty to quit Polish bases by the end of 1993.

7 On 20 November 1984; presented by Neil MacFarlane, Minister of Sport.

8 Yorkshire Post 8 May 1984.

9 RAF News No 598 18-31 March 1984.

10 President Yeltsin confirmed that production of the new Backfire bomber had ended and at the end of 1992 it was thought that there were some forty or fifty Backfires based in the east.

Chapter 29 - Operation is the Gulf 1990-1991

1. This somewhat bland title was simply the next one in the list of British Operation code names. I am grateful to F/Lt D. M. Pleasant WRAF, Community Relations Officer, RAF Leeming, for details of aircraft disposition during Operation Granby.

2 This was W/Cdr Nigel Elsdon's Tornado flying from Muharraq against the former RAF base at Shaibah near Basra. Four Tornadoes took part in the attack but none of the crews saw Elsdon's aircraft strike the ground. The precise reason for the crash, in which both crewmen died, is unknown.

3 By 28 January 1991 about 100 Iraqi aircraft had fled to Iran whose government promised that none would be permitted to leave before the end of hostilities.

4. Forty-one Iraqi aircraft were destroyed in combat, including nine Mirage F9s, eight MiG-23s, five MiG-29, four MiG-21s, two MiG-25s, two Su-25s and four Su-7/17/22s. Those specified were all aerial victories most of which were won by the successful use of AIM-7, AIM-8 and AIM-9 air to air missiles.

5. Paul Jackson, Gulf Air War Debrief (ed. Stan Morse), Aerospace Publishing, 1991, p 144.

6. This had been a Royal Navy requirement for underwater survival.

7. The quotations are from S/Ldr R. Phillips' Royal Aeronautical Society lecture "Buccaneer Design and Gulf Operations."

Bibliography

Abbott, Patrick, The British Airship at War 1914-18, Terence Dalton 1989

Adams, C., 578 Squadron Operations 1944-45, YAM 1990

Allen, W/Cdr., Who Won the Battle of Britain? Arthur Barker Ltd 1974

BAe, From Blackburn to British Aerospace 1909-1985, British Aerospace 1986

Barker, The Thousand Plan, Airlife 1992

Barnes, C.H., Handley Page Aircraft since 1907, Putnam 1987
—— Shorts Aircraft since 1900, Putnam 1989

Barnett, Corelli, Engage the Enemy More Closely, Hodder & Stoughton 1991

Bekker, Cajus, The Luftwaffe War Diaries, Macdonald 1964

Bennett, D., Pathfinder, Goodall 1983

Bingham, V., Halifax - second to none, Airlife/Yorkshire Air Museum 1986

Blanchett, C., From Hull, Hell and Halifax, Midland Counties 1992

Boot, Roy, From Spitfire to Eurofighter, Airlife 1990

Boughton, Terence, The Story of the British Light Aeroplane, John Murray 1963

Bourgain, Louis, Nuits du Feu sur l'Allemagne, Panda, 1991
—— Sarabande Nocturne, Georges Thomas (Nancy) 1951

Bowyer, Chaz, The Mosquito at War, Ian Allan 1976
—— Hampden Special, Ian Allan 1975
—— Guns in the Sky, Dent 1979/Corgi 1981

Boyd, A., The Soviet Air Force since 1918, Macdonald & Jane's 1977

Boyle, A., No Passing Glory, Collins/Reprint Society 1955/57

Braddon, R., Cheshire VC, Evans/CBC 1956

Braybrook, R., Air Power - the Coalition and Iraqi Air Forces, Osprey 1991
—— Military Training Aircraft of Today, Haynes 1987

Bridson, Amy, From Needles-Sewing to Irons-Soldering, Merlin 1989

Brooks, Geoffrey, Hitler's Nuclear Weapons, Leo Cooper 1992

Brookes, A., V-Force, Jane's 1982

Brown, A.J., Ground Staff, Eyre & Spottiswoode 1943

Burge, C.G., Encyclopaedia of Aviation, Pitman, 1936

Bushby, John, Air Defence of Great Britain, Ian Allan 1973

Buttlar, von, Zeppelins over England, Harrap 1931

Caldwell, L., JG 26, Orion, New York 1991

Campbell, J., The Bombing of Nuremberg, Futura 1974

Castle, H.G., Fire over England, Secker & Warburg, Leo Cooper 1982

Catchpole, B., Twentieth Century Germany, Oxford 1965

Cook, R.C. & Nesbit, R.C., Target: Hitler's Oil, William Kimber 1985

Cooper, A.W., Bombers over Berlin, PSL 1989

Charlwood, Don, Journeys into Night, Hudson Australia 1991

Chartres, John, Fly for their Lives, Airlife 1988

Cheshire, Leonard, Bomber Pilot, Goodall 1988

Chorley, W.R., To See the Dawn Breaking, Chorley Publications 1981
—— In Brave Company, Chorley Publications 1990

Churchill, W.S., The Gathering Storm, Cassell 1948
—— Their Finest Hour, Cassell 1949
—— The Grand Alliance, Cassell 1950
—— The Hinge of Fate, Cassell 1951
—— Closing the Ring, Cassell 1952
—— Triumph and Tragedy, Cassell 1954

Cole, C., & Cheesman, E., The Air Defence of Britain 1914-1918, Putnam 1984

Dean, Sir Maurice, The Royal Air Force and Two World Wars, Cassell, 1979

Deighton, L., & Hastings, M., Battle of Britain, Michael Joseph 1990

Dodsworth, Ted, Wings over Yorkshire, Hutton Press 1988

Donnelly, G. L. 'Larry', The Whitley Boys, Air Research Publications 1991

Dundas, Hugh, Flying Start, Stanley Paul 1988

Dunmore, S. & Carter, W., Reap the Whirlwind, McClelland & Stewart Inc (Canada) 1991

Escott, Beryl E., Women in Air Force Blue, PSL 1989

Fairlie, G., & Cayley, E., The Life of a Genius, Hodder & Stoughton 1965

Foster, I.D., RAF East Moor 1942-1946, YAM 1991

Freeman, R. A., Mighty Eighth War Diary, Jane's 1981
—— The British Airman, Arms & Armour 1989

Galland, Adolf, The First and the Last, Methuen 1955

Gardner, Charles, British Aircraft Corporation, Batsford 1981

Gardner, R., & Longstaff, R., British Service Helicopters, Hale 1985

Gerbïg, Werner, Six Months to Oblivion, Ian Allan 1975

Gibbs-Smith, C.H., Sir George Cayley's Aeronautics, HMSO 1962
—— Early Flying Machines, Eyre Methuen 1976
—— The Rebirth of European Aviation, HMSO 1974

Goebbels, Josef, The Goebbels Diaries, Hamish Hamilton 1948
—— The Goebbels Diaries: the last days, Secker & Warburg 1978

Golley, J., (ed) So Few, W.H.Smith Ltd 1992

Garnett, David, The Grasshoppers Come & A Rabbit in the Air, Chatto & Windus, 1941

Green, G., British Aerospace - A Proud Heritage, Green Publications, 1988

Green, William, Famous Fighters of the Second World War, Macdonald & Jane's 1975

Griehl, M., & Dressel, J., Zeppelin! Arms and Armour 1990

Griehl, M., Do 217-317-417, Airlife 1991

Gunston, Bill, World Encyclopaedia of Aero Engines. PSL 1986
—— F-4 Phantom, Ian Allan 1977

Hallam, T.D., The Spider Webb, Arms & Armour 1979

Halpenny, Bruce, Action Stations 4: Military Airfields of Yorkshire, PSL 1982

Hamilton, Tim, The Life and Times of Pilot Officer Prune, HMSO 1991

Harris, Sir Arthur, Bomber Offensive, Collins 1947

Harrison, Tom, Living through the Blitz, Schocken Books (NY) 1976

Harvey, J.D., Boys, Bombs and Brussels Sprouts, McClelland & Stewart 1981

Harvey, M., The Allied Bomber War 1939-1945, Spellmount/BCA 1992

Hastings, Bomber Command, Michael Joseph 1980

Hough, R., & Richards, D., The Battle of Britain, Hodder & Stoughton 1989

Haugland, V., The Eagle Squadrons, David & Charles 1979

Irving, D., The Mare's Nest, William Kimber 1964
—— The Destruction of Dresden, William Kimber 1963

Jackson, A.J., Avro Aircraft since 1908, Putnam 1990
——— Blackburn Aircraft since 1909, Putnam 1989
Jackson, R., Aces' Twilight, Sphere 1988
——— Air Force - The RAF in the 1990s, Airlife 1990
Jakab, P.L., Visions of a Flying Machine, Airlife 1990
Jary, C., Portrait of a Bomber Pilot, Jary Publications 1990
Johnson, F., (ed) RAAF over Europe, Eyre & Spotiswoode 1946
Johnson, R. (ed), 434 Squadron History, The Hangar Bookshelf (Canada) 1984
Jones, A.H., The War in the Air Vol III, OUP 1928-1931
Jones, Geoffrey, Raider - the Halifax and its Flyers, William Kimber 1978
Jones, R.V., Most Secret War, Hamish Hamilton 1978
Lacey-Johnson, L., Point Blank and Beyond, Airlife 1991
Lee, A.G., The Flying Cathedral, Methuen 1965
Lee, Sir David, Flight from the Middle East, HMSO 1980
Liddle, P. H., The Airman's War 1914-1918, Blandford 1987
Lucas, Laddie (ed) Out of the Blue, Hutchinson, 1985
——— Wings of War, Hutchinson 1983
Lyall, G., The War in the Air, Hutchinson 1968
MacBean, J., & Hogben, S., Bombs Gone, PSL 1990
Macleod, R. & Kelly, D., The Ironside Diaries, Constable 1962
Mason, P.D., 'Fighting' Church Fenton, Fenton Enterprises 1992
McKee, A., Dresden 1945 : The Devil's Tinderbox, Souvenir Press 1982
Merrick, K.A., The Handley Page Halifax, Aston 1990
Middlebrook M., & Everitt, C., The Bomber Command War Diaries, Viking 1985
Middlebrook, M., The Berlin Raids, Penguin 1990
——— The Peenemünde Raid 1943, Penguin 1988
——— The Battle of Hamburg, Penguin 1984
——— The Nuremberg Raid, Allen Lane 1980
Middleton, D.H., Airspeed, Terence Dalton 1982
Milward, Alan, The German Economy at War, London University 1965
Moyes, P., Bomber Squadrons of the RAF and their Aircraft, Macdonald/PBS 1976
Morse, Stan (ed), Gulf Air War Debrief, Aerospace Publishing 1991
Musgrove, Gordon, Operation Gomorrah, Jane's 1981
Ogley, Bob, Doodlebugs and Rockets, Froglets Publications, 1992
Ormes, I., & Ormes, R., Clipped Wings, William Kimber 1973
Overton, Bill, Blackburn Beverley, Midland Counties 1990
Parry, Simon, Intruders over Britain, Air Research Publications 1987
Partridge, R.T., Operation Skua, FAA Museum 1983
Penrose, Harald, Architect of Wings, Airlife 1985
Poolman, Zeppelins over England, Evans 1960
Powers, Thomas, Heisenberg's War, Jonathan Cape, 1993
Price, Alfred, Battle over the Reich, Ian Allan 1973
——— Blitz on Britain 1939-1945, Ian Allan 1977
——— Instruments of Darkness, Macdonald & Jane's/ Granada Panther 1979
——— The Battle of Britain: The Hardest Day, Macdonald & Jane's 1979
Pudney, J., A Pride of Unicorns, Oldbourne 1960
Ransom, S. & Fairclough, R., English Electric Aircraft, Putnam, 1987

Rapier, Brian, White Rose Base, Aero Litho, 1972
——— Halifax at War, Ian Allan 1987
——— Melbourne Ten, Air Museum Publications 1982
Rawlings, J., Fighter Squadrons of the RAF and their Aircraft, PBS 1976
——— Coastal Support Aircraft and Special Squadrons, Jane's 1982
Redman, R.N., Yorkshire's Early Flying Days, Dalesman Books 1981
Revie, Alasdair, The Lost Command, Bruce & Watson 1971
Richards, D., Portal of Hungerford, Heinemann 1977
Rimell, R.L., Zeppelin! A Battle for Air Supremacy in World War I, Conway Maritime Press 1984
Rivett, L. & Matthew, J., Sir George Cayley, Yorkshire Air Museum Publications 1991
Robertson, Bruce, Halifax Special, Ian Allan 1980
Robinson, Peter, Then the War Came, Hutton Press 1989
Rolt, L.T.C., The Aeronauts, Longmans 1966
Rothnie, N., The Baedeker Blitz, Ian Allan 1992
Saward, D., 'Bomber' Harris, Sphere 1986
Sawyer, Tom, Only Owls and Bloody Fools Fly at Night, Goodall 1982
Searby, John, The Bomber Battle for Berlin, Airlife 1991
Shepherd, Dolly (with Peter Hearn in collaboration with Molly Sedgwick), When the 'Chute went up: the Adventures of an Edwardian Lady Parachutist, Hale, 1984
Shute, Nevil, Slide Rule, Heinemann 1954
Simpson, R.W., Airlife's General Aviation, Airlife 1991
Smith, Constance Babington, Evidence in Camera, Penguin 1961
Smith, J.R., & Kay, Antony, German Aircraft of the Second World War, Putnam 1976
Speer, A., Inside the Third Reich, Weidenfeld & Nicolson 1970
——— Spandau: the Secret Diaries, Collins 1976
Steetly, Martin, Confound and Destroy, Macdonald & Jane's 1978
Taylor, E., Operation Millennium, Hale 1987
Terraine, John, The Right of the Line, Hodder & Stoughton 1985
Thetford, Owen, British Naval Aircraft since 1912, Putnam 1977
——— Aircraft of the Royal Air Force since 1919, Putnam 1979
Townsend, P., Time and Chance, Collins 1978
Vergnagno, P., I Caccia Fiat, Intyrama 1968
Watson, B. (ed.), Military Lessons of the Gulf War, Greenhill 1991
Webb, E., & Duncan, J., Blitz over Britain, Spellmount 1990
Webster, C., & Frankland, N., The Strategic Air Offensive against Germany 1939-1945 (four Volumes), HMSO 1961 ('The Official History')
Whitbread, Helena (ed), The Diary of Anne Lister 1791-1840, Virago 1988
Winslow, T.E., Forewarned is Forearmed, William Hodge 1948
Winterbotham, F.W., The Ultra Secret, Weidenfeld & Nicolson 1974
Wood, Alan, History of the World's Glider Forces, PSL 1990
Wood, D., & Dempster D., The Narrow Margin, Arrow 1969
Wright, T., 'Knights Templar' - the Copmanthorpe Squadrons 1916-18, Yorkshire Air Museum Publications 1990

Index

'Doodlebug' (Fieseler Fi 103 VI) 209-10, 232
Dornberger, Walter 146
Döring, Lt Arnold 220
Dowding, Air Marshal 81, 85
Driffield 24, 59, 67, 76, 87, 89, 104, 131, 159, 182, 185-6, 193, 200, 215, 220, 228, 239, 242
Dubeski, F/O 171
Dumbarton 195
Dundas, Hugh 86
Dungate, S/Ldr John 266
Dunkirk 82
Dutrieux, Mlle Hélène 11

Eagle Squadrons 96
Eaker, General 153
Eisenhower, General 174, 180, 234
Easington 28
East Fortune 40
East Moor 122, 166, 183, 218, 229
Edwards, Michael 280
Elder, F/Sgt 143
Ellington, Sir Edward 65-66
Elvington 22, 135, 144, 154, 160, 162, 178, 183, 189, 191, 213. 220, 225, 228, 237-8, 240, 280-2
Emeson, F/Lt 223
Empire Air Training Scheme 99
Empson, Jack 20-21
Esmonde, Lt Commander E. 113
Espie, F/Sgt 185
Evere (1914-18) 24
Evere-Melsbroek (1944-5) 187-9

Farnborough 117, 244
Farsley 28
Fauquier, F/Lt 108
Fewlass, Bob 131-2, 257
Finland 64
Finningley 67-8, 236-7, 242, 266-267
Flamborough 24, 86, 212
Flood, G/Capt 243
Foers, F/O 118
Foreman, Trevor 280
Frankland, Dr Noble 232
Forsdike, F/Lt 142
Foster, P/O 161
Fowler, R 61
Fox, F/Lt P 167
Freeman, Roger 197
'Friday the Thirteenth' 228, 233
Fritz, KptLt Hans 24
Full Sutton 182, 186-7, 212, 228, 238-9, 244
Fussell, Sgt 131
Fylingdales 22, 244

Gale, Lt G. B. 1
Galland, Adolf 227
'Gardening' 212-4
Gaudron, Capt. A 21-2
Gibson, F/Lt Julie 267-8
Gilchrist, S/Ldr 92, 97
Giles, F/O 222
'Gisela' 210, 219-222
Goebbels, Josef 116, 136, 139, 142, 145, 209, 226, 229
Gontrode 24
Goodyear, Harry 13-14
Göring, Hermann 82, 87, 89-90, 149, 209
Graf Zeppelin I 56-7
Graf Zeppelin II 58
Graham-White, Claude 11
Grandy, Air Marshal 242
Great Yarmouth 24
Green, Charles 5-6
Greensted, Capt 245
Gregory, 'Sticks' 87
Grimsby 25

Hacking, P/O 108
Hage 24
Halifax 5, 10
Hall, Jack 201
Hamel, Gustav 15
Hamilton, Dr Helena 282
Hamilton, W/Cdr David 271
Handley Page Halifax, BI, BII modifications 123, 155
BIII 155
Handley Page, Sir Frederick 118
Hartlepool 24, 27
Harris, Sir Arthur 77, 124-5, 132-45, 152-5, 160-3, 174, 176, 179, 182, 184-6, 189, 201, 211, 216, 218-219, 234, 237, 247-50
Harris, W/Cdr 149
Harrogate 14-15, 21, 229
Hart, Sgt 131
Hart, Gerry 197
Harvey, Doug 158
Harvey, Sgt R. 187
Hassan, Sgt 108
Hautecoeure, Capitaine 228
Haxey 5
Hayton 154
Hazard, Sgt 131
Heckingen 215
Hedon 12, 50
Helperby 30-32
Henry, F/O 92
Henson, William Samuel 7
Heron, Ralph 5

Heseltine, Michael 250
Hethel 186
Hicks, F/Lt Stephen 273
Hickson, Capt Ken 250
High Ercall 228
Higgins, Major T. C. R. 33
Hill, S/Ldr 171
Himmelbett Line 110-1, 121
Hipper, Admiral 24
Hirst, Stuart 14, 16, 22
Hislop, S/Ldr 273
Hitler, Adolf 61, 73, 82-3, 90, 116, 145-5, 149, 160, 175, 205, 209
Hockey, G/Capt 245
Hogg Turnour, F/Lt 37-38
Holme-upon-Spalding-Moor 122, 144, 152, 161, 179, 185, 193, 200, 203, 218-9, 234, 237, 247-250
Holmes, Sgt 89
Holmes, S/Ldr 227
Holt, David 254
Hornby, Rev. W. B. 4,5
Hornsea 27, 29, 32
Hornsea Mere 34
Horrocks, General Sir Brian 180
Hotham 267
Howden 37-38, 43, 55-7
Hucks, Bentfield 14-16
Huddersfield 6
Hull 1, 5, 6, 8-11, 25-28, 50, 52, 54-5, 58, 102-103, 202, 207, 209, 249, 255
Hulshoff. Hpt 94
Humberside Airport (see Kirmington)
Humber-Forth gap 262
Hutton Cranswick 193
Hutton Henry 29
Hyams, Sub-Lt Gordon 34

Ipswich 71
Ironside, Field Marshal 81
Ismay, Lord 232
Itford Hill 47

Jackson, Paul 271
Jarron, W/Cdr Jake 263
Jefferson, Bernard 280
Jefferson, Guy 234
Jeffrey, F/Lt Ralph 233
Jenkins, Conway 15
Jeschonnek, General 149
Johnen, Wilhelm 143-4
Johnson, Amy 51-52
Jones, Dr. R. V. 146

Kammhuber, Josef 109, 121
Kammhuber Kinemas 141